92
C443

THE LIFE OF
JOSEPH CHAMBERLAIN

CHAMBERLAIN IN SOUTH AFRICA
(DECEMBER 1902)

THE LIFE OF
JOSEPH
CHAMBERLAIN

BY
JULIAN AMERY

VOLUME FOUR
1901 – 1903

AT THE HEIGHT OF HIS POWER

MACMILLAN AND CO., LIMITED
ST. MARTIN'S STREET, LONDON
1951

PRINTED IN GREAT BRITAIN

THIS AND THE SUCCEEDING VOLUME OF
THE LIFE OF JOSEPH CHAMBERLAIN
ARE DEDICATED TO
MY FATHER
LEOPOLD STENNETT AMERY

PREFACE

SOME six months after Joseph Chamberlain's death, my father came home, on leave from the Western Front, to find the following communications.

AUSTEN CHAMBERLAIN TO L. S. AMERY

January 19, 1915.—. . . Please let me know when you return home. I am most anxious to have a talk with you . . . that I may sound you as to the feasibility of a project for which I am anxious to enlist your sympathy.

January 28, 1915.—Mrs. Chamberlain and I are both very anxious to induce Lord Milner to write my father's Life. Lord Milner is, I think, much attracted by the idea but is afraid that the work of preparing the material, of gathering illustrative extracts from his papers and correspondence, and so forth, would require more time than he can give and more labour than he is equal to. It is clear to me that, if he is to undertake the work, he would need something more than the assistance of the ordinary secretarial type, and it has occurred to me that you might possibly be willing to give your assistance in the matter. . . .

The transaction proposed in these letters was discussed, a few days later, by the three men concerned. It was then agreed that my father should write the Life of Joseph Chamberlain under Lord Milner's general supervision.

But the fates decided otherwise. As the military operations in France settled down to the long deadlock of trench warfare, the prospects of an early peace began to fade. This was no time to write biography. Before long, Lord Milner and my father, who was soon to be ordered to the Balkans on special service, felt bound to tell Austen Chamberlain that it might be two or three years before they could even begin upon their task. The

vii

Chamberlains were concerned at the prospect of so long a delay. Accordingly, the joint authors offered to release them from their agreement. This offer was accepted. Alternative biographers were approached; and, not long afterwards, the writing of the Life was entrusted to Mr. J. L. Garvin.

In the course of the next twenty years Mr. Garvin presented three massive volumes to the public. The third of these, published in 1934, carried Joseph Chamberlain's story to the close of the year 1900. But the last and, in many ways, the most interesting phase of that story was never told. The exacting editorship of *The Observer*, the growing crisis in international affairs, and, finally, the Second World War itself so absorbed even Mr. Garvin's energies that he never finished what he had often described as his life's work.

For some years, indeed, he continued his researches for the final volumes. In 1946, however, realising that he had reached the end of his strength, he told the Chamberlain trustees that they must find another biographer. Soundings were made in different quarters; and, by a curious twist of fate, the task, from which my father had withdrawn more than thirty years earlier, devolved upon his son.

Most of the materials required for this volume had already been assembled by Mr. Garvin. They reached me, indeed, in some disarray. The Auxiliary Service, which had used his library during the war, had taken them from the shelves and tables, where they were marshalled, and dumped them into trunks and boxes without much regard for their previous and complicated arrangement. Worse still, Mr. Garvin's secretary, who alone had understood that arrangement, as well as the full significance of her employer's hieroglyphics, had died. But, though disordered, the vital documents were there; and I have thus been spared much of the labour of research. Mr. Garvin also left drafts of six chapters. I have not found it possible to include these in this volume. I am, however, indebted to them for many interesting indications and, more often than not, have accepted the conclusions at which they had arrived. Like his copious notes, they have aided me in my task more than I can adequately express.

The account, given here, of men and of affairs inevitably

lacks that contemporary understanding which Mr. Garvin would have brought to bear upon them. I have, however, profited much from conversation with Mrs. Carnegie (formerly Mrs. Joseph Chamberlain), Miss Hilda Chamberlain, Mr. Byng Kenrick, and many others who have been kind enough to recall their personal impressions of Joseph Chamberlain. Above all, I have found in my father an unfailing source of information on the policies and personalities of the time, as well as the best of counsellors.

I hope that I may also have learnt something from the advice upon the writing of biography which I sought and received from Professor Keith Feiling, Professor R. C. K. Ensor, Colonel F. W. Deakin and Lord Birkenhead. I should like to express my thanks to them, as to Sir Hubert Henderson, Sir Charles Petrie and Mr. Randolph Churchill who read my proofs and contributed many valuable suggestions.

After much patient reading of the Lives of Chamberlain's contemporaries, I am of the opinion that none has surpassed, nor, perhaps, even equalled the range or insight of Mr. Garvin's first three volumes. It has not been easy to follow in his footsteps. But, though I cannot hope to have maintained the quality of his work, I have at least endeavoured to preserve its scale, so that the proportion of the whole should not suffer. This will explain and, I hope, excuse the length at which I have felt bound to write.

My first volume, the fourth in the series, covers the period from the "Khaki" election, at the end of 1900, to Joseph Chamberlain's departure from South Africa in the spring of 1903. These were the years of Chamberlain's supremacy in our domestic, imperial and foreign affairs. My account of them is divided into five books, which at times, inevitably, overlap. The first of these relates to the final phase of the Boer War, the making of peace and the reconstruction of South Africa. The second describes the failure of Chamberlain's last effort to reach an understanding with Germany, and his subsequent negotiations with France which led up to the *Entente Cordiale*. A third book is devoted to some of Chamberlain's achievements which lie removed from the main stream of events: his work for the West Indies and for the study and application of Tropical

Medicine, his part in the founding of Birmingham University and his experiment in Zionism. The fourth book tells of his memorable visit to South Africa in the spring of 1903. The fifth and last seeks to analyse the issues and events which formed the prelude, as it were, to the movement for Imperial Preference and Tariff Reform.

The subsequent course of that movement and its revolutionary effects upon British political life will form the subject of a final volume. This I hope to submit to the public as soon as the preoccupations of contemporary politics may allow.

JULIAN AMERY

112 EATON SQUARE,
LONDON, S.W.1
July 31, 1950

CONTENTS

BOOK XVI (1901–1902)
WAR AND PEACE IN SOUTH AFRICA

BOOK XVII (SEPTEMBER 1900–JANUARY 1903)
THE DIPLOMATIC REVOLUTION

CHAPTER XC

CHAPTER XCI

BOOK XX (1901–1903)

THE ORIGINS OF TARIFF REFORM

CHAPTER XCII

CHAPTER XCIII

CHAPTER XCIV

CHAPTER XCV

CHAPTER XCVI

CHAPTER XCVII

LIST OF ILLUSTRATIONS

MAP

BOOK XVI

WAR AND PEACE IN SOUTH AFRICA
(1901–1902)

CHAPTER LXXVI

THE POLITICAL BACKGROUND

(1901)

ENGLAND after the Khaki Election—Chamberlain's Supremacy—
The Queen's Death—Chamberlain and King Edward—The Royal
Titles Act—Prince George's Empire Tour—A Waiting Mood—West
African Affairs—The Pacific Cable—"The war to the knife and
fork"—An All-night Sitting—The Blenheim Demonstration—Irish
"Over-representation"—Chamberlain or Rosebery?—The Chester-
field Speech—The Lloyd George Riot—Foreshadowings in Domestic
Policy.

I

IN the third volume of this work, Mr. Garvin carried the
tale of Chamberlain's career to the close of the nineteenth
century. The Unionist parties had returned from the Khaki
Election victorious and undiminished. With a majority of
134 in the Commons and an unchallengeable supremacy
in the Lords, their supporters might well expect to endure
the cares of office, or enjoy its sweets, for the full term of
seven years. The political prospect was fair for the proud
and massive coalition. No controversial issues disturbed the
placid surface of domestic affairs. The momentous revolution
in our foreign policy went forward behind closed doors. The
prolongation of the war in South Africa excused the absence
of reforms. Above all, the harsh dissensions of Liberalism
forbade the marshalling of an effective Opposition, let alone of
an alternative Government.

The balance of power within Unionism, reckoned in terms of
seats in Parliament and in the Cabinet, inclined more than
ever towards the Conservatives. By a compensating circumstance, however, the centre of personal influence had passed

3

from Hatfield to Highbury. Salisbury was still Prime Minister, but his influence, with his strength, was waning fast. Much of his time was spent in milder climates abroad; and his colleagues already speculated freely both on these holidays and on his impending retirement. Balfour, his nephew and the Leader of the House, was generally accepted as his chosen successor. But, though beloved of Society and admired in Parliament, he was still little known in the constituencies. For all his great gifts, no man was ever less a democratic leader. In the eyes of the British Democracy, of their brothers overseas, and of the world at large, it was Chamberlain who spoke for England. He had saved the United Kingdom from disruption. It was his blend of Imperialism and Social Reform which had revived the failing forces of Conservatism. His South African policy was the paramount issue of the day. Above all, he had been the Organiser of Victory in the Khaki Election; and few believed that Unionism could keep its hold on the country without him.

Winston Churchill, then a newly elected member for Oldham, would recall his own contemporary estimate of Chamberlain's position in these vivid terms:

At the time when I looked out of my regimental cradle and was thrilled by politics, Mr. Chamberlain was incomparably the most live, sparkling, insurgent, compulsive figure in British affairs. Above him in the House of Lords reigned venerable, august Lord Salisbury, Prime Minister since God knew when. Beside him on the Government Bench, wise, cautious, polished, comprehending, airily fearless, Arthur Balfour led the House of Commons. But "Joe" was the one who made the weather. He was the man the masses knew. He it was who had solutions for social problems; who was ready to advance, sword in hand if need be, upon the foes of Britain; and whose accents rang in the ears of all the young peoples of the Empire and of lots of young people at its heart.[1]

As yet, Chamberlain's predominance aroused but little resentment. Most Conservatives had been conciliated by his conduct of Imperial affairs, and, while the war continued, all were grateful for his leadership. Nevertheless, certain sections of the Gentlemen of England regarded the future with concern. They feared that Balfour would lack the authority to restrain his

---

[1] Winston S. Churchill, *Great Contemporaries*, p. 72.

impetuous colleague. They jibbed at the idea of entrusting their ancient interest to the care of this Birmingham manufacturer, with his Radical and Dissenting background. Not least, they suspected Chamberlain of meditating new departures in policy, costly in themselves and disruptive of the settled scheme of things.

In this they were not altogether mistaken. Chamberlain's first concern was to bring the war to a successful conclusion. His second was to put an end to our precarious diplomatic isolation by coming to terms with one or other of the rival European alliances. Nevertheless, he was already looking further ahead to the future when peace should have returned. It was not his way to lose the initiative; and there is little doubt that he had begun to revolve plans for fresh advances in Social Reform and towards the Unity of the Empire, already the transcendent cause of his life. These plans, however, and the clash of principles and personalities which they foreshadowed, were postponed for close on two years by the unexpected prolongation of the struggle in South Africa.

The conduct of Imperial policy is conditioned by the interplay of domestic and external forces. It expresses, with varying degrees of accuracy, the relation between what is deemed desirable and what is reckoned possible. Much of this volume will be devoted to Chamberlain's endeavours in South African and in Foreign Affairs. The full significance, however, of his achievements in these spheres can only be understood in relation to the background of day-to-day administration and of party politics against which they were enacted. This we must now consider.

II

The twentieth century opened with a solemn portent. Swiftly upon the nominal division of the years came a real break with the historic past. Before January was out, the Queen was dead; and the Victorian Age was over.

We cannot easily recapture, in these revolutionary times, the sense of awe which fell upon the nations, nor the void that was left in English life. For more than sixty years she had reigned at the summit of the world, mistress of a power and wealth unexampled in history. Her subjects, except a few, had never known another sovereign. In an age of continuous change, she had become the one enduring symbol of the State, the Nation and the Empire.

Amid the pomp and ceremony of her funeral, men took stock of the past and questioned the future more closely. Looking back on an era of fabulous prosperity, they felt strange forebodings of dangers to come. The fabric of things was changing. The supremacy of the Royal Navy and of British Capitalism was no longer unchallenged. The ruling principles of Splendid Isolation and of Free Trade were no longer universally accepted. The letters of the time show that, in this solemn hour, a complacent generation felt a pang of doubt about the wider destiny beyond. Well they might; for the death of a woman marked the death of an age.

As it happened, Chamberlain was the last Minister she saw; the last in the long succession of her statesmen since Melbourne had first kissed hands. From Melbourne to Chamberlain: there was the measure of her reign. She had sent for the Colonial Secretary to learn of the situation in South Africa. Later he wrote this brief and bare account of this last audience.[1]

I was the last Minister to see the Queen before her death. I went to Osborne by Command on the 10th. Sir A. Bigge [*her private secretary, afterwards Lord Stamfordham*] told me of the Queen's serious indisposition when she first came to Osborne, but said she was better and had desired him to say I must not suppose she was seriously ill.

My interview lasted about 20 minutes. I was much relieved to find the Queen looking much better than I expected with bright eyes and clear complexion.

Her voice was distinct as usual and she showed not the slightest sign of failing intelligence. She spoke about the War, regretting its prolongation and the loss of life which this entailed, but said earnestly, "I am not anxious about the result".

Her chief concern was as to the proposed enquiry into the conduct of the War, which she said could do no good, would lead to recrimination and might lower the Army in the eyes of Foreign Nations. When I said

[1] Dated January 25, 1901—three days after her death and a fortnight after the interview.

that the enquiry had been promised in Parliament and reminded Her that the refusal of an enquiry had brought about the fall of Lord Aberdeen's Government in the time of the Crimean War, she said emphatically "I do not want that, of course". She proceeded to ask whether, if it could not be abandoned, the enquiry might not be postponed, and I replied that this would be reasonable in view of the fact that the war was not yet over.

She desired me to repeat Her views to the Cabinet at its next meeting—which I did on January 18th.

Some reference was made to the visit of the Duke of York to Australia, and I said how Her assent was appreciated in the Colonies. She said that she knew that was so or words to that effect.

She was most gracious and when I took leave Her last words were "I am very glad to have had the pleasure of seeing you".

She was thinner than when I had previously seen Her [1] and there was a certain look of delicacy but, as I told Sir A. Bigge afterwards, I should not have known that She had been ill from Her appearance.

Sir A. Bigge attributed her indisposition to the strain of the Irish visit and subsequent visit to London which was not perceptible at the time but which was followed by a reaction.

On January 18, at the first Cabinet of the new century, Chamberlain, as he had promised, reported her views to his colleagues. None of them suspected that it was the Queen's last communication with her Ministers. That same night, however, the doctors issued the warning bulletin from Osborne. Four days later she was dead.

In Chamberlain the news must have stirred strange emotions. He could remember, what most had forgotten, the years of self-indulging sorrow and retirement which had offended her people and not least the class to which he belonged. He could remember too her abhorrence of his theoretical Republicanism and of his earlier Radical courses. But these antipathies belonged to a distant past. The great Imperialist had become her most-admired, perhaps her favourite Minister. Experience of her devotion to duty had taught him to return her admiration. Soon afterwards he wrote of her:

[1] This seems to have been six months before, on June 27, when the Colonial Secretary and Mrs. Chamberlain dined with the Queen at Windsor.

CHAMBERLAIN TO MILNER

January 25, 1901.—She was the greatest of Englishwomen—I had almost said of Englishmen—for she added the highest of manly qualities to the personal delicacy of the woman. I will tell you one anecdote of her. In the black week of 1899 and during the worst stage of the war, some of the Court were talking of the situation with great discouragement. She interrupted and said "I will tell you one thing. I will have no depression in my house."

III

On the morning after the Queen's death Chamberlain kissed hands at the Privy Council summoned in "His Majesty's" name. A few days later he had a private interview with the King. In his punctual way he made a short note of their conversation. It deserves to be given here.

FIRST INTERVIEW WITH KING EDWARD

Colonial Office, January 29, 1901.—I had my first private interview with the King at Marlborough House this afternoon. He was most kind. As to the Duke of York's visit to Australia he said rather pathetically that he was quite alone but for his brother the Duke of Connaught who had his duties in Ireland and his only son the Duke of York—that it would be a sacrifice to part with him, but that he had already told Lord Salisbury that if it was his duty he would not let his private feelings interpose any obstacles. He would like a few days more to think it out and would give his decision after the Funeral.

He accepted with pleasure the idea of a separate Proclamation and Declaration to the Colonies and asked me to prepare some suggestions as to the wording.

He also approved the idea of adding to the Titles of the Sovereign some such phrase as King of Greater Britain across the Seas and assented to my proposal to consult the principal colonies confidentially as to their wishes in the matter.

He spoke with regret of the prolongation of the War and wished that it were possible to do something to hasten its termination. He is evidently thinking of the possibility of some personal intervention and I told him that I had been considering whether, in view of the personal loyalty expressed by both Dutch and Boers to the Queen, it might not be possible to make an appeal to those in arms to recognise the futility of further contest and to accept the opportunities of securing the welfare of themselves and South Africa under free institutions, which we were anxious to be able to accord to them. He entirely agreed and I promised to consult Sir A. Milner.

In the course of conversation he said—You and Lord Roberts were the last persons outside the family to see the Queen—He added: "You know my Mother had a great regard for you and valued your services. I hope the same relation will continue between us. We are old friends you know, and I am sure we shall continue so." [1]

The King's relations with his powerful Minister were "always very warm and cordial".[2] The Court, however, seems to have been less well disposed; and Lord Knollys [3] in particular "never liked Mr. C." [4] This antipathy may have been due in part to Chamberlain's excursions into Foreign Affairs, still regarded as something of a royal preserve. Perhaps there was also some resentment of the almost royal position which Chamberlain enjoyed in the eyes of Colonials and foreigners. Whatever the causes, the fact is worth retaining. The influence of the Palace still counted, not least with Balfour. There is no evidence that it was ever exercised against Chamberlain. It is certain, however, that, when he came to the supreme crisis of his life, it was not exercised in his favour.

IV

From his first audience of the King, Chamberlain went to the Colonial Office and initiated confidential enquiries into the feelings of the Colonies regarding the Royal Titles. A quarter of a century earlier, when Disraeli had moved the "Empress of India" Bill, Forster had appealed for some recognition of the

[1] Some weeks afterwards, in memory of Queen Victoria, King Edward presented to Chamberlain a little Sèvres travelling clock which she had been accustomed to use. With it the King wrote: "As you were the last of my beloved Mother's Ministers who had an audience before Her Majesty became so seriously ill and knowing the high regard in which she held you . . ." The

Colonial Secretary replied that "This memento will be one of my most treasured possessions . . . to be handed down as an heirloom".

[2] Lord Monkbretton to Mr. Garvin, November 5, 1920.

[3] King Edward's Private Secretary, and a man of some influence.

[4] Lord Monkbretton to Mr. Garvin, November 5, 1920.

Colonial Empire. Disraeli had replied that the time for this had not yet come, though he did not despair that it would. In 1887 the first Colonial Conference had repeated Forster's plea. It was left to Chamberlain to fulfil it. His own suggestion was to add the words "and of Greater Britain beyond the Seas". *Greater Britain* was the title of Dilke's book which had first stirred his interest in the Empire; but the Canadian Ministers, mindful of the French part of their people, preferred: "of all the British Dominions beyond the Seas". This expression finally prevailed and brought to the new recital of the Royal Titles a majesty which could be matched by no other monarch in the world— "Edward the Seventh, by the Grace of God of the United Kingdom of Great Britain and Ireland and of all the British Dominions beyond the Seas, King, Defender of the Faith, Emperor of India".[1]

No British statesman has done more than Chamberlain to enhance the Monarchy's association with the Colonies. The Empire Tour, undertaken that year by the Prince and Princess of Wales, is another example of his constant care for the strengthening of this bond of unity. But for his initiative and skilful management, it would never have happened. It had been his idea from the start, and he it was who overcame the natural hesitations first of the Queen in her old age, and later of the King in his bereavement. As Chamberlain had planned, the tour embraced all the self-governing Colonies. Through the Mediterranean and the Indian Ocean to Australia; thence to New Zealand and far westward to the Cape; thence again by the length of the Atlantic to Canada, where the Royal Visitors journeyed overland from ocean to ocean and back again to return by the old track from Newfoundland to Portsmouth Harbour.

The homecoming of the royal pair was celebrated by a lunch at the Guildhall,[2] where Chamberlain and Rosebery were prominent among the guests. In his speech the Prince described how

---

[1] Some abbreviated inscription was required for the new coinage. This was more in the province of the Chancellor of the Exchequer who consulted classical and numismatic authorities. They recommended: "Edwardus VII, D.G., Britt: Omn: Rex, Fid. Def: Ind: Imp."—"I understand I have to obtain the concurrence of the Lord Chancellor. Will you approve if he does?" (Hicks Beach to Chamberlain, September 20, 1901.)

[2] December 5, 1901.

he had travelled 45,000 miles without setting foot on any land—
with the technical exception of Port Said—where the Union
Jack did not fly. One sentence in particular attracted attention.
The Prince repeated the opinion of the Colonies that, if Britain
intended to maintain her position in the world, "the old country
must wake up".

Rosebery proposed the toast of the Colonies and paid a
generous tribute to Chamberlain, rather to the latter's surprise.

He has many friends—and he has also many enemies—but, whatever
his friends or his enemies may think of his political career, they must all
of them, if they be candid, recognise the fact that to the duties of his high
office he has brought an energy and industry and an ability and above
all a sympathy which is invaluable in the head of so great a department.

Chamberlain, in his turn, dwelt on the growing unity of the
Empire engendered by the struggle with the Boers. He recalled
that Canada and the two Australasian Colonies had already sent
18,000 men to the war and that 50,000 more had been raised on
the British side in South Africa itself. From these figures he
drew the moral,

The British Empire is said to be loosely compacted. Yes; but the
invisible nerves of sympathy which run throughout that great organism
now beat in unison. The same spirit animates us all. A common patriotism binds us together . . . we may look forward with confidence to the
future.[1]

The Guildhall lunch after the voyage of the *Ophir* was not a
party occasion, but it was a red-letter day for the dominant
Imperial movement of the early century.

As always, Chamberlain lost no opportunity, that year, of
upholding the ideal of a United Empire. His principal speech
on this theme was made at the Canadian banquet on Dominion
Day:

Sir Wilfrid Laurier . . . is reported to have said . . . that if we
wanted their help we should call them to our councils. Well, Sir, of one
thing I am convinced—that in this movement which I think is progress-
ing, nothing could be more fatal than to be premature. The movement is
one which must come from our colonies and must not be unduly pressed

[1] *Daily News*, December 6, 1901.

upon them by us. But if they desire this closer connexion, if they are willing to assist us, not merely with their arms but also with their counsel and their advice, I believe that there is nothing that the people of this country will more readily welcome.[1]

For the time being he made no proposals as to the means whereby closer Imperial Unity might be attained. He had thrown out several suggestions in the past. Now he was content that the war should do his work for him; believing that, when peace returned, the initiative might come from the Colonies. If it did, then he would support it with all his strength.

He had explained this waiting and almost passive mood in a conversation with Dr. G. R. Parkin,[2] a Canadian champion of Imperial Federation. Parkin had observed that English statesmen ought not to let the wider patriotism kindled in the war die down without taking some practical steps towards consolidating the Empire. Chamberlain replied

that he was prepared to go just as far in that direction as Canada and Australia would go; but that he and his colleagues feared to spoil all by appearing to drive the Colonies into taking a share of the burdens of Empire.[3]

Meanwhile the work and spirit of his Imperial administration went forward. In the early part of the year he was much engaged with the affairs of West Africa, whence Colonel Willcocks had just returned from his masterly, if miniature, campaign in the last of the Ashanti wars. Chamberlain's intentions were fulfilled. Ashanti was annexed and enjoyed henceforth more peace and progress than it had ever known. In private conversation, Willcocks was full of enthusiasm for the way he had been backed up by the Colonial Office and personally encouraged by Chamberlain.

I have served many years under the War Office but, if ever I have a difficult job to do again, I know who the man is I want to serve under.[4]

Chamberlain had Chatham's gift, rare in politicians, of exciting devotion; and we soon find him pressing Willcocks' claims upon a harassed War Office with annoying tenacity. It was the same

[1] The Times, July 2, 1901.
[2] Afterwards Sir George Parkin of the Rhodes Scholarship Trust.
[3] The Times, March 28, 1901.
[4] Mrs. Chamberlain's letters to America, March 8, 1901.

almost paternal interest in the welfare of his lieutenants which
led him to write to Milner, then showing signs of strain:

> You do not say how you are getting on yourself. . . . Do not hesitate
> to ask for anything or anybody that will strengthen your hands.[1]

The cost of the Boer War and the insistence of the Treasury
compelled him to abandon many of his plans for the development of West Africa. His railway construction programme,
which he regarded as the surest means of advancing the march
of civilisation, had to be drastically curtailed. Nevertheless,
when he defended his West African administration in debate, one
admirer described him as dancing round his critics and then
dancing on them.

> What is the theory of the hon. member? It is that all these colonies
> were enjoying a kind of Elysian happiness. . . . And then upon this
> picture a baleful shadow is cast—the shadow of the Colonial Secretary.
> . . . What are the customs of the native with which we are interfering?
> Human sacrifice is one, fetishism of all kinds is another, and slavery is
> another.[2]

His efforts to improve communications were more successful
in another sphere. The project of the Pacific Cable, for many
years a dream, was now fulfilled by Chamberlain's decision.[3] The
enabling Act, piloted through the House by Austen Chamberlain, was passed at the end of this session.[4] It provided for a
line connecting Canada, and Britain also, with Australasia.
The Mother Country and the Colonies concerned went shares
in the cost of the joint undertaking. Before another year was
out, the cable was made and laid; and the line opened for traffic.
The Empire's intelligence was cheapened and quickened, as well
as extended. For the first time the Mother Country and the
Colonies "had combined to improve their means of intercourse".

The addition of a new province to the Empire, and the
creation of modern means of correspondence between its greatest
Colonies were respectable achievements for a single year. Yet in
a general view of Chamberlain's activities they are but minor
incidents. Most of his energies that year, as we shall see, were

---

[1] Chamberlain to Milner, December
30, 1901.
[2] Hansard, Fourth Series, vol. xci.
cols. 349-352 (March 18, 1901).

[3] Cf. Vol. III. of this work, p. 175.
[4] Hansard, Fourth Series, vol. xcix.
cols. 491-495 (August 12, 1901).

absorbed by South African and Foreign Affairs. Of the residue, the greater part was inevitably expended in the frequent contests of party politics.

V

In the summer of this year, Chamberlain saw his old party plunge into orgies of discord unparalleled since 1886. Campbell-Bannerman, seeking to conciliate Lloyd George and the Radical Left, accused the Government, over the concentration camps, of waging war by "methods of barbarism".[1] A few days later, Asquith and the Liberal Imperialists dissociated themselves from his remark. Acrimonious exchanges followed; and, since public dinners were the chief occasion of their utterance, the conflict within Liberalism came to be derided as "the war to the knife and fork". The sections met at the Reform Club to proclaim their formal unity despite their temporary differences. But the effect of this gesture was soon marred by Rosebery, who declared in repeated speeches that there could be no Liberal unity on present terms. Chamberlain was not far wrong when he remarked to those about him that Liberalism had no principle of union but antipathy to himself.

The chaos of the official opposition was deepened by the association of its Radical wing with the Irish party. Throughout the session, the Nationalist phalanx pursued tactics of defiance and obstruction seldom seen since the old days of the Home Rule convulsion. They denounced the British Army. They prayed God to strengthen Boer resistance. They proclaimed themselves a hostile body in a foreign legislature. One of them tried to address the House in Erse. Another had to be carried out by its police. They voted against the grant to Lord Roberts and compelled the Government to carry it by closure. Procedure was tightened; but their filibustering ingenuity was inexhaustible; and, in many a sitting, Chamberlain, like other Ministers, had to sit the benches and tramp the lobbies up to 3 A.M. and later. One night, near the end of the session, his wife noted that he had not got to bed until seven in the morning.

Two hours and a half sleep is not much of a night, is it? But it was all that he had, for there was a Cabinet meeting.[2]

[1] June 14, 1901.   [2] Mrs. Chamberlain to her mother, August 9, 1901.

The climax of confusion came in the debate of August 2.[1] South Africa was the subject, and Chamberlain the Government's chief spokesman. Much of his speech was conciliatory, but some scathing passages provoked repeated interruptions from the Irish benches. Lloyd George, in his turn, was assailed by the Ministerialists with cries of "divide, divide". By way of retaliation on behalf of the Radical leader, the Nationalists then refused to give Grey a hearing, although parts of his speech were critical of Chamberlain. Next, John Redmond prayed that South Africa might take vengeance one day by separating altogether from the British Empire; a sentiment which alienated many moderate pro-Boers.

It was an all-night sitting and grew more disorderly as the night advanced. Rarely had Chamberlain been more luridly denounced. An excited member described his speech as "one of the most cruel, the most un-English, the most infamous speeches ever delivered in the House of Commons". Another moved to reduce his salary but ran away from his own motion, when Campbell-Bannerman, who had been expected to support it, disappeared with the other Liberal leaders. Labouchere then moved to abolish the salary altogether. Complete confusion followed; and, in repeated divisions, the number of Liberals voting with the Irish phalanx sank to less than half a dozen.

H. W. Massingham, watching from the gallery, drew this pen picture of Chamberlain during the debate:

> While Mr. Labouchere in the most direct terms I have ever heard used in the House of Commons was accusing him between one and two in the morning of guilty complicity in Mr. Rhodes's plots, he looked steadily up at the ceiling, his features fixed as if they were cast in stone. When Mr. Ronald was discussing the Malta question a few minutes later, who so smooth, so affable, so tolerant as the Figure of Wrath of a few hours earlier.[2]

The controlled contrast of moods is typical. The same chronicler, then the best on the Liberal Left, wrote of this long sitting that it marked "the last stage of humiliation for the Liberal party".[3]

---

[1] Hansard, Fourth Series, vol. xcviii. cols. 1103-1126 (August 2, 1901).
[2] H. W. Massingham in the *Daily News*, August 6, 1901.

[3] *Daily News*, August 3; *The Times*, August 3 and 5, 1901; and James F. Hope (Lord Rankeillour), *History of the 1900 Parliament*, pp. 294-295.

Such lamentable proceedings could only redound to the Government's advantage; but the personal inconvenience which they caused determined Chamberlain to strike back. Before the House rose, he incited his colleagues to organise a great counter-demonstration.

This was held at Blenheim on August 10, a hot and shining Saturday afternoon. A hundred M.P.s and a score of other dignitaries sat upon the platform constructed beneath the Corinthian portico of the palace. The crowd of some thousands of people was gathered on the lawn. It was like a scene out of Disraeli.

Balfour, more ingenious than stirring, was betrayed into the witticism: "We will neither sacrifice our Empire to the Boers nor our Constitution to the bores". Chamberlain by contrast was at his most forceful. He made rude sport of Rosebery's humourless suggestion that his adherents should form a "Liberal (Imperialist) League", with the word "Imperialist" in brackets! Next he described the dissensions within the Liberal party as the inevitable consequence of Gladstone's Home Rule Policy and the complete vindication of his own attitude.

Fifteen years ago they were a great and powerful and a united party, and they were led by Mr. Gladstone. Today they are a Rump and they are led by Sir Henry Campbell-Bannerman.

But Chamberlain had not organised the Blenheim demonstration merely to indulge in political invective. He had a new issue to bring forward; a proposal to sap the influence of the Irish party by reducing the representation of Ireland at Westminster.

Great Britain is strong enough to be contemptuous of this toyshop treason which takes advantage of our toleration in order to shout for the Mahdi or King Prempeh or President Kruger or anyone else with whom we may happen to be engaged in hostilities. . . . It is my conviction that the nation is taking note of these proceedings. I think they expect that the Mother of Parliaments will know how to defend herself against these attacks—attacks by men who come to us in numbers altogether disproportionate to the wealth, to the intelligence and to the population which they represent.[1]

[1] *The Times*, August 12, 1901.

Public attention fastened on this passage; and, for some time, the Unionist press resounded with a clamour against the in- justice of Irish "over-representation". Two months later, at Edinburgh, Chamberlain repeated and enforced his argument. But it was not to be. For one thing, his colleagues were unenthusi- astic; and George Wyndham, the new Chief Secretary, was already working towards a policy of conciliation. For another, the agitation failed to catch on in the constituencies. It was too frankly partisan. Ireland had been as much under-represented at the time of the Union as she had become over-represented since; and her population had diminished for reasons miserable to recall. Besides the necessary redistribution bill could not have taken effect until after the next General Election; and this might still be as much as six years ahead. Accordingly, Chamberlain agreed to postpone the issue until nearer election time. It never arose again. Long before the nation went to the polls, the whole political scene was revolutionised by Chamberlain's own action.

Nevertheless, the Blenheim meeting deserves our attention. A decade and a half after Gladstone's bid for Home Rule and Chamberlain's secession, it was the last full-blooded demonstra- tion of the old style in the Unionist Age. Never again would the great constitutional alliance present so united a front, nor glory with such arrogant assurance in the dissensions of its opponents. The greatest triumphs were still ahead, but, already with the autumn, would come the first warning symptoms of approaching disintegration. Blenheim marked the meridian, not indeed of Unionist achievement, but of Unionist political power.

VI

For Chamberlain's personal career the Blenheim meeting had one significant consequence. His speech that afternoon had shown a quality of leadership not to be found in Balfour's dilettante remarks. The inevitable comparison between the two men and their speeches gave rise to the first rumours that Chamberlain, not Balfour, would succeed to the Premiership. The view was not yet shared by serious observers; but, that winter, Chamberlain's personal prestige was still further en- hanced by two notable triumphs over his chief opponents.

Imperialism was the dominant movement of the day; and Chamberlain was regarded by many as its chief exponent. A rising backbencher like young Winston Churchill declared that he and his friends pinned their faith to the triumphant Birmingham school. A veteran like Lord George Hamilton asked another audience what the Colonies would say to Lloyd George's cry that Chamberlain "should go". He answered his own question by asserting that in the judgment of those Colonies "Mr. Chamberlain was by far the ablest Colonial Minister that the country had produced for a century and they would never consent to swop him for the whole of the Liberal Imperialists bag and baggage".[1]

The very ardour of these declarations suggests that Chamberlain's leadership of the Imperial movement was not unchallenged. Rosebery was his rival; and he too had powerful claims. He had been Prime Minister. His oratory reached to greater heights than Chamberlain's. He carried none of the responsibility for the mistakes of the Government nor for the disappointments of the war. As the autumn advanced and the prospect of victory came no nearer, many men of independent views asked themselves whether Rosebery might not form some broader and more inspiring kind of National Government than the stale forces of Unionism could offer. There was talk of a ministry of all the talents with a sailor and a soldier as political heads of the fighting services, and Cromer called from Cairo to become a great Foreign Secretary. In the Liberal party, a few ardent souls dreamed that Rosebery might "imperialise" Liberalism. Others, more prosaic, judged that he might at least supersede Campbell-Bannerman in the leadership and make the party an effective Opposition once again.

The latent issue between Chamberlain and Rosebery was brought to a head that winter. Rosebery was to make a speech at Chesterfield; and the political world, shaken by the repeated setbacks on the veld, awaited his words with unconcealed excitement. Interest was universal; speculation was rife; and in some quarters hopes were high. Would the great man return at last to the political arena and give the Empire a new lead?

[1] By an odd chance these references to statements by Mr. Churchill and Lord George Hamilton (then Secretary for India) are found in the *Westminster* *Gazette* of December 7, 1901, under the title, "Notes for Mr. Chamberlain's Biographer"!

Chamberlain had never liked Rosebery, nor did he greatly respect him. It is the vainest of regrets to lament, as did many of their contemporaries, that the two men never joined forces. In politics, as in love, there is no enemy so bitter as a rival; and Chamberlain was far more hostile to the Liberal Imperialists than to the pro-Boers. He had once said in conversation with Walter Long:

I don't hate the Irish, I don't hate the Little Englanders, but I hate the Imperialist Liberals who profess to be so patriotic and are always ready to embarrass the Government. The line they should have taken was to support the Government while the country was in difficulties . . . then they would have made their position clear as the alternative to the Government, presently. They would have dominated the Little Englanders entirely. If Rosebery had had any courage he would have done that. The only one of them who has any courage is Grey and he is too idle.[1]

This had been at the beginning of the year. Now he awaited Rosebery's speech with complete unconcern. A few weeks before the Chesterfield meeting he wrote to his old comrade Morley, also an enemy of the Liberal Imperialists though for different reasons.

CHAMBERLAIN TO MORLEY

November 10, 1901.—Are you excited to know what Rosebery will say? *I am not*—and I think I know beforehand the ballad which the lonely one is likely to sing.

The real fact is that there is now, as there always has been since the war, only one policy on which a "Great United Liberal Party" can agree, and that is to "give Master Joe another fall".

Meanwhile "Master Joe" would give anything to be free of the work and worry, at least for a year or two.

The event justified his anticipations.

In mid-December, when all the roads to Chesterfield were white with snow, an imposing audience assembled to hear the long-awaited oration. They listened for two hours to a brilliant, stirring, but enigmatic performance. Rosebery's negative injunc-

---

[1] From a contemporary note of the conversation taken by Chamberlain's   Parliamentary Private Secretary, J. Parker Smith (December 1900).

tions were definite enough. He told his party to "clean its slate" of its past errors and especially of Gladstonian Home Rule, pro-Boerism and anti-Imperialism of every kind. But his positives were more nebulous. He condemned Chamberlain and Milner, but justified the war, and bade the nation put its trust in Kitchener. He would make no overtures to the Boers, but peace might begin "with an apparently casual meeting of two travellers in a neutral inn". Looking to the future, he announced that the secret of good Government in peace and war was "efficiency", a platitude which, as one observer remarked, is as significant as pronouncing *abracadabra*.

The meaning of the speech seemed to be yea-and-nay; but the skill and forcefulness of its delivery won it, in the first instance, a favourable reception. Had Rosebery followed it up with something more constructive, Liberal Imperialism might have become a force to reckon with; and its leader might have intervened with decisive effect in the South African peace settlement and the Imperial conference. Instead, he waited for the response that never came.

Waiting to be called is the negation of leadership. In the absence of any further explanation of his policy, Rosebery's admirers had to content themselves with his Chesterfield speech. The more they studied it, the more their scepticism grew. There was no message in it. Rosebery's legend was dissipated. It never revived; and the dream of Liberal Imperialism faded into nothing. Many, especially the young men hitherto impatient of the party system, now turned for the first time to Chamberlain. Henceforth to the end of his life he would be the unchallenged leader of Imperialism.

VII

The political demise of Chamberlain's rival was followed closely by the discomfiture of his foremost opponent. Two days after Rosebery's speech at Chesterfield came the Lloyd George riot in Birmingham.

The Birmingham Liberal Association had invited the young Radical leader to address their last great meeting of the year in Birmingham Town Hall. It was an imprudent invitation; and Lloyd George was imprudent to accept it. Birmingham had neither forgiven nor forgotten the Kynoch debate. Chamberlain was their first citizen, and, in this very year, had crowned thirty years of civic achievement by the formal inauguration of Birmingham University. The Unionists, accordingly, decided that the man who had slandered Chamberlain's private honour and who now led the agitation that "Chamberlain should go", would not be heard in their city. It was not, as has often been said, an attack by Jingoism on pro-Boerism, but rather a demonstration of outraged civic pride.

Admission to the meeting was to be by ticket, but the original issue was cancelled when a free circulation of counterfeits was discovered. The new tickets were of no avail. Huge crowds heaved outside the Town Hall. When the doors were opened a hostile majority crushed in with the rest. From the beginning the scene was pandemonium. The Chairman's remarks were drowned. Far worse was Lloyd George's ordeal. For forty minutes or so he faced the roars of his opponents and the surge of Union Jacks, but his speech was dumb-show to the audience. Not a syllable could be heard except by a few reporters pressing close. The tumult within the Hall worked on the crowds outside. They hurled stones through the windows and beat against the doors. As glass crashed down on the audience, passions rose, until a sudden furious rush was made for the platform. The assailants were held off by the police, but only with difficulty; and the Chief Constable had to persuade Lloyd George to retire into a room behind the platform. There he changed clothes with an officer of slight build, and, thus disguised, was marched with a squad of constables from the Town Hall to a suburban police station. Thanks to this ruse, he escaped without a scratch. But, meanwhile, in the scuffles between the police and the mob in the Square, a youth fell against the kerbstone and was killed.[1]

Chamberlain deplored the young man's death, but otherwise took a grim pleasure in the whole affair. He was especially delighted when the Liberal Association had to pay for the damages to the Town Hall. One of his jests at the time shocked some of his contemporaries. Asked in the lobbies how Lloyd George had escaped with his life from Birmingham, he answered, "What is everybody's business is nobody's business".

[1] *The Times*, December 19 and 20, 1901.

In the longer run the riot had a healing consequence. Lloyd George bore no malice for quits; and Chamberlain regarded the Kynoch account as closed. When Lloyd George next spoke in Birmingham Town Hall, it was as Britain's Prime Minister and the Empire's war leader. On that occasion he waited until the applause had subsided, and then, with a twinkle in his eye, remarked that the Hall seemed "somehow familiar".

VIII

The Unionist administration stood at the height of its power. Chamberlain's influence in the nation's councils continually increased. His colonial policies went forward. Such was the general background to the greater issues which we shall presently survey. Meanwhile, beneath a smiling surface, the faint pull of strange new undercurrents could already be felt.

We have still, of course, our greatest fence before us when we get to the Budget and the heavy additional taxation we shall have to impose.[1]

So Chamberlain wrote at the beginning of April. Hicks Beach's gloom indeed had become contagious in the Cabinet. How to raise £190,000,000 in a single year and yet survive? To a generation, scarcely conscious of its immeasurable resources, the problem seemed insoluble; and, indeed, it was insoluble within the limitations of Gladstonian principles of sound finance. The pundits harped on the need for "broadening the basis of taxation" to meet the growth of ordinary expenditure. But how was this to be done without deviating from the straight and narrow path of economic orthodoxy?

The Chancellor's response was neither original nor inspiring. The deficit of £55,000,000 was to be met mostly by loan. Only a fifth of it was to come from increased taxation. The income-tax was raised from a shilling to fourteen pence; a sacrifice, regarded as a great gesture of patriotism on the part of property. In an attempt to "broaden the basis of taxation", the revenue duty on sugar was also raised, but so little that the retail price was not increased by more than a halfpenny a pound.

The only surprise of the budget was the revival of a strange and antiquated device, the levy of a shilling a ton on the export

[1] Chamberlain to Milner, April 1, 1901.

of British coal. Hicks Beach maintained that British coal was a necessity to other countries and that the foreign consumer would therefore pay the tax. The argument was uncertain; but the coal- mining interests complained with so little restraint that they lost the sympathy of the public. The miners threatened to stop the pits; the owners prophesied ruin; and the cries of Croesus from two Liberal millionaires caused widespread merriment. Chamberlain had never forgiven the coal owners for their opposition to the Workmen's Compensation Bill. The opportunity to pay off this old score was irresistible; and, in a speech at Birmingham,[1] he mocked them in the tone of his Radical days.

It seems to me that the richer a man is, the more frightened he is lest even a penny should be taken from him.

Hicks Beach's budget solved the immediate financial problem, but it contained no ideas for the future. Everything pointed to a continuing increase in the scale of state expenditure; and this could not indefinitely be met by loans. Unionist critics, in the House and outside, began to discuss the various advantages of a tariff. Some urged it purely as a means of raising revenue; others to reinforce home industries against foreign rivals; yet others as a step towards colonial development. With Sir Francis Mowatt and the "Gladstonian garrison" at the Treasury behind him, the Chancellor stood unalterably opposed to anything which savoured of protectionism. He repudiated the notion of a duty on foreign manufactured imports. To Chamberlain's regret, he also rejected the plea of a handful of Unionist members to exempt colonial sugar from the sugar-tax. As he saw it, retrenchment was the only cure for the nation's financial ills; and the need for it obsessed him more and more as the year advanced. But in vain. State expenditure only continued to increase; and the problem of how to meet it became correspondingly more insistent.

Army policy cast another ominous shadow. The campaigns in South Africa had shown the urgent need for a reform of our military system. St. John Brodrick, the Secretary for War, had accordingly drafted a scheme for the creation of an army of six army corps organised on the continental model. This was to

[1] Birmingham Town Hall, May 10, 1901.

come into force after the return of peace; but the more Brodrick's plans were studied, the less they were liked; and back-
bench discontent with the conduct of the war was deepened
seriously by misgivings over the army scheme.

More ominous still for Unionism was the unexpected revival
of the education controversy. The so-called Cockerton judgment [1] declared that the school boards were only empowered to
conduct primary education and that their higher educational
activities were a breach of the law. Immediate legislation was
required if higher education throughout the country was not
to be brought to a standstill. But Ministers mismanaged their
procedure. A first bill satisfied no one, and was handled by
Gorst with more wit than tact. It had to be dropped. A second
bill merely legalised the existing situation, but for one year only.
The issue was thus postponed; not resolved. A cloud had
appeared on the horizon, and a storm threatened for the next
session.

After the Cockerton judgment came another legal pronouncement destined to have a still more far-reaching effect. The Taff
Vale judgment declared that a Trade Union might be sued for
the actions committed by its agents and forced to pay damages.
The immunity assumed for thirty years was swept away; and
Organised Labour was hamstrung at a time of growing strain
in industrial relations. The Government underestimated the
political significance of the decision and declined to intervene. It was a grave miscalculation. Their inaction alienated
many supporters of Unionism in the Labour movement. It
drove the Unions into alliance with the Opposition and powerfully stimulated the development of the political Labour
party.

These developments were destined to exercise a powerful
influence on Chamberlain's further career. As yet, however, he
had little to do with them. There was a limit even to his
capacity for work. Once or twice, indeed, he spoke on Temper-
ance and Old Age Pensions.[2] But his utterances were more
practical than inspiring; and the critics accused him of having

[1] April 1, 1901. For the details of
how the Cockerton case was engineered
see *Sir Robert Morant*, by Bernard M.
Allen, pp. 133, 143-145 and 150.

[2] Notably at Birmingham, May 29
and October 14, 1901, and at Edinburgh, October 25, 1901.

put up his shutters as a Social Reformer. For the time being he could afford to disregard these charges. The desire for Social Reform might grow all the stronger for being pent up; but public opinion was still agreed that the first task was to win the war.

CHAPTER LXXVII

THE ENDLESS WAR

(1901)

A FALSE Prospectus?—"Shovelling fleas across a barn"—Kitchener's Strategy—The Political Danger—The Parties and the War—The Middelburg Negotiations—Independence the Real Issue—Milner's Triumphal Return—He urges Reconstruction under Arms—The Concentration Camps—The Banishment Proclamation—The Unionist Revolt—Chamberlain and the Conduct of the War—Milner's Bid to oust Kitchener—More Colonial Contingents.

I

AT the Khaki Election, Chamberlain had announced that the war against the Boers was won. Such, indeed, had been the opinion of the military chiefs at home and in South Africa. The event, however, belied their estimate of the situation, and lent some colour to the Opposition's charge that Chamberlain had won the election on a false prospectus. No victory on the veld followed the victory at the polls. Far from being over, the war was not yet half-way through.

From the beginning of 1901 to the end, the struggle in South Africa was tedious, thankless and frustrating. It called for endless patience. It involved heavy expenditure and some loss of life. It offered no gleam of glory. Yet, while it lasted, no constructive work could be done. The year opened with the stinging little reverse at Helvetia. It closed with the fiasco at Tweefontein. In between, the tale of disappointment and humiliation—of "disasters" as contemporary opinion had it—was unrelieved.

Looking back, we can see that there was nothing surprising in these setbacks. The Boers were still well equipped, and their morale was sustained by continued hope of foreign intervention.

26

We could not defend the whole length of our lines of communication. They could strike where they chose. No early victory was possible over an enemy who could not be brought to battle; and chasing commandos from one part of the veld to another was, in Abraham Lincoln's words, "like shovelling fleas across a barn".

It is never easy to suppress a guerilla. Kitchener's efforts to do so fell into two parts. He covered the whole country with a network of corrugated-iron block-houses linked together by barbed wire. Having thus confined the commandos to limited areas, he proceeded to burn down the farms on which they depended for shelter and supplies. These were sound tactics, but they were costly and took time to tell.

Meanwhile the best chance for the Boers was that British opinion might waver in its determination to see the thing through. Sickened by an expensive and inglorious struggle, the public might have been tempted to call for peace on terms which would have left the South African problem unresolved. This was what Milner meant when he wrote: "The only thing I ever really fear is a 'wobble' in British opinion".[1]

Chamberlain's reply to the letter in which Milner used this phrase deserves to be quoted. It is the frankest contemporary estimate of the political dangers inherent in the South African situation.

CHAMBERLAIN TO MILNER

Colonial Office, February 7, 1901.—*Secret*—I have received your letter of January 17. I continue firmly of the opinion that there is no fear of any "wobble" on the part of the British public provided that our policy is firm, clear and consistent, and that in carrying it out we do not raise new questions of a deeply controversial character. . . .[2]

You must bear in mind that nothing at the present time can exceed the bitterness of the Opposition. In one sense they are contemptible because they have no trusted leader, no cohesion, and no common policy. But they are as cross as a bear with a sore head at their own impotency, at the defeat which they recently sustained at the elections, and at the

[1] Milner to Chamberlain, January 17, 1901.

[2] Chamberlain is alluding to Milner's renewed proposal to suspend the Cape Constitution. See ch. lxxx.

failure of all their attacks upon the Government. It would be much better for us if they *were* all agreed—even upon an extreme policy. We should then know how to meet them. As it is we have to expect assaults from every section; but the only matter on which we can reckon on the unanimity of the Opposition is a personal attack upon the Colonial Secretary. . . .

As regards the military situation I admit to having been more depressed the last week or two than ever before. The way in which De Wet and the various commandos escape our men, do mischief all over the place, and prevent any approach towards a permanent administration is most discouraging. No one here dares any longer to fix a limit to the war and its expenditure which is going on at the rate of at least a million a week. The country is denuded of troops—fortunately we can count upon the Navy, for if an invasion were possible I do not see how humanly speaking we could resist it. Nevertheless in view of the staleness of the troops and the necessity of the war, a new effort has been resolved upon and 30,000 more mounted men are to be sent to the seat of war.[1]

But if some progress is not made before long I think public dissatisfaction may become serious and threaten the existence of the Government in spite of the enormous majority.[2] I do not believe that our opponents would be able seriously to alter the policy although they would no doubt change the persons; but even then a defeat at the present time would encourage the Boers and increase the chances—now almost infinitesimal—of foreign intervention. . . .

This letter reveals Chamberlain's innermost anxieties with unusual candour. Perhaps he overdrew them deliberately to give Milner pause; but we must remember that beneath the mask he was often liable to moods of dark depression. As a rule, he found hard work the only remedy; but, while the war lasted, the real control of South Africa rested with the War Office; and, unless invited or compelled, he would not meddle with the affairs of a department where he could not command. Meantime there were no funds available to get things done elsewhere; and he had no choice but to champ the bit.

In public, of course, he admitted nothing of these inward

[1] The reinforcements officially announced on the date of this letter consisted of 10,000 Imperial Yeomanry, 8000 police, 5000 new colonial contingents, with 7000 cavalry and mounted infantry from the home establishment.

[2] My italics.—J. A.

doubts; rather the reverse. The worse things were, the harder he CHAP.
pressed his attacks on his political opponents until a note of LXXVII.
bravado invaded his speeches. This was sound tactics. By keep- ÆT. 64.
ing up the political temperature, he kept the nation's courage
and his colleagues' screwed "to the sticking point". It was not
his least contribution to the final victory. As Lord Roberts
would write a year later: "Few, perhaps, know better than I do
how different the position in South Africa would have been . . .
had there been any vacillation in our policy at home".[1]

II

Chamberlain was challenged over South African affairs as soon
as Parliament reassembled. On this subject the Opposition was
split into three sections. The Irish Nationalists waged a steady
guerilla at Westminster in support of the guerilla on the veld.
The Liberal Imperialists held to a course not easily distinguishable from the Government's save that, for personal reasons,
they combined support of Milner with criticism of Chamberlain.
Between these extremes, but, as it were, in front of the main
body of pro-Boer Liberalism, stood the Radicals. Lloyd George
was already their established champion, more sparkling than
Chamberlain but never as deadly in his thrusts. Campbell-
Bannerman, the official leader of the Opposition, bestrode these
warring sections with little grace but some skill. He reckoned
shrewdly that as long as the electors wanted Imperialism they
would look to the Unionists not to the Liberals. Accordingly, he
leaned more and more to the Left waiting for the pendulum to
swing. Chamberlain, for his part, had the Unionists solidly
behind him, though an influential element was alarmed by the
mounting costs of the war.

In the debate on the Address, Campbell-Bannerman contended
that, while our military fist must no doubt be iron, we should
hold out the olive branch with the other hand. He urged that
the demand for unconditional surrender be withdrawn. Lloyd
George went further. He denounced farm-burning; accused
some British Commanders by name of cruelty; and advocated
that full self-government should be given to the ex-Republics

---

[1] Roberts to Chamberlain, February 16, 1902.

immediately on the cessation of hostilities. But he neither moved the amendment he had announced nor challenged a division. Chamberlain mocked this discretion which prevented the opinion of the House from being taken at once in the lobbies. He and his colleagues were prepared to grant full self-government to the ex-Republics at the earliest reasonable moment. But there must first be an interval of direct rule, both to undertake material reconstruction and to establish those equal rights between the British and Boer races for which the war had been fought. "The country", he said,

"will grudge no sacrifice which is necessary to carry the war to a successful conclusion and . . . it will forgive no Government and no party which attempts to stultify the objects with which it has been undertaken." [1]

The same night, Winston Churchill made his maiden speech. The text still reads well, but he had not yet acquired the art of delivery. Recalling a friendship of other years, Chamberlain voiced his hope "that we may see the gifts of the father repeated in the son".

III

Very soon Chamberlain was called upon to define his views on the question of peace terms more precisely. The veld had been the grave of many reputations; and Kitchener earnestly desired to exchange South Africa for India as soon as honour would allow. Accordingly, he sent a verbal message to Botha, through Mrs. Botha, proposing discussions. Botha accepted the chance of sounding the British Government's intentions; and, at the end of February, the two men met at Middelburg.

Chamberlain was by no means ill-disposed to these negotiations. Before the meeting, he cabled to Milner:

Do not reject any proposal which Botha may make without communicating with us. Reserve all doubtful points.[2]

In his original message Kitchener had explained that there could be no question of the Boers retaining their independence. The very discussion of this question was to be excluded. At Middelburg, however, Botha said "that he was not sure of being able

---

[1] Hansard, Fourth Series, vol. lxxxix. cols. 397-434 (February 18, 1901).
[2] February 26, 1901.

to bring about peace without independence. He tried very hard for some kind of independence." [1] This was the crux, as we shall see. But Kitchener believed that he could get round it by making concessions on other points. He relied chiefly on a promise of amnesty for the Cape rebels; and on financial grants to restore the devastated farms.

On these two points Chamberlain refused to accommodate him. He held that to promise amnesty to the rebels, before peace was assured, would be unfair to the Loyalists, and might well encourage further rebellion should the negotiations break down. He also held that, as a general principle, financial assistance to restore Boer farms should be "by loan" and not by gift. Even Milner demurred to "by loan", but Chamberlain stuck to his view that gifts should be acts of grace rather than articles of settlement. "It would not do to allow the Boers to think that they could escape all loss in consequence of the war." [2]

His final terms to the Boers were communicated to Botha on March 7. They may be summarised as follows:

1. Progress by stages towards complete self-government.
2. A grant of £1,000,000 towards compensating burghers for supplies requisitioned from them by their late Governments.
3. Loans to renew destroyed farms.
4. Subordination of the natives.
5. Equality of the English and Dutch languages.
6. Full amnesty for burghers of the late Republics, but not for Cape rebels who would be liable for trial according to the law of that Colony.

In mid-March Botha curtly rejected this offer. [3]

Kitchener, convinced that he knew the statesman's business as well as the soldier's, held that a golden opportunity of making peace had been lost. He blamed Chamberlain and Milner for refusing to concede, in advance, an amnesty for the Cape rebels and grants for the restoration of the farms. He thought their attitude narrow and vindictive. [4] In this he was not alone, as the subsequent debate in the House showed. [5]

[1] Cd. 528, p. 2 (Kitchener to Brodrick, February 28, 1901).
[2] Ibid. p. 3 (Chamberlain to Milner, March 6, 1901).
[3] Ibid. p. 7 (Botha to Kitchener, March 16, 1901).
[4] Sir George Arthur, Life of Lord Kitchener, vol. ii. pp. 25-26.
[5] Hansard, Fourth Series, vol. xcii. cols. 123-138 (March 28, 1901).

The event, however, proved that Kitchener was wrong and Chamberlain right. The Boers rejected the terms for one reason and one reason only. They were not interested in amnesty or financial grants. They wanted independence. This was made perfectly clear in the next few months by their chief men in South Africa and in Europe. Botha proclaimed it to all officers and burghers:

I informed Lord Kitchener that we were only fighting for our independence.

De Wet repeated it in the Orange Free State:

What is the use of examining all the points, as the only object for which we are fighting is the independence of our Republics and our national existence?

As late as July, a final declaration in the same sense was issued in the names of President Kruger and the delegation in Europe; of Steyn and Schalk Burger, the political leaders in South Africa; and of the chief Commandants including Botha, De La Rey and De Wet.[1]

The truth is that the Boers never took the negotiations seriously. Once their independence had been excluded, they looked on them only as a means of sounding British intentions. Judged from this standpoint, all concessions were signs of weakness. Chamberlain had seen this at once. Kitchener had not. The result of the negotiations was almost certainly to encourage the Boers to fight on. As Botha put it to his burghers at Ermelo, the rejected peace terms contained "nothing more but rather less than what the British Government will be obliged to do should our cause go wrong".[2]

IV

Milner came home in May at his own urgent request. He needed a change both to recover from the strain of the past two years and to prepare for the work of peace-making and reconstruction. He also judged that the time had come to discuss his ideas for the future personally with Chamberlain.

---

[1] Cd. 633, relating to the sequel to the Middelburg negotiations.
[2] *Ibid.* p. 3, March 15, 1901.

CHAP.
LXXVII.

Æt. 64.

In advance the pro-Boers spread a rumour that his return meant permanent recall and veiled disgrace. This was the purest wishful thinking, but it stung Chamberlain into counter-measures which would strike the imagination of the whole Empire. He proposed that Milner should enjoy a Roman triumph, and cabled his plans to Madeira. Milner, astonished and incredulous, replied:

I have received telegram from you concerning arrangements for my return. Bearing in mind hoax attempted on previous occasion feel some doubt as to its genuineness. If genuine I am of course much honoured by H.M.'s commands and thank you for your other kind proposals.

It was no hoax. At Waterloo he was met not only by Chamberlain but by Salisbury, Balfour, Lansdowne, the Lord Chancellor, the Secretary of State for War, and Lord Roberts.

Salisbury's presence came about in a curious way. Hating ceremonies of all kinds, he had not at first intended to take part in the welcome. At Chamberlain's instance, however, he had proposed to the King that a royal carriage might be sent to meet Milner.

SALISBURY TO CHAMBERLAIN

May 16, 1901.—. . . The King it appears craned at the idea of sending a royal carriage to meet Milner—but suggested—it was a queer alternative—that I should send *my* carriage to meet him. It would have been rather a bumptious proceeding on my part in any case—but the King's idea seems to have been that my carriage, *empty*, was to meet him. With all deference to H.M. I think this would be a bit of bad manners on my part, and therefore inadmissible. It seemed to me possible that we might both meet him at the station.

So it was arranged.

From the station Milner was driven straight to Marlborough House, where the King raised him to the peerage in the presence of the Prime Minister and the Colonial Secretary. Next day Chamberlain and his wife gave a luncheon in his honour at Claridge's, where a distinguished company included the Duke of Cambridge, the Prime Minister and half the Cabinet. In proposing Milner's health, Chamberlain looked to the future.

A greater work lies before him after his return to South Africa. Although we may have many disappointments, I am sanguine that, when that time comes, the smouldering embers of war—which has long ceased to be a war in the true sense of the word . . . will have been extinguished. Then he will be able to take up this work, more arduous than any which he has hitherto confronted—which I believe will be more congenial to himself—and after the chaos of war and conflict he will found a new order of things in South Africa, and establish the administrative machinery which we confidently believe will unite and reconcile the two races in that country. . . . You all will join me in the hope that Lord Milner, strengthened by a short respite from the strain of the last few years, and heartened and encouraged by the proof that he still has the support of his fellow countrymen, will be able to crown the work which he has undertaken, laying broad and deep the foundations of a united South Africa, as free, as prosperous and as loyal as the sister federations of Canada and Australia.[1]

Milner's reply dispelled the illusion, fostered by the Liberal Imperialists, that he and Chamberlain were at loggerheads.

. . . I feel bound to take this opportunity, especially in view of the remarks which have been made in certain quarters, to express my deep sense of gratitude for the manner in which His Majesty's Government, and especially my immediate chief, have shown me great forbearance and have given me support, most prompt at the moment when it was most needed, without which I should have been helpless indeed. . . .

He went on to deal with the pro-Boers in sounding words much noted at the time:

I do not know whether I feel more inclined to laugh or cry when I have to listen for the hundredth time to these dear delusions, this Utopian dogmatising, that it only required a little more time, a little more patience, a little more meekness, a little more of all these gentle virtues of which I know I am so conspicuously devoid in order to conciliate—to conciliate what?—panoplied hatred, insensate ambitions, invincible ignorance.

These welcoming scenes were only the beginning. There were to be other honours to mark Milner's merits and Chamberlain's determination. Before his return to South Africa, Milner was

[1] *The Times*, Saturday, May 25, 1901.

created a Privy Councillor; and Chamberlain was present when he received the freedom of the City. These things are notable, not so much in themselves, as because they illustrate the public support which Chamberlain never failed to give his great proconsul.

Milner's mind, that summer, was a power-house of constructive thinking. Within a week of his return, he went to Highbury, where, from morning until midnight for three strenuous days,[1] he and Chamberlain ranged over South African affairs. Immediately afterwards Chamberlain wrote down the substance of these conversations in a long memorandum, later circulated to the Cabinet. This we must briefly summarise.[2]

Milner urged that, if Kitchener's war of attrition had not brought success by early autumn, a new plan would have to be tried. The basis of such a plan, as he saw it, would be the creation and extension of protected areas around the principal towns. The reconstruction of industry and the development of agriculture might go ahead in these areas; and, provided they were well protected, it would not matter much if the guerilla persisted in the sparsely-peopled ranges of the backveld.

Milner believed that reconstruction under arms was possible. He also looked on it as a means to his main end. This had always been the establishment of British supremacy in South Africa. To achieve it required, first, the rehabilitation of the gold industry, and, second, some British settlement on the land. In both cases Milner thought it best to make a start, while the Boers were still our enemies.

Chamberlain sympathised with these main purposes and, to prepare the ground for their acceptance, arranged that Milner should be summoned before the Cabinet "to make a short statement and submit himself for examination".[3] This happened on June 21, when Chamberlain, to his vexation, was kept away by an attack of gout.

Milner's view called as yet for no decision. He proposed to raise the matter again in the autumn, if the war were not over before. Meanwhile, as a practical step towards reconstruction, Chamberlain carried a vote of £6,500,000 to finance Milner's

[1] May 31–June 2, 1901.
[2] Dated by Chamberlain, June 3, 1901—circulated to the Cabinet, June 12, 1901.
[3] Chamberlain to Salisbury, June 6, 1901.

plans for the rehabilitation of railways, mines and agriculture in the new colonies.[1]

V

All that summer the Government was under fire over an issue at once miserable and tragic. Conditions in the South African concentration camps, set up by the Army, had become a crying scandal; and the Opposition made the most of it. At the time, Chamberlain was often denounced as the instigator of these camps. It was a lie; but the legend has persisted; and something must be said, here, of his part in the matter.

Concentration, in a phrase of the time, was a natural corollary of devastation. Having burned down the Boer farms, it was the practice of the Army to intern the women and children who had lived in them. For one thing, they could not, in humanity, leave them out on the veld to starve. For another, it was believed that, by interning their families, the burghers in the field would be induced to surrender. This second idea was altogether mistaken. By relieving the burghers of their most anxious responsibilities, the camps enabled them to fight to the bitter end.[2] The humanitarian conception was sounder, but it was largely defeated by the conditions in which the camps were kept; conditions which fostered disease and led to terrible loss of life.

The gravity of the situation was exposed in June by Miss Emily Hobhouse. The Government then sent out a Committee of Ladies under the chairmanship of Mrs. Fawcett. Their report confirmed the worst fears. Congestion, pollution and infection were rife. Some of the camp sites had no proper water supply; and the Boer women themselves, in their ignorance, practised insanitary habits "to an extent which would probably not be credited except by those who have seen it". Worst of all, the supply of doctors and nurses was quite inadequate in face of persistent epidemics.[3]

Until this time the camps had been run entirely by the

---

[1] Hansard, Fourth Series, vol. xcviii. cols. 1454-1493 (August 6, 1901).

[2] In December 1901 Kitchener recognised that this policy was militarily a mistake. Concentration ceased, and the Boer women and children were left to fend for themselves. The wretched state to which they were soon reduced was not the least cause of the eventual submission at Vereeniging. ("*The Times*" *History of the War in South Africa*, vol. v. p. 404.)

[3] Cd. 893, 1901, pp. 1-21.

military. It was not until after the visit of the Fawcett committee that they were transferred to the civilian administration
and thus became, for the first time, Chamberlain's responsibility.
A few extracts from his correspondence with Milner show in
what spirit he grappled this Augean task.

CHAMBERLAIN TO MILNER

October 1, 1901.—Then as to concentration camps, the death rate in
which is causing much anxiety here, have you discussed possibility of
removing them to the coast? Personally I think those in camps, perhaps
with some defined exceptions, might have option to leave them.

November 5.—The mortality in the Concentration Camps has undoubtedly roused deep feeling among people who cannot be classed with
the pro-Boers . . . personally as you know I have always doubted the
wisdom or necessity of this concentration, but, be that as it may, we
ought to give some evidence of exceptional measures. . . .

December 12, 1901.—As regards the camps I am glad to see that its
last returns are a little better. I shall not be happy until you can inform
me that some of them have been broken up and considerable numbers of
their inmates sent to other camps or dispersed.

From the late autumn, when Chamberlain and Milner took
over practical control, the death-rate was rapidly reduced. In
October it had been 344 per 1000. By January it had fallen to
160; and, by the time peace was concluded, it had come down
to 20, a figure well below the ordinary death-rate on the veld.
At Vereeniging, indeed, Botha acknowledged this improvement
and admitted that the burghers had been only too thankful for
British protection of their women and children.[1]

VI

Chamberlain had been unfairly blamed for the tragedy of the
concentration camps. But now he made an undoubted mistake. At the beginning of August he authorised Kitchener to
issue a Banishment Proclamation. This decreed that all Boer

[1] "It is also worth noting that
valuable educational work was carried
out in the camps by British and
Canadian teachers." ("*The Times*"
History of the War in South Africa,
vol. v. p. 405.)

leaders of armed bands, large and small, not surrendering before mid-September, would be banished for life from South Africa. It also warned all ordinary burghers that, if they did not submit by the same date, the cost of maintaining their families would be charged on their property.

The origins and results of this move must be examined. For months past a growing section of opinion, in South Africa and at home, had been calling for sterner measures to put an end to a guerilla, deemed unworthy of the name of war. They wanted political measures which would correspond to the more ruthless tactics already employed in the field. Kitchener and Milner shared this view, and pressed it upon the Government. Kitchener, indeed, went beyond Milner and insisted that "everyone here considers confiscation the only chance of bringing these people to their senses".[1] He also asked for power to threaten still more drastic punishments. Chamberlain regarded these proposals as impracticable and absurd.

CHAMBERLAIN TO BRODRICK

August 20, 1901.—. . . I do not blame him [Kitchener] for these absurd proposals but they show that he was too much occupied with military matters to be able to give his mind to other things, and we poor civilians have therefore to think for him. . . .

It was the last part of this [Kitchener's letter] that we chiefly objected to. We did not believe that they [the Boers] *would* come in . . . and if they did not, we felt that we had no power to carry out any threats of wholesale punishment of a severer kind, and should only make ourselves ridiculous by threatening what we could not perform. I am afraid Lord Kitchener attaches too much importance to "bluff", but it is a very dangerous game when you do not hold the cards.

Despite Chamberlain's objections, Kitchener continued to press for more vigorous political measures; and British opinion in South Africa supported him with growing warmth. It was at last officially expressed by the Government of Natal. At the end of July, the Premier of that colony asked specifically for the banishment of the Boer leaders and the confiscation of the property of the rank and file, unless they laid down their arms

---

[1] *Milner Papers*, vol. ii. p. 257 (Kitchener to Milner, July 4, 1901).

by a certain date.[1] Milner, who was still at home, supported this proposal. His intervention seems to have been decisive with Chamberlain; and on August 7 the Proclamation was issued.[2]

Having taken his decision, Chamberlain held fast to it. As one of his civil servants said:

If he was wrong he was hopelessly wrong. He never hedged. . . .

Just before the recess, he defended the Proclamation vigorously in the House. He blamed the Boer leaders for senselessly prolonging the war, and added:

If we can bring home to these people [the leaders] that they personally will suffer by continuing longer in the field we may—and that is the greatest advantage we can hope for—so influence them as to bring about an immediate end of the war. That is worth trying.[3]

The Boers, however, paid no attention to the Proclamation. They thought it ridiculous. In a series of no less than seven "whereases", they were solemnly informed that they ought to surrender because for all serious and legitimate military purposes they had been annihilated. As a matter of fact, they were almost as numerous and, in their own way, more effectively organised than ever before. Besides they guessed shrewdly that the terms announced on paper would not mean much in practice.

Threats with a time-limit are always dangerous. For military purposes the Proclamation was worse than a fiasco; it was a boomerang. Botha, Steyn and De Wet not only determined to fight on. The threatened penalties gave them a fresh impulse. They struck right and left. Smuts invaded and traversed Cape Colony, stimulating rebellion so that martial law had to be extended to the whole country. Botha attacked the Natal frontier. The British Forces were the victims of frequent "regrettable incidents". At home these setbacks led people to believe that worse might come. Such fears were exaggerated, but the truth is that, until this time, the Boers had been underestimated, physically and morally, both in South Africa and in London. It was not until they faced the third year of war that their fighting qualities were at last fully appreciated.

[1] Cd. 732. July 24, 1901 (Governor of Natal to Colonial Office. Telegram.)
[2] *Ibid.* p. 6.
[3] Hansard, Fourth Series, vol. xcix. cols. 995-1002 (August 15, 1901).

VII

The sorry tragedy of the concentration camps, the fiasco of the Proclamation and the continued reverses in the field combined to produce a revolt of Unionist opinion. It broke out first in *The Times*, during the early autumn; and was soon supported by the whole London press. In the circumstances it is hardly surprising that the public should have lost patience with the Government. The third year of war was beginning; and there was still no end to be seen. The cry of "inefficiency" was raised against the War Office; and there was some substance in the accusation. Kitchener himself was known to have said that many of the mounted reinforcements sent him from England could neither ride nor shoot. Nor did the critics overlook his famous order of the day informing officers that to carry about "kitchen ranges, pianos and harmoniums" was not an aid to pursuit!

The revolt soon spread from the press to the Parliamentary party. Fortunately for Ministers the House would not meet till after the New Year; but letters of protest rained. The following is a good example:

WINSTON CHURCHILL TO CHAMBERLAIN

105 *Mount Street, October* 14, 1901.—*Private.*—I am afraid you will not approve of the series of speeches I am making in the country, if you should happen to see them in the papers; but I should like you to know what my line is.

It is not enough for the government to say: "We have handed the war over to the Military: they must settle it: all we can do is to supply them as they require!" I protest against that view. Nothing can relieve the Govt. of their responsibility. If Kitchener cannot settle the question you will have to interfere.

The situation is not getting better at all, according to every letter I get from South Africa . . .

K. is overworked, exhausts himself on many unimportant details, and is now showing signs of the prolonged strain. There is no plan worth speaking of in the operations except hammer, hammer, at random. The troops, which are numerous everywhere, are overwhelming nowhere. The thousands of superior men are intermingled with and consequently

reduced to the level of the inferior soldiers. The mobility of the Army is
that of the slowest mounted man.

Moreover they are being bucketed to pieces with almost ceaseless
trekking. Remount and Intelligence Departments are both very badly
managed: there is neither bold design nor clear business calculation but
only indiscriminate, methodless and haphazard energy.

How much longer is it going to last?

What I want is that the Govt. should localise, delimit and assign the
functions of the C. in C. in Africa. Should reorganise the Remount and
Intelligence Depts. Should lay the army by for a short period of rest and
refreshment. Should organise a picked force. Should make some sort of
peace: and make sure that we end the matter with the next bitter
weather, whatever happens.

As a Minister, Chamberlain seldom showed much appreciation
of the independence of the press or of Members, save when it was
exercised in support of his own policies. This time he had more
than usual justification for annoyance. For some time past he
had planned to take a much-needed holiday in the West Indies
with Hicks Beach. The state of public feeling now forced him
to abandon this project. Hicks Beach wrote:

So far as our West Indian trip is concerned, I do not see a chance for
it now. Your leaving the country would give rise to more "misconstruc-
tion" than my policy of economy.[1]

The Chancellor, indeed, was so alarmed by the growing
expenditure of the state that he threatened to demand a
December session; a prospect which filled his colleagues with
horror.

In his private talk and correspondence, Chamberlain praised
the *Scotsman*'s rebuke of the "Cockney panic" among the
London papers, and denounced "this periodical fit of pessimistic
shrieking by editors, correspondents and disgruntled M.P.'s
alike". But his censure of mutinous editors and backbenchers
was matched by his drastic strictures on Kitchener's conduct of
the war. He was particularly critical of that General's interventions in politics, as, for instance, when he forced the Cape
Ministers to extend martial law. The following extracts from his

[1] Hicks Beach to Chamberlain, October 2, 1901.

letters to the Secretary for War give some indication of his mood.

CHAMBERLAIN TO BRODRICK

August 24, 1901.—Only K. himself has faith in threats to bring the Boers to their knees. . . . But I beg you to consider with Lord Roberts whether the proper answer to Botha's bluff is not the *corps d'élite* of which we have talked so often and which K. is so slow in forming. It must be a real *corps d'élite*—picked from the whole army— . . . If K. could organise such a force . . . I believe he would do more to bring the war to an end than all the Proclamations that can possibly be devised.

September 17, 1901.—I am much annoyed at Kitchener's proceeding . . . he has no business to threaten the Cape Government. . . . I object to the policy as at present advised but above all I object to the method. Let him stick to his military work and catch Botha or de Wet and leave us to decide political questions.

September 19, 1901.—Your last telegram just received is a sickener. [Botha had cut up Major Gough's force at Blood River Poort.] Surely Botha ought not to have been able to collect a large force without our scouts or spies knowing all about it. I judge that this affair was an attack by Boers not a defence. It is heartrending to find that with inferior numbers they could hold defensive positions against masses of our troops and yet that we are not infrequently surprised and defeated in similar positions. If this goes on I suppose a December session will be certain and then Heaven help us.

By mid-October he could contain himself no longer and made his only serious attempt to intervene in the military conduct of the war. His plan, which he pressed on the Cabinet, the War Office and Milner, fell into two parts. First, he urged the formation of "flying columns" of picked men designed to capture or destroy the Boer leaders. Second, he called for the adoption of Milner's scheme of resuming civilian life and work inside protected areas. His views are best expressed in the following telegram:

CHAMBERLAIN TO MILNER

October 31.—*Secret and Personal.*—When you left I believe we were perfectly agreed as to the military policy which should be pursued, and

you intended to discuss it fully with Lord Kitchener. . . . Your idea,
concurred in by us,[1] was that the drives over large districts were becoming ineffective—that we should endeavour to confine ourselves to areas,
where the resumption of agriculture and industry was most important
and which might be guarded by the Constabulary assisted by block-
houses and by garrisons and bases of supplies at principal centres. That
we should also form mobile columns to be employed in dispersing any
concentrations outside these areas and thus to extend their limits from
time to time.

I do not gather that this has been done. I have no account of any such
protected areas where industry is being resumed on a large scale. The
drives still continue, in many cases with disproportionate results, and
we still employ 200,000 troops and 500 guns to deal with 10,000 [2] men
without any guns at all.

Secondly, I suggested, with Lord Roberts' entire approval, that one or
more flying columns of 1,000 or at most, 2,000 men should be formed
with the special object of catching Steyn, Botha and other leaders. We
are informed that six such bodies have been formed and hitherto they
have failed in their principal purpose. Each man in such a corps should
be specially selected—their baggage should be restricted to what they
can carry on their horses and they should have as many horses as they
can manage. They should, in fact, be more mobile than the Boers. . . .

As the great difficulty will be correct intelligence, they should be
accompanied by scouts in sufficient numbers, probably natives who
would never lose sight of the detachments which are the objects of the
operations. No money should be spared in this part of the business and
large rewards should be offered to all who give information which results
in the surprise and capture of the leaders. We might use this plan, which
I do not think has been fully grasped, to catch one leader, say Botha or
Steyn, and if successful we could then try it with another. We think the
war will never end till the leaders are captured, and the surrender of
one would be more important than all the drives which only secure
unimportant persons.

This telegram precipitated a curious crisis. At the moment
Milner's own cup was full. A natural dictator himself, he found
Kitchener's military dictatorship intolerable. He longed to get

---

[1] This telegram was sent from Whittingehame, where the Colonial Secretary, after speaking at Edin-burgh, was visiting Arthur Balfour.

[2] The Boers, in fact, still had nearly 30,000 men under arms.

down to the work of reconstruction even if the guerilla still flickered on the backveld. But Kitchener would not have it. Accordingly, in his drastic way, Milner decided that Kitchener must be removed to make room for a more amenable General. Chamberlain's telegram reached him in this mood. With only two hours to spare before the courier left, he dashed off the following sweeping letter:

Private and Confidential.—No copy kept.

LADYSMITH,
Nov. 1, 1901.

MY DEAR MR. CHAMBERLAIN—Your long telegram (secret and personal) has just reached me and I have two hours before the mail goes in which to answer it. You will make allowances especially for length, as I have no time to condense my remarks.

I have not in any way altered my views about the conduct of the war since I was in England; and to my lay mind the present methods are not those calculated to bring it most easily to a conclusion, or, assuming that no definite conclusion is possible, to enable us to make the most of the conquered territories while the war is burning itself out. But I do not think that my opinions, frequently expressed, have any weight with the Commander in Chief, nor to be quite frank do I believe that any man's would. . . . He may, under great pressure, appear to bow to instructions from home. But in matters military he will, I am convinced, never take anything but his own line.

The remedy and the only remedy if results seem inadequate is to change the command.[1] The difficulty of this course appears to be that K. does not want to go until he has "finished the war". To remove him, against his will, seems to me, in view of the great services he has undoubtedly rendered, to be next door to an impossibility, and, more than that, what assurance have we that his successor will do better?

Kitchener, be it observed, has not done badly. On the contrary he has done, in some ways, exceedingly well. He is a very able man and his energy is enormous. He has reduced the numbers of the enemy till they are quite insignificant. He has harried the country till there are large tracts in which no enemy can possibly live. He has reduced the supplies and munitions of war to such an extent that it now takes the best of the Boer Generals weeks to collect even a small fighting force.

[1] My italics.—J. A.

The great drawback to him is that he will look at the problem as a purely military one. It is not now purely or even mainly military. . . . He has not the smallest sympathy with the "revival of industry and agriculture". All that is, in his view, something to come "after the war is over". In my view it is more important than the relics of the war.

But as I say no military man will ever take that view. The successor might lack his vigour and genius, without being devoid of his professional narrow-mindedness.

For all that I think, if it can possibly be done without a huge commotion, it would be better to try Lyttelton [General N. G. Lyttelton, G.O.C. Natal], especially if he was distinctly told at starting, that it was the determination of H.M.'s Govt. to restore the British population to the Transvaal, and to protect them in carrying on their work and that the chivying of the remaining Boers was subsidiary to that.

If I may make a suggestion: Is it not possible to tell K. that he is wanted in India. . .? I feel sure we should get on better without him, not because anyone else will conduct the war better, but because someone else may, if put in on that distinct understanding, obstruct the work of reconstruction less. I should not make the suggestion if we had not got Lyttelton. With any other General we might be only out of the frying pan into the fire. But I have seen enough of L. to feel sure that if our relations are put on the right footing to begin with, it will be possible to do *something* in the direction of settling the country tho' perhaps not all I might wish. Under the present regime I can do nothing of importance. . . .

As I read your telegram you wished me to tell you privately the whole of my mind. I have done this with great frankness and in extreme confidence. The other part of the business viz. the *publishable* statement, I will try to send by next mail.

Once more apologizing for a letter written without time to choose or to censor my phrases.—I am, Yours very sincerely,

MILNER.

As soon as he received it, Chamberlain circulated Milner's letter to the Cabinet. There is no doubt that he leaned towards its main argument, but at this stage he made no comment. One section of Ministers held strongly to Milner's views. Another as strongly dissented. Yet others feared that Kitchener's removal would shake public confidence too severely. Salisbury applied all the skill of his dissolvent method of criticism to Milner's proposal.

SALISBURY TO CHAMBERLAIN

November 26, 1901.—Most Confidential.—I have read Milner's letter with care—but I have not derived any clear idea of what policy it is that he wishes to carry out. His letter leaves no impression on the mind except that in some points not clearly indicated he prefers Lyttelton to Kitchener. He does not tell you distinctly what is the evil that K. has done or how L. will do the work better. The counts of the indictment against K. are very vague; the superiority of L. is left to the imagination. It is scarcely possible—not possible—that the change should be affected without conveying to the outside mind the belief that we are blaming K. severely and placing unbounded confidence in L. . . . We must know much more fully in detail what it is that Milner has asked in vain of K. before we make it a ground for superseding K. by a commander chosen by Milner.

If you desire to move in the direction in which Milner is pressing, you must make him set down his demands and—if we approve of them—urge them on K. I do not say that the results of this mode of action will be free from embarrassment, but any other course, adverse to K., seems to me in the present state of affairs impossible. . . .

I am not in the least inferring from your brief note that you are urging any action of this kind: but Milner's letter can hardly be interpreted except in that sense.

The old Prime Minister's negative irony was unanswerable, and Chamberlain reluctantly gave way.

CHAMBERLAIN TO SALISBURY

November 26, 1901.—I agree entirely with your view. Nothing can be done to give the impression that we have lost confidence in Kitchener, but I thought it possible that the India Office might claim him under circumstances that would make his transfer natural.

Reconstruction under arms was a great conception. But it came too late. Kitchener's ponderous strategy was just beginning to yield results. To have changed horses at this point would have been neither prudent nor popular.

Meanwhile the Unionist revolt was dying down. With Parlia-

ment adjourned there could be no debates to feed fuel to its
flames. Moreover, the holiday season approached. On Christmas
Day, indeed, De Wet appeared to inflict the final humiliation of
this depressing year. At Tweefontein he stormed the Yeomanry
Camp and made a clean sweep. But the nation only grumbled.
In comparison with the earlier agitation, the consequences of
Tweefontein were politically negligible.

The final assurance of victory for the public at large, as for
Chamberlain, was the renewed support of the self-governing
Colonies. At the end of November, Canada's offer of a third
fighting contingent, completely equipped, had been accepted. In
mid-December, New Zealand, still outstripping Britain itself in
proportion of sacrifice, added an eighth contingent to those
already sent. Australia would have done the same, but Barton,
the Premier of the new Commonwealth, felt, as a matter of
form, that he should wait until he was asked for troops by
the Imperial Government. At this the Premiers of some of the
states threatened to raise men on their own. The sequel might
have been awkward; but, with his usual contempt for false
punctilio, Chamberlain cut the knot and released the hands of
the Commonwealth Government. Just before Christmas he
cabled that, in view of the prolongation of the war, the Imperial
Government would gladly accept another Australian contingent
of a thousand men. Barton replied at once that Australia would
be proud to send this reinforcement and a larger one if desired.

Once again, in all three Colonies, the men who offered their
services far exceeded the numbers that could be accepted. Yet
these early Colonial contingents were small, even compared to
the slender resources of the countries where they were raised. The
world noted this, but not the spirit which had sent them forth.
But here was the beginning of the process, which, in the lifetime
of many who then volunteered, would make the British Empire a
great military Power in two titanic wars.

CHAPTER LXXVIII

VICTORY AND PEACE

(1902)

CHAMBERLAIN routs the Opposition—Methuen captured—Still more
Colonial Contingents—The National Scouts—"A good judge of
traitors"—The Boers face Defeat—First Peace Feelers—The Dutch
Premier's Mission—Schalk Burger's Ride—The Klerksdorp Conference—Rhodes Dies—Peace Terms and the Cabinet—The Vereeniging Conference—Kitchener *versus* Milner—The Final Terms—
Vereeniging votes "Yes"—Chamberlain and the Boer War.

I

THE House met again on January 9, 1902, for a session destined
to be among the longest in its annals. It opened well for
Chamberlain. At the outset he scored one of the most notable
triumphs in his parliamentary career.

As their main amendment to the Address, Campbell-
Bannerman and his advisers had framed a pious formula,
designed to enable the rival sections of a divided party to present
"a united face". This was its text:

> That this House while prepared to support all proper measures for the
> effective prosecution of the war in South Africa is of opinion that the
> course pursued by your Majesty's Ministers and their attitude with
> regard to a settlement have not conduced to the early termination of the
> war and the establishment of a durable peace.

Chamberlain made devastating play of this amendment,
awkwardly moved and transparent in intent. Who could
reconcile sincerely its two parts? How could pro-Boers vote
honestly for the first part? Or Liberal Imperialists for the
second? He showed that the Boer leaders, by their guerilla

48

tactics, had forced the policy of the concentration camps upon Kitchener. If, according to the general practice of belligerents, we had refused to take care of the women and children, the war might have been over long ago. He quoted Rosebery, Asquith and Grey to prove that the terms of peace advocated by the Liberal Imperialists—all of them supporters both of Kitchener and Milner—were not to be distinguished from those pursued by the Government. Much had been made of the phrase "unconditional surrender", but nothing sinister was intended by it. He implied plainly that Ministers did not bind themselves to the letter of that phrase but wanted only to keep their hands free. They had no thought of imposing vindictive conditions, and were prepared to receive overtures from any Boer quarter found competent to treat. They were bent on securing a magnanimous peace. But, if it was to be a solid peace also, it must be preceded by an undisputed victory.[1]

The manner of this speech claims our attention. No separate passage or sentence in it was remarkable. It will not bear quotation. He had relied wholly on power of argument expressed in ordinary words. And yet it was a triumph. The truth is that, in parliamentary speaking, he had arrived at a perfection of efficiency, more telling than any oratorical flight.

The speech worked on the Opposition like a "break-through" by a charge of cavalry. The defenders fell back in different directions. Lloyd George exposed the sham of the amendment and covered his own leader with ridicule. Along with his Radical following and with the Irish members, he abstained in contempt. The Liberal Imperialists likewise abstained—Asquith, Grey and Haldane among them. They could see no sufficient difference between the Government's policy and their own. Thus it happened that the official amendment which was to have manœuvred all the sections of the Opposition into one lobby was defeated by 333 votes to 123—a majority of 210.

From the beginning Chamberlain had had to fight a war on two fronts; against the Boers in Africa and against the Opposition at home. Now the Opposition had been routed; and, while the war lasted, they would not return to the attack.

[1] Hansard, Fourth Series, vol. ci. cols. 360-383 (January 20, 1902).

II

On the same day that Chamberlain routed the Opposition, he wrote to Milner in an optimistic strain. The final sentences, quoted here, confirm that, by "unconditional surrender", he meant nothing but absolute acceptance of annexation.

CHAMBERLAIN TO MILNER

January 20, 1902.—. . . I do not know whether strain which you indicate affects your view of the situation but in any case we are much more optimistic here than you appear to be. The Session has opened and on the whole I think we are stronger than ever . . . . As far as I can learn, the representatives of the Boers in this country and in Holland are almost in despair. They know that the game is up and, although they may not openly say so, they have practically admitted their defeat. . . . There seems to be a flavour of mediaeval cruelty about unconditional surrender from which men shrink, but after all they mean the same thing as we do. . . . You may rely upon me to refuse any terms which seem likely to embarrass us hereafter.

This optimism was premature. The most stinging reverse of the war was still to come. On March 7, De La Rey cut up a British mounted column at Tweebosch, capturing a senior general, Lord Methuen. Hopes of an early peace again receded; and for a few days Chamberlain relapsed into his old depression.

CHAMBERLAIN TO MILNER

March 12, 1902.—I am at least as anxious as you are to see the civil administration substituted for the Military Dictatorship, but as you yourself say, the latter seems to be necessary and it is impossible for me here to attempt to put a limit to it. Our late reverses, and especially the disastrous misfortune of Lord Methuen, seem to throw much further off than I had hoped the prospect of something like a satisfactory settlement. We have therefore to make the best of the situation and I cordially recognise and approve your determination not to allow any differences of opinion to develop into active antagonism or to become known to the outside public. . . . On the whole I see nothing for it but patience and a stiff upper lip. . . .

But Chamberlain's depression, like the nation's, soon passed. The humiliation of Methuen's capture stung the British people and the whole Empire to renewed activity. It steeled their determination to make an end of it. From New Zealand, Seddon offered a tenth contingent of 1000 men. It was gratefully accepted; and Chamberlain then invited both Canada and Australia to follow this example. Both responded and, within a week, had promised to raise fresh contingents of 2000 men each.

Meanwhile another unexpected element had rallied to the British flag and brought a powerful reinforcement. Growing numbers of Boers were becoming convinced that to prolong the struggle was to court race-suicide. Many, indeed, felt this so strongly that they were prepared to fight in the British Army against their own kith and kin in order to hasten the restoration of peace. The line between "collaboration" and treason is not easily drawn; and the employment of these National Scouts, as they were called, was deeply resented by the pro-Boers at home. It led to a bitter scene in the House, when Chamberlain exacted a cutting revenge for the insults he had so often endured at the hands of the Irish Nationalists.

MR. CHAMBERLAIN: "At this moment we have between 3,000 and 4,000 of these men, Boers, burghers, fighting with us against the burghers in the field. You may read the accounts of what they are doing in almost every telegram. . . . And you may read it in the very interesting communication which General Vilonel has addressed I think to De Wet or to Louis Botha, in which he says that the enemies of the country are those who are continuing a hopeless struggle."

MR. DILLON: "Yes, but he is a traitor." (*Cheers.*)

MR. CHAMBERLAIN: "No. The hon. gentleman is a good judge of traitors." (*Loud cheers.*)

MR. DILLON (*rising amid loud Nationalist cheers*): "I want to know, Sir, whether that is a parliamentary expression."

THE SPEAKER: "The hon. member himself interrupted the right hon. gentleman by crying out that the soldiers who were serving under the British Crown were traitors. (*Ministerial cheers.*) I deprecate interruptions; I deprecate retorts. If the hon. gentleman will not interrupt he will not be subjected to retorts."

MR. DILLON: "Then I desire to say that the right hon. gentleman is a damned liar." [1]

[1] Hansard, Fourth Series, vol. cv. cols. 577-595 (March 20, 1902).

Forthwith, by a majority of 200, Dillon was suspended from
the service of the House. As he passed down the floor a
number of his compatriots cheered and waved their hats. Then
Chamberlain was heard again. "I was commenting when I was
interrupted . . ."

This incident was much discussed at the time. It is a good
example of Chamberlain's caustic irony; but we have recorded
it here for another reason. It marked a point in parliamentary
history. Sixteen years after the first Home Rule conflict, it was
the last of many bitter exchanges between Chamberlain and the
Irish members.

Methuen's capture was the worst affair of its kind. It was also
the last. The Boers could not follow up their success. For some
weeks now, Kitchener's plan of continuous drives within his
perfected system of block-houses had been in full operation.
The main chains of forts, linked together by barbed wire,
secured the uninterrupted working of the railways. The subsidiary cross-country chains subdivided the veld into manage-
able compartments. Within these barbed-wire pens mounted
columns harassed the commandos, wore down their numbers
and swept away their supplies. The Boers were in fact besieged
upon the veld; and the lines of circumvallation had been completed. There was no hope of relief. Stocks of food and munitions
were running out. Casualties could no longer be made good.
Desertions were increasing. In a strict military view, the end had
come. As Napoleon had said, an army which cannot reinforce
itself must perish.

Botha and many of his colleagues recognised the gravity of
their situation. The offer of fresh contingents from the Colonies
was their warning. Methuen's capture was their opportunity.
They could never hope to secure such a success again. Now,
therefore, was the time, while they still enjoyed some prestige
from this last victory, to sue for an honourable peace. British
Ministers might speak of "unconditional surrender", but Botha
shrewdly conjectured that they would still be ready to treat in
the spirit of the terms offered at Middelburg.

III

Since the time of those abortive negotiations, there had been some curious peace feelers. One had been put forward as early as July 1901.

SALISBURY TO CHAMBERLAIN

Downing Street, S.W., July 28, 1901.—You will remember that on Friday week I spoke to you about a communication from Rosebery—proposing to open negotiations through a German gentleman who had been introduced to him by an unnamed M.P. in whom he had confidence. The only salient point in his communication was hostility to Milner. He hinted at more conciliatory terms of peace but specified nothing. I did not write to him after having spoken to you; I did not understand him to wish it. But on Thursday I received a letter from him asking if there was any answer. I replied with an apology for not having answered before—and saying that under existing circumstances it was better to adhere to the beaten track of negotiation.

Rosebery's German informant was Herr Lippert, the former holder of Kruger's dynamite concession in the Transvaal and then in touch both with the Boer leaders in Holland and with pro-Boer advocates in London. Nothing could result from this sort of approach; nor from similar advances by Sir Thomas Lipton and Mr. Leo Weinthal. But they were straws in the wind.

Six months passed. Then Rosebery, at Chesterfield, suggested that the first step to peace might be "an apparently casual meeting of two travellers in a neutral inn". Dr. Kuyper, the Dutch Premier, was impressed by this passage, and sounded ex-President Kruger and other Boer delegates in exile. He represented that intervention by any European Power on their behalf was now totally excluded. Had not the time come to treat? Encouraged by their response, Kuyper paid a short and discreet visit to London. He made no official *démarche*; but on January 25, after his return, the Netherlands Minister called at the Foreign Office and formally proposed mediation. His suggestion was that some of the Boer delegates in Holland should be allowed to go to South Africa to seek full powers from the burghers in the field to undertake peace negotiations in Europe.

These would be held under the auspices of the Dutch Government, which would confine itself to keeping the parties in touch.

Lansdowne very courteously replied that no foreign intervention could be accepted; that the Boer delegates in Europe had
no adequate status; and that any peace negotiations must take
place not in Europe but in South Africa itself. "The quickest and
most satisfactory means of arranging a settlement would be by
direct communication between the leaders of the Boer Forces
in South Africa and the Commander-in-Chief of His Majesty's
Forces." [1]

But the Cabinet did not let the matter rest there. A few weeks
later Kitchener was authorised to hint skilfully to his opponents
that the door to peace stood open. A note to this effect was
forwarded without comment to the Transvaal leaders. Curiously
enough this was done on March 7, the very day of Methuen's
capture, still unknown to Kitchener. Like Chamberlain in
London, Kitchener feared that this reverse would "of course put
off the end of the war". Not so. Schalk Burger, the Acting President of the Transvaal, replied to Kitchener's message that he
was ready to make peace proposals but wished first to consult
President Steyn of the Free State. He asked, therefore, for a safe
conduct through the British lines and back. This was readily
granted; and, on March 22, Schalk Burger rode through our lines
to Kroonstadt to communicate with the Free Staters. They disliked his procedure, but there could be no question of holding off.

As a result of the meeting in Kroonstadt, delegates of both
Republics came together at Klerksdorp, on April 9, to discuss the
proposals which they would lay before Kitchener.

IV

At this juncture, by a solemn coincidence, Cecil Rhodes died
at Muizenberg.[2] The prophet of a United British South Africa
would never see the fulfilment of his vision. But he knew that
it was at hand. His friend Lord Grey wrote to Chamberlain:

He did look forward to helping you to carry out your policy of fusing
the British and Dutch into one people.[3]

[1] January 29, 1902 (Cd. 906).   [3] Grey to Chamberlain, March 31,
[2] March 26, 1902.   1902.

The majestic simplicity of Rhodes' burial in the Matoppos, and the publication of his will, drawn in the spirit of an Emperor, caught the imagination of the world. At the time Chamberlain wrote this judgment:

CHAMBERLAIN TO COLLINGS

Highbury, March 27, 1902.—. . . I agree with you about Rhodes. He was a great man in his way and not unhappy in his death. Nothing can take from him the credit of having kept Rhodesia for the British Empire, and posterity will think of this long after they have forgotten the mistake of the Raid.

V

The prospect of peace negotiations revealed certain differences of opinion in the British camp. Kitchener and three-quarters of the Cabinet, with Hicks Beach at their head, were prepared to make wide concessions to bring the war to an end. The General longed to escape to the Indian command. The Chancellor was obsessed by the need to reduce expenditure. Other Ministers, shaken by the Unionist revolt in the autumn, dared not contemplate a prolongation of hostilities. The King sympathised with their view. At the other end of the scale, Milner held out for the spirit and the letter of "unconditional surrender".

Between these two extremes Chamberlain and Salisbury kept the balance. Throughout the seven weeks of negotiation leading up to the signature of the treaty they worked in close alliance. On the whole they inclined to Milner's attitude, though caring less for verbal consistency. They had always meant to grant generous terms but were equally determined not to make concessions which would make their victory less complete. The following exchange of letters gives some idea both of the pressures to which they were subjected and of the intimacy of their alliance.

SALISBURY AND CHAMBERLAIN

Salisbury to J. C.—March 29, 1902.—I have a letter from Beach in which he forecasts the possibility of proposals of some kind coming by telegraph in the next few days and strongly urges that "if they do, at whatever inconvenience to ourselves, a Cabinet will be summoned to consider the matter before any reply is sent". This seems to me [a] matter of course—but as he has written I send a line to warn you of the possibility, so as to make the inconvenience of which he speaks as small as possible. . . .

I do not myself see the possibility of an early issue. The King is in a fuss about the matter and talks about the length of the war emulating the thirty years war in Germany. I assured him of your pacific desires— if peace could be obtained without sacrificing the main object of the war.

J. C. to Salisbury—April 1.—. . . The King with his Coronation and Beach with his Budget are both too eager for "peace of a sort". I have spoken several times to the King and thought each time that I had satisfied him that while we were all most anxious to finish the War, nothing would be more dangerous for the Country and for his own popularity than that any responsible person should appear ready to sacrifice essential points and show weakness at this stage.

I have an idea that the Rosebery clique, and perhaps Rosebery himself, have been assuring him that an honourable peace was possible if only we were rid of Milner—and perhaps—although he did not say so—of the Colonial Secretary.

Chamberlain's attitude to the peace negotiations was settled in the second week of April. He would not seriously depart from it. The inwardness of his mind is revealed in the following letter, written on the eve of Kitchener's first meeting with the Boer leaders.

CHAMBERLAIN TO MILNER

April 9, 1902.—. . . I imagine that before this reaches you the peace negotiations—if that is the right name for them—will have been undertaken and probably concluded. My expectation is that the terms offered by the Boers will be on the face of them impracticable. If, however, they were moderate and in the main satisfactory we should find ourselves in a difficult position if they were broken off on what would appear to be a detail. Personally I believe, as I have always done, that anything short of unconditional surrender will be most dangerous and may lead to further trouble but this is not the opinion of everyone. . . .

Money alone ought certainly not to be an obstacle to peace. . . .

Amnesty is more difficult. . . . I do not suppose that in any case we should wish to press hardly upon the rebels who had fought fairly. . . . We might give the most positive assurance as to our intentions in regard to ultimate colonial self-government, but it seems to me that it would be impossible and in any case most dangerous to fix an exact date when free institutions should come into operation.

This letter is important. It lays down for the first time the broad principles on which the final agreement would be based. Money was not to be an obstacle. Over amnesty there was room for a compromise short of proclaiming complete impunity for rebellion. As to self-government, Chamberlain was ready to promise its ultimate restoration, though refusing to bind himself to a date for its introduction.

VI

As Chamberlain had foretold, the Boer representatives began, for form's sake, by advancing impossible proposals. They demanded the independence of the Republics but offered to concede franchise for Uitlanders, equality of languages, dismantling of forts, and arbitration excluding European interference. These proposals closely resembled those which Chamberlain himself had urged on Kruger in the autumn of 1899; but the Boers could not hope to obtain, in the hour of defeat, the conditions which Britain had once put forward to avoid the war. Chamberlain had already written to Brodrick:

The only instruction we can give at this time is a negative one— that is to say that they [Milner and Kitchener] are not to listen to any proposals which do not accept the annexation as final.[1]

The Boer leaders, however, declared that they were not empowered to accept this overriding condition. They could not surrender independence and accept annexation without first consulting the burghers in the field. Accordingly, they asked for an armistice for that very purpose. Meanwhile they pressed for a statement of the terms, which they would be granted, if they relinquished independence.[2]

[1] April 11. Chamberlain to Brodrick, transmitted to Pretoria, on April 13. (Cd. 1096) Brodrick to Kitchener.

[2] Cd. 1096, April 14, 1902 (Kitchener to Secretary for War).

This was the crux of the business, as the whole Cabinet knew. Nor was the answer easy to give. Britain's general intention would have to be made known, but Ministers naturally wanted to reserve the discussion of details until the Boers had abandoned hostilities. The matter was considered at two successive Cabinets. For the second, Chamberlain prepared a telegram which was to prove decisive. The draft in his own handwriting still exists. With only two or three slight alterations in phrasing, it was adopted as it stood and dispatched to Kitchener in the name of the Secretary for War. Its theme was that the British Government, though disappointed by the delay of the Boer leaders in renouncing independence, still adhered to the spirit of the Middelburg terms. One passage read as follows:

We are, however, as we have been from the first, anxious to spare the effusion of further blood, and to hasten the restoration of peace and prosperity to the Countries afflicted by the war, and you and Lord Milner are therefore authorised to refer the Boer leaders to the offer made by you to General Botha more than twelve months ago, and to inform them that although the subsequent great reduction in the strength of the forces opposed to us and the additional sacrifices thrown upon us by the refusal of that offer would justify us in imposing far more onerous terms, we are still prepared, in the hope of a permanent peace and reconciliation, to accept a general surrender on the lines of that offer, but with such modifications in detail as may be agreed upon mutually.[1]

The same day a similar telegram was sent to Milner. It contained an important reservation also approved by the Cabinet.

In further discussion with the Boer leaders you should avoid showing your hand, as far as possible, while they remain absolutely unpledged. The concessions we are willing to make . . . are very great and represent I think the extreme limit.

On the main difference between Milner and Kitchener, the Cabinet decided for Milner.

[1] Sent through Brodrick to Kitchener immediately after the Cabinet of April 16. It is a mistake to regard this document as a paraphrase of Milner's mind. A comparison with the High Commissioner's suggestions will show a wide difference in tone (see *Milner Papers*, vol. ii. pp. 334-335). The remark that the reduction of Boer strength would justify "more onerous terms" is adopted from Milner. But the main point is that the Middelburg offer should be the basis of the new agreement. This had been suggested by Chamberlain himself to Milner in a cable of April 13.

No date can be fixed for the introduction of self-government. It is
our interest as well as our desire that it shall be as early as possible.[1]

That Chamberlain was in earnest in drafting this last sentence was shown a few days later when he cabled to Milner: "Would it be possible from the first to nominate such men as Botha and De La Rey on Executive Council?"[2] But Milner regarded this as evidence of what he once described as Chamberlain's "incorrigible optimism".

VII

The Boer representatives left Pretoria on April 18, 1902, to convene the conference which was to decide their nation's fate. Thirty delegates were to be elected to it from each of the Republics. Kitchener had refused a full armistice; but the leaders were given every facility for consulting the scattered commandos; and the railway and telegraph were placed at their disposal. Smuts, for instance, was summoned from six hundred miles away in Cape Colony and joined the conference by gun-boat and train. Apart from these immunities, the war pounded on until the conference itself assembled. Seldom in history can elections have been conducted in such circumstances.

By mid-May the election was over, and the delegates met at Vereeniging, a Transvaal village just across the river from the Free State. The spokesmen of each Republic camped separately, under canvas, on their respective sides of a hollow square. In the middle stood a larger tent for the plenary sessions of the conference. There were bitter and tragic dissensions between the leaders of the Free State and of the Transvaal. At the outset it had been the Transvaal's quarrel; but now the Free Staters, with Steyn and De Wet at their head, were the diehards. The moderates were mostly in the Transvaal tents.

The opening debates at Vereeniging lasted through three days and went on till late at night. On the Transvaal side, Botha led the case for peace even at the cost of accepting the hard fact of annexation. He argued that casualties and lack of supplies would in any case soon compel surrender without terms. More and more burghers would break away; and in the end more

---

[1] Chamberlain to Milner, April 16 (*Milner Papers*, vol. ii. pp. 335-336). [2] Chamberlain to Milner, April 19, 1902.

Boers might be fighting with the British than against them. Schalk Burger then explained that there was no longer any hope of foreign intervention; and Smuts admitted that there was no prospect of a general revolt in Cape Colony.

On the Free State side, Steyn was too ill to exert his full influence, but De Wet stood for resistance to the death. Yet even he had to admit that he was guided in this course not by facts but by faith. It was a war of religion. Others replied that it was a war of miscalculation. They had presumed too much on the sanction of God. "We can understand the answer God has given to our prayer—that prayer which we offered with the Mausers in our hands when the war began." It was left to De La Rey to reach to the heart of the matter. As yet he had reserved himself in the debate. Now he said in his quiet grave voice, "There has been talk about fighting to the bitter end, but has not the bitter end already come?" [1]

On the third day the delegates resolved to send a deputation of five men to British headquarters. They were instructed to ask for a limited independence but they were now also empowered to discuss any other basis of peace. The five men chosen for the task were Botha, De La Rey, De Wet, and the two lawyers Smuts and Hertzog.

While the delegates wrestled at Vereeniging, Chamberlain spoke in Birmingham with unrelenting firmness. He hushed his vast and eager audience when he said of the peace negotiations, "I am hopeful but I am not sanguine". Then, as he went on, the cheers came like crashes of artillery:

One thing you may be assured of. So long as this Government lasts the mistake of Majuba will not be repeated. (*Great cheering.*) . . . The main lines are settled. As far as we are concerned they are settled for all time. (*Great cheering.*) We think we interpret the opinion of this people when we say that, although we are not vindictive, although the idea of revenge upon those who have opposed us does not enter our heads, yet we recognise that we are trustees in this war as well as principals. . . . We owe something to those self-governing colonies who have come to our aid in this matter. . . . We owe something to ourselves, something to this people which has borne so many sacrifices

---

[1] De Wet, *Three Years' War*, p. 429.

with such great cheerfulness; something to the men who have died for their country. We owe it to all of these that their sacrifices shall not be in vain. Never again shall there be a chance of a renewal of this conflict.[1]

It was the harsh strain of the conqueror, but it had its purpose. Over the heads of his Birmingham audience, Chamberlain had spoken to the delegates at Vereeniging.

VIII

The scene now shifts to Pretoria. There the Boer plenipotentiaries began by pleading for limited independence with British control of foreign relations, and Home Rule for the Rand. They were told at once that these proposals had no hope of acceptance. Kitchener said bluntly that they would mean "war again in a year". At Milner's suggestion the parties then settled down to draft a document excluding independence, which might be put to the burghers for a "Yes" or "No" vote.

This was no easy task. Over two main issues, amnesty and money, the negotiations came near to breakdown. The Boer leaders could not in honour abandon their allies, the rebels of the Cape and Natal, to the mercies of the courts martial. Nor could they hope to preserve their political influence if they signed a treaty which did not provide for the repayment of war debts due to their own followers. On this score, indeed, they asked for a high figure—£3,000,000.

On both these points Kitchener sympathised with the Boers. He liked them as men. He wished to seem magnanimous in victory. Above all he wanted to leave South Africa and dreaded a renewal of the war. Milner took a sterner view. He was convinced that the Boers would never fight again, and saw no need to make any concessions. He remembered, too, that while Kitchener rested on his laurels at Simla, he would have to carry out the treaty in South Africa. Accordingly, he aimed at reducing the Boers to a position where they could not interrupt the work of reconstruction during the necessarily brief but decisive period of Crown Colony rule.

This difference of approach ran so deep that it sometimes seemed to the Cabinet as if the real contest was not between the

---

[1] Birmingham, May 16, 1902 (*Birmingham Post*).

Boer and the British delegations, but between Kitchener and Milner. It did not show at the conference table, but it emerged clearly from the telegrams.

MILNER TO CHAMBERLAIN

May 21.—The negotiations . . . have now taken a turn for the worse and the Boers are making what appear to me preposterous proposals. I am in a weak position as Kitchener does not always support me even in the presence of Boers.

May 21.— . . . Clause II [war-debts to burghers] is detestable and in my opinion in the nature of an audacious try-on. I fought hard, but unsupported, to induce them to drop it or at least not to seek to advance upon original Million [the Middelburg figure]. As the clause stands we shall be virtually paying for conduct of war against us. . . . I foresee that we are not by any means at the end of their dodges. . . .

May 24.—. . . It is not merely a question of money. Of all ways of giving money this is the worst. I should attach more weight to Kitchener's view that it is vital to peace, if he had not used the same argument with regard to every other Boer demand to which I especially objected. . . .

Most of the Cabinet felt like Kitchener. Chamberlain, for his part, defended his lieutenant, though often not wholly agreeing. But he insisted that there must not be a breakdown over money:

CHAMBERLAIN TO MILNER

May 23.—Cabinet has not met but I send you my personal impression on terms which appear satisfactory on the whole. . . . In accordance with my views in previous telegrams, I do not think a mere question of money should prevent termination of war which costs more than a million per week. . . .

May 23.—(later). Cabinet had the suggested terms of surrender before them at meeting today and agree that they are an improvement on terms offered to Botha, 7th March, 1901.

Between them, Chamberlain and Milner worked out a financial solution. There was to be no formal acceptance of liability for the burghers' war debts, but these were to rank, in practice, for compensation with other war losses. Beyond this, the Boers were to receive a free grant of £3,000,000 to restore homeless or ruined burghers to their homes and means of livelihood. Loans on easy terms were also to be advanced for the same purpose.

The generosity of this financial solution was matched by the remaining terms. The Dutch language was to be used where desired in the schools and courts. Representative institutions were to be established, as soon as circumstances allowed, as a first step towards the restoration of self-government. In return, the Boers were asked to renounce their old independence and embrace a new allegiance. By a collateral understanding with the Cape and Natal Governments, it was further agreed that no rebels would suffer more than disfranchisement for clean treason and that in no case would the death penalty be imposed.

The burgher forces in the field will forthwith lay down their arms . . . and desist from any further resistance to the authority of His Majesty King Edward VII whom they recognise as their lawful sovereign.

Chamberlain telegraphed these terms to Pretoria on May 27. They represented the British Government's last word to be taken or left. On this Kitchener and Milner were already at one. They must now have "a definite answer to an unalterable proposal". Accordingly, the terms were read next day to the Boer delegates, with the request that the burghers at Vereeniging should vote upon them "Yes" or "No". This procedure was accepted; and Milner telegraphed to Chamberlain:

They asked us to give them until Saturday night for their answer, to which we agreed. We then shook hands and parted.[1]

The burghers at Vereeniging had the last three days of May to decide between these terms of peace and suicidal resistance. Steyn, spent but still intransigent, inveighed against acceptance, resigned his Presidency and went away. But De La Rey compelled his comrades to face up to the inevitable when he said "You may say what you will, resolve what you will; but whatever you do, here, in this meeting, is the end of the war".

It was plain enough that the last hope of united resistance was dead. On the morning of the final day De Wet rallied to

[1] Cd. 1096, May 28, 1902.

Botha, and declared for unity and peace. That settled it. Of the sixty delegates in the conference tent, only six voted "No".

Late on that Saturday night, May 31, 1902, the Boer representatives arrived at Kitchener's house in Pretoria. Milner had been summoned. In silence, just before eleven o'clock, the Treaty of Vereeniging was signed. The war was over.

IX

Next day, the first of June, was one of relief and rejoicing for Britain and the whole Empire. The long struggle was ended at last. It had cost some £220,000,000 and more than 20,000 lives. These were high figures by the standards of the time; but the victory was cheap at the price. Two new Colonies had been brought within the circle of the Crown; and one of them contained the richest gold mines in the world. Above all, the foundations had been laid upon which a new British nation would be built; the union of all South Africa up to the Zambesi.

Chamberlain was the chief architect of this work. Milner had been his indispensable adviser and executive; Roberts and Kitchener his swords; Rhodes, in some ways, his prophet. Each had played a great part, but neither they nor his colleagues in the Cabinet could have won through without him. It was his firm yet conciliatory leadership which had kept public opinion staunch through all delays and disappointments. It was his imaginative vision which had drawn the self-governing Colonies into the struggle to make it something more creative than a mere war of colonial expansion. Not least, it was his tactical genius and relentless determination which had forced through the Khaki Election at the critical moment. Thanks to that stroke, the Government had been upheld by a powerful majority through all the inevitable vicissitudes of war. For once, the end had justified the means.

It has sometimes been said that, in his conduct of South African affairs, Chamberlain allowed matters with Kruger to come to a head before our military preparations were equal to a war. There is a grain of truth in this criticism, though it may be doubted whether some such discrepancy can ever be avoided under our easy-going dispensation. Yet, if Chamberlain miscalculated on this point, it was a fortunate miscalculation. The reverses on the veld led to far-reaching Army Reforms. They were not perhaps far-reaching enough; but, without them, we should have faced the German Army, twelve years later, in Crimean order. Above all, it was well for the Empire that we did not delay conclusions with the Boers until 1914.

Chamberlain received the news that Vereeniging had voted for peace late on the night of May 31. The details of the Treaty were not available at Prince's Gardens until next day. At the time he only said that he was "satisfied", but we can guess the relief that he must have felt. For six years, from the time of the Jameson Raid, he had carried his political life in his hands. Had he failed in South Africa, his political ruin must have been final; and, in the eyes of his enemies, this would almost have compensated for national defeat itself. Now, at last, the ship of his policy was safe in harbour. Bitterness would remain, but it could no longer undo his work.

Congratulations rained upon him. The most significant politically was the letter which we print below. It was from John Hay, the American Secretary of State and a staunch friend of the Chamberlain household:

June 15th.

MY DEAR CHAMBERLAIN—I have little time at my disposal and write very few letters. My congratulations over the return of peace are therefore belated, but are none the less cordial. I think nobody out of England has heard the good news with more genuine gratification than I have felt. Great Britain once more has wrought a great work for the world —and she is too wise to complain of blindness and ingratitude. These are in the day's work.

I have myself learned in the last few years that in politics the lower motive is the one more immediately effective. But in the long run it is an immense advantage to have taken the long view and to have adhered to it in spite of flurries and squalls.

Once more I congratulate you and your colleagues who have brought this great task to completion. I shall always be glad to remember— during what remains to me of life—that some of the men who did the work were my friends. My wife sends her regards to Mrs. Chamberlain and I am always faithfully yours,

JOHN HAY.

Chamberlain's papers contain little record of his own reflections at this time. But all his actions in the months to come suggest that he came out of the war with a new issue dominant in his mind. The struggle with the Boers had offered an unprecedented example of Imperial Unity in action. Was that unity now to be dissolved or could a man devise some means of giving it permanent expression? The reconstruction of South Africa would engross his main energies for some months to come; but already, as often before in his life, we see him moving from a great to a still greater task. As he wrote to one of his congratulators after the Treaty of Vereeniging: "Now a new chapter begins—not a very easy one to write".

CHAPTER LXXIX

THE AFTERMATH—A GREAT GESTURE—CHAMBERLAIN AND THE BOER GENERALS

(1902)

MILNER's Task and Chamberlain's—"A Charter of South African reconstruction"—Chamberlain decides to Visit South Africa—Mission of the Boer Generals—The Naval Review Incident—The Generals and Kruger—A New Peace Treaty?—"I shall keep them kicking their heels in London"—The Generals Climb Down—Their Conference with Chamberlain—His Attitude Generally Approved—The "Appeal to the civilised world"—An Unsuccessful Lecture Tour —"Kruger's millions"—Chamberlain Rebukes the Generals—His Speech in the House and Botha's Change of Heart.

I

THE reconstruction of South Africa after the Boer War remains one of the greatest achievements in the history of British Imperialism. Milner had laid his plans at an early date. He had discussed them in detail with Chamberlain, and their significance had been carefully explained to the responsible officials at the Colonial Office. A strong organisation had been created in South Africa; the right men had been chosen for the jobs to be done; and both the system and the individuals who worked it had been tested in the peculiar circumstances of the guerilla war.

So long, indeed, as the guerilla had lasted, the work of the civil government had been repeatedly frustrated by the proceedings of the military. Theirs had been the first priority; but Milner, though often chafing at their abuse of it, had not wasted his time. His administrative machine was in working order; and, as soon as the peace was signed, the reconstruction of a devastated country went forward at top speed.

The details of the story belong to Milner's life more than to

Chamberlain's. The plans were Milner's for the most part; but on Chamberlain lay the responsibility of approving them or disapproving, of ensuring their conformity with the Government's wider policies, and of obtaining the funds for their fulfilment. It was also his part to secure the indispensable support of the Cabinet, of the House of Commons, and of public opinion.

Milner knew these things better than anyone, and recognised them frankly. The following telegram shows how much he relied on Chamberlain's support.

MILNER TO CHAMBERLAIN
(Telegram)

June 10, 1902.—*Private and Personal.*—. . . My sole reliance is on you personally for obtaining the amount of loan which we require for our purposes. *The Treasury is certain to try and pinch us and if this is done it will be an irretrievable mistake.* The next year or eighteen months may well decide the whole future. Our aim should be to get on as fast as possible with all recuperative work. This will both keep up prestige of Government and help to keep in this country thousands of splendid and willing British settlers who are anxious to find employment here. . . .

The Treasury is always on the alert to cut down irrespective of requirements and consequences, and unless you take the matter up personally I am greatly afraid that they will cripple us.

To avoid giving offence to the Chancellor, Chamberlain excised the words shown above in italics and circulated the telegram to the Cabinet. Meanwhile he telegraphed to Milner:

CHAMBERLAIN TO MILNER

June 10, 1902.—*Private and Secret.*—. . . I will do my best and hope to succeed.

This exchange of telegrams provides, perhaps, the best epitome of the relationship between these two great Empire-builders.

II

On July 29 Chamberlain sketched the broad outline of his plans in a speech which still reads like a charter of South African reconstruction. It was his first appearance in the House since a serious cab accident suffered a few days earlier, and the

natural sympathy with which he was received was sustained,
throughout the debate, by his generous and forward-looking
declarations. Even Labouchere congratulated him on "the conciliatory tone of his speech".[1]

He compressed into a few lines the immense problem
confronting Britain in South Africa.

> . . . A more tremendous task was never placed on a Government
> than that connected with the present condition of things in South
> Africa—to evolve order out of what has hitherto been chaos, to bury
> the animosities of the past, which we regret as much as any on the
> other side can do; to restore the country to a condition of prosperity
> which, we are confident enough to believe, will be greater than any that
> has been known in its past history; to carry out all that is required to
> establish a new Administration; to build up Courts of justice; to secure
> sympathy between those who hitherto have been bitterly opposed;
> to repatriate the greater part of the Boer population; to restore to their
> homes those settlers who were refugees from the country, and to re-
> arrange a system of taxation. . . . To do all these things, and to do
> them all . . . at once, is a task so great that we may well solicit all
> the assistance that hon. members opposite can give us. . . .

While the war lasted, Chamberlain's attitude towards the
Boers had been intransigent. But with victory, clemency and
conciliation became his watchwords. He still maintained, indeed, that the unpopular Banishment Proclamation had been
justified as a war measure; but he now made it perfectly clear
that he had no intention of proceeding against any of those who
were directly touched by it. The sole discriminatory power
which he reserved for the Government was that of deporting or
excluding from South Africa "persons who may by their actions
show themselves to be undesirable citizens". This was aimed
chiefly at the irreconcilables who had fled to Holland with
Kruger. It was applied with studied moderation; and the
few who suffered under the ban received but little sympathy
from Boer opinion, which accepted the inevitability and the
statesmanship, if not always the justice, of Vereeniging.

The most urgent problem confronting Chamberlain and
Milner was the resettlement of the enemy. Thousands of

---

[1] Hansard, Fourth Series, vol. cxii. col. 36 (July 29, 1902).

prisoners of war were interned in British possessions from Ceylon to the West Indies, and a still larger burgher population remained in the South African concentration camps. The first aim and interest of the British Government was to return these people to their homes; but many material difficulties had first to be overcome. The prisoners and internees could not simply be turned out on to the veld to rebuild their burnt farmsteads with bare hands, amid a hostile native population. The essentials of life had first to be provided—seed, ploughs, oxen, and sufficient food to support life until the first harvest. The purchase of these essentials was financed by the British Government. But it was left to local commissions of Boers to assess, assemble and distribute the requirements of their several districts. The rate of Boer repatriation and resettlement was thus made to depend upon the speed and success with which the Boer commissioners discharged their functions.

From the practical tasks of resettlement and repatriation Chamberlain went on to define the Government's plans for the constitutional development of the former Republics.

. . . We are entitled under the terms of surrender to establish and we have established at the present moment a Crown colony government of the strictest form and character. It is a government which is carried on by the Governor . . . as the Chairman and President of the Executive Council and of the Legislative Council, in which he has the assistance of certain officials who constitute with him the Executive Government. That is the first step. But we have always, from the first, declared that that was only the first step, that we should go on gradually, and that the next advance would be to add to the official element a non-official element which would be in the first instance a nominated non-official element. Then we should go on from that, probably, to substitute for the nominative element an elective element; and after that nothing would separate us, but the circumstances of the time, from that full self-government which is, and always has been, our ultimate goal. (*Hear, hear.*) I cannot understand how any person in his senses can believe that it will be the interest or the object of the Government, or of any one in their place, to delay that consummation one day longer than it can safely be granted. (*Cheers.*). . . .

[1] Hansard, Fourth Series, vol. cxii. col. 40 (July 29, 1902).

Chamberlain turned next to the more controversial question
of South African finance. While fighting lasted, victory had been
the foremost aim; but, now that the war was over, Members
began to count the cost. The burden of immediate taxation
loomed larger in their minds than the long-term benefits which
might accrue to their children from the development of the new
Colonies. Self-sacrificing zeal for the cause of Empire now gave
way to the claims of individual and sectional interests; and many
began to wonder if they might not recover from South Africa
itself some part of the treasure which they had lavished on its
conquest. To lay an indemnity upon the beaten enemy would
have been impossible even if it had been politic. The Boers had
no substance left. But there remained the great industry of the
Rand: the very cause of the conflict and a source of immeasurable wealth. What more natural, therefore, than that a vocal
section of opinion in all parties should have clamoured for a
heavy tax upon the gold mines?

Chamberlain sympathised with this demand. Nearly a year
before, he had replied as follows to an appeal from Hicks Beach
for greater economy:

CHAMBERLAIN TO HICKS BEACH

September 30, 1901.—. . . I observe that in your estimates you
take no credit for any repayment of debt by the Transvaal. I can only
say that I remain firmly of opinion that the Colony can well bear a
contribution of 50 millions. Note that Egypt, a smaller and much
poorer country, bears easily a debt of over 100 millions, and I have no
doubt that with good government and a capital expenditure of some
millions on development the Transvaal can without difficulty sustain
a still larger liability.

Since then he had imposed upon the mines a profit tax of 10 per
cent. For the time being, however, he was inhibited from going
further by weighty considerations. On the one hand, he hoped
to obtain a large but voluntary contribution from the Rand
towards the cost of the war. On the other hand, it was fundamental to his and Milner's vision that the reconstruction of
South Africa should be financed out of the expanding prosperity
of the gold industry. Could the Rand bear the double burden

and still prosper? In his own mind the dilemma was not yet resolved.

> ... The fact is that shareholders and investors in this country and other countries are willing to speculate in mines if they can get 10 per cent, and they will not speculate for less. ... Now if by your policy you cut down this 10 per cent, there will, of course, be no investment in mines, and if there is no investment in mines there will be no development of the country and no revenue. You will not have the vast sums that we expect to acquire in order to carry out the schemes of irrigation, improvement of agriculture, public works, and development of railways, all of which will make South Africa, I firmly believe, one of the very richest countries on the face of the earth ... we will do nothing which will in any way interfere with the quick and complete development of the mines. (*Cheers.*) But, subject to that, there is no man in this House more anxious to recover a considerable proportion of the expenses of the war from South Africa than I am myself ... in my opinion it is perfectly fair to lay upon the industry of the Transvaal, the main and principal industry of the Transvaal, a fair proportion of the cost of the war. . . .[1]

As a statement of principle this was beyond cavil. The rub came in deciding its practical application.

> ... What is a fair proportion? If we say too much we are killing the goose that lays the golden eggs. That would be a foolish and ridiculous policy. If we say ... too little, or if we fix a sum at all, how do we know but that in a year or two we may altogether revise our judgment? How is it possible for any one to predict exactly what will be the extent of the prosperity to which these new countries may look forward. . . .[2]

For the time being these generalisations satisfied the House; but Chamberlain already sensed that the popularity of his South African policies would largely depend upon his success in inducing the Rand to contribute to the cost of the war.

Meanwhile another cloud had appeared on the horizon. It was still no bigger than a man's hand, though in time it would darken the whole political sky. The shortage of native labour on the Rand was already causing concern to the mining interests. Chamberlain judged that this was only a temporary phenomenon, attributable to the dislocation of life caused by the war

---

[1] Hansard, Fourth Series, vol. cxii. col. 44 (July 29, 1902).   [2] *Ibid.* col. 45.

and to the relative prosperity of the native. To overcome it he favoured measures calculated to induce the native, though without compelling him, to seek work in modern industry. In this he steered a middle course between the reactionaries who advocated compulsory labour and the sentimentalists who dreamed of leaving the native in his natural state. The passage of his speech, which Chamberlain devoted to this subject, deserves quoting. It is a representative expression of the more progressive Imperialist opinion of his time.

. . . An impression exists . . . that it is altogether wrong and improper, not merely to force or compel the black man to labour, but even to induce him to labour by indirect means. I differ entirely from that. In my opinion the future of the coloured race in Africa depends entirely upon our success and the success of other white nations in inducing them to labour. What has been the history of Africa hitherto? We know that labour has been impossible because . . . the fruits of labour were not secured to the labourer, because the different tribes were engaged in internecine strife and struggles, and there was no possibility of anything in the nature of peaceful industry. But now that that is all being stopped . . . by the progress of the white race in Africa; now that peace is secured, the future of the black is an impossible future unless he will work for his living, unless like every other man he is content to do something which affords a sufficient subsistence. . . . Of course, as I said, that is not to be taken as supporting in any way whatever the idea of compulsory or forced labour. That is a totally different thing. All men are forced to labour in one sense by necessity of providing for their subsistence or by the competition which exists. I do desire that the negro may be forced to labour in that sense, but not in the sense of actual physical compulsion brought to bear upon him. . . .[1]

Interesting, in the light of subsequent events, was a reference to the agitation just beginning in favour of the employment of white labour in the mines.

. . . I see that a movement is going on, to which I heartily wish success, for introducing a much larger quantity of white labour into the conduct of mining operations. (Hear, hear) . . . certainly any assistance or encouragement which the Government can give to proposals to secure that result will be readily accorded. . . .[2]

[1] Hansard, Fourth Series, vol. cxii. col. 47 (July 29, 1902).   [2] Ibid.

At the end of his speech Chamberlain turned to the question of British settlement in South Africa, regarded by Milner as the key to his dream of British supremacy. Chamberlain, indeed, disclaimed any idea of packing the country with British immigrants solely for political reasons. He represented that large-scale, if gradual, British land settlement was just as essential from the economic point of view. In this he may have been influenced overmuch by Willcocks' too sanguine report of the potentialities of South Africa.[1] But the real issue then, as in the war, was between the patriarchal pastoralism of the Boer and the modern methods of British Imperialism. One or the other must prevail; and on that question Chamberlain had long ago made up his mind.

. . . There is no doubt whatever that you have a country there, where there is latent wealth to an enormous amount, and at the present time in the Transvaal there are, I believe, only 5,000 farmers. . . . What are these farms? They are generally dry farms—enormous ranches, used only for the raising of cattle and a certain number of horses and animals of that kind. Tillage in the true sense of the word has hardly been known over a vast extent of country, but it is capable of being put into operation. There is no earthly reason why the country should not be a great grain-producing country, and why a great number of other most valuable products should not be produced. In order to bring about that result you must increase very largely the number of people upon the land, and you must improve the methods of cultivation. How is that to be done? You cannot increase the number of Boers. We cannot make more Boers than exist . . . we can only do it by bringing in settlers, who must be British settlers either from the Colonies across the seas or from this country. That is the policy which Lord Milner favours, and which we, the Home Government, entirely support. We believe it will be possible gradually—the thing cannot be done in a moment—to place upon the land a considerable number of effective settlers, who will themselves be examples and models which the Boers may ultimately follow. Their mere presence will tend to improve the practice of agriculture in the country, to secure a very much greater production than has hitherto obtained. The emigration of settlers into these Colonies

---

[1] In fairness to Willcocks it should be remembered that he recommended in his report the pursuit of a vigorous policy against soil erosion. The full importance of this recommendation is only now beginning to receive the recognition it deserves.

will be mainly an economic factor. I do not deny that it has a political importance. . . .[1]

The speech, as we have said, was well received on all sides; but, in his reply to the debate, Chamberlain stressed that it involved no new departure. He claimed, with justice, that it was of a piece with the policy he had consistently followed from the beginning.

. . . While I am glad that my earlier speech should have been considered by the House generally as a conciliatory speech, I do not admit that it differed either in manner or in matter from scores of other speeches which I have made on South African affairs. (*Cheers.*) I have always desired conciliation; I have always desired the absence of those racial feelings or animosities which at other times have existed in South Africa; but I have always thought that the opportunity for such reconciliation could not come until certain questions had been once for all settled. The fight has been fought out. Now is the time to shake hands, now is the time for reconciliation. . . .[2]

III

The sincerity of his words was soon attested by a gesture as dramatic as it was imaginative.

In a telegram to Chamberlain of June 10, 1902, Milner had written:

. . . If you could come to this country and see for yourself both its splendid opportunities and its total lack of equipment for use of them . . . you would be altogether on our side. There is nothing I wish more than that you could come.

These words may have sown the seed. Certainly by the end of August Chamberlain had made up his mind to go to South Africa.[3] The motives behind this decision were many. Some of the weightiest we shall consider in another context. Here we must confine ourselves to those directly concerned with South African affairs. They were weighty enough. At the beginning of September Chamberlain put his plan to Milner.

CHAMBERLAIN TO MILNER

Colonial Office.—Private and Personal.—September 4, 1902.—I am seri-

[1] Hansard, Fourth Series, vol. cxii. col. 49 (July 29, 1902).
[2] *Ibid.* col. 85.
[3] Mrs. Chamberlain's diary states that the visit to South Africa was first "seriously" discussed on August 25, 1902.

ously contemplating an early visit to South Africa and I want your frank opinion on the subject. I am led to this intention by several reasons. . . .

I am very anxious to see you and personally to discuss with you the very critical situation at which we have arrived. There are many questions of principle which might be settled between us in conversation but which it is almost impossible to arrange by correspondence at long intervals.

I should like to see for myself and to make the acquaintance of representative men of both parties and of both races. For more reasons than one I should desire as far as that was possible to avoid any platform speaking, although probably before leaving I might accept an invitation and endeavour to impress the views at which I had arrived upon the people. I should leave, however, all question as to this until I had seen you and Sir Walter Hutchinson [Sir W. F. Hely-Hutchinson, Governor of Cape Colony], as I certainly should not desire to commit myself to any premature expression of opinion. Even if I did not speak at all my chief object would be secured by having been brought into contact with the men who are chiefly responsible for the future of South Africa, and learning something of their characters and relative importance.

. . . I could leave without disadvantage, probably about the end of November. I should visit all the Colonies including if possible Rhodesia and would give two or even three months if necessary to the job.

Now I want you on receipt of this to consider the subject and to telegraph to me immediately what you think of the proposal. I rely on you to speak frankly and if you disapprove I shall not come.

Milner replied:

Colonial Office.—Decypher from Lord Milner, received 1.43 *p.m.* 27 *September,* 1902.—*Secret and Personal.*—Sept. 26. Your letter private and personal. Only one opinion is possible. It would be the best thing that could happen for all of us and I earnestly urge you to carry out your plan. MILNER.

Having thus obtained Milner's approval, Chamberlain told Balfour of his intention. The new Prime Minister [1] replied at once:

BALFOUR TO CHAMBERLAIN

Whittingehame, October 4, 1902.—I most sincerely hope you will be able to carry out your plan of going to South Africa in the winter. I am sure it

[1] Balfour had succeeded Salisbury as Prime Minister on July 11, 1902. This important transaction is fully discussed in another context. See ch. xcv.

would do a great deal of good to the colony; and you certainly deserve something in the nature of a rest and change of scene. . . .

The proposed visit was discussed and approved by the Cabinet on October 21; and a few days later Mrs. Chamberlain could write:

MRS. CHAMBERLAIN TO HER MOTHER

October 25, 1902.—. . . You will be glad to hear that both Mr. Balfour and Lord George [Hamilton] spoke most sympathetically about our South African plan. Any doubts as to its feasibility from the practical point of view *here* seem to have vanished and so far as South Africa is concerned they have but one opinion as to the advantage it will be. Lord George said quite frankly that he had been taken by surprise with the proposition, and that his first impression was one of doubt. But, on thinking it over, he had become convinced that it was a splendid idea, and he was very glad that we were going.

Yesterday Joe saw the King about it, and he "entirely approves"—"a very good idea"—and so our fate seems to be sealed and the only question is how soon we go. The announcement about it is to be made on Monday, and I am curious to see how the public takes it.

There was no need for anxiety.

The news was received with acclamation by the Liberal, as well as by the Unionist, press. The leaders of the Opposition joined in the general praise; the chorus of approval swelled throughout the Empire; and even the pro-Boer press abroad could not conceal its admiration. Chamberlain's gesture had caught the imagination of the world.

Once again Mrs. Chamberlain's letters give the best description of the contemporary mood:

MRS. CHAMBERLAIN TO HER MOTHER

October 28, 1902.—. . . Yesterday the announcement was made of Joe's visit to South Africa . . . and it has been received with a chorus of approval on all sides. Even the Opposition papers give him their blessings, and only one or two feeble dissentient squeaks are heard in the land. . . . Seriously, it is *most* satisfactory to find that everyone sees in it a new policy, and a real effort to deal with the situation, and any fear we may have had of misapprehension has vanished, and there is no disposition to cavil anywhere. The result is that Joe is full of interest in it—it has had the same effect as the original plan at Highbury did, and I see that all his thoughts revert to it at once, as soon as any other affairs which crop up are disposed of. He is today *inundated* with offers of Members of Parliament, middle-aged Diplomatists, and young men, etc., etc., to go as unpaid private secretaries—so does the idea appeal to them all. But in this respect they are doomed to disappointment. Lord Monk Bretton and a Member of the South African Department of the Colonial Office, and Mr. Wilson, his private Private Secretary, go with us and that completes his staff.

There is another delightful thing—how do you think we are to go? His Majesty has expressed a desire that one of his Cruisers should take us out, and the Board of Admiralty have placed at Joe's disposal the "Good Hope", one of the newest and biggest Cruisers, built with the money voted by the Cape Parliament. A very appropriate ship in which to set sail. . . .

November 1, 1902.—. . . [The reception of the news] continues to be most satisfactory!!! Even the Opposition bless Joe. Sir H. Campbell-Bannerman is pleased to say he considers it an excellent thing, and Sir Robert Reid, to whom Joe is anathema maranatha, said to one of the Whips: "This is the best thing you fellows have done yet". I must say I did not expect this, and one must give them full credit for it. It makes the going quite easy.

We are now deep in preparations. . . .

Meanwhile another remarkable journey was in progress. The Boer Generals, Botha, De Wet and De La Rey, had visited London and were touring the capitals of Europe. Their proceedings demand our attention.

IV

The war in South Africa, especially the guerilla war, had been waged with almost modern ruthlessness. Tens of thousands of farms had been burnt. Vast tracts of land had been systematically laid waste; and whole populations had been herded into concentration camps. Even away from the battle-front, the sub-continent had endured for more than two years the harsh operation of martial law. At home, indeed, the Boers were regarded with more admiration than hatred; but, in South Africa, the casualties and devastations, inflicted and suffered by both sides, had left a weighty legacy of bitterness.

Nevertheless, the peace, when it came, was a real peace. There was no blood-stained aftermath to Vereeniging. A blessed oblivion was drawn over recent events; in law, at least, if not in men's hearts. No charges of war-guilt were brought against the vanquished leaders. With few exceptions, prosecutions for atrocities inflicted in the heat of combat were abandoned. Even in the Cape and Natal, the commandos, whose rebel status was undeniable, were punished only by disfranchisement. Under the terms of the surrender, the burghers became British subjects, and, with the obligations, also received the privileges of a condition, so long and fiercely resisted. For two years they had been hunted men and, since the Proclamation, virtually outlaws. Now they were free men, free to come and go wherever they pleased; and, in an age when the passport was a rarity and the visa unknown, this meant over the whole world.

While the war lasted, the political direction of the Boer cause had remained in the hands of President Kruger and the Delegation at the Hague. At Vereeniging, however, the same act, which had dissolved the commandos, had created a new political constellation among the burghers. By appearing, on their own authority, as contracting parties to a conditional surrender, Botha, De Wet and De La Rey had superseded Kruger and the Delegation as the political leaders of the Boer people. There could be no turning back. Henceforth their feet were set along political paths; for they were under an inescapable obligation, to their own people, to ensure that the terms of surrender were administered in the spirit in which they had concluded them.

At Vereeniging, the three Generals had arranged with the other burgher representatives, and with Kitchener, to visit Europe in the summer. The declared object of their mission was to raise funds for the relief of the disabled burghers and their widows and orphans. Nor was such a plan unreasonable. The Generals knew the British as stern enemies. They had found Milner a hard man in negotiation. They had, as yet, no experience of British magnanimity in victory. But their mission was also inspired by political motives. They had acknowledged their military defeat, but they were still determined to resist the establishment of British supremacy by political means. For the moment their political influence rested only upon the precarious foundation of their past achievements. But, if they could raise and administer a large fund for the relief of their people, they might hope to consolidate that influence upon a more enduring basis. They also hoped that their friends, in England and on the Continent, would give them powerful moral support. This might enable them to win from Chamberlain, concessions which they had failed to extract from Milner.

Their decision was also influenced by a natural though no longer avowable allegiance. The Generals had surrendered on their own responsibility, but they were plainly under a moral obligation to explain their conduct to the exiled Government which had appointed them. Moreover, as soldiers so long cut off from the outside world, they felt it to be their interest, as well as their duty, to consult with the men to whose political judgment they had trusted in the past.

V

Chamberlain recognised, from the first, the political importance acquired by the Generals. He wanted them to work with him, and was, therefore, much concerned by reports that they intended to travel direct to Germany without first visiting England.

CHAMBERLAIN AND MILNER

(Telegrams)

J. C. to Milner.—*July* 1, 1902.—It is reported in the newspapers that De La Rey, Botha and De Wet are to leave very soon for Germany in order to address meetings under the auspices of the Pan-Germanic League on behalf of the Distressed Burghers' Fund. From our point of view such proceedings are likely to have the most undesirable results. Feeling in Germany is still strongly anti-British. The Boer leaders could not fail to be influenced by it and reports more or less inaccurate of their meetings would get to South Africa and might have a most mischievous influence. To enlist these men on our side is of the first importance. . . .

. . . The matter is a delicate one and we cannot, of course, forbid their going, but if they persist perhaps we might induce them to visit this country first . . . we could ensure them a cordial reception which might reduce the danger of a subsequent visit to Germany or even altogether prevent it.

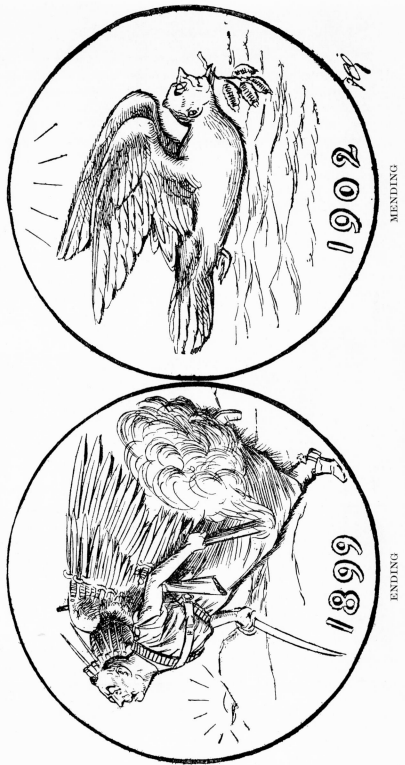

ENDING   MENDING

From the cartoon by F. Carruthers Gould in the *Westminster Gazette*, November 25, 1902

J. C. to Milner.—July 15, 1902.—Kitchener thinks strong effort should be made to induce any of Boer Generals who have not abandoned idea of visiting Europe to come direct to England in the first place, under our auspices, by offering facilities for passage and making it cheaper for them to come that way. What are the intentions of Botha or of any who may already have left?

Milner to J. C.—July 17, 1902.—Three leading Boer Generals are I think quite determined to sail for Europe at the end of the present month. . . . Botha, De Wet and De La Rey think . . . that they have no choice in the matter but are bound to collect funds for their people by the instructions of the Vereeniging Conference. At present they intend to visit England first. I will do what I can to confirm them in this intention and, of course, I should not stick at a trifle like providing passages for them. You will see, however, that to coax them to go to England without exciting their suspicions is rather a delicate matter.

Policy and inclination combined to prepare a cordial welcome for the Generals. While they were still on the high seas, Chamberlain and Milner decided to offer seats on the projected Legislative Council at least to Botha and De La Rey. Roberts and Kitchener proposed to offer hospitality and entertainment.

Kitchener's proposal was dramatic. The Generals were due to dock on August 16, the day of the Coronation Naval Review. He suggested that they should at once be conducted to the Colonial Secretary's ship *Nigeria* to watch the review as his guests. The Generals, so Kitchener reckoned in his oriental way, would appreciate this show of hospitality and must be suitably impressed by the evolutions of the greatest navy in the world.

The Generals were duly welcomed on the quay by Kitchener. A launch swept them out to *Nigeria*. There, on the deck, they came face to face, for the first time, with Chamberlain. The Colonial Secretary, immaculately dressed as ever, was accompanied by Roberts and the colonial dignitaries assembled for the Coronation. Behind him the battle fleet of Britain stretched out in four grey lines to the horizon. Amid the pageantry of Empire, the Generals seemed awkward in their crumpled, country clothes. For all their valour and cunning, they were only simple farmers, seeing the world for the first time.

When the formal introductions had been done, Chamberlain stretched out his hand towards the ships, inviting the Generals to watch the Review as his guests. "Now that you have sworn to be loyal British subjects," he said, "they are your ships as well as ours." An embarrassed silence followed, but presently the Generals were understood to decline the invitation.

Chamberlain was piqued by this rebuff. In conversation a few days later he declared:

Now about the visit to the Fleet. That was all Kitchener's doing. He said there was no doubt but that they would come to see the Fleet. When the gentlemen came on board my ship, I asked them to come and see the ships, saying that they were their ships now, as well as ours, as they had sworn to be loyal British subjects. They made a lot of excuses and finally said their clothes would not do. That, of course, was only an excuse but it shows their mind. They are only waiting an opportunity, and I am not going to trust them while they are in that frame of mind.[1]

From Southampton the Generals went to London, where, for the first time, they came in contact with the extraordinary nation which had conquered them. Their arrival was expected, and they were greeted by cheering crowds shouting, "Bravo, Botha!" and "Good old De Wet!" London's welcome astonished and confused these earnest veterans. In their long and desperate fight, they had learned to hate their English enemies and had assumed that this hatred would be reciprocated in Britain, as it undoubtedly was by the British element in South Africa. They could not understand that, at the heart of the Empire where the war had scarcely been felt at all, they had acquired a type of popularity then usually reserved for the stars of the cricket field or the music-hall. In their ignorance, as Milner had feared, they interpreted these friendly demonstrations as striking evidence of political support.

At the King's request, they returned to Southampton on the next day and were received in audience on the royal yacht, *Victoria & Albert*. Kitchener, evidently trying to efface the unfortunate impression created by the incident on board

[1] From the shorthand notes of a conversation with a Mr. McHugh, who came to see Chamberlain at Highbury, on September 1, 1902, on behalf of Mr. Le Sage, the editor of the *Daily Telegraph*.

Nigeria, sent Chamberlain the following account of this second and more successful visit to the fleet:

KITCHENER TO CHAMBERLAIN

August 18, 1902.—The Boer Generals went off to town to get clothes and came down on Sunday beautifully got up in ready made garments and top hats.

Botha told me they intended leaving to-day for Brussels to attend Meyer's funeral[1] and that they were coming back again in a week and were anxious to see you—Lord Roberts said he would write to you on this subject.

Botha assured me they intended to behave quite loyally and do their utmost to make all their people do so. He said there was no fear of their being influenced by foreign intrigues.

The interview with the King went off very well, it was quite short and I think they were much impressed.

I afterwards showed them the Fleet.

I send you herewith a Transvaal and Orange Free State flag which I hope you will accept. . . .

From Brussels the Generals formally solicited an interview with Chamberlain. His reply was significant.

CHAMBERLAIN TO THE BOER GENERALS

(Telegram)

August 21, 1902.—I had hoped to have preliminary discussions with Generals on board "Nigeria" if they had been able to accept invitation; failing this, Lord Roberts undertook to arrange interview at Colonial Office on 2nd September at 3 o'clock. If convenient to them, I will come up to London to meet them.

I should like to know beforehand the subjects on which they wish to see me. If they will send list to Colonial Office, I will get all information and shall be able to deal with them without delay, which would be necessary if I have no knowledge of their wishes beforehand.

On board *Nigeria* he would have set no limit to the range of their informal discussions, but his offer had been rejected. Now

---

[1] Lukas Meyer was a prominent Boer General, who had arrived in England some weeks before the triumvirate. The Chamberlain Papers show that he had an interview with Chamberlain on August 2, and that the Colonial Office made arrangements for him and his wife to see the Coronation.

he was determined, before risking an interview, to probe their intentions further. Nevertheless, in a final attempt to establish cordial personal relations, he sent the Generals an invitation to dine with him after their talks at the Colonial Office. This reached them at the Hague; but, there, they had already come under other influences.

VI

At the Hague, the Generals were conducted by Leyds and Wolmarans to President Kruger. The embittered old patriarch and the gallant men who had fought to the bitter end were at last united in defeat. There was no recrimination. All was over. This mournful meeting in a distant European capital was only an epilogue to the tragedy on the veld.

Kruger and his advisers knew that they could no longer play a direct part in South African politics. They still hoped, however, to exercise indirect influence through the Generals. It was their last card, and, with characteristic obstinacy, they overplayed it.

The Generals had little political experience and were soon entirely under the influence of the Delegation at the Hague. They now entrusted to its members the drafting of their reply [1] to Chamberlain's request for a statement of the subjects which they wished to discuss with him. These proved to be a list of fourteen separate demands, which may be summarised as follows:

(1) Total amnesty for the Dutch rebels in Cape Colony and Natal.

(2) The financial support of Burghers' orphans and widows to be a yearly charge on the Imperial Exchequer.

(3) Equal rights for English and Dutch languages in schools and law courts.

(4) British citizenship and the right to return to South Africa to be accorded to all members of the Boer Delegation abroad who complied with the terms of surrender.

(5) Reinstatement in the State Service of former Burgher officials, or their compensation for loss of office.

(6) Compensation to Burghers for all losses occasioned to their property by the British Army.

[1] The Boer Generals to Chamberlain, August 23, 1902 (published in Cd. 1284 of September 1902).

(7) Reinstatement of Burghers in the ownership of farms confiscated under the Proclamation of August 7, 1901.

(8) Compensation to Burghers for the use of their property by the British authorities during the War.

(9) Payment of the pre-war and war-time debts of the Republics.

(10) Return to the Transvaal of the districts ceded to Natal.

(11) Moratorium on Burgher debts due to the late Republic.

(12) Abolition of the compulsory administration to Burghers of the Oath of Allegiance.

(13) Removal of the National Scouts from the Resettlement Commissions.

(14) The free grant of £3,000,000 to be made available solely to Burgher prisoners-of-war and Burghers in the field at the time of the surrender, *i.e.* not to the National Scouts, or "Hands-uppers".[1]

These remarkable demands amounted to nothing less than a proposal to set aside the Treaty of Vereeniging and negotiate an altogether new agreement in every way more favourable to the Boers. This was sheer bluff, but, as if to underline how far they were in earnest, the Generals also declined Chamberlain's invitation to dinner. The language of their refusal was courteous and dignified, but its effect, in his mind, was to add insult to injury. He had been anxious from the first to show them that they were fully accepted as equal fellow-subjects of the Crown. Hence his proposals for their entertainment which, if a trifle crude, were perfectly sincere. But the Generals misunderstood his purpose. They were suspicious of an enemy's hospitality and preferred to nurse their grievances. One sentence reveals their mood.

In view of the many grave questions which we have before us . . . we have resolved that . . . it would best become us, as it best accords with our own feelings, not to accept any hospitality that may, in no matter how remote a degree, be construed as partaking of pleasant social functions whilst problems fraught with such terribly serious issues to our people are as yet hanging in the balance.[2]

Nothing was in the balance as far as Chamberlain was con-

[1] The "Hands-Uppers" were those burghers who had accepted the fact of British victory and taken an oath of neutrality or of allegiance to the British Crown.

[2] Generals Botha, De Wet and De La Rey to J. C., August 23, 1902.

cerned. He was quite prepared to discuss the application or even the interpretation of the terms of surrender, but nothing would induce him to reopen questions which had been settled at Vereeniging. His official reply[1] was unyielding but admirably calm. His private feelings and intentions were more forcefully expressed in letters to Roberts and to Austen.

CHAMBERLAIN ON THE BOER GENERALS

J. C. to Roberts.—August 28, 1902.—The Boer Generals have sent me a list of 14 subjects which they desire to discuss with me.

The general effect of their proposals would be to set aside the terms of surrender and to substitute a new Treaty of Peace whereby the only losers in the late war would be the British.

I think that the "loyalty" of these gentlemen is about as real as that of Mr. Kruger when he accepted office from us in 1878.

I have written to say that I will have no discussion on any matters already settled by the terms of surrender and have asked if they accept the interview on these conditions. It is therefore doubtful whether we shall meet on the 2nd or not, but I will inform you of their reply.

J. C. to Austen Chamberlain.—September 1, 1902.—. . . I am having trouble with the Boer generals. The correspondence will be sent to the King and the Cabinet but the position is this. I asked for details of the subjects they wished to discuss with me tomorrow. In return they sent me a list of 14 which together would constitute an entirely new agreement in substitution for the terms of surrender. I have absolutely refused to reopen that agreement and have postponed meeting until they accept my conditions. I have come to the conclusion that they are thoroughly untrustworthy.

We are ready to be friends but the friendship must be on both sides and frankly declared. With them it is all take and no give. I shall no doubt hear from them again to-day but I shall keep them kicking their heels in London till I have a satisfactory statement in writing as to their intentions.

Back in London, the Generals denied "claiming the right to contract a new or to substitute a modified agreement for the existing one",[2] and described themselves merely as "subjects of

---

[1] J. C. to the Boer Generals, August 28, 1902 (published in Cd. 1284 of September 1902).

[2] Boer Generals to J. C., September 1, 1902 (published as No. 7 of Cd. 1284, September 1902).

His Majesty, seeking to obtain a fair hearing and as we respectfully submit, clemency and justice".[1] Nevertheless, they went
on to say that the subjects which they wished to discuss with
Chamberlain were precisely those contained in the 14 points.

Chamberlain was not to be moved. He remained entrenched
at Highbury, declining to come to London until he had received
the necessary assurances.

CHAMBERLAIN TO THE BOER GENERALS [2]

September 1, 1902.—. . . I regret to find that you do not accept the
condition which I felt it my duty to make as a necessary preliminary to
any official interview, namely, that there should be no attempt to reopen
the agreement which was signed in Pretoria only 3 months ago.

On that occasion, actuated by motives of humanity, His Majesty's
Government authorised Lord Kitchener and Lord Milner to agree to
terms of unprecedented liberality, and it would be unfair to you to allow
you for one moment to suppose that any good result could follow from
an attempt to obtain better terms than were then conceded. As you yourselves remind me the conditions were in the nature of an ultimatum,
which it was open to you to accept or refuse, but which His Majesty's
Government were in no case prepared to alter. . . . In any case I feel obliged
to adhere to my former decision, and . . . to ask you for a formal assurance
that you will not raise any subject inconsistent with the settlement arrived
at in Pretoria.

On receipt of such an assurance I would endeavour to arrange for the
presence of Lord Kitchener at an interview to be subsequently arranged
at a time to suit your convenience, and which I should make it my special
duty to attend, but I could not accept a meeting under circumstances
which could only lead to disappointment and misunderstanding.

Next day, he wrote to Austen:

CHAMBERLAIN TO AUSTEN

September 2, 1902.—Your letter to London received this afternoon has
crossed mine about the Boer Generals. I entirely agree with the King
about them. I . . . do not mean to give way. They must come to my terms
or I will not see them.

[1] Boer Generals to J. C., September 1, 1902 (published as No. 7 of Cd. 1284, September 1902).   [2] Published as No. 8 of Cd. 1284, September 5, 1902.

I intend to get Kitchener to meet them if the interview comes off—meanwhile they are kicking their heels in London.

Before I have done with them they will perhaps be sorry they did not come on board the Nigeria. In any case they will learn that while we are ready to be friends we shall expect them to prove their friendship for us by something better than words.

In haste to catch the post. . . . Here the rain it raineth every day.

Chamberlain's position was impregnable. He had the full support of the Prime Minister, and, by publishing his correspondence with the Generals, could at any moment rally the whole of public opinion to his side. Meanwhile, with the House of Commons adjourned and London empty for the holidays, they had no means of bringing pressure to bear upon him. He was thus playing from strength and knew that sooner or later they must climb down. He had not long to wait. Within twenty-four hours of receiving his last letter, they supplied the necessary assurances.[1]

The meeting, thrice postponed, at last took place at the Colonial Office on the afternoon of September 5. With Chamberlain were Kitchener, Lord Onslow (the Parliamentary Under Secretary), and Mr. Graham of the permanent staff. The discussion was confined within the limits previously imposed by Chamberlain and, in consequence, was dull though prolonged. The tone of it was accurately described in the telegraphic report made the same day to the King.

CHAMBERLAIN TO THE KING

September 5, 1902.—The three Boer Generals met Lord Kitchener and myself this afternoon.

The meeting lasted $2\frac{1}{2}$ hours and was quite satisfactory. Their attitude was perfectly correct and even friendly, and the explanation given them on the points raised appeared to satisfy them. One or two small points were reserved for consideration by Lord Milner but no concessions have been made, and they expressed themselves fully determined to abide loyally by the terms of peace. . . .

The verbatim report of the conversation [2] covers some twelve

---

[1] Published as No. 9 of Cd. 1284, September 5, 1902.   [2] Published as No. 10 of Cd. 1284, September 5, 1902.

pages of printed foolscap. Most of it is taken up with points of detail, but Chamberlain's closing statement deserves quoting.

GENERAL BOTHA: "Of course we look to you for help. . . . Something might be done with regard to the widows and orphans. . . . You have got so many assets in the country."

CHAMBERLAIN: "Well, I think we had better not enter upon discussion in detail upon points of that kind. I would only remind the General that we have undertaken many obligations already, more than has ever been undertaken before in similar circumstances. . . . The General suggests that we might make provision for the widows and orphans of those who have been killed, of those who have fought against us. Well, in my time I recollect very well the great Civil War in America, and I appeal to that, because that stands out as a case in which, more than ever before or, indeed, ever since, the victor showed a magnanimous and generous feeling to the conquered. There was good reason for it because they were brothers, of the same race, the same religion, the same everything. It was a Civil War, but, even in that case, the Northern side, that is to say the victorious side, made no provision whatever, either by way of grant or pension or allowances, to people who had been wounded—to the side that had been conquered. They gave them their lives, they gave them their liberties, and after a period of about ten years they gave them their votes, but they did not give them any money compensation. But we have gone one step beyond that, because we have contributed, in addition to all our own enormous expenses, a very large sum to relieve those who are really destitute in our new Colonies. We have done more than, I think, was expected of us, and we have done all that we can afford to do, and I think it would be undesirable that the Generals should press us any further in the matter either now or in writing.

As regards the general statement which he [Botha] has made, I desire to reciprocate it. We want, in this country at any rate, to forget and to forgive, because if you think, as you well may, that you have something to forgive, we also think that we have a great deal to forgive; but we want to put all that on one side. The war is over. We each of us fought as well as we knew how during the war. Now there is peace. All we want is to recognise you as fellow-subjects with ourselves, working, as we shall work, for the prosperity and the liberty of South Africa. . . . We shall certainly show trust in you whenever you will show trust in us. We shall be very glad of your co-operation, and of the co-operation of men like yourselves who have loyally accepted the new situation. . . . We want South Africa to be a happy abiding place for all who live in it, not for one class alone, not for one section, for one race, or for one political party, but for all. . . . I am sure that if you meet us half way you will find us to be in the future quite as good friends as we have been, I hope, loyal enemies in the past."

Next day, Chamberlain saw Botha alone at the Colonial Office. He invited him, and through him, De La Rey, to join the Legislative Council. The Chamberlain Papers suggest that he would have liked to extend the invitation to De Wet as well; but Milner would not hear of it. Botha received the proposal kindly but asked for time to think it over.

A few days later [1] Chamberlain's correspondence with the Boer Generals and the Minutes of their meeting were made public. The Colonial Secretary's attitude was approved by the great majority of his countrymen at home and in the Empire. Foreign comment, too, was, for the most part, favourable. The *New York Evening Post*, not always a friendly critic, characterised the Boer Generals' demands as "extraordinarily presuming, puerile and preposterous". It went on to commend Chamberlain's "admirably calm reply". [2]

VII

Chamberlain now believed that the visit of the Boer Generals would have no further political consequences.

CHAMBERLAIN TO BALFOUR

September 9, 1902.—. . . As regards South Africa, you will I think see from the papers that the demands of the Boer Generals have fizzled out, and on the whole I hope we shall have no further trouble from this source.

This hope was doomed to an early disappointment. Sense of duty and political interest still impelled the Generals to try and raise a fund. They dared not return home with empty hands, at least until they had exhausted every possible source of supply. Nevertheless, they missed a great opportunity. Had they issued

---

[1] September 10, 1902 (Cd. 1284).
[2] *New York Evening Post*, September 10, 1902.

an appeal to the British public, based on the frank acceptance of the fact that the burghers were now fellow-subjects of the King, they might well have raised large sums of money and gained political influence besides. But they had timed their visit badly. They had few real friends in London; and those Englishmen who counselled them, mostly professional pro-Boers, never considered an idea which would have involved beating Chamberlain at his own game. The Liberal Imperialists might have done it, but they were away on holiday.

With no one to advise them, and embittered by their failure to wring concessions from Chamberlain, the Generals returned to the Hague. There, with the help of the Delegation, they issued the famous "Appeal of the Boer Generals to the Civilised World".[1] A few extracts will suffice to show its general character.

APPEAL OF THE BOER GENERALS TO THE CIVILISED WORLD

. . . As we have up to the present not succeeded in inducing the British Government to grant further assistance to our people, and as the needs are indescribably great, no other course is open to us but to apply to the peoples of Europe and America.

. . . The people of the two Republics were prepared to sacrifice everything for their independence; and now that the struggle is over they stand totally ruined . . . at least thirty thousand houses of the Boer farms, and, further, a number of villages, were burned or destroyed by the British.

. . . In this great distress we now turn to the World with our appeal to help. . . .

. . . The small amount which England will contribute, according to the terms of surrender, would, even if multiplied tenfold, be totally insufficient to cover even the war losses.

The widows and orphans, the maimed and destitute, and our children, for whom alone we make this appeal, will, therefore, receive little, and in the most cases nothing, from this source. . . .

British sympathy was chilled by the hostile tone, by the implication that the Free Grant was of little use, and by the omission of any reference to the work that was being done by

[1] September 25, 1902. According to one report reaching Chamberlain from the Foreign Office, Fischer was the author of the Appeal.

British officials for resettlement and education. The unfortunate impression made by the Appeal was only confirmed by the
incidents which marked the Generals' subsequent lecture tour.
To their credit, they several times insisted that they were loyal
subjects of the King, but they could not prevent their friends
on the Continent from turning the meetings into anti-British
demonstrations. As a result, British opinion was alienated; not
to be fully reconciled until the first World War.

These regrettable effects of the tour were compensated by
no material advantages. Admiration or curiosity might still
produce a crowded meeting, but contributions were small.
Throughout the war, the Generals had been sustained by the
strong pro-Boer sentiments manifested in Europe. Then, they
had hoped for foreign intervention. Now, they counted, at least,
on a generous response to their appeal. They expected a sum
which would have dwarfed the £3,000,000 given by the British
Government. They were profoundly disillusioned by the result.
When the fund closed, it amounted to only £105,000, or little
more than 3 per cent of the Free Grant. Towards the end of
October, the Generals returned to London, "sad and worse", as
their friend Leonard Courtney described them.[1]

Chamberlain was not unnaturally incensed by the appeal. He
addressed a firm remonstrance to Botha,[2] and made a stinging
suggestion. If the Generals would help him to recover the
balance of the state treasure which Kruger had brought to
Europe, he would be very glad to add it to their relief fund.

CHAMBERLAIN TO BOTHA

November 6, 1902.—. . . His Majesty's Government are aware that
large sums were remitted from the Transvaal to Europe during the war
to be expended in the interests of the South African Republic.

They have no desire to question the expenditure of this money so far
as it was legitimately devoted to the purposes for which it was intended,
but they cannot doubt that a large balance still remains which would
properly come to them as the successors of the late South African Republic, and which they would be prepared to add to the fund provided

[1] Gooch, *The Life of Lord Courtney*,
p. 480.
[2] Chamberlain to Botha, November

6, 1902 (published as No. 1 of Cd. 1329
November 1902).

for the relief of the distressed burghers and their families. I venture to think that in this matter your wishes will coincide with mine, and that you will give me any assistance in your power to discover the persons to whom the money was entrusted, and to obtain from them a statement of account showing the expenditure and the amount of the balance which remains over.

The monies referred to were popularly known as "Kruger's millions" and were reputed to total an enormous sum. There was always a danger that they might be used to finance anti-British activities; and Chamberlain was, therefore, concerned to gain control of them. He sent secret agents to nose them out. He offered to let members of the Delegation go back to South Africa, if they would tell him where the money was. In vain. The mystery remained impenetrable. Accordingly, in a second interview with the Generals, Chamberlain asked them, once more, to help him recover these Transvaal funds.[1] They resented his suggestion and firmly declined to be drawn. Botha declared:

You cannot expect that we will go and act as a kind of detectives [*sic*] against people who have been our friends all our life.

The ultimate disposal of "Kruger's millions" is still uncertain. The Chamberlain Papers, however, contain the fragment of a letter in Lord Onslow's handwriting which suggest that Botha finally obtained control of them.

FRAGMENT OF LETTER FROM ONSLOW TO CHAMBERLAIN [2]

. . . Botha and Fischer came to see me to-day. They have been over in Holland and have been making inquiries into the disposition of the monies sent from the T.V. I enclose a copy of the short-hand notes of the interview.[3]

I felt that, as they have got the money and we cannot get hold of it, it was better to take what they would offer than to risk the charge of imposing conditions which they would not comply with.

---

[1] At the Colonial Office, November 11, 1902—General De Wet was not present at this interview.

[2] The letter was evidently written after Chamberlain had left for South Africa and while the Generals were still in London. This would fix its date between November 26 and December 13, 1902.

[3] These, unfortunately, are not among the Chamberlain Papers.

It amounts to this, that they will hand over a small sum to the widows and orphans, but will not disclose the total amount remitted or give an account of how it was spent.

I think we must do what we can to find out and obtain proof of the amount of money sent out of the country, and compare the smallness of the balance with the amount expended.

Botha, you will see, declared that there was never any ship chartered, that no sum was sent by a French or other steamer to Naples, and that the amount sent out of the T.V. was a trifle to the sums that have been named.

If we can prove these statements to be incorrect, I think we shall damage the generals very much in the eyes of their countrymen. I am trying to press Botha to say what was the sum that was sent to Europe.

Beyond this the records are silent. The *Milner Papers* give the total sum remitted to Europe as some £750,000.[3] It is possible, therefore, that, after two years of war, the remaining balance was inconsiderable. Equally it may have provided the war-chest with which Botha later launched his political movement, *Het Volk*.

VIII

Apart from the exchanges over the Transvaal funds, the Minutes of the second inverview between Chamberlain and the Generals show the latter chastened and crestfallen. Botha, indeed, virtually admitted that their visit had been in many ways unfortunate:

I am thankful you have given me an opportunity of seeing you. I think the last interview [*i.e.* that of September 5] was unfortunate. There was a misunderstanding. I hope to remove any misunderstanding that has occurred.

Chamberlain was courteous, kindly, but immovable. He heard and answered their grievances and suggestions with extraordinary patience. Then, in measured terms, savouring of a magisterial admonition, he rebuked them for their Appeal and told them that it obliged him to withdraw his invitation to them to join the Legislative Council.[1]

---

[1] *Milner Papers* (*South Africa*), vol. ii. p. 78.

The Generals set sail for home a month later. Their mission had been a failure. They returned empty-handed, without political concessions or substantial funds. But the lesson of this humiliating experience was not lost on so shrewd an observer as Botha. The tour of the Continent had taught him that it was useless to look to the nations of Europe for support. Henceforth, for better or for worse, the destiny of the Boers would lie within the British Empire, and it was there, and not outside it, that he must look for help.

In coming to this conclusion, Botha seems to have been powerfully influenced by hearing a speech of Chamberlain's on South African affairs. It was the Colonial Secretary's last important statement on this subject before he left for South Africa, and was mainly a report on the progress of resettlement. The record of achievement was impressive, and deserves to be briefly summarised:

Concentration Camps

. . . At the close of the war the number of persons in concentration camps was about 103,000—men, women and children. At the present moment . . . the number is 34,000 . . . these camps, which are costing us £200,000 a month, are camps the dispersal of which we should see with the greatest satisfaction. We would have closed the camps the day the war was over, had we not known that, as a matter of certainty, it would have involved the deaths of thousands and tens of thousands of women and children.[2]

Prisoners of War

. . . Originally there were 24,000 prisoners from South Africa. Fourteen thousand have already returned and 7,000 are bound to be repatriated before the end of the year, and the remainder in a very short time after. . . .[3]

[1] Despite his firm handling of the triumvirate, Chamberlain was by no means inaccessible to other Boer leaders. His Papers show that he gave interviews among others to Generals Kritzinger and Viljoen (the former had lain for a time under sentence of death for atrocities against natives), as well as to Schalk Burger and to the Dele- gates Wessels and Fischer. Although granted interviews the last two were by no means *persona grata* and were not allowed to return to South Africa until some months later.

[2] Hansard, Fourth Series, vol. cxiv. col. 232 (November 5, 1902).

[3] *Ibid.* col. 234.

Free Grant of £3,000,000

Chamberlain reminded the House that the British Government had originally intended that this grant should be raised on the security of the Transvaal. The Boer Generals, however, claimed that they had expected it to be a charge on the Imperial Exchequer; and, in this case, the Government had decided to defer to their opinion. He explained that the Free Grant would be used solely for the resettlement of those who were utterly destitute, but added,

. . . If the money which we are to devote to that purpose should be insufficient, I for one, should not hesitate to come for more.[1]

Compensation for Loyalists

Chamberlain had spoken with pride of the work that was being done for the relief of the defeated burghers. He stressed, however, that even more must be done for those who had been friends to the British Empire. He therefore asked the House to vote a grant of £2,000,000 for the compensation of Dutch and British loyalists.

Sir, the defeated party in a war must suffer more than the victors; that, it appears to me is commonsense and cannot be contravened. . . . We are going to do a great deal for those who were recently our opponents but I sincerely hope, as long as I have anything to do with the matter, to do more for those who have been with us.[2]

He was at his best in the peroration. It set the tone for his approaching visit to South Africa.

. . . In actually giving, I will not call it compensation, but assistance to those who were our former enemies we should clearly state what are the reasons. The reasons are humanity and policy. (*Cheers.*) Humanity first, because we do not wish, under the British flag, that any one should be subjected to the misery which these people would otherwise have to suffer. (*Cheers.*) But policy, because, as we have said over and over again, we have got to live together and want to live together. We hope that we shall live together as friends. (*Cheers.*) We have absolutely no vindictive

feelings towards those who, by superior force, we have conquered, but
whose merits and qualities we are the first to recognize. (*Cheers.*) We say
it is good policy that these men should not be discontented, but that, as
far as possible, we should enable them . . . to place themselves in a position
in which they may recover their former prosperity. . . .

Let us believe in the future, and the future will answer our anticipations. (*Loud cheers.*) I do believe in the future. To my mind what has
been done, in the short period that has elapsed since this desolating war
was brought to an end, is the greatest encouragement that we could possibly have. (*Hear, hear.*) . . . The results of our efforts at resettlement and
repatriation have exceeded my most sanguine estimate. And I hope I
may have even greater cause for congratulation when I go to South
Africa, going, as I shall do, with the most earnest desire to forget all that
is controversial, all that is unhappy in regard to the recollections of the
past, and with the one sole desire to bring together the people, a kindred
people after all, separated only by the circumstances of recent times—to
bring together this kindred people in one great South African nation
under the British Crown.[1]

We may be sure that the Boer General listening in the gallery
did not fail to mark either the record of practical achievement
or the expression of the firm but generous spirit by which it
was inspired. From this speech, perhaps, dates the beginning of
a change of heart destined one day to lead to consequences
momentous for the British Empire, as for Botha.

[1] Hansard, Fourth Series, vol. cxiv. col. 241.

CHAPTER LXXX

THE SUSPENSION CRISIS AND MILNER'S RESIGNATION

(1902)

A CLASH between Colleagues—How the Issue arose—Milner's Attitude
and Chamberlain's—Milner Rallies the Suspension Movement—
The Suspension Petition and Milner's Indiscretion—Chamberlain in
the Dark—He Rebukes Milner—Suspension and the Cabinet—The
Colonial Premiers Consulted—Turning the Crisis to Good Account—
Chamberlain Defends Milner in the House—Sprigg and Martial Law
—Chamberlain Fails to Dismiss Sprigg—Verdict on the Suspension
Crisis—Milner's Resignation—Chamberlain Fails to Dissuade him—
A Successor Chosen—Milner and Chamberlain Compared.

I

BOOK
XVI.
1902.

WE saw in the last chapter how, from the moment peace was signed, Chamberlain and Milner had thrown themselves into the work of South African reconstruction. Minister and pro-consul had now worked together for five years. They knew each other's minds. They were inspired by the same general conceptions. They strove towards the same goal. Yet, almost at once, they clashed with results nearly fatal to their collaboration and to the South African settlement.

The greatest political conflicts are those between the champions of opposite and irreconcilable principles. But a peculiar interest attaches to those collisions between colleagues over the means of achieving an agreed end. The fate of a common strategy is seen to hang upon a choice of tactics; and the exponents of the rival courses hold to their own convictions so tenaciously that normal restraints are disregarded and an open breach ensues. The crisis brought about by the Suspension

98

Movement in Cape Colony was of such a kind. It was obscured
from the general view by more dramatic events and attenuated
by the long delays in the mail service between England and
South Africa. It was, nevertheless, an event of the deepest
significance to the whole Empire. It will deserve our careful
attention for the light which it throws both upon the characters
of Chamberlain and Milner, and upon the nature of British
Imperialism.

II

Until the conclusion of peace, wide tracts of Cape Colony—
the midland, western and north-western districts—were in more
or less open rebellion against the Government in Cape Town.
To meet the dangers of this situation, the Premier, Sir Gordon
Sprigg, was persuaded to govern under martial law; and his
proceedings remained unchallenged, thanks to the continued
prorogation of the Cape Parliament. This form of government
served well enough while the war lasted; but it was evident that
the return of peace must raise delicate constitutional issues. If
parliamentary government was to be resumed, the Ministry
would require immediate legislation to indemnify them for their
administration of martial law and to confirm the sentences
passed by the military courts. They would also require to pass a
new Registration Bill before elections could be held. Above all,
if the British element in the Colony was to receive a just representation, they would need a Redistribution Bill as well.
Loyalist opinion, moreover, thought it necessary for the future
peace of the Colony to tighten up the laws regarding sedition and
the possession of arms.

But, if the existing Parliament were to be recalled, the
balance between the parties would be a very near thing. For
certain purposes, Sprigg might claim a bare majority; but most
observers judged that he could only maintain himself with the
support of the Bond. Now the Bond was the great Dutch party.
Many of its members had fought in the rebel Commandos, and
all of them sympathised with the cause of the Republics. The
prospect of the Bond in power, on the morrow of a British
victory, was intolerable to the whole British population at the
Cape; as, indeed, to those Dutchmen who had remained loyal to

the Crown. Pro-Boers would be promoted to high posts in the administration; British officials would receive no support from the Government; and British colonists, especially in the up-country districts, would suffer from every kind of discrimination open and concealed. Rebellion would go unpunished; loyalty unrewarded; and Afrikander racialism would regain in Parliament the supremacy it had lost on the battlefield. There seemed to be only one way to avert this harsh fate. This was for the Imperial Parliament to suspend the constitution and place the Cape under Crown Colony government until British supremacy had been firmly established. This idea of Suspension was frequently discussed among the leaders of the "Progressive" (British) party, and, as peace approached, it became a widespread political aspiration.

Milner had always been for Suspension.[1] His genius was of the autocratic kind, and in his heart he never recognised with much good humour the right of opposition. To judge, indeed, from his private letters, there were moments when he would have thought the suspension of the British constitution itself a wholesome step towards the more efficient development of the Empire.[2] But, where Cape Colony was concerned, he had a strong case. The war had been fought to bring South Africa inside the British Empire; and Milner was convinced that it would only be kept there by the establishment of British supremacy. To achieve that supremacy would require large-scale British immigration, the spread of the English language, and the general inculcation of British standards in every sphere of life. All these things would require considerable encouragement from the Cape authorities, and this was hardly to be expected from a government controlled by the Dutch:

[1] For previous refs. to his attitude on this subject, see this work, Vol. III. pp. 538, 573-574, 577-578, 621-622.

[2] Cf. following extract from one of his letters written on May 30, 1902 (just before signing the surrender at Vereeniging) and published in *Milner Papers (South Africa)*, vol. ii. p. 364. ". . . What with our sentimentality, our party system, our Government by Committee, our 'Mandarins', our 'Society', our Generals . . . the game is just hopeless. It's rather hard on the nation, a sound-hearted nation as ever was, but that's not enough. . . . Our political organisation is thoroughly rotten, almost non-existent. It is Carthaginian—really the only comparison I can think of. Never was there such an absurd waste of power, such ridiculous inconsequence of policy—not for want of men, but for want of any effective central authority or dominant idea, to make them work together."

It is an important consideration that even a short period of Crown
Government would, by encouraging immigration, materially quicken the
Anglicisation of this country, which is our only ultimate security. It is
probably the greatest of all the objections to self-government of the Cape
Colony on the old lines that no Cape Ministry depending on Parliament
will dare really to encourage, though for the benefit of the British public
they may talk about, the introduction of a fresh British population into
that portion of South Africa. Indeed we may think ourselves lucky if they
do not actually put obstacles in the way of it. A Bond Government
certainly would.[1]

There were other considerations besides. To plunge the Cape
into a general election would be to widen the breach between
Dutch and British:

At present there is no possible dividing line of parties but race, no possible subject of political controversy but the war. But it will not be many
years before . . . new problems will begin to agitate and divide opinion;
and unless the old party-divisions are *revived and stereotyped at once*, they
may never be revived at all.[2]

There was also the question of the future constitution of
South Africa as a whole. Milner's heart, like Chamberlain's,
was set on South African Federation. The Transvaal and the
Orange River were already under Crown Colony government.
If the same regime were applied to the Cape, might it not ease
the task of setting up common federal institutions for the whole
sub-continent?

At the root of these weighty arguments festered a personal
antagonism. Milner disliked and despised Sprigg.

MILNER TO CHAMBERLAIN

Johannesburg, September 20, 1901.—*Private and Confidential.*—. . .
The difficulty is immensely heightened by personalities. Sprigg is the
most hopeless man, weak, obstinate and vain. He has never given us the
least help or shown the least strength in dealing with treason, but he
takes a delight in displaying his independence of Governors and Com-
manders-in-Chief, and has always a side-glance at his position in Parliament, and the chance of conciliating a little "Bond" support by recounting
his exploits in resisting the "Imperial factor".

---

[1] Milner to Chamberlain: Secret   [2] Milner to Chamberlain: Secret
Dispatch of May 31, 1902 (25279/3).   Dispatch of May 10, 1902 (21682/5).

Sprigg was, indeed, the very antithesis of Milner. He was, essentially, an adroit party manager. No great principles guided his political course; nor was it illumined by any broad conception of the future. His only aim was to maintain himself in power; a state of things which he identified, and rightly as it proved, with the principle of self-government. To preserve it he would make whatever concessions had to be made. He saw things as they were, not as they might be; and, since he wished above all to remain Prime Minister, preferred to be it with the help of the Bond than not to be Prime Minister at all.

Chamberlain, as we have seen, had always been against Suspension. Milner once wrote of him, "Joe is a strong man. Under other stars he might be as big as Cavour or Bismarck."[1] Chamberlain certainly believed in strong government, but he believed in self-government too. It was in his blood, part of the democratic tradition of Dissent; and a generation spent in the House of Commons had only confirmed his faith in it. His genius was more empirical than Milner's. As an English statesman, he accepted the limitations of his rôle. It was no use to kick against the pricks. Self-government was the accepted British way. Its suspension even in South Africa would come as a great shock to opinion at Home and in the Empire. It would also give precious ammunition to his political opponents. He was determined, therefore, not to resort to it unless he was compelled to by events. It was a step not to be contemplated until he had an incontrovertible case to lay before the House of Commons.

III

Milner had discussed the whole question with Chamberlain during his visit to England the year before. He was well aware of his chief's objections to Suspension but utterly unmoved by them.

MILNER TO HELY-HUTCHINSON

Johannesburg, March 3, 1902.—Secret and personal.—. . . I am absolutely convinced myself of the necessity of intervention from home to put the Cape Colony straight and prevent its being a drag on all South African progress. And I am not the least afraid of "bearding Joe" about it, tho' he hates it, and loses his temper with me when I tell him what he

---

[1] *Milner Papers (South Africa)*, vol. ii. p. 364.

is in for. It is the only point in connection with South Africa about which
he and I are at cross purposes. . . . At the same time I feel that, if I am
right in my diagnosis of the state of public feeling at the Cape, viz., that
virtually all the British (except a few office holders) and not a few of the
modern Afrikanders *in their hearts*, long for a period of Crown Colony
government, *Joe ought to know it.* . . .[1]

Convinced that he was right, Milner now determined to provide Chamberlain with proofs that the great majority at least of
the Loyalist population at the Cape wanted Suspension. This
would lead him to intervene directly in Cape politics.

Rhodes, already a sick man, had returned to South Africa
at the beginning of the year. To him, to Jameson and to other
Progressive leaders, Milner spoke in favour of Suspension. He
stressed, however, "that there was no chance of the Imperial
Parliament intervening . . . unless there was a strong and
fairly unanimous appeal by the loyalists to Great Britain".[2]
Rhodes took the hint and proceeded to organise a petition
urging the temporary suspension of the constitution. He had
intended that all the members of the Progressive party should
sign this petition, and, when his last illness came upon him, he
had already secured forty-three out of some fifty signatures.
Had he lived he would almost certainly have compelled even the
Cape Ministry's support. As it was, his death left the petitioners
leaderless. With characteristic adroitness, Sprigg proceeded to
sow the seeds of dissension among them, until, as Jameson put
it, they "broke up into small squads".[3]

Milner had disliked the form which the Suspension agitation
had taken, but he was infuriated by Sprigg's manœuvres to
thwart its aim. Determined to have his way on an issue which
he regarded as vital, he left Johannesburg, towards the end of
April, for the Cape, ostensibly on a few days' holiday. There he
met the Progressive leaders and revived the waning Suspensionist movement by the assurance of his support.

Fortified, by Milner's advice, the Progressive leaders duly [4]

---

[1] Quoted from *Milner Papers* (*South Africa*), vol. ii. p. 408.

[2] *Ibid.* p. 406, paraphrase of letter from Milner to Rhodes of January 30, 1902.

[3] *Ibid.* p. 413.

[4] The Petition was presented on May 10, 1902. The Colonial Office was informed by telegram on May 12, but did not receive the text of the Petition, sent by mail, until June 2.

presented the Petition for Suspension to Hely-Hutchinson, the Governor, requiring him to lay it before the Imperial Government. They also asked him to forward a copy to Milner:

... as they desire his guidance and advice in the present difficult position. They feel most strongly that Lord Milner who was so recently their Governor and ... showed much foresight and so complete a knowledge of the political conditions prevailing, could, if he would, give some expression of opinion which would be of assistance to them not only in regard to the present proposal, but also in regard to the probable position of the colony during the time when their Parliamentary institutions would be inoperative.[1]

This was a concerted manœuvre designed to enable Milner to make a public statement which would reassure doubters among the Progressives and rally Loyalist opinion to the Suspension policy.

Milner replied in a letter to the Governor, which was communicated to the petitioners and made public. In this he expressed himself whole-heartedly in favour of Suspension and sought to allay the anxieties which some Loyalists still felt at the thought of surrendering self-government.

MILNER TO HELY-HUTCHINSON

Sunnyside (Johannesburg),—May 19, 1902.—. . . Speaking, then, unofficially, and as to old friends, I may say that I entirely sympathize with their desire to preserve the Colony from the disastrous consequences which are likely to result from the resumption of Parliamentary and party strife before the bitter passions excited by the war have had even a little time to subside. . . . It does not follow that an interim Colonial Government, because it was not based on popular election, would, therefore, not be representative. On the contrary it would be the interest, as well as the duty, of the Imperial Government to make it so, just as it would be its interest and its duty to see fair play between the various colonies in any federal arrangements.

IV

Nothing is harder to define than the limits in which an official representative may give expression to personal opinions when

[1] Messrs. F. Schermbrucker, A. Wilmot and Amos Bailey (organisers of the Petition) to the Governor of Cape Colony, May 10, 1902.

these are at variance with the policies of his government. The same rule can hardly be applied to a great proconsul as to a junior secretary; and judgment in each case must largely depend upon the circumstances and the man. But, whatever the proper limits may be, there is no doubt that, on this occasion, Milner exceeded them. He knew perfectly well that his action did not conform with Chamberlain's wishes. But so deep-seated was his conviction that he determined to stop at nothing to get his policy accepted. His letters show clearly enough what was his attitude.

MILNER TO CHAMBERLAIN

June 27, 1902.—. . . My principal object in writing was to make it quite clear what the real issue was; and the effect of my words no doubt has been to separate men according to their opinions on the fundamental question, unclouded by a number of imaginary or irrelevant considerations. In doing this, I necessarily showed to which side I personally inclined. It was impossible to avoid this, if I was to give people the guidance they were seeking for in considering the question. Rightly or wrongly there are a number of Cape Colonists, who think that my experience of the inner working of the constitutional system is unique, and who would rather take my view than any man's as to the probable results of a given political situation. If the meeting of Parliament was, in my opinion, likely to result in certain consequences, which they intensely dread, they were prepared to take any steps in their power to prevent its meeting. Thinking, as I did and do, that these consequences must result, was I justified in withholding my opinion? I thought not. I was quite aware of the unusual, and grave nature of the step. But with men, to whom I owed so much and who trusted me so completely, turning to me, in a crisis, for advice, and seeing them, as I thought exposed to the danger of being grossly misled by their natural leaders, I thought one of those rare cases had arisen, in which the formally incorrect course was the substantially right one. I still think so. At the same time I am conscious of the grave complication introduced by my official position. But I did all that was possible to make it clear that I spoke in my private character, and I did make it quite clear that I did not speak on behalf of H.M.'s Govt."

He expressed the same ideas more bluntly to a friend:

MILNER TO JAMES RENDEL

August 2, 1902.—. . . My letter was not an "indiscretion", if by that is meant a piece of thoughtlessness. It was a *very deliberate*, desperate, perhaps questionable attempt to prevent a tremendous blunder.[1]

Milner may well have hoped that his public intervention would compel Sprigg and his colleagues to fall into line with the main body of the Progressive party and support the Petition. He would thus have produced that "overwhelming case" in the form of the "clearly expressed desires of the great majority of the white population" which Chamberlain had declared to be the only possible justification of Suspension. If this was indeed Milner's hope, it was disappointed. Sprigg stood his ground with unexpected courage. With the single exception of Dr. Smartt, he persuaded his reluctant colleagues to declare against Suspension. He even prevailed on a few of the signatories to withdraw their names from the Petition. Having survived the first shock of the attack, Sprigg left for London to attend the Colonial Conference. There, he could put his case personally to Chamberlain and might hope besides to enlist the support of the other Colonial Premiers. Milner had thus failed to obtain a clear-cut decision, and was already outmanœuvred.

v

The scene now shifts to London. There Chamberlain remained, for more than a month, in total ignorance of what had happened. Milner neither warned him beforehand nor afterwards informed him of the grave step which he had taken. Moreover, by a curious oversight, the news of it was communicated to the London press not by cable but by the slow motion of the ocean mail.

While this political dynamite slumbered in the mail-bag, Chamberlain was busy exploring alternatives to Suspension. In a letter to Milner [2] he urged a compromise between moderate elements of the Progressives and the Bond which might enable the constitution to be maintained. Ironically enough, this letter

---

[1] *Milner Papers (South Africa)*, vol. ii. p. 424.

[2] Chamberlain to Milner, May 19, 1902.

was written on the same day as Milner committed his calculated indiscretion.

On June 2 Chamberlain received the text of the Petition in favour of Suspension. The same mail brought a detailed dispatch from Milner[1] advocating a Suspensionist policy. Chamberlain still knew nothing of Milner's public action. He sensed, however, that the Petition might bring matters to a head and telegraphed precise instructions to the Cape and to Johannesburg.

CHAMBERLAIN TO HELY-HUTCHINSON[2]

June 10, 1902.—*Strictly secret.* I shall consider carefully your despatches on the political situation in the Cape Colony. Meanwhile I would ask you to be very careful not to commit yourself in any way to the policy of suspending the Constitution and to stand outside any agitation.

His Majesty's Government could not for a moment entertain such a policy without incontrovertible proof that British interests are seriously threatened and that for their maintenance this policy is absolutely necessary. The Cape Colonists must not be allowed to think that they can appeal to the Imperial Government for the purpose of impressing on a majority the views of a minority.

Meanwhile, rumours of Milner's action reached London. On June 12 Chamberlain was asked in the House whether Milner had publicly recommended the Suspension of the Cape Constitution. He replied, in all good faith, that he had no reason to believe it. Nevertheless, he judged a further word of warning timely:

CHAMBERLAIN TO MILNER
(Telegram)

June 20, 1902.—*Confidential.*—. . . The more I consider the subject the more strongly I feel that suspension of Constitution by Act of Imperial Government is most undesirable and under present circumstances almost impossible.

Every other course should be exhausted, and I am most anxious for some kind of concordat between moderate men of both sections. . . .

All these instructions, issued in the dark, were, of course, without effect. Milner had already spilt the milk. They served,

[1] S.21682 of May 10, 1902.
[2] This telegram was repeated to Milner on June 15, as an answer to his dispatch of May 10. See previous footnote.

however, to deepen the imbroglio and to underline the questionable nature of Milner's action, when at last the truth came out. This was no longer delayed.

The mail from South Africa was received in London on June 23. Next morning a bulky dispatch[1] from Milner lay on the Colonial Secretary's desk. This contained a powerful plea for Suspension, but written as if the whole matter was still under discussion. Yet that same morning Chamberlain read in *The Times* the text, made public at the Cape a month before, of Milner's letter commenting on the Suspension petition. He was cut to the quick. Milner's action seemed to him at once disloyal and indiscreet. His rebuke was stinging.

CHAMBERLAIN TO MILNER

(Telegram)

June 24, 1902.—Secret and Personal.—I have received your despatch of 31st May. I certainly do not complain of full expression of your views in Confidential despatch, but am grateful for opinions which are most useful to me. I am, however, dismayed and seriously embarrassed by publication in this country of your letter of 19th May to Sir W. Hely-Hutchinson, apparently intended for publication, and in which you argue at length in favour of Suspension. When you visited England the question of possible Suspension was mentioned, and I explained the numerous objections to such a step, both from the point of view of the Home Government and from that of the situation in South Africa, and I stated that an overwhelming case would be required before I should feel justified in calling on the Imperial Government to intervene in order to suspend the Constitution of a self-governing Colony. Nothing but the safety of the State or the clearly-expressed desire of a great majority of the white population would, in my opinion, justify such a step.

I assumed that after this conversation nothing would be said or done in favour of Suspension without previous communication with me.

Throughout the difficult and complicated situation which has existed during the last few years in South Africa, I am sure you will admit that I have supported you with absolute loyalty, and that I have done my best to shield you from criticism and to avoid worrying you

[1] S.25279 of May 31, 1902.

unnecessarily to explain your action at a time when you have been
overwhelmed with the work of your most responsible office.

In these circumstances, I am deeply hurt to find that, in a matter
of cardinal importance, on which I desired the utmost caution, you
should have fully expressed your views to private individuals without
giving me the opportunity of considering them beforehand.

It is impossible for the public to dissociate the views expressed by
you, unofficially but publicly, from your official and representative
position as High Commissioner; and, accordingly, the Government is
already being asked whether your letter was written and published
with their sanction, and I cannot now avoid comment on the divergence
of views which seems to exist at present between us.

In your Secret telegram on 1st May you promised a Confidential
despatch on the situation, but did not give me the slightest intimation
that you contemplated any public pronouncement, and I observe that,
in your Secret despatch of 10th May, you stated that you did not even
at that time propose to draw inferences or obtrude advice, but that
you would return to the subject, and, meanwhile, your object was to
describe a situation and not to propound a policy.

I did not think it necessary, therefore, to warn you not in any way
to commit yourself or His Majesty's Government. The unfortunate
publication of your letter of 19th May seems to prejudge the matter,
but I still hope that the spirit which has been universally shown since
the surrender may give you an opportunity to modify your views. . . .

Milner felt Chamberlain's words keenly but nothing would
modify his views.

MILNER TO CHAMBERLAIN
(Telegram)

June 28, 1902.—*Secret and Personal.*—. . . I am deeply grieved
to cause you annoyance or embarrassment as I fully recognise all I owe
to your support in the past critical years. But for it I must have failed
and I shall always feel grateful to you.

As regards the action you complain of I was more than careful not
to commit H.M. Govt. I risked only myself and that I did deliberately,
though reluctantly, because I felt bound in honour to help those Cape
Loyalists who, deprived of their real leader, were being given away by
their nominal chiefs. Attempt on the part of Cape Ministry to stifle

expression of opinion on the part of their followers was intolerable, and, in view of fables freely put about as to my attitude, I had no choice but to state my true opinion. Details by letter too long for telegram will I hope greatly modify your view of personal aspect of matter. But nothing can alter fact that on this important question my action has been disapproved by you.

It is impossible for me to go back on opinions which I have expressed and which I hold as strongly as ever. But I shall of course abstain from further expression of them or from any dealing whatever with political questions at the Cape. I shall gladly devote myself to urgent business up here which by itself threatens to overtax my strength. My view of ultimate consequences of incident are fully stated in my letter of next mail.

This letter is among the most interesting documents in all the Chamberlain Papers. It belongs more to Milner's biography than to Chamberlain's, but no study of the Suspension crisis can be complete without it. It is a frank and fascinating account of the conflict in Milner's mind between his personal loyalty to Chamberlain and his deep conviction of what was politically right. It must be quoted here:

MILNER TO CHAMBERLAIN

Johannesburg, June 27, 1902.—*Private and Confidential.*—As usual, I am writing against time. There are a number of things I ought to write about, but there is one which claims attention as more important than all the rest, your "secret and personal" telegram of July [evidently an error for June] 24th.

It is by far the most painful thing which has befallen me during all this long business. Not that I mind much an official snub. In revolutionary times, when one has to take a number of decisions and do many things "off one's own bat", which would not be justified, or indeed required, under ordinary circumstances, there is always a chance of going too far, and of being pulled up for it. What affects me is the personal aspect of the matter. I feel more towards you than a sense of official duty—viz. personal respect and gratitude, and I am sorry to have given you cause to think that I acted without proper consideration for you.

I have no wish to argue as to the rights and wrongs of the case, but will confine myself simply to a record of what happened. You will see from it that, though my judgment may have been wrong, I certainly never forgot my obligations to you, and that the action I took was the result of a very exceptional, almost incredible complication.

I have all along been fully conscious of the great aversion you had for anything like interference with the constitutional machinery at the Cape, but I have also felt—perhaps I have not pointed out sufficiently, tho' I meant to—that a situation must arise, in which, whatever you might decide to do or not to do, the question must be faced. My great anxiety has been that the difficulties should be realised in time, and things not simply allowed to slide till we were over the precipice. When, therefore, I found, soon after my return to South Africa, that my anxieties were shared by nearly all the men, at the Cape, who have made great efforts and run substantial risks on our side, and on whom alone we can, in my opinion, really rely in the future, and when they incessantly appealed to me for advice and assistance, I felt it was impossible, having regard to the responsibility which their past support and continued confidence placed me under, to take up a strictly official "can't discuss the matter" attitude. But what I steadily impressed upon them all was (1) that anything I said was my personal opinion only, and (2) that H.M.'s Government was averse to interference in their affairs, and that a very strong case indeed would have to be made out, before any action whatever could be taken on your side. It was and is difficult for them to realise that they would not count for more, man for man, in the hour of victory than the people who, in the struggle, have been against us. But it is not for want of illumination from me that they fail to grasp the unpleasant fact. Of course, personally, I take their view. I have never concealed it. I think it unfortunate that public opinion in England . . . is capable of regarding it as tolerable that, within six months of the end of the struggle for British supremacy in South Africa, the men who have fought for that supremacy at the Cape should by any possibility be allowed to fall under the control of its bitter and treacherous enemies. . . . But that is neither here nor there. I knew it to be possible and that I myself could do little to avert it. But it seemed to me not only permissible for me, but my plain duty, to tell them that, unless they could themselves, and through the regular channels, bring their fears and necessities and the true state of the case before the British Govt. and people, judgment might go against them by default.

So far, there was certainly nothing in my action inconsistent with what I understood to be the limits placed upon me by your instructions. And as a matter of fact the suspension movement, when it came, not only originated in a manner which I never contemplated, but took a form, of which personally I should not have approved and which I have always regarded as unfortunate.

But there was one feature about it, however ill-advised the conduct of it, which seemed and still seems to me to have been invaluable, and which may yet help to save the situation, and certainly, in my opinion, strengthens instead of weakening the position of H.M.'s Govt. in any action it may take. That feature is the dissipation of the false security, the absurd illusions, which Sir Gordon Sprigg's blind self-confidence has led him to cherish. . . .

The agitation, when it came, revealed several things of importance. One was the fact that ministerial assurances that all was well . . . could not stand examination for a moment. Another was, that, with the exception of ministers themselves and a perfectly insignificant number of "mugwumps", the loyal population was prepared, and even anxious, to forego for a time its own privileges. . . . And, still more remarkable, it became evident that at least a considerable section of the Afrikander Party were equally willing.

I maintain, and I shall always think, that these are facts which it was absolutely necessary to bring to the notice of the public at home and of H.M. Govt., especially when it was done in a manner which in no possible way committed the latter, and that, if I had allowed the existence of such a state of feeling to be hidden away or lied out of court, I should have failed in my duty. . . .

VI

This letter, like the one which it explained, was long delayed on the high seas. Meanwhile Sprigg had arrived in London. He assured Chamberlain that he had a sufficient majority to carry an Indemnity Act and to confirm the sentences passed by the military courts. Chamberlain resolved to put him to the test. Only if Sprigg failed would he contemplate more drastic measures. He laid his views before the Cabinet in a memorandum [1]

[1] June 25, 1902.

which summarises with admirable clearness and impartiality
the history of the crisis and the contrary opinions of Milner and
of Sprigg. His own recommendation and comment was reserved
for the end.

I imagine that it would take a month or more to pass an Act (sus-pending the Cape constitution) in the Imperial Parliament, and I have reason to know that it would be opposed strongly by the so-called Liberal Imperialists. I doubt if we could count on our own supporters without a much stronger case than I can make; and I am, therefore, of opinion that we should make an early announcement that the Cape Parliament will be shortly called together.

It cannot have been easy for Chamberlain to recommend that his High Commissioner's categorical and published advice be overruled. Milner's prestige was immense; he was the man on the spot; and his conviction was shared by the Governor of the Cape and the most loyal elements in that Colony. The Chamberlain Papers show that, in their first reactions at least, the Cabinet were not unanimous. James and Balfour of Burleigh gave Chamberlain their whole-hearted support.

BALFOUR OF BURLEIGH TO CHAMBERLAIN

June 27, 1902.—*Private.*—. . . I recognise in what a delicate and difficult situation you have been placed. I wish to say, however, that I incerely trust you will be able to stand to your own view.

We really cannot *now* suspend the Constitution in the light of the way the Boers have behaved since the surrender. Events might make such a step necessary. It would be suicidal now in my humble opinion. . . .

JAMES TO CHAMBERLAIN

June 27, 1902.—. . . Milner's monstrous indiscretion seems to render it necessary that complete firmness should be shown here. . . . I am *strongly* opposed to any suspension until it can be shown that the loyal Colonists cannot obtain justice by constitutional action.

Selborne, always under Milner's influence, was less convinced. He was astonished at Milner's proceeding but hesitated to go contrary to his advice.

SELBORNE TO CHAMBERLAIN

June 27, 1902.—I have read with dismay and distress your corre-spondence with Milner about the suspension of the Cape Constitution.

It would be nothing less than a national disaster that there should be any breach of your mutual confidence and cooperation.

I have not seen the letter Milner appears to have written to Hely-Hutchinson. I must have missed it. But I feel convinced there must be some misunderstanding. It is utterly unlike Milner to write such a letter, without your knowledge, *for publication* or *to allow it to be published.*

Do High Commissioners write letters to Governors for publication and do High Commissioners or Governors publish such letters without the approval of the Secretary of State? I cannot believe it.

In respect of your memorandum I follow all the train of argument and see the full force of it. But, before coming to a final decision, must we not ask ourselves what the position will be if Milner's prognostications turn out correct and Sprigg's optimistic forecasts all moonshine?

In that case will the consequences be such as Milner fears? If so what steps will it then be open for us to take? . . . Instinctively I . . . distrust the Bond leaders in Cape Colony far more than I do the Boer leaders in the new Colonies.

Before reaching a final decision, Chamberlain referred the question to what, in his mind at least, was the supreme court of appeal. With Sprigg's consent he consulted the Colonial Premiers, assembled in London for the Coronation.

CHAMBERLAIN TO MILNER

July 24, 1902.—I took an opportunity, before finally coming to a decision, to submit the question to the Prime Ministers now in England. I gave them no indication of my own views, but I found that they were unanimously of the opinion that such a drastic step would be regarded with grave anxiety in the Colonies, unless we could produce evidence of serious and urgent danger to British interests or of a desire expressed through the usual constitutional channels on the part of the majority of the constituencies.[1]

The Colonial Premiers felt strongly on the subject. Barton, indeed, went so far as to declare publicly that

[1] In this letter Chamberlain states that the Premiers were "unanimously" opposed to Suspension. There is certainly nothing in the Chamberlain Papers to support Professor Eric Walker's assertion (*Lord de Villiers and his Times,* p. 402) that Seddon and Hime wanted Suspension. Professor Walker also seems to imply, in the same context, that Chamberlain was, himself, in favour of Suspension. All the evidence cited here suggests that this is a misapprehension.

there was not a self-governing part of the Empire which had not been
in sympathy with Sir Gordon Sprigg in his earnest deprecation of any
interference with the political liberties of the Cape Colony.[1]

Meanwhile, Chamberlain received support from an unexpected quarter. Asquith sent on to him a letter from de Villiers, the Chief Justice of the Cape, earnestly advising against Suspension. De Villiers was the most influential of the loyal Dutch, and his views weighed heavily with Chamberlain. Asquith's own letter must also have counted for much. He was a close friend of Milner; and it had long been the dream of the Liberal Imperialists to find an opportunity of supporting Milner against Chamberlain.

ASQUITH TO CHAMBERLAIN

June 28, 1902.—*Confidential.*—. . . For my own part . . . I cannot but think that the conclusion of peace and the disfranchisement of the Cape rebels . . . make it of the highest moment to try the experiment of governing by means of the Cape Parliament, before giving any countenance to the suggestions of the Rhodes-Jameson party. I should hope that Milner himself will see that this is, in the altered circumstances, the course of wisdom.

These exchanges only confirmed Chamberlain's resolution. On July 1 he persuaded the Cabinet to reject the Suspensionist Petition.

Having carried his point, Chamberlain's first care was to try and repair the breach with Milner.

CHAMBERLAIN TO MILNER
(Telegram)

July 2, 1902.—*Secret and Personal.*—I deeply regret that any serious difference should have arisen between us as to policy and hope that time and progress of events will remove it. I rely on your cooperation as far as you can honestly give it to prevent ill consequences to public interest.

I am communicating decision of Cabinet with regard to Suspension to Governor of Cape where it will be published immediately. I have tried to minimise difference and to follow as far as possible spirit of your suggestions. . . .

[1] At a banquet of the Primrose League, July 7, 1902.

The last sentence is important. Chamberlain was resolved to turn the crisis to good account. He had resisted Suspension. He would, however, keep the threat of it in the background to admonish the Bond leaders of the wisdom of moderation. In this spirit he prepared the official reply to the Petition.

Considering the whole question of the proposed Suspension broadly, His Majesty's Government cannot but feel that to deprive the Cape Colonists, even for a time, of their constitutional rights by imposing a system of Crown Colony Government, without giving to the present representatives of the people the opportunity of expressing their opinions on such a great change, is likely rather to produce discontent and agitation than to pacify race hatred. It does not appear to them justifiable to assume *beforehand* that the Colonial Parliament will refuse to pass the necessary measures for the pacification of the country; and His Majesty's Government agree, therefore, with your Ministers that it is proper, *in the first place*, that the Colonial Parliament should be called together as soon as possible, and that the requisite legislation should be *at once* introduced.[1]

The words shown here in italics were used advisedly. Elsewhere, indeed, in the dispatch Chamberlain made it plain that he was determined that the necessary acts of Indemnity, confirmation of Martial Law sentences, and Redistribution should be passed:

Such legislation, which might be passed either by the Imperial or by the Cape Parliament, is no doubt indispensable for the maintenance of British interests, but His Majesty's Government entertain the hope that the Cape Parliament will not fail in its evident duty; and will be prepared to take all the steps necessary for the security of the Colony and for discouraging racial and political controversy likely to interfere with the restoration of its prosperity.

It is only in the event, which His Majesty's Government do not contemplate as probable, of refusal by the Cape Parliament to fulfil its obligations that serious danger would arise to Imperial interests.[2]

His meaning was unmistakable. The Imperial Government wished to see the Cape Parliament reassemble; but if that

[1] Chamberlain to the Governor of the Cape, dispatch telegraphed July 2, 1902 (published in Cd. 1162, July 1902). My italics.—J. A.
[2] *Ibid.*

Parliament should fail to pass the legislation required for the
 protection of British interests, then, though only then, the Government might feel compelled to resort to Suspension.

Chamberlain's decision was generally approved by public opinion at Home and in the Colonies. The Suspensionists at the Cape were naturally disappointed but adjusted themselves to the new situation with commendable realism. Mistrusting Sprigg more than ever, they kept their organisation in being to press, no longer indeed for Suspension, but for the passage of those measures for which Suspension had at first been thought necessary.

The Cape Parliament was accordingly summoned to meet on August 20. Sprigg abandoned the Colonial Conference to prepare for a stormy session. Before sailing, he acknowledged his debt.

SPRIGG TO CHAMBERLAIN

July 12, 1902.—On the point of starting I must write to thank you for the magnificent service rendered to the Colony I represent and South Africa at large by the clear and decisive Dispatch regarding the Suspension of the Constitution. . . .

VII

The crisis was over. Chamberlain had had his way, but it would have been a bitter triumph unless followed by reconciliation with Milner. Milner's letter of explanation was by now to hand. Chamberlain could not accept its arguments, but his reply was frank, generous and healing.

CHAMBERLAIN TO MILNER

July 24, 1902.—*Secret.*—. . . I wish you to feel that I do not attach exaggerated importance to the difference of opinion which has arisen between us on a matter of policy. It seems to me that such differences are inevitable in the situation in which we find ourselves. It is hardly possible that two men separated by great distances should arrive uniformly at exactly the same conclusions on the hundred and one important questions which come up for settlement. Where, as in our case, there exists mutual confidence and respect, we can well be content to regard the policy as a whole and not to allow a general agreement to be in any way disturbed by occasional divergences. In such a case it is our duty, as I am sure it is our wish, to minimise the difference and above all to give no cause to the enemy to blaspheme, or to separate our positions and to sow dissensions amongst our followers.

The principle which should govern our relations is that which governs all Cabinets, namely, that there should be absolute frankness in our private relations and full discussion of all matters of common interest, and that, then, the decisions finally arrived at should be loyally supported and considered as the decisions of the whole of the Government or of the parties concerned in the discussion. Of course there may be occasions in which the difference is of so vital a character that it is impossible for the minority or the party whose views are rejected to continue their support, and in this case the Ministry breaks up or the minority member or members resigns.

But this is certainly not our case at present. Important as is the policy to be pursued in Cape Colony it is not an absolutely essential part of your general administration. On all the main lines of the latter I believe we are in entire agreement, or at all events, if there are differences they are of no great importance, and either of us might give way to the other without difficulty. Whatever happens in the Cape, we have practically a free hand in the two Colonies and can lay securely the foundations for their future.

As regards the merits of the particular subject in dispute, I do not think it necessary to add much to what I have said in previous letters. . . .

I must, however, take exception to one paragraph in your letter in which you say that those who have fought or sided with us do not count for more, man for man, in the hour of victory than the people who in the struggle have been against us. This is certainly not the case, and on the contrary it has been a guiding principle with me to pay special attention to the views of our friends and whenever possible to accept them. At the same time I do not admit that they can claim to dictate Imperial policy. I find, in all such cases, that those on the spot are not necessarily the best advisers. They take too limited and too parochial a view of the situation and are unable to make allowances for broader considerations which are present to our minds. . . . I doubt whether . . . it would have been possible, even with our nominal majority, to carry such a measure through the House of Commons without much greater evidence of necessity than we at present possess. What then would have been the result in South Africa of a discussion carried on, it may be for months, in the British House of Commons and echoing throughout the whole British Empire, in which a most serious division of opinion would have been manifested even amongst the strongest Imperialists? In my opinion it would have reacted most mischievously on South African politics and would have stimulated and encouraged the enemies of British rule to further agitation of the most dangerous kind.

At the same time I am not unaware of all that is to be said on the other side. On the contrary, I am deeply impressed with the difficulties of the situation and by your forecast of the kind of political agitation that we may have to face. But, so long as it is merely political, I do not fear it. The worst that could happen would be that in the words of the pro-Boers we should have an "Ireland in South Africa". That would be a most undesirable and annoying result, but its importance should not be exaggerated. After all, what is the situation in Ireland? We have constant agitation promoted by the most insincere and impracticable politicians in the world. We are hampered in the House of Commons, and our time, which might be devoted to matters of much greater interest to the Empire, is wasted on imaginary Irish grievances. After all, however, the annoyance is personal and does not constitute any real danger. We have always been told that England's difficulty would be Ireland's opportunity. Well, we have been in the greatest difficulty that we have had to face during a century. We have denuded the country of almost the whole of its reliable military forces, and yet Ireland has been perfectly quiet, and there has never been a time in which it has given us the slightest serious anxiety. So I hope it will be, at the worst, in South Africa. We may have political agitation and obstruction, but, as long as the physical force is under our control, British rule will be firmly established and nothing can touch our more important interests. Time alone will show whether you or I are right in our forecast. In my experience political decisions are always a choice of evils, and I firmly believe that your alternative would have involved us in greater difficulties than the worst we have to anticipate under present conditions.

I want you, however, to understand that in regard to this I am not dogmatic and recognise the possibility that I may have been mistaken. I have acted under a very strong conviction and must take full responsibility for the consequences whatever they are. I repeat, then, that I do not attach serious importance to the fact that on one point our judgments differ. What I do regret, and must in all frankness impress upon you, is that you should have thought it necessary publicly to declare your opinions before I had had the opportunity of discussing them with you. I quite appreciate the difficulty in which you were placed and the obligations under which you felt yourself to those who had consistently supported your policy. But, when they asked you to give an opinion on a matter of such great importance, I still think that you should have telegraphed the situation to me and waited for my opinion before taking action which could not be recalled. It is this which has made the present difficulty and which has compelled a public disclosure of differences which I should have liked to have kept entirely private.

I will say no more under this head except to assure you that it has not lessened my general confidence in your able and loyal cooperation and that I hope it will not interfere in any way with our cordial relations in the future.

A few days later [1] Milner's conduct was sharply censured in the House of Commons by the leader of the Opposition. Chamberlain defended Milner in generous terms.

. . . The right hon. gentleman has offered some criticism on the action of Lord Milner in regard to this matter. . . . I wish he would take into consideration the debt that we owe to Lord Milner (*cheers*), the enormous work he has been performing, the unstinted labour that he has given, the great ability he has brought to bear, even, as I fear, to the detriment of his own health, and that under these circumstances he had thought it unnecessary to bring up to public criticism any details in connexion with this great public servant. (*Cheers.*) As he has done so, I will say that I think that injustice has been done to Lord Milner with regard to his real action . . . What does it all amount to? . . . We have differed from him, it is true, upon an important point, but that does not in the slightest degree lessen our confidence in him, that he will carry out loyally the policy in which we have instructed him, and we believe that there is no one who can give that policy so much effect and emphasis as he can. (*Cheers.*) . . . We do not look to the past, we look to the future, and, for the future, we regard Lord Milner as the most effective instrument in our possession (*cheers*), and we hope that the House of Commons

[1] July 29, 1902.

will extend to him the consideration and confidence which we are so glad to show him. . . .[1]

VIII

The Cape Parliament met on August 20. The Bond proved to have an effective majority whenever they cared to exercise it; and the Sprigg Government only existed on sufferance. But the Dutch acknowledged their military defeat by the caution of their political manœuvres. They spoke with violence. They voted with restraint. The Act of Indemnity was duly passed, and the estimates were approved, including the increased naval contribution promised by Sprigg at the Colonial Conference. Sprigg in return abandoned all idea of introducing a stricter Sedition Bill or any legislation to limit the purchase and possession of firearms.

The thorny task of reviewing the major sentences imposed under martial law was by consent entrusted to a Royal Commission under the Lord Chief Justice, Lord Alverstone, who accepted the charge at Chamberlain's request. The Commissioners spent two months in South Africa and reviewed 794 cases. With few exceptions they upheld the verdicts of the military courts but scaled down the sentences in accordance with the Government's declared policy of clemency.

Thus far Sprigg had walked his tight-rope with some skill; but it was precisely over this question of martial law sentences that he all but overbalanced. The appointment of the Alverstone Commission had removed the graver cases from the political arena. There remained the minor cases and the sentences already served. The British element was disinclined to allow such cases to be reopened, but the Bond, seeing an excellent opportunity for smearing the British record, pressed for their re-examination. Sprigg prepared to yield. He proposed that a local commission should be appointed to review the minor sentences or, alternatively, that the terms of reference of the Royal Commission should be extended. Chamberlain was strongly opposed to either proposal. He regarded them as a breach of the assurances which Sprigg had given in London and seriously contemplated dismissing him.

[1] Hansard, Fourth Series, vol. cxii. col. 52 (July 29, 1902).

CHAMBERLAIN TO GOVERNOR HELY-HUTCHINSON
(Telegram)

August 26, 1902.—Secret.—. . . As you know, I have strongest objection to either a Local Commission or to an extension of Lord Alverstone's Commission . . . The enquiry will in any case be accompanied by . . . grave evils . . . and to prevent them I am ready to contemplate a quarrel with Sprigg provided that there is an alternative Government who could hold the new elections. It will depend on the present Parliamentary proceedings whether I should or should not instruct you to withhold your signature from such a Commission and try a change of Government. If Smartt's party as a whole are also in favour of a Commission, nothing would be gained by getting rid of Sprigg. But, if the Government is opposed by all the Progressives outside the Ministry, the case is different.

The point is that we must, if we quarrel with Sprigg, have a united Progressive party to fall back upon. I fear there would be little chance of this commanding a majority in the present Parliament, but I assume that, if Smartt could form a Ministry, he would at once dissolve.

I shall be glad if you will let me have your views as to what the probable composition of the new Parliament would be in such case, and whether the Progressives and Moderates would be likely to hold their own. . . .

But Sprigg had judged the situation to a nicety. No alternative government was possible.

GOVERNOR HELY-HUTCHINSON TO CHAMBERLAIN
(Telegram)

*August 28, 1902.—Secret.—*As regards an alternative government . . . I cannot say that it is likely that Progressives and Moderates would be likely to hold their own. I am at present, therefore, disposed to the opinion that it will be better not to quarrel with Sprigg. But further developments may take place.

Further developments, however, tended to Sprigg's favour. The Progressives were far from united under Smartt; and a few days later an important fraction rallied to the Premier. In the circumstances Chamberlain could do nothing. It was a galling situation, and he gave vent to his irritation in private talk at Highbury.

At any moment most important events may arise in South Africa. I cannot trust Sprigg, you see what he is doing. If I could get anyone to replace him, I would dismiss him to-morrow. . . . I have reports which show that I cannot trust the Progressives. They are holding "pot" meetings. Only the other day they held one at which they discussed rescinding their vote of censure on Sprigg and rejoining him again. The parties at the Cape are not clearly divided into Bond and Progressive. If they were I would know what to do. Sprigg is a clever little politician who will do anything to be Premier. He would sell himself to the Bond or to any other group in order to be that![1]

How Milner would have smiled, if he had overheard!

For a further eighteen months Sprigg governed the Cape by a policy of balance which favoured the "rebels" at least as much as the "loyalists".[2] Like a beginner on a bicycle he swerved erratically from side to side but was for a long time preserved from the inevitable fall. In the end both sides abandoned him; and at the general election he would be rejected even by his own constituents.

Nevertheless, Sprigg deserves greater credit than he has generally been given. He was not a great statesman, but he was a firm believer in parliamentary self-government, if only for the very practical reason that it was his trade. Yet, in the circumstances of 1902, there seemed but little hope of reviving parliamentary government at the Cape. The essential measure of understanding between the opposing parties did not exist. They were separated by all the bitter passions of a civil and racial war. The Progressives thought of themselves as "loyalists", of the Bond as "rebels". The Bond, judging their opponents by themselves, saw in the agitation for Suspension nothing but an attempt to establish a British racial domination, comparable to their own dream of Dutch supremacy. The gulf between them seemed impassable. But for Sprigg, it might well have remained so. By a happy accident Sprigg's personal interest coincided with that of the State. To preserve the constitution he threw to the

[1] From the shorthand notes of a conversation at Highbury, September 1, 1902, taken down by a Mr. McHugh for Mr. Le Sage the editor of the *Daily Telegraph*.

[2] Sprigg's proposal for extending the enquiry into the martial law sentences remained under discussion for some months. It was finally abandoned in January 1903 during Chamberlain's visit to South Africa.

winds most of the prejudices and many of the principles in the name of which the war had been fought. His ends may have been unworthy and his methods questionable; but he bridged the gap. It was no mean achievement.

What is to be our verdict on the Suspension crisis? Was Chamberlain right and Milner wrong? The question admits of no such easy answer. The subsequent history of South Africa suggests that Chamberlain's decision was wise. Yet it does not necessarily follow from this that Milner was mistaken. But for Milner, the Suspensionist movement might have died with Rhodes; and, but for their fear of Suspension, the Bond might have thrown all self-restraint to the winds and wrecked the constitution. Moreover, it was the Suspension movement, however unsuccessful in attaining its original purpose, which gave a new lease of life to the Progressive party. It contributed more than anything else to Jameson's victory at the elections of 1904, and so gave the Cape a predominantly British Government in a critical period of its history.

We may thus conclude that, examined objectively, Milner's policy was not the opposite of Chamberlain's, but its essential complement. Their letters show that they did not at once see things in this light. Chamberlain undoubtedly thought Milner guilty of a grave indiscretion; and Milner, as we shall see, judged Chamberlain's disapproval fatal to their partnership. But Chamberlain deserves great credit for the skill with which he presently turned Milner's action to his own account. With consummate statesmanship he combined his policy and Milner's in their true proportion. The lure of the carrot was enhanced by the crack of the whip; and Chamberlain's resolve to preserve self-government at the Cape was made compatible with British interests chiefly by Milner's efforts to prevent its restoration. Thus incalculably did the clash between these leaders of Imperialism subserve their common purpose.

IX

But, for our story, the most significant aspect of the Suspension crisis was its effect upon Chamberlain's relations with Milner. Chamberlain, at the summit of affairs, saw matters in their true proportion. He had resented Milner's indiscretion CHAP. keenly, but he held it of small account against the value which LXXX. he set upon their partnership. Milner, confined to the South Æт. 66. African horizon, brooded upon the incident and exaggerated its importance. Tired and intensely lonely in the uncongenial crowd of Rand magnates and Boer attorneys, he read into it a fundamental difference between his and Chamberlain's conception of South Africa's future. Besides, having played for high stakes and lost, he was determined to pay his forfeit. These things led him to a dramatic decision. He would resign.

His telegram of June 28 had already contained a hint of resignation; and Chamberlain, sensing the danger, had sounded Selborne's opinion:

SELBORNE TO MILNER

July 7, 1902.—. . . Chamberlain asked me if you would resign. I said I would bet my last dollar you would not because your duty to the Empire was the only thing you thought of, never your personal feelings, and that your great life's work in South Africa is not yet done, you know full well. Now I have told you everything, except that Chamberlain also judged you so. . . .[1]

But Selborne and Chamberlain were wrong. Milner's mind was made up. In the fateful exchanges which followed, it will be best to leave the protagonists to speak for themselves. The absorbing interest of their correspondence must excuse its length. It provides a comparison between two powerful characters worthy almost of Plutarch.

MILNER TO CHAMBERLAIN

June 27, 1902.—*Private and Confidential.*—. . . The incident, and your udgment of it (the rightness of which I don't dispute, tho' personally, feeling strongly as I do on the matter, I am unable to sympathise with it) strengthens a doubt, which has been growing in my mind for some months, whether I am any longer the right man to represent H.M.'s Govt. in S. Africa. Clearly I am out of touch about Cape matters. That could be remedied by simply leaving them alone. But they won't leave me alone. The S. African question is *one* question. In different shapes, the problem throughout is an identical one. The political developments

---

[1] Quoted from *Milner Papers* (*South Africa*), vol. ii. p. 418.

at the Cape will profoundly affect the future of the new Colonies. I am afraid that my views on the subject are diverging more and more from the average views of those who, *during the struggle,* have in the main sympathized with my line of action. You may say, "what does that matter. It is not your business to decide policy. We are content if you loyally carry it out." And, of course, I quite recognise that. But the efficiency of an agent, certainly of *this* agent, is enormously affected by the question whether he is *in the main*—of course there must be constant differences about details—in cordial agreement with the work he is set to do. Let me speak quite frankly. I do not think any one can quite realise what the strain of these last 3 years has been to me. What has carried me through has been my sense of your complete confidence in me, and my own absolute conviction that we were on the right road. I cannot help feeling that your confidence is somewhat shaken, and, on my side, I am no longer equally convinced that we are on the right tack. In this Cape matter I do not think we are. No doubt, it would show an imperfect sense of proportion to make too much of that one point. The world won't come to an end even if the Cape Colony relapses into something like its old condition. But the state of public information and feeling at home, the attitude of the public mind, which makes it *impracticable* to take the bull by the horns in Cape Colony, will, I foresee, make it equally impracticable to fight the Bond, or its analogues, when it spreads to the new Colonies, as I think it ought to be fought, tooth and nail. Even if we were so to fight it, I don't think I am the best man for the job. I am suspected . . . of being too little disposed to *conciliate* our late enemies. I think the idea mistaken, but I recognise that it is very natural.

The immediate problem up here—I mean in the new Colonies . . . causes me no alarm.

I am sure that I shall be in complete accord with you about this. The only danger here is narrow-mindedness and parsimony. You will protect us against these. But with the wider political problem which lies beyond . . . I feel less fitted to cope. . . .

Speaking after much reflection, I think you should begin to consider whether some new man cannot be found to take up the task. Under the most favourable circumstances, I am not sure whether I could last the course. It is a five years job and I am not good for five years of such work and anxiety as those of the last five. My health has never been satisfactory since my return and it does not improve. There is only one good side to this and that is that, whenever a change was thought desirable, it would be easy to effect it on grounds of health. . . . And as I do not desire any other public employment, there would not be the difficulty, so common in these cases, of finding something else for me to do.

I have not the slightest idea of embarrassing the Government by asking to be relieved immediately. It would be a mistake, and I should be very sorry, to make the change, until the Govt. of the two new Colonies was a going concern. This may take 6 or 9 months— perhaps a year, not, I think, longer. . . .

How would it do to say, that I should put in one complete year of the new system, which begins its first twelvemonth to-morrow? I do not mean to say that you should not relieve me sooner if you desired it. Neither do I propose to let anyone know that I have asked to be retired at the end of the year. It would greatly weaken me, and embarrass you, if a change were announced or suspected too long beforehand. On the other hand, if this date were provisionally fixed *between you and me*, you would have plenty of time to make the not easy choice of a new man.

CHAMBERLAIN TO MILNER

July 24, 1902.—*Secret.*—. . . Turning now to the latter part of your letter and to a consideration of the future, I think you will have understood from what precedes that I do not think our present divergence should make any difference at all in regard to your plans and position. There is a great work to be done for the Empire in South Africa—greater even than all that has arisen in connection with the war, and there is nobody who by natural ability and local experience can better perform that work than yourself. It seems to me therefore that, apart from all personal considerations, it is your duty to remain and to carry this work as far as your health will permit. It has fallen to you to lay the foundations on which British supremacy must ultimately rest. You have all the strings in your hand and you have—all the more perhaps because of the views you have taken in the recent controversy—the confidence of those whose loyal and strenuous co-operation is necessary to success. You can do more than anyone else to moderate the extreme views of the loyalists in South Africa and at the same time to maintain a firm control over anti-British agitation and opposition.

I hope, therefore, you will allow me to consider the latter part of your letter as still unwritten. Of course, if at any time the question of health becomes a serious one, I should be the last to press upon you the continuance of labours which have become too heavy for you to bear; but on no other ground could I assent, either in the interests of the Empire or of your own reputation, to any curtailment of the services which have hitherto been so efficiently rendered. . . . I shall be glad to know by return that you are able to accept this view of the situation which, in that case, I shall consider as entirely unchanged by recent events, leaving us to count as before on your loyal cooperation in the difficult work which still lies before us.

MILNER TO CHAMBERLAIN

September 6, 1902.—*Secret and Personal.*—. . . I regret that I cannot alter the opinion expressed in my letter of June 27th, tho' perhaps, at this distance of time, I should alter certain expressions.

I am most anxious that you should not think that opinion was formed in any "huff" about an incident, for which I am to some extent to blame, but to which I do not attach, indeed could not attach after your letter, exaggerated importance.

I never had the childish idea of resigning, leaving everything here at sixes and sevens, and seriously embarrassing the Government because I was over-ruled even on an important matter. As you say, differences of opinion must arise, and I cannot expect always to have my own way.

But a thing, which is not in itself of first rate moment, may be significant as a symptom and a warning. What my failure to prevent the Cape relapsing into the hands of the Bond—not of itself, but coming on the top of a series of events all teaching the same lesson, has brought home to me, is that I am out of touch with the predominant sentiment of my countrymen, the trend of opinion which ultimately determines policy, on the S. African question. This has not always been the case, nor is the divergence, of which I have been increasingly conscious for some time past and which is perhaps as much due to a change in my views as to a change elsewhere, as yet generally recognised. It is highly desirable that it never should be. It is for this reason that I am anxious to quit the field, while I can do so in peace, without discredit, and with a really good pretext. The last 3 years have really told upon me physically, and this can occasion no surprise.

In private, and between ourselves, I look at the question entirely on public grounds. Personally, I have always been unfortunate in disliking

my life and surroundings here. On that ground I should have sought
escape before, but, of course, in the thick of a great struggle, it was
not to be thought of. I can honestly say I have put personal considerations absolutely on one side, and I would not let any such consideration,
even that of health, weigh at all, if I thought my staying on here indefinitely was in the public interest. But I am sure it is not. . . . A
new man will have immense advantages. He will not be "stale". . . . He
will not excite the same hostility as I do among the Boers or their friends
at home. He will be able to take "conciliation" seriously. If he does not
trust the Boers (which I pray he may not do) he will be better able to
pretend to trust them than I am, weary as I feel of their eternal dupli-
city. As regards the English, he will, no doubt, at first not have anything
like my influence. But, on the other hand, that influence cannot always,
or long, remain what it is to-day. Indeed I have already drawn heavily
on my capital in that respect, and shall have to draw more in the immediate future. I do not complain of this. I feel that my popularity is not
being wasted, but is being legitimately *used up* in securing public objects
of importance. . . . My successor will be able to face the next set of
problems with much better heart than I, because he will, presumably,
have some sort of belief in what he is doing. I assume that he will have
that robust faith in self-governing institutions which is the birth-right
of every sound-hearted Briton, but which in my case has been unfortunately dissipated by experiences which I trust are exceptional. What I
have seen of the working of "responsible government" in S. Africa
makes it totally impossible for me to labour for its extension with any
sort of zeal, even if I do not absolutely show the cloven hoof of political
heresy in connection with it. Of course, I know it must come—and pretty
soon. Our own people are as determined to have it as they will be sorry
for themselves when they have it. But it is surely better that the way
should be paved for its establishment by some one who regards it as a
desirable thing in itself, and not simply as a deplorable necessity.

. . . When you have fixed on him (my successor), I only ask for so
much notice as may enable me to take the first step, by applying for my
release (on the ground of my need of a prolonged rest), and to look after
people, to whom I am under special obligations and whom I would not
like to have suddenly to turn adrift. In the meanwhile I shall say absolutely nothing. There was some rumour (pure conjecture) at the time of
your constitution despatch, that I was going, but it has *entirely subsided.*

I am working on quietly and I shall work with all the more cheerfulness and energy because I believe that relief is somewhere in the offing.

Milner's decision seemed irrevocable. Chamberlain had done all he could to heal the breach. He now faced the necessity of choosing a successor.

CHAMBERLAIN TO BALFOUR

Highbury, September 29, 1902.—*Secret.*—"I am afraid you must wade through the enclosed correspondence.

The papers . . . contain all that has passed since the question of the Cape Constitution was decided in reference to Milner's own position.

I do not think I can do more than I have done to keep him and I fear we must consider the question of his successor who will have to go out next year—say any time after July.

I should like a few words with you about this before or after the Cabinet. . . .

Chamberlain and Balfour discussed this delicate question when they met again in October at the end of the recess. They decided that Chamberlain should make a last effort to change Milner's mind, when he reached South Africa. They also agreed, meanwhile, to offer the provisional succession to Balfour of Burleigh, the Secretary of State for Scotland. They sounded him together in the Prime Minister's room at the House on October 28. He accepted their offer, though reluctantly.

BALFOUR OF BURLEIGH TO CHAMBERLAIN

October 29, 1902.—*Private.*—On thinking over our conversation yesterday, I am half afraid I may have left on your mind the impression that I let the personal element to myself bulk too largely.

I know I spoke of that, and perhaps I did not say enough to give you a proper idea of how highly I value your having spoken to me as you did, nor perhaps enough of the magnitude and responsibility of the task which lies before anyone in South Africa.

I should be ungracious indeed were I not gratified by the former, and as to the latter, I can only say I think the task the greatest the Empire has to offer, outside the British Islands, and there are not many in the islands worthy to be compared with it.

I still hope that events will not make a change necessary. I read the letters you sent round with care. Nothing could be kinder than your own, and the combination of responsibility with isolation must try the grit and nerve of any man.

If a change comes I would with diffidence and not without fear do my best to take up the burden.

Balfour of Burleigh was a genial fellow, though ponderous and rather deaf, and had gleaned a considerable knowledge of the Empire in the course of a lifetime of service on Royal Commissions. It is, however, hard to believe that he would have had the vitality, the resourcefulness or the intellectual powers to take Milner's place in the critical years of reconstruction.

X

Thus, on the eve of Chamberlain's departure for South Africa, his great partnership with Milner seemed to be drawing to a close. Together they had thwarted Kruger's policy of Dutch supremacy, and had waged a bitter but finally victorious war. Now they were to be sundered before completing the greatest task of all, the reconstruction and unification of South Africa. Fortunately for the Empire the gods decided otherwise; though they would grant only a short respite.

The names of Chamberlain and Milner are written large across the pages of South African history. Both men were great Imperialists, but they came to that faith by very different paths. Milner was above all things an intellectual. For him the British Empire was a political conception of absolute value not, as for most Englishmen, a mere projection of British energies and interests. Reasoning from first principles, he enjoyed a larger perspective of affairs than most, perhaps than any, of his contemporaries. But this quality had its own defect. His very grasp of the broad trends seemed to make his handling of details awkward. As a result, his incomparable political strategy was sometimes cheated of its full reward by rigid or clumsy tactics. This was perhaps a natural failing in a great idealist always more intent upon his objectives than on the means of securing them. Another fact contributed to it. Milner knew the problems of the Imperial dependencies better than those of the Mother Country. In Egypt and in South Africa he had gone to the heart of things. At home, he had watched and studied but had never shouldered the responsibilities of domestic politics. He was thus always more aware of what the Empire needed than of what the British people could be brought to accept. This weakness in his armament would, one day, be made good. At this time, it led him to underrate certain realities in the Imperial situation. Already a great Imperial thinker and administrator, he was not yet a great Imperial statesman.

Chamberlain was more than Milner's equal in administration and as much his superior in statecraft as he was his senior in years. His genius, like his blood and background, was English through and through. His Imperialism was essentially organic not intellectual. Over the years the circle of his experience had slowly widened from the Town Council to Parliament, and from the Cabinet to the Imperial Conference. He knew the constituencies, the Commons and the Colonies equally well; but he had come to know them in that order. He may never have attained to the fullness of Milner's conception of what the Empire might be; but he knew better than any man alive what it was and what it could be made to give.

BOOK XVII

THE DIPLOMATIC REVOLUTION
(September 1900–January 1903)

CHAPTER LXXXI

CHAMBERLAIN'S LAST BID FOR A GERMAN ALLIANCE

(SEPTEMBER 1900–JULY 1901)

RETROSPECT—The International Scene in the Summer of 1900—The China Crisis and the Cabinet—Chamberlain Leads the pro-German Faction—His Memorandum of September 10—The Yangtse Agreement—Does it apply to Manchuria?—Chamberlain's Offer at Chatsworth—The Kaiser in England—Bülow denies Chamberlain's "alternative"—A Golden Opportunity Lost—Bülow Flouts Britain over Manchuria—Failure of Chamberlain's Offer—Eckardstein initiates Alliance Negotiations—"Froth" not "Business"—Judgment on Chamberlain's Last Bid.

I

THE building of a new Empire in South Africa was, perhaps, the greatest of Chamberlain's achievements. No less important, however, if less tangible, was his influence in these years upon the course of British foreign policy. Here, then, we must resume the zigzag thread of the negotiations through which it was exerted.

In the previous volume, Mr. Garvin described how Chamberlain became convinced that splendid isolation was a bankrupt policy.[1] Developments in Africa and the Far East showed that the British Empire had outgrown its strength in relation to its potential foes. It was time, therefore, to come to terms with one or other of the rival diplomatic systems: the Triple or the Dual Alliance.

The immediate threat to British interests arose from the expansionist policies of France and Russia. Germany, therefore, seemed indicated as Britain's most natural ally. Accordingly, with more zeal, perhaps, than caution, Chamberlain had thrown

[1] See Vol. III. of this work, ch. lvii.

himself into the task of fashioning an Anglo-German alliance. The world supremacy of this new constellation was to be assured by a general understanding with the United States, seconded in the Far East by an agreement with Japan.

Chamberlain's first bid for an Anglo-German alliance had come to nothing.[1] His second had seemed, at first, more promising.[2] The Kaiser had received his proposals in a friendly spirit, and Bülow had been distinctly encouraging. It had, indeed, been at Bülow's instance and on the understanding that Bülow would reciprocate, that Chamberlain had declared himself at Leicester for "a new Triple Alliance" between England, Germany and the United States. But the wording of his speech had been unfortunate; nor had opinion been in any way prepared for its message. Its reception had been chilly in England, as abroad; and Bülow, with short-sighted caution, had left Chamberlain in the lurch. A more honourable or more generous statesman must at least have acknowledged the intention of the Leicester speech. He had ignored it.

The incident had cooled Chamberlain's ardour for his self-appointed task. For one thing, it had momentarily weakened his position in the Cabinet. For another, it had undermined his confidence in Bülow. Nevertheless, in the spring of 1900, as we saw,[3] he had repeated to Metternich his settled belief that an understanding between England, Germany and the United States offered "the surest basis for the future development of our peoples".

But through the first half of the year the outlook for such an understanding was gloomy. The dominant forces on both sides were unfavourable. In England, as the sequel to the Leicester speech had shown, Salisbury, not Chamberlain, was the master of British foreign policy; and his dislike of foreign entanglements was proverbial. In Germany, Bülow and Holstein were almost equally reluctant to bind themselves by a British alliance. They needed Anglophobia, inside the Reich, to ensure the passage of the sinister Navy Bill then in preparation. At the same time they were working to separate Russia from France, and feared that an engagement with Britain would only consolidate

---

[1] See Vol. III. chs. lviii., lix. (1898).   [2] See Vol. III. ch. lxix. (1899).
[3] See Vol. III. ch. lxix. pp. 514-515.

the Dual Alliance. Above all, they were convinced that mounting difficulties in every quarter of the globe would presently compel the British to pay a higher price for German support than they were yet prepared to contemplate. As the German leaders saw it, it was a case of "everything comes to him who waits".

Such were the general circumstances when, in the last summer of the nineteenth century, events in China decided Chamberlain to make a last bid for an Anglo-German alliance.[1]

II

The Boxer rebellion had momentarily united the Great Powers of Europe among themselves and with the United States and Japan. But, with the relief of the Legations, the semblance of unity soon disappeared. Count Waldersee, the German Generalissimo of the International Relieving Force, found himself in an invidious position. The Russians determined to dissolve his command by withdrawing their troops from Peking. Their French allies could hardly be expected to act differently; and the United States, on the eve of a Presidential election, wanted only to escape from the unpopular Chinese entanglement. The Germans, from the start, had been the moving spirits of the International Force. But they had plunged into the adventure with more greed than caution; and their whole position in China now depended on the attitude of the British. With British support they might maintain themselves, but, if the British withdrew, they would be compelled to a humiliating retreat in a land where "prestige was fifty per cent of power".

As the Minister responsible for Malaya and Hongkong, Chamberlain was directly concerned with policy in China. His advisers on Chinese affairs expected a virtual break-up of the

[1] The Chamberlain Papers contain no trace of these final negotiations with Germany. The chief sources used in this account are *Grosse Politik*, vols. xvi. and xvii.; Eckardstein, *Lebenserinnerungen*, especially vol. ii. chs. xii.-xvi.; Bülow, *Denkwürdigkeiten*, vol. i., covering 1897–1903 (English translation, 1932); Fischer, *Holstein's Grosses Nein*; *British Documents* (edited by Gooch and Temperley), vol. ii.; *Documents diplomatiques français*, série 2, vols. 2 and 3. See also works on Friedrich von Holstein by Helmuth Rogge and Freiherr von Trotha; and Johannes Haller, *Die Aera Bülow*. The translations of German and French documents are my own.—J. A.

Chinese Empire. They urged that steps be taken to protect British interests, especially in the Yangtse Valley. But, while the South African war lasted, there could be no question of assuming fresh commitments in the Far East. In these circumstances, Chamberlain made up his mind that only by a firm combination with Germany could we hope to prevent the Russians from consolidating their occupation of Manchuria and exercising a growing ascendancy over China within the Wall.

Several members of the Cabinet, notably Devonshire and Balfour, shared Chamberlain's view. They dissented strongly from Salisbury's obstinate coldness towards Germany and from his patient, if sullen, acceptance of Russian encroachments. In particular, they criticised his failure to give more sympathetic support to Waldersee, whose difficulty, in their view, was Britain's opportunity of improving relations with Berlin. The following letters give some idea of the feeling in the Cabinet.

THE CABINET AND CHINA

Goschen to J. C.—*Confidential.*—*Hawkhurst, September* 1, 1900.—I sent you a telegram, thinking you would be wondering whether any attempt was being made to induce Salisbury to reciprocate to some extent the Emperor's advances. [*I.e.* requests for support for Waldersee.]

. . . I enclose his reply to the letter. It makes one despair. A *non-possumus* in every direction. It is quite possible the Emperor has some designs that are not clear: but we shall not thwart them by standing aloof.

I do not know that more can be done. If some policy is forced on Salisbury, which he disapproves of, it breaks down in the execution.

. . . The latest Russian move as to retreating from Peking which is distasteful to Germany, furnishes a good opportunity for opening of conversations and exchange of ideas with the Emperor, but we hang back, are open with nobody, and shall practically stand alone, or come in at the tail of other Powers on every occasion.

If I see any opening that may be utilized I would ask you and Balfour to come to London to meet Lansdowne and G. Hamilton, who, like myself, are in despair of our present attitude. But the difficulty lies not in any one step which we might jointly persuade Salisbury to take, but

in his whole attitude in this question. He himself views the situation,
as he wrote to me, "with the gravest apprehension".

I never like Lascelles' [British Ambassador in Berlin] treatment of the
Emperor. He tries to score and to prove the Emperor in the wrong, and
assumes a complaining tone.

Meanwhile Monson [British Ambassador in Paris] can't get on with
Delcassé. It is a pretty kettle of fish.

P.S.—Please burn this very frank letter, but which I thought I ought
to write, as I know the interest you always take in our relations with
Germany.

Lansdowne and the W.O. are strongly in favour of retiring from
Peking to Tient-sin.

So is Beach.

Goschen to J. C.—Secret.—Admiralty, September 2, 1900.—I am
troubled about much graver things. Salisbury, as you will have seen,
sent some kind of an answer to Berlin, but it was almost worse than
silence.

. . . Whatever harm might come from pourparlers at Berlin, our
present attitude does more harm; but pressure on Salisbury does not
produce any real change of attitude, though he may take some small step.

I cannot help expressing myself strongly. . . .

Absolute isolation is playing the devil . . .

Goschen to J. C.—Sunday, September 4, 1900.—. . . Salisbury's answer
to our joint telegram was not satisfactory. He agrees to our troops not
being withdrawn from Peking, but will make no capital out of it.

And, so far as I can see, he has not notified this decision to Germany
or to any other Power. . . .

Brodrick to J. C.—Dartmouth, September 7.—Yacht Mera.—Private.
—One line to say Arthur [Balfour] generally concurs with you re
Peking and Germany. I have sent his letter to Goschen with a request
to forward to you. . . .[1]

The latter part of Salisbury's reply is characteristic and I think
unlucky. We do what is needed and get nothing for it. We could surely
get some credit, if nothing else.

[1] Not among the Chamberlain Papers.

I feel assured we shall ultimately have to make some overtures to Germany when the grace of them is past. . . .

These and other communications led Chamberlain to state the views of the dissident Ministers in a trenchant Cabinet memorandum (September 10). Too long to quote, this paper must be summarised:

Russia by withdrawing her troops from Peking would place the Kaiser in a weak and humiliating position. If Britain stood by him, however, his position would become tenable; and, in that case, he might also count on the support of Japan. We, thus, had it in our power to do a signal service to Germany and should obtain satisfactory assurances in return. Britain was certainly not strong enough by herself to maintain the integrity of the Chinese Empire or to enforce the principle of the Open Door for Trade. In the long run Britain and the United States must work together in China, but this would take time. Meanwhile, to resist the immediate threat of Russian expansion, we should work closely with Germany and Japan, supporting the special claims of these two Powers in Shantung and Korea.

But in return, we should obtain written assurances recognising our claim to predominant interest and influence in the Yangtse valley.

Salisbury yielded reluctantly to the pressure of his colleagues. Negotiations began for the conclusion of an Anglo-German agreement to maintain the principle of the Open Door. But their course only seemed to confirm the old Prime Minister's misgivings. The Germans proposed that the agreement should be confined to the Yangtse Valley. Their meaning was plain enough. They were not prepared to resist the advance of Russia in the Northern provinces. Instead they proposed, by a rigid but purely local application of the Open Door principle, to exclude any kind of British predominance in Central China. This was to deny the very essence of Chamberlain's conception; and Salisbury had the whole Cabinet behind him when he refused to accept a limited transaction. In the end,[1] the two Governments contracted to maintain the principle of the Open Door throughout the territories of the Chinese Empire, "so far as they can exercise influence". This was a Delphic formula and

[1] October 17, 1900.

aroused suspicion from the start. Its true meaning would be
manifested sooner than anyone expected.

The New Year brought graver news from the Far East. *The
Times* published a startling revelation from its Peking correspondent, "Chinese Morrison". Russia had extorted a secret
agreement[1] from the Chinese Government for the virtual
annexation of Manchuria under the thin guise of a temporary
Protectorate.

Britain now had every right to expect that Germany would
join her in a protest. It was less than three months since the two
Powers had engaged, not only to maintain the Open Door, "so
far as they can exercise influence", but also "to direct their
policy toward maintaining undiminished the territorial condition of the Chinese Empire". Instead, an inspired statement in
the German press suggested that Germany had no interests in
Manchuria and that "it is a matter of perfect indifference to
her who governs it".[2]

The unfortunate impression created in London by this statement was only heightened by Waldersee's conduct. Embroiled in
disputes over the military use of the Chinese northern railways,
he leaned consistently to Russian interests at the expense of
British. Meanwhile, it was also rumoured that Russia's new
settlement at Tientsin was to be fortified so as to dominate
communications between Peking and the sea.

Contemporary opinion, including Chamberlain's Far Eastern
advisers, might exaggerate this or that detail of the situation.
But, plainly, nothing less was at stake than the whole Empire
of China; and upon its fate depended both the safety of
massive British interests and the balance of power throughout
the world.

The grave and urgent nature of the crisis in the Far East
determined Chamberlain to bring to a head the decisive issue in
British Foreign Policy. He would make a final bid for an alliance
with Germany. If he failed, then, without much further delay,
Britain must seek other means of escaping from her precarious

---

[1] This was the Alexieff-Tseng agreement of January 3, 1901, signed at
Mukden. Morrison somewhat exaggerated its purport; but, by giving
Russia control of the Manchurian railway system, it brought about a considerable extension of Russian influence.
[2] *The Times*, January 7, 1901.

isolation. He disliked the alternative, but he had kept it steadily in view since his first project of an Anglo-German alliance three years before.

Two incidental considerations seem to have encouraged Chamberlain in his decision. After a rapturous welcome in France, President Kruger had reached Germany in the first week of December 1900. Anglophobia throughout the Reich exploded in his favour; and he proceeded triumphantly to Berlin for an Imperial audience. But at the capital he got another and very different "Kruger telegram". The Kaiser had gone hunting and could not receive him. To avoid giving offence to Britain, the Kaiser and Bülow had incurred unpopularity at home. It seemed to Chamberlain a good omen.

The second consideration concerned the day-to-day conduct of British foreign policy. At the end of October, Salisbury had at last relinquished the Foreign Office; and Lansdowne, his successor, was known to sympathise with the pro-German section of the Cabinet.

But these, we must repeat, were only incidental circumstances. The immediate cause of his decision was the crisis in China. His deeper motive, then as previously, was the urgent need for Britain to escape from an isolation, no longer splendid nor secure.

III

Devonshire was of the same mind as Chamberlain. Together they now prepared an informal but none the less significant communication to the German Government. Eckardstein was again chosen as their intermediary. He was then in active charge of the Embassy, owing to the long illness of his chief, and commended himself to the British statesmen on two counts. He was sincerely anxious to bring Britain and Germany together; and his zeal for the general interest was stimulated by his personal ambition to succeed Hatzfeldt as Ambassador. He was accordingly bidden to Chatsworth. The Duchess—she was a Hanoverian—wrote:

Please come at all events for the Duke wants to discuss with you some urgent political questions. Jos. Chamberlain also you will meet with us. As a large party of about fifty guests will be staying at Chatsworth for the theatricals, you will have opportunity for conversation with the Duke and Jos. without attracting any notice. Indeed, Asquith also, and perhaps some other leading members of the Opposition will be with us. That does no harm for there are more than enough rooms in the *schloss* where you can speak alone with Jos. without being remarked by anyone.[1]

This seemed pressing indeed; and Eckardstein might well hope for official approval in accepting. It was after all only a few months since Bülow had written about "Herr Chamberlain without whose vigorous co-operation we have got nothing and shall get nothing under the present English regime".[2]

The holiday season was still at its height when the Baron reached Chatsworth. A round of house-parties was in full swing. The Prince of Wales had just left. No one dreamed of the Queen's death. The amateur theatricals were more admired than ever.

Such was the background to Eckardstein's mission. With the momentous communication confided to him we shall presently deal, but first we may record a more trivial incident which followed it. Among the guests at Chatsworth were two young people much in love. On the very night of the Baron's talk with Chamberlain, they arranged to meet in *her* room when the company had retired. But Chatsworth, as Dr. Johnson once remarked, is "a very fine house"; and the young man, fearing to mistake another room for his lady's, asked her to leave a sign to show which was her door. On the spur of the moment, she promised to drop a large sandwich on the floor outside. Now Eckardstein was a voracious eater, accustomed to devour a whole cold chicken before retiring. That evening, however, the prolonged discussion of foreign affairs had intercepted his hopes of lighter refreshment. Hungry and morose he was retiring to bed, when, as he walked along the passage to his room, he saw a sandwich lying on the floor. Making sure that he was alone, he pounced upon this dusty prey. In an instant it was devoured; and the course of true love was made less smooth than ever.[3]

[1] Eckardstein, vol. ii. pp. 235-251.
[2] *Grosse Politik*, vol. xvii. p. 332 (Bülow to Hatzfeldt, June 13, 1900).
[3] Related to Brigadier Fitzroy Maclean, M.P., by Mrs. George Keppel.

Apparently the Baron told the story against himself at breakfast next morning, though without realising the sentimental complications he had unwittingly caused.

IV

The conversation between Chamberlain and Eckardstein, for which the German guest had been invited, took place in the library after dinner on the evening of January 16. Devonshire was also present. No note of what passed is to be found in his or Chamberlain's papers. We are dependent for our knowledge on a compact version framed within forty-eight hours by Eckardstein in consultation with Hatzfeldt.[1]

COUNT VON HATZFELDT TO THE FOREIGN MINISTRY

(Telegram)

London, January 18, 1901.—*Secret.*—At a recent meeting between Baron Eckardstein and Mr. Chamberlain, at the Duke of Devonshire's country seat, the Colonial Secretary made the following significant remarks.

He and his friends in the Cabinet are now clear about one thing. The days of "splendid isolation" are over for England. With an eye on the future, they must look round for allies. The choice lies between Russia with France, or the Triple Alliance. Within the Cabinet, as in the nation, there are zealous advocates of a settlement and of long-term cooperation with Russia. They are ready to pay a very high price for that object. He himself does not belong to those who desire an alliance with Russia. Instead he is convinced that cooperation with Germany and adherence to the Triple Alliance are preferable. Personally, he would do everything in his power to pave the way gradually in this direction. *He would begin with a secret agreement between England and Germany over Morocco on the basis he had formerly explained.*[2] His advice was to take up the matter as soon as Lord Salisbury went South and then to discuss details with Lord Lansdowne and himself. So long as he [Chamberlain] is convinced that a lasting partnership with Germany is possible, he will resist to the utmost the idea of an arrangement with Russia. Nevertheless, should it become evident that a permanent junction with Germany is not practicable, then he too would advocate a settlement with Russia, despite the enormous price that England must expect to pay for it

---

[1] To make the conversation seem more informal and so avoid arousing the suspicions of Holstein, Hatzfeldt thought it more prudent to omit any mention of Devonshire's part in his report (Eckardstein, vol. ii. p. 237).

[2] *I.e.* at the Windsor meeting with the Kaiser and Bülow, Vol. III. ch. lxix.

(including eventual concessions in China and the Persian Gulf). He CHAP.
begged that his remarks, *except as to Morocco*, should be regarded, for LXXXI.
the time being, not as a proposal, but merely as an academic exposition ÆT. 64.
of his views . . .[1]

This report shows that Chamberlain's long-term aim was
nothing less than the adherence of the British Empire to the
Triple Alliance. But he knew that, for the time being, so far-
reaching a commitment was impracticable. For one thing,
Salisbury was still Prime Minister. For another, the South
African War had stirred up too much hostility between the
British and German peoples. Accordingly, he had asked that his
remarks on that subject should be treated as "academic". They
were merely intended as the background against which his
immediate and practical proposal should be examined: this was
for a secret agreement over Morocco; a transaction to which he
and Lansdowne could bring the Cabinet, at least in Salisbury's
absence, and about which public opinion need never be consulted. He had no desire to brusque this great business, but
contemplated a gradual procedure. The general alliance between
Britain and Germany would grow by degrees out of particular
and local understandings. In its mixture of guiding principle
and empirical method, the conception was typical of the man.

Significant also was his choice of Morocco rather than China
to illustrate his plan. His purpose was, almost certainly, to stress
that his approach was the result of a deliberate and long-
matured policy; not a mere attempt to make Germany pull
Britain's chestnuts out of the Far Eastern fire. Nevertheless,
there is no doubt that China was uppermost in his mind. It was
there, rather than in Morocco, that he first expected to see the
German Government's reply to his proposal. He could not know,
of course, that, on the very day of his conversation with Eckardstein, the Kaiser's Ambassador at St. Petersburg had assured
Count Lamsdorff that Germany would leave the Tsardom a free
hand in Manchuria.

V

Full of his message Eckardstein returned to London and, with
his ailing chief, concerted the report quoted above. To it they

[1] *Grosse Politik*, vol. xvii. pp. 14-16. (My italics.—J. A.)

added a private telegram designed to anticipate the objections of the dreaded Holstein.

HATZFELDT TO HOLSTEIN

(Private Telegram)

London, January 18, 1901.—You and I are entirely in agreement that the idea of an Alliance is still premature. Chamberlain, however, seems to share this view, desiring that particular agreements about Morocco etc. shall lead up to the later general understanding. That might suit us. Meanwhile, it is to be hoped that the coolness between England and America, resulting from the growing intimacy of the latter with Russia, will still increase, and that then, more and more, England will have to depend on us.

The hope Chamberlain almost openly expresses of soon becoming free of Lord Salisbury and remaining master of the situation is worthy of careful note. It seems likely that when Salisbury goes South, as he will for several months, Chamberlain and his friends—and Lansdowne is one of the chief—will take the initiative.[1]

This telegram is important. It expresses by far the shrewdest approach to Chamberlain's proposal that would ever be made on the German side. Hatzfeldt appreciated the Wilhelmstrasse's view that Germany would secure the British alliance on better terms if only she waited for Britain's difficulties to increase. But he was also convinced that Chamberlain's declared alternative of a Russian alliance was no empty threat. As he saw it, Chamberlain's proposal excluded the Russian alternative and was consistent with both British and German aims. There was no question of rushing into a full alliance. Local agreements would be of advantage to both sides. There would be plenty of time for reflection; and, if Britain's world position suffered meanwhile, as Holstein expected, Germany could raise her terms before entering upon the final contract.

But Bülow only saw the difficulties of the proposal. His first reply to it was evasive. It is too full of allusions to contemporary events to be quoted, but this is the gist of it:

---

[1] *Grosse Politik*, vol. xvii. p. 17.

BÜLOW TO HATZFELDT
(Paraphrase)

January 20, 1901.—Better wait and leave the initiative to the English. CHAP.
The frustration of the former agreement about the Portuguese colonies LXXXI.
raises doubts about the value of entering into a similar agreement on ÆT. 64.
Morocco before a crisis actually arises in that quarter. There is no hurry.
"I don't believe in an agreement between England and the Dual Alliance
until England has lost all hope—and there is no ground for supposing
she has—of Germany's eventual support." While the American illusion
lasts she will hardly be brought to pay the price of an alliance acceptable
to Germany. It looks, however, as if English hopes of America will be
sobered pretty soon. Then perhaps will be the right moment for negotiating with an England driven nearer to us. Meanwhile the English should
be listened to with a friendly ear and with an admission that the two
nations may yet be called to make a common stand for vital interests.
At the same time they should be warned that German mistrust engendered by the Boer war and the Samoa episode has been increased
by the Anglo-Portuguese rapprochement.[1]

Bülow doubted the possibility of an understanding between
Britain and the Franco-Russian alliance and was therefore more
anxious than Hatzfeldt to play for time. But his telegram,
though negative, left the matter open. At this juncture, however, an unexpected incident compelled the Wilhelmstrasse to
crystallise its policy.

VI

While Chamberlain and Devonshire deliberated at Chatsworth, the Kaiser was celebrating in Berlin the bicentenary of
the Prussian Kingdom, raised in those two hundred years from
minor rank to the headship of Europe. He had just proclaimed
his fixed resolve to make the German Navy "as mighty an
instrument" as the Army, when the news came that his grand-
mother, the Queen of England, was dying. She was the only
human being whom he reverenced. With a surge of genuine
affection as well as of dramatic impulse, he broke off his celebrations and hastened across the sea. All about him were against it.

[1] *Grosse Politik*, vol. xvii. pp. 17-18.

They knew that the journey would be bitterly unpopular with the German people; but he was not to be moved.

He reached the Queen's bedside before the end. The British people were touched to the heart by his gesture; and many who had come to regard him with distrust were melted and disarmed. All contemporary accounts of those days are stamped with one ineffaceable impression which must have been shared by the hushed crowds lining the funeral route through London. Three horsemen in red cloaks followed the gun-carriage. The Kaiser rode on the King's right hand. That day and for some days to come, he was the centre of the nation's affection; more almost than the King himself.

In London the Kaiser learned, for the first time, of the Chatsworth proposal. Moved by the warmth of his reception and by the reconciling influences of the hour, his whole inclination was to grasp the hand which Chamberlain had proffered. He wired to Bülow:

THE KAISER TO BÜLOW
(Telegram)

January 20, 1901.—. . . Baron von Eckardstein tells me of Chamberlain's confidential intimation that it is all over with splendid isolation; England must choose between Triple Alliance and France-Russia. He is *à tout prix* for the former, part of the Cabinet for the latter. Foreign Office for the former. Only if we are not willing, then the swing to the Dual Alliance. The understanding about Morocco again desired by him [Chamberlain] can come about as soon as Lord Salisbury goes to Cannes. So "they come" it seems. This is what *we* have waited for.[1]

But this enthusiastic telegram threw the Wilhelmstrasse into consternation. Afraid that the Kaiser might commit himself, especially against Russia, they poured water into his wine and drowned it. They denied categorically that Chamberlain's alternative was possible.

HOLSTEIN TO METTERNICH [2]

Berlin, January 21, 1901.—I am very distrustful of this storm of friendship on the part of Chamberlain and his friends; all the more so as

---

[1] *Grosse Politik*, vol. xvii. p. 19.
[2] The senior diplomat in the Kaiser's suite.

the threatened understanding with Russia and France is a patent fraud. Concessions (to France and Russia) might postpone Britain's fight for existence for a few years, but it would only make it the more inevitable by strengthening her opponents and diminishing the power and prestige of the British. We can wait. Time is on our side. As I see it, a rational agreement with England—that is to say, one where the almost certain risk of war, which we should have to assume, would be paid off by suitable concessions—will only come within reach when England feels the pinch more acutely than she does to-day.[1]

Thus Holstein, the opinionated *éminence grise* of the Wilhelmstrasse. Bülow worked in the same sense, manipulating his Imperial master with a blend of sting and sycophancy.

BÜLOW TO THE KAISER

Berlin, 21 *January*, 1901.—. . . Your Majesty is quite right in the feeling that the English must come to us. South Africa has cost them dear; America shows itself uncertain; Japan unreliable; France full of hatred; Russia faithless; public opinion hostile in all countries. At the Diamond Jubilee in 1897 English self-conceit reached its highest point; the English peacock spread its proudest display, and preened itself in splendid isolation. . . . Now it begins to dawn gradually on the consciousness of the English that, by their own strength alone, they will not be able to maintain their world-empire against so many antagonists.

Everything now depends upon neither discouraging the English nor allowing ourselves to be prematurely tied by them. English troubles will increase in the next months, and with them the price that we can demand will rise. . . .

In view of the general world-situation, as of our own vital interests, your Majesty will execute a very master-coup, if your All-Highness can succeed in leaving leading English personages with the hope of a future firm relationship with us, but without your All-Highness being at present prematurely bound or committed. The understanding threatened with the Dual Alliance is nothing but a scarecrow made up to intimidate us in the way the English have already practised for years. . . . Your Majesty will of course know just how to rub their noses gently but firmly in this truth.[2]

---

[1] See also his telegram to Eckardstein of the same date (*Grosse Politik*, vol. xvii. p. 22).   [2] *Ibid*. pp. 20-21.

The Kaiser, against his earlier instinct, took the cue. In a long conversation at Osborne with Lansdowne, he traversed the whole order of Chamberlain's ideas. Russia, he argued, was perfidious and insatiable; America egotistical and ruthless. Britain could never make a safe settlement with the one or expect practical friendship from the other. The only way of salvation was for "Europe"—including Britain and France—to pull together against both Russian and American aggrandisement. The old English notion of holding the balance of power between the Continental nations was exploded. With twenty-two German army-corps "I am the balance of power in Europe".

Lansdowne listened with perfect deference and dry judgment. The Kaiser had rejected the possibility of an Anglo-Russian agreement and in almost the same breath had spoken of a general understanding between Germany, Britain and France. These remarks suggested that he was in no hurry to take up Chamberlain's proposal for an Anglo-German agreement, least of all in Morocco. Moreover, he was evidently intent on driving a wedge between Britain and the United States. Lansdowne no doubt told Chamberlain of this conversation; and both must have drawn the gloomiest conclusions.

Nevertheless, the Kaiser seems to have been troubled by the part he had been instructed to play. At Windsor, on the day when Queen Victoria's body was laid in the grave, he turned to Metternich, the cold diplomatic guardian placed by the Wilhelmstrasse at his elbow, and said with a flash of insight, "I cannot wobble for ever between Russia and England; I would find myself at last trying to sit between two stools." [1]

The mentor told him that he was right in principle, but that the right time had not yet come. It would not come until England was brought by sheer necessity to the point of proposing a Defensive Alliance, to be accepted by Parliament and only to come into operation if either of the contracting Powers were attacked by two others. Such terms assumed the inevitability of Britain's rapid decline. Here was the fundamental error in the Wilhelmstrasse's judgment; and Metternich underlined it by the following illustration of his theme.

[1] *Grosse Politik*, vol. xvi. p. 295 (Metternich to the Wilhelmstrasse).

I reminded his Majesty of yesterday's spectacle [the funeral procession through London]. The military ranks stretched for miles. A muster of troops morally degraded, idiots, undersized and pitiable beings. The dregs of the population. With astonishment and affright we beheld yesterday that the English have reached the end of their military capacity.[1]

Next day the Kaiser left England. His visit marked, perhaps, the turning-point in this fateful transaction. Had he followed his own instinct and encouraged Chamberlain's proposal, a beginning might have been made. Powerful forces were at work in both countries to prevent the alliance. But Chamberlain and the Kaiser were powerful too. Had they reached a good understanding, then, gradually, by way of China and Morocco, they might have gone on to build a full alliance. Here, at least, was the golden opportunity.

So much for what might have been. As it was, the Kaiser's visit had just the contrary effect. His first enthusiasm for the Chatsworth offer compelled the Wilhelmstrasse to take a decision. They decided against it, and would never bring themselves to change their minds until it was too late. Deterred by their advice, the Kaiser made no move to see Chamberlain, though he was a whole fortnight in England. After their cordial talks at Windsor the year before and Chamberlain's latest advance, the omission must have seemed a rebuff. There would never be a chance to repair it.

VII

When the Kaiser had gone, Hatzfeldt besought the Wilhelmstrasse to give Chamberlain's proposals more serious consideration. He wrote to Holstein,[2] as frankly as he dared, that they were not dishonestly meant.

The English ministers and Chamberlain, in particular, are not so stupid as not to recognise that Germany cannot and will not give them her help in China without the assurance of compensation elsewhere and above all of protection against the danger of a Franco-Russian attack.

The Ambassador further begged the Wilhelmstrasse not to

[1] Grosse Politik, vol. xvi. p. 296 (Metternich to the Wilhelmstrasse).   [2] Hatzfeldt to Holstein, February 10, 1901 (private telegram) (Grosse Politik, vol. xvii. pp. 30-32).

underestimate the possibility of an Anglo-Russian agreement, adding that he felt it his bounden duty to give this warning "before the door is shut"—a word as prophetic as can be found in the whole range of the German archives.

It was in vain. Holstein, with Bülow's express consent, replied that an alliance with Britain would be repugnant to the German people; that Salisbury would never give the concessions and the guarantees required; and that Britain could drive the Russians back from China by acting in concert with Japan. Germany, as matters stood, could offer nothing but neutrality.

A project of Anglo-German neutrality was in fact elaborated in the Wilhelmstrasse. Bülow prided himself upon it, as his memoirs relate. But it was too evidently framed solely in German interests, and, on Hatzfeldt's advice, was never presented to the British Government. It would have been to offer not bread but a stone.

Meanwhile, Russian demands at Peking threw a lengthening shadow over the Far East. The critical hour approached when Bülow would be compelled to make public the German Government's attitude towards events in Manchuria. His statement on this subject was made in the Reichstag on March 15.[1] Amid loud acclamation, and some irony at Britain's expense, the Chancellor declared:

The Anglo-German Agreement has no bearing on Manchuria. . . . What may become of Manchuria? Why, gentlemen, I cannot really conceive what could be more indifferent to us.

This declaration flouted the British interpretation of the Anglo-German agreement and showed that German support was not available in the only quarter where it was immediately required. In Chamberlain's view, it knocked the bottom out of his last project for an alliance between Britain and Germany.

VIII

Curiously enough, it was in these belated and unpropitious circumstances that the two Governments entered into direct negotiations for an alliance. The responsibility for this singular

[1] For full text of this speech see Penzler's *Fürst Bülow's Reden*, vol. i. pp. 194-210.

development rests, almost certainly, upon Eckardstein. Hoping,

at best to rescue Anglo-German relations from the abyss, at
worst to avert a settlement between Britain and Russia, he took
a personal initiative. His intentions were sincere. His methods
were more dubious. His first step was to seek another meeting
with Chamberlain, whom he had not seen since their talk at
Chatsworth. After some cool delay on that statesman's part, the
interview took place at the Colonial Office at noon on March
18. The conversation was of little comfort to the visitor.[1]

ECKARDSTEIN TO HOLSTEIN
(Telegram)

March 18, 1901.—. . . How they are working officially on the Russian
side may be gathered well enough from the following remarks which
Chamberlain made to me to-day. "We would gladly approach Germany
with far-reaching proposals which would offer her at the least the same
advantages as to ourselves, if not greater. But, as we now know for
certain that everything Berlin learns is at once passed on to Petersburg,
no one can be surprised, if we impose on ourselves the greatest reserve
towards Berlin in future." Later in the conversation Chamberlain remarked that, so far as Germany was concerned, he holds the same views
in principle as he expressed to the Kaiser and Count Bülow [over] a year
ago at Windsor; but he has no desire to burn his fingers again, especially
in the above-mentioned circumstances.

The Chamberlain Papers show that the Colonial Secretary's
information about leakages from Berlin to St. Petersburg was
not derived privately from pro-Russian agents, as Eckardstein
supposed, but from the Foreign Office itself.

From this disconcerting interview, Eckardstein went on to
lunch with Lansdowne. Their private conversation at table was
followed by an official interview at the Foreign Office. There,
representing that he spoke only for himself, Eckardstein
suggested that

The German Government . . . would entertain favourably the idea
. . . of a purely defensive alliance between the two powers, directed solely
against France and Russia. So long as Germany or England were attacked
by one only of the other two Powers the Alliance would not operate.[2]

[1] Eckardstein, vol. ii. p. 278.
[2] Lansdowne to Lascelles (copy to Chamberlain), March 18, 1901.

Lansdowne's account of the conversation states plainly that it was Eckardstein who advanced the idea of an Alliance. He concludes with the words, "I have no doubt that he had been desired to sound me".[1] But Eckardstein, in his official report [2] to the Wilhelmstrasse, represented that the initiative had come from Lansdowne. The Baron's memoirs leave no doubt that Lansdowne's version is correct. In these he admits, or rather claims, that he himself made the suggestion to Lansdowne in the course of lunch. He also shows that the idea of a Defensive Alliance had been conveyed to him a few days before in a private letter from Holstein.[3] Holstein, however, had written that it was on no account to be mentioned to the British Government for the present. His purpose in writing had been merely to explain the kind of proposal he hoped one day to receive from London.

Eckardstein's deception misled both sides into believing that an alliance was eagerly desired by the other. In London, indeed, the prospect aroused little enthusiasm. The Cabinet could see few advantages in a Defensive Alliance which would not apply to Manchuria and might not operate in any quarter where British interests, but not British territory, were threatened. The Wilhelmstrasse, however, were convinced that British policy was conforming to their preconceptions with almost mathematical exactitude. No sooner did they learn of Lansdowne's supposed initiative than they raised their terms. They stipulated that Britain should adhere to the Triple Alliance and that this compact should be ratified by Parliament. This was no more, indeed, than the ultimate goal which Chamberlain had set before them. But, at Chatsworth, he had been careful to stress that it could only be approached by gradual, local and secret arrangements.

Full and public junction with the Triple Alliance was impracticable in the circumstances of the time. The very idea of it was made derisory by an extraordinary condition added by Bülow and Holstein. This was that the British Government, instead of dealing with Germany direct, should conduct the

---

[1] Lansdowne to Lascelles (copy to Chamberlain), March 18, 1901.
[2] *Grosse Politik*, vol. xvii. p. 41.

[3] Eckardstein, vol. ii. pp. 314-315 (Holstein to Eckardstein, March 9, 1901).

further negotiations through Vienna. Holstein's letter containing the first suggestion of this change of venue is a capital piece
in our diplomatic dossier.

HOLSTEIN TO ECKARDSTEIN
(Telegram in cipher)

Secret.—Berlin, 20th March, 1901.—. . . The practical way would be
to stamp the rapprochement not as a German-English alliance but as the
adhesion of England to the Triple Alliance. Count von Goluchowski will
be for this policy which is entirely in his own line. . . . Lord Lansdowne
should not breathe a word to Rome if he does not want it to be known
in St. Petersburg. What Chamberlain says about indiscretion on our side
is a mere pretext in order to disguise that Chamberlain is now hindered
by Salisbury from making proposals. If, against expectation, Salisbury
lets himself move so broadly as to countenance positive proposals for
an alliance, then I truly believe that the roundabout road through
Vienna will lead to something useful and tenable. I cannot see why
Japan also should not be drawn into the defensive alliance. That
would facilitate the combination in various respects, for Japan is
popular in Germany. . . . The road through Vienna, I believe, is
the right road.[1]

Negotiation with Germany through Austria was an impossible
condition. Even if the avowed object had been attainable,
this was not the way. Politically, a guarantee of the internally
discordant Habsburg Empire would have been unacceptable
to Parliament. Diplomatically, the mere fact of negotiations in
Vienna must have embroiled Britain still more deeply with
Russia, thus making her more dependent on Germany and still
less secure. It is, indeed, hard to believe that this was not the
main object of Bülow and Holstein.

Eckardstein prudently kept Vienna in the background. Even
then, the course of negotiations was bedevilled by bickering over
such smaller questions as the claims to compensation of German
subjects in South Africa, and German efforts to exact a large
war-indemnity from China.

From time to time, in his conversations with Lansdowne,
Eckardstein revived the theme of Alliance. In mid-April the
Foreign Secretary told him that he was consulting Chamberlain

[1] Eckardstein, vol. ii. p. 283 (Holstein to Eckardstein, March 9, 1901).

and Devonshire. Eckardstein, already impatient, sought to "feel his teeth"; and the following dialogue ensued:

ECKARDSTEIN: "Would it not be better to drop the idea of an alliance since there does not seem to be any likelihood of Lord Salisbury coming to a decision?"

LANSDOWNE: "Devonshire, Chamberlain and I are for it. As for Lord Salisbury I do not doubt that he will also decide in favour. Times have changed." [1]

This was the nearest thing to encouragement which he was to receive; and its authenticity is uncertain. Having embarked on a course of deception, Eckardstein was bound to paint the picture for his chiefs in Berlin in more favourable colours than the facts warranted. Lansdowne, no doubt, was careful to guard himself and his colleagues against any charge of rebuffing German approaches. It is, none the less, certain that by this time the British Cabinet, Chamberlain included, had become wholly sceptical about the worth of these negotiations. They no longer even regarded poor Eckardstein with much respect. Lansdowne on one occasion calls him "that person ".[2]

IX

The final crisis came in May. Old Hatzfeldt, lately returned to London, thought himself well enough to take personal control of the negotiations. He knew that it would be fatal to ask the Foreign Office to work through Vienna instead of Berlin. At the same time he appreciated the insistence of the Wilhelmstrasse [3] that Britain should publicly adhere to the Triple Alliance.

Hatzfeldt, accordingly, called at the Foreign Office and suggested a full discussion of the alliance project.[4] Lansdowne returned his call on May 23; and an earnest but fruitless conversation took place. Hatzfeldt argued strenuously that Britain should join the Triple Alliance and undertake the guarantee of Austria. This was the *conditio sine qua non* of an alliance. With-

---

[1] Eckardstein, vol. ii. p. 337 (April 13, 1901).
[2] *British Documents*, vol. ii. p. 63.
[3] For the best exposition of the German views on this subject see

Richthofen's letter to Hatzfeldt of May 18, 1901 (*Grosse Politik*, vol. xvii. p. 60).
[4] May 15, 1901.

out it Germany would be compelled to look to Russia which could easily be "squared".[1]

Hatzfeldt's terms proved unacceptable to the inner Cabinet to which these matters were referred. It consisted of Salisbury, Lansdowne, Chamberlain, Balfour, Devonshire and Hicks Beach.[2] Salisbury, prophetically pessimistic of the Habsburg Empire's prospects, would not accept a liability for its defence. Devonshire gruffly surmised that Bülow was not in earnest. Chamberlain's view does not seem to have been very different. He had been prepared to accept eventual adherence to the Triple Alliance, but he had stressed from the first that this must come as the result of practical co-operation, not as its starting-point. Besides, he could have had little faith in an arrangement which, while committing Britain to the most dubious of European obligations, would not have provided for the defence of British interests in China or elsewhere outside of British territory proper. It was becoming clear to him that Germany did not want the alliance for his purposes. In that case he did not want it for theirs.

This was the real end of Eckardstein's attempt to revive the Alliance project. For some time to come negotiations flickered on, but henceforth there was no substance in them. Bülow and Holstein, still under the delusion that the initiative had come from London, continued to press their arguments with grim absurdity. Lansdowne met them with flawless courtesy, but in the Cabinet, as he afterwards put it, "the subject had been dropped".

In June Chamberlain dined with Alfred Rothschild and must have spoken with his usual caustic trenchancy. Rothschild was a close friend of Eckardstein; and his letter, which we quote below, makes a pungent epitaph to these ill-fated negotiations.

ALFRED ROTHSCHILD TO ECKARDSTEIN

June 14, 1901.—Your negotiations in March and April were *tacheles* [business] but what is going on now is only *schabbeshmus* [froth]. No one in England can put trust again in Bülow's fine, meaningless phrases. Frank Lascelles laughs at the clumsiness with which Berlin handles the

---

[1] Hatzfeldt to the Wilhelmstrasse, May 23, 1901 (*Grosse Politik*, vol. xvii. p. 65).   [2] *British Documents*, vol. ii. pp. 64-71.

matter. Apart from that, your Government today no longer seems to know what it wants. . . . Joe, who dined with me, has quite lost heart and will have nothing more to do with the people in Berlin. If they are so short-sighted, he says, as not to see that a quite new grouping of the world [*Weltkonstellation*] is at stake, they cannot be helped.[1]

X

Chamberlain's last bid for a German alliance marks one of the great turning-points in history. Had it prospered, the fate of mankind from that time to this might have been altered immeasurably and for the better. The greatest sea-power in the world would have been allied to the greatest military power. Their joint industrial might would have been beyond challenge. Behind Germany would have stood her two allies of the Triplice: behind the British Empire, the reborn nation of the East, Japan. The general support of the United States would scarcely have been withheld. Such a constellation would have been inclined by its interests and enabled by its power to maintain the peace of nations and to control the inevitable revolutions in the world's affairs. The golden era of the nineteenth century might have been indefinitely prolonged; and the advancing forces of civilisation might have continued to hold off the horsemen of the Apocalypse. This prospect of what might have been is so compelling, that we must pause a moment to consider how it was that Germany's statesmen took the road to ruin instead.

The failure of the negotiations, which we have described, had many causes; and it is not easy to impose a pattern upon them. Foremost, however, was the unbridgeable gap that separated the aims and conceptions of the British and the German protagonists.

Chamberlain believed that the time had come when the British Empire must seek allies to maintain its supremacy in a hostile and jealous world. He never for a moment regarded Britain as a declining Power, nor contemplated the sacrifice of her supremacy as the price of an alliance. His purpose in approaching the Germans had been twofold. First, he wanted German support for British interests in those regions where the

---

[1] Eckardstein, vol. ii. pp. 300-301.

future seemed most uncertain; in China, in the Middle East and
in the crumbling Moorish Empire. Second, he wanted a German
alliance to prevent the formation of a hostile coalition of
Russia, Germany and France against Britain. CHAP.
LXXXI.
Æt. 64.

... Both in China and elsewhere it is our interest that Germany should
throw herself across the path of Russia. An alliance between Germany
and Russia, entailing, as it would, the cooperation of France, is the one
thing we have to dread, and the clash of German and Russian interests,
whether in China or Asia Minor, would be a guarantee for our safety.

I think, then, our policy clearly is to encourage good relations between
ourselves and Germany, as well as between ourselves and Japan and the
United States, and we should endeavour to emphasise the breach between Russia and Germany, and Russia and Japan. ... [1]

This passage shows that Chamberlain wanted the alliance, as
the Wilhelmstrasse feared, in order to pursue the traditional
Imperial policy of divide and rule. He wanted the Germans to
"pull Britain's chestnuts out of the fire". Holstein and Bülow
were right to recognise this aspect of his purpose. They were
wrong in believing that it was the whole of it. The Colonial
Secretary was far too practical a statesman ever to believe that
Germany would work for British interests for nothing. From
the beginning, therefore, as he had told Eckardstein at Chatsworth, he had looked on a full junction between the British
Empire and the Triple Alliance as the ultimate goal.

Here we come to the crux of the whole affair. Chamberlain was
not master of the British Government when events in China
brought the crisis in British foreign policy to a head. He was,
thus, not in a position to grant the full alliance for which the
Germans asked. All that he could do, instead, was to suggest
those local arrangements in Morocco and China, which he knew
the Foreign Office would support and which he believed would
lead up to the wider agreement. In asking the Germans to act
on his suggestions, he was, therefore, asking them to take two
things on trust. First, that he was sincere in declaring for the
full alliance. Second, that the British Government would come
to share his view. As he saw it, his speech at Leicester was the
guarantee of the first; the evident self-interest of Britain of the

[1] Memorandum by Chamberlain written for the Cabinet, September 10, 1900.

second. To have accepted his proposals in these circumstances would have required a great act of faith on the part of the Germans. In retrospect we can see that it would also have been a great act of statesmanship. The Kaiser was inclined, for a moment, to attempt it, but his counsellors stayed his hand. Mistrust was one of their motives. It was not the chief.

The truth is that the Germans never really wanted a British alliance; certainly not for Chamberlain's purposes. Their aim, unavowed but ill-concealed, was to supersede Britain at the summit of the world. They already commanded the strongest of armies, the most powerful of industries and a nation virile and disciplined. They were also building a fleet. Once it was launched, the Kaiser would indeed become *arbiter mundi*. But this would still take some years. Meanwhile, they were determined to keep their hands free and to avoid any commitment or adventure which might embroil them in war with France or Russia. Hence their reluctance to take up Chamberlain's suggestion over Morocco, or to stand by Britain in Manchuria. They were playing for time; time to build the fleet.

The Kaiser and his *camarilla* were confirmed in the pursuit of this fundamental policy by a number of more tactical considerations. They conceived themselves to be safe from any hostile combination of Powers and so felt no need of new allies. They had deliberately stirred up Anglophobia in Germany to popularise the Navy Law, a course which must have made an English alliance politically embarrassing. Obsessed, moreover, by the myth of British decadence, they were convinced that Britain's difficulties would steadily increase and that, in time, they might exact immense concessions as the price of an eventual alliance. Above all, they denied the possibility of Chamberlain's alternative. Britain would never bring herself to pay the price of an understanding with the Dual Alliance; never at least while she could hope for Germany's friendship. As Bülow wrote, revealing the very inwardness of his mind:

We must let hope shimmer on the horizon. In this hope lies after all the surest guarantee that the English will not surrender to the Russians.[1]

The German conviction that Britain could never come to

[1] *Grosse Politik*, vol. xvii. p. 109. Bülow's marginal note on Holstein's memorandum dated October 31, 1901.

terms with France and Russia was "worse than a crime. It was
a blunder." For this one miscalculation Bülow and Holstein have
deserved the lasting censure of their countrymen. It wrecked
the fabric of their master's dreams, and brought the Reich, like
a bull in the arena, to encirclement and inescapable doom.

Englishmen, however, may find some consolation in Holstein's
error of judgment. Had the Wilhelmstrasse followed Hatzfeldt's advice and changed their tactics while sticking to their
strategy, they might have gained in peace the supremacy which
they would fail to win in war. Had they taken their share of
China, Morocco and the Middle East, in concert with Britain,
they must have finally cut off our line of retreat to the Dual
Alliance. Meanwhile, their fleet would have increased and their
trade expanded to a point where Germany might have become
the dominant partner in the Anglo-German combination.

It must always be dangerous for Britain to ally itself with
the strongest power in Europe; and Chamberlain was wrong,
as the event would show, to believe that Imperial Germany
could be made to serve our own Imperial purposes. Yet, when
we consider what afterwards befell the Kaiser and his Chancellor, his Field-Marshals and his Grand Admirals, and what became of their dreams of sea power and expansion, of Baghdad
and China, and of the arbitership of the world, we may justly
conclude that that prince and his counsellors would have been
well advised, had they responded with warmth to Chamberlain's
proposals.

CHAPTER LXXXII

CHAMBERLAIN BREAKS WITH BÜLOW

(March 1901–February 1902)

PRELUDE to the Entente Cordiale—Conclusion of the Anglo-Japanese Alliance—Its International Significance—Chamberlain's Edinburgh Speech and the Teutonic Fury—Bülow seeks an Apology—Formal Abandonment of Negotiations for an Anglo-German Alliance—Bülow attacks Chamberlain in the Reichstag—"What I have said, I have said"—Chamberlain Honoured by the City—Germany becomes the Enemy—The Effect on Anglo-Italian Relations and the "Maltese Language Question".

I

BOOK XVII.

1901.

WE saw in the last chapter how Bülow's refusal to support British policy in Manchuria wrecked Chamberlain's final proposal for an alliance with Germany. Here we must begin by examining a further consequence of Bülow's action. Its significance was not misunderstood at the Quai d'Orsay. Delcassé and his ambassador in London, Paul Cambon, had for some time been working quietly towards a *rapprochement* with Britain. They now saw, in Germany's rebuff of her would-be ally, an unexpected but golden opportunity for France.

Chamberlain's advice at Chatsworth had been to begin with a practical agreement on Morocco and to make it lead up to a general alliance. The Germans never even tried this gambit counselled by a born chess-player of politics. It was not that they failed to understand it. Hatzfeldt's telegrams explained its meaning clearly enough. But Bülow and Holstein suffered from a morbid fear that in Morocco, as in Manchuria, Britain meant to use them "to pull her chestnuts out of the fire". They had nightmares of being embroiled with France and Russia merely to help Britain seize Tangier. As Bülow wrote:

We must avoid every sort of appearance of being taken in tow by England in the Moroccan affair. . . . In this affair, pending further developments, we must maintain complete reserve and play the Sphinx.[1]

A few weeks later he impressed upon the Kaiser that no French success in Morocco could be as objectionable as "the danger of our being pushed forward by England against other powers *pour les beaux yeux de l'Angleterre*".[2]

The French were more acute and adroit. They understood the empiricism of British Foreign Policy, inevitable under our constitution. In those same days of March that Bülow announced his refusal to support Britain in Manchuria, Cambon took a significant initiative. He suggested that such causes of friction as the everlasting dispute about fishing-rights on the Newfoundland shore might be resolved, if the British Government could bring itself to make concessions on the Niger or the Gambia, or to countenance French expansion in Morocco. Lansdowne at once communicated this suggestion to Chamberlain. His reply introduces a new theme into our story.

CHAMBERLAIN TO LANSDOWNE

House of Commons, 17 March, 1901.—I had already thought of the Sokoto boundary as offering the possibility of a territorial compensation to France for the Treaty Shore.

It is of very great importance to France and she must pay well for it if we are to give it up.

I do not know its value to us but I will at once make enquiries.

Meanwhile, I may say that the surrender of the "enclaves" on the Niger must be part of any consideration. I have never liked them and they will be a source of trouble to us in the future.

If we are to discuss such a large question as Morocco please bear in mind that the Germans will have something to say—and both they and we will want compensation.

A more useful arrangement—if it were in any way possible, would be the exchange of Dahomey and its hinterland either for the Gambia or for territory in Borneo.

This would really be a good thing as it would immensely lessen the

---

[1] *Grosse Politik*, vol. xvii. p. 332 (June 20, 1901).
[2] *Ibid.* p. 341 (August 9, 1901).

territory where our boundaries are co-terminous with the French, but I do not know if they would listen to it.

The letter shows Chamberlain determined not to be worsted in a bargain. It also shows him moving for the first time, though very cautiously, towards the ideas that would ripen one day into the Entente Cordiale. He was still anxious to keep the door open for Germany in Morocco. But he was no longer averse, in principle, to a large transaction with France.

A few days later Cambon broached such a transaction in more definite terms. But it was still too early. Lansdowne answered that he would rather not discuss a proposal on that scale, especially not as regards Morocco.[1] The British Government, though disappointed by the Germans, had not yet been finally alienated.

II

Chamberlain's hopes of a German Alliance had failed, but the immediate danger, against which he had sought that alliance, remained. The Tsardom's expansion into Manchuria was still unchecked; and it became the first task of British statesmanship to find an alternative barrier against it. In the nature of things this could now only be Japan.

The preceding volume of this biography has shown that Chamberlain, among British statesmen, was the initiator of the historic compact with the new Power in the Far East.[2] At first, indeed, he had hoped that it would be part of a wider system, including a full alliance with Germany and close association with the United States. But, though the Germans refused their part in this larger scheme, they were none the less ardent supporters of an Anglo-Japanese alliance. For one thing, they thought it would embroil Britain still more deeply with Russia. For another, they hoped that the new combination would pull their own Chinese "chestnuts" out of the fire. Thus it happened that it was Eckardstein who, in April of 1901, first brought Hayashi, the Japanese Minister in London, to broach the subject of an alliance with Lansdowne.[3]

[1] March 20, 1901, Lansdowne to the Ambassador in Paris (dispatch copied for Chamberlain).
[2] Vol. III. of this work, pp. 96, 249-

250, 287.
[3] See *Memoirs of Count Hayashi*, pp. 114-196; also Eckardstein, vol. ii. pp. 272-374.

Chamberlain for one had no doubt as to what should be the result; and by midsummer the Cabinet were of the same opinion. They recognised that Japan was in the same predicament as they were themselves. If she could not obtain an alliance with Britain, then, at whatever cost, she must come to terms with the Tsardom.[1]

The negotiations were not completed for another six months. In the interval, Chamberlain strove to extend Japan's reciprocal guarantee to cover not only British interests in the Far East but in the rest of Asia as well and particularly in India.[2] Tokio, however, was unwilling to be formally bound, and the Cabinet thought it unnecessary to insist. Hayashi, moreover, pointed out that the Japanese would be sure to attack Russia on their own account, if Britain were drawn into war with her in defence of our interests in Asia.

The treaty was finally signed on January 30, 1902. Its conclusion was followed by a cordial exchange of messages between Chamberlain and Lansdowne.

CHAMBERLAIN TO LANSDOWNE

House of Commons, February 21, 1902.—Now I want to write one line to say with how much pleasure I have followed your success at the Foreign Office, and especially the popularity of the *coup* you have made in the Japanese Treaty. It required some courage to carry it through, and no one could be certain beforehand how it would be taken. The main credit is yours and recognised as yours, and I sincerely hope that this will be some compensation for the long torture of an almost hopeless task at the War Office.

LANSDOWNE TO CHAMBERLAIN

Foreign Office, February 21, 1902.—A great many thanks for your note which gave me much pleasure. I had no idea the Treaty would be taken so well, and I am glad to have had a hand in it, without pretending to so large a share in its paternity as you generously gave me.

No one could then be sure how far Japan was capable of barring the way to Russian expansion. The event would prove that Chamberlain had built even better than he knew. For over

[1] *British Documents*, vol. ii., especially on Far Eastern Affairs, pp. 26-59, and pp. 89-122.

[2] *Memoirs of Count Hayashi*, pp. 183-185.

three years he had sought to buttress Britain's position at its weakest point by enlisting the support of a military power. So far from failing in this purpose, he realised it in an unexpected way. He had looked chiefly to Germany, regarding Japan as an incidental reinforcement. As it turned out, the Japanese factor enabled Britain to dispense altogether with the German.

The Wilhelmstrasse, in their blindness, welcomed the Japanese Alliance. It led the Kaiser, in conversation with the British Ambassador in Berlin, to say of Chamberlain and his colleagues, "The Noodles seem to have had a lucid interval." [1] He could not see, any more than his counsellors, that by taking Germany's place in the Far East, Japan had made Britain temporarily independent of the need for a German alliance. Nor could he guess that the military power of Japan would force the Russians to abandon their Far Eastern dreams and turn back their energies against his Habsburg ally.

One further consequence of the Anglo-Japanese alliance must be noted. Though seldom recognised, it was of fundamental importance. Russia and Japan glared at each other across the Manchurian steppes. France was allied to Russia; Britain to Japan. The danger of war was plain; and the highest statesmanship would be required, if the seconds were not to be drawn into the conflict between the principals. Henceforth, therefore, a *rapprochement* between Britain and France became a necessity for the preservation of European peace. The ground was thus prepared for the new diplomatic constellation. The French desired it eagerly. Our slower statesmen still required a psychological shock to bring them to the point of decision. It was not long delayed.

III

In the last week of October, Chamberlain crossed the Border into Scotland to defend the Government's South African policy. In the course of a short but strenuous visit he spent a few days with Balfour at Whittingehame. Balfour, who delighted in new inventions, was already an enthusiastic motorist, and Chamberlain, with his wife, was whisked about the country at the surprising speed of twenty miles an hour. It was his first experience of motoring.

[1] Newton, *Lord Lansdowne*, p. 247.

Edinburgh was the scene of the main speech of this Scottish tour. He had not been there for a long time; and imposing preparations had been made in his honour. As once for Gladstone, the huge Waverley Market had been adapted for the meeting and roofed with draperies of red, white and blue. The audience numbered some 8000 persons and gave him a mighty welcome. Despite a heavy cold, his voice held for an hour and seventeen minutes; and he was plainly heard thanks to a web of telephone wires—there were said to be eight miles of them— radiating from over his head to the furthest corners of the building.

The manner of his speech was graphically described by one of his hearers: "He moves with the force of a steam puncher manufacturing rivets. But every bit of the machinery tells. There is no waste and the driving-power never ceases."

His matter was the stock-in-trade of contemporary party politics. He exulted in the Unionist triumph north of Tweed at the Khaki Election. He inveighed against Irish over-representation. He defended his South African policy against its assailants, foreign and domestic. It was good fighting stuff, but the effect would soon have been lost in the general din of platform oratory, save for the furious misinterpretation, in Germany, of a single sentence.

British and foreign criticism, just then, had fastened on farm-burning and other anti-guerilla tactics, already stigmatised by Campbell-Bannerman as "methods of barbarism". In reply to these attacks, Chamberlain cited the practice of other nations in recent wars, as precedents justifying Kitchener's resort to sterner measures. There was nothing irresponsible in this; and, considering the abuse which foreigners were hurling at the British Army, he was justified in pointing out that they had reacted far more rigorously against irregular resistance than ever Kitchener had. Moreover, though he spoke in defence of the Army's methods, he was careful to guard against the demand for blind and wholesale reprisals.

I think that the time has come—is coming—when measures of greater severity may be necessary, and, if that time comes, we may find precedents for anything we may do in the action of those nations who now criticise our "barbarity" and "cruelty" but whose example, in Poland, in the Caucasus, in Algeria, in Tongking, in Bosnia, in the Franco-German war, we have never even approached. . . . We would rather be blamed for being too slow than for being too fast, and, when I read some of the demands that are made upon us for wholesale confiscation, for wholesale execution, I confess I have not up to the present time been able to convince myself that these measures would conduce either to a speedy termination of the war or to a satisfactory peace at the end of it.[1]

Had there been any offence in these words, other nations would have had as much right as Germany to be offended. But the storm of indignation, which now broke out, was confined to Germany alone. Abuse began in the leading dailies. They attacked Chamberlain for daring to compare the German "heroes" of the Franco-Prussian war with Kitchener's "butchers". The agitation soon spread to the universities and to the professional associations. Meetings of protest were held throughout the Fatherland and culminated in a Grand Remonstrance by the Evangelical clergy of the Rhine.

These paroxysms were received in England, first with bewilderment, then with growing anger. Campbell-Bannerman might hold Chamberlain responsible for them, but the bulk of opinion took the opposite view. These virulent attacks against the man, who had been pre-eminent as Germany's friend, convinced a growing section that there could be no sincere understanding between the two countries.

At the end of November the uproar in Germany began to subside. But, despite Metternich's warnings [2] that the situation was dangerous, the Kaiser's Ministers now prepared to exceed the folly of his people. Chamberlain had watched the agitation with astonishment and regret. Presently, in an effort to pour oil on the troubled waters, he wrote, through his secretary, to a correspondent [3] that no sensible German could be offended by his words. This well-meant gesture was regarded in Berlin as a sign of weakness; and Bülow was tempted to seek a personal triumph by extracting an apology from Chamberlain. Metternich was instructed to make a formal protest at the Foreign Office.

[1] *The Times*, October 26, 1901.
[2] *Grosse Politik*, vol. xvii. p. 194 (November 19, 1901).
[3] Letter to Mr. A. A. Marriner, November 18, 1901.

Lansdowne replied that he saw no ground for protest and no prospect of an apology "for a speech which in our opinion did not call for one".[1] A further request from Metternich for some expression of regret, which Bülow could use in the Reichstag, met with a further refusal.[2]

Meanwhile, in a friendly talk with the Austrian Ambassador, Count Deym, Chamberlain had given his own warning that there would be no apology. The following is the report of this conversation sent to Bülow by Metternich:

. . . Count Deym tells me in the strictest confidence that, in a talk with Chamberlain yesterday, he told him that he [Deym] had foreseen from the start the storm which Chamberlain's remarks would arouse in Germany. Chamberlain answered that there had been no warmer advocate than himself of England's adherence to the Triple Alliance and that he had pursued this goal consistently. Two years ago, in his interview with Count Bülow, he was able to affirm that no insuperable hindrances lay in the way. It was, no doubt, the fact that the ordinary ideas of the English people made it not easy to gain them for alliances; but he had believed firmly that, in time, he could overcome this obstacle and lead English public opinion towards adherence to the Triple Alliance.

But, now that he saw German hatred becoming more and more intense, he was naturally beginning to despair of attaining his ideal. He feared, indeed, that, even if the excitement in Germany should die down later, the remembrance of the outburst of German hatred during the Boer War would remain deep-rooted in the English people. . . .

When Count Deym suggested that the Minister might make a public explanation putting intentional insult out of the question, he answered that he would have done this gladly soon after his Edinburgh speech, if he could have foreseen the impression it would make in Germany. He could not at first bring himself to conceive that such an agitation could arise. Now that he had been subjected for three weeks to measureless abuse and attack, he could give no further explanation since it would be interpreted as an apology. Since no insult had been meant no apology would be given.[3]

[1] Lansdowne to Buchanan, November 26, 1901.
[2] December 3, 1901.
[3] Grosse Politik, vol. xvii. pp. 198-200. The Austrian Ambassador's confidential account reported by Metternich to Bülow, November 26, 1901.

IV

The storm created over Chamberlain's speech led to the final wreck of Bülow and Holstein's British policy. By a polite fiction of diplomacy, the negotiations initiated by Eckardstein, as a sequel to the Chatsworth meeting, were supposed to be suspended but not extinct. Conscious of the growing estrangement between the two countries, the Cabinet now decided that a frank statement of the real position must be made to the German Ambassador. Otherwise they might soon find themselves accused of double-dealing. Accordingly, on December 19, 1901, Lansdowne formally intimated to Metternich that the alliance project was at an end.[1] It had been dead for some months. It was now buried for ever.

The event was of more than purely formal significance. It dispelled the last faint hope of an eventual Anglo-German alliance, the hope which Bülow himself had been so anxious to keep "shimmering on the horizon".[2] With it disappeared the last slender obstacle to a *rapprochement* between Britain and the Dual Alliance. The road was open now which was to lead to the founding of the Entente and the encirclement of Germany. The failure of the Wilhelmstrasse's diplomacy was complete; but there was still just time to make matters worse; and Bülow was just the man to do it. In a single speech he destroyed the last remnants of Bismarck's system of security and turned Chamberlain into his most implacable foe. All this before the anniversary of the Chatsworth proposals came round.

V

Bülow had failed to extract an apology from Chamberlain for his Edinburgh speech. He had been assured, however, by the Foreign Office that no offence had been intended; and Metternich had warned him against attempting any reply in the Reichstag that might antagonise Germany's best friend in the British Cabinet.[3] In this delicate, even critical, conjuncture of Anglo-German relations, the Chancellor would have been well

---

[1] *British Documents*, vol. ii. pp. 79-83.
[2] *Grosse Politik*, vol. xvii. p. 109
(November 1, 1901).
[3] *Ibid.* p. 198 (Metternich to Bülow, November 26, 1901).

advised to let the matter drop. Nor was there any pressure upon
him to pursue it. The agitation in Germany was dying down;
and the Reichstag had dispersed in December without even
debating its cause.

But Bülow was moved by other considerations, partly
tactical, partly personal. His influence and position rested on
precarious foundations. Repeated personal successes were the
surest key to the Kaiser's favour. Pandering to Anglophobia
was the surest means of rallying the Reichstag in support of new
taxes and of the Naval Programme. The Chancellor was also very
vain. He loved to display his skill in the parliamentary arena.
The applause of the deputies was, perhaps, his only compensation
for outward servility to his sovereign and inner subservience to
Holstein. He, therefore, decided to reopen the subject of the
Edinburgh speech, already more than two months old, and to
secure a facile but striking personal triumph by repelling the
supposed insults of a foreign politician to the honour of the
German Army. Considering what was at stake for Germany, this
pursuit of tactical advantage was more than irresponsible. We
understand why a German wit wrote of the Byzantine flatterer
who sat in Bismarck's chair: "Take him for all in all, this was
no man".

The Reichstag reassembled on January 8. In a prearranged
interpellation, a Conservative spokesman, Count Stolberg,
declared, amid applause, that whoever insulted the German
Army insulted the German people. Bülow then rose. He had
prepared his effects with unusual care. His speech ranged
over the whole field of international affairs. But he began
with Chamberlain. He explained that the English had assured
him that no offence had been meant, and hinted that there
had been apologies. These were accepted, but the wounding
of German feelings was none the less to be deplored.
Foreign statesmen would do well to leave other countries out
of their comparisons. Then came a rebuke clearly addressed to
Chamberlain:

But the German Army stands far too high and its escutcheon is far too
stainless for warped judgments to affect it. (*Bravo!*) This business recalls
Frederick the Great's remark when told that someone had been attacking him and the Prussian Army. "Let the man alone," said the great

King, "and don't get excited; he is biting granite." (*Laughter. Very good!*)[1]

It was a bad day's work. Bülow had lied in hinting at a British apology. He had then added injury to falsehood by coupling his acceptance of that apology with a rebuke. The Reichstag might applaud, but the British public was outraged. There was something about the speech which flicked them in the face. Chamberlain was alienated for ever; and he had the whole country behind him.

He did not hurry his reply. Too much was at stake, and the least loss of restraint would have played into Bülow's hands. Public opinion was concerned for his dignity; and friends who knew his natural pugnacity were uneasy. They might have spared their anxiety.

He had a long-standing engagement to speak, two days later, in the familiar company of the Birmingham Jewellers at their annual dinner. He was never more sure of himself than when he rose that night. The compact and controlled style was his best. His speech was a full-length address upon the greatness of the Imperial ideal, the honour of British policy and arms, and the assurance of victory in South Africa. Some of it was prophetic:

This war has enabled the British Empire to find itself. It has united the British race throughout the world. . . . If ever again we have, as we have done in the past, to fight for our very existence against a world in arms—we shall not be alone, we shall be supported by the sons of Britain in every quarter of the globe.

But only one passage of the whole was remembered. With consummate skill he coupled his domestic with his foreign enemies and answered both in a dozen sentences. First he dealt with the Liberals.

I understand a good party fight. I am myself a party man. When I am struck I try to strike again; but I cannot appreciate the position of those who, inflamed by party passion, are not content with fighting the battle here at home on fair and reasonable lines but must go out of their way to impute methods of barbarism to our soldiers in the field—to imply that

[1] "Lasst den Mann gewähren und regt euch nicht auf; er beisst auf Granit" (Penzler, *Bülow's Reden*, vol. i. pp. 241-242). Historians, however, believe that Frederick made the remark in French.

His Majesty's Ministers, who are Britons like themselves, can by any

possibility be guilty of deliberate cruelty and inhumanity, and who laud the Boers while they slander the Britons, and then profess to be astonished and surprised at the growing hostility of foreign nations. They have helped to create an animosity which we all deplore.

Then came Bülow's turn in words which excluded a retort. They were cheered until the ceiling shook:

I am well aware that in some quarters this animosity is attributed to another cause. It is said to be due to the indiscreet oratory of the Colonial Secretary. Gentlemen, what I have said, I have said. I withdraw nothing. I qualify nothing. I defend nothing. As I read history, no British Minister has ever served his country faithfully and at the same time enjoyed popularity abroad. I make allowance for foreign criticism. I will not follow the example that has been set me. I do not want to give lessons to a Foreign Minister, and I will not accept any at his hands. I am responsible only to my own Sovereign and my own Country-men. . . .

I would ask you gentlemen how it can be due to a few words in a speech, that was delivered only a few weeks ago, that for months and for years, from the very beginning of this war, the foreign press has teemed with abuse of this country? How can the Colonial Secretary be responsible for what Sir Edward Grey has called "the foul and filthy lies", for what Lord Rosebery has described as "the foul and infamous falsehoods" which have been disseminated in foreign countries without a syllable of protest, without the slightest interference by the responsible authorities? No, Gentlemen, my opponents must find some other scapegoat.[1]

The steely restraint of this reply raised Chamberlain to new heights in the esteem of his compatriots. The fortune of his speech was that it had expressed exactly both the pent-up feeling of the nation and its strength of character. From the depths of their nature, ordinary Englishmen, at home and in the Colonies, had wanted someone to stand up to Bülow, but to do it with better manners and yet tougher fibre. Chamberlain had fulfilled their need.

VI

Praises rained upon him from every quarter, but one tribute was especially grateful. At its first meeting after the reply to

[1] Birmingham, January 11, 1902.

Bülow, the Corporation of the City of London unanimously resolved to present him with an address, in recognition, as they said, of his patriotic statesmanship and his work in consolidating the Empire. They could not give him the City's freedom; for, like his forebears, he already had it. As a member of the Cord-wainers' Company, he had been a freeman and a liveryman since he came of age. Thus the highest honour in their power was to present him with an address in "a suitable gold-box". In such matters, Chamberlain was more apt to be quizzical than com-placent, but, this time, he made no effort to deny his pleasure. He had always hoped to be honoured by the city of his birth.

Another notable tribute came from *The Times*. That news-paper had long been cool towards him on account of his pro-German proclivities. It now commended the Corporation on their decision, and drew the moral for domestic politics:

Lord Rosebery is fond of preaching efficiency, therefore he ought to have a very high appreciation of Mr. Chamberlain. For this nation is convinced, the Colonies are convinced, foreign nations are angrily con-vinced, that Mr. Chamberlain stands for efficiency. He knows what he wants, and he knows how to set to work to get it. . . . By a sound instinct the nation desires to be led by someone who has a mind, who knows how to handle facts and who can go to the root of the matter while others are fumbling with words or losing themselves among non-essentials. We do not want to disparage any servants of the Crown, but it is mere plain fact that at home and abroad Mr. Chamberlain is recognised as the one amongst them who pre-eminently stands for efficiency of national effort.[1]

The Guildhall ceremony on February 13 was one of the out-standing scenes of Chamberlain's career. With the memories of his early life crowding in upon him, and with the thought of five generations of faithful City tradition behind him, he might well be moved. As he drove with his wife through the streets in an open carriage, he was cheered all the way. The crowd round Guildhall raised storms of cheers, and the ovation was taken up within, when the trumpets sounded his arrival. Half the Cabinet were there and the chief magnates of a capitalist society in its golden age. The Lord Mayor, in presenting the casket and address, hailed Chamberlain as one who had

[1] *The Times*, January 17, 1902.

Stood for his Country's glory fast
And nailed her colours to the mast.

When he rose to reply, he was under strong emotion but mastered it. He made no reference to his duel with Bülow, which was the real occasion of his honour. Instead he looked to the future.

Can we hold for ourselves and can we transmit to our descendants this great heritage of a united Empire? . . . Our enemies of yesterday, if they surrender today, will be welcomed tomorrow as friends. The danger is of a different kind. We have to take care lest our sensibility should run away with our sense. . . . I believe we shall show to the World, in a period of time which is a mere moment in the history of a nation, a South Africa as strong, as prosperous, and as free as any other part of His Majesty's Dominions.

The presentation was followed by a luncheon at the Mansion House. There Chamberlain made a second speech, but the surprise of the afternoon came from another quarter. With his usual grace, but with unexpected warmth, Balfour paid a remarkable tribute to his colleague. He declared that, in his work for the Empire, Chamberlain had united genius with opportunity in a way that won for him "a position on the roll of statesmen of this country second to none".

We must mark these words in view of what the relative positions of Balfour and Chamberlain were then and were afterwards to become. Nothing could have given more unaffected pleasure to Chamberlain and to his family. They long remembered Balfour's gesture that day; and it would count in times of strain not yet foreseen.

When the guests left the Mansion House late in the afternoon, the crowds were still thick and the cheering tremendous. It was Chamberlain's first triumph in what was to be his year of triumphs. Next morning he might read in *The Times*:

Mr. Chamberlain is at this moment the most popular and trusted man in England.

VII

Chamberlain's duel with Bülow led to a lasting breach between Britain and Germany. Characteristically, its first effects

were seen in the mutual relations of the reigning families. Just
before the reopening of the Reichstag, the Kaiser had written
to his Uncle that "sharp repartees" might be expected to the
"overbearing bluff" of the "most ill-advised Colonial Secretary". As royally as Queen Victoria had once defended Salisbury
against a worse attack, King Edward had defended Chamberlain
and now condemned Bülow.[1] He seriously considered cancelling
the Prince of Wales' impending visit to Berlin; and it was only
at the Kaiser's earnest request that this finally took place as
arranged. In Berlin the Prince tried to explain to Bülow what
Chamberlain's name and work meant to the British people.[2]
But it was already too late.

The British people have a curious way of coming suddenly
to immovable conclusions after a slow-working process of
uneasy instinct. Bülow's attack on Chamberlain finally convinced them that Germany was the enemy. "You would be
interested," wrote a shrewd observer not long afterwards,

to see the effect created in England by the German treatment of us.
The change is extraordinary. Every one, in the [Foreign] Office and out,
talks as if we had but one enemy in the world, and that Germany. It
is no manner of good trying to assure us unofficially or officially that
they are really our friends. No one believes it now, and the only effect is
to disgust. The change in Chamberlain's mind is most remarkable. The
last time I saw him he was a mad philogerman, and now! . . .[3]

VIII

The breach between Britain and Germany had an immediate
and significant consequence.

During most of his term of office, Chamberlain was troubled
by agitations in Malta. These centred upon the so-called
language question. Maltese, derived from Arabic, was the
language of the island's inhabitants. Italian, however, had long
been the second language of the educated classes and an official
medium in the law courts. In 1899, to foster British influence
and remove glaring legal anomalies, Chamberlain had an

---

[1] Sir Sidney Lee, *King Edward VII*,
vol. ii. pp. 136-140.
[2] *Bülow's Memoirs*, vol. i. pp. 548-
550.

[3] Letter of Spring Rice, of April 17,
1902, quoted from *The Letters and
Friendships of Sir Cecil Spring Rice*,
edited by Stephen Gwynn.

MR. C. (*apostrophising portrait of William Pitt*). "IT'S WONDERFUL, WILLIAM, HOW MUCH ALIKE ALL WE GREAT MINISTERS ARE. YOU WERE HATED IN EUROPE IN YOUR TIME AS I AM HATED TODAY."

"Read your history, and you find the younger Pitt, one of the greatest of English Ministers; you find Lord Melbourne, you find the Duke of Wellington, you find Lord Palmerston—you find all those great Ministers who in their time upheld the honour and interests of the British Empire—you find them all complaining that they had not a friend in Europe ... sometimes that is a consolation to me."—Mr. Chamberlain at Birmingham, January 6, 1902. *Westminster Gazette*, January 8, 1902

From the cartoon by F. Carruthers Gould in the *Westminster Gazette*, January 8, 1902

ordinance issued, placing English on an equal footing with Italian in the Maltese courts, and declaring that in 1914 English would be substituted for Italian entirely. This ordinance aroused fierce opposition in an influential section of the educated classes. Many saw in it an extension of British influence at the expense of their national identity. The lawyers, who were most directly affected, dreaded an influx of British competitors. The powerful and obscurantist clergy feared the spread of heretical ideas. Chamberlain, however, held resolutely to his course and defended it vigorously in Parliament.

There is no doubt today that he was right on the merits of the case; and a later Government had to return to his policy. Nevertheless, the ordinance produced a painful feeling in Italy. Chamberlain was made aware of this when he passed through Rome after the Khaki Election. On that occasion, Wickham Steed, then Rome Correspondent of *The Times*, persuaded the British Ambassador to invite Visconti Venosta, the Foreign Minister, and Sonnino, the powerful leader of the Italian Right, to meet Chamberlain at lunch. He hoped that a frank discussion of the Maltese question might lead to better relations between the two countries.

At the beginning, the conversation took an unfortunate turn. Chamberlain, who was sitting next to Sonnino, began discoursing on racial characteristics and disparaged the Jews as "physical cowards". Now Sonnino was a Jew. He reacted vigorously; and Steed, seeing his hopes of a *rapprochement* in danger, gave Chamberlain a vigorous kick under the table. Chamberlain literally jumped with pain, but took in the position at once. With great dexterity he retracted his *gaffe* and admitted the force of Sonnino's reply. He then led him into a discussion of the Maltese language question which lasted until four o'clock. On leaving, he said to Steed: "Thank you for that friendly kick. It hurt, but I twigged, and now we have had it out." By "it" he meant the Maltese language question.[1]

Sonnino's arguments made a considerable impression on Chamberlain. At the time, however, he saw no reason to yield to them. For one thing, he was convinced that his policy was intrinsically sound. For another, he was already planning his

[1] See Wickham Steed's *Through Thirty Years*, vol. i. pp. 161-165.

last approach to the senior partner in the Triple Alliance. Had he secured an understanding with Germany, there would have been no need for concessions to Italy.

A year later he saw the matter in a very different light. The breach with Germany made it expedient to improve relations with the Mediterranean Powers. Accordingly, in January 1902, a few days after Bülow's attack upon him in the Reichstag, he announced the withdrawal of the language proclamation.

A good feeling between Italy and this country is I think for both peoples a national asset. . . . Our relations with Italy have always been friendly. Our interests and theirs are, in many cases and especially in the Mediterranean, mutual interests. . . . It would be deplorable if any misapprehension were to alter or to diminish in any way the sympathies which have existed and which I hope may long continue to exist between the two nations.[1]

There was no voice of dissent from the Opposition benches. Campbell-Bannerman praised the "force and grace" of this conciliatory retreat; and Steed wrote in *The Times*:

Mr. Chamberlain's speech on the Maltese language question has gone straight to the core of Italian feeling and is earning for him heartier approval in Italy than anything he ever said or did.[2]

This incident has a deep significance. Geography made friendship between Britain and Italy necessary to both Powers. If Chamberlain's Chatsworth proposals had prospered, that friendship would have bound Italy securely to the Triple Alliance. As it was, it contributed, more than anything else, to detach her from it. Here was a further consequence of Bülow's miscalculations.

[1] Hansard, Fourth Series, vol. vi. cols. 1182-1206 (January 28, 1902).
[2] Chamberlain wrote in generous terms to Sonnino to say that if a settlement had been found it was due to his exposition of the Italian case at lunch a year before.

CHAPTER LXXXIII

TOWARDS THE ENTENTE CORDIALE

(January 1902–January 1903)

CHAMBERLAIN turns to France—First Negotiations with Cambon—
Continued through "the usual channels"—Chamberlain, Lansdowne
and Morocco—Anglo-French Relations in Siam—Kelantan and
Trengganu—Swettenham's Dispatch and Chamberlain's Intervention
—A Tacit Understanding with France—The Breach with Germany
Widens—Bülow drives a Wedge between Britain and U.S.A.—Folly
of his Policy of Pin-pricks—Chamberlain's Frank Talk with Eckard-
stein—Bülow, the Kaiser and the Boer Generals—The Kaiser at
Sandringham—His Eyes opened by Chamberlain—Germany Tries to
Retrieve the Position—the Venezuelan Fiasco—Setbacks to Anglo-
French *Rapprochement*—Chamberlain proposes an *Entente*—Cambon's
Estimate of Chamberlain.

I

CHAMBERLAIN never forgave Bülow's attack upon him in the
Reichstag. It convinced him finally that there could be no
friendship with the German Government. But its effect went
further. It turned and spurred him on decisively towards his
alternative goal: the settlement of Britain's traditional disputes
with the Dual Alliance.

CHAP.
LXXXIII.
Æt. 65.

The Chamberlain Papers contain no account of the part
which he played in this momentous process. The German
records, however, show plainly that, on the British side, he was
the initiator of the French alliance project, just as he had been
of the German alliance project before it. This time, taught by
experience, he moved more cautiously.

Within a few weeks of Bülow's attack on Chamberlain,
Metternich telegraphed in alarm to the Wilhelmstrasse.

179

METTERNICH TO THE FOREIGN MINISTRY
(Telegram)

London, January 30, 1902.—*Secret.*—In the strictest confidence I hear that negotiations have been going on for the last ten days between Chamberlain and the French ambassador for the settlement of all differences in colonial matters between the two powers. Chamberlain has proposed to the French Ambassador that the outstanding colonial differences between the two powers should be treated not one by one but as a whole. Newfoundland, the Niger, the New Hebrides, as well as commercial rights in Madagascar and extra territoriality in Zanzibar, are apparently among the so-called Colonial questions which Chamberlain wishes to settle. Cambon seems to be very keen to secure a definite agreement with the British Government upon these questions. Moreover, according to one of the officials in closest touch with Chamberlain at the Colonial Office, the Ambassador, as a consequence of the recent Franco-Italian Mediterranean Agreement, has raised the Moroccan question here and has hinted that his Government would not be unwilling to negotiate a Franco-British understanding over Morocco. On this subject, Chamberlain apparently answered that he would gladly encourage the discussion of the question and the pursuit of an agreement satisfactory to both sides. Nevertheless he proposed that the Moroccan question should be handled separately from the other so-called Colonial questions.[1]

A few days later, Eckardstein attended an official function at Marlborough House. There, after dinner, he saw Chamberlain and Cambon go off together to the billiard room, where they remained in lively conversation for exactly twenty-eight minutes by the Baron's watch. He could not overhear their talk but caught the words "Egypt" and "Morocco". Later in the evening, he had some talk with Chamberlain himself who said to him:

Count Bülow has already attacked me once before in the Reichstag [a reference to the sequel to the Leicester speech]. I've had enough now of such treatment. There can be no question any longer of an alliance between Germany and England.

Before going home that night, Eckardstein had a short conversation with King Edward, who repeated that there could be no question of an Anglo-German alliance for a long time to

[1] *Grosse Politik*, vol. xvii. p. 342.

come. The King also told him that a *rapprochement* with France
was now inevitable.[1]

A few days later Eckardstein went to Berlin, where his sombre
impressions were confirmed by other evidence. Passing through
that capital, the Austro-Hungarian Ambassador in London,
Count Albert Mensdorff, warned the Wilhelmstrasse that
Bülow's attack had only strengthened Chamberlain's position
and increased his popularity. About the same time Metternich
wrote from London, in a private letter, that he "wouldn't give
twopence for Anglo-German relations" and that the Colonial
Secretary was very embittered. But the sleek and florid
Chancellor had convinced himself that a serious *rapprochement* between Britain and the Dual Alliance was impossible.
He found no better answer, therefore, to these warnings than
to say that Germany had received all the provocation, and that
Chamberlain, as a reasonable statesman, should now return to a
more sober frame of mind.[2]

At that very time Chamberlain was discussing with Lansdowne, and the latter with Cambon, the details of an Anglo-
French settlement. A memorandum of Chamberlain's shows
that he was determined to do everything in his power to bring
it about. He wrote of Newfoundland, West Africa, the New
Hebrides and Siam, and contemplated facilitating the general
settlement by an understanding over Morocco. Lansdowne's
reply speaks of "the value of what we have to sell and its
immense importance to the French".[3] Chamberlain's alternative
was coming into play.

II

Chamberlain's talks with Cambon in the early weeks of 1902
mark the beginning of the decisive reorientation in British
Foreign Policy. The Colonial Secretary was, thus, the initiator
of the negotiations which would lead to the Entente Cordiale.
Their subsequent control, however, would not lie in his hands.
There was, indeed, no reason why he should continue to intervene in the conduct, as distinct from the formulation, of foreign

---

[1] Eckardstein, vol. ii. pp. 376-380.
[2] *Grosse Politik*, vol. xvii. pp. 149-
152 (Bülow to Metternich, March 13,
1902).

[3] Chamberlain's memorandum is
undated but clearly belongs to March
1902. Lansdowne's note is dated
March 11.

policy. The situation was now very different from what it had been at the beginning of 1897. Then, he had taken the leading part in negotiations with the German Embassy, precisely because Salisbury, as Foreign Secretary, had not, himself, been prepared to discuss a Continental alliance. But, by 1902, all that was changed. Salisbury was no longer at the Foreign Office; "Splendid Isolation" was dead; all hope of a German alliance had been abandoned; and Balfour and Lansdowne were at one with Chamberlain in wanting a *rapprochement* with France. There was thus no further need to conduct negotiations outside the usual diplomatic channels. Nevertheless, Chamberlain's Papers show that his vigilance in foreign affairs was unsleeping. He was consulted at every step in Lansdowne's delicate exchanges with Cambon, and his influence was decisive in bringing about the first practical solution of a serious difference between France and Britain.

III

On the French side, Delcassé and Cambon looked, in the first place, for agreements with Britain over Morocco and Siam. At Windsor and at Chatsworth, Chamberlain had spoken of Morocco as a possible starting-point for an alliance with Germany. In the same spirit, though in different circumstances, he had welcomed Cambon's suggestion that Morocco might be the subject of an agreement between Britain and France. In this he was supported by a school of thought in the Admiralty [1] which favoured a deliberate partition of Morocco designed to give the French a free hand in most of the territory, but specifically excluding them from the regions around Tangier. Lansdowne, however, was more reserved. He was not convinced that the disintegration of the Shereefian Empire was inevitable, and, as yet, gave no encouragement to Cambon's proposals for hastening that process.

Chamberlain had no special reason for pressing his view of the Moroccan affair against Lansdowne's. In Siam, on the other

[1] "Let France have what she will and Spain have what she can, but neither they nor any other power should have the country west of and south of and including the city of Tangier, a division the more to be desired seeing that it is the best part of the country, the richest and most fertile province of that interesting land." (Dispatch from Captain Troubridge, Naval Attaché, British Embassy, Madrid, April 9, 1902.)

hand, there was a more practical coincidence between his aims
and those of the Quai d'Orsay.

Anglo-French relations in Siam were governed, at this time, by the Convention of 1896. This guaranteed the independence of the Menam Valley, "the middle of the [Siamese] artichoke",[1] but recognised the "special interests" of France in the Mekong Valley adjoining Indo-China, and of Britain in the Malay Peninsula. France had always sought to interpret the phrase, "special interests" to mean "zones of influence"; but the Foreign Office had resisted this interpretation, for a solid but unavowable reason. They had already secured what was, in effect, a "zone of influence" for British interests by a secret treaty concluded with Siam in 1897.

Now it so happened that the working of this secret treaty had proved unsatisfactory to Britain. Contrary to its spirit, though not to its letter, the Siamese had sought to revive their shadowy claims of suzerainty over certain of the Malay States. The Rajah of Patani had been imprisoned and deposed; and a similar fate threatened the rulers of Kelantan and Trengganu. Sir Frank Swettenham, Chamberlain's vigorous Governor of the Straits Settlement, had accordingly prepared the draft of a revised secret treaty designed "to secure British interests and put matters on a definite footing".[2] The King of Siam, however, had rejected Swettenham's treaty; and the Foreign Office were disinclined to press it upon him, lest the French should hear of it and demand counter-concessions in the Mekong Valley.

Thus matters stood when, on August 6, Cambon, on Delcassé's instructions, proposed to Lansdowne that Britain and France should define their "zones of influence" in Siam. The Foreign Secretary answered non-committally. The summer holidays had begun, and he could not easily consult his colleagues. A few days later, however, Chamberlain received a strongly worded dispatch from Swettenham, urging that, if the Siamese continued to refuse his draft treaty, he should be allowed to negotiate direct agreements with the Rajahs of Kelantan and Trengganu. Chamberlain, who already knew of Cambon's proposal, now forwarded Swettenham's dispatch to

[1] Draft dispatch from Lord Lansdowne to Sir E. Monson, July 30, 1902.   [2] Letter from Swettenham to J. C. of July 15, 1902.

Lansdowne, indicating his agreement with its recommendations. Lansdowne saw at once that, by adopting Swettenham's
policy, he would put himself into a position where he could
hardly avoid accepting Cambon's proposal for a definition of
"zones of influence". He disliked the prospect but saw no
alternative to it.

LANSDOWNE TO CHAMBERLAIN

August 23, 1902.—Thanks for your letter of the 20th. I return Swettenham's. His policy would be plain sailing enough, if there were no risk of
complications with other Powers—that risk and the existence of the
Secret agreement are the real trouble.

But the conduct of the Siamese is forcing us more and more towards
the adoption of Swettenham's policy. . . .

If the Siamese answer is obdurate, I see nothing for it but to send
Swettenham at once to negotiate direct agreements with the Rajas—the
conditions should be as simple as possible, and we should represent them
as neighbourly arrangements between us and the Malay States, reserving
fully any rights actually exercised by the Siamese Govt.—rights which,
if Swettenham is correct (V. his letter to you), amount to nothing.

But there will be wigs on the green over all this, and the Secret
Agreement, which is probably known to the French already, will come
out.

I am inclined to think that we should make a virtue of necessity and
tell them all about it, and about our difficulties with Siam in regard to
the Malay States. We shall, in that case, of course have to be prepared for
a corresponding assertion of French influence in the Mekong Valley, and
I for one do not believe it would hurt us.

We might send Swettenham forms of agreement with the Rajas so
that he might be prepared at any moment and clinch matters with
them.

I wish the whole business could stand still till October, but I fear it
will not, and we must be prepared. . . .

Chamberlain was determined "to clinch matters" in the
interests of relations with France as well as of Malaya. Accordingly, he sent on the papers to Balfour with the following terse
and categorical comment:

CHAMBERLAIN TO BALFOUR

August 24, 1902.—The enclosed letter and Papers from Lansdowne explain themselves.

The situation is critical and urgent.

I . . . agree strongly as to the propriety of making a clean breast to the French and I do not object to giving them a free hand in the Mekong Valley which is worthless to us.

Balfour concurred. Swettenham's policy was accepted; and a few days later Chamberlain wrote to him.

CHAMBERLAIN TO SWETTENHAM

September 15, 1902.—. . . I hope that the Siamese Government, who have shown themselves masters of diplomatic delays, do at last understand the gravity of the situation, and that the draft agreement will be immediately signed. If not, we have prepared your instructions and I think you will find them satisfactory.

I am fully aware of the importance of maintaining our legitimate influence with the two States of Kelantan and Trengganu, and, subject to the necessity of keeping faith in regard to the unfortunate Secret Treaty, I am prepared to give every support to your policy.

England and France were thus pursuing parallel though unconcerted policies in their respective zones of Siam. The Siamese, who had planned to play them off one against the other, now saw no alternative but to come to terms with both. By the Franco-Siamese Convention of October 7, the King of Siam recognised a considerable extension of French influence in the Mekong Valley. Meanwhile, he resumed negotiations with the British Government on the basis of Swettenham's draft treaty.

On October 15, Cambon called on Lansdowne to explain the purpose of the new Franco-Siamese Treaty. Lansdowne raised no objections to it and did not deny Cambon's remark that the negotiation of an Anglo-Siamese arrangement with regard to Kelantan and Trengganu was "a matter of notoriety". At the end of the conversation, Cambon said that it was the desire of the Quai d'Orsay "that the two Governments should treat one another with the fullest confidence". Lansdowne replied that

that was my feeling also and that I hoped before long to place the whole of my cards upon the table. I could not do so yet, partly because the matter had not been fully considered by my colleagues and also because our arrangements as to Kelantan and Trengganu, which concerned the Malay Rajahs as well as the Siamese Government, were not actually concluded.[1]

To keep faith with Siam, it was decided not to disclose the existence of the Anglo-Siamese Secret Treaty until Siam's new treaty with France had been ratified. The signing of a new Anglo-French convention was, therefore, delayed for some time. But the substance of France's claims had, in effect, been already granted. In accepting the Franco-Siamese Treaty, Lansdowne had waived the British Government's previous objections to an extension of French influence in Siam. He had also admitted that England had decided to pursue a similar policy in her zone. This was tantamount to acceptance of Cambon's original proposal. Thus, it was in the swamps of the Mekong and the jungles of Kelantan and Trengganu that the Entente first began to take shape. It would still take time for such local arrangements to ripen into a full alliance. Nevertheless, this tacit agreement between Britain and France over Siam marked a turning-point in the diplomatic revolution. Henceforth British policy entered on a new but settled course. There was still to be a moment's hesitation, against Chamberlain's advice, but there would be no turning back.

IV

All this time the breach between Germany and Britain had been growing wider. Naïvely confident that he alone held the diplomatic initiative, Bülow proceeded on his way with a blind disregard for British interests or susceptibilities. His first aim was to create a Continental bloc under German leadership. To this end, the Triple Alliance was renewed. An attempt was made at Reval to repair "the wire to St. Petersburg"; and relations with France were informed by a new spirit of conciliation.

Thus far Bülow's policy was in the Bismarck tradition and rested upon the sure foundation of the German Army. But it was midsummer madness to believe that the formation of a

‾‾‾‾‾
[1] Lansdowne to Sir E. Monson, October 15, 1902.

Continental bloc could be combined with an anti-British policy, at least until the German fleet was built. Nevertheless, Bülow chose this critical year to challenge British interests in every quarter of the globe. He began with a blatant and gratuitous attempt to drive a wedge between Britain and the United States.

In January the German Ambassador in Washington disclosed that, during the Spanish-American War of 1898, Lord Pauncefote had suggested, "A collective step on the part of the Powers in disapproval of the American policy in Cuba". He also announced that "this step was abandoned in consequence of the decisive refusal of Germany".[1] This "collective step" was, of course, none other than the unfortunate "moral protest" from which Chamberlain himself had wisely dissuaded the British Government at the time.[2]

The details of the German disclosure were rebutted by Cranborne, the Under-Secretary of State for Foreign Affairs. Chamberlain, however, thought that some stronger action was needed. He wanted to teach the Germans a lesson and, at the same time, to convince American opinion that Britain's attitude in 1898 had been "uniformly friendly" to the United States. He suggested, therefore, that the Foreign Office should publish the relevant contemporary dispatches. The technical difficulties attending this course were explained in a letter from Cranborne. It deserves quotation for the interesting light which it throws on the opinions held at this time, both by Chamberlain and in the Foreign Office.

CRANBORNE TO CHAMBERLAIN

Foreign Office—February 15, 1902.—I have had all the papers on the American controversy put together, and Lord Lansdowne has gone through them with Sanderson and myself this afternoon. Ld. L. thinks that, at the present moment, our declarations have given us the best of the position and that it is not likely to be bettered by any publication. The fact is that our ordinary practice of doctoring papers for publication is not open to us in the present instance, where we should be under an honourable obligation not to publish anything which is not rigidly

[1] From published dispatch of Dr. Hollanden, the German Ambassador in Washington. See *Annual Register*, *1903*, p. 303.
[2] See Vol. III. of this work, pp. 298-301.

genuine, and there are several expressions which would not look very well in public. (What private communications are there of which that cannot be said?) . . .

May I add, in reference to what you said to me the other night, that though I think it is very possible that the Germans will behave better after our telegram to Lascelles of yesterday, yet I am afraid there will never be any security in any close relations with the Emperor.

It may so well be true that, as you said, he wishes to supplant us with the Americans, and there is no doubt he wishes to oust our commerce and probably our naval supremacy.

I am afraid I have no confidence that the closest alliance would necessarily make him forego these objects.

He might even extend his efforts not merely to separate us from the United States but also from our Colonies, and, if we were committed to his party in Europe and therefore definitely estranged from the other party, we should be hampered in resisting his mischief-making lest we should fall between the two stools.

Yet perhaps our only hope lies in the friendship of our Colonies.

The Germans, as Chamberlain had feared, mistook the British Government's silence for weakness and "returned to the charge". They presented our Ambassador in Berlin with a memorandum recapitulating their accusation. On this Chamberlain commented.

CHAMBERLAIN TO LANSDOWNE

February 25, 1902.—. . . I hope you can make an effective answer to this German (*i.e.* rather insolent) communication.

The situation in the United States is rather critical. Our friends want us to show the Germans up. If we do not do so, they will be discouraged and the anti-British party proportionately elated.

I have gathered from Cranborne that there is some weakness in Lord Pauncefote's despatches at the time of the proposal for intervention. If so, cannot we spring something else on the Germans?

We know, 1st, That we were uniformly friendly; 2nd, That the Emperor and the German Government were itching to intervene.

Cannot we, under this provocation, at least suggest the truth?

I do not care a "twopenny damn" (*vide* Duke of Wellington) for the Germans but I do care a great deal about the Americans.

Chamberlain's suggestion, to "spring something else" is typical of the man. It was a golden rule with him, in all forms of controversy, not to waste energy defending uncertain positions, but always to "change the issue" by counter-attacking. Lansdowne, however, preferred to let the matter drop; unfortunately, as it proved, for British interests. A few days later Chamberlain sent the following word of warning:

CHAMBERLAIN TO LANSDOWNE
(Memorandum)

March 7, 1902.—. . . I gather that the present series of Memoranda may not be published.

If so, I regret it on account of American feeling which is at present wavering or even inclining to Germany in this controversy.

I am certain that, if we are unable to set ourselves right with the American people, we shall suffer in the future in any change in the Government of that country.

In this he was prophetic. Elections were approaching in the United States; and President Roosevelt needed an issue on which he could "stand up to Britain" and so conciliate the anti-British current of opinion aroused by the German disclosures. Differences over the delimitation of the Alaska boundary would provide just such an issue; and a few weeks later Spring-Rice, who knew the United States better than most Englishmen, would write from Washington:

SPRING-RICE TO CHAMBERLAIN

Washington—May 7, 1902.—I am convinced of my host's [*i.e.* Theodore Roosevelt] friendliness to England, or rather to the Anglo-Saxon idea, and he has consistently told his Boer friends that their true interest lies with the Empire, and in the English language.

At the same time the cry that he is pro-British (fomented by the Germans here) is strong; and, in view of the weakness of the administration in the November elections, he will be forced to do something apparently anti-English—when he conceives he is in the right as against us. He will not have arbitration as to the Alaskan frontier. . . .

On the last point Spring-Rice was to prove too pessimistic. Thanks to Chamberlain's efforts there would be at least a show of arbitration; but though the form might be improved, the substance of Roosevelt's policy would remain unchanged.

This incident of the German disclosures in Washington is significant for our story. From the beginning, Chamberlain had regarded a good understanding with America as an essential feature of British Foreign Policy. He thought it second only in importance to a European alliance. Bülow's attempt to drive a wedge between the two Anglo-Saxon Powers confirmed his belief that an understanding with the Kaiser's Government was no longer possible. It did more, it led him to propose counter-measures. These, as we saw, were not adopted by the Foreign Office. Nevertheless, their mere proposal had brought Chamberlain from a negatively to a positively anti-German position.

v

Encouraged, perhaps, by the short-term success of the disclosures in Washington, the Germans pursued anti-British courses in other regions. In the Far East, they sought to exploit international differences at Shanghai so as to undermine Britain's special position in the Yangtse Valley. In the Near East, they pressed on with their plans to build the Baghdad railway without British participation. More ominous still, they seemed to encourage Russian manœuvres to reopen the Straits to Russian warships.

The folly of these diplomatic pin-pricks is apparent. In themselves they were unimportant, but they inflamed British opinion and drew its attention to two more sinister trends in German policy. The first was the growing German threat to British trade, emphasised that year by the agreement between the chief German and American Atlantic shipping companies. The second was the German naval construction programme, the full extent of which only now began to dawn upon the British Government and public. Bülow's one chance of success in his ambitious designs lay in lulling Britain's suspicions until a strong German Navy had come into being. In a mood of mad insouciance he threw the chance away, playing his hand as if the navy was already built. Had they been paid *agents provocateurs* of the British Government, Bülow and Holstein could hardly have served our interests better.

Amid the growing tension induced by the German Government's proceedings, Eckardstein went to Highbury. He already
despaired of Anglo-German understanding and was preparing
to resign from the diplomatic service.[1] Before taking this step,
however, he wanted to have a last frank talk with Chamberlain,
on whose goodwill towards Germany he had set such high hopes.

After dinner on the night of September 1, the two men sat up
late "over some old port", as the Baron recalls in his memoirs.
The Chamberlain Papers contain no note of their remarkable
conversation. The German, however, after revolving Chamberlain's words for a fortnight, reported them in detail to Berlin.
He had staked his career on reaching an understanding with
Britain through Chamberlain. He had failed, through no fault
of his own or of Chamberlain's, and was determined that the
Wilhelmstrasse's responsibility for his failure should be placed
on record. His letter is his apologia. It may also serve as
Chamberlain's.

ECKARDSTEIN TO BULOW [2]

Secret.—London, September 14, 1902.—I recently paid a visit to the
Colonial Secretary at his estate near Birmingham. There, one evening,
Mr. Chamberlain gave free course to his rancour against Germany. For
some time now, I had only had fleeting talks with him. I knew that he
had abandoned his former pro-German inclinations, but I had thought
that his resentment against us was only temporary, and that, in altered
circumstances, it would not be difficult for us to correct it. The vehemence, however, with which he expressed himself to me, leaves no doubt
in my mind that his repugnance to Germany has struck deeper roots and
bears a far more dangerous character than I had thought hitherto.

Mr. Chamberlain spoke of the attitude of German public opinion and
of the German press during the Boer War. He remarked that he, as well
as his colleagues in the Cabinet, had been slow to recognise the real
significance of the unrestrained outbreak of German hatred against
England. The German people had apparently formed the fixed idea that,
in a matter of years, Germany would easily succeed in bringing down

---

[1] Eckardstein to Chamberlain, *August* 29, 1902.—". . . I shall be now in charge of the Embassy again till October 15th. Then I am leaving the diplomatic service altogether and shall embark on a large Parliamentary undertaking in Germany. . . ."

Eckardstein's visit to Highbury was on September 1, 1902.

[2] *Grosse Politik,* vol. xvii. p. 221.

England and its Colonial Empire and so become the heir to the whole. [*Kaiser's marginal note:* (!)]. For his part, he was convinced that such fantastic ideas were wholly impracticable and that any attempt to translate them into action would have fatal consequences for Germany. Nevertheless English policy would, henceforth, have to reckon with the seemingly incorrigible hatred of the German nation. No British Minister had ever been more convinced than he had been of the value to both countries of Anglo-German cooperation in all the great political problems of the world. He had made no secret of this view, either in Cabinet or in public, but rather had tried to convert British opinion to it by every means in his power. But he now saw that he had deceived himself. He had, therefore, altogether broken with his former tendency.

He did not wish to speak of the way he had been treated personally either by German public opinion or by the Imperial Government. These were side issues. But all classes of the English people, in the Colonies as well as in the Motherland, were filled with such a hatred against Germany that any Government, even the strongest, would have to reckon with this factor, for a long time to come. It was self-evident that no English statesman in his senses would think of a sudden war of passion with Germany. Nevertheless continued German provocation, such as they had experienced in the last ten years, would end by putting John Bull into such a temper that no English Cabinet would be in a position to resist him. At the time of the Kruger telegram, as well as of the subsequent Zanzibar affair in 1896, the two nations had stood near to war. But that had only been hysterical impulse, as far as public opinion had been concerned. To-day, the situation was far more grave. Resentment and mistrust of Germany were so widespread and deep that much lesser challenges than those of 1896 would be enough to set everything ablaze. He hoped for his part that it would never come to that; for he was clear in his own mind that in the long run an Anglo-German conflict would have injurious results for England as well as for Germany. Nevertheless the belief, widespread on the Continent and especially in Germany, about England's isolation was a myth. Just as in 1896 England could count with certainty on France, so in the future she would still be in a position at the last moment to find one or more allies. [*Kaiser's marginal note:* "Very interesting for Petersburg".]

I objected that during the South African War, England had been, to all appearances, completely isolated, and that, as he knew himself, repeated efforts had been made in certain quarters to build up a coalition against

England; efforts, which were only prevented by the friendly and unselfish
attitude of His Majesty the Kaiser and the Imperial Government. The
Colonial Secretary replied, "I am very far from underestimating the
attitude of the Kaiser during the South African War, but the British
Empire would not have gone down, even if the German Government had
been hostile to us instead of friendly. [*Kaiser's marginal note:* (!).] When,
in the summer of 1899, I made up my mind, even against the opinion of
some of my colleagues, to take 'the bull by the horns' in South Africa,
I did so because it was my conviction that it was the only possible way
of saving South Africa for the British Empire. Nevertheless before reaching my decision, I reflected like a practical politician on all the pros and
cons. Some of my colleagues repeatedly expressed the fear that certain
European powers would not fail to exploit the opportunity of England's
entanglement in South Africa and might even intervene. I replied that
we had no need to fear, because the mutual jealousies of the Continental
powers would always make it possible for English policy, in case of need,
to come to an understanding with one power or another, or with a group
of powers on the basis of political or colonial concessions. [*Kaiser's marginal note:* "No, there he is very wrong. We are no longer jealous. The
two great Continental coalitions have just reached an understanding."]
Even Russia could have been won over at any moment. The price in that
case would indeed have been higher, but, if it had been absolutely necessary, we would have paid it."

I objected that the friendly attitude of the German Government had at
least enabled England to localise the South African War, and had saved
her from being compelled to weaken her power by just such concessions.
Mr. Chamberlain replied that he could not contradict this argument.

Later in the conversation the Colonial Secretary referred to His
Majesty the Kaiser's forthcoming visit to England. He remarked that he
himself naturally welcomed a private visit, which showed that the best
relations prevailed between His Majesty the Kaiser and King Edward.
But he did not believe that the visit would have any political consequences. In view of the private character of the Kaiser's visit, the British
press would naturally bear itself with tact and courtesy, but it would be
a great mistake to draw the conclusion that English opinion could be
suddenly swung back into a pro-German mood. The resentment against
the German nation in all classes of the people was already too deeply
rooted. [*Kaiser's marginal note:* "And he has contributed more than anyone to this result".]

Towards the end, Mr. Chamberlain referred once again to the attitude of the German Press and German public opinion. I remarked that the pro-Boer leanings of the German press had certainly not been more aggressive than those of other Continental countries, and that the Imperial Government had done everything in its power to restrain the outbreaks of the more extreme elements. I suggested, moreover, that it was hardly surprising that, in spite of the efforts of wise men, public opinion on the Continent should have developed pro-Boer and anti-British tendencies, seeing that the English pro-Boers, and among them such men as Sir Henry Campbell-Bannerman, had given just such a lead in their speeches. This reference gave Mr. Chamberlain the opportunity to break out in strong language against his enemy Campbell-Bannerman and other opponents.

As your Excellency is aware, Mr. Chamberlain, in the new Cabinet even more perhaps than in the old,—is the Minister who exercises relentlessly the dominant influence on British policy. He also enjoys in the broad masses of the people a reputation which secures for him a position of almost unchallengeable supremacy. So long as we have to reckon with Mr. Chamberlain's antagonism, it would seem to be out of the question to improve our relations with England to a point where we can work, with any prospect of success, against the movement of mistrust and resentment of Germany, which is steadily growing among the English people. Mr. Chamberlain controls a great part of the press; and it follows, even more unhesitatingly than in the past, the suggestions which he throws out to it.

I gained a definite impression, however, from this conversation that it would not be out of the question to turn the Colonial Secretary from his present threatening mood towards us. But Mr. Chamberlain's character is of so firm a kind that only by cautious exertions on our side, and then only gradually, could we succeed in bringing him once more to a mood in our favour. . . .

[*Kaiser's concluding note:* "Well written! However wildly this *must* ferments it will become a wine".]

A copy of Eckardstein's letter was sent to Count von Schlieffen, the Chief of the General Staff. On meeting Eckardstein, a few weeks later, he remarked:

If what you assume as to the future attitude of England is correct, I should have to alter my whole plan of campaign, but I cannot possibly believe that you are right. I think you are much too pessimistic.[1]

---

[1] Eckardstein, *Ten Years at the Court of St. James*, p. 240.

Whom the gods would destroy . . .!

Chamberlain's words confirmed Eckardstein's worst fears and clinched his decision to resign. Here, then, we may take leave of him. For some years yet his name will figure in Chamberlain's Visitors' Book; but he will no longer play a leading part in our story. As an intermediary he was more zealous perhaps than accurate, but he bears no responsibility for the failure of the alliance proposals. If, behind Eckardstein, there had stood a Bismarck, all might have been well. At least there would have been mutual respect. But it was the tragedy of the situation that, from first to last, there was no responsible statesman in Germany on whom Chamberlain could rely.

Further light was thrown on Chamberlain's attitude that summer by another foreign diplomat. Later in September, Soveral, the Portuguese Ambassador, also visited Highbury.[1] His main purpose was to discuss the Barotseland frontier dispute with Chamberlain; but their conversation seems to have ranged beyond the African sphere. Certainly, on his return to Lisbon a few days later, Soveral would tell the French Minister in that capital that "M. Chamberlain est aujourd'hui partisan d'un rapprochement avec la Russie et d'une entente cordiale avec la France".[2]

VI

Bülow was fully informed of Eckardstein's talk with Chamberlain and had wind of the negotiations in progress between Britain and France.[3] Nevertheless, he chose precisely these critical September days to commit one of the most ridiculous blunders of the whole Wilhelmic era.

The Boer Generals, then in Europe, had let it be known that they meant to include Berlin in the course of their lecture tour. Bülow was anxious that their visit should not be made the occasion for anti-British demonstrations. At the same time, he advised the Kaiser to receive the Generals in audience, believing that such a gesture would conciliate pro-Boer opinion in Germany and abroad. The British Government, he thought, could have no reason to object, seeing that the Generals had

[1] September 18, 1902.
[2] *Documents diplomatiques français*, série 2, vol. 2, No. 423 (M. Rouvier to M. Delcassé, October 5, 1902).
[3] See *Grosse Politik*, vol. xvii. Nos. 5188, 5190 and 5191, pp. 344-347.

been received by King Edward and had been given a most friendly welcome by the London crowd. As Bülow saw it, the audience would be *"ein guter Coup"*.[1] At worst, it was a somewhat irresponsible attempt "to have the cake and eat it". The Kaiser accepted his advice and duly appointed a date for the audience. His footnote, "let them be presented by Lascelles", shows clearly that no anti-British demonstration was intended.

Thus far there was no great danger in this proceeding; but, a few days later,[2] the Generals published their "Appeal to the Civilised World". British sympathy for them was changed overnight to stern disapproval. Henceforth their tour was regarded in London as part of an anti-British campaign designed to raise funds for renewed agitation in South Africa.

It should have been clear to Bülow that, in the changed circumstances, the audience would have to be abandoned. But despite warnings from London,[3] he pressed on with the arrangements for it, and, on September 29, publicly announced its date. There was an immediate outcry from the whole British press; and King Edward sent a curt warning to his nephew that he might have to cancel his visit to England, if he insisted on granting the proposed audience. Bülow's position now became extremely invidious. He could not honourably withdraw in the face of British popular clamour; nor could he go ahead with the audience without risking a serious incident. To make matters worse his own colleagues, including Holstein, turned against him. Fortunately for the Chancellor, the initiative lay with London. The Generals were to have been presented to the Kaiser by Lascelles, the British Ambassador in Berlin. It was up to the Foreign Office, therefore, to decide whether the audience should take place. What instructions would be sent to Lascelles?

On this point Chamberlain had no doubts. The Boer Generals were his special responsibility, and his opinion on the matter was decisive.

CHAMBERLAIN TO DEVONSHIRE

October 3, 1902.—As at present advised I am against asking for an audience for the Boers.

---

[1] "A good stroke of policy" (*Grosse Politik*, No. 5093, September 17, p. 219).
[2] September 25, 1902. *V.* p. 91 of this volume.
[3] *Grosse Politik*, vol. xvii. No. 5095, p. 225, September 28, 1902.

It would certainly be strongly objected to by our people here and in S. Africa. . . .

He wrote in a similar strain to Lansdowne, who replied that he "did not think there could be two opinions as to the Boer Generals". Lascelles was accordingly instructed "not to move"; and the audience was allowed to lapse on a point of protocol.

But the damage had been done. The Generals presently arrived in Berlin and were received with extravagant demonstrations by the Pan-Germans. The Kaiser was much criticised in Germany for not granting them an audience, but his forbearance gained him no credit in England.

One other aspect of this incident must be noted. A few days before their visit to Berlin, the Generals went to Paris. There they had a private audience of President Loubet, and were received officially by Combes, the Prime Minister, and by Delcassé. No word of protest, of any kind, was heard in England. Here was the writing on the wall.

In those same October days, while the Boer Generals were fêted in Berlin, Selborne, the First Lord of the Admiralty, circulated a historic memorandum to the Cabinet. In this he wrote:

Since . . . last autumn, I have studied the naval policy of Germany more closely than I had previously done. The result of my study is that I am convinced that the new German Navy is being carefully built up from the point of view of a war with us. This is also the opinion of Sir Frank Lascelles and he has authorised me to say it. The more the position of the new German Fleet is examined, the clearer it becomes that it is designed for a possible conflict with the British Fleet.[1]

To this momentous statement he added the practical recommendation, soon to be adopted, of building a new naval base on the Firth of Forth, to confront the new danger from across the North Sea.

VII

The Kaiser's visit to Sandringham, a month later, forms an epilogue to Chamberlain's ill-fated endeavours to bring about the alliance with Germany. It was a purely private visit to

[1] Memorandum of October 17, 1902, explaining the Navy Estimates for 1903.

BOOK
XVII.
1902.

celebrate King Edward's sixty-first Birthday; but English opinion had grown so hostile to Germany, that Balfour had publicly to deny that it had any political significance.[1]

Chamberlain was bidden to Sandringham, along with Balfour, Lansdowne and Roberts, to meet the Imperial guest.

MRS. CHAMBERLAIN TO HER MOTHER

November 11, 1902.—. . . After removing the stains of travel . . . we came down to tea in the Hall and there found the Queen presiding at the tea-table. . . . The four children of the Prince of Wales were playing about, and very soon Joe was to be seen, having made friends with the baby, a delicate-looking, dear little sensitive boy of three, and dragging him about seated on a wooden engine. The King soon joined the group, looking extremely well and very gracious. After a little while the King and his son . . . went off to the station, and soon returned with the Emperor and his Suite. The Queen and the Princess Victoria greeted him near the door, and, while they did so, we naturally formed in a circle. The Emperor walked round it, the King presenting the gentlemen and the Queen presenting the ladies. When he reached me, he showed that he was the possessor of the traditional Royal memory, for, on this point, there could have been no one to prompt him. He at once said: "The last time I met you was at Hatfield!" We were all much impressed by the force of his grip (it was "the mailed fist" indeed!), and my poor fingers were much punished by my rings. He has changed a good deal in appearance and not, I think, for the better—he is stouter and his hair is darker and his moustache is altered in shape. He is wonderfully like the English Royal Family in his manner, and especially round the mouth. His smile is bright and the shape of his teeth very like Queen Victoria's. . . .

That night at dinner I . . . sat next His Imperial Majesty, an honour due no doubt to the scarcity of ladies among the guests. . . . I found him most agreeable, and conversation flowed with the greatest ease. Of course, he talked a good deal to the Queen, but she is so deaf that I got my full share of him. He told me about Prince Henry's visit to America. . . . He betrayed a knowledge of Bret Harte and Mark Twain, and showed much discrimination in preferring the writings of the former, I thought —and altogether I had a most pleasant dinner. My only embarrassment was caused by his persisting in addressing me as "Ma'am" which, in consideration of the presence of Royalty, was very trying. However, it

[1] Guildhall, November 10, 1902.

was natural enough for him, as a direct translation of *Madame*—and was not my affair. . . .

In the course of the visit, Chamberlain had at least one serious talk with the Kaiser. His Papers contain no mention of it, but Admiral Fawkes, with whom he was to sail to South Africa a few days later, made the following entry in his diary.

Sunday 30*th* (*November*).—. . . I had a very interesting talk with Mr. Chamberlain. He told me how straight he had spoken to the German Emperor at Sandringham. He commenced his conversation by saying "I suppose Your Majesty would wish me to say exactly what I think" about the way His Ministers and People had behaved when we were a bit down,—that he [the Kaiser] knew that he [Chamberlain] had been one of the greatest friends of Germany—but that now no statesman could propose an alliance or anything of that sort—He said the Emperor did not like it much.

Some years later the Kaiser told Haldane that he had tried on the visit "to get on with Mr. Chamberlain but had found it extremely difficult".[1] At the time he reported the following impressions to Bülow.

THE KAISER TO BÜLOW

Sandringham—November 12, 1902.—Best thanks for your two telegrams. The data were familiar to me and enabled me to tell Chamberlain that you were attacked in Germany as pro-English and were even called "Lord Bülow". But all that was no use. He is intensely irritated with your Excellency and the "Ministers" in general, and is under the supposed impression that he has been personally duped in the grossest manner. It is in this humour that he judges the whole of our policy and proceedings. His irritation is also reflected in the newspaper articles which he inspires directly or indirectly, and it has taken possession of an obstinate section of the people. It is all most unfortunate but cannot, for the moment, be changed. He is absolutely dominant and all-powerful in England and has the absolute support of all classes of the people. The Ministry dances to his tune and does little that is important without him; nothing against him. In these circumstances it is of urgent necessity, first, to keep a firm restraint upon our press—for they won't stand for much more here—; second, in foreign affairs, to do nothing further that can bring us unnecessarily into friction or dissension with England. We

[1] Sidney Lee, *King Edward VII*, vol. ii. p. 150.

must give them all possible information, where suitable, about what is happening and trust to reciprocity. . . .

My reception here was hearty and affectionate as ever. The people warm, responsive and very courteous, so that I was personally well pleased. But I believe that they draw a distinction here between "The Kaiser" and "The German Government", wishing the latter to the Devil; just as we do in Germany between the King and Chamberlain, for whom also a hot place is desired. . . .

This is the true report of the impressions I have received here. They are politically discouraging and must be overcome with much patience and tact,—not least in the Wilhelmstrasse, and by our press "holding its jaw". If this is not done, there may be very serious consequences not yet foreseen. Therefore caution! Here they have 53 ironclads in service and we 8!! About the year 1905, England, counting battleships, cruisers and armed cruisers, will have 196 ready for service against 46 on our side! [1]

At last the gravity of the situation was beginning, though only beginning, to dawn on the rulers of Germany. The vision of *arbiter mundi* was receding. In its place came the growing consciousness of their increasing isolation. They now made a desperate last effort to recapture the position and the opportunities which they had lost. With Chamberlain away, Fate seemed at first to smile upon them. But it was too late.

VIII

Repeated injuries to their interests in Venezuela had led Britain and Germany to demand compensation from the Venezuelan Government. This demand had been rejected, and discussions had, therefore, begun between London and Berlin over the next step to be taken in support of their claims. These were still in progress, when the Kaiser reached Sandringham and formed the gloomy opinions which we have noted above. In his anxiety to improve relations with Britain, he saw in the Venezuelan crisis an excellent opportunity for a dramatic gesture of Anglo-German co-operation. Accordingly, he urged joint action by the two countries upon King Edward and Lansdowne. His arguments, with those of the Wilhelmstrasse, were accepted in London; and on December 7, 1902, Britain and Germany

[1] *Grosse Politik*, vol. xvii. p. 115.

declared a belligerent blockade of Venezuela.
This action produced an immediate outcry at home, where
opinion was unanimous in condemning any form of co-operation
with Germany. It also aroused the resentment of the United
States, which saw in it a threat to the Monroe Doctrine. In the
face of this opposition, domestic and foreign, the British
Government was glad enough to comply with President Roosevelt's peremptory request that the whole affair be submitted
to arbitration. The blockade was, thus, abandoned, and this
last effort to secure Anglo-German co-operation ended in a
humiliating fiasco.

Chamberlain had already left for South Africa when the
blockade was imposed. His marginal notes, however, on earlier
Cabinet papers relating to the Venezuelan crisis show that he
never approved of the idea. He advocated, instead, the seizing
of Venezuelan ships "which does not interfere with the Monroe
doctrine or any foreign power. We should hold the vessels till
satisfaction was given by present or any future Venezuelan
government."[1] He was also opposed from the beginning to
joint action with Germany. "I warned Lansdowne that joint
action with Germany would be unpopular and I very much
regret that we did not go into the matter alone."[2]

IX

Chamberlain exercised little or no influence on the course of
the Venezuelan crisis, but this attitude towards it is significant.
Two years earlier, he might have welcomed the blockade as an
instance of the very kind of local Anglo-German arrangement
which he had envisaged in his Chatsworth proposal. As it was,
he saw in this joint action with Germany only an obstacle in the
way of securing a good understanding with France. That this
was now his dominant purpose is attested by an unusual but
significant communication which he made to the French
Government on the very day that the blockade of Venezuela
was declared.

Cromer was a close friend of Chamberlain's and, when on

[1] Marginal note on Lansdowne's
Cabinet, memorandum of October 17,
1902. [2] Chamberlain to Austen, Johannesburg, January 9, 1903.

leave that summer, had discussed the international situation with him more than once. On his return to Egypt, he had sought to impress upon his French colleagues that British foreign policy, and more especially Chamberlain's conception of it, had undergone far-reaching changes. He now proposed that M. Lecomte, the French *chargé d'affaires*, should meet Chamberlain for a private talk, when the latter passed through Cairo on his way to South Africa. The Frenchman at once accepted; but Chamberlain's ship was delayed in the Mediterranean by engine trouble; and, before he reached Cairo, Lecomte had to leave it to attend the ceremonial inauguration of the Assouan dam. The two men were thus prevented from meeting; but this accident was partially repaired by an unusual manœuvre on the British side. Chamberlain made a statement to Cromer on British foreign policy, intended expressly for communication to Lecomte. The gist of it is contained in the following extract from Lecomte's subsequent report to Paris.[1]

LECOMTE TO DELCASSÉ

Cairo, December 12, 1902.—Most Confidential.—. . . Mr. Chamberlain said that the experience of recent years had convinced him that the time had passed when England could take pride or profit in "splendid isolation". Henceforth she would have to count on the friendship of one or other of the Continental Powers. At first he had looked to Germany. It was not long, however, before he realised that the violence of German Anglo-phobia, engendered by the Boer war and sustained by the jealousy and greed of Germany's rapidly expanding commerce, would make any understanding with that Power impossible for a long time to come. There remained Russia and France. From the former there was nothing to be hoped for. Britain and Russia were too incurably suspicious of each other and their mutual resentment was of too long standing. There were, besides, too many points of contact between their Empires which were the cause of soreness and irritation. Any effort to arrive at mutual understanding was thus foredoomed to failure.

[1] *Documents diplomatiques français,* série 2, vol. 2, No. 524. The published version of Lecomte's dispatch nowhere mentions Cromer, but speaks instead of "un fonctionnaire anglais en Égypte, ami personnel du Secrétaire Colonial et avec qui je suis lié depuis longtemps par de cordiales relations . . ." It seems almost certain, however, that Cromer was meant by this description. There was no one else in Cairo to whom it could easily have been applied.

It was otherwise with France. For one thing, the French Government's policies were not opposed to a conciliatory course. For another, French opinion, once so inflamed against England, seemed to have returned to a mood of calm and quasi-neutrality which would allow prudent leaders to give it a new orientation, without arousing too much resistance. Such an evolution on the part of France does not seem to him to be impossible. He has good reason to know just how easy it would be for him to bring it about in England with the spontaneous and sympathetic support of the public.

Taught by experience of Britain's need for foreign support; led by reason to hope for that of France; he now believes that the time is ripe to enter into negotiations. At the least, if the desire for an entente is reciprocated, the task of making it fruitful should begin by an exchange of obligations. Although not personally responsible for the Foreign Office, Mr. Chamberlain has already thought it right to expound this conception of his to the Cabinet of which he is a member. . . .

This communication is of outstanding interest. It contains the first clear suggestion ever made to the French Government by a responsible British statesman that the time had come to begin negotiations for an "entente". It also suggests the broad lines which these might follow. The phrase "exchange of obligations" (French: *échanger des arrhes*) is obscure. We may conjecture, however, with some confidence, that Chamberlain had in mind those local arrangements which he had envisaged in the earlier negotiations with Germany as the natural preliminaries to a full alliance.

The form of the communication underlines the importance of its content. It is most unlikely that Cromer would have arranged for a private conversation between Chamberlain and a relatively junior French diplomat without being first assured of Chamberlain's approval. It is unthinkable that Chamberlain should have gone to the length of making a statement expressly for communication to that diplomat, unless he had some very definite purpose in view. What was that purpose?

The choice of venue suggests two sets of motives, and both may have had their influence. Despite the tacit understanding over Siam, negotiations with the French had made little headway. In the spring Chamberlain had been sanguine enough to hope for an early settlement of all outstanding points of friction in the colonial sphere. In particular, he had looked forward to an exchange of concessions in Newfoundland and on the Niger.[1] But a letter to Fielding, the Canadian Finance Minister, written in the autumn shows that he could report no progress in this direction.

CHAMBERLAIN TO FIELDING

Private.—September 19, 1902.—. . . I cannot hold out hopes that any considerable territorial compensation can ever be given for the abrogation of the French rights [in Newfoundland]. We cannot rob Peter to pay Paul, or in other words give up the rights and territory of one British Colony in order to assist the negotiations of another.

As I told you I have had in view a concession in Africa which might be of great importance to the French and at the same time would not involve too great a sacrifice on our part, but up to the present time no hint of this has been given on either side. The French are too far off for us to approach them.

Since then the prospect of an Anglo-French *rapprochement* had been darkened by the joint action of Britain and Germany against Venezuela. This was naturally seen in Paris as a setback to Delcassé's hopes of an *entente*. A British relapse into the German camp was feared; and Chamberlain was widely rumoured to be the author of this development. It was even said—we now know how absurdly—that at Sandringham he had again succumbed to the Kaiser's blandishments.

In these circumstances, Chamberlain must have wished to reassure the French Government as to the general trend of British policy, to advance the progress of negotiations, and to contradict the rumours of his own return to a pro-German position. He could not, however, dissociate himself from the Venezuelan policy without disloyalty to his colleagues. Nor could he have made direct proposals to Cambon in London without an unwarrantable invasion of Lansdowne's sphere of action. No such disadvantage, however, could attach to an informal conversation in Cairo. Indeed, the full significance of Chamberlain's *démarche* might well have been overlooked but for the unusual form which circumstances forced upon it.

These considerations may explain Chamberlain's motives in

[1] See pp. 163 and 180.

this matter. Cromer's part in it, however, suggests that it may
have had a further aspect. The reader will recall how, at the
beginning of the year, Eckardstein had watched Cambon and
Chamberlain talking together in the billiard room at Marlborough House and had overheard the words "Morocco" and
"Egypt". There is no further reference to Egypt in Cambon's
many talks with Lansdowne in the course of 1902. It seems
probable, however, that Cromer, when on leave in London, discussed the Egyptian aspect of Anglo-French relations with
Chamberlain among others. Certainly, on his return to Cairo,
he began to work for a local *rapprochement* with the French.
He may have judged, therefore, that a conversation between
Chamberlain and Lecomte would promote his local purpose as
well as the British Government's broader policy. Chamberlain's
words might well influence the attitude of the French representatives in Cairo; and they, in turn, might gradually draw the
Quai d'Orsay's attention to the advantages of introducing
Egypt into the negotiations with Britain.

Be this as it may, Lecomte's report of Chamberlain's statements was duly communicated to Cambon in London. The copy
preserved in the archives of the French Embassy still bears the
following marginal note in the Ambassador's own hand.

INTÉRESSANT

Il est certain que M. Chamberlain a été déçu du côté de l'Allemagne—
qu'ayant pris trop au sérieux les amabilités de l'empereur Guillaume et
ayant parlé à la légère d'une alliance anglo-allemande, il se produit chez
lui une réaction qui le rapproche de nous. J'en ai la confirmation de mon
côté—mais il ne faut pas oublier que M. Chamberlain n'a aucun principe
politique, qu'il est l'homme du moment présent et qu'il varie d'opinions
avec une facilité incroyable; il ne s'embarrasse pas le moins du monde de
ses propres déclarations et se dément lui-même avec une facilité prodi-
gieuse. Il a le sentiment très juste des exigences de l'opinion, il en suit
toutes les fluctuations en ayant l'air de les diriger—de là sa popularité.

En ce moment, l'opinion anglaise est soulevée contre l'Allemagne;
l'affaire du Venezuela, où l'Angleterre a été entraînée par le roi, exaspère
le sentiment public. M. Chamberlain fera donc de la politique anti-alle-
mande. Mais c'est un réaliste et il ne nous offrirait rien que donnant
donnant, s'il était en état de nous offrir quelque chose.

La conversation relatée par M. Lecomte est bonne à noter et je crois à la sincérité actuelle de M. Chamberlain, mais il ne faut pas trop faire fonds sur des déclarations qui peuvent être emportées au vent par le premier courant de l'opinion publique, si elle change de direction.[1]

Cambon was a shrewd judge of men and knew England well. Nevertheless, this estimate of Chamberlain is myopic. It shows a just appreciation of the master of political tactics. It betrays a complete failure to understand the statesman who was the chief author of the revolution in British foreign policy.

Notwithstanding his qualifications of Chamberlain's sincerity, Cambon must have rejoiced in the knowledge that the powerful Colonial Secretary was his ally. He, and his chief, might have been still more encouraged, if they could have read the following comment in one of Chamberlain's private letters:

CHAMBERLAIN TO AUSTEN

Johannesburg—January 9, 1903.—. . . I am sorry to hear that Delcassé is likely to go.[2] He seems to me to have done much to make possible an "entente cordiale" with France, which is what I should now like. I wonder whether Lansdowne has ever considered the possibility of the King asking the President to England this year. . . .

[1] "INTERESTING.—Mr. Chamberlain has undoubtedly been disillusioned about Germany. Having taken the Emperor William's blandishments too seriously and having thrown out the idea of an Anglo-German alliance, he is now reacting in a way which brings him nearer to us. I have confirmation of this on my side. But we must not forget that Mr. Chamberlain has no political principles. He lives in the present and changes his opinions with incredible facility. He is not in the least embarrassed by his own previous statements and goes back on what he has said with extraordinary ease. He has a very accurate sense of what public opinion requires, and follows all its fluctuations, seeming, the while, to guide them. Hence his popularity.

Just now, English opinion has turned against Germany. The Venezuelan affair into which England has been drawn by the King has exasperated public opinion. Mr. Chamberlain will, therefore, pursue an anti-German policy. He is a realist, however, and if he were in a position to give us some-thing, would not give it to us for nothing.

The conversation described by M. Lecomte is worthy of note. I believe in Mr. Chamberlain's present sincerity, but we must not build too much upon statements which can be blown to the wind by the first gust of a changing public opinion."

This marginal note is published here for the first time by kind permission of H.E. M. René Massigli, the French Ambassador. It is evident from a comparison of the texts that it served as the draft of Cambon's dispatch to Delcassé of January 22, 1903, published in *Documents diplomatiques français*, série 2, vol. 3, No. 37.

M. Cambon's phrase, "J'en ai la confirmation de mon côté", is worthy of note. It has not been possible to have access to the Cambon Papers, but when these are eventually made public they may throw further much-needed light on Chamberlain's relations with the Ambassador in the course of 1902.

[2] Austen had heard this rumour from Clemenceau and reported it to his father in an earlier letter.

BOOK XVIII

STUDIES IN POLICY AND ADMINISTRATION
(1895–1903)

CHAPTER LXXXIV

BIRMINGHAM UNIVERSITY

(1897–1903)

CHAMBERLAIN and Higher Education—Mason's College and Seeley's
Lecture—"A University of my own"—Breaking away from the
Federal Model—Chamberlain the First Chancellor—His Conception
of a University—Higher Education and National Progress—The
Choice of Professors—How the Money was raised?—Carnegie's Con-
tribution—"The School of Brewing"—"A landmark of the Midlands"
—Chamberlain and Haldane.

I

CHAMBERLAIN's biography, at this stage, is not easy to construct.
Later the main narrative will brook but little interruption.
Here, then, we must turn to those aspects of his achievement and
endeavour which lay removed from the central issues of international or party politics. They show that, at the zenith of his
career as an Imperial statesman, he was still the practical
reformer and creative administrator of his Mayoralty days.

In these years of his Colonial Secretaryship, when he already
carried responsibilities enough to break any other statesman,
he embarked on four subsidiary but remarkable ventures. He
founded Birmingham University. He organised the equipped
study of Tropical Medicine. He raised the West Indies from
desolation to prosperity. He drew the Zionist movement into
the orbit of British Imperial policy. These things would by
themselves have constituted a respectable record for any statesman. For Chamberlain they only filled the intervals of his main
business: the union of South Africa under the Crown, the
buttressing of Britain's world position by a foreign alliance,
and the maintenance of the Unionist regime. To ask how he

found the extra time and energy required is merely to point to one of the secrets of his greatness.

II

Chamberlain's public life, from the beginning, had been bound up with questions of education. His work for the National Education League had led directly to his entry into national politics and indirectly to his leadership of the new Radicalism. Twenty years later, the extension of free education to the whole country had been his doing. It had been the proof, as he claimed, that, in changing sides after the Home Rule split, he had not recanted his past beliefs but was pursuing the same aims as ever, though by different means. In a later chapter, we shall see how an unexpected and awkward revival of the education controversy threatened his political position in the country and helped to bring on his last and greatest campaign.

Chamberlain's interest in education was neither accidental nor merely personal. The spread of education had been an essential accompaniment, part cause and part effect, of the ascent in the nation of the Nonconformist middle class to which he belonged. Political controversy on the subject was confined to primary and secondary education; but, in Chamberlain's mind, university education was no less important. We must remember that Oxford and Cambridge had still been closed to Nonconformists when he had left school. Nor should we forget how he had once exclaimed to Morley, as they walked through Balliol quad, "Ah, how I wish that I could have had a training in this place".[1]

Personal experience and sectarian interest thus combined with civic pride to implant in him the idea that Birmingham should have a university. It was some time before the idea became a clear conception and longer still before he accomplished it; but his interest in it dated from the days of his municipal career.

While Chamberlain was still Mayor, Josiah Mason founded in Birmingham the college that bore his name. Birmingham's band of civic reformers set great hopes on this foundation. But Mason's design was only to spread scientific and technical

[1] See Vol. I. of this work, pp. 36 ff.

instruction; and he provided neither space nor funds for the humanities. About the same time, however, Owens College, in the North, had developed into Victoria University, a federal body affiliating Leeds and Liverpool as well as Manchester. What had been done in Manchester could be done in Birmingham; and a few local thinkers, with Chamberlain's friend Dr. Crosskey at their head, began to canvass the idea of a federal university for the Midlands. A decisive impetus was given to this idea by J. R. Seeley, who came over from Cambridge in 1887 and delivered an address [1] on the true purpose and form of a provincial university.

Seeley said, in effect, that, were such new seats of learning widely created in the country, the movement "would be one of the grandest in the history of English culture". Let the provinces not seek to imitate the splendid colleges of Oxford and Cambridge. Those "great boarding houses" had grown out of historic circumstances. But time and expense made it impossible to follow their example. Let them rather follow the Scottish and German models. Colleges were not essential to the organisation of study and knowledge, of teaching and research. "A university consists of class-rooms and professors." If that simple idea were once grasped, every great town like Birmingham might have, and should have, its complete corps of professors; its general staff of culture.

Seeley's address, reprinted as a pamphlet, set its impress on Chamberlain's civic policy, just as the *Expansion of England* had already done on his broader conception of the Empire. He now determined that Birmingham should have a university, and, in the following year, proclaimed his ultimate purpose. When opening new board schools in 1888 he asked his audience not to rest content with progress in elementary education. They should cherish the vision of a Jacob's ladder of democracy,

enabling the poorest amongst us, if he has but the ability, if God has given him these gifts, to rise to the greatest height of culture ... I desire that we may crown the edifice by establishing here in Birmingham a true Midland University. I hope that every Birmingham man will keep it before him as one of the great objects of his life.[2]

[1] Town Hall, Birmingham, October 10, 1887.
[2] May 28, 1888, Birmingham.

He never forgot; but he had to wait. Nearly a decade passed before circumstances combined to create his opportunity. In 1897, the year of Queen Victoria's second Jubilee, Mason College was enlarged by the addition of a medical department. Chamberlain was its President, and Parliament had passed an Act to constitute it a University College. But its resources were below its new name. To equip it suitably even for its existing functions would require a large new endowment. Could the necessary sums be raised for a second-class purpose, or had the time come, at last, to absorb Mason College in a wider and nobler plan?

It so happened that, in that same year, Chamberlain had been elected Lord Rector of Glasgow University. In the winter he travelled north to deliver his rectorial address.[1] The proceedings made a deep impression on him, and, just before leaving Glasgow, he remarked: "When I go back to Birmingham, I mean to have a University of my own."

III

This was in November 1897. Before a month was out, he had framed his plans and started his campaign. Early in December, his kinsman, George Kenrick, wrote:

Chamberlain's power and the boldness of his ideas have triumphed over everything and people are now actually being canvassed for the half-preliminary list which is essential to a scheme of this kind.[2]

George Kenrick's letter was written to congratulate Professor Sonnenschein, who had advocated a Midland University affiliating the colleges of other Midland towns. Such, indeed, had been Chamberlain's original design, but, already, he had superseded it with one more ambitious. For the sake of freedom and concentration, he decided to break away from the federal model of the North and to set up instead a fully independent City University.

Within a year of launching his campaign he had received enough support to justify a petition for a Royal Charter. The

[1] Vol. III. of this work, pp. 199-200.   *of a University: a passage in the life*
[2] December 9, 1897. See *The Birth*   *of E. A. Sonnenschein.*

first draft of it was unsatisfactory. It subjected the academic body too much to the lay council. Accordingly, at the urging of Professor Sonnenschein and others, Chamberlain intervened and cut it to pieces. In its new form, it secured for the academic body the freedom and influence which form the spirit of a university. Thus amended, the Petition was duly presented and the Charter granted; and Chamberlain was appointed the first Chancellor of the new University. The Court of Governors met under his chairmanship for the first time in May 1900. A year later, while the Boer war was still at its height, the University celebrated its first congregation. A procession marched to the Town Hall, where the degrees were conferred; and Chamberlain officiated in his Chancellor's robes of black and gold. A new chapter had opened in the story of Birmingham, and of English education.

That "nothing could have been done without Chamberlain" was the general view. A Liberal observer, who had watched the work closely and with growing admiration, paid him this tribute:

While the contributions of many minds have been of value, that of Mr. Chamberlain is unique. To him the University of Birmingham indisputably owes its existence. By his energy and initiative the idea was lifted out of the weary region of discussion into that of inspiring action; to his boldness and judgment the institution owes its wise breadth and the admirable representative constitution secured to it by Charter; to his clearness of view and statesmanlike insight, its avoidance of the many dangers which it has been fortunate enough to escape. No man has ever more abundantly earned the right to be head of a university than the first Chancellor of the University of Birmingham.[1]

This quotation may stand for innumerable congratulations which poured in from Birmingham and from all parts of the country. But deeds speak louder than words; and the most valued tribute was still to come. The cities of the North had shown the provinces the way to higher education by setting up Victoria University on the federal model. Their achievement had been Birmingham's inspiration; but it was now their turn to follow the Midland capital's lead. Within the next few years, Manchester, Liverpool and Leeds abandoned the federal model

[1] *New Liberal Review*, March 1901.

to set up independent universities. They were treading in Chamberlain's footsteps.

IV

We must look closer at Chamberlain's work for Birmingham University. At first sight, it seems a dry subject; but the way he matched his methods to his aims throws a flood of light upon his character. It shows that he was still Birmingham's greatest "executive citizen". Let us take separately the conception and the execution of his plan.

What did he mean by a university? His speeches on this subject, delivered over seven years, show the gradual unfolding of his purpose. He explained his general view at the meeting called to authorise the petition for a Royal Charter.

Our ideal may be stated, in a few words, to be the creation in Birmingham of a great school of universal teaching—an institution which shall provide for the intellectual cultivation of the mind in the broadest possible sense and shall maintain for ever in this city the highest standard of intellectual eminence.[1]

They could not and they would not imitate Oxford and Cambridge. The humanities—what he called "the older branches of learning"—must have their due place. But he insisted always that the new seats of learning ought to adapt themselves to newer needs. Birmingham, in particular, ought to lead the world in applying the highest knowledge to industry, trade and transport. His conception of a Faculty of Commerce included the study of economics and the technical processes of particular industries; but it also provided for instruction in modern languages and the relevant parts of geography, history and law. This is now accepted doctrine; but then he was a pioneer.

Nor, for all his townsman's background, did he stop at urban industry. Experts, still pleading today for more support in one long-neglected branch of learning, may be interested to find him writing to his wife that he has arranged to establish "a school of Veterinary Science and Research, a thing much needed in agriculture and I think quite new".[2] On a later occasion he remarked prophetically, "Whatever improvement may take place

[1] November 18, 1898.   [2] October 20, 1900.

in agriculture hereafter, one thing is certain, that it will not be the agriculture of generations ago. It will be a new industry conducted on the most scientific principles." [1]

Like many contemporary thinkers he held that our commercial future in the new century depended on the spread of higher education. American and German competition was growing daily; and the rapid industrial progress of these two nations was widely ascribed to the excellence of their provincial universities. The Consular reports, like the newspapers, were full of this topic; and, when Chamberlain spoke of it at the first meeting of the Court of Governors, his speech aroused more than local interest.

... No one can read the reports, which have recently appeared, of the progress of manufacture in the United States ... without being fully aware that we have somewhat fallen behind—that we have reached a critical stage, and that it depends very much upon what we are doing now at the beginning of the twentieth century, whether at its end we shall continue to maintain our supremacy, or even equality, with our great commercial and manufacturing rivals. ...

During the last generation, the last thirty years, we have practically established, on a firm and broad basis, primary education which is now within the reach of every child in the country. We have reorganised our secondary education, we have made a beginning with technical training ... but ... upon the highest education our national expenditure is less than 1% of our total expenditure on education. For my own part, and I have no doubt I speak your views also, I do not grudge one penny of the money which has been spent on primary education. ... But we should make a great mistake, if we think that, as a commercial investment, this expenditure is likely to bring a great return. Its return is ... in the general happiness of the nation, but it does not secure our commercial position. I should like to make that perfectly clear, and I would remind you that all history shows that national progress of every kind depends upon certain individuals rather than upon the mass. Whether you take religion, or literature, or political government, or art, or commerce, in all these cases the new ideas, the great steps, have been made by individuals of superior quality and genius, who have, as it were, dragged the

---

[1] January 28, 1904—speech at the fourth annual meeting of the Court of Governors.

mass of the nation up one step to a higher level. And so it must be in regard to material progress.

The position of the nation to-day is due to the efforts of men like Watt, Arkwright, or in our own time, the Armstrongs, the Whitworths, the Kelvins, the Siemenses. These are the men who, by their discoveries, by their remarkable genius, have produced the ideas upon which others have acted, and which have permeated the whole mass of the nation and the whole of its proceedings. And, therefore, what we have to do, and this is our special task and object, is to make, to produce more of these great men. It may be that this is impossible. It may be said, very likely truly, that genius is born and not made; but, then, at least we can do this, we can multiply tenfold the number of those who are qualified to be the assistants and the interpreters of these men, who can take their ideas and carry them into practical operation. . . . That is the object . . . which I think the University of Birmingham must . . . deliberately set itself. [1]

These words are significant in a wider context than the foundation of Birmingham University. They constitute the clearest exposition to be found of Chamberlain's view of the relation of the individual to the mass, and of the effect of their interaction upon the forward march of the human race.

One more speech on this subject must be noted. More prosaic than that quoted above, it nevertheless contains a more systematic statement of his academic ideal. On the first Degree Day he demanded that the new University should fulfil four conditions. It should be, a place; first, where all existing knowledge is taught, embracing the full range of science but not neglecting the older studies. Second, where the knowledge acquired is tested by strict standards of proficiency. Third, where knowledge is ceaselessly extended by the original research of teachers continuing to learn and of students uniting with them in "the eternal quest". Fourth, a place where the students should learn to apply the knowledge they have acquired.[2] Like many of his Colonial Office Minutes this statement is too business-like to be inspiring; but it is not easily improved.

From the very beginning Chamberlain recognised that the spirit of a university depends upon its professors. His opening appeal in 1898 went to the root of the matter.

[1] January 17, 1901.   [2] July 6, 1901.

But, at the very first, the one thing which is essential, the one thing we must do, is to put the University in a position to attract the best teachers, to attract the men of the highest reputation and to keep them here, when we have induced them to come.[1]

In his appointments, he and Birmingham were singularly fortunate. Sir Oliver Lodge, the scientist and philosopher, came from Liverpool to become the first principal. Sir William Ashley, an English economist of international mark with invaluable experience of things American, came from Harvard to organise the Faculty of Commerce. Later a Chair of Music was endowed, and its first incumbent was Sir Edward Elgar. Chamberlain held that the remuneration of teaching was deplorably low by comparison with the rewards of success in other spheres of life; and he strove, not without effect, to improve the status and salaries of his professors. The list of scholars who have filled Chairs in Birmingham, since then, forms not the least distinguished page in the annals of that city.

V

But the strangest part of this story has yet to be told. Only with money could his ideal become reality. How much would he need and how would he raise it? At the outset he asked Professor Bertram Windle what was the least sum which would justify Birmingham in applying for a Charter. Windle said £100,000. This, as Chamberlain saw, would only be enough to give Mason College some inadequate additions and a false name, and he replied that he would have "no pauper university, no starved university". Accordingly, at the meeting called to launch the campaign for the University, he appealed for a quarter of a million pounds. Many thought him over-sanguine, but, within twelve months, half that sum had been obtained by his public appeals to local patriotism and by his private canvass of local wealth. But that was too slow for him; and he, therefore, threw all his personal prestige into the scales in order to reach his target.

Mr. Charles Holcroft, a local admirer, was persuaded to give £20,000. Next, "an anonymous donor" was induced to contribute,

[1] January 13, 1898.

by degrees, another £50,000. This latter benefactor was Lord Strathcona, the Canadian High Commissioner and Chamberlain's friend.

STRATHCONA TO CHAMBERLAIN

October 30, 1899.—I should just say to you that, notwithstanding the interest I take in higher education, I should hardly have been led to move in the matter in the case of a town or city less attached to the cause of union and the unity of the Empire than Birmingham has happily been under your guidance.

In a final bid to raise the full £250,000 before the century expired, Chamberlain approached Andrew Carnegie, the Scottish-American magnate and philanthropist. Carnegie at once agreed to subscribe £50,000 for the endowment of the sciences. This gift had unexpected consequences. At the donor's request, a deputation from Birmingham crossed the Atlantic to study the provincial universities of the United States. When they reported what they had seen,—the scale of endowment, the extent of building and the provision of equipment—Chamberlain's ideas were revolutionised. His whole conception seemed suddenly too small.

Up to this time, Chamberlain had only contemplated,—what Seeley had advised,—the formation of a more complete corps of professors. He now decided that building would have to be undertaken on the grand scale. When the Royal Charter was received at the end of May 1900, he startled his audience by telling them that, though the fund had now risen to £330,000, a further quarter of a million would have to be raised. It was the least sum he could ask for in the new circumstances, and "we must get it". In this speech he used a vivid simile:

We are like those who ascend mountains. Again and again we think we see the summit before us and, when we top the eminence, we find there is still something further beyond.

Two more generous gifts were offered in response. Sir James Chance gave £50,000; and, at Chamberlain's suggestion, Lord Calthorpe and his son presented twenty-five acres of land, an excellent site on the Bournbrook side of the Edgbaston estate.[1]

[1] July 1900.

Chamberlain was already sure that every inch of that space would have to be "covered with buildings"; and Calthorpe afterwards increased the area by twenty more acres. But still it was not enough. At the first Congregation of the University, when more than £400,000 was already assured, their Chancellor announced that more was wanted. "Half a million of money. What is it in view of the object?"[1]

Six months later he took Birmingham's breath away, when he told the second yearly meeting of the Court of Governors that they must aspire to a university "second to none". It would cost, he said, not less than a million sterling.[2]

This last vision was more than even he was destined to accomplish. But he pressed towards it by methods conventional and otherwise. One incident is typical of his shamelessness in begging for a good cause. When he read in the newspapers that an individual, whom he had never met nor heard of, had been left a fortune, that worthy man found himself honoured with an invitation to Highbury. The sequel to his visit can be readily imagined.

But, in the end, voluntary generosity had to be supplemented. Following a suggestion of Chamberlain's to the Lord Mayor, the City Council decided to make an annual grant from the rates. The County Councils of Staffordshire and Worcestershire followed suit; and by these means a further income of £7000 was provided.

This was Chamberlain's final effort in the cause. His interest in the University would continue as long as he was in public life and after. But, presently, the battle for Tariff Reform would absorb all his energies, and leave him neither time nor strength for other things. In little more, however, than four years, he had already created for his City a university, the first of its type in England. In the same period he had also secured for it direct endowments amounting to £450,000, as well as an annual income equivalent, at that time, to the interest on another £200,000 of capital. Out of his own diminished means he had given £2000; and it was more than he could afford.

[1] July 6, 1901. [2] January 8, 1902.

VI

The achievement was not without its humorous side. Facetious journalists in London wrote that, if Chamberlain wanted a glorified technical school for Birmingham, by all means let him have it, but why call it a university. Others, more concerned for the repute of learning, feared that academic standards would be degraded by Brummagem degrees. The inclusion of a School of Brewing caused scandal in some quarters; but the brewers had been among the best donors to the University; and Chamberlain jestingly remarked that "a School for Cocoa" could also be founded, subject to endowment. But, as the work advanced, the critics were disarmed; and the press, irrespective of party, wrote with growing admiration.

Among statesmen Haldane was Chamberlain's most fervent supporter in the cause of higher education. He, for one, never thought that Chamberlain was unqualified for his self-appointed task nor that he approached it with insufficient reverence. Out of a number of letters, which passed between them in these years, one sentence gives the tone:

HALDANE TO CHAMBERLAIN

March 13, 1903.—On this matter of highest education I feel that I am wholly at one with you—and that you are the only man in this country who has the combination of keenness and of power that can make it live.

Both men were deeply discontented with the meagre amount of Government aid given to the new universities.

The University buildings are the greatest of Chamberlain's visible memorials in his city. The Tower was raised in his especial honour. At his own wish, the design was taken in essentials from the famous Torre del Mangia which soars above the Piazza del Campo in Siena. The Birmingham model has sometimes been derided as a "landmark of the Midlands". But they might have a worse. Without him, they might have had none at all. Great is architecture among the arts; but, as Ruskin suggests, not the least question about a building is what does it contain or enshrine. Birmingham will never rival the beauty of the older Universities, but, already, its spirit at least approaches theirs. Years later, Haldane once recalled a talk about All Souls and other Oxford colleges.

I shall never forget Chamberlain's earnestness, when he turned to me and said almost in a whisper, "Haldane, it may take us in Birmingham generations to create a spirit equal to that, but, if it does, one thing I can promise you—we will never lower the standard.[1]

[1] Note of a conversation (undated) between Lord Haldane and Mr. Garvin.

CHAPTER LXXXV

TROPICAL MEDICINE

(1895–1903)

THE "Dark problem" of the Empire—The Colonial Nursing Association—The Tsetse Committee—Manson becomes Medical Adviser—Ronald Ross Discovers the Cause of Malaria— Chamberlain Founds the London School of Tropical Medicine—The Liverpool School—Further Consequences at Home and Abroad—Co-operation with the Royal Society—The Malaria Committee—The Practical Achievement—Ross takes Offence—Money and the War against Disease.

I

IN the forward march of Man, the statesman's part is principally executive. Others, by meditation or research, open new horizons to the human race. His duty is to assess the worth of their successive discoveries, and to find the means, among the mass of competing claims, to put them into practice. In none of his many-sided activities did Chamberlain discharge this part of the statesman's function more successfully than in the field of Tropical Medicine. Indeed, when the final account comes to be drawn, it may well be judged that he did here his greatest service to humanity.

When Chamberlain came to the Colonial Office, the Bight of Benin and the coasts of Ivory and Gold were still the White Man's Grave. Nor were conditions much more wholesome in many other of Britain's tropical Dependencies. Malaria, blackwater fever, yellow fever, and other afflictions brought death, sickness, and debility, at an appalling rate, to the Empire's officials and traders, as to the hapless natives. Sudden burials, repeated invalidings, and chronic enfeeblement made regular administration difficult and continuous policy impossible. There

was a grim but familiar story of a dispatch sent from a West
African territory to the Colonial Office. Before it reached that
quarter, the secretary who drafted it, the clerk who copied it
and the Governor who signed it, were all dead.

The "dark problem" of Empire-building in the Tropics was
brought to Chamberlain's attention at the outset of his long
term of office. The war against King Prempeh ended in bloodless
victory. No British soldier fell to the Ashanti spears. But
malaria took its toll. For once, however, that part of the price
was not taken for granted; and, just as the Mayor had cleansed
the slums of Birmingham, so now the Colonial Secretary determined to apply the spirit of sanitation to the tropical Empire.

II

In the first eighteen months of his administration, Chamberlain took two important steps to promote the war against
disease. The Colonial Nursing Association began its work in
1896. It was a voluntary organisation, but it owed much to
Chamberlain's support. He recommended it to Governors in a
special dispatch. He appealed for funds on its behalf; and Mrs.
Chamberlain became one of its most active Vice-Presidents.
Later, at his instance, the nurses sent to the Tropics received a
special training.

His second step was to lead to still more significant results.
From Zululand, Surgeon-Major David Bruce sent home a report
upon the ravages of the cattle-killing and horse-killing tsetse
flies. These insects infest millions of square miles in tropical
Africa. Their area was then still spreading; and, as the tribes
departed before them, wide tracts returned to wilderness. On
the strength of Bruce's report, Chamberlain invited the Royal
Society to set up a Committee to investigate the activities of the
tsetse fly. This was a form of enquiry never before attempted.
It led to momentous consequences.

In 1902, after five years of research, the Committee discovered that the mysterious terror of sleeping-sickness is
spread among human beings by a species of the same blood-
sucking insect. The cause of Africa's cruellest scourge was known
at last, and, with the knowledge, came at least the hope of its

prevention. One remedy, adopted at an early stage, was to destroy the haunts where the flies breed in relatively narrow belts of scrub along the rivers. This, however, could be but partially effective; and it is only now, nearly half a century later, that immunisation against the tsetse peril seems at last to be in sight. Cure and prevention have followed very slowly on discovery; but discovery was the first step.

III

In 1897, Chamberlain's hand was providentially strengthened by the appearance of an unknown ally. The post of Medical Adviser to the Colonial Office became vacant, and applications were invited from would-be successors. The time-limit for these applications had expired and the choice was about to be made, when Lord Lister moved on behalf of a Mr. Patrick Manson. Impressed by Lister's recommendation, Chamberlain broke the rule and gave Manson time to collect the necessary credentials. A few weeks later, on July 14, 1897, he was appointed Medical Adviser. Thus began the association between Manson and Chamberlain: the man who had the knowledge to suggest and the man who had the power to act.

Patrick Manson was the initiator of the revolution, then beginning, in the vast and terrible study of tropical disease. He had practised for years in China, where he had pursued an experiment of the utmost significance. He had found that the filarial worms associated with elephantiasis and related afflictions are conveyed by a biting mosquito. The epoch-making character of this discovery was not at once recognised. In retrospect, however, we can see plainly that, if interaction between insect and man were the cause of one disease, it might well be the cause of others. Here was a wholly new approach to the solution of the "dark problem".

In due course, Manson had returned to London. Conditions there were hopeless for the further pursuit of his experiment, and he devoted himself instead to lecturing on tropical disease. One of his students, however, Ronald Ross, was then in India, searching into the nature of malaria. In August 1897, a few weeks after Manson first came to Downing Street, Ross, after

innumerable failures, came at last in sure sight of the truth. CHAP.
Shaken with agitation, as he himself describes, he identified the LXXXV.
parasite of malaria in the tissue of the *anopheles* mosquito. Æт. 59–66.
Before long he showed how the disease is transmitted by this
mosquito from bird to bird; and, soon afterwards, how it is
carried in exactly the same way from man to man.

Since the days of antiquity malaria had been among the most
devastating enemies of the human race. It is probable, indeed,
that it had claimed more victims than had fallen to famine,
fire, flood, earthquake or war. It had emptied cities, desolated
farming communities and reduced whole provinces to a sparse
remnant of miserable inhabitants. The blight had fallen on such
scenes of fame as the plains of Marathon and the Roman
Campagna. In India and in vast regions of the Tropics, one-
third of the whole population were infected and permanently
weakened by it. In a word, malaria and related fevers had been
the principal cause of death, disease, enfeeblement and social
stagnation in some of the most fertile regions of the earth.

Until Ross's discovery, however, the origin of the disease was
still almost universally attributed—as the medical works of that
day show—to emanations from marshy ground; literally to
mala aria. This ancient theory and the helpless fatalism connected with it were now swept away for ever. Henceforth, for
countless millions of human beings—and for a large proportion
of the inhabitants of the British Empire—the fight against the
disease became the fight of Man against certain mosquitoes. A
secret of ages was out at last; and, with it, came a new hope for
mankind.

IV

Manson was kept informed by Ross of every stage in the
progress of the momentous experiment at Secunderabad. He
did not, at first, accept all his disciple's conclusions, but he saw,
at once, that a new and vast field of research had been opened
to science. For seven years, Manson had publicly and privately
deplored the absence of all facilities for the study of Tropical
Medicine. "No teaching, no special opportunities for study, no
guidance." Now, under the powerful inspiration of Ross's
discovery, he determined to press for action. Accordingly, three

months after his appointment to the Colonial Office, he called for a new deal for Tropical Medicine in an address delivered at St. George's Hospital. He spoke of the dire need of our tropical Colonies; he explained the recent progress of medicine in the diagnosis, cure and prevention of tropical disease; and he inveighed against the inertia and indifference which had hitherto prevented the application of this knowledge to the relief of human suffering.

This address, and the private representations that no doubt accompanied it, made a deep impression upon Chamberlain. Looking back, he wrote that it was, at this time, that "my attention was more definitely directed to the importance of scientific enquiry into the causes of malaria, and of special education in tropical medicine for the medical officers of the Crown Colonies".[1]

With Chamberlain, to know was to act. As Manson himself put it, "This far-seeing statesman at once . . . took prompt action".[2] He saw that the first step must be to form a training centre where medical officers, newly appointed to posts in the Colonies and Protectorates, might be given

systematic instruction, with special facilities for clinical study, before leaving England; and where doctors already in the Services might, when on leave, have opportunities of bringing their professional knowledge up to date.[3]

Having determined his aim, Chamberlain cast about for means of achieving it. Here again, a lucky coincidence pointed the way. The Seamen's Hospital at the Albert Dock was due to be enlarged. Standing at the dock gates, it admitted, straight from the ships, patients arriving from every part of the world; Lascars, Chinese, Negroes, as well as Europeans. They would provide the indispensable cases for clinical research. The Seamen's Hospital, moreover, had another advantage. The Medical Adviser to the Colonial Office was already closely connected with it. He would, thus, be able to supervise personally any

[1] Cd. 1598, *Establishment of Schools of Tropical Medicine*, containing Chamberlain's dispatch of May 28, 1903, to the Governors of all Colonies. Too long to quote here, it is an indispensable document to the closer study of this subject.
[2] Manson's *Life*, p. 211.
[3] Cd. 1598, 1903, Chamberlain's retrospective dispatch to the Governors of all Colonies.

scheme for the study of Tropical Medicine developed under its auspices.

Chamberlain, accordingly, suggested to the Committee of the Seamen's Hospital Society [1] that their proposed enlargements at the Albert Dock might be extended to include a School of Tropical Medicine. Their consent was soon obtained; but money had to be raised, before the idea could become a reality. The cost of the school buildings was estimated at £3550. After some months of negotiation, the Treasury was persuaded to make, what was rather grandiloquently termed, an Imperial Grant of half that sum. The remaining half had to be provided jointly by the poverty-stricken tropical Colonies and Protectorates. But this sum was by no means enough. The buildings had to be suitably equipped; and Chamberlain insisted that travelling scholarships should be endowed to extend the range of research. He took the lead, therefore, in begging for contributions to this great cause.

His most conspicuous appeal was made at the festival dinner of the Seamen's Hospital Society.[2] The gathering included leading men in shipping and other interests connected with the Empire. One characteristic and much applauded passage from his speech caught the attention of the public.

The man who shall successfully grapple with this foe of humanity and find the cure for malaria, for the fevers desolating our colonies and dependencies in many tropical countries, and shall make the tropics livable for white men—who shall reduce the risk of disease to something like an ordinary average—will do more for the world, more for the British Empire, than the man who adds a new province to the wide dominions of the Queen. All those who co-operate in securing this result, whether by their personal service or by some pecuniary sacrifice, will be entitled to share the honour and to add their names to the golden record of the benefactors of mankind.

About £12,000 of private money was raised in response to his speech. With this sum his purpose was firmly founded; and, in the autumn, Manson inaugurated the London School.[3] Its first session was attended by only twenty-seven students, but it was

---

[1] Cd. 1598, February 2, 1898. [2] Hotel Cecil, May 10, 1899.
[3] October 2, 1899.

to become one of the great teaching centres of the world. Its facilities were soon opened not only to students intended for official service, but to all medical graduates who might wish to avail themselves of it. Many missionaries were trained there for what has often proved to be the most convincing form of their activities. Foreign students were admitted on equal terms; and the non-official entrances became the majority.

Meanwhile, there had been an unexpected parallel development. To his astonishment and pleasure, Chamberlain found that his efforts had created not one school but two. In March 1898, he had sent out a letter to the General Medical Council and to the leading medical schools of the United Kingdom urging them all to promote the study of Tropical Medicine. Liverpool had replied that there were exceptional facilities for this purpose in its hospitals and that recommendations for action would be made. These were discussed by a strong local committee. Its driving force was Sir Alfred Jones, of the Elder Dempster line, who had large interests in West Africa and the West Indies. His expert adviser—his Manson as we might say— was Professor Boyce. These two men determined that Liverpool, as well as London, should have its School of Tropical Medicine. Having laid his plans, Jones approached the Colonial Office for a financial grant; but Chamberlain was forced to explain that there were no funds available. Nothing daunted, the Liverpool Committee decided to go on independently; and Jones himself offered to contribute £350 a year.

Chamberlain welcomed their decision but naturally supposed that their school would be subordinate to his own. As it happened, however, Liverpool outstripped the efforts of London. Having no Treasury to contend with, they were able to begin teaching in May 1899, a few months ahead of the London School. By a masterstroke, moreover, they secured, at a modest salary, no less an expert than Ronald Ross, just returned from India. Chamberlain was filled with admiration for this achievement, conceived in the spirit of his policy but carried out independently of all Government assistance. He recognised the Liverpool School as equal in status to the London School, and presently accorded equal value to its credentials in considering applicants for colonial appointments.

Liverpool's was the most spectacular response to Chamberlain's initiative. But it was not the only one. Before the century was out, the Universities of Cambridge, Edinburgh, Aberdeen and Queen's College, Belfast, had all extended their medical faculties to make possible the study of tropical disease.

No less notable was the active interest aroused abroad. The British movement to tackle "the dark problem" was followed with admiration by the authorities in France; and schools of tropical medicine were duly opened at Paris, Bordeaux and Marseilles. Belgium, too, started its State School; for no one grasped the significance of the medical revolution quicker, nor with shrewder anticipation of profit, than King Leopold. The Germans proved even more zealous. The Hamburg Institute was founded; and the Reich, though only a beginner in colonisation, was soon spending five times as much as Britain to promote the war against tropical disease. In this great humanitarian crusade, it was Chamberlain, among statesmen, who had given the lead to Britain and to the world.

v

The foundation of the London School and the inspiration of similar projects at home and abroad were Chamberlain's main achievements in the cause of Tropical Medicine. But there were others hardly less important. When the plans for the London School had been completed, he wrote to Lord Lister to explain them but added, "I am not satisfied to rest at this point". For the next stage, he invited the co-operation of the Royal Society.

I went on to suggest that a thorough investigation should be undertaken by scientific experts on the spot into "the origin, the transmission and the possible preventives and remedies of tropical diseases, especially of such deadly forms of sickness as the malarial and blackwater fevers prevalent on the West African coast, and that the enquirers should be appointed by and take instructions from the Royal Society".

He asked for a grant from the resources of that institution, promising to provide an equal amount from Colonial funds.[1] Negotiations followed, and the Royal Society decided to appoint

---

[1] Cd. 1598 (Chamberlain to Lister, July 6, 1898).

a Malaria Committee. This was formed on similar lines to the Tsetse Committee already appointed at Chamberlain's instance. The Malaria Committee superintended researches by investigators both in Africa and India. It found that Ross had been right both as to the origins and as to the prevention of malaria. It also established that the deadly blackwater fever was essentially malarial in its nature and could be countered by identical means. When the reports of the two Committees were completed and published, the Royal Society judged that the money and labour spent had been well repaid.[1] It proceeded, therefore, to form a permanent Tropical Diseases Committee, charged with the continuous investigation of all tropical pests afflicting both human beings and animals.

Chamberlain naturally welcomed the appointment of this permanent Committee and determined to further its researches. To this end he persuaded the Treasury, the Foreign Office, the India Office, and the Crown Colonies and Protectorates to contribute to a Tropical Disease Research Fund. The creation of this war-chest was his last important initiative in the crusade against the "dark problem". Undertaken at the end of his long administration, it was not formally effected until after he had resigned.

By extending the activities of the Royal Society into the field of Tropical Medicine, Chamberlain achieved a result second only in importance to the foundation of the London School. He had done as much as could be done in the circumstances of the time; yet his interest in the question was by no means confined to these two broad initiatives. The records show that he was personally attentive to the smallest details of the campaign against disease. In one circular dispatch to Governors, we find him asking, at Manson's request, that collections of biting insects should be made and sent home for examination by the Natural History Museum. In another, he urged reinvestigation of the properties of drugs and herbs used by the natives but too often despised by European doctors. No less important was an administrative reform requiring the medical reports from the Colonies to be drawn up on a uniform model, designed to throw light on the cause, prevention and cure of disease. In this way,

[1] Cd. 1598, April 24, 1903, p. 16.

knowledge gained in any one of the Colonies was made available to them all and to the medical profession everywhere. The reports, thus compiled, provided data of considerable signifi- cance; and one witness, who watched these things closely, recorded that a decade later they still furnished "abundant evidences of the impetus given to the local study of endemic and epidemic diseases by Mr. Chamberlain's administration".[1]

VI

Before Chamberlain left Downing Street, full light had been thrown on the truths afterwards packed into one vivid sentence by Boyce of Liverpool.

No tsetse, no sleeping sickness; just as no anophelines, no malaria; no stegomyia, no yellow fever.[2]

But the progress was not merely theoretical. Already in Chamberlain's time far-reaching practical results had been obtained. Ross led successive expeditions to Sierra Leone, where his sanitary brigades attacked the anophelines by draining their breeding-places—or by filming pools with oil. Organised by the Liverpool School and supported by Chamberlain's instructions to the Governor, these were the first campaigns of the mosquito war.

In 1902, Ross went to Ismailia, at the invitation of the Suez Canal Company. The Company adopted his methods, and the Canal region was soon freed from the curse of malaria. Still further east, similar tactics led to similar victories in territories under the Colonial Office. In the Malay States, malaria had almost forced us to abandon Klang and the adjoining Port Swettenham. In 1901, however, the new methods were introduced, and within a few months the number of serious cases, demanding admission to hospital, fell by nine-tenths. In Hongkong, despite more difficult conditions, both the death-rate and the incidence of sickness were sharply reduced. Most remarkable of all, the careful application of Ross's methods virtually eliminated malarial casualties during the South African War.

[1] Sir Charles Bruce, *The Broad Stone of Empire*, vol. i. p. 451.
[2] *Mosquito or Man?*, p. 200.

Meanwhile, following in Ross's footsteps, the American scientist Reed had discovered that yellow fever is transmitted in the same way as malaria, though by another species of mosquito. This discovery led to the great American campaigns which purified Havana, New Orleans and Panama. Reed's methods were soon adopted by the British authorities; and the terror, which had overhung the West Indies since the days of the buccaneers, was soon little more to be feared than in England.

VII

Unfortunately for its artistic perfection, the tale of this humanitarian crusade is marred by personal jealousies. Chamberlain's loyalty to Manson earned him the rancour of Ross, who indulged it freely in his *Memoirs*. On returning from India, Ross had hoped that Manson would secure for him the command of an Imperial anti-mosquito war. He had also expected a substantial donative, such as Jenner had received for his discovery of vaccination. In the event, neither was forthcoming; and Ross was permanently embittered. His sourness was not merely selfish. He dreamed of anti-malarial action on a scale worthy of the British Empire. But he knew nothing of the financial anxieties pressing upon the Cabinet, nor of the restrictions which the Treasury imposed on the most enterprising Ministers. In March 1901, as a member of a deputation to the Colonial Office, Ross urged sweeping plans for the cleansing of West Africa, but with little regard to expense. Chamberlain asked him to give further consideration to that aspect of his plans and to explain how funds were to be furnished. "If you could tell me how to make West African administration cheaper and better, I would be eternally grateful." [1] Ross took mortal offence. In his *Memoirs* he blames Chamberlain for the parsimony of the Treasury. But this was not his only, nor perhaps his deepest, grievance against the Colonial Secretary. When he wrote of jealousy, secret influences and a "dead-pull" against him at the Colonial Office, he meant Manson; and he never forgave Chamberlain for not making him Medical Adviser in Manson's stead.

[1] March 15, 1901.

No one, of course, wished more heartily for unlimited funds
than Chamberlain; nor did more to raise such limited sums as
were in fact supplied. This part of his work, indeed, continued
after he had left office. As he said himself, his interest in Tropical
Medicine was "unexhausted and unabated" even then. On
May 10, 1905,—six years to a day since the inaugural banquet—
he presided over another dinner to appeal once more on behalf
of the London School. The London Committee were asking for
£100,000 to enlarge their buildings and improve their labora-
tories. Chamberlain described that total as "a mere drop in the
bucket" by comparison with the resources of London and the
public spirit already shown by Liverpool. Only some £10,000
were subscribed that night; but Austen Chamberlain raised over
£70,000 more in his father's lifetime. After the first World War
Milner carried on the work; but, in 1926, all previous efforts were
eclipsed, when the Rockefeller Trustees gave £2,000,000 towards
the great new institute which now includes all branches of
preventive medicine. Appropriately enough its foundation stone
was laid by Chamberlain's son Neville, then Minister of Health.

Chamberlain's initiatives against the "Dark Problem"
changed the face of vast regions of the earth. Within the
British Empire by his action, and beyond it by his example,
life was saved, suffering lessened, vigour renewed and efficiency
increased. Almost immeasurable things still remain to be done;
and the modern world, with all its resources, lags far behind its
duty and its opportunity. But here, in Chamberlain's association
with Manson and in their application of Ross's momentous
discovery, was the beginning of a new era in Man's fight against
Pestilence.

CHAPTER LXXXVI

THE WEST INDIES AND THE SUGAR WAR

(1895–1903)

"The Empire's darkest slum"—The West Indian Crisis and the European Sugar Bounties—Chamberlain investigates—The Royal Commission and its Report—Disagreement on the Main Issue—Palliative or Cure?—The Cabinet Postpones a Decision—Chamberlain's Constructive Programme—Peasant Proprietors—The First Department of Tropical Agriculture—Subsidised Shipping Lines—The Constitutional Aspect—Jamaica and Barbados—Chamberlain and West Indian Federation—The Bounties Again—A Flanking Manœuvre—Chamberlain *versus* Hicks Beach—Free Exchange or Free Imports? Overthrow of the Bounty System—The West Indies Saved—Foreshadowings of the Fiscal Revolution.

I

BOOK
XVIII.
1895.

In the gradual revolution of events, the West Indies, once our most treasured possessions, had become the Empire's darkest slum. The course of this melancholy transition must be briefly recalled. All through the eighteenth century, capital and negro slaves had been poured into the islands to develop the great sugar plantations. Assured of a protected market in Britain and of a widespread demand elsewhere, the sugar industry had steadily expanded. The islands had prospered; and the wealth derived from them provided the solid foundation of many of the stately homes of England. Those were the days when British and French Ministers had thought a single West Indian island worth the whole of Canada; when the great Chatham had provoked and silenced the merriment of the House in a famous opening sentence: "Sugar, Mr. Speaker, sugar (*loud laughter*); who dares to laugh at sugar?"

234

But, after the Napoleonic wars, all this had changed. Slavery had been abolished but without making provision for the working of the plantations. Then, at the beginning of the Free-Trade era, had come the abolition of the preference which assured the supremacy of West Indian sugar in the home market. These two measures had seriously discouraged British investment in the West Indies; and the resulting depression had been aggravated by the high tariffs with which most European nations protected the local production of beet sugar. Nevertheless, the West Indies continued to hold their own in the British market. Some of the plantations, indeed, were backward in their methods of cultivation; but West Indian labour was cheaper than European; and, in Trinidad, for instance, as in British Guiana—included in this subject though technically on "The Main"—, the sugar estates were the most efficient in the world. In 1880, however, West Indian sugar received a death blow. France began to subsidise her beet-sugar industry by a system of export bounties.[1] Her example was soon followed by the chief Powers of Europe; and the bounties were progressively increased. The immediate result was that West Indian cane sugar was displaced at a sweeping rate from Britain's open market by the subsidised beet sugar of Europe. By the end of the century, indeed, West Indian sugar provided less than a tenth of Britain's total sugar import.

Here was a classic instance of the strength and weakness of Britain's policy of free imports. It assured the British public the cheapest sugar in the world. For the West Indies, however, the ruin of their staple industry—all-important in some islands and predominant in most—meant disaster. Many plantations were abandoned. All were crippled. Wages fell. Unemployment rose. Riots threatened. Investment ceased altogether, and with it all hope of future progress. Meanwhile, the revenues steadily declined, until most of the island governments were faced with bankruptcy.

Such were the general circumstances in this historic quarter of the Empire, when Chamberlain became Secretary of State for the Colonies. His predecessor, Lord Ripon, had replied to the

[1] The production of beet sugar was first encouraged on a large scale by Napoleon. The beet crop is, in any case, a valuable element in the whole cycle of agriculture, especially for cattle feed, and the possibility of producing sugar from it as well made it worth protecting and subsidising it.

petitions and entreaties of the islands that nothing could be done. The Liberal Government of the day considered that the principle of "Free Trade" precluded them from any attempt to retaliate against that worst of economic perversions—in a strict Free-Trade view—the export bounty system of the European Powers.

Chamberlain never accepted this interpretation of Free Trade. He had sought the Colonial Office for the very purpose of substituting a policy of active management for the old regime of *laissez-aller*. Indeed, in one of his first speeches as Secretary of State, he had struck the keynote of his whole administration.

I regard many of our colonies as being in the condition of undeveloped estates, and estates which can never be developed without Imperial assistance.[1]

The West Indies were not exactly an "undeveloped estate", for they had once been prosperous. They were rather a neglected estate, fallen into ruin through administrative inertia and economic pedantry. To rescue this estate was to be one of Chamberlain's greatest achievements.

II

Chamberlain gave himself, from the very beginning of his term of office, to the problems of the West Indies. He had been keenly interested in the islands since the time of his venture in sisal-planting; and its unfortunate outcome may have given him a personal sympathy with the difficulties of the islanders. He, certainly, took extraordinary pains to master the subject. One of his little black books, a pattern of neatness, contains, in his own handwriting, a complete analysis of the essentials of the West Indian question. The principal Colonies are separately entered, and there is even an index in alphabetical order. How did he make time for it? Yet it betrays no sign of hurry.

This notebook shows that he was especially struck by our utter failure to develop the fertile island of Dominica. Later he cited it, in the House of Commons, as a telling illustration of the effects of two generations of neglect.

[1] August 22, 1895. See Vol. III. of this work, p. 19.

The condition of Dominica is hardly creditable to the Imperial Government. Here is one of the most fertile islands in the whole of the West Indies; magnificent land, suitable for all kinds of cultivation; and, although we ourselves possess in the shape of Crown lands more than 90,000 acres of this fertile territory, we have never made a single road to open up the territory, and at present it is just as distant from all profitable cultivation as though it were in the centre of Africa. When I contrast what we have done with what the French have done in the neighbouring colonies, I confess the comparison is not to our advantage.[1]

It was some time, however, before he took effective action. For one thing, he was delayed in this, as in many other matters, by the Jameson Raid and its political consequences. For another, he needed more information to build up his policy and a good opportunity to present it. The information began to accumulate from the time he took office. The opportunity came at the end of 1896.

In the autumn of that year, France doubled her sugar bounties; and Germany, with other countries, prepared to follow suit. Sugar prices fell to the lowest level yet. The market for West Indian sugar disappeared; and the Governors warned that more estates were about to abandon cultivation and that grave economic and social consequences must ensue.

Chamberlain was already convinced that the European sugar bounties were the main cause of the West Indies' depression. He also regarded the imposition, or at least the threat, of countervailing duties as the only effective means of combating the bounty system. At the same time he doubted whether any purely departmental case, however well presented, could prevail against the doctrinal objections of the Treasury and the electorate's vested interest in cheap sugar. He resolved, therefore, upon an intermediate step, and asked for the appointment of a Royal Commission to enquire into the situation in the West Indies and make definite recommendations as to future policy.

COLONIAL OFFICE TO THE TREASURY

November 9, 1896.—. . . The position of affairs being as indicated, Mr. Chamberlain is not prepared, as Secretary of State for the Colonies, to accept the responsibility of allowing matters to take their course and

[1] Hansard, Fourth Series, vol. lxiii. col. 876 (August 2, 1898).

to acquiesce in the policy hitherto pursued in regard to the Bounties, without having satisfied himself as to what such a policy may entail, as regards both the Colonies and the Exchequer; nor would he think it right that Her Majesty's Government should adhere to their present attitude on this question without knowing, as clearly as possible, at what cost it may be to the welfare and stability of an important part of the Empire, and to industries in which British Capital is largely involved.[1]

No Cabinet could refuse a Commission requested in these terms, and it was at once secured. The Chancellor of the Exchequer was the only Minister who might have made reservations, but he gave his consent without attempting to prejudge the main issue.

HICKS BEACH TO CHAMBERLAIN

November 22, 1896.—. . . If your Commission shows that the West Indies must be aided by our taxpayers, if the bounties continue, the taxpayers will have to choose whether they think (temporarily) cheap sugar is worth the subsidies which they would have to pay.

Hicks Beach could hardly have stated the alternatives with greater clearness. In the event, however, as we shall see, large sums of public money would have to be spent on subsidiary purposes, before this rigorous guardian of the public purse could be brought to adopt the obvious economy of cutting at the root of the mischief.

III

The choice of the Commissioners was well calculated to ensure respect for their findings. Sir Henry Norman, the Chairman, had been Governor of Jamaica in the course of a long and distinguished colonial career. Sir David Barbour had been Finance Minister in India and was held in high regard by the Treasury. Finally, to raise the Commission above any charge of party, Chamberlain sought and secured the services of Edward Grey as third member. Mr. Sydney Olivier, a member of the Colonial Office staff but also an advocate of Fabian socialism, was chosen as Secretary.

One other appointment deserves our attention. With his passionate interest in flowers, Chamberlain had made friends

[1] Cd. 8359, 1897, pp. 100-102.

with Dr. Morris,[1] the Assistant Director of Kew Gardens. He
now decided that Morris should accompany the Commission as
expert adviser on botanical and agricultural questions. This
appointment would lead to far-reaching results not confined to
the West Indies. These we shall presently examine. Here it is
enough to note that the creation of the post and the choice
of its incumbent were directly attributable to the Colonial
Secretary's hobby.

As a Liberal leader, Grey could hardly be expected, except in
the presence of "imperative necessity", to recommend a policy
of retaliation against the sugar bounties. Chamberlain, accordingly, wrote to safeguard his position on this controversial issue.
The Colonial Secretary's letter implied that retaliation in some
form was perhaps the only solution for the West Indies. But it
also recognised the deep-seated objections to such a course from
the British point of view.

CHAMBERLAIN TO GREY

Colonial Office—December 16, 1896.—The objections either to prohibition, countervailing duties, or equivalent duties, are very strong. . . . No
Government will attempt anything in this direction, except in the presence of an imperative necessity. Whether such a necessity, which can be
truly described as "Imperative", has arisen will appear in the course of
your enquiries. For myself, while hoping that other and more easy alternatives may be found, I shall endeavour to keep an open mind, being
assured that the Commission, as now formed, will ascertain the true facts
and will not make recommendations without overwhelming reasons in
their support.

The Commissioners left England in January 1897. In the
course of hearings and enquiries lasting through several months,
they visited British Guiana, Grenada, St. Vincent, Barbados,
Trinidad, Tobago, St. Lucia, Dominica, Montserrat, Antigua,
St. Kitts, Nevis, and Jamaica.[2] They returned to England at
the beginning of May and, after taking further evidence in
London, presented their report at the end of August.

It was a remarkable document, and its pages still breathe the
tragic contrast between the ancient prosperity of the Antilles

[1] Later Sir Daniel Morris.
[2] Cd. 8655, 1897, report of the West Indian Commission.

and the dire poverty to which their peoples had been reduced.
On all points but one the Commissioners were unanimous; but
this one point was the most important. They agreed that the
sugar bounties were at the root of the West Indian crisis. They
disagreed, however, on purely theoretical grounds, over the
means of tackling them.

Chamberlain was disappointed by their failure to face the
main issue. But his hands were powerfully strengthened by the
rest of the report. Its conclusions must be briefly summarised:

1. *The Crisis and its Consequences.*—The Commissioners
found that the sugar industry was suffering from a severe
decline which, in some Colonies, might well end in its extinction.
Left to itself, this decline would lead to mass unemployment and
displacement of the coloured workers, including the large
element of East Indian coolies; to the bankruptcy of the public
finances; and the collapse of the standards of civilised administration.

2. *Causes.*—The crisis was not due in the main to backward
methods. These were, indeed, all too prevalent, but the best
equipment and management could not hold their own under
the conditions prevailing. The root cause of the trouble was the
abnormal competition of subsidised beet. While this continued,
existing plantations must run at a loss, and there could be no
fresh investment.

3. *Bounties and Countervailing Duties.*—The Commissioners
were unanimous that the abolition of the bounty system on
the Continent would make it possible to cultivate profitably a
large part of the existing sugar-cane plantations. They recommended, therefore, that the Government should try to persuade
the Powers to abandon that system. But, though they willed the
end, a majority would not will the means. Barbour and Grey
declined to recommend the imposition of countervailing duties,
or other measures of retaliation, because of "the danger direct
and indirect, of departing from what has hitherto been considered to be the settled policy of the United Kingdom".
Norman, the Chairman, dissented vigorously from this view.
He held that, without action against beet bounties, other
reforms would prove costly to Britain without solving the
problems of the West Indies.

4. *Measures of Relief.*—In default of a unanimous recommendation upon the essential issue of the bounties, the Commission proceeded to recommend certain measures of relief. These were: the creation of a peasant proprietary; the improvement of methods of cultivation; the development of better communications between the islands; the encouragement of the fruit trade as an alternative to the sugar industry; and the establishment of central sugar factories in Barbados. The minimum cost of these measures was estimated at £460,000, to take the form of grants spread over several years. The building of the central sugar factories would also call for a loan of £120,000.

The significance of the Report was plain. The British Government had the choice of attacking the cause of the disease or of treating its symptoms. Either they must take active measures to protect our sugar Colonies from the operation of the bounty system at least in the home market, or they must apply large direct subsidies to relieve them from its worst effects. The Commissioners could not agree to recommend the former course. They settled, therefore, upon the latter, but with important reservations. They admitted that it would be an expensive policy; that it would take time; and that it offered no certain or complete solution of the West Indian crisis.

Armed with the findings of the Commission, Chamberlain confronted his colleagues with their alternative. In a trenchant Cabinet memorandum [1] he argued that the failure of the Commissioners to agree upon the main issue left the responsibility for taking a decision to the Government. As Colonial Secretary, he maintained that "The bounty-system is indefensible, and it is absolutely wrong that the United Kingdom should profit by the ruin of its oldest colonies". He urged his colleagues, therefore, to seek the abolition of the bounty system by entering into diplomatic negotiations seconded by the threat to impose countervailing duties. Countervailing duties, indeed, would mean dearer sugar; but he met the political objections to this result in words which closely foreshadow one of the main arguments of his subsequent tariff reform campaign. "It would be possible for instance to accompany any duty on sugar with, at

[1] November 8, 1897.

R

least, a corresponding reduction of the duty on tea, and in this way the working class would not suffer from the change." He agreed that the measures of relief recommended by the Commission would be valuable. But he represented that the Commissioners had altogether underestimated their expense and that they could not serve as an effective alternative to bold action against the beet bounties. The latter policy, however, "will undoubtedly provoke violent opposition and it is for the Cabinet to say if they will face it".

The Cabinet did not "face it". The Chancellor of the Exchequer disliked both horns of the dilemma, but, at the pinch, preferred to find grants than touch retaliation with its risks of fiscal heresy. At Chamberlain's instance, however, Salisbury agreed to call another international conference to discuss the bounty system. It met at Brussels in the summer of 1898 and failed, as it was bound to do, seeing that the British delegation was not armed with the one weapon necessary—the power to threaten retaliation unless the abuse were redressed. Nevertheless, the Conference was not altogether vain. It brought home to the Powers the extent of British concern over the bounties. They realised that they had already twisted the Lion's tail too far. It also taught the British Government that they could not hope to abolish the bounty system solely by persuasion. There must be some sanction at the back of their arguments.

The Cabinet's decision had gone against Chamberlain, but he refused to regard it as final. He told the House that the Government's hands were in no way tied. Ministers had not judged the moment opportune for raising the issue of retaliation, but they had not been influenced by the theory that countervailing duties would conflict with the proper principles of Free Trade. In his opinion, indeed, they would restore true Free Trade and "secure the natural condition of ordinary competition which it is an effect of the bounty to destroy".[1]

IV

Overruled upon the main issue, Chamberlain resolved to turn his defeat to good account. Immediately after the Cabinet

---

[1] Hansard, Fourth Series, vol. lxiii. cols. 887-889 (August 2, 1898).

decision, therefore, he informed the Treasury that, so long as the fundamental problem of the sugar bounties was not tackled, he could set no limit to the demands which he might have to make for the relief of the West Indies. In March 1898, he carried, with Grey's support, a first vote of £120,000. A supplementary vote of £41,500 followed in August. By the standards of the day, these were high figures, though only a beginning.

Chamberlain's speeches on these two occasions will not bear quotation, but they are of far more than debating importance. They are essential documents in the history of Imperial policy. Taken together, they form the blueprint of what was, in effect, a five-year plan for the reconstruction of the West Indies.[1] This was a method unprecedented in the Free-Trade era; and the precision, with which the subsequent practice conformed to the conception, marks these two speeches as the first examples of Imperial Planning in the modern sense.

Chamberlain claimed that the interest of the West Indies was inseparable from that of Britain. He denied that the prejudiced word "doles" should be applied to the grants for which he asked. They should be considered as "necessary expenses of Empire". Despite the sugar crisis, the West Indies still supported British production and employment by buying £3,000,000 worth of British goods a year. But, though it was Britain's interest and duty to come to the help of her Colonies, the acceptance of financial liability must be accompanied by political control. Accordingly, he laid it down, as a principle of his remedial policy, that "It is the intention of the Government in every case in which a grant is made to any of these islands, to see that we have full and absolute control over the taxation and the expenditure".

Some two-thirds of the original grants had to be spent on wiping out deficits in some of the island budgets. With the remainder, however, and with larger sums voted later, Chamberlain began the constructive programme recommended by the Commissioners. His fulfilment of it must be briefly recounted under its three main heads: the establishment of a peasant

---

[1] Hansard, Fourth Series, vol. liv. cols. 1538-1547 (March 14, 1898); vol. lxiii. cols. 871-899 (August 2, 1898).

proprietary; the improvement of methods of cultivation; and the development of communications.

Peasant Proprietors

Chamberlain's first efforts to establish a peasant proprietary were undertaken in two islands where conditions were exceptional. In St. Vincent, wages had fallen almost to starvation point and many sugar estates had been abandoned. Experts were, therefore, sent to buy those lands and distribute them among the peasants.

The situation in Dominica was of a different order. There was no need, there, to buy land for settlement. The Crown already owned 90,000 acres, among the most fertile in the West Indies. But there were no roads to those acres; and, without roads, the peasants could neither begin cultivation nor hope to sell their produce. Chamberlain, at once, gave orders for roads to be built, and, in a few years, the island—as he had said long before of Birmingham—"did not know itself". In the light of these two "pilot" experiments, he afterwards directed that, in other islands where the Crown owned land, measures were to be taken to give the peasants access to it and to settle them upon it on easy terms.

Improved Methods of Cultivation

The establishment of a peasant proprietary advanced swiftly. But these coloured peasants were very ignorant and very poor. By themselves they could not make the best use of their holdings nor develop the cultivation of alternative crops to sugar. They had to be taught and helped. For this purpose Chamberlain secured a vote to found the Agricultural Department of the West Indies. In his speech he paid a well-deserved tribute to Kew Gardens,[1] "the botanical headquarters of the Empire"; and Dr. Morris of Kew, who had travelled with the Royal Commission as its botanical adviser, was appointed the first director of the new Department. Its headquarters were set up at Barbados, and the staff included specialists in several

---

[1] Hansard, Fourth Series, vol. lxiii. col. 882 (August 2, 1898). "Thousands of letters pass every year between the authorities of Kew and the Colonies, and they are able to place at the service of those colonies not only the best advice and experience but seeds and samples of economic plants."

branches of botany and a travelling superintendent. Barbados
was the main centre of research and experiment, but, in due
course, supplementary botanical stations were also set up in each
of the other islands.

The knowledge acquired by the Agricultural Department was
popularised by officials who toured the islands, exchanging
information with their colleagues, giving courses of lectures in
the schools, and offering practical advice to individual culti-
vators. A number of elementary school teachers were trained in
agricultural instruction; and, while Chamberlain was still in
office, agricultural schools were opened in Dominica, St. Vincent,
St. Lucia and St. Kitts. As a result, the general level of hus-
bandry was raised; new sugar-canes more resistant to disease
were introduced; the cultivation of fruit began on a considerable scale; and sea-island cotton was planted with success,
especially in St. Vincent. The Agricultural Department of the
West Indies was the first of its kind in the tropical Colonies; but
the West Indian example was soon followed by other parts of
the Empire. Within Chamberlain's lifetime, though after his
resignation, similar departments were formed in India, Ceylon,
Malaya, Mauritius, Fiji and the African Dependencies.

Improved Communications

The third object of the constructive policy was to improve
communications. This was a double task. The Royal Commission had recorded that the journey by mail route from British
Guiana to Jamaica took eight days. To bring the islands in
closer touch with each other, Chamberlain subsidised fortnightly
steamer services. This was the first step. The second and more
decisive was to improve West Indian traffic with Britain
and with the American Continent. Hitherto, with no prospect
of a subsidy, this had seemed to be a hopeless task. Now
Chamberlain had the means, but, even so, it proved difficult
to accomplish.

He began by negotiating with the Royal Mail Company which
had the postal contract. But this came to nothing. Next, he
reached an understanding with Sir Alfred Jones, the self-made
head of the Elder Dempster Line. This firm was already experienced in the kind of traffic required; and its chairman saw great

possibilities both in the fruit trade with the West Indies and in the development of tourism. Jones had boundless energy and imagination; and Chamberlain thought that "of all men in the United Kingdom he was the best able to carry the scheme to success".

But there were rough hitches with the Treasury. Jones broke off. Efforts to find a substitute failed. Then, at the end of December 1899, negotiations were resumed; and Chamberlain and Jones reached a provisional agreement. The British Government was to provide an annual subsidy of £40,000, half being paid by Jamaica. Jones, on his side, was to undertake a fortnightly service for passengers and fruit between Jamaica and Bristol. This time, Chamberlain was determined to avoid a break-off. Accordingly, he clinched the deal on his own responsibility and wrote to Hicks Beach, in a reasonable but decided letter, that, unless his action was supported by the Treasury and the Cabinet, "I cannot possibly be responsible for the future of the West Indies".[1] This drastic step settled the business. Coming, as it did, at the end of months of patient interdepartmental negotiation, it is typical of Chamberlain's administrative tactics. It was like a charge after a long and sometimes deceptively desultory bombardment.

In the event Jones accomplished more than Chamberlain had ever hoped from him. He raised £500,000 of new capital; built splendid steamers for the traffic; and converted the Service, at his own cost, from a fortnightly to a weekly one. By 1901 all was under way; yet, in the end, Jones got out of it more glory than gain.

Meanwhile, with Chamberlain's encouragement, better communications had also been developed between the West Indies and Canada. This too was an assisted service, the Dominion and the Mother Country each paying half the subsidy. Its success led American shipping interests to develop yet other links with the West Indies, to the great advantage of the tropical fruit trade which, by 1914, had become the largest in the world.

In addition to subsidised shipping lines, Chamberlain secured direct cable connection with Jamaica via Bermuda. He also proposed to set up wireless communication between Trinidad

[1] Chamberlain to Hicks Beach, January 11, 1900.

and Tobago and between Antigua and Montserrat. Doubts about patents prevented the fulfilment of this plan. It shows, however, the freshness of mind that marked Chamberlain's whole colonial administration. He was one of the first of British statesmen to appreciate the potentialities of Marconi's revolutionary invention.

Chamberlain's constructive policy was often interrupted and sometimes even thrown back by natural disasters. Hurricanes swept the islands; and, in 1903, a tempest destroyed the whole Jamaican banana crop. More terrible was the eruption, in 1902, of the Soufrière Volcano on St. Vincent, when 2000 people perished and half the island was devastated.[1] Lord Mayors' funds were raised repeatedly to help the victims of these elemental catastrophes; and Chamberlain saw to it that they were supplemented by Imperial grants and loans. Thus, in spite of everything, the remedial plan went forward.

v

Chamberlain's policies for the economic relief of the West Indies were accompanied by the extension of his control over their Governments. He held this course desirable both for the sake of efficiency and on the ground of the principle that responsibility must go with supply. Some of the islands were already under Crown Colony administration. In others, hybrid constitutions were now replaced by direct rule. Almost everywhere, the change proved to the advantage of the Colonies and passed unnoticed by the mass of their peoples. Only in Jamaica and Barbados were the constitutional aspects of Chamberlain's policy in any way remarkable.

Jamaica is by far the largest of the British islands, and its population approached that of the others put together. Thanks to some previous development of the fruit trade, it had suffered less from the sugar crisis than the other islands. It also stood to gain more than all of them from the remedial policy which made it the terminus of the new shipping services. Nevertheless, its finances had fallen into chaos through mismanagement and

[1] The eruption of Soufrière was simultaneous with the far more dreadful explosion of Mont Pelé in the neighbouring French island of Martinique.

misfortune. The mismanagement was chiefly the fault of the elective members who used their influence over the finances to oblige their friends. The misfortune was the failure of an unremunerative railway which the Colony had felt bound to take over from the bankrupt speculators. In addition to these defects, the one endemic and the other perhaps inevitable, the island's financial policy had been imprudent. The sugar crisis had gravely impaired the revenue; but, instead of enforcing economies, the Government had only increased its expenditure. As a result, Jamaica was confronted, by the end of 1898, with a deficit of £150,000; a figure judged astronomic by the standards then accepted in Whitehall.

In these circumstances, Chamberlain acted as a benevolent dictator. He dispatched Sir David Barbour to Jamaica to investigate the situation. Armed with that expert's report,[1] he, then, asked for an Imperial loan to Jamaica of £450,000, to cover existing deficits, to put the railway on a sound basis, and to undertake other public works. He assured the House that Britain would not lose a penny by the transaction, and that Jamaica would one day repay the whole amount. Moreover, to confirm this assurance, he announced that he would take command until the island could pay its way again.[2]

To do this, he had to alter the Colony's constitution so that the Jamaican Government could be assured of a permanent majority in the Legislative Council. Accordingly, he instructed the Governor to nominate sufficient additional members. His arguments were conclusive and pithily expressed.

CHAMBERLAIN TO SIR A. W. L. HEMMING[3]

August 22, 1899.—Two plain facts in connection with this matter must force themselves upon the attention of all who study the question, still more of all who are called upon to find a solution of it.

The first is that the "Home Government", in Sir David Barbour's words, "are in the last resort responsible for the financial condition of Jamaica".

The second is that, as a "working compromise", the existing system has failed. It is a compromise but it has not worked. I am not now so much

---

[1] Cd. 9412, 1899.
[2] Hansard, Fourth Series, vol. lxxv.
cols. 1157-1159, August 2, 1899.
[3] Cd. 125, 1900, p. 15.

concerned with principle as with practice. As a machine for doing the
work which has to be done, the present system has failed.

It is in fact impossible, except where tact and good will and friendly
feeling exist in an unusual degree, for the Government of a country to
be carried on, when those who are responsible for it are in a permanent
minority in the legislature. I decline to allow the Jamaica Government
to remain in that position any longer, not merely because it is unfair
to them, but also because, recognising the ultimate responsibility
of Her Majesty's Government for the solvency of the colony, I must
ensure that the measures which they may consider necessary are carried
out.

I must instruct you, therefore, before the Legislative Council is again
summoned, to fill up the full number of nominated members and to
retain them, using at your discretion the power given you by the Constitution to declare measures to be of paramount importance. You will give
the Council and the public to understand that this step is taken by my
express instructions.

The restoration of Imperial rule led to a prolonged agitation on
the part of the elected members. While the nominees held the
balance, they refused to take part in the Council. But their
boycott of it was unavailing. The mass of coloured people were
wholly indifferent; and Chamberlain was not to be moved. The
Constitutional Struggle, as it was grandly called, bubbled
and simmered for several years. At an early stage, however,
Chamberlain removed its chief sting by authorising the Governor to excuse the attendance of official and nominated
members, whenever he thought fit.

Chamberlain, indeed, was never pedantic in his insistence that
political control must accompany financial responsibility. In
Barbados, for instance, an ancient constitution, more than two
hundred years old, had worked well. Accordingly, when further
aid was needed for Barbados, and Hicks Beach suggested that,
here too, control should go with supply, Chamberlain disagreed.
He had his way; and the island received the grants while
retaining its liberties.

One result of his assumption of direct rule over the West
Indies was to instil a more humane influence into their administration. His determined and successful efforts to reduce

flogging, especially in Jamaica, were worthy of his long record on that subject. He several times disallowed laws which would have extended flogging, and, on one occasion, bluntly overruled a proposal of this kind, though it was backed by the Governor and the Legislative Council.

For all his autocratic temper, he was a firm upholder of human dignity. One incident, out of many, bears witness to this side of his nature. A Governor of Barbados had kicked his under-gardener downstairs in a moment of temper not wholly un-provoked. The story was brought to Chamberlain's notice by an anonymous correspondent; and, when the Governor next came on leave, Chamberlain refused to see him until he had submitted an explanation of his conduct. In a short written statement, that embarrassed official admitted the kick and described the provocation. Chamberlain read it and minuted coldly, "Yes, I will see him. But gentlemen do not kick their servants, and there is no excuse for such conduct." It must have been a painful interview.

One other constitutional issue must be mentioned. It concerns what is still a subject of controversy. Long before Chamberlain went to the Colonial Office, there were zealous advocates of Federation as a remedy for the ills of the West Indies. At first sight this is always an attractive idea. The number of separate Governments means more officials and more expense; and Federation suggests the means of effecting a substantial economy. Chamberlain looked into the question, when he first took office, but judged that the possibility of practical combination did not exist and that the objections outweighed the advantages. He held that the best chance for the smaller Colonies was to have their own Governors or administrators, each of whom could give his whole attention to his island and act with more spirit and initiative than a dependent federation could allow. As he saw it, to cut down the number of high officials would be to make a false economy. These arguments against Federation are weighty; but West Indian Federalists might well reply that Chamberlain's administrative mind was in itself a kind of federation. He is certainly the only statesman who has ever applied a comprehensive policy for the aid and advancement of the West Indies as a whole.

VI

The remedial policies, which we have described, did much to improve conditions in the West Indies. But they were not enough. There could be no return to prosperity so long as West Indian sugar was excluded from the British market by the bounty-fed exports of the beet-producing powers. Thus the main work—the abolition or neutralisation of the bounty system —had still to be done.

Chamberlain, as we saw, had failed in his first and direct attempt to make the Cabinet "face" this decisive issue. He now sought to advance his purpose by a flank manœuvre. This movement, executed with consummate skill, pivoted upon the case of Mauritius. Though not of the West Indies, that island was also entirely dependent upon its sugar crop, and had suffered as much from the beet bounties as any other Colony. Now Mauritius, though dependent on the Colonial Office, was closely associated with India both in population and in business interests. Chamberlain, therefore, suggested to the Government of India that they should impose countervailing duties upon their imports of subsidised beet sugar in defence of Indian interests in Mauritius. Elgin, the Liberal Viceroy, demurred; but Curzon, his successor, proved more responsive. The Secretary of State for India, Lord George Hamilton, was gained for Chamberlain's view; and early in 1899 Curzon telegraphed:

CURZON TO LORD GEORGE HAMILTON

February 25, 1899.—*Private.*—Sugar Bounties. We propose to take immediate legislative action giving authority to Government to impose countervailing duties.

At home, the Cabinet raised no objection to the Viceroy's proposal. It was given immediate effect; and a key position was thus captured in the fight against the bounty system.

In Europe, meanwhile, the chief exporting Powers were already tiring of the expensive competition in bounties. They now saw, in the Indian reprisals, a warning of the steps that Britain herself might take, unless they moderated their policies. Accordingly, in the autumn of 1900, France, Germany and

Austria-Hungary came to a conditional agreement to reduce their bounties. Next, in February 1901, the Belgian Government proposed another international conference to discuss the whole question of the bounty system. This proposal was accepted; and, in December 1901, delegates of all the Powers concerned, except Russia, met in Brussels.

It was generally expected that the conference would lead to some reduction of the bounties. But the beet producers were a powerful pressure group in their own countries. How far the bounty system would, in fact, be dismantled depended mainly upon the attitude of the British Government. The issue to be decided in London was simple enough. Was the British delegation at Brussels to be empowered to threaten retaliation against a continuance of the subsidies, or was it to be unarmed as in the past?

This question led to a suppressed crisis in the Cabinet. Chamberlain insisted on retaliation. Hicks Beach, as stubbornly, resisted it. In view of what was to come, it is interesting to note that both men took their stand upon the orthodox doctrine of Free Trade. It is clear, however, that by Free Trade each meant something very different. Chamberlain had already told the House of Commons that in his view the vital element in Free Trade was free exchange.

I read in the speeches of Cobden and Bright and other great authorities on the subject that the main object of free trade is to secure the natural course of production and exchange . . . a countervailing duty would only restore free trade and secure the natural condition of ordinary competition which it is the effect of a bounty to destroy.[1]

Hicks Beach, by contrast, maintained that the essential element in Free Trade was not free exchange but free imports. As he saw it, the cheapest imports were the best, whatever their effect might be on our Colonies or our agriculture. As a result, he was far from deploring the bounty system. Rather he welcomed it, because it provided the British public with still cheaper sugar. The point emerges clearly from the following letter which shows the real nature of the difference in the Cabinet.

[1] Hansard, Fourth Series, vol. lxiii. cols. 888-889 (August 2, 1898).

LANSDOWNE TO CHAMBERLAIN

December 27, 1901.—. . . I cannot help believing that if, as Beach desires, we preclude ourselves from resorting to countervailing duties, we shall find that we have parted with the only really serviceable weapon at our disposal. Now that sugar is taxed the main objection to these duties disappears.

Beach makes no secret of his belief that it will be a misfortune to us if the bounties are got rid of.[1] I ventured to tell him that, if we honestly entertain this view, we have no business at the conference. It seems to me scarcely honest to go there and then to ride for a fall.

A majority of the Cabinet leaned to Chamberlain's view; but, in the face of the redoubtable Chancellor's opposition, the Cabinet committee, to which the matter had been referred, shrank from taking a decision. Thereupon, Chamberlain told them that, if the Conference failed and the bounty system continued, he would demand that the existing sugar-tax be remitted in favour of the West Indies to an extent counter-balancing the bounties.[2]

Hicks Beach substantially accepted this demand. That it implied admission of the principle of Imperial Preference does not seem to have disturbed him unduly at this time. But the main issue had still to be decided. What course was the British delegation to pursue at the Conference? Lansdowne advised the Cabinet that countervailing duties would never have to be imposed. He urged, therefore, that there was no danger in threatening them. But Hicks Beach still protested that this was "a policy which leads straight to general retaliation on foreign protective duties, and to protection to our home industries".[3] So strong, indeed, was the Chancellor's dislike of countervailing duties, that he preferred to threaten a total prohibition as an alternative sanction.

The respective merits of duties and prohibitions were still under discussion, when Lansdowne, on his own responsibility, cut the knot. He telegraphed to the British delegation that if,

[1] My italics.—J. A.
[2] January 14, 1902. Chamberlain's memorandum for the Cabinet Committee.
[3] February 20, 1902. Memorandum for the Cabinet Committee (Lady Victoria Hicks Beach, *Life of Sir Michael Hicks Beach*, vol. ii. pp. 161-163).

unfortunately, the Conference failed, His Majesty's Government would certainly take steps, though they were not prepared to say beforehand what those steps would be.[1] This veiled threat was enough. Ignorant of the dissension in the Cabinet, the Powers gave way; and a five-year convention was signed at Brussels on March 5, 1902. It provided for the total abolition of the former system of bounties.[2] Britain, on her side, had to give a formal assurance that she would not grant any preference to sugar from her Colonies during the term of the Convention. Chamberlain could hardly have liked this restriction, but it was nothing to the gain.

Congratulations flowed in upon him from all sides. The Convention was recognised as his work and one of the notable successes of his career. The Governor of Mauritius, and no one was more anxiously concerned, thought that "the energy of Mr. Chamberlain achieved the impossible".[3]

VII

Chamberlain had won his five-year battle; and a sure prospect of recovery opened at last before the West Indies. But there was still a gap to be bridged. The Convention would not come into operation until September 1903; and, for the intervening eighteen months, the bounty system would continue. How were the West Indies to carry on meanwhile? Governments often forget that human beings live from day to day; but Chamberlain rendered the island peoples a last service by obtaining from Parliament a grant of £250,000 to tide them over the interval. He told the House that, when the bounties ceased, confidence would return and new energy and capital would be attracted to the sugar industry. With the restoration of equal access to the British market, the islands would hold their own once more.[4]

Time proved kinder to this prophecy than to most mortal forecasts. With the abolition of the bounties, capital flowed back into the plantations. Cane sugar recovered its predominance in the world market; and the islands regained something of their

[1] Cd. 1013, February 21, 1902. *Brussels Sugar Bounty Conference.*
[2] Russia was not a party to the Convention, but her exception was of negligible practical importance.
[3] Sir Charles Bruce, *Broad Stone of Empire,* vol. ii. p. 129.
[4] Hansard, Fourth Series, vol. cxii. cols. 290–300 (July 31, 1902).

ancient prosperity. Five years after Chamberlain had left office, their finances were so well repaired that no West Indian Colony was any longer dependent upon grants-in-aid. Instead, they had all accumulated reserves against the emergencies of the future. Chamberlain had saved the West Indies from utter ruin and had set them on the road to recovery. Many of the seeds, which he had planted, were not seen growing until after his resignation. But the harvest was reaped in his lifetime, and it was abundant.

The story of the West Indies and the sugar war has engaged our attention at some length. It is a remarkable page in British Imperial history. It is also of exceptional significance for the purpose of this study. It illustrates Chamberlain's flexibility and tenacity in Cabinet, his persuasiveness in the House, and his autocratic yet progressive ways in administration. Taken together, its different episodes throw a flood of light on the many-sided personality of this constructive reformer, humanitarian, and natural dictator.

Chamberlain's influence decided the recovery of the West Indies. No less decisive, perhaps, was the influence of the West Indian struggle on the development of his own ideas. The long-drawn difference with Hicks Beach over the need for counter-vailing duties undermined his faith in the traditional policies of the Treasury. It taught him, too, that the principle of Free Imports could not always be reconciled with the prosperity or the development of the Empire. Reports from the West Indies were on his desk almost every day for five years; and the moral to which they pointed must have sunk deep into his mind.

CHAPTER LXXXVII

ZIONISM

(1902–1903)

CHAMBERLAIN, the Empire and the Jews—Origins of the Zionist Movement—Herzl turns to Britain—His First Meeting with Chamberlain and its Consequences—The Sinai Project—Chamberlain in East Africa—He offers Herzl a Settlement there—Kenya not Uganda—The Kishinev Pogrom and the Failure of the Sinai Project—Herzl's Plight—Chamberlain renews his Offer—The Draft Agreement—Zionist Opposition to "the Uganda Project"—Death of Herzl—The Zionist Movement abandons "Uganda"—Chamberlain and the Jewish Territorial Organisation—Chamberlain, Balfour and Zionism.

I

BOOK
XVIII.
1902–3.

IN another aspect of Imperial policy, Chamberlain was both prophet and pioneer. He was the first among British statesmen to see in Zionism both an end to the ancient Jewish problem and a means of advancing the interests of the British Empire. His efforts to combine these two forces ended in failure. Nevertheless, they deserve our study. The calculations which informed them proved enduring. They played their part in the process which led to the Balfour Declaration and so, ultimately, to the creation of the State of Israel.

For all his Liberal background, Chamberlain was not uninfluenced by the racial theories of his time. Wickham Steed records having heard him say:

I have been called the apostle of the Anglo-Saxon race, and I am proud of the title. I think the Anglo-Saxon race is as fine as any on earth. Not that I despise other races. They have their several virtues and aptitudes, though I admit that the aptitudes of my own race appeal to me most strongly. There is, in fact, only one race that I despise—the Jews, sir. They are physical cowards.[1]

Nevertheless, Chamberlain's Papers show that he was intimate with Alfred Rothschild and maintained extensive Jewish connections. Reasons of policy, indeed, naturally drew him towards the Jews. Jewish influence was still predominant in the City; and, under the economic system of the day, his plans for the development of the Empire depended for their realisation upon the support of the big finance houses. The Rand, in particular, was mainly in Jewish hands; and, as we saw, it was upon its prosperity that Chamberlain and Milner counted for the reconstruction and future progress of South Africa. Thus, whatever his personal prejudices may have been, political interests led him to regard the Jews as potential allies of the British Empire. This rational but calculating approach was humanised by a natural sympathy for the victims of religious or racial persecution. The resulting outlook was well expressed in a public statement, which he made, condemning anti-Semitic legislation introduced by the Roumanian Government.

I am consistently opposed to all persecution on account of religious belief, and deeply regret the unreasoning prejudices in so many countries directed against the Jewish people.

History shows that, while preserving with extraordinary tenacity their national characteristics and the tenets of their religion, the Jews have been amongst the most loyal subjects of the States in which they have found a home, and the impolicy of persecution in such a case is almost greater than its cruelty.[2]

Such was Chamberlain's general attitude to the Jewish question, when, at the beginning of the century, the Russian Government began a systematic persecution of the millions of Jewish subjects of the Tsar, already confined within the so-called Pale of Settlement. Von Plehve's anti-Semitic decrees shocked the nations of Europe. They also confronted them with an awkward problem. Hundreds of thousands of Russian Jews fled from the pogroms into Europe; and their numbers threatened

[1] H. Wickham Steed, *Through Thirty Years*, p. 163.
[2] Extract of letter from Chamberlain to the editor of the *Roumanian Bulletin*, July 24, 1902.

to impose a serious strain upon the hospitality of their hosts. Nearly 100,000 Russian Jews settled in Britain alone in the first years of the century. The Unions began to fear the competition of cheap foreign labour. Some anti-Semitic prejudice was aroused; and there was pressure on the Government to restrict alien immigration.[1]

II

The rising tide of persecution in Russia called for some immediate plan to resettle the growing numbers of fugitives. This practical need, combined with the age-old yearning of the Jewish race to return to Palestine, produced the Zionist Movement. Its founder and leader was Theodor Herzl, the author of the Zionist blueprint, *Der Judenstaat*, and, at this time, a Paris correspondent of the *Neue Freie Presse*.

Herzl had vision, enthusiasm, and the gift of persuasion. His conception of the Zionist Movement's task was extremely simple; over-simple perhaps. As he saw it, there were poor Jews who needed help and rich Jews who could be persuaded to help them. This help should take the form of money to buy land in Palestine on which the poor Jews might be settled. Now Palestine belonged to the Sultan who was proverbially short of money. Herzl's plan, therefore, was to induce that ruler to grant a charter to the Zionist Movement authorising them to undertake the Jewish settlement of Palestine. In practice, however, his negotiations with the Sultan came to nothing and his efforts to exert pressure on him, through the German Government, were equally unsuccessful. He decided, therefore, to seek British support. From Cyprus and from Sinai, Britain commanded the western and southern approaches to Palestine. She was, thus, in a strong position to influence the Turks, and might even assist the formation of a Zionist base at El Arish, on the Egyptian side of the Palestine border. Accordingly, in July 1902, Herzl came to London to discuss these ideas with Rothschild. Rothschild spoke of them in general terms to Chamberlain, who suggested that Herzl should come back to see him after the summer recess.

---

[1] A Royal Commission was appointed, in 1902, to enquire into the problem. It reported in 1903 but the Bill then introduced by the Government was rejected. A second Bill was introduced and passed in 1905 ((5 Edw. 7 c. 13), "*an act to amend the law with regard to Aliens*").

The first meeting between Chamberlain and Herzl took place at the Colonial Office on October 22, 1902. We are dependent on Herzl's account for our knowledge of what passed between them. Never intended for publication, this seems at times strangely naïve and self-important. It has, however, an authentic ring and gives a very live picture of Chamberlain. Some of it must be quoted here.

London, October 23, 1902.—Talked yesterday for an hour with the famous master of England, Joe Chamberlain. . . . I explained . . . everything to him just as I had intended, and he listened well. Unfortunately my voice trembled a little at first, which at the time annoyed me very much. After a few minutes, however, things . . . improved, and I talked quietly and emphatically, so far as I could in my shaky English.

I expounded to the immovable mask of Joe Chamberlain the entire Jewish Question . . . my relations with Turkey, etc.

"I am in negotiation with the Sultan," I said. "But you know how it is with Turkish negotiations. If you want to buy a carpet, you must first drink half-a-dozen cups of coffee and smoke a hundred cigarettes; then you proceed to family-gossip; and, from time to time, you throw in a few words about the carpet. Now, I may have time to negotiate, but my People have not. They are starving in the Pale. I must bring them immediate succour . . ." and so on.

At the bit concerning the carpet, the Mask laughed.

I then came to the territory which I want to get from England: Cyprus, El Arish and the Sinai Peninsula.

Chamberlain began by saying that he was only at liberty to discuss Cyprus. The rest concerned not him but the Foreign Office. But, as to Cyprus, this was how the matter stood. That island was inhabited by Greeks and Moslems, whom he could not evict for the sake of new-comers. On the contrary, he was in duty bound to take their side. If the Greeks —encouraged perhaps by Greece and Russia—were to resist Jewish immigration, the deadlock would be complete. He personally had nothing against the Jews. And, had there been a drop of Jewish blood in his veins, he would have been proud of it. But, *voilà*, he had no such drop. He was, however, willing to help if he could; he liked the Zionist idea, etc. Ah, if I could show him a spot in the British Dominions where there was no white population yet, then we could talk! . . .

. . . He denied the existence of anti-Semitism in England. Perhaps an intensified Jewish immigration would lead to restrictive legislation—that was evidently a hint to me, the gipsy-chieftain, to warn off my hordes —but the race-question did not enter into the matter; it was solely a trades-union question. . . .

. . . It was not for him to speak about El Arish and Sinai. The Government would first wish to consult Lord Cromer, whom they held in great esteem. What a pity that Lord Cromer had . . . already gone back to Egypt. . . . I drew El Arish for him upon a bit of paper that lay on his desk and also my Haifa-Hinterland idea. I said that I hoped to induce the Turks to come more speedily to terms with me, if I also turned up by the brook of Egypt. I might then be able to get the Haifa district cheaper.

At this, the smooth-shaven mask laughed once more and dropped his eye-glass.

But he had no idea where El Arish was, and so we went over to a big table, where he hunted out an atlas, among other big books, and looked in it for Egypt. As he did so, he said, "In Egypt, you know, we should have the same difficulties with the natives (as in Cyprus)."

"No," said I, "we won't go to Egypt. We have been there before."

At this he laughed again, stooping low . . . over the book. It was only now that he understood fully my wish to have a place of assembly for the Jewish people in the neighbourhood of Palestine.

In El Arish and Sinai, the country is untenanted. England can give it to us. In return she would gain an increase of her power and the gratitude of ten million Jews. All this . . . impressed him.

I summed up:

"Would you agree to our founding a Jewish colony on the Sinai Peninsula?"

"Yes!" he replied, "if Lord Cromer is in favour." . . .

In the hall, strangely enough, I met the South African Langermann. I expected that Chamberlain would ask him about me and gave him "the good tip" to say that he was a Zionist. I met him afterwards, at the Hotel, and he told me that, as I had foreseen, Chamberlain had actually asked him about me. Langermann declares that his own reply was: "You and Dr. Herzl are my two *chiefs*."

In any case it must have made a certain impression on Chamberlain that this South African promoter should also be one of my men.

The impression left by Chamberlain is not brilliant. Not a man of imagination—a sober screw-manufacturer who wishes to extend the business. A mind without literary or artistic resources, a man of affairs; but an absolutely clear, unclouded head.

The most wonderful feature of the interview was that he did not completely know his way about the British possessions, of which he is at present the undisputed master. It was, as though the manager in a big dry-goods store were not quite sure whether some slightly uncommon article happened to be in stock.

The main result, a tremendous one, which I achieved yesterday, is that Joe Chamberlain does not reject *a limine* the idea of founding a self-governing Jewish colony in the South-Eastern corner of the Mediterranean. . . .[1]

At the end of their conversation, Chamberlain suggested that Herzl should see Lansdowne. He agreed to arrange the appointment and asked the Jewish leader to come back to the Colonial Office next day.

Herzl's arguments had undoubtedly made a deep impression on Chamberlain. Hitherto his interest in Zionism had been chiefly humanitarian. He now saw in it more positive opportunities for British policy. By supporting Zionism, Britain would enlist the sympathies of world Jewry on her behalf. She would also secure Jewish capital and settlers for the development of what was virtually British territory. Looking, moreover, to the future, a Jewish colony in Sinai might prove a useful instrument for extending British influence into Palestine proper, when the time came for the inevitable dismemberment of the Ottoman Empire.

When Herzl returned to the Colonial Office on the following morning (October 23), he found "the Mask" far more genial than at the first encounter. He saw Lansdowne the same afternoon, and next day, on the boat between Folkestone and Boulogne, wrote in his diary:

Yesterday, I believe, was a great day in Jewish history. . . . At 2.15 I entered Chamberlain's office-salon. For that is what the Colonial-Secretary's office reminds you of: the drawing-room of some shipping-magnate.

Chamberlain rose, very busy. He could only spare me a few minutes. But he said it in the most engaging manner. . . .

[1] Theodor Herzl's *Tagebücher*, vol. ii. pp. 295 *seq*. (My translation.—J. A.)

He said to me:

"I have arranged a meeting between you and Lord Lansdowne. He expects you at half-past four in the afternoon. I have already prepared the way for you. Put the whole matter before him, but do not mention Cyprus. The Cyprus part of it is my concern. Be careful to tell him that your projected settlement is not a jumping-off place with the point directed at the Sultan's dominions."

He positively beamed as he said that. Altogether, the Mask was amazingly alive to-day and full of sustained mirth.

I said:

"Of course there can be no question of that, as I want to go to Palestine only with the Sultan's consent."

He looked at me with amusement, as if to say: "The deuce you do." But aloud he said:

"Reassure Lord Lansdowne that you are not intending a Jameson raid from El Arish upon Palestine."

"I shall reassure him, Mr. Chamberlain!" said I, laughing in my turn. . . .[1]

As a result of Herzl's talks with Chamberlain and Lansdowne, a Zionist Commission was sent to Egypt to investigate the practical possibilities of colonising the coastal region near El Arish. Cromer was instructed to give them his support; and Chamberlain spoke to him sympathetically of Herzl's plans, when he passed through Cairo, in December, on his way to South Africa.

III

Beyond Cairo, Chamberlain broke his journey, once more, to visit the East African Protectorates. In the course of his travels there, he was much attracted by the idea of settling a European population in the country between Nairobi and the Mau Escarpment. But to make this idea a reality would require both capital and immigrants. Where were they to be found? It was with this question in his mind that we find him making the following entry into his diary:

December 21, 1902.—If Dr. Herzl were at all inclined to transfer his efforts to East Africa, there would be no difficulty in finding suitable land

[1] Theodor Herzl's Tagebücher, vol. ii. pp. 304 seq. (My translation.—J. A.)

for Jewish settlers. But I assume that this country is too far removed from Palestine to have any attractions for him.

This is the first mention, in the Chamberlain Papers, of the possibility of Jewish settlement in East Africa. We know, indeed, that, at their first meeting, Chamberlain had spoken in general terms to Herzl of settling Jews "on a spot in the British Dominions, where there was no white population". The last sentence, however, of the diary entry quoted above suggests that, then or subsequently, Herzl had explained that he was only interested in Palestine. Nevertheless, the idea of a settlement in East Africa remained in Chamberlain's mind, and was strengthened by the Zionist Commission's rather gloomy report of the prospects in Sinai. He put it tentatively to Herzl, when the latter came to London to see him soon after his return from South Africa. Here again, we may let the Jewish leader describe their conversation in his own words.

London, April 24, 1903.—Yesterday at noon, I was with Chamberlain. He received me cordially like an old acquaintance.

He looked a good deal older, and careworn, but mentally alert. "Since we last met, I have seen a good bit of the world," he began. . . . "I spoke about your affair to Lord Cromer, when I was in Egypt. What have you done?"

I referred him to the Commission's report which I had sent him on the previous day, and which lay on the desk in front of him.

"That is not a favourable report," he remarked.

"Yes," I said, "it is a very poor country, but we mean to make something of it."

"In the course of my journey I saw the very country for you," said the great Chamberlain. "That's Uganda. The coast-region is hot, but the farther you get into the interior the more excellent the climate becomes, for Europeans too. You can plant sugar there, and cotton. So I thought to myself: that would be just the country for Dr. Herzl. But then, of course, *he* only wants to go to Palestine, or somewhere near."

"I can't help myself," I replied. "Our starting-point must be in or near Palestine. Later on we could also colonize Uganda; for we have vast numbers of human beings who are prepared to emigrate. We must, however, build upon a national foundation; that is why the political attraction of El Arish is indispensable to us. . . . As a land-speculation the thing would be bad. No one would give a penny for country of that sort. No one but ourselves, because of that underlying political purpose of ours. But, be it well understood,—we are not going to place ourselves under Egyptian, but only under British rule."

He: "I expect that that is how matters will remain. *We shall not leave Egypt.*[1] Originally that was our intention. I know what I'm saying, for I was in the Government at the time. In the 'Eighties, we thought we should relinquish Egypt. But we have had to sink so much money in the country, and we have so many interests there, at the present time, that we can no longer get away. Thus, you with your Settlement will be sharing the fortunes of a British Dependency. Should things change in Egypt at some future time, and your Colony be strong enough, I am sure it will not fail to assert itself."

We went on to talk about various matters.

"In Asia Minor," said Chamberlain, "our interests are continually growing less. There, some day, an argument will blaze up between France, Germany and Russia. . . . I ask myself, what would, in such a case, be the fate of your Colony, supposing that meanwhile you succeed in establishing it?"

I said: "I believe in that case our chances would be even better. For we shall be used as a small buffer-state. *We shall get what we want not from the good-will but from the jealousies of the Powers.* And when we are under the Union Jack at El Arish, then Palestine too, will *be in the British sphere of influence.*"

He seemed to take pretty kindly to that argument.

I next spoke of the money to be raised. . . . The country would have to be made attractive, and then he (Joe Ch.) would be entitled to the credit of having added another Colony to England.

He received that in a friendly enough spirit. He said, however, that we must have Rothschild with us whatever happened, for the British Government counted on him. . . .

In conclusion, he promised me that he would speak to Lansdowne in the sense of urging Cromer to speed the matter up. . . .

It will be noted that, in describing this conversation, Herzl writes of "Uganda". His use of this name is at the origin of a curious confusion. It is clear from subsequent letters that the territory suggested by Chamberlain for Jewish settle-

[1] The italics indicate that the words appear in English in Herzl's diary.

ment was situated between Nairobi and the Mau Escarpment. CHAP.
Now this territory is in Kenya: not in Uganda. How then did LXXXVII.
the confusion arise? It seems likely that, in his talk with Herzl, ÆT. 66.
Chamberlain either spoke loosely of Uganda or—more accurately perhaps but to a foreigner no less confusingly—of land
which he had seen from the Uganda Railway. Be this as it may,
Herzl certainly went away under the impression that the territory offered to him was called Uganda. The term is never used
in official correspondence, but henceforward Chamberlain's
proposal was popularly known as "the Uganda offer".

This terminological confusion has done little good to
Chamberlain's reputation. Uganda is not suitable for white
settlement; and the "Uganda offer" has often been derided
on this score. In fact, however, Chamberlain's offer was of the
Kenya highlands, and there is no better white man's country
anywhere in the Tropics.

The conversation quoted above was the third and last
between Chamberlain and Herzl. It was also the first occasion
on which they discussed East Africa. Herzl's account leaves no
doubt that he was not yet attracted by Chamberlain's offer.
His mind, as Chamberlain had half expected, was still set on
Palestine. Events, however, were already combining to put in
question what had been hitherto the basic assumption of
Zionism.

IV

That spring, the anti-Semitic policy of the Tsardom entered on
a new and still more vicious phase, exemplified by the Kishinev
pogrom. Persecution swelled the flood of refugees from Russia;
and the problem of their resettlement became more urgent even
than before. Herzl, in his impulsive way, had pinned all his hopes
of solving this problem on obtaining a charter from the British
to found a preliminary colony in Sinai. A few days, however,
after his last talk with Chamberlain, these hopes received a
death blow. Cromer reported to the Foreign Office that his water
engineers judged the Sinai scheme to be impracticable. Some
Zionists still believe that it might have been worth pursuing on
a small scale.[1] It was clear, however, that Sinai offered no

---

[1] Chaim Weizmann, *Trial and Error*, p. 120.

immediate solution to the problems of the Jewish refugees from Russia.

The substance of Cromer's report was duly communicated to Leopold Greenberg, the editor of the *Jewish Chronicle*, who acted as Herzl's representative in London. In despair, Greenberg went to see Chamberlain,[1] who told him that he could do no more where Sinai was concerned, but that he would gladly renew his offer of a settlement in East Africa.

Greenberg's report to Herzl of this conversation found the Zionist leader confronted by a serious crisis. On the one hand, the failure of the Sinai proposal left no hope of an early re-settlement of Jews in Palestine. On the other hand, the intensi-fied persecutions made the need for resettlement more urgent than ever. As Herzl put it in a dramatic phrase, "the lower strata of the Jewish edifice were already inundated". In these circum-stances, tragic for his race and critical for his movement, Herzl clutched at Chamberlain's offer of a settlement in East Africa. Negotiations were begun at once.

CHAMBERLAIN AND GREENBERG

Greenberg to Chamberlain—May 25, 1903.—I have communicated to Dr. Herzl the suggestion you were good enough to make to me . . . as to the formation of a Jewish Settlement in South East Africa. Dr. Herzl desires me to express to you his sincere thanks for your continued interest in the matter, and to ask you, if you will be so kind as to let me have particulars as to the exact territory to which you referred, as well as any details you are able to supply, as to the extent and nature of its present population.

In view especially of the difficulties that have arisen in respect to the proposed settlement in the Sinai Peninsula, Dr. Herzl is anxious to give to your suggestion his immediate earnest consideration. . . .

The Colonial Office to Greenberg—May 30, 1903.—. . . Mr. Chamberlain wishes me to say that he did not refer to any particular place, but that, in his view, the most favourable territory is between Nairobi and the top of the Mau Escarpment, but that, if Dr. Herzl is disposed to consider the matter, it would be necessary that his Agents should visit the Protectorate and make their own report on the most suitable spots.

[1] May 20, 1903.

Greenberg to Chamberlain—June 7, 1903.—. . . Dr. Herzl is most anxious
to consider at the earliest possible moment the suggestion you were so
good as to make, for the establishment of a Jewish Settlement in the
British East Africa Protectorate, and, with that in view, is willing at once
to despatch a Commission of Enquiry to the Protectorate to report on
the most suitable locale for the purpose.

Dr. Herzl will be glad to know, if he may now send to you, for submission to the Government, the form of a Preliminary Agreement which
he would suggest should be entered into prior to the setting out of the
proposed Commission of enquiry. . . .

Colonial Office to Greenberg—June 1903.—I am desired by Mr. Chamberlain . . . to say that Dr. Herzl may send the draft if he wishes to, but,
as he has already informed Dr. Herzl, the matter is in the Department of
the Foreign Office, and the result must depend on their decision. Still he
is quite willing to do his best to secure their consideration.

In its original form, the draft agreement submitted by Herzl
presumed the establishment of a virtually independent Jewish
State; and Lansdowne minuted on it, "I fear it is throughout an
imperium in imperio". After some modification, however, by
the Foreign Office, a more suitable text was agreed. This provided for the settlement in East Africa of a Jewish community
to be organised under a Jewish "Super-Mayor" with a wide
measure of "municipal" autonomy.

On the strength of this understanding, Herzl laid his "Uganda"
project before the Sixth Zionist Congress which assembled in the
last week of August 1903.[1] Long and heated debates followed;
and powerful opposition was organised, chiefly by Chaim Weizmann, a brilliant young chemist from the Pale, destined to play
the leading part in the fulfilment of the Zionist vision. Weizmann held that Zionism could never be a short-cut solution to
the Jewish problem. The National Home would take years to
build; but it must be in Palestine; and to start settlements elsewhere, even for the relief of the refugees, would only be to
divert the energies of the movement from its true aim. In the
end, Herzl's proposal to send a Commission of Enquiry to East
Africa was carried; but the size of the opposition vote made the

[1] For a full account of this Congress see *Trial and Error*, by Chaim Weizmann, ch. vi.

fulfilment of the project doubtful from the start. Its fate was soon sealed. A few weeks after the Congress, Chamberlain left the Government. Within a year, Herzl died in Vienna. Some months later the Commission of Enquiry returned an unfavourable report.

V

The Zionist Movement formally abandoned the "Uganda" project at the Congress of 1905. A number of Zionists, however, remained "Ugandists" and, under the leadership of Zangwill, broke away from the main body of the movement to form the Jewish Territorial Organisation. Their purpose was to revive the project or, should this prove impracticable, to find some other territory, where the British Government would assist the settlement of a Jewish colony. As a first step, Langermann, Zangwill's representative in London, wrote to Chamberlain asking for advice and support. Chamberlain's reply is worth quoting. It is the fullest public statement he ever made on his relations with the Zionist Movement.

CHAMBERLAIN TO LANGERMANN

November 11, 1905.—I beg . . . to assure you of my sincere and continued sympathy with the Jewish people so cruelly oppressed at the present time, and of my readiness to give all the support in my power to any scheme that offers a hope of practical relief from their sufferings. When I first saw the late Dr. Herzl some years ago, while I was still Colonial Secretary, he greatly impressed me not only by his intense enthusiasm, but also by his practical appreciation of the difficulties in his way and of the means of overcoming them. His idea then was to appeal to the national sentiments of the Jews and to organize a great settlement on a sufficient area of vacant land somewhere under the British Flag, where with the help of large funds at the disposal of Jewish organizations and under a system of extended municipal institutions. which would allow full play for Jewish aspirations without actually creating an *imperium in imperio,* the Jewish refugees from tyranny and persecution might develop the resources of a British colony and find a home for themselves. This conception of Dr. Herzl strongly appeals to me, as being the first promising attempt to solve a problem the existence of which, in its present form, is a disgrace and a danger to European

civilization. I was sorry when I learned that the report of the commission
sent out to examine the territory offered by the British Government was
unfavourable, and still more to notice the decision of the Basel Zionist
Congress, after Dr. Herzl's death, to abandon the project altogether.
Now, I understand that you and your friends have determined to renew
the efforts on the lines suggested by Dr. Herzl, and, although the delay
has certainly increased the difficulties in the way, all that has since
occurred, and particularly the recent terrible persecution of the Jews in
the east of Europe, has intensified the necessity for finding some immediate remedy for the existing state of things, and has added to the responsibility of Christian nations in regard to it. I should, therefore, most gladly
give any aid and influence that I can command in support of any
application that may now be made by a responsible organization to the
British Government to consider favourably the scheme prepared by
Dr. Herzl, or any amendment of it which experience has shown to be
desirable. . . .

This was written on the eve of the 1906 election. Chamberlain's interest in the question, however, continued even after
the Unionist defeat, and a few weeks before the end of his
active political life we find him writing to Zangwill: [1]

. . . The fact that I am now out of office necessarily lessens any prospect
of usefulness that I might have had, but, if at any time I see an opportunity for rendering practical service to a practical scheme, I shall not be
unwilling to come forward. . . .

VI

Many British experts, who knew East Africa well, always
regarded the East Africa project as chimerical. [2] Nevertheless,
it is hard to deny that material conditions in East Africa were
at least as favourable as those in Palestine. It is, in any case,
important to remember that Chamberlain was never for East
Africa as against Palestine. It was only when circumstances
made Zionist plans for Palestine temporarily impracticable, that
he urged East Africa upon Herzl as a practical alternative
solution for an urgent human problem. In this his view was,
perhaps, too materialist. He did not fully realise that a refugee

[1] April 20, 1906.
[2] See Weizmann's *Trial and Error*, p. 118.

settlement in East Africa would never attract the necessary
capital and immigrants in the same way as a National Home
in Palestine.

Balfour had approved the motives and the course of Chamberlain's initiative from the start. It was not, however, until the
"Uganda offer" was refused that his interest in Zionism was
really aroused.[1] His first conversation with Weizmann, during
the election of 1906,[2] threw a new light for him on the aims of
the Zionist Movement. Subtler than Chamberlain and of a more
speculative cast of mind, he was quicker to appreciate the
mystical appeal which Palestine had for the Jews. He understood that Zionism was Nationalism in the full sense of the
word, and not a mere relief operation. This understanding,
however, only strengthened his belief that Zionism could serve
the interests of the British Empire. But Palestine remained
under the Turk; Balfour was in Opposition; and for a decade
there was nothing to be done. It was not until the first World
War led, at last, to the dismemberment of the Ottoman Empire,
that Balfour was able to fulfil the policy which Chamberlain
had initiated.

The following conversation between Herzl and the King of
Italy may serve as a postscript to this story.[3] It took place in
January of 1904.

HERZL: "Napoleon had plans for the resettlement of the Jewish
nation."

THE KING OF ITALY: "No, he only wanted to turn the scattered peoples
of the world into his agents."

HERZL: "That is an idea which I also found in Chamberlain."

Herzl's comment is penetrating but over-cynical. Chamberlain undoubtedly hoped by his support of Zionism to enlist the
sympathies of world Jewry on Britain's behalf. He also sought
to divert part of the golden rain of Jewish capital to the development of the British Empire. These aims were statesmanlike in
themselves. They were ennobled and acquired moral force by
the humanitarian purpose which they also served.

[1] See *Arthur James Balfour*, by
Blanche Dugdale, vol. i. pp. 434-435,
and *Trial and Error*, by Chaim Weizmann, pp. 142-145.
[2] *Ibid.*
[3] Herzl's *Tagebücher*, vol. iii. p. 54.

CHAPTER LXXXVIII

THE PERSONAL SIDE

(1900–1903)

DOMESTIC Harmony—Mrs. Chamberlain's Influence—"I would rather take the ten years and the Champagne"—At Highbury—His First Grandchild—Literary Ventures—A Strange Prophecy—Joseph and Austen—No Comrades—*Rapprochement* with Morley—A Hard Man —The Heart beneath the Mask.

I

IN our study of the statesman we had almost overlooked the man. Nor is this surprising. The very harmony of Chamberlain's private life, in these years, robs it of interest. But, then, private life, like the life of nations, is often happiest when it has no history. Certainly he had earned his share of personal happiness by the tragedies of his early years; and he would pay for it again at the latter end.

The author of this domestic harmony was his wife, a gentle influence but vital. Her youth made him feel younger in her company, and, at the same time, made her seem the sister, more than the stepmother, of his children. She brought them closer to him, making a home, where for a long time there had only been a house. Also—and it was not the least of her achievements —she bridged the gap, as perhaps only a foreigner could, between their Birmingham background and the aristocratic world into which the changes of political life had thrown them. Chamberlain himself was of the stuff which, in every age, transcends social distinctions; but, for his children, these things might have presented problems. How lightly they were over-come is suggested by the following letter.

271

MRS. CHAMBERLAIN TO HER MOTHER

October 25, 1902.—Last night we had such a pleasant informal little dinner—comprised chiefly of the Cecil and Chamberlain families—for there were the three girls and Austen besides ourselves, Mr. Balfour and Mr. Gerald Balfour, Lord and Lady Cranborne, and Lord and Lady George Hamilton . . . the talk was more or less general at times and always interesting—with much laughter and good fellowship.

The reader may well wonder whether these personal relationships would have been quite so easy without Mary Chamberlain's influence.

Lady Dorothy Nevill, no bad judge, described her as

a woman in a thousand and one who is above all thoroughly feminine, not clouding one's appreciation of a cultured and clever intellect by advocacy of any fad or theory likely to cause a sensation—a true woman . . . while assisting her husband in every possible manner, and constantly attending political meetings with him, Mrs. Chamberlain is the very opposite of the so-called advanced woman who dabbles in politics; indeed I feel sure that her husband would never have countenanced anything of that kind.[1]

Woman's suffrage was already finding its advocates, and Lady Dorothy goes on to write:

With reference to the question of woman's suffrage and the ultimate possibility of female members of Parliament, he [Chamberlain] once said to me: "Thank goodness there are none! Of the two evils I prefer Parnellites to petticoats." [2]

He was certainly no feminist.

There was little change in his habits and no concession to advancing years. He still sat up into the small hours, chainsmoked his long black cigars, and ate and drank whatever was placed before him. He made no effort to conserve his strength, and justified himself in this by a dubious but amusing argument.

I have always believed that if Gladstone had been ten years younger in 1886, he would never have made the mistake of taking up Irish Home Rule. I do not want to live until my judgement fails. My doctor warned me lately that he would not give me another ten years to live if I con-

_____
[1] *The Reminiscences of Lady Dorothy Nevill*, p. 195.   [2] *Ibid.*

tinued to drink champagne with my dinner. When I asked him how long he would give me if I gave it up, he said "an extra five years at least." But I told him I would rather take the ten years and the champagne! . . .[1]

He was never, indeed, a "clubbable man", but he loved good company. Besides, hospitality provided an agreeable means of keeping his wide connections in repair. There was Society and the world of Politics, in those days still very much the same thing. There were visitors from the Colonies, Governors on leave and business men whose help he needed to develop the Empire. Not least exacting were his territorial base in Birmingham and his kinsmen through whom he held it firm. The entertainment of these varied elements involved an unceasing round of dinners and receptions, as his diaries show; and when, on Good Friday, 1902, he and his wife dined alone, she would note it as "a most unusual occurrence". Meanwhile, the volume of his work was steadily expanding. It was a killing pace.

He had enjoyed an all too brief Mediterranean cruise after the Khaki Election. But, in 1901 and 1902, he escaped no further than to Highbury. These interludes from London were hardly holidays. The messenger from the Colonial Office was an almost daily visitor; and there was no escaping the burden of correspondence, private as well as official. Several times urgent affairs required his presence in London; and visitors to Highbury came, as often as not, on business. The Midland capital, too, had its claims. Still, even to work at home was a relief after the rigours of the session, and sometimes "the Italian climate of Birmingham", as he called it, allowed him to enjoy "the usual routine you know so well—coffee under the oak tree and tea at the dairy or more often among the rosebeds or near the house".[2]

The lights and shadows of the domestic pattern were very normal in these years. His first grandchild was born in 1901; and Mrs. Chamberlain's letters show the statesman in an unfamiliar light:

I wish you could have walked into the drawing-room on Wednesday at tea time and seen the family idyl. "The Cherub" sitting in state on the

[1] Wickham Steed, *Through Thirty Years*, vol. i. pp. 162-163. This conversation is ascribed to the autumn of 1900 in Rome.

[2] Mrs. Chamberlain to her mother, August 23, 1901.

hearthrug,—Grandpa with his legs crossed sitting beside her—"the Cherub's" arm leaning on his knee while she stretched up with the other to pull his glass out of his eye—then Grandpa replaced it solemnly and the performance was repeated ad infinitum . . . as Lord Selborne unsympathetically said: "I see you have all got it very badly." [1]

A few months later the baby needed more vigorous entertainment.

When she catches sight of Joe she starts on the run after him with shrieks of glee, and a regular romp takes place at tea time when he appears on the scene. You should see him on all fours, with the baby on his back in the seventh heaven of delight, while he rushes about with her, an agonised Aunt trying to keep pace with his gyrations and hold the baby on. [2]

The darkest shadow was the long-drawn illness of Ethel, his youngest child; and the spring of 1902 was marred by operations and the consulting of specialists. With the summer she mended enough to take a little house at Eastbourne; but the doctors could not pronounce her cured; and her condition was a constant anxiety.

His mother-in-law, Mrs. Endicott, came over for the Coronation and spent the summer at Highbury. A sequel to this visit shows another facet of the man. Mr. Choate, the American Ambassador, had written a short memoir of her husband, Judge Endicott. Mrs. Chamberlain showed it to Chamberlain, saying that it lacked understanding on the personal side. He returned it next morning with a few extra paragraphs, drafted in the night to make good the deficiency which had troubled her. In itself this is a trivial incident, but it is easy to understand the pleasure that it must have given, and harder to guess how he found the time and energy to spare.

It was not his only literary venture. At a function, in the spring of 1902, he had confessed to Mrs. Beerbohm Tree that he had once written a play. She begged him to show her the manuscript, and went so far as to read it to a theatre management with a view to its production. In the end nothing came of this project; perhaps because he insisted that the authorship must remain "a profound secret".

[1] Mrs. Chamberlain to her mother, March 8, 1902.
[2] Ibid. October 7, 1902.

A few months later we find him corresponding with the young member for Oldham. Winston Churchill had just begun work on the *Life of Lord Randolph*, and wrote asking for letters which might help him in his task. Chamberlain's archives were kept with meticulous care, and, in little more than a week, he had dispatched the father's letters to the son; an example which may well excite the envy of less fortunate biographers.

II

Chamberlain's deepest source of personal satisfaction was Austen's progress in the public career. They had sat ten years together in the House and, in 1902, were at last united in the Cabinet. Little has been recorded of Chamberlain's opinion of his sons, but, on the night of Schalk Burger's ride to Kroon-stadt, he let fall a prophetic comment.[1] He was staying at Westonbirt, the home of Sir George Holford, a great collector of orchids. That night, young Mr. Grenfell, then a clerk in Morgans,[2] sat up late with him hoping for news of the peace negotiations. On this subject Chamberlain would not be drawn, but he talked with great freedom of political personalities at home. He thought that Austen had as good a chance as anyone of heading a government, but added:

You know of my two boys Neville is really the clever one, but he isn't interested in politics; if he was, I would back him to be Prime Minister.[3]

But, for all the harmony of his family life, there was a lack which none of them could supply. He had no comrades, such as Dilke and Morley had been in the past; and for a man of action all else is second best. Austen came the nearest to it; but the son was too respectful, and the father too conscious of his responsibility for that free clash of minds which is the essence of comradeship. Besides, for all their mutual devotion, they were made of very different stuff. Chamberlain was a revolutionary, steadfast to a few great political principles, but a supreme opportunist in his tactics. Austen was a born Conservative, punctilious to a fault. He was a capable administrator, but,

[1] March 23, 1902.
[2] Now Colonel A. M. Grenfell, D.S.O.
[3] From a letter to the author from Lieutenant-Colonel A. M. Grenfell, D.S.O.

like many who have no clear vision of the end, he was ever preoccupied about the means. He copied his father in every detail of dress and manner, till he seemed almost to be his caricature. But the resemblance was only on the surface; even their bodies denied it. Chamberlain's features were questing and aggressive; Austen's were calm and smooth. The father's frame was taut and wiry; the son's upright and relaxed. It might have been better for Austen, if he had asserted his own individuality by growing a beard and wearing horn-rimmed spectacles. As it was, the surface similarities only served to underline the differences between the two men. Nor was Austen wholly unaware of them. He was intensely proud of his father, but sometimes he seemed embarrassed by a lingering doubt whether "Joe" was really quite a gentleman.

Taking it all in all, the loss of comrades was the cruellest forfeit which Chamberlain paid, when he changed sides in politics. As far as he could, he kept in touch with his old associates, but, at best, it was the silver of friendship, not the gold of comradeship. Dilke was no longer the same man. His tragedy had dulled him. Besides, their friendship had been rooted in their causes, and now the roots had withered. Sympathy remained, but there was little contact. With Morley it was easier. For some time, indeed, their relations had been strained. But, early in 1901, Morley paid a visit to Highbury. The news of it leaked out and caused some stir in the press. Chamberlain seized the opportunity to set a seal on their reconciliation.

Feb. 10, 1901.

MY DEAR MORLEY—. . . I should like you to know that, as far as I am concerned, I do not object to the whole world knowing the fact—if, as I hope, it is a fact—that our long friendship, which was somewhat in abeyance during the Home Rule crisis, has been revived, and that we do and shall meet as often as we like, and without the slightest regard to politics and politicians. . . .

If you agree with me, we will go on our way rejoicing—and hoping that the demand created by the modern journalism has been supplied in an 8th circle of Hell provided with the latest machinery and the newest torments.—Yours ever,

J. CHAMBERLAIN.

Characteristically, it was only to his former comrades of
Radical days that he signed himself "Yours ever". His Whig and
Tory colleagues were seldom favoured with any but the chilling
form, "Yours very truly".

In the autumn, Morley came again to Highbury and told
Chamberlain of his labours on the *Life of Gladstone*, which
included the sorting of some 300,000 letters carefully preserved
by Gladstone himself. This time their reconciliation proved
enduring; and a year later we find Chamberlain writing:

CHAMBERLAIN TO MORLEY

October 16, 1902.—If you will kindly look into my room, I shall be glad
to see you any time that I am alone. But you must do more than this.
You and I have made up our minds that, for the rest of our mortal lives,
we may differ in politics but we will remain friends. I hope, therefore, I
may see as much of you as is possible in our busy lives. Would you be
inclined to dine here quietly next Sunday at 8? If so we shall be delighted.

The letter shows his hunger for friendship.

III

The world at large thought Chamberlain a hard man, incap-
able of feeling. To his enemies, he was the callous middle-class
magnate of the caricature. In fairness it must be said that his
pugnacity and tendency to sneer sometimes lent colour to these
misconceptions. One example will suffice to illustrate this
darker side.

The legislative programme of 1902 included certain proposals
for the reform of parliamentary procedure. Their main objects
were to strengthen the authority of the Chair and to reserve
more of the time of the House for Government business. A fixed
dinner hour, during which the House would not divide, was
also proposed for the convenience of members wishing to dine
out. There was no malice in this new rule, but it was inevitably
more attractive to the wealthier Conservative party than to the
Radicals or Irish Nationalists.[1]

[1] It was likewise proposed to give parliamentary sanction to the rapid though still recent growth of the week-end habit by holding the weekly early sitting on Friday instead of Wednesday.

Chamberlain replied for the Government in the debate upon these changes of procedure. His speech was, in the main, a business-like defence of practical measures. He urged the importance of maintaining the authority of the Chair and vigorously upheld the proposal to exact an apology from any member who had defied it. "We are only asking an offender to do what every gentleman would volunteer to do." But the smoothness of the performance was marred by an ugly outburst into which he was betrayed, while defending the proposed dinner hour.

MR. CHAMBERLAIN: "Is it to be represented as a crime that a member . . . should prefer on the whole, much as he likes the House of Commons, to spend, if he can, an hour or two with his family and to spend that time at dinner, or that he should prefer, if he has no family, to dine with his friends? (*Cheers.*) I have heard gentlemen on this side of the House called 'the dinner party'."

MR. MACNEILL: "Hear, Hear."

MR. CHAMBERLAIN: "Yes I think it was the hon. gentleman. (*Laughter.*) Well they have a right to dine and I do not complain, on their account, of their being called 'the dinner party'. But remember there is more than one dinner party in the House of Commons. The hon. member himself belongs to one."

MR. MACNEILL: "I dine in the House."

MR. CHAMBERLAIN: "Yes, a dinner party in the House. The convenience of the hon. member and his friends is a matter for consideration, as well as the convenience of those other hon. members who, having friends or families, prefer to dine with them outside. There are members in this House who find that they can get a good dinner in this House cheaper than they can get it elsewhere." (*Laughter and interruption. The Speaker intervened but his words were not audible in the gallery amid the uproar.*)[1]

It was a corrosive sneer, and must have made his friends shudder. Even the ceaseless provocation of the Irish members could hardly excuse it; and the House shook with laughter, when a Conservative critic [2] of the new rules sarcastically remarked:

The Colonial Secretary said that to apologise was only what every gentleman would do, but he [Mr. Bowles] was not sure what meaning the

---

[1] *The Times*, February 8, 1902.   [2] Mr. Gibson Bowles.

Right Hon. Gentleman attached to the word gentleman. (*Laughter.*)
. . . George IV was considered the first gentleman in Europe, and the
Colonial Secretary was undoubtedly the first gentleman in Birmingham.
(*Great laughter.*)

Most statesmen have been guilty of such lapses at one time
or another; but in him they were doubly damaging, because
uncompensated. None has equalled him in debate; few have
rivalled his power of arousing enthusiasm or compelling assent;
but there was no pathos in his make-up, none of the quality
which plucks at the heartstrings of an audience. As Lord Salisbury said, about this time, comparing Chamberlain with
Gladstone:

"There is a difference. Mr. Gladstone was hated, but he was
very much loved. Does anyone love Mr. Chamberlain?" [1]

And yet, beneath the cold, ironic mask, he was capable of a
warmth and depth of emotion beyond most of his contemporaries. It was not given to many, but, where it was given, it was
without stint. Few of his numerous acquaintances would have
thought him capable of the letter we print below.

Poor Jesse Collings, his devoted henchman, had been out of
sorts since Balfour had dropped him from office in the summer
of 1902. For all practical purposes, Collings had long been a
spent force; but Chamberlain loved the man. He made a
determined and, as it proved, successful effort to pull his old
comrade together.

40 PRINCE'S GARDENS, S.W.,
November 21, 1902.

MY DEAR COLLINGS—If you love me, do as I tell you and all will be well
for both of us.

Hand over your beastly business, such as it is, to Harry Field who will
attend to it better than you can do yourself and start for Egypt or elsewhere *not later than a fortnight hence.*

Come back when I do, with recovered strength and new ideas. All will
then be easy to you, and we will live happily ever afterwards.

I joke—but I am most serious. If you stay muddling here you will get
ill, really ill, and we shall not be able, as I hope still, to exchange
memories for many years, when we have both "retired from business".

[1] *Autobiography of Margot Asquith*, vol. i. p. 156.

As your oldest friend I beg you, with all my heart, to try my prescription.

I have been telling Mary of our conversation—I did not say anything to her before—but now she joins me in hoping earnestly that, when you have talked the matter over with Mrs. Collings, you and she will settle details, which may be anything you like, provided that you take a change and seek new surroundings for a few months.

God bless you, old fellow! May we meet again full of fight still, even though we are both "getting on in years".—Yours ever,

J. CHAMBERLAIN.

This was homely advice to a very old friend. But he could also write with feeling to a young man in trouble. His secretary, Lord Monkbretton, was bereaved that year. Here is Chamberlain's letter of condolence to him. It is full of the memory of his own early tragedies.

COLONIAL OFFICE,
August 22, 1902.

MY DEAR MONKBRETTON—I am very sorry to hear of your trouble.

When such things come to a man, he must set his teeth and worry through, but it takes time, and I am glad you are going away to new scenes and associations.

I hope you will come back—I will not say cured—but able to bear the pain and do the work that is nearest.

In fact I have found that work is the only anodyne.—Yours truly,

J. CHAMBERLAIN.

Twenty years later Monkbretton would still regard it as "the best letter I ever received from a friend".[1]

[1] Lord Monkbretton to Mr. Garvin (undated).

BOOK XIX

CHAMBERLAIN IN SOUTH AFRICA
(November 1902–March 1903)

CHAPTER LXXXIX

BIRMINGHAM TO PRETORIA

(November 1902–January 1903)

BIRMINGHAM's Send-off—H.M.S. *Good Hope*—A Stormy Passage—
Egyptian Interlude—Crossing the Line—Chamberlain in East Africa
—Zanzibar—Durban—Two Important Speeches—"The first of
many deputations"—Natal Contributes a Million Pounds—Through
the Battlefields—With Milner in the Transvaal—Pretoria—Botha's
Return—Boer and British Sit Down Together—The Meeting in the
Raadzaal—Smuts *versus* Chamberlain—First Steps Towards "active
loyalty".

I

WE must here resume the main thread of our story and prepare
to follow Chamberlain on his momentous journey to South
Africa. Only one engagement now delayed his departure.
He had still to take leave of Birmingham: a leave-taking
destined to be the crowning demonstration of this year of
triumphs.

When the news of his journey had been first announced, the
constituents of West Birmingham had planned to give their
member a hearty send-off. But the Government supporters in
the rest of the city refused to admit that this honour should fall
on West Birmingham alone. It was, accordingly, decided to hold
a great demonstration of the Liberal Unionists and Conservatives of the whole city. But even this would not satisfy Birmingham. For once in all these strenuous years the bitterness of
party was laid aside. The local Liberal leaders announced their
intention of joining in the celebrations, explaining in six solemn
theses the reasons which had decided them "not to allow their
strong disapproval of much of Mr. Chamberlain's party strategy
. . . to prevent their supporting him in a policy, which may be

283

fraught with lasting consequences to the peace and prosperity of South Africa".

As the number and variety of Chamberlain's hosts increased, so the programme of the celebrations was expanded. After much deliberation, it was finally decided to hold a banquet in the Town Hall, to be followed by a triumphal torchlight procession culminating in a grand display of fireworks. Honours such as these had never yet been paid in Birmingham even to Royalty.

On learning of the torchlight procession, Mrs. Chamberlain took a wise precaution:

> To-day the beloved "Meteor", that well conducted and ancient horse, is travelling down from London to join "Comet" and so ensure a steady pair of animals for the carriage. "Sin" I think is hardly adapted for the the occasion.[1]

The banquet was held on the evening of November 17. It was "a cold, clear, wintry night", but the square outside the Town Hall was already thronged when Chamberlain and his wife drove up. At the entrance, veterans of the Crimea and the Mutiny formed a guard of honour. Within, the Town Hall had been transformed into a vast dining-room elaborately decorated with floral garlands and monograms and with clusters of tropical fruits. Some three hundred guests were gathered; clergy of the established Church, Nonconformist ministers, city fathers, justices of the peace, university professors, foreign Consuls and prominent business men; the élite of the Midland capital.

As Chamberlain entered, the whole assembly rose to its feet and cheered, while the strains of "Auld lang syne" rolled out from the great organ. An immense meal was served, after the fashion of the time; and conversation was supplemented or drowned by a selection of nautical airs judged appropriate to the occasion.

Chamberlain's speech, after the banquet, was one of the few in his long career in which he sought to strike a personal note. It was not a medium in which he excelled; but, that night, the suppressed emotion in his voice made up for any lack of inspiration in his words. He began with a tribute to his wife:

[1] Mrs. Chamberlain to her mother, November 15, 1902.

. . . I can never say, certainly not in a public gathering, what I owe to her; but I know that, during fourteen years of arduous and sometimes excessive strain, she has sustained me by her courage, cheered me by her gracious companionship and I have found in her my best and truest counsellor.[1]

There is no magic in this sentence and still less in those that preceded it. Yet all the eye-witness accounts agree that the audience was deeply moved. The best of them comes from his wife herself:

. . . Joe rose to reply—very pale, but he always is under emotion, and before I could realise whither his words were leading him, I found his voice was almost breaking as he paid a tribute to his wife. . . . For a moment I trembled lest he would not be able to finish what he had set himself to say, for he paused to command his voice; but he did command it, and the audience was so sympathetic and so responsive that a sort of thrill of emotion passed through it as he pronounced the few sentences in which he spoke of me. They came so unexpectedly, and, coming from him who so rarely shows his feeling, meant so much, that I think everyone present was touched. For me it was a real ordeal. . . .[2]

He went on to recall the comrades of his early struggles for municipal reform—"a band of men who would have been remarkable in any society". Then, in a few short sentences that tower above the rest of the speech, he spoke of his love for Birmingham.

How should I do otherwise than love it? Here is my home, here is my family life, and no man owes more than I do to the blessings of a family life. Here I have been happy, here also I have sorrowed; and through good and evil, through all the vicissitudes of my career, the sympathy and the goodwill of the people have followed me and have bound me to them by links of steel and by the share which they have had in the precious memories of my life.[3]

But a wider audience than Birmingham would read the speech next morning. What would he say of the journey that lay before him? It was a dramatic occasion, but he deliberately

[1] *Birmingham Post*, November 18, 1902.
[2] Mrs. Chamberlain to her mother, November 19, 1902.
[3] *Birmingham Post*, November 18, 1902.

avoided dramatic phrases. He called it "a business trip and not a mere parade".

> I go to South Africa . . . to see every representative of every class and race and section who may desire to see me. My ears will be open to all that they have to say to me. My eyes to all that they will show me and, in this way, I cannot help thinking . . . I shall learn more in a few days . . . than I could possibly gain by months of study of Blue Books and official despatches. . . . Going as I do, in this spirit and with these intentions, I hope and believe to be met halfway. . . .[1]

The proceedings in the Town Hall lasted some three hours. Outside the night was bitterly cold; but, when Chamberlain emerged into the square, the "tens of thousands" of the Birmingham democracy welcomed their hero with volley upon volley of thundering "hurrahs". He climbed into his carriage bowing and raising his hat, while the vast and surging crowds chanted "For he's a jolly good fellow". Slowly the carriage moved off, escorted by a detachment of the Naval Reserve and the Warwickshire Imperial Yeomanry, while 4000 torch-bearers from the University and the Birmingham constituencies lined the route.

> . . . We found ourselves driving, at a foot pace, between a long avenue of torch bearers who kept the road—behind them, on both sides, was an enormous crowd of people, in some places eight to ten deep, and a solid mass at every corner of the street. Bands were stationed at intervals, and from time to time the glare of the torches was rendered even more effective by the burning of coloured lights. Every window was full,[2] and, as we got towards the houses, many were decorated in honour of the occasion. As the Procession passed, the torch bearers fell in behind the carriages, and, as we drove down the steep hill of Suffolk Street and then looked back, the scene was wildly picturesque. An avenue of torches on either side of us, and, behind, a great solid mass of flame following us. The crowd never ceased to cheer, and the same personal note rang through it which had pervaded the audience in the Town Hall. What they had come to see was Joe,—and, as now and then he stood up in the carriage to look at the great gathering, it was striking to notice how every eye was

---

[1] *Birmingham Post*, November 18, 1902.

[2] As much as £5 was paid for the rent of a single window that night.

lifted to his face. "There's Joey!"—"Look at 'im now!" " 'Ere comes *our* Joe!"—"Wish you a pleasant journey, Joe!". . . .[1]

It was a personal triumph; but it was also something more. It was a demonstration that his policy had been raised above party. On South African affairs he could speak for England.

II

Chamberlain left London on the morning of November 25. He travelled in the Royal train; and Balfour, Roberts and half the Cabinet came down to Victoria to see him off. At Portsmouth he went on board H.M.S. *Good Hope*. She was a 14,000-ton cruiser of the latest type, and this was to be her maiden voyage. Admiral Fawkes surrendered his quarters to the Chamberlains, who were thus provided with a dining-room and drawing-room as well as their cabins, all specially carpeted and furnished for the occasion. This was to be their home for the best part of a month.

Austen and a few friends accompanied his father on board, returning after lunch. A few minutes later, *Good Hope* was under way, "the sun lighting up the ships in the harbour, marines in their scarlet uniforms saluting from the deck of a man-of-war, our band playing and theirs responding . . ."[1] Chamberlain and Mrs. Chamberlain stood on the upper bridge with Admiral Fawkes. This time there were no cheers; but, as the ship glided away, the crowd on the jetty raised their hats. Chamberlain raised his in reply. He was still on the bridge when *Good Hope* steamed out of sight.

III

They had started in fair weather, but ran into a violent storm as they approached the Bay of Biscay.

Soup and bottles of claret emptied themselves into people's laps . . . it was bang, bang, crash, crash all day, the ship drenched and everything thoroughly uncomfortable everywhere![1]

The description is Mrs. Chamberlain's. But even the Admiral had to admit that "it was horrid".[2] Out of the twenty officers in

[1] Mrs. Chamberlain to her mother, November 29, 1902.
[2] Admiral Fawkes to his wife, November 28, 1902.

the ward-room, only six appeared at dinner. But Chamberlain never turned a hair. That night, he kept his usual late hours, sitting right aft, in the Admiral's cabin, and smoking his long, black cigars. According to one account, "the senior Naval Officers wished to keep Mr. Chamberlain company, but they could not stand the motion. He alone did not mind it a bit."[1]

Besides Mrs. Chamberlain, the party consisted of Monk-bretton, H. W. St. Just of the Colonial Office, and Wilson, the private secretary. Every day the Admiral had one or two officers to dinner or to breakfast, so that gradually Chamberlain made the acquaintance of them all. By an interesting chance, these officers included Captain Madden and Mr. Chatfield, both destined in due time to become First Sea Lords. Once or twice Chamberlain and his wife dined in the ward-room. One day, he also inspected one of the ship's stokeholds, a hot enough business even in winter. He had done this out of curiosity, but, hearing casually that the men in the other stokeholds were disappointed not to have seen him, he insisted on visiting them all.

The Admiral found him "most interesting to talk to" and "very frank about everything".[2] One conversation in particular deserves recording. One evening, Chamberlain recalled the crisis caused by the Russo-Turkish War of 1876–78, and Gladstone's subsequent Midlothian Campaign. He admitted that, like most of the Liberal party, he had been carried away at the time by horror of the Bulgarian atrocities. In retrospect, however, he thought Gladstone had been unpatriotic in exploiting the massacres for party purposes to the extent that he did. At the same time, he thought that Disraeli had been unwise in going against the moral sense of the public and making light of them. The proper course, in his view, would have been to appoint a commission of enquiry and, meanwhile, to have educated the public about the real issues at stake. It is perhaps as good a judgment as any yet delivered on that memorable crisis.

So much for reminiscences. Most of Chamberlain's time was

[1] Information supplied to Commander Locker-Lampson (September 5, 1920) by Captain Charles Coke, S.N.O. Cape Town, at the time of Chamberlain's journey.
[2] Admiral Fawkes to his wife, December 11, 1902.

JOSEPH BEFORE THE SPHINX.

MR. C. "REALLY! WHAT A FAMILY LIKENESS!"

(Mr. Chamberlain has visited Egypt on his way to South Africa)

spent in the study of books and papers on South Africa. As Mrs. Chamberlain wrote:

Joe . . . is sitting beside me reading the inevitable South African book. . . . He came on board a week ago looking tired but that is much better now and he begins to-day to have a good colour. He is doing rather more work than I like, but much is done in the open air and all done without any rush. . . .[1]

The party landed at Port Said on December 4, continuing by special train to Cairo. Chamberlain and Cromer were old friends, and plunged at once into a long political discussion, while the others went off to watch the sunset from the citadel. On the next two days, there were visits to the new museum and the Barrage, and an audience of the Khedive. Later Chamberlain would write to King Edward:

We spent two days at Cairo, where I once more had the opportunity of noticing the marvellous growth in the prosperity of the country under Lord Cromer's wise administration. When we are also able to get rid of the "Caisse" and the last vestiges of international control, I can see no limits to the development of Egypt on its present lines.[2]

The Chamberlains rejoined *Good Hope* at Suez on December 7, and started, next morning, on the second lap of their journey down the Red Sea and into the Indian Ocean. They crossed the line on December 13; Monkbretton and the rest of the staff being unceremoniously ducked, though Chamberlain escaped with a salt-water baptism. One of the crew, disguised as Neptune, also conferred on him the Order of the Bloater, a decoration which, as Chamberlain remarked, "even His Majesty of Germany does not possess".[3]

Two days later they reached Mombasa, the chief port of the East African Protectorates.

IV

At Mombasa, Chamberlain was received by Sir Charles Eliot, the gifted and independent-minded High Commis-

---

[1] Mrs. Chamberlain to her mother, December 2, 1902.
[2] January 4, 1903.

[3] Admiral Fawkes to his wife (undated).

sioner.[1] The native dignitaries, "a stately group of dignified Arabs, some Somalis and some Gozos ",[2] were first presented to him. Afterwards there was a lunch given by the European community. It was very hot and the Admiral thought it "such a long affair".[3] But Mrs. Chamberlain wrote, "It was extremely well done and we were a little ashamed of the ignorance which had made us imagine the place much smaller and less important".[4]

From Mombasa, the party proceeded by train towards Nairobi, halting for the night on the uplands of the Taru desert. In the course of this journey, they saw much game: hartebeest, wildebeest, ostriches, zebras and a rhinoceros. They also passed lions, but "of course we were looking on the other side and, when the servants came rushing in to tell us, it was too late. Five lions in all we failed to see, the one disappointment of the tour." [5]

A day and a night were spent in Nairobi. It had only been in existence four years, "a mushroom town of

corrugated roofs . . . bungalows on the higher ground . . . and a long straight road, a sea of mud after the heavy rain . . . lined with police (Indians in khaki uniform and red turbans) and wild, half-naked savages, the Masai. . . . I got into a ramshackly vehicle with Sir Charles Eliot. . . . About half-way down the road the motley procession of mule carts, horses, jin-rickshas, handcarts, etc. came to a standstill. A lady from an outlying district rode up on horseback and presented me with a bouquet . . . and the Indian community, merchants, etc. presented Joe with an address in a silver casket. . . ."[6]

Next day, the train journey was continued inland in the hope of reaching Fort Ternan for a distant view of Lake Victoria

[1] Sir Charles N. E. Eliot. Eliot had previously been Chargé d'Affaires in Morocco, Bulgaria and Serbia. He had served in the British Embassy in Washington and had been High Commissioner in Samoa. He resigned from the Foreign Office soon after Chamberlain's visit to East Africa, as a result of a disagreement with his departmental chiefs over policy. He was subsequently Vice-Chancellor of Sheffield University, and served on a Royal Commission. In 1918 he rejoined the Foreign Office and became High Commissioner in Siberia. The following year he was appointed Ambassador to Japan, where he was converted to Buddhism. He died in 1931 in a Buddhist monastery. Apart from this very varied career he wrote a number of books, of which his *Turkey in Europe* is deservedly the most famous. This remarkable man really deserves a biography to himself.

[2] Mrs. Chamberlain to her mother, December 20, 1902.
[3] Admiral Fawkes to his wife, December 21, 1902.
[4] Mrs. Chamberlain to her mother, December 20, 1902.
[5] *Ibid.*
[6] *Ibid.*

Nyanza. Much of the time, Chamberlain rode on a special seat constructed on the engine buffer to get a clearer view of the country. The train passed through the rolling plains, where the Masai graze their humped cattle and the sheep which, Chamberlain noted quaintly, "do not appear to be of the woolly kind".[1] Beyond, it crossed the Kikuyu and Mau escarpments. These, Chamberlain thought, would make good ranching land. "The whole country", he wrote in his diary, "bears considerable resemblance to the Sussex downs and, in parts, to an English park." [2]

At midday on December 18, they reached Mile 521 of the railway, but could go no further, as part of the track had been washed away in a rainstorm. They turned back, therefore, and two days later were again in Mombasa.

At a farewell dinner, there, Chamberlain advised the Colonists to give every encouragement to Asiatic as well as to European settlers. He coupled this advice with a humorous and frank appeal to their commercial instincts. "It was ridiculous to try to confine the

country to Europeans. There were many and enormous parts of it suitable only for Asiatics and they should be given these parts freely. The presence of such settlers here would soon have the desired effect on the Natives. He had been very much struck by the fine physique of the men, but there was a lamentable paucity in their clothing, and he thought that one of the earliest effects of the presence of settlers amongst them would be to create a great demand for Manchester cottons and that, in time, would lead also to a demand for Birmingham jewellery, to our mutual benefit (*laughter*)." [3]

East Africa came at this time under the jurisdiction of the Foreign Office not the Colonial Office. Chamberlain's diary, however, shows that his talks with Sir Charles Eliot, Sir George Whitehouse and other members of the European community led him to make certain recommendations to Lansdowne for the improved administration of the Protectorate. He advocated increasing both the number and the salary of British officials. He also proposed "the immediate formation of a scientific agri-

[1] Chamberlain's Business Diary, vol. i. p. 2.
[2] *Ibid.* p. 3.
[3] *African Standard*, December 24, 1902.

cultural department, similar to that which had been established in the West Indies under Dr. Morris, . . . to prospect the country and to establish model plantations in different parts".[1] His general conclusion was that "the promise of the future seems to me to be good, provided the money is not spared at the outset in the experiments necessary to secure a rapid increase of population and cultivation".[2]

The only note of criticism in the diary was for the conditions prevailing in Mombasa itself and in the ten-mile coastal strip. Slavery still flourished in this region, in accordance with an earlier British undertaking to the native chiefs; and Chamberlain noted: "The state of things in Mombasa and the ten-mile strip could not be defended in Parliament . . . something will have to be done quickly".[3]

A night's journey from Mombasa brought the party to Zanzibar, where Chamberlain went ashore for a "Baraza", or audience of the Sultan. Mrs. Chamberlain was first received in private by that ruler, "a boy fresh from four years at Harrow . . . dressed in white with a gorgeous red and gold belt in which was stuck a gold-hilted dagger . . ."[4]

She withdrew before the public Baraza began, but

from a corner behind a venetian blind we were able to look into the long room where the audience were assembled. The Sultan sat in the middle with Joe on his right and all the Europeans, . . . on his left the Arabs. These sat motionless in silence while coffee and sherbet were served to the Europeans. It being the Fast of Ramadan, none of the natives took anything.[5]

Chamberlain afterwards wrote to the King that the Sultan "has an intelligent face and good manners but is said to be going the way of all Asiatics . . ."[6]

After the audience there was a lunch given by the British community. Chamberlain had been studying the trade statistics of Zanzibar and was concerned at the weak position of British shipping and exports. According to Admiral Fawkes:

[1] Chamberlain's Business Diary, vol. i. p. 7.
[2] Ibid. p. 10.
[3] Ibid. p. 13.
[4] Mrs. Chamberlain to her mother,

December 25, 1902.
[5] Ibid.
[6] Chamberlain to King Edward, January 4, 1903.

He went for the people and said, "They tell me you are afraid of German competition. That's not English. They tell me you want bounties. That's not English. They say you want Government help. That's not English." A gentleman near me got quite excited and kept repeating, "That's the way to talk to us"; and they all cheered.

The waters of Zanzibar are treacherous, and *Good Hope* had to stand nine miles out to sea. Chamberlain and his party were, accordingly, rowed back in the Sultan's barge "by twenty black oarsmen dressed in crimson and green and gold". It was a slow crossing, and, as the brief tropic twilight faded into night, the Colonial Secretary amused himself trying to pick out the constellations in the unfamiliar order of the southern sky.]

This brief visit to East Africa made a profound impression on Chamberlain.

Eager as Joe was to see what had been done here, his anticipation fell far short of the reality. . . . All our ideas about equatorial regions have been revolutionised. . . . Joe has always taken an interest in it [*i.e.* East Africa]—in fact he was one of the first and most strenuous advocates of the construction of the railway—he had read a great deal about it, and yet to him, as to me, it was a revelation.[1]

Beyond Zanzibar, they came into heavier seas, but Christmas Eve found them running smoothly along the coast north of Delagoa Bay. That night they dined in the ward-room, where the junior officers sang "Poor old Joe", and Chamberlain replied with a short speech, beginning, "Unaccustomed as I am to public speaking . . ." On Christmas Day, the anniversary of its discovery, they came in sight of Natal. Early next morning *Good Hope* cast anchor off Durban.

Chamberlain now discarded the white "ducks" he had worn in the Tropics and appeared in a grey frock-coat, and top-hat. According to one of the midshipmen, "he looked a dream"; but Mrs. Chamberlain had visions of sunstroke and insisted that he should wear a sun-helmet. A frantic search on board at first seemed fruitless, but, eventually, the ship's carpenter produced a rather battered naval topee, which the immaculate statesman good naturedly assumed.[2] Thus attired, he left *Good Hope*

[1] Mrs. Chamberlain to her mother, December 20, 1902.
[2] Captain Charles Coke to Com-

mander Locker-Lampson, September 5, 1920.

while the ship's company cheered and the band struck up "Auld lang syne".

V

Chamberlain was welcomed on the jetty by the Governor of Natal, Sir Henry McCallum, and by the Premier, Sir Albert Hime. Together they drove away to the Town Hall to receive the first of many addresses of welcome. Durban, reputed apathetic by comparison with the rest of the Colony, surprised itself by its unbounded enthusiasm. The streets were blocked with cheering crowds, and the air was filled with cries of "Good old Brummagem!" and "How are you, Joe?" Inside the Town Hall, the welcome was scarcely more restrained. They might have been back in the Midlands. The warmth and sincerity of his first South African audience stirred Chamberlain deeply. It also moved him to utter a timely word of warning.

I would deprecate any notion that, by the waving of a magician's wand, I could settle in my sole capacity all these difficult questions. No; time is wanted, the great healer of all wrongs, the great remover of all bitterness; time and patience, and, above all, local goodwill.[1]

Chamberlain delivered two important speeches in Durban. All sides in South Africa scanned them closely; and they still deserve our careful attention. In them he struck the keynotes of almost every public statement he would make throughout the tour.

The first was delivered at an official luncheon on the same day that he landed. It was carefully studied and ranks among his best performances. In essence, it was a broad plea for the reconciliation of the two white races under the British flag.

At one time Dutch and English have been fighting shoulder to shoulder for the cause of civilisation against barbarism. At another time Dutch and English have been fighting one against the other in a courageous rivalry. May we not hope that out of these experiences, different as they are, may yet grow . . . the mutual respect and appreciation which is the only sound foundation upon which you can build up a lasting friendship. (*Cheering.*) And, when the smoke of the great war in which we have been engaged has cleared away, may we not hope that both sides will be

[1] *Natal Mercury*, December 27, 1902.

content to forget all that we ought not to remember, to seek to work cordially for the common good.

Ladies and gentlemen, two proud and kindred races have come to stay in South Africa. (*Hear, hear.*) They are kindred races, kindred in origin, alike in the great qualities which both nations have throughout their glorious history constantly displayed. The love of freedom, of endurance, of tenacity and resolution; of independence and self-reliance; these are the qualities that we find in the nation which honours a Van Tromp, a De Ruyter amongst its leaders, which claims William the Silent amongst its statesmen. These are the qualities which we also love to associate with the names of Drake, of Frobisher, of Nelson and Marlborough and Wellington, Pitt and Chatham. (*Hear, hear.*) Out of these very qualities have sprung some of our greatest difficulties. Between such people there must be a struggle, a rivalry. As long as human nature is what it is, it was inevitable that, in the clash of interests, there should be this struggle for supremacy; and it had to be fought out. (*Hear, hear.*) We are neither of us nations to surrender without a fight; and, in my opinion, this terrible war, which we all deplore, was in the nature of things inevitable (*hear, hear*)—and no statesmanship could have permanently prevented it. (*Loud applause.*) Neither would yield but to a trial of strength.

Now the issue has been decided once for all (*applause*)—the trial has come, and the British flag is, will be, and must be paramount in South Africa. (*Applause.*) But then, gentlemen, if that is granted, . . . what is there any longer to separate us? Why should not reconciliation be easy? Victor and vanquished alike have bravely played their parts. We, on our part, would scorn to glory in our triumph. They need feel no humiliation in their defeat. And, therefore, when the wounds which have been made are healed over, when the scars which have been left begin to fade, then let us see to it as Englishmen worthy of the name—let us see to it that we do nothing to recall much to be regretted animosities of the past. We must show our readiness to welcome our new fellow-subjects to all the privileges of a greater and a freer Empire than the world has ever known. We must give to them equality in all things with ourselves, and we must ask of them something in return. It is with them, now, that the future lies. We hold out the hand to them; we ask them to take it (*hear, hear*)—and to take it without any *arrière-pensée*, but frankly and in the spirit in which it is offered.

Let us try whether out of these two great and kindred races we cannot make a fusion—a nation stronger in its unity than either of its parts would be alone. . . .[1]

In the peroration he returned to this theme but from a different angle. Talk of South African federation was widespread, and many saw in it a cure for all ills. On this controversial issue, Chamberlain gave a clear lead. There could be no federation until self-government had been given to the new Colonies; and self-government could not be given until there was genuine reconciliation.

I come then in a spirit of conciliation, in a spirit of firmness also. The losses we have suffered, the sacrifices we have made, they must not be thrown away. . . . Yes, gentlemen, federation is now a thing to which we look forward with the most favourable anticipation; but a federation pre-supposes that it will be safe for us to concede to the new colonies the self-government which you enjoy. When that time will come, depends upon the spirit in which our advances are met. I hope it will come soon. On the other hand, no mistake would be greater than to hasten it prematurely. . . .[2]

On the following evening, Chamberlain was entertained to dinner at the Marine Hotel by members of the Natal Government. There were to have been no speeches, but, as the night advanced, a dense crowd gathered outside. They clamoured insistently for "a few words"; and, in the end, Chamberlain came out to them on the balcony of the hotel. He spoke impromptu and very briefly, but his words rang among the British community from one end of South Africa to the other. They were a direct appeal to the colonists to remember the obligations as well as the privileges of Empire.

The apathy or indifference which some years ago attended our Colonial policy has entirely disappeared, and, to-day, the people of the Motherland have their kinsmen o'er the sea ever present in their thoughts. (*Loud cheers.*) They are grateful to you for the assistance which you have given. They are ready to do their part in the work of Empire, and they call upon you to accept your obligations. (*Cheers.*)

You are a small Colony; you are a comparatively poor Colony in regard to the wealth of the rest of the Empire; but not the less on that account

---

[1] *Natal Mercury*, December 27, 1902.   [2] *Ibid.*

must you take your share and do your part. It is an obligation on the part of all of you to see that the foundation of a permanent empire will be laid; and no empire can be permanent, if it is not based upon a readiness on the part of all its members to make sacrifices for the common good. (*Loud applause.*)

Let me speak to you freely—and what I say to you I shall say to any other Colony similarly situated—that, up to the present time, you have not done your full share; you have left the larger part of the burden upon the shoulders of the Mother Country. As long as a Colony is weak and dependent and in its infancy, well, it is the duty of the Mother Country to protect it and bear the burden. But as it grows to manhood—and you are growing to the full stature of manhood—it becomes you to relieve the Motherland, and to take your full share of the burden—to accept the obligations as well as the privileges of Empire.[1]

Such, then, were his two fundamental themes: The reconciliation of the two white races under the British flag; The duty of the Colonies to bear their share of the burden of Empire.

For the rest, Chamberlain was "kept on the run"[2] during the two days he spent in Durban. Immediately after his first speech, he received the first of the many deputations which would wait on him everywhere in South Africa. Their members represented different social, economic or political interests. They came not for any formal welcome but to bring their grievances to the Colonial Secretary's attention and talk over their problems with him, man to man. For seven years Chamberlain had surveyed the South African scene from the commanding, but relatively secluded, eminence of the Colonial Office. Now, within a few hours of setting foot in South Africa, he was plunged into the practical discussion of all the varied issues which stirred its restless populations: War Damage Compensation, Amnesty, Trade and Railway Policies, Shipping Subsidies, and Native and Indian Rights. Henceforth, almost every moment of the day not devoted to public functions would be filled with such interviews. It was like an election campaign prolonged over two months. Never before had a British Minister of comparable standing opened himself to such direct, intimate and continuous contact with the forces of public opinion. It was an object lesson in

[1] *Natal Mercury*, December 29, 1902.　　[2] Mrs. Chamberlain to her mother, January 5, 1903.

democratic statesmanship. Alas for Chamberlain, the Colonials, though blunt, were seldom brief. At times the strain would be almost unbearable.

VI

On December 28, the Chamberlains left Durban for Pietermaritzburg, the capital of Natal. Their train journey was a triumphal progress, but with flowers this time, not torches, as its motif.

The journey up from Durban was really charming, and we were embowered in flowers all the way. . . . At every station the people had gathered and, even when we did not stop, bouquets were thrown in; and when the train paused, I generally received three or four. . . . Half-way, we stopped at a place called Inchanga, where the station was turned into a bower and . . . flowers, especially wild orchids were showered upon us. In these first three days in Natal, I counted 36 floral offerings. . . . I still have bouquets everywhere I go.[1]

Pietermaritzburg offered the same unbroken round of functions, interviews and deputations as Durban.

A large reception at Government House, a garden party by the Mayor and Mayoress . . . and a huge banquet in the Town Hall were the principal events of that visit, while every hour of the day, from breakfast to dinner, was occupied for Joe by interviews with all sorts of representative people from the Ministers of State to the natives. It was desperately hard work, and I began to wonder how he would stand it. . . .[2]

In his talks with the Natal Ministers, Chamberlain scored the first practical success of the tour. Responding to his plea to bear their share of the burden of Empire, the Natal Government agreed to abandon important claims on the Imperial Exchequer. These were for War Expenditure amounting to nearly a million pounds. This was no small sum for a small Colony, and, in accepting it as a charge on their finances, the Natal Ministers were doubling Natal's total contribution to the cost of the war. Chamberlain announced their decision at a public banquet[3] given in his honour. Seldom in history can the announcement of

---

[1] Mrs. Chamberlain to her mother, January 5, 1903.
[2] *Ibid.*
[3] Pietermaritzburg Town Hall, December 30, 1902.

increased taxation have been greeted with such tremendous
cheers. When he stood to speak, "for nearly two minutes by the
watch the whole audience, both diners and spectators seemed to
lose all control over themselves. The ladies waved their handkerchiefs, while the men stood on their chairs and yelled, cheered,
and shouted until the hall rang again." [1]

Then, as so often during the tour, he rose to the occasion. His
South African speeches seldom touched the heights, but they
have a breadth of vision and full-blooded vigour which the
colder and more critical audiences at home could not always
evoke. His speech, that night, was only a variation on the twin
themes he had already sounded in Durban, but one appeal in
particular caught the imagination of the public. He called on
the Dutch to convert their "passive loyalty" into an "active
loyalty".

From Pietermaritzburg, Chamberlain and his party travelled
northwards through the Natal battlefields. At Chievely, they
stood for a moment by the grave of Lord Roberts' son. Thence
to Colenso, where they slept in a "ramshackly shanty", and
drove out next day, in a "huge waggon drawn by ten mules", to
visit the scene of Buller's defeat. New Year's Day saw them
in Ladysmith. They visited the landmarks of the siege; and
Chamberlain, dressed in riding boots and breeches, rode out to
Spion Kop to see "the long sad lines of trenches, now huge
graves of those who perished there". [2] This is the only recorded
occasion of his whole career when he took to horse.

At wayside stations, by the road, and in scattered farms near
the battlefields, Chamberlain stopped for frequent talks with
local leaders, Dutch and British, and with many humbler folk
as well. The first-hand knowledge gained from these talks soon
gave a more concrete cast to his speeches. In an enthusiastic
meeting in the shell-shattered Town Hall at Ladysmith, he
spoke for the first time on local grievances. [3] He appealed to the
Dutch to stop boycotting the British and the "Hands-Uppers".
He pledged himself to see that the receipts issued by the
military would be honoured.

Beyond Ladysmith, the journey was continued towards the

[1] *The Times*, January 1, 1903.   January 5, 1903.
[2] Mrs. Chamberlain to her mother,   [3] January 2, 1903.

Transvaal with "frequent stops and crowds and speeches". Natal's reception had been wonderful, "and so we go, amid shouts and cheers, smiles and sometimes tears, as more than once I have seen on some rugged face when Joe has appealed to their patriotism and their love for the land of their fathers as well as of their adoption".[1]

At Charlestown, the last station in Natal, they were joined by Milner. After the letters which had passed between them over the Suspension crisis, this might have been an awkward meeting. Mrs. Chamberlain, however, noted that "Milner seemed much better than in England . . . looking as if the strain had been relieved and life were easier".

The train passed close under Majuba and through the tunnel under Lang's Nek into the Transvaal. They were now on the veld, in what had been enemy country, and amid the ruins of the guerilla war.

The houses are destroyed, but the tents which replace them and the flocks and herds grazing nearby soften the ravages of war. Occasionally, block houses and rows and rows of tin cans strung on a wire, which were used to give the alarm when the enemy tried to cross the railway, also had their tale to tell. . . .

At Volksrust, the first station in the Transvaal, they left the train to meet a group of local Boer dignitaries. Among them was a son of General Joubert, Kruger's Commandant-General at the beginning of the war. Chamberlain shook hands with him and said: "I am pleased to meet the son of so brave a man".

In the Transvaal, as in Natal, the train stopped at almost every station. The crowds were now, perhaps, more curious than enthusiastic, but, everywhere, Chamberlain's reception was cordial. It was past midnight when he reached Pretoria; but a large crowd was still waiting at the station, and much of it was Dutch.

Next day, Chamberlain summed up his impressions of this first stage of the tour in the following letter.

CHAMBERLAIN TO THE KING

January 4, 1903.—. . . We arrived at Durban on the 26th, and since then there has been a constant rush of addresses, banquets and meetings

[1] Mrs. Chamberlain to her mother, January 5, 1903.

of all kinds. The Colony is especially British and most loyal. The Dutch are still sullen, but there is not the slightest sign of further trouble, and, if we can only get the Compensation claims, which have been terribly mismanaged by the Military Courts, fairly and finally settled, the population will settle down and I believe the former satisfactory relations between Boer and British will be restored. Altogether, I anticipate no difficulty in the future in connection with this Colony and there are every signs [*sic*] of an approaching era of great prosperity. I cabled home the satisfactory arrangements which I have been able to make with regard to the Colony's share in the cost of the war. It has been well received in the Colony and is creditable to their patriotism and sense of Imperial responsibility.

We visited the battle fields of Colenso, Wagon Hill, and Spion Kop where the long lines of graves show the severity of the fighting. I am not competent to criticise military operations, but, even to the eye of a civilian, it seems evident that the most inexcusable mistakes were made by the Generals in command, and I find the opinion universally expressed that they failed altogether to take advantage of the local knowledge that might have been at their disposal. Our intelligence was very bad, and the suggestions of men who knew every inch of the country were either not asked, or, if given, were curtly rejected. This applies of course to the early stages of the war in Natal, and I believe our generals learned wisdom later.

VII

At the wayside stations in the Transvaal, Chamberlain's reception had been cordial enough. The Boer farmers were weary of strife and genuinely grateful for the Government's efforts to help them make a fresh start. It was otherwise in Pretoria. There, the Boer intelligentsia cherished their grievances, unemployed and despairing of the future. They had suffered less material loss than the farmers but they had lost power; and there is no greater cause of bitterness.

It was generally supposed that the Dutch in the capital would boycott functions held in Chamberlain's honour. This, indeed, had been their original intention. But, meanwhile, Botha had returned to South Africa. His first public statement, on landing at the Cape, was remarkable for its friendly references to Chamberlain.

I have broken off my mission in Europe and have hurried back here expressly that I may if possible cooperate with him. I believe Mr. Chamberlain sincerely desires a good understanding between the two peoples and, to that end, any helpful offices on my part and on that of my colleagues will, of course, always be ready. Nothing but good can come of his expressed resolution to see things in this country with his own eyes and form his own opinions. . . . I certainly consider him the strongest man I have met in England. It is not only that he thinks for himself, but his mind has also a practical bent.[1]

From Cape Town, Botha hurried to Pretoria and begged his compatriots to abandon a boycott which must be thought discourteous and, perhaps, disloyal. He was by now convinced that the Boer interest would best be served by a frank acceptance of the new situation and, therefore, of the social obligations which followed from it. His arguments prevailed; and the Boer leaders agreed to make a show of courtesy, though many, perhaps most, were still unreconciled at heart. It was an important first step.

The British community were well pleased with the situation. On the surface, however, they chafed against "Downing Street control", and clamoured for self-government. They also loudly complained that the Boers were "coddled" and "spoonfed" with grants, while "loyalist" claims remained unsettled. But, though their speeches on these topics were extreme, it was a superficial agitation. They knew that they were still too weak to maintain their newly won supremacy by themselves. There was always the danger of a Boer rising.

Chamberlain was soon made aware of these different currents of opinion by talks with leading citizens, British and Dutch. The details of these interviews are no longer of much interest, though one of them may be noted in passing. It is a good example of the way in which Chamberlain gradually disarmed Boer prejudice.

Among his visitors was the Reverend Bosman, a leading *predikant*, reputed wholly irreconcilable. Bosman spoke "with the evidence of restrained feeling and bitterness";[2] but, for some time, Chamberlain could not reach to the root of his grievance. At length, after much patient prodding, the *predikant*

---

[1] *South African News*, December 31, 1902.   [2] Chamberlain's Business Diary, vol. i. p. 57.

explained his anxiety lest the new Department of Education should neglect the teaching of the Dutch language and undermine the influence of the parents and of the Church in the management of the schools. No one knew better than Chamberlain how high passions can run over questions of education. He, at once, showed understanding of Bosman's fears. The tone of their conversation softened; and the two men were soon concerting practical measures for giving the Church and the parents a just say in the control of the schools.

The first public function in the capital was a garden-party given by the Lieutenant-Governor. Several of the Boer leaders were present, including Botha, De La Rey, Smuts and "old Piet Cronje who stood and gazed at Joe, notwithstanding the term he had served at St. Helena as prisoner of war".[1] The Chamberlains were expected to shake hands with each of the guests, and Mrs. Chamberlain might well complain, "my supply of gloves is coming to an end, to say nothing of my hand, for the Colonial grip is strong".[2] A few days later, indeed, her hand was so sprained from repeated handshakes that she had to resort to bowing instead.

The garden-party was followed by a public banquet, where, for the first time since the war, the leaders of the Boer and the British communities sat down to table together. That such a thing could happen, within a bare six months of the "cease fire", was of the utmost significance. It was due, at bottom, to two sets of circumstances. First, to the generosity of the terms of the peace and to the free constitution of the Empire, in which the Republics were now included. Second, to the magnanimity and broad-minded acceptance of the situation shown by Botha and his followers. These things made such a communion possible. But to make it happen required a gesture as imaginative as Chamberlain's journey to South Africa. It was not the least of his achievements that he brought Briton and Boer to the same board.

At the banquet the Boers behaved with that dignified courtesy, which Milner admired and at times regretted above all their other qualities. It was left to the spokesman of the "loyalists" to strike a jarring note by lecturing Chamberlain on

---

[1] Mrs. Chamberlain to her mother, January 13, 1903.   [2] *Ibid.*

the shortcomings of "Downing Street rule". Chamberlain, however, prudently declined to be drawn. He dismissed the criticism with some irony, pretending to have forgotten the "loyalist"
speaker's name. Then, he turned to his theme of conciliating
the two white races. With one eye on the Boer guests, he
stressed that conciliation must not be misinterpreted.

> The policy of His Majesty's Government must be a policy of union
> and a policy of conciliation, so far as conciliation leads to union. Now
> that is a somewhat important qualification. Conciliation we all desire,
> but it is not conciliation to attempt to meet the views of your opponents,
> if at the same time you alienate your friends; and it is no use to make
> concessions, if they are to be interpreted as a sign of weakness and are
> merely to be the prelude to further demands. . . . The leaders of the
> Boers have accepted, in terms as frank as any of us could desire, the
> results of the war and the terms of settlement by which the war was
> concluded. I absolutely accept their assurances which I believe are made
> in perfect sincerity. We are going to carry out the terms of that settle-
> ment in spirit and in letter, and we expect . . . that they will do the
> same. . . .[1]

Events would soon show that this warning was not uncalled
for.

VIII

On the next morning, January 8, Chamberlain met the
members of the Boer Delegation[2] in the Raadzaal, the chamber
where the Lower House of the old Transvaal Legislature used to
meet. The Delegates filled the rows of seats and desks arranged
in semicircles facing the Speaker's chair. Among them were
Schalk Burger, who had acted as President after Kruger's flight,
Botha, De Wet, De La Rey, Cronje and Smuts. The remainder
represented every section of the burgher community from "the
carefully dressed man of the world to the rough farmer from
the distant veld with his unkempt beard and haystack head
and shabby ill-fitting clothes".[3] But one seat was conspicuously
empty. On the floor of the House, to one side of the Speaker's

---

[1] *Rand Daily Mail* (Johannesburg),
January 7, 1903.
[2] The Delegation which had approved the terms of the Treaty of
Vereeniging.
[3] Mrs. Chamberlain to her mother,
January 13, 1903.

A N S V A A L

PRETORIA

Elandsfontein

Standerton

SWAZI-
LAND

Volksrust

Charlestown

ER

N A T A L

LADYSMITH
Colenso

AND

INDIAN OCEAN

PIETERMARITZBURG

Inchanga

DURBAN
(Chamberlain landed here
from H.M.S. Good Hope)

CHAMBERLAIN'S JOURNEY
IN
SOUTH AFRICA
December 26th to February 25th, 1903

0   100   200 miles

Chamberlain's Route { by rail
                      by waggon

chair, an ordinary chair stood alone. It was there that Kruger used to sit. As President, the grim old patriarch had no right to speak in the Lower Assembly, but, in a crisis, he would come down to listen to the debates and overawe the Opposition by his presence. In some mysterious way, a rumour had gone round that Chamberlain meant to sit in Kruger's chair. There was never any truth in it; but it was believed by many of the Delegates; and there was a murmur of relief when Chamberlain, flanked by Milner and Lawley, took his seat on the dais where the Raad officials had sat in the past.

The Delegates had assembled to present Chamberlain with a memorial. In this they put forward six main demands:

1. A complete amnesty for the Cape and Natal rebels.
2. Provision for the more efficient teaching of the Dutch language and for some measure of parent's control in the management of the schools.
3. A firmer policy towards the Natives.
4. No war indemnity to be exacted until self-government had been introduced.
5. Permission for former members of the Boer Delegation in Europe to return to South Africa.
6. The return to the Transvaal of the districts of Vryheid and Utrecht annexed to Natal.

These demands were substantially the same as those made by the three Boer Generals, during their visit to London. To have accepted them would have been to reopen the main questions settled at Vereeniging. It is, indeed, difficult to believe that Botha and his colleagues seriously expected Chamberlain to concede in Pretoria what he had refused at the Colonial Office. It seems more likely that they were trying to disarm the criticism of their own extremists, by subjecting them to the same experience which they had themselves endured.

The memorial was introduced, in a skilful speech, by Smuts, "a trim, young-looking man".[1] In terms which seemed to echo Chamberlain's own plea for reconciliation, he began by denying any suggestion that the Boers were reluctant to co-operate with the new Government.

---

[1] Mrs. Chamberlain to her mother, January 13, 1903.

We are here to-day to prove by our presence that that is incorrect ...
The people have come from all parts to show their desire to cooperate.
Our interests are so firmly connected with the country, and the land is
so dear to us that we cannot stand aside but must work together for the
welfare and benefit of the country. It is, however, our desire that this
cooperation should rest upon a proper basis, a basis of confidence and
respect. It has been the curse of South Africa in the past that there has
been so much mutual disrespect, and one of the virtues of the war is
that we can now see each other face to face and that we can press the
hands of each other, as white men, and cooperate on a basis of respect
which has hitherto not existed.[1]

He went on to make an eloquent appeal for total amnesty to
the Cape and Natal rebels.

We do not minimise the crime of these people, but we say the crime is
ours and that the burden should rest upon us. The people in Natal and
the Cape Colony nowhere rose of their own accord, but everywhere, when
we came and encouraged them, they joined us; and therefore I say the
burden rests upon us, not only upon our honour, but also upon our
conscience.

He closed with a moving plea for confidence in the loyalty of
the Boers.

The deep characteristic of the Boer is his loyalty, his loyalty to his
Government; not that loyalty which calls out to the house-tops, or the
loyalty that hangs, but that loyalty which is true till death. We now
come to our new Government and offer them that loyalty, but we ask
them again to think that we have been a free people,—that we have been
the freest people upon earth. We ask them to respect our feelings and our
traditions, to cause justice to be given us. And they will then find out
that there is no portion of the British Empire more loyal than the people
of the Transvaal.

These words were well calculated to appeal to English ears,
but they could not hide the fact that to have accepted the
demands set out in the memorial would have meant to undo
the settlement made at Vereeniging. This Chamberlain was
determined to refuse; not, as his critics have suggested, on
narrow legalistic grounds, but on grounds of political realism.

[1] *Rand Daily Mail*, January 9, 1903.

Looking back, there can be little doubt that he was right. Whatever the merits of each individual case, further concessions, at that time, would have been regarded by the "loyalists" as a breach of faith, and might have been understood by the Boers as yielding to pressure. But the task of refusal is always invidious; and, here, it was made more difficult by the admirable manner and matter of Smuts' speech. For a less practised debater than Chamberlain, this might well have been an encounter between David and Goliath.

Chamberlain prefaced his reply with a few friendly sentences. He deplored his inability to speak Dutch and hoped that the Delegates were beginning to see "that, however bad I may be, I am not quite so black as I have been painted". The ice thus broken, he struck a more ominous note. "You have spoken very frankly to me. That is what I like, and I intend to reciprocate by speaking just as plainly to you."

Only that morning, he had read in the papers the text of Botha's statement, thanking the pro-Boers in Europe for the £100,000 which they had raised in response to the "Appeal to the Civilised World". He began, therefore, by contrasting the eloquence of this message with the silence in which the Boers had received the infinitely greater sums spent by the British Government on their rehabilitation.[1]

I say that never in the history of the world has a conquering nation done so much for those who were so recently their opponents, and I think that, when you gave thanks for £100,000, you might also in your hearts, at any rate, have recognised that we, who have given 150 times as much, are not altogether undeserving of your regard.[2]

This claim wrung from his audience reluctant murmurs of assent.

After this preliminary rebuke, Chamberlain went on to underline the finality of the terms of the Vereeniging Treaty.

There is an impression that, while the Boer leaders are most excellent people at a bargain, they fail to recognise our desire that, when a bargain is once made, it should be stuck to. The terms of the peace at Vereeniging were the subject of long discussions. . . . I do not pretend that they gave

[1] Estimated by Chamberlain at this time as between £10 and £15 million.   [2] *Rand Daily Mail*, January 9, 1903.

to the Boers everything that the Boers desired to have, but, such as they were, they were the best we could offer and they were frankly and loyally accepted; and it is a little too early to try now to go behind, or to go further than the terms which were then conceded. *The terms at Vereeniging are the charter of the Boer people.* You have every right to call upon us to fulfil them in the spirit and in the letter and, if in any respect you think that we have failed or that in the future we do fail in carrying out these terms, bring your complaints to us and they shall be redressed.[1]

Chamberlain turned next to the demand for a total amnesty for the Cape and Natal rebels. It was easy enough to say that their punishment was in strict accordance with the terms of the Treaty, but so purely legalistic an argument was no sufficient answer. Smuts' appeal to honour and conscience could only be parried by a more elemental counter-attack. It ranks amongst the shrewdest blows which Chamberlain ever delivered.

He began by speaking of the generosity with which the rebels had been treated, and the extensive measures of amnesty already granted. Then he led up to his attack.

... You ..., who value a free constitution and free liberties, must feel with me that there is no more serious political offence—I am not speaking of moral offences,—than rebellion against a free government; and now you come to me and you ask me to act, as if I thought this offence, which cuts at the root of all government, were a venial one. I ask you to bear in mind what was your own action. How did you treat your rebels?

He paused and slowly looked round the Raadzaal at the Delegates. Then, the words came with the staccato crack of a pistol:

You shot them. You imprisoned them. You sjamboked them. You fined them.

He paused again and then continued more gently:

I do not say that you were wrong. You were, as you thought then, protecting your own government. I ask you, as reasonable men, to justify us when we try to protect ours. ... I do not wish you to understand that I close the door absolutely to further Amnesty. But it will not come as a result of pressure.

The Delegates winced under this punishment; but the worst was still to come. Dismissing the question of Amnesty, Chamber-

[1] *Rand Daily Mail*, January 9, 1903. (My italics.—J. A.)

lain took up the demand that members of the Boer Delegation in Europe be allowed to return to South Africa. "Each
case", he said, "must be considered on its merits." The men
concerned had declared their loyalty to the British Government.
He had offered them a chance to prove that loyalty, but they
had refused to avail themselves of it. He had asked that they
should disclose the whereabouts of the money sent to Europe by
the Transvaal Republic, or, at least, the account of how this
money had been spent.

We do not want this money for ourselves, we have promised that when
we receive it, we will hand it over to a Committee on which the Boer
leaders shall themselves be placed, and that the whole of the money shall
be spent in relieving the widows, orphans and destitute.

It was a ruthless thrust, degrading to both parties like all
quarrels over money; but it went home. As so often in defeat,
the final disposal of the war-chest was a sore subject among the
Boers. When Chamberlain spoke of using the money for the
relief of widows and orphans, the Boer leaders shifted uneasily,
but from the back benches there were cheers.

This was the unkindest cut; and now Chamberlain prepared
to apply the salve. He could not reverse the annexations of
Vryheid and Utrecht to Natal, but on the subjects of education
and of native policy he was frankly conciliatory. He also
welcomed a suggestion made by Smuts that he should extend
his visit to the districts of the backveld. He closed on a note
of friendship and of hope.

Now let me say how heartily I agree with Mr. Smuts when he said that
we must all stand together, and that you as a people cannot stand aside
in the work of restoration and resettlement. . . . In the centuries long ago
we were kinsfolk, and now, although we have been separated for so long,
the resemblances between us are greater than our differences. . . . I believe, then, that with consideration on both sides, with strict observance
of agreements on both sides, with a readiness to give as well as to take,
before many years are over, probably sooner than any of us now can
anticipate, we shall be a free people under one flag.

The proceedings now came to an end. Chamberlain rose to go;
and, at a signal from Botha, the Delegates gave him a hearty
cheer. Thus, only six months after their annexation, the

conqueror of the Boer Republics left the Raadzaal amid the applause of his former enemies.

Chamberlain's speech made a deep impression on the Boer leaders. It marks their last direct effort to reverse the terms of peace. When Chamberlain had gone, Schalk Burger addressed the assembled Delegates. He told them that they had met a man who was firm and absolutely determined to stand by the terms of the Vereeniging Treaty. "It is no use", he continued, "for us to hold these meetings to ask for more assistance, and to put forward more demands." His advice was to be loyal in spirit as well as in conduct and to abide strictly by the terms of peace. Then they could "watch and see what the British Government is prepared to do for us". The first step had been taken in the transition from passive to active loyalty.

CHAPTER XC

THE JOHANNESBURG CONFERENCE

(January 1903)

CHAMBERLAIN at "Sunnyside"—War Damage Compensation—The Investment Loan—The Transvaal Contribution—Speech at the Wanderers' Ground—The Contribution Agreed—Self-Government and Federation—The Labour Famine—Cresswell's White Labour Plan—Chamberlain, Milner and Chinese Labour—Chamberlain and Johannesburg—He sums up his Impressions of the Transvaal—Milner's Resignation withdrawn—Relations between Chamberlain and Milner.

I

CHAMBERLAIN left Pretoria immediately after the meeting in the Raadzaal. He broke the short train journey at Elandsfontein, where, in a memorable phrase, he described himself as "a missionary of Empire". The same afternoon he reached Johannesburg, or "Joesburg" as the local wits had already rechristened their city. Here, at last, he found time to send a hurried account of his doings to Austen.

CHAMBERLAIN TO AUSTEN

Johannesburg, January 9, 1903.—I have just recd. your two letters . . . and am sending you a few words in reply, taking advantage of what are literally the first moments I have had to myself since I landed in this country. I knew I was not going to have a holiday but even I was not prepared for the tremendous pressure and strain. Six hours sleep and 18 hours work—and such work! Deputations and interviews all day, interspersed with banquets, deputations, and addresses without number. I find that, since I left England, I have already made 23 speeches of sorts —all the time skating on thin ice and in deadly terror lest I should fall through. But I may say at once that we have both kept very well and, although I am certainly getting thinner, I have practically no headache and sleep and eat well.

311

I have only seen extracts from the London papers and do not know, therefore, how my proceedings are regarded at home, although I gather not unfavourably.

As regards opinion here, my tour hitherto has been an unqualified success. I have been supported by a united Press—even the Boer papers being not unfriendly, and my reception by the people has been a continued triumph.

I am well satisfied with the situation as far as the Boers are concerned. Some are still bitter but, I think, not irreconcilable. There is a general consensus of opinion that they will never fight again, and, with good and sympathetic government, they may and I believe they will become really loyal. You will have seen that I had a straight talk to them yesterday which I believe has done good. They seem, by the reports of what passed at their meeting after I left, to have taken my speech very well and to have accepted it as final for the present. . . . If I can get Milner to assent to certain suggestions I have made on the language and education question which involve no sacrifice of principle—I think we may look forward with confidence to a restoration of good feeling. . . .

I had a tremendous reception here yesterday. . . .

Thus far, Chamberlain's progress had been swift and triumphal. The British had acclaimed him with unrestrained enthusiasm. The Boers had been courteous, even friendly. Both had come together to do him honour. As yet, indeed, there had been more "parade" than "business" in the tour. But this was only natural, for he had still been feeling his way among the thorny questions which agitated South African opinion. In private interviews he had shown himself more anxious to learn than to teach. In public speeches he had refused to be drawn on controversial issues. Nevertheless, his broad appeals for reconciliation between Boer and British, and for acceptance by both of the obligations of Empire, had called forth a powerful, if emotional response. Within a fortnight, Chamberlain had transformed the whole political climate of South Africa. He had created an atmosphere in which he might hope to enlist popular support for the policies he was now to hammer out with Milner. The first phase of the tour—the phase of psychological preparation—was over; the time had come for practical decisions.

From Pretoria to Johannesburg is a short journey, but Kruger's capital and the Golden City were worlds apart; then even more than today. Chamberlain had insisted, against Milner, that Pretoria should remain the seat of government; but, for all practical purposes, Johannesburg had become the seat of power. It was there that Milner lived and worked. It was the chief centre of British population in the Transvaal. Above all, it was the centre of the gold industry, upon the prosperity and expansion of which Chamberlain and Milner had founded their hopes of a United British South Africa. It was natural, therefore, that Johannesburg should be the scene of their deliberations.

For the next fortnight, Chamberlain was Milner's guest at "Sunnyside". These were strenuous days even in the bracing climate of Johannesburg, but it was all to some purpose; and after four days of it Mrs. Chamberlain could write:

Joe is very hard at work, but I see signs that he is getting hold of things. Last week he was rather low in his mind but now he is in full swing and sees day-light, I think. . . . The regular routine is that in the morning there are several appointments, at lunch there are generally one or two people whom he wants or is wanted to see, then more deputations and appointments. I invade his room at tea-time and make him come out on the piazza. Then despatches and telegrams have to be written. Every night there is either a big or small party at dinner of the important people and, when that is over, his unfortunate private secretaries are summoned for more work. . . .[1]

II

On landing at Durban, Chamberlain had received a letter from Milner twenty-three foolscap pages long. "This", as its author wrote, "may look formidable, but its real object is to save time." It was to serve as the agenda of what may well be called the Johannesburg Conference. The discussion of this agenda was prolonged over a fortnight, and the consideration of its several items inevitably overlapped with private inter-views and public speeches. Here it will be more convenient to consider them, each under its own head.

[1] Mrs. Chamberlain to her mother, January 13, 1903.

Compensation

By the time Chamberlain had reached South Africa, most of the problems directly created by the war were well on the way to solution. The vast majority of the prisoners of war had been repatriated. All but a very small number of the inmates of the concentration camps had been restored to their homes. Supplies had been distributed on a generous scale, and Milner was confident that there would not be "a single case of starvation and very few even of want".[1] The restrictions of martial law had been lifted. The freedom of the press had been restored; and some of the more obnoxious wartime taxes had been withdrawn. There remained, however, one wartime legacy which threatened to undermine the confidence of both Boer and Briton in their new Government. This was the failure to settle the claims for compensation of those whose property had been damaged by the British Army.

During the war, the military had often commandeered private property for their own use or destroyed it to deny its use to the enemy. These inevitable but arbitrary transactions had sometimes, though not always, been accompanied by the issue of a promise to pay or at least of a receipt. Now, it so happened that the greater part of the property thus commandeered had belonged to those burghers who had taken the oath of neutrality in accordance with Lord Roberts' proclamation. By its terms they had been promised that their property would be protected and that they would be compensated for any damage inflicted upon it. Accordingly, when the war was over, the holders of receipts or promises to pay, and others, who had suffered loss or damage, had come forward to claim compensation. Their rights had been recognised in principle, and special commissions had been set up by the Army to examine and settle each individual claim. But, in practice, the operation of these commissions was slow, inefficient and unjust. Many claims were disallowed on somewhat specious grounds. Others were shelved; and, by the time that Chamberlain reached South Africa, less than a third had been settled.

These proceedings inevitably caused great bitterness, as Chamberlain was soon made aware. His diary, indeed, shows

[1] Milner to Chamberlain, December 26, 1902.

that failure to obtain settlement of compensation claims was
the most common grievance of the many individuals and
deputations that came to see him. More shocking still was the
"evidence . . . incontrovertible of great injustice and breach
of faith by the Military Commissions".[1]

He saw at once that nothing less was at stake than the confidence of South Africa in the good faith of the British Government. This he was determined to maintain at all costs. At
Ladysmith, therefore, before he could even consult with Milner,
he made the following categorical statement:

> I have had good evidence laid before me which goes to show that, in
> some cases, the receipts given by British Officers or officials on behalf of
> their Government have been disallowed. That is an entire misapprehen-
> sion. . . . I say nothing of the kind will be permitted. Those who hold
> these receipts and who can show they are legitimate owners of them and
> who have not . . . acted against us in the field or elsewhere may rely on it
> that the receipt of a British Officer must be always and will be always as
> good as a bank-note.[2]

The injustice of the situation was made plain by a deputation
of National Scouts, who came to see Chamberlain in Johannesburg.[3] Its leaders, Andries Cronje and Piet De Wet, told a
pathetic tale. They had taken the oath of allegiance, and fought
for the British. They had failed, however, to obtain compensation for their damaged property and were now no better off, and
in many cases worse off, than the burghers who had fought
against Britain to the bitter end. These were laughing at them
and saying that they would have done better, if they had also
fought to the last and so shared in the terms of Vereeniging.

By this time, indeed, Chamberlain already regarded the
settlement of the compensation claims as "the most urgent of
all the practical questions with which we have to deal . . .[4]
He and Milner, therefore, sat down to work out a solution. They
started from the assumption that, while the War Office was only
concerned to economise now that the war was won, the Colonial
Office was chiefly interested in bringing about a settlement that

[1] Chamberlain to Onslow, telegram
of December 30, 1902, from Pietermaritzburg.
[2] Speech in Ladysmith Town Hall,
January 2, 1903 (*Johannesburg Star,*

January 3, 1903).
[3] January 14, 1903.
[4] Pretoria, January 6, 1903, speech
in the banqueting hall.

would be fair and swift. They, accordingly, proposed that the War Office should transfer £3,000,000 to the Government of the Transvaal, who would take over the total settlement of the claims. These were estimated at something under £4,000,000; and the Colonial Office undertook to find the difference. This proposal was embodied in a forcible telegram intended for circulation to the Cabinet. It was approved within a week.

In the event, Chamberlain's settlement worked well enough, though it would end by costing not £3,000,000 but £5,000,000.[1] It had, however, an important political advantage. By making possible a generous settlement of the claims of the National Scouts and Hands-Uppers, it left the whole of the Free Grant of £3,000,000, promised at Vereeniging, available to those Boers who had fought to the bitter end. In this way all parties were satisfied.

For these payments and for the substantial sums later advanced to them from the Transvaal revenue, the Boers showed little gratitude. They accepted them as of right. But the gratitude of a people is not always the best test of the wisdom of a policy. The generosity of the British Government averted serious economic distress, in the months immediately after the war, and so removed a fertile source of discontent. It gave the individual Boer a good chance of building up his life again within the framework of the British Empire. As the historian of the South African War has written, "True magnanimity does not always meet with immediate response, but it always has its reward".[2]

III

The Investment Loan

With the settlement of the compensation claims, the way was open for the discussion of more constructive policies. The conception of South Africa's future was Milner's more than Chamberlain's. But something must be said of it here; for, without the backing of a Colonial Secretary of Chamberlain's stature, Milner's policies, already well ahead of their time, would hardly

[1] This £5,000,000 was allocated as follows:

Burgher claims	.	£3,000,000
British & foreign	.	1,700,000
Natives	. .	300,000

[2] L. S. Amery, *"The Times" History of the War in South Africa*, vol. vi. p. 84.

have received the sanction of the British Government. It was not the least of Chamberlain's qualities that he knew how to listen and to learn. To the end of his active life, he would preserve the power of absorbing as well as of expounding ideas.

As Milner saw it, the building of a United South Africa must rest upon three material foundations. First and most important was the expansion of the gold industry. This would attract a growing urban and technical population, chiefly of British stock; and the "overspill" of its wealth, whether flowing directly to the market or siphoned off by taxation, would fertilise all South Africa. Second was the settlement of a British population on the land. This might never be large enough to establish British supremacy on the veld, but it would at least leaven the Boer lump. British settlers, moreover, would tend to improve agricultural methods and so bring down the price of food and with it the cost of living on the Rand. The third foundation of a United South Africa was to be its railway system. Milner meant to extend it in order to open up the country. He also meant to nationalise it, as an easy and certain method of collecting and increasing revenue.

The gold industry might attract the capital necessary to its expansion by the prospects which it offered to the investor. But the plans for land settlement and for the acquisition of the railways would require government expenditure far in excess of the revenues of the Transvaal. For these basic policies, and for the discharge of existing liabilities, Milner needed a loan. Nor could he draw up his plans for reconstruction, until he knew how big that loan would be.

This question of a loan had been under discussion for some time, but the ordinary difficulties of reaching a settlement by correspondence between London and Johannesburg had been aggravated by the repeated objections of the Treasury. Left to the departments, the question might well have dragged on for months, perhaps until Milner's visit to England in the autumn. At "Sunnyside" it was settled in a few days.

On January 12, Chamberlain telegraphed proposing that the British Government should guarantee a £30,000,000 loan, issued at 3 per cent on the security of the revenues of the Transvaal. He urged the importance of striking "while the iron

is hot",[1] and called for the immediate approval of the Prime
Minister and the Chancellor of the Exchequer. This was received
four days later. On the following evening, at a public banquet,
Chamberlain announced the decision as a "unique and unprecedented act on the part of the Imperial Government".[2]

The size of the loan fell short of Milner's hopes. But it was a
beginning, and he looked to the swift expansion of the gold
industry to provide him with a steadily increasing revenue. In
those days, moreover, £35,000,000 was a substantial sum, worth
nearly £100,000,000 of our present money.

IV

The War Contribution

The British Government's decision to guarantee the Investment Loan was conditional upon a second arrangement. This
concerned the payment by the Transvaal Government of a
contribution towards the cost of the war. Chamberlain, as we
have seen, had supported the idea of such a contribution both
in Cabinet and before the House. Now, therefore, that he was in
South Africa, the time had come to put the Transvaal's capacity
to pay to the test.

For Chamberlain the question was one of principle. He held

---

[1] Chamberlain to Onslow, telegram of January 12, 1903.
[2] At the banquet in the Wanderers' Rink, Johannesburg, January 17, 1903.
At Chamberlain's discretion, the figure of the loan was raised from £30,000,000 to
£35,000,000 so as to include the Orange River Colony as well as the Transvaal.
Its final allocation was settled between Chamberlain and Milner as follows:

1. Existing liabilities:
    (*a*) Deficit 1901–1902 .   . £1,500,000
    (*b*) Former debt of South Afri-
        can Republic .   2,500,000
    (*c*) Compensation to loyalists
        in Cape and Natal . 2,000,000
                          ————— £6,000,000
2. Acquisition of existing railways . . 14,000,000
3. Compensation and repatriation:
    (*a*) Advances by way of loan . £3,000,000
    (*b*) Other charges . . 2,000,000
                          ————— 5,000,000
4. New development:
    (*a*) New railways . . £5,000,000
    (*b*) Land settlement . . 3,000,000
    (*c*) Other public works . 2,000,000
                          ————— 10,000,000
                                £35,000,000

Chamberlain to Onslow, telegram, January 22, 1903.

that the gold industry, which would profit most from the war, could and should contribute to its cost. But it was a question of great political importance also. If he could bring back a substantial contribution, the credit of his South African policy would be upheld, especially against those Conservatives who already criticised it as a cause of high taxation. The event, moreover, would strengthen his personal position in the Cabinet and especially his relations with the Chancellor of the Exchequer. He would no longer be the "spendthrift" of the Treasury's morbid imagination, but a large-scale contributor with a special claim on that department's gratitude. To secure the contribution was thus a matter of great moment. It was not, indeed, the chief cause of Chamberlain's journey to South Africa. But, once embarked upon that journey, it undoubtedly became his main practical objective. This was no secret; and, in many minds, the contribution had become the touchstone by which the success of his mission would be judged. It was essential, therefore, that he should not return empty-handed.

There could, of course, be no question of arbitrarily decreeing the size of the contribution or the method of its payment. The Transvaal was only temporarily a Crown Colony, and Chamberlain had wisely laid down that it must be governed with the most scrupulous regard for public opinion. Any other policy, indeed, must have raised the cry of "No taxation without representation" and might well have discredited the Imperial connection. The extent and nature of the contribution would, therefore, have to be agreed with the chief men in the Transvaal, and more especially with the representatives of the great mining interests, upon which the financial burden would fall most heavily.

In this delicate task, Chamberlain required the support of public opinion. The Rand, however, had been thoroughly alarmed by reports in the London press that they would be asked for an astronomic figure; and, indeed, as late as August, Chamberlain had told Alfred Beit, in private conversation, that he expected "as an ultimate contribution to the war, £100,000,000".[1] Nor was the general uneasiness allayed by the insistence with which Chamberlain had dwelt, in all his speeches,

[1] Chamberlain to Milner, telegram of August 5, 1902.

on the Colonies' duty to bear their share of the burden of Empire. The significance of this appeal had not been misunderstood; but it had called forth little response. On the question of contribution, Johannesburg was very much on the defensive.

On arriving in Johannesburg, Chamberlain was driven straight from the station to the great Wanderers' Ground. A crowd over 10,000 strong had come to hear him; but Mr. Lionel Curtis, Milner's observant Town Clerk, noted that its prevalent mood was "a somewhat cynical curiosity" to see how he would handle the question of contribution. Some of the crowd, indeed, may have remembered that the Wanderers' Ground had been the scene of their greatest demonstrations against Kruger's claim to tax the British community without granting it representation.

For Chamberlain this mass meeting was of the utmost importance. Its success or failure would determine the atmosphere in which he would have to conduct his negotiations with the magnates of the Rand. It will be best to quote Mr. Curtis's eyewitness account of what followed:

Chamberlain, as he mounted the platform, had the air of a man whose faculties were concentrated for the moment on a single purpose. The proceedings were opened by the reading of addresses of welcome from the Municipality, the Australian Association, the Birmingham residents and the Jewish community. . . . The crowd listened with attention until the Municipal address had been read; but, as the following addresses could not be heard by so large a concourse, they quickly began to get out of hand. The Jewish address, which came last, was greeted with hoots, and cries of "Sheeny". . . . When at length Chamberlain rose to speak, the hubbub was so great and the crowd so out of control that it seemed doubtful whether even he would obtain a hearing. He stood confronting them, holding in his hand a used envelope on the back of which were scrawled a few words, the only notes he used in the course of his speech.

Through all the uproar, the reed-note of his wonderful voice seemed to penetrate till it reached and silenced the most distant members of his vast audience. In a few minutes the shouting had died away, and his 10,000 auditors were listening with close but still cynical attention.

He began by thanking the deputations *en masse*, devoting some special words to the Birmingham residents only. He then referred briefly

to Milner and dwelt on the magnitude of the task before them all. The
crowd listened, expectant, with scarcely a cheer, till he paused and said
to them "I come to you as a friend". At this the cheers were a little more
general, but still with a certain note of hesitancy. "In the darkest days
of your adversity", he continued, "when you were subject to oppression
and insult, I supported your appeal for the intervention of the Imperial
Government. . . . I have never joined in the calumnies which were levelled
against you." A voice cried out "We know that", and the cheers began
to swell. "You have been accused in Johannesburg of clamouring for war
in order to fill your pockets. (*Laughter.*) That is a false accusation.
(*Cheers.*) It has been shown to be so, for you risked everything in order
to preserve those rights which no self-respecting Briton could surrender
without humiliation. (*Cheers.*) You have been accused of unwillingness
to share in the dangers of the war—a war you have provoked. That
reproach, ladies and gentlemen, has been wiped out by the Imperial
Light Horse at Ladysmith (*cheers*) and by the gallantry of the contingents which you sent from this city to fight (*cheers*) and to die in many
of the fiercest encounters that took place throughout the war (*cheers*)—
and at the same time the courage and cheerfulness with which men, and
women too, driven from their homes, and exposed to want and suffering,
bore their troubles, deserves the recognition of their fellow countrymen
throughout the world. (*Cheers.*) What you did in war, I well believe you
are prepared to do in peace. (*Cheers.*) You will be prepared in peace to
take your part, if ever again the call should be made upon you."

His audience had by now forgotten the critical temper in which they
had come to listen. Ten thousand hearers were literally rocking with
enthusiasm and self-admiration. Mr. Chamberlain waited in silence for
several minutes till the crowd, hoarse with cheering, would allow him to
proceed. At last he began to speak again in a voice which sounded 'like
amber beads falling into a silver bowl'. "But there is still another
calumny in store for you, for it has been said that you are prepared to
repudiate your share of the expenditure which has been incurred in this
war." The crowd gasped a little, and then began to titter, largely in
admiration of the skill with which it had been lured into a trap by his
sheer dexterity. "There are people", continued Chamberlain, "who say
that you, whose interests came first in the matter, while not only the
Motherland but your sister colonies have made sacrifices to maintain
them, that you and you alone in the British Empire, will fail in your

CHAP.
XC.

Æt. 66.

duty." A voice: "Never". "I will wait and see." He stood waiting to hear the response, while a hair might have turned the scale back to cynicism or up to enthusiasm. Suddenly, a man on the edge of the crowd threw his hat in the air and cheered vociferously. The cheer acted like a match dropped into the dry grass of the veld. In a second it was running like fire through the whole crowd. Johannesburg was swept with a blaze of enthusiasm which continued to burn as long as Chamberlain remained there. Those who were watching from the platform felt that, for once in their lives, they had seen the feat of Mark Antony realised in actual life. . . .

Chamberlain was now in a position to open negotiations with the chief men of the Rand. He had a strong case to plead. He appealed to their patriotism and sense of justice. He offered an Imperial guarantee for the Investment Loan as an inducement. Finally, he hinted that, without a contribution, Parliament might refuse to maintain the British garrison in the Transvaal. These powerful arguments admonished the Rand leaders that some contribution must be made. It remained to decide the method of raising it and the amount.

Chamberlain and Milner had originally thought in terms of an annual payment, extending over a number of years and representing an agreed proportion of any surplus in the Transvaal revenues. The advantage of this plan was that each annual instalment, being by definition a proportion of the budget surplus, would always have been within the means of the Colony. Chamberlain had already spoken in this sense to representatives of the mining houses before leaving London.[1] The men on the spot, however, were flatly opposed to such a plan. They argued that a payment, dragging on over several years, would almost certainly be attacked as a tribute and might even be repudiated when self-government was granted. They would much prefer to raise a lump sum, perhaps by loan, and so pay off their whole contribution in two or three years at the most.

How large was this lump sum to be? In the summer of 1901, Chamberlain had provisionally arranged with Milner that the contribution should total some £50,000,000. But he was now

[1] Interview at Colonial Office, October 23, 1902. Present: Mr. Chamberlain, Lord Harris, Mr. Wernher, Mr. Neumann, Mr. Goldman, Mr. Christopherson, Mr. S. Farrer.

faced with a serious dilemma. The more the gold industry expanded, the bigger would be the contribution which the Transvaal could afford. On the other hand, a large contribution would mean high taxation, and this, in turn, would discourage the investor on whom the industry depended for its expansion. Accordingly, though with extreme reluctance, Chamberlain allowed himself to be persuaded that the Transvaal could not raise more than £30,000,000.

The final agreement was reached at a meeting between Chamberlain and a deputation representing the biggest interests on the Rand, including Ecksteins, Barnatos, Consolidated Gold Fields and Neumanns. Their leader, Sir Percy Fitzpatrick, proposed that the contribution of £30,000,000 be raised in the form of a loan secured on the assets of the Transvaal. This loan would be called up in three annual instalments each of £10,000,000. To create the necessary confidence, the mining groups were prepared to guarantee the whole of the first instalment themselves. Chamberlain's reply to this offer is best given in his own words dictated to a secretary immediately after the interview.

I replied thanking them for the spirit they had shown, but saying that I could not help a certain feeling of disappointment as to the amount. My opinion was that, if, when they made the appeal for the intervention of H.M. Government, we had asked for a guarantee of expenditure, they would have promised almost anything.

This they admitted. I said that, although at the present time they could not spare more without a deficit, yet that the future contained infinite possibilities, and the time might come when the present contribution would appear small in comparison to their means.

On the other hand, I felt that the good will, with which the contribution was made, was of more importance than the amount, while finality was of the essence of a satisfactory solution. I felt that, if they offered a larger sum now, involving payments spread over a long term of years, it was quite possible that the political agitators of the future might make it a serious grievance and endeavour to repudiate. Therefore, although the amount was less than I hoped and at one time anticipated, I was prepared to recommend its acceptance as a full and satisfactory settlement of all claims.[1]

[1] Chamberlain's Business Diary, vol. i. p. 34.

The same evening he telegraphed to Onslow at the Colonial Office that he was

forced to the conclusion that it would be better to accept a smaller sum, which would be payable at once and as to which no question could possibly arise in the future, than to fix a much larger maximum, which in practice might never be reached and which even at the present time would undoubtedly be accorded unwillingly.[1]

Chamberlain's agreement with the mining houses was accepted by the Prime Minister and the Chancellor on January 16. Next day, Chamberlain made it public, amid tumultuous applause, at a public banquet in the Wanderers' Rink.

The thorny question of the contribution was thus settled to the satisfaction of both parties. Chamberlain obtained less than he had hoped for; but £30,000,000 was a substantial sum, all the more so as it was to be payable almost at once. Seemingly, he had secured a triumph.

V

Self-government and Federation

The Investment Loan and the Contribution would increase the burden on the Transvaal taxpayer and, more especially, upon the prosperous British community centred on the Rand. Now, there is an inseparable association in the Anglo-Saxon mind between the concepts of taxation and representation. Already, indeed, the mood of frustration, induced by the problems of the aftermath of war, had found an outlet in a fluctuating and half-hearted clamour for self-government. It was, as we have seen, a superficial agitation. The Rand was stirred by no deep discontents; and the wiser heads in the British community were still too frightened of the Boers to feel confident that they could manage their affairs alone. Nor were the Boers themselves at all eager for the grant of a constitution which would have made them accept responsibility for the reconstruction of their devastated country. Botha, indeed, in private conversation with Milner,[2] went so far as to say that "the time has not come for popular government" and that he hoped the Colonial Office would keep power in their own hands.

[1] Chamberlain to Onslow, January 12, 1903.
[2] January 18, 1903, recorded in

Chamberlain's Business Diary, vol. i. p. 124.

Chamberlain was satisfied that the British community was not sufficiently organised nor the Dutch sufficiently reconciled to make the Transvaal safe for self-government. He looked forward to the time when it could be granted; but, meanwhile, his first task was to lay the material foundations of a United South Africa and create its administrative framework. This would require a period of Crown Colony government. But how long could such a system be maintained?

MILNER TO CHAMBERLAIN

December 26, 1902.—. . . It is inevitable that a Crown Government should be unpopular in a community like this, and that its accumulated unpopularity must ultimately lead to a change. The whole question is, at what pace the unpopularity accumulates? If it grows sufficiently slowly to tide the country over the next three or four years, a point may have been reached when popular institutions may be granted with safety. It is therefore of supreme importance—not, indeed, to make Crown Government popular, which is impossible, but to make its unpopularity grow as slowly as possible, or, in other words, not to use up faster than necessary the influence, which is still considerable, of its principal agents.

Obviously the best, and only means, of compassing this end, as well as of promoting that influx of British population which is the only ultimate safeguard of our position in South Africa, is to go ahead as hard as possible, drums beating and colours flying, with the development of the country and its resources, and with the work of building up an administration so competent and so imposing as to enforce an unwilling respect —a system which self-government, when it comes, is not likely altogether to destroy.

Sound and constructive administration was, thus, Chamberlain's immediate aim rather than self-government. He was, nevertheless, convinced that his work would only endure, if it was done with popular consent. This view recurs constantly in his letters to Milner and his instructions to the Colonial Office. He gave public expression to it at Johannesburg, and added a warning that irresponsible agitation for self-government might well cause the British Government to lay down its burden prematurely.

It is our duty and our desire that in every act of legislation we shall follow the trend of that underlying public opinion which should govern the actions of a self-governing colony. After all, you are only in name a Crown colony. If you have not at this moment the full privileges of self-government, they are only withheld in the interests of your own security. I hope the day is not far distant, when you will, like your predecessors, attain to this much coveted position.

But of one thing you may be sure, the Home Government have no interest whatever in delaying that consummation. The fear is all the other way. The fear is lest this Government or lest its successor, tired of the responsibility and the heavy burden of the task, should too hastily relinquish it, before the objects of such government have been fully accomplished. . . . Downing Street is ready to abdicate (*laughter*), but unless I mistake your opinion, you desire, before you ask it to do so, to know what is to follow. . . . You do not desire to put in the hands of your opponents the power to gain by political agitation what they have failed to secure by the sword. You do not desire, I imagine, to reproduce the position which, in a neighbouring colony, has induced the majority of British subjects to pray to be relieved from the privileges which they consider have been abused.[1] And, lastly, Gentlemen, if I interpret your sentiments aright, neither Boer nor Briton, in the Transvaal, would wish to get rid of Downing Street in order to substitute Park Lane (*loud laughter and cheers*). Now, Gentlemen, I take your cheers to mean that you would sooner bear the ills you have than fly to others that you wot not of. . . .[2]

In order to govern and to be seen to govern in accordance with public opinion, Chamberlain and Milner had decided some time before to set up a Legislative Council. Its composition was settled during Chamberlain's visit to Johannesburg. It would be nominated, not elected; but it was not to be a mere puppet. In addition to sixteen official, there were to be fourteen unofficial members. These were to include representatives of the chief interests and communities in the Colony: capital and labour in the mines, the British community in Pretoria, the National Scouts and Hands-Uppers, and even the burghers who had fought to the bitter end.

[1] This is, of course, a reference to the Suspension movement at the Cape.
[2] Speech at banquet in Wanderers'

Rink, reported in *Johannesburg Star*, January 17, 1903.

We have already seen how Chamberlain had at first wished to
include the Boer Generals in the Legislative Council, but had
changed his mind after the issue of their "Appeal to the Civilised
World". This decision was now once more reversed; and Botha,
De La Rey and Smuts were invited to join the Council. After
long parley, however, they declined. They knew that the final
responsibility for the Government would rest with Milner and
the Colonial Office. In these circumstances, they preferred to
keep their hands free to organise their own people into an
effective opposition. Politically, they were right.

A further step towards self-government was the decision to
set up elected municipalities. The constitution of these municipalities was left to the Legislative Council. Chamberlain, as
Secretary of State, had no say in it, but, as a former Lord
Mayor of Birmingham, he received the members of the
existing Johannesburg Town Council and gave them shrewd
advice.[1]

The political reconstruction of the two Colonies was thus
begun on a basis of elected municipalities and of temporarily
nominated legislatures. But the fundamental constitutional
issue was federation. There could, of course, be no federation, as
Chamberlain had repeatedly pointed out, until the two new
Colonies were ready for self-government. Nevertheless, if
federation was the aim, it was important to lay its foundations
while the situation was still fluid. As Milner wrote:

MILNER TO CHAMBERLAIN

December 26, 1902.—. . . Meanwhile, with everybody declaiming
in favour of federation, we are in fact rather drifting away from it.
I will not here consider whether this is for good or evil. All I urge is
that the time has come when we ought to make up our minds. I do
not say to work deliberately for federation or against it, but *in which
direction we are consistently to lean* on all occasions, and occasions are
numerous, when our action can either favour federal tendencies or the
contrary. *To have no policy* or, let me say, *to do nothing* is, in my opinion,
to lean against federation. . . . There are some friends of federation
who, nevertheless, favour inaction. . . . On the other hand there are
those who desire to cling tenaciously to whatever nucleus of common

[1] January 16, Chamberlain's Business Diary.

institutions already exists and would wish to see the Imperial Government exercise its influence to strengthen and multiply them. . . .

From the beginning of the war, and perhaps even before it, Chamberlain had regarded the federation of South Africa under the British Crown as the ultimate aim of his policy. In this he and Milner were at one. They now decided on two practical steps towards it. The first was a decision to set up an "Inter-Colonial Council". This was to be a joint organ of the Transvaal and the Orange River Colony, designed to administer both territories as a single unit for the allotment of the Investment Loan and the maintenance of the Constabulary. It was to be financed from the revenues of the railways. As Chamberlain wrote, it was deliberately intended as "a step towards the union of the two colonies, in anticipation of the ultimate federation of South Africa".[1]

The second step was the decision to summon a Conference of all the South African Colonies. They were to meet, in March, at Bloemfontein to consider the establishment of a customs union, the preparation of a new tariff, and common policies for native administration, the shortage of native labour, alien immigration, and railways.

On most of these questions, Chamberlain was content to be guided by Milner, only restraining him, when the implacable logic of the latter's policies seemed in danger of outrunning the current of public opinion in South Africa or at home. On one issue, however, the Colonial Secretary took a definite initiative. At the Colonial Conference, that summer, the representatives of Cape Colony and of Natal had agreed to recommend that their Governments should grant a tariff preference to British goods. Chamberlain now proposed to Milner that the Transvaal and the Orange River Colony should follow suit. Milner agreed wholeheartedly. In a later chapter we shall discuss the details of their first talk on this subject, preserved by a curious accident. Here, it is enough to quote the bare entry, in Chamberlain's diary, recording the decision at which they arrived.

Preferential Trade.—Lord Milner will undertake that this question shall be raised at the Inter-Colonial Conference which he has invited

---

[1] Chamberlain's Business Diary, vol. i. p. 107, January 15, 1903.

to meet at Bloemfontein. He is inclined to suggest a preference of
25% in favour of the products of the British Empire.[1]

VI

The Labour famine

The problem of finding labour for the mines hung like a
question mark over the future of the Transvaal. It was to
assume such important political proportions that we must treat
of it here in some detail. Chamberlain's and Milner's hopes of
establishing British supremacy in South Africa depended on the
rapid expansion of the gold industry. But the Rand was desperately short of labour. Before the war, the mines had employed
nearly 100,000 Kaffirs. When hostilities came to an end, a
bare 30,000 were back at work; and, by the time Chamberlain
reached Johannesburg, this number had only with difficulty
been increased to some 50,000.

There were several reasons for this labour famine. Many of the
Kaffirs had earned considerable sums during the war and would
not return to work until these had been spent. Others had taken
up more congenial employment on the railways or the farms.
But, in the first instance at least, the mine magnates had chiefly
themselves to blame. In their anxiety to attract more capital in
the London market, they had selected a moment when labour
was naturally scarce to reduce wages by nearly a third. At
Chamberlain's instance, this imprudent policy had been modified
that autumn and for a time the recruitment of labour had
improved. It soon appeared, however, that, whatever the level
of wages, the supply of Kaffir labour available in the Transvaal
was wholly inadequate to the demands of the Rand. Scores of
new companies had been floated since the war; immense sums
of money had been invested; and it was reckoned that the gold
mines would soon require between two and three hundred

---

[1] Chamberlain's Business Diary,
vol. i., January 21. In addition to the
major problems considered above,
Chamberlain and Milner also discussed
a number of important but subsidiary
questions. Among these were Asiatic
immigration and the status of British
Indians in South Africa; the administration of Swaziland; the means of
reducing the cost of living in the new
Colonies; railway and shipping rates;
education; the immigration of women;
and the organisation of the Secret
Service. Decisions were not taken
on all these questions, but their discussion, even when inconclusive,
"saved infinite explanatory correspondence and vexatious delays in the
future" ("*The Times*" *History of the
South African War*, vol. vi. p. 93).

thousand miners;[1] a figure far in excess of the most optimistic estimate of the Transvaal's surplus labour force.

Until the labour strength of the Rand had returned to its pre-war level, the problem could hardly be considered urgent. Nevertheless, it was already engaging the deepest interest of the mining community, as well as of others occupied in agriculture and secondary industries. Many different solutions were advocated. A small but resolute group led by Mr. F. H. P. Creswell, the manager of Village Main Reef, urged the substitution of unskilled white labour for Kaffirs. He had put his idea to the test in his own mine and was convinced that the increased costs of the innovation would soon be balanced by increased output. The scheme had the added political attraction that it would soon double or treble the size of the British population in the Transvaal. But the majority of the mining community opposed it. The magnates were sceptical of the prospects of increased productivity, especially in the lower-grade mines, and feared that higher wages would only curtail profits and so discourage investment. The skilled white workers were also opposed to Creswell's scheme. They were highly paid. They feared further white competition; and they had grown accustomed to the employment of black assistants.

Another school of thought looked to the lands north of the Zambesi as a new source of Kaffir labour. This view was popular; but those, who knew best, doubted whether Central or East Africa could provide any substantial supplies of man-power. The mine magnates, indeed, were coming more and more to believe that the labour shortage could only be overcome by importing coolies from India or China. They had already begun to canvass this solution; but the reactions of the public showed that all sections of Transvaal opinion were resolutely opposed to anything of the kind. Prejudice against Asiatics was very strong, and there was a widespread fear that, whatever the terms of their contracts, the coolies would remain as settlers, as they had done in Natal. At home, there were even stronger objections to this proposal, though on very different grounds. Indentured labour seemed a form of slavery; and the very idea that the

[1] Foreign Office Memorandum prepared for the Cabinet, February 18, 1903.

Government might tolerate such a thing, in a Crown Colony, called forth a number of indignant letters to the newspapers.

Chamberlain discussed the labour question with the representatives of the different interests concerned. Like Milner before him, he inclined at first to Creswell's white labour plan. It seemed the swiftest way to build up a large British population. But he was soon forced to recognise that, whatever its merits, this solution would never be accepted by the largest mining interests and their technicians. He came, moreover, to have doubts about its political desirability. The presence of a growing native population was a fact not to be overlooked; and it was only by participating in the economic life of the country that this population could be integrated into the structure of the new South Africa.

I will go further and I will say even if it were possible [to substitute white for black unskilled labour] I am not clear that it would be desirable. After all, you have got the black man to deal with. He is increasing . . . and unless in some way or other he can be settled in regular industry he will create a danger and a difficulty of the first class. But if we could . . . increase the proportion of white labour that would be a great benefit. . . .[1]

In particular, he stressed the importance of increasing the numbers of skilled as opposed to unskilled white labour. It was with this end in view that he pleaded for the "immediate provision of a High School, efficient in every respect, and of a Scientific University, specialised according to the needs of the great industries of the community . . ."[2]

Chamberlain agreed to support the efforts of the mining interests to recruit labour from north of the Zambesi, but subject to important reservations. He would not allow any recruitment which might hinder the development of Central and East Africa, as, for instance, in the districts adjoining the East African Railway. He also insisted on the need for careful precautions to prevent Central African labour from spreading sleeping sickness and other tropical diseases in the Transvaal. His diary, indeed, shows that he did not expect to find any substantial surplus of man-power in Tropical Africa.

[1] Speech at banquet at Wanderers' Rink, from *The Star*, January 17, 1903.
[2] *Ibid.*

The mining interests shared this pessimism and urged that the only effective solution to the labour problem lay in importing Chinese coolies. But they found him deliberately discouraging. He regarded the proposal as premature, so long as the Kaffir labour force had not returned to its pre-war strength. He also refused to support it, so long as the great majority of South Africans, Dutch and British, remained opposed to it. Only if public opinion changed radically, would he reconsider his view.

Milner, by contrast, already supported the mine-owners on this issue. He suggested, as a first step, that coolie labour should be tried out in Rhodesia, where the labour shortage was even more acute than on the Rand. Chamberlain's refusal was categorical.

Lord Milner would be inclined to favour an experiment in the importation of Chinese labour. . . . I consider that such action would be extremely unpopular and would raise a storm at home. . . . The feeling at present all over South Africa is against such a policy, and, as long as this continues, it is not likely that the Home Government would give its assent.[1]

Nevertheless, a rumour spread that Chamberlain had agreed to the introduction of Chinese labour, in return for the acceptance by the mining interests of his Contribution proposal. The press, at this time, was naturally teeming with rumoured versions of his opinions. Most of them were disregarded. But this one he thought it essential to contradict.

There is one rumour so extravagant that I think it necessary formally to refer to it. . . . Apparently it has been rumoured in London that, outside and beyond this arrangement [the Investment Loan and Contribution], there is an ignoble bargain between my friends who represent the mining interests and myself that, if they consent to be taxed, I, on my part and on behalf of the Imperial Government, will agree and approve of a proposal to introduce Chinese labour. . . . Anything of that sort would be discreditable to the mining interests; it would be almost treasonable on my part, and I destroy it in a sentence.[2]

[1] Chamberlain's Business Diary, p. 131, January 21, 1903; see also the Milner Papers, vol. ii. p. 438. The diary entry is evidently a copy of the previous day's minute.

[2] The Star, January 17, 1903. Report of Chamberlain's speech at the Wanderers' Rink banquet.

Thus far Chamberlain's contribution to the discussion of the labour problem had been chiefly negative. His positive advice to the mining groups was to make the best of the labour locally available. He was not yet convinced that the South African supplies were exhausted and suggested a policy of economic inducements and pressures to attract the Kaffirs back to the mines. Among the inducements proposed were higher wages, the establishment of married quarters in the Kaffir compounds, and the sale of controlled supplies of Kaffir beer. Among the negative pressures were an increase in existing taxation and the introduction of a new tax on polygamy.[1]

Chamberlain was all in favour of inducing the native to work, but he was as strongly opposed to any suggestion of forced labour. One deputation urged the Government to administer the natives with a firmer hand and, in particular, to reintroduce the penalty of flogging for minor offences. At this, all Chamberlain's old hatred of brutality blazed forth:

If a Kaffir commits offences of an outrageous, violent, brutal nature, he is liable to be flogged, and I for one would make no objection to that punishment; but, if it is suggested that a Kaffir must be flogged for a breach of contract etc., then I protest against it as being contrary to the English character, unworthy of the English, and inhuman. Anything like universal flogging, at the mercy of whomsoever might happen to sit upon a bench, is out of the question.[2]

When Chamberlain left Johannesburg, the problem of the labour shortage was still unresolved. In the next few months,

[1] In his speech at the banquet on January 17, Chamberlain advanced the ingenious argument that polygamy was a form of slave labour and that, in discouraging it by taxation, the Government could claim to be serving the cause of freedom. This is an almost classical example of self-interest masquerading as altruism. But it is clear from the context that Chamberlain advanced the thesis in a jesting tone. We cannot acquit him of cynicism, but he was certainly not guilty of hypocrisy.

On March 24, 1903, when he had returned to London, the question of Native Labour was raised in the House of Commons, and Sir William Har-

court made some play with the proposed tax on polygamy. Chamberlain pricked his balloon with the bland statement: "Let me say at once that although the discouragement of polygamy may very fairly be an object, I do not think it has ever been put forward as an important or principal ground for the tax. The Kaffir's wealth", he continued, "is often indicated by the number of his wives, and in taxing polygamy the Transvaal Government would only be emulating Sir William Harcourt's own principle of graduated taxation." (*The Times*, March 25, 1903.)

[2] Chamberlain's Business Diary, vol. ii. p. 249, January 16, 1903.

however, the advocates of Chinese labour made some headway. Milner became wholly converted to the idea; and, at the Bloemfontein Conference in March, it was decided that the introduction of indentured coolies might be "permissible". Chamberlain, however, held fast to the view that the experiment could not be approved, so long as the majority of South African opinion was against it.

CHAMBERLAIN TO MILNER

April 27, 1903.—. . . I am quite prepared to find a change in regard to the importation of Asiatics in South African public opinion. When it comes, and the vast majority are in favour of such policy, I have already told the House of Commons that they cannot prevent its adoption. . . . At present, however, the surface indications are all the other way. The big meeting against Asiatic labour has not been and cannot be at present balanced by any meetings on the other side; and, so long as the mass of the working men are against the importation, there is not the least chance of its being permitted by public opinion here. . . .

But Milner's mind was already made up. In a letter which crossed Chamberlain's quoted above, he wrote, "I believe we shall not be able to get through without some reinforcements from Asia".[1] A few weeks later he would describe Chinese labour as "a temporary bridge, though an absolutely necessary one to the development of South Africa".[2]

By this time, indeed, he was convinced not merely that his policy was right, but that opinion in the Transvaal had come round to it. He was also sure that the commission appointed to investigate the labour situation would report in the same sense. With almost German thoroughness, he had already worked out his plan of campaign and appended it as a postscript to his letter of July 13.

My conjectural time-table is as follows:—

October: Report of Commission establishing inadequacy of African supply.

December: Transvaal Legislature passes Ordinance providing for importation of indentured Asiatics.

January or February: Chinese begin to arrive if they can be got.

[1] Milner to Chamberlain, April 20, 1903.   [2] Milner to Chamberlain, July 13, 1903.

Deeply embroiled in graver issues, Chamberlain thought this excess of zeal. He wrote on the covering docket of Milner's letter:

I fear he is inclined to move too much. I must discuss with him in October. J. C.

But by October many things would have happened.

Chamberlain's handling of the Chinese labour question in many ways resembles his handling of the earlier Suspension crisis at the Cape. On both occasions, he understood the full strength of Milner's arguments; but he would not accept them until events, as well as logic, should force him to do so. He knew that Chinese labour would be unpopular. He was never quite convinced that it was necessary. As he saw it, therefore, it was far better to wait until he had "incontrovertible proof" that South African public opinion insisted upon it. Only then, could he hope to persuade the House of Commons and opinion at home to allow its introduction.

It is impossible to say what Chamberlain would have done had he still been in office when the Labour crisis came to a head in the spring of 1904. We may conjecture, however, that, on purely political grounds, he would still have delayed giving his assent to the import of the Chinese coolies. Despite Milner's insistence, he would have waited until the House of Commons was convinced that the pressure of South African opinion left the Imperial Government no other choice. To the Rand, it would have meant a tiresome delay of a few weeks or at most a few months. But it might have made all the difference to the struggle of the parties at home and to the outcome of momentous issues then at stake between them.

VII

The fortnight which Chamberlain spent in Johannesburg wrought a remarkable change in his attitude towards the city and its people. He had come with a strong prejudice against this money-making, cosmopolitan community and especially against the magnates of the Rand. He left convinced of its inherent soundness and patriotism. It was almost as if he had come to see in Johannesburg the Birmingham of South Africa.

This rapid evolution of ideas shows that, for all his breadth of mind, Chamberlain was still capable of prejudice and susceptible to the influence of environment. It also shows that he could still profit from experience. The whole development throws an interesting light on his character and is worth tracing in his own words and Milner's.

On arriving in the Transvaal, but before setting foot in Johannesburg, Chamberlain had expressed the following view of its inhabitants:

CHAMBERLAIN TO THE KING

Pretoria, January 4, 1903.—. . . I arrived here[1] last night and do not at all like the task before me. The key of the South African situation is here, and the men, who hold it in their hands, are a cosmopolitan population, devoted to money making and their own interests and apparently indifferent to the higher claims of the Empire. They are unmindful of the sacrifices that we have made and clamorous for further benefits; impatient of the slightest restraint and discontented if all their demands are not immediately complied with.

The one hope of the position appears to be the unlimited confidence inspired by Lord Milner. I found this feeling invariably expressed in Natal, and it is evidently as strong here and in the Cape. His early resignation would be a calamity and I must do my best to prevail on him to give up his intention of early retirement.

The strictures in this letter were directed against the magnates of the Rand. But, after his first talks with them, he would pass a more charitable judgment.

CHAMBERLAIN TO AUSTEN

Johannesburg, January 9, 1903.—. . . All the magnates I have hitherto seen are a good sort and compare most favourably with the Park Lane millionaires. The worst of them is that they are timid, as almost all rich men are, Rhodes being a notable exception. If they would go to the working people and consult them freely, they might gain their confidence and lead them to their advantage. I am preaching salvation in public work and find not unwilling listeners. . . .

[1] It is clear from the context, that although the letter was written from Pretoria, "here" means the Transvaal in general.

But this was only the beginning. Ten days later Milner wrote:

MILNER TO LADY EDWARD CECIL

January 18, 1903.—Jo'burg has quietly succeeded in enlightening Joe. He does not say much, but I can see from things he constantly lets slip that he is beginning to realise its potential greatness and thoroughly British character. He will always think about it differently from what he has done, without being in the least aware that he has changed. I chuckle inwardly at this but say nothing. Indeed, it amuses me occasionally to "draw" him by running the place down and see him bridle and begin in his incisive way to take up arms for it. He is a wonderfully vital sexagenarian. Mrs. Chamberlain continues to behave like an absolute angel. . . .[1]

The final stage in the evolution of Chamberlain's ideas on Johannesburg is shown in the following letter to the King. It was written on his last evening at "Sunnyside" and summarises his impressions of the Transvaal as a whole. As such, it is worth quoting in full.

CHAMBERLAIN TO THE KING

January 21, 1903.—I venture, on the eve of my depature from Johannesburg, to submit to Your Majesty the impressions I have formed of the situation in the Transvaal. On the whole they are most favourable and I am convinced that the country is settling down with greater rapidity than I could possibly have anticipated 6 months ago. If the baneful influence of political agitation can be excluded, I believe that the Boers will loyally accept the new order of things and will make excellent subjects.

Emissaries from the Cape Dutch have been here, but at present have had little success with the leaders or the people. The "Predikants" of the Dutch Reformed Church are divided, but the majority are still bitter. If however they find that their religion is respected, I hope that the party of conciliation will grow.

Meanwhile, they are very sore with the "hands-uppers" who surrendered early in the war, and still more with the National Scouts who assisted us. This may not be a bad thing for us in the end, and I have made it perfectly clear that we shall stand by all those who gave us help,

[1] *Milner Papers* (*South Africa*), vol. ii. p. 435.

and that, in the end, it will be seen that those who supported the British will be the gainers. Much dissatisfaction has been caused by the delay in settling claims for compensation and by the extraordinary decisions of some of the Military Commissioners. Now, however, that the Government have agreed to place the matter entirely in the hands of the Civil Administration, we shall be able to hasten matters greatly and to proceed on some definite and consistent lines. I anticipate great good from the decision.

Johannesburg is destined to be the commercial centre of South Africa and must always exercise a powerful political influence.

If the Transvaal is contented and loyal, it will matter very little what Cape Colony does or thinks, as the prevailing sentiment will be dictated from here. *At present the population of the City is essentially British with a large sprinkling from the Australian Colonies and New Zealand. It is keen, intelligent and responsive, with an inclination to be too impatient and critical, but still at bottom intensely loyal and Imperialist.*[1]

They want delicate handling, and Lord Milner has secured their confidence in an extraordinary degree; so that I am more than ever convinced that his stay here, for some time longer, is a matter of the highest importance.

They have behaved extremely well in the question of the War contribution. All classes have cheerfully accepted the obligation to pay their share, and the only doubt has been as to the ability of the Country to find money at the present stage of its development. Unfortunately, the supply of native labour is very short and the mines are only running about half their stamps. The immediate future depends entirely on this question of unskilled labour, and I am afraid it will take time to solve it. The Mine Managers believe that it will be impossible to work the lower grade mines with white labour and, although they may be inclined to exaggerate the difficulties, it is evident that the conditions here are different from anything that prevails in America or the Colonies.

The white man who has been accustomed to the lower forms of manual labour at home, when he arrives here and finds black men doing the work, instantly conceives a dislike to it. It is humiliating to him to work side by side with a Kaffir on equal terms, and he expects the "nigger" to do all the unskilled work. Unfortunately, the "nigger" has

[1] My italics.—J. A. Compare these lines with the views expressed on the same subject in Chamberlain's letter to the King of January 4, printed above, p. 336.

his own views on the subject. He prefers not to work at all, but, if he must work, he chooses any task rather than labour in a mine. There is no large surplus population in South Africa to draw upon, and so the problem is one of infinite difficulty. I have no doubt that it will be overcome in time but I can seen no ground to expect that early "boom" for which the speculators are waiting so impatiently.

An inter-colonial Conference will meet in March to consider this and other subjects of common interest. In the same month the new Legislative Council with nominated representative members will begin its sittings, and shortly afterwards a Town Council will be elected for the City and its suburbs. In this way preparation is being made for free institutions but I am strongly of opinion that full representative Government could not be granted for some time to come without danger.

Thus, in those crowded days in Johannesburg, Chamberlain and Milner laid the foundations of the South African Union. Much would happen before the edifice was completed but here was the beginning. As Chamberlain had said in the peroration with which he brought his last speech in Johannesburg to a close.

You are a great city, but what you are now is nothing to what you may speedily hope to be. Your growth will proceed according to all human foresight in a kind of geometrical progression and you are destined to become a powerful element in that federation of free states shortly to be established, and then to constitute one in the group of free nations gathered round the motherland. I think that is an inspiring thought. The day of small kingdoms with their petty jealousies has passed. The future is with the great empires and there is no greater empire than the British Empire. Am I not justified in the hope that there will be none more united?[1]

VIII

One further consequence of these deliberations must be noted. The reader will recall that, after their sharp disagreement over the Suspension crisis, Milner had expressed his unalterable

---

[1] *The Star*, January 17, 1903. Report of Chamberlain's speech at the banquet in the Wanderers' Rink.

decision to resign. This resignation was now withdrawn. In the course of their talks, Milner came to see that he had over-dramatised their differences and under-estimated how much they were at one.

Chamberlain explained the circumstances of this change of heart in a private letter to Balfour of Burleigh, who was to have been Milner's successor.

CHAMBERLAIN TO BALFOUR OF BURLEIGH

Johannesburg (undated).—As I spoke to you confidentially before leaving about the possibilities of Milner's resignation I think you may be interested to know how I have found matters.

He is determined not to stay on indefinitely for reasons partly personal and partly political. He is sensitive, lonely and misses very much the intellectual environment to which he has been accustomed. Yet he admits the importance of the work, the great opportunity of making an undying reputation as one of our Empire-builders, and he recognises that his resignation at this moment would be almost an act of cowardice. His influence is extraordinary, and his successor will at any time have a hard task to gain in equal measure the confidence of the people.

Things, however, are moving very fast and what would be a National disaster to-day may in a year's time be accepted as natural and necessary.

His present offer is to get through certain pressing work and then take a holiday of which he stands much in need. After a rest he would return with the definite statement that he would only remain 12 months longer.

I am clear that we must accept this as a present settlement, although it is possible that it may be altered if owing to the state of his health he should ask for earlier relief.

If I were in his place I would stop as long as there was work to do, for I find it all intensely interesting and I like the fight with all the strong conflicting elements in this new community which has the making of a great people and with all its faults is essentially British, loyal and patriotic.

I am putting a week's work into every 24 hours, but both my wife and I keep well. . . .

Chamberlain could scarcely convey in this letter the full satisfaction which he felt at Milner's decision. It was after all an intimation to Balfour of Burleigh that his services would no longer be required. His two letters to the King, however, printed above, show how much importance he attached to keeping Milner. He knew that no one else combined the necessary drive, knowledge and authority to fulfil the hopes which he had founded upon the period of Crown Colony rule. If ever a man was indispensable, it was Milner in the aftermath of the Boer war. In persuading him to stay at his post Chamberlain achieved the most enduring single result of the whole South African tour.

For a Minister of the Crown to visit his proconsul's territory is always a delicate undertaking. If they consult over every trifle the personal authority of each will suffer. If they fail to consult enough, their enemies are sure to drive a wedge between them. The difference between Chamberlain and Milner over the Suspension crisis was well known; but neither Boer nor Briton succeeded in shaking their solidarity. As Chamberlain had said in a memorable phrase: "You have confidence in Lord Milner. So have we." [1]

In the course of the tour he paid many tributes to Milner and his work. The finest was in his farewell speech at Cape Town.

I know there are people who talk of Lord Milner, whom perhaps they have never seen, and with whom I am sure they are not personally acquainted, as if he were a hard man, inclined always to arbitrary and even tyrannical methods. There can be no greater travesty of the truth than that—and if these people had seen him, as I have had the privilege of seeing him, at work; if they could have seen his patient and personal attention to every grievance that was brought to his knowledge, his devotion to the details of every branch of his administration—his constant endeavour to find new methods of benefiting every class of the population—his earnest desire to help the needs of those who are in trouble, to restore those who have suffered during the war to their old prosperity—I say, if they could have seen this they would themselves have been the first to be ashamed of their suspicions. [2]

What Milner thought of Chamberlain is best shown by the following extract from one of his letters. It was written some

[1] Speech in the Market Hall, Pretoria, January 6, 1903 (*Rand Daily Mail*, January 7, 1903).

[2] Speech in the Drill Hall, February 24, 1903 (*Cape Times*, February 25, 1903).

months after Chamberlain had left South Africa, but, evidently, with the memory of the visit still fresh in the writer's mind.

MILNER TO LADY EDWARD CECIL

May 16, 1903.—. . . Joe is an extraordinary man—quite absolutely on the big lines. Under a different system, he really might federate the Empire effectively and live in history with the Richelieus. He has most comical weaknesses,—look at his impressionability. The most ridiculous incidents—and people—temporarily affect him, and may cause him to make great mistakes. But the effect is only temporary. In the long run, he is swayed by big permanent ideas, and they are not external to him, but, wherever he gets them from, *they have roots inside him*, which alone can ensure any vitality to a policy or any greatness to its possessor. Still, even Joe can make nothing great with this *system*, and what do you expect of lesser men? . . .[1]

---

[1] *Milner Papers* (*South Africa*), vol. ii. p. 447.

CHAPTER XCI

CHAMBERLAIN ON THE VELD—THE CAMPAIGN IN CAPE COLONY

January–February 1903

CHAMBERLAIN's first Trek—With De La Rey at Lichtenburg—Mafeking and Kimberley—A Tribute to Rhodes—Trekking through the Orange River Colony—Bloemfontein—"A stormy interview"—Milner's Fears—Chamberlain's Campaign in Cape Colony—Its Aims and Strategy—The Appeal to the Bond—A Hostile Reception at Graaff Reinet—De Waal Joins the Train—His Private Talk and Public Statement—At the Paarl—"A prophetic remark"—In Cape Town—Chamberlain and Hofmeyr—Contribution and Amnesty—Hofmeyr's Assurance—Chamberlain Persuades the Progressives to Reciprocate—Hofmeyr's Circular—Progress of Reconciliation—The Bond Refuse a Contribution—Chamberlain's Other Aims Achieved—A Farewell Speech—Verdict on the Tour.

I

CHAMBERLAIN left Johannesburg on January 22. He would fulfil the promise made to the Boer leaders in the Raadzaal and visit the backveld districts of the Transvaal and the Orange River.

His first halt, on the train journey north-west, was at Krugersdorp, where the Boers had been offended by the defacing of a monument commemorating their victory at Majuba. Chamberlain was told of this incident by a Boer farmer, and agreed at once that the monument should be restored. He also suggested that an inscription be added to it in remembrance "of the brave men on both sides who had lost their lives during the present war".[1]

Beyond Krugersdorp, the party stopped for the night at Potchefstroom, the ancient capital of the Transvaal. Potchef-

CHAP.
XCI.

ÆT. 66.

[1] Chamberlain's Business Diary, vol. i. p. 135, January 22, 1903.

stroom had been the scene of fierce encounters in many wars; but
Mrs. Chamberlain described it as

> a quiet little town with a sort of village green in the centre, surrounded
> by oak trees. One of the Dutch inhabitants lent us his house, which over-
> looked this green and had a broad pleasant piazza.[1]

Replying to the inevitable address of welcome, Chamberlain
renewed his plea of reconciliation. But he did not stop at words.
The local authorities seemed to him too cold towards the Boers,
and we find Mrs. Chamberlain writing:

> Every night we were there [i.e. in Potchefstroom], the local magistrate
> . . . entertained us and some of the principal residents, but he did not
> include enough of the Dutch, so, the last day we were there, we had
> Mr. & Mrs. de Jooste [who had lent the house] on our own account and
> a Mr. & Mrs. Karliss who have taken a leading part in the Dutch land
> settlement which has been established there.[2]

In the course of his visit Chamberlain reviewed the garrison
and inspected a Boer settlement, where General Andries Cronje,
one of the leaders of the National Scouts, had settled a number
of his men. These gave Chamberlain an unexpectedly cordial
reception.

> Quantities of Boers met us on the borders of the farm and we drove under
> a triumphal arch of welcome, escorted by a cavalcade. We drove on, and
> then fancy our astonishment, when we found them removing the horses
> and we made the final stage of the drive drawn by Boers, old and young,
> all smiling and waving and enthusiastic. Who could have foreseen that
> such a thing could ever happen to Joe and me?[3]

There were also visits to an experimental British settlement
and to the Kaffir location, where Chamberlain was greeted with
a banner bearing the inscription, "welcome *Moathodi*". This,
being interpreted, means, "He who puts things straight". The
press seized on the name, and it stuck to Chamberlain to the
end of the tour.

At Potchefstroom, the party left the railway and began the
trek across the high veld to Mafeking. Lawley, the Lieutenant-
Governor, and Baden-Powell went with them. The Chamberlains travelled in "a sprung waggon drawn by a grand team of

---

[1] Mrs. Chamberlain to her mother, January 26, 1903.   [2] *Ibid.*   [3] *Ibid.*

grey mules". This team was expected to travel as fast as ten miles an hour; but rainstorms had spoiled the track; and it took the whole day to cover the thirty-two miles to Ventersdorp. As they drew near the *dorp*, British and Boers rode out to meet them and returned caracoling about the waggon. De La Rey awaited them on the village green. He shook hands warmly with Chamberlain, who told the cheering crowd:

I am very glad to see General De La Rey here. I think many of you fought under him, and I congratulate you on having been comrades of so brave and gallant a man. I met your friend General De La Rey in London and now I hope he is my friend also. I hope that we are all friends.[1]

Next day, January 25, the trek was continued for forty-two miles across the veld to Lichtenburg. There was no house in the village judged suitable for Chamberlain, and instead a camp was pitched

in the market square, an open grassy space with fine old weeping willows at one end of it. It was extremely effective as a setting to our little town of tents; for you would be astonished how large a group it takes to provide for the needs of two people, and their modest party.[2]

Lichtenburg was De La Rey's home, and he made himself the party's host.

At Lichtenburg . . . General De La Rey is a great personage, and he and his wife showed us much courtesy. . . . He is, I think, the one of all the leaders who gives one a sense of confidence. He appears straightforward and reasonable in his aims and ideas and he impresses one with the idea that, left to himself, he will be easy to deal with and can be of great assistance to the Government. . . . But time only will show whether he will be able to resist the pressure, which undoubtedly exists in some quarters.

Mrs. De La Rey is a typical Boer in appearance, of the rather French type —short, thick and genial—, and, after talking to her for a couple of hours, I came to the conclusion that she was a woman of much ability. These Boer women, unlike "the world" as their appearance may be, have great power over their men, and it seems to me almost more important in the interests of the country to make friends with them than with the men.

[1] From report in *Transvaal Leader*, January 26, 1903. [2] Mrs. Chamberlain to her mother, February 5, 1903.

If their goodwill can be won, many problems will become easier. Of course most of them feel strongly and cannot be expected to fall upon our necks; but . . . the wonderful thing is to find how ready they all are to talk of the War and how little bitterness they show in speaking of their losses.[1]

In the morning, the whole population gathered under the willow trees in front of De La Rey's house. There the General who had fought to the bitter end and Piet De Wet, the General of the National Scouts, presented Chamberlain with a joint address of welcome.

Chamberlain's reply to this almost entirely Boer audience was among the happiest of the tour.

War is always a bad thing, and the sufferings from this war have been great. In my own country there is hardly a home . . . in which the people are not mourning for the loss of some relative or friend; and, as I have travelled through the country, I have seen the graves of British soldiers in many places and, very often by the side of them, graves of the Boers who fought against them. Now they lie together in peace. Let us who live, live also in peace.

Your sufferings have perhaps been even greater than ours. . . . The war was brought about, as I believe, by misunderstanding between us. You were suspicious of us and we were suspicious of you. Now let us try to trust each other and, if there come among you any mischief makers from outside, tell them to mind their own business. Tell them that you are grown men and that you are able to take care of yourselves. . . . You must not look backwards; you must look forward; you must be a united people; you must not only be united with the British, but you must be united among yourselves. You must not carry forward any of the ill-feeling which may have been caused by the war. Remember that this land wants the services of everyone of its sons.[2]

At first the audience had seemed rather sullen, but the tension relaxed, as Chamberlain spoke, and they cheered loudly at the close. De La Rey then stood up. He had not been expected to speak again that day; but, in a few sentences, he worked the

[1] Mrs. Chamberlain to her mother, February 5, 1903. Mrs. De La Rey must have been a remarkable woman. For some months during the guerilla war she had followed her husband's commando with a bullock waggon, often driving it through the British lines.

[2] Report from the *Diamond Fields Advertiser*, January 27, 1903.

crowd up to the full pitch of enthusiasm. "It is my wish", he said,

that you will serve the new Government with equal honesty and equally faithfully as you served the old Government. . . . I, for myself, want to offer up my personal feelings and everything for the prosperity of South Africa. I do not know how far my new Government trusts me, but that is a matter for the future and our deeds will have to prove it. . . . I hope that, as Mr. Chamberlain is one of the biggest statesmen, it will be his greatest policy to see South Africa restored to its former state of prosperity. I must make you understand that Mr. Chamberlain in Europe is a very strong man. He has the key and he can lock or unlock [*laughter*]; and I trust that, when it is the time, he will do the right thing and come out triumphantly in South Africa.[1]

Here was a beginning of the "Active Loyalty" for which Chamberlain had called.

After the meeting, Chamberlain walked across the green to the schoolhouse, where the *predikants* of the western Transvaal had gathered to meet him. As often happens with a people conquered in war, and especially with a peasant people, the Church had become the rallying-point of the spirit of resistance among the Boers. In their fight to foster Afrikander nationalism, the *predikants* deliberately kept alive ill-feeling against the National Scouts and the "Hands-Uppers". A pastoral letter, issued by the Synod, had exhorted the National Scouts to make public confession of their guilt in fighting for the British; and Chamberlain had even found cases where National Scouts had been refused communion until they "should repent of their sin".

Pressed by Chamberlain, the *predikants* admitted to practising such discrimination. They explained that it was necessary to prevent the rival sections from creating disorder in the Church. Chamberlain rejected this explanation. He had no desire to intervene in religious affairs, but he would not tolerate the persecution of burghers who had fought for the British.

If the church is going to throw all its strength on to the side of the burghers who were not National Scouts and if you make it a condition that these people shall say "we repent of what we have done", the British

---

[1] Report from the *Diamond Fields Advertiser*, January 27, 1903.

Government must take sides too, and we shall take sides with the National Scouts. . . . We do not want to take sides, but we must put forth all the strength we possess to prevent the persecution of those who helped us.[1]

II

From Lichtenburg the trek was continued to Ottoshoop with its vast underground caves, which some have held to be the site of King Solomon's fabulous mines. A day later, the party crossed into Cape Colony. At the border, Chamberlain was welcomed by Governor Hely-Hutchinson, and Prime Minister Sprigg. Together they returned amid cheering crowds to Mafeking.

. . . As we drove in, General Baden-Powell pointed out the various lines of the investment forces and the lines of defence. A triumphal arch, gay with flags, was erected, and all the streets were full of bunting and decorations. . . . The enthusiasm was unbounded when the crowd caught sight of Joe. Even the "tommies" could hardly repress their desire to join in the acclamations. . . . Mafeking is not a pretty town but a halo still rests upon it.[2]

Mafeking was buzzing with resentment against the Bond-controlled Government in Cape Town. Its citizens, almost aggressively loyal, had been whole-hearted supporters of the Suspensionist Movement. Now that Suspension had been dropped, they favoured annexation to the Transvaal instead. This, at least, would bring them under Crown Colony rule. The day before Chamberlain's arrival, the same crowds, which were to cheer him so enthusiastically, had given Sprigg a most chilling welcome. Several leading citizens had refused to shake hands with him, and a banner inscribed with the words "We Want to be Annexed" had been hoisted in front of his window.

A petition in favour of annexation was duly presented to Chamberlain. He heard the deputation sympathetically but declined to intervene. They had self-government, and the matter was one to be settled locally by majority decision. As he would say, a few days later, to a similar deputation at Kimber-

[1] Chamberlain's Business Diary, vol. i. pp. 149-155, January 26, 1903.   [2] Mrs. Chamberlain to her mother, February 5, 1903.

ley: "It is like marriage. You take self-government for better or for worse." [1]

At Mafeking Chamberlain attended a great *Indaba* of Bechuana chiefs. Among them were his old friends, Khama, Sebele and Bathoen, who had come to London to plead for the Queen's protection in the anxious months before the Jameson Raid, when Rhodes had sought to annex the whole of Bechuana-land.[2] Tribal matters were discussed at length; and Chamberlain then addressed the assembly in a traditional strain:

I recognise that the Baralongs have been loyal to the King and that they have done good service against the King's enemies. They have been friends of the English; and the English do not forget friends.[3]

As Chamberlain left the *Indaba*, the Chiefs shouted after him the traditional Bechuana greeting, "Pula! Pula!"—"May you have rain!"

Their wish was only too speedily fulfilled. Chamberlain was due to make the chief speech of his visit at an open-air meeting that same evening. It was delivered in a heavy downpour. Mafeking's appreciation of it must have been drowned by the rain, but the printed word, next day, caught the imagination of the whole Empire.

Now the great war is over, we have peace—for which God be thanked—; and we hope it will be an enduring peace. I believe, and I say it in no spirit of boasting, . . . that there is no other nation on the face of the earth that could have accomplished what we had to do. We have shown in this war the strength and the power of the British Empire. We have done more. We have shown its cohesion and its union. We have tested and proved British brotherhood . . . and, for the first time in our history, men of the British race have poured in from all quarters to join with the Motherland in her time of trial and stress. They joined to prove that blood is thicker than water. . . . Let the spectacle speak for itself. We are bound together by threads which to the unobservant man may seem as light as a gossamer web; but let an enemy try to break through and he will find them strong as tempered steel.[4]

[1] Chamberlain's Business Diary, vol. i. p. 190, January 30, 1903.
[2] See Vol. III. p. 40 of the present work.
[3] *Diamond Fields Advertiser*, January 29, 1903.
[4] *Ibid.*

Chamberlain left Mafeking on January 29, and arrived the same evening in Kimberley. The welcome of the Diamond City was, if possible, even more enthusiastic than Mafeking's.

We arrived after a long day of thirteen hours in the train, and found the station crowded with people, many of them in evening dress. Greenery and flags and arches began on the platform and extended to the streets, where a dense crowd raised cheer upon cheer. We were driven in an open carriage with four white horses . . . and, with a splendid escort of Cape Police, accompanied by torch-bearers—running, cheering, jumping about us—we passed down the gaily decorated and illuminated streets, amid crowds which seemed to spring out of the ground. It was a most animated scene and truly a surprise, for, though everywhere there has been enthusiasm, the preparations here were on a larger scale than usual and we were much pleased. . . .

We stopped at the Sanatorium, a sort of hotel built by the De Beers Company. It was here that Julia MacGuire, Mr. Rhodes, and his party were during the siege.[1]

Next morning, there was a presentation of diamonds to Mrs. Chamberlain, the inevitable deputations and addresses of welcome, and a visit to de Beers' diamond mines. At a banquet in the evening, Chamberlain paid a tribute to the memory of Rhodes. It is not among the best examples of his oratory—he never had Asquith's gift for paying tributes; but we quote it here, as an epilogue to the tangled story of his relations with the great Empire-builder.

It would be ungrateful of us to forget the man who sleeps now in the Matoppo hills and whose name will always be identified with this town. . . . My personal acquaintance with Mr. Rhodes was a very slight one. I do not think I had more than, perhaps, half a dozen conversations with him from first to last, but I can speak of him therefore impartially. . . . He was not infallible, he made mistakes which at this time I do not care to dwell upon, but he was a great Englishman. There was nothing mean or petty about him. He had great ideas. He was careless of many of those things which attract the ordinary man. Careless of those things in the way of luxury and the pleasures which wealth can purchase. But he was ambitious of power, ambitious of power because he believed that he

[1] Mrs. Chamberlain to her mother, February 12, 1903.

could use it for the benefit of South Africa and for the advantage of the Empire. Mr. Rhodes gave a new state to the Empire and he has imprinted upon South Africa his own large conception of its future destiny . . . the union of South Africa in one great free state under the British flag. That was the desire of his life.

From Kimberley began a second trek through the Orange River Colony to Bloemfontein. The party travelled once again by waggon, this time drawn by horses, and, despite violent dust storms, followed the broken trail across the veld until sunset. Every now and then their way led past lonely farmsteads, ruined by war.

> We stopped [wrote Mrs. Chamberlain] at almost every farm we passed and had a few words with the farmer and his wife. Everywhere we met with hospitality and, even when at first they seemed a little glum, we always parted the best of friends.[1]

A whole day was spent at Paardeberg, where the battlefield was still strewn with relics of the fight. Chamberlain climbed the knoll known as Kitchener's Kop, spending some hours there with an officer who had taken part in the battle and could explain the operations to him. Next day, they trekked on across almost wholly uninhabited country to the isolated farmstead of Abraham's Kraal in the fertile valley of the Modder River. On the evening of February 3 they reached the capital of the Orange River Colony.

> The entrance into Bloemfontein was quite unlike any we have had in the way of welcome. Nearly all the white population, Boer as well as Briton, came out to Spitz Kop to meet us, four miles from the town. . . . We knew that some were sure to come, but were entirely taken by surprise when we saw the vast concourse of vehicles of every kind and description—from bicycles and cape carts to landaus and victorias—while ladies, men and boys, by the hundred, were mounted on horses and ponies. When we reached Spitz Kop, we alighted and were received by the Mayor and Mayoress, and the inevitable bouquet was given to me. Then we got back into the carriage again, and our six horses were quite frisky, in spite of the forty miles they had travelled, when they found themselves surrounded by all this great cavalcade, which spread itself

[1] Mrs. Chamberlain to her mother, February 12, 1903.

out over the veld and escorted us into the town. The sun was nearly setting, and it was extraordinarily picturesque to see the company driving
and riding around us. . . .[1]

That night they slept in the Governor's house, once the
official residence of President Steyn.

III

Bloemfontein's welcome was remarkable, when it is remembered that this was the capital of a conquered state, and that
Chamberlain was its conqueror. But the Orange River Colony
suffered from few of the problems which beset the Transvaal,
and from none of them with the same acuteness. It was an
almost entirely agricultural country. Farm labour, indeed, was
short; but, with the confidence inspired by British administration, land values had risen steeply; and the farmers, despite their
war losses, were growing rich. There was, besides, a tradition of
good neighbourship between the Dutch and the British of the
Orange River, such as had never existed between the dourer
descendants of the *Voortrekkers* and the pushful *Rooineks* of the
gold-fields. This tradition, the effect no doubt of more equal
circumstances, dated from the days of President Brand, "that
good and great man", as Chamberlain called him, "whose
character, whose wisdom and whose liberality secured for him
the admiration and esteem of every Englishman as much as of
his own compatriots".[2]

Relations might be cordial between British and Dutch; but
the Dutch themselves were bitterly divided. Of the two republics,
the Orange Free State had been the more reluctant to enter the
struggle; but once engaged, its leaders, Steyn and De Wet, had
proved the most uncompromising of all the burghers. Their
followers were now divided into a moderate and an extremist
section; and these, in turn, were sundered by feuds of varying
bitterness from the burghers who had joined the National
Scouts under De Wet's own brother, Piet De Wet. Chamberlain
had, therefore, to receive three separate deputations, each
claiming to represent a majority of Dutch opinion in the Colony.

[1] Mrs. Chamberlain to her mother,
February 12, 1903.
[2] Speech in reply to an address of
welcome (*Bloemfontein Post*, February
5, 1903).

CHAMBERLAIN TALKING TO GENERAL PIET DE WET
AT LICHTENBURG

The deputations from the National Scouts and from the more moderate section of burghers came and were met in the most friendly spirit. But the petition presented by the extremists led to a "stormy interview".[1] It was under twelve heads. Of these, three alleged violations of the peace terms by the British Government; four repeated grievances already settled; while the remainder related to matters altogether outside the terms of peace. Chamberlain was incensed by this document, and particularly by the charges of violating the terms of peace, which, in his view, reflected on the honour of the British Government.

He received the deputation in the ballroom at Government House.[2] It was led by De Wet, with General Hertzog as chief spokesman. De Wet had come prepared with a traditional speech of welcome; but, before he could deliver it or even introduce his colleagues, Chamberlain rounded on the deputation. In cold but scathing terms he tore the contentions of their memorial to shreds and sternly rebuked them for its irresponsibility and for their discourtesy to him as their guest. Old De Wet sulked in silence; but Hertzog, trusting to his lawyer's skill, tried to trap Chamberlain in legalistic argument. The dialogue that followed was bitter and prolonged. One exchange gives its whole tone. Hertzog had sought to draw a distinction between the intentions of the Colonial Secretary and the actions of the officials on the spot.

GEN. HERTZOG: "We cannot expect that you will remain with us for ever to attend to these points."

CHAMBERLAIN: "The British Government remains for ever."[3]

The best description of this encounter comes from Mrs. Chamberlain. The reader may suspect her of a natural partiality, but the verbatim transcript of the interview, lying before the author, fully bears out her account.

. . . The deputations were extremely interesting, and I stowed myself away in a corner of the Ball-room with Lord Milner (who came to camp there) to listen to them. . . . The one of chief interest was that in which General Christian De Wet took part. The Address was framed in the

---

[1] *The Friend*, February 7, 1903.
[2] February 6, 1903.
[3] "Report of the proceedings at a meeting held in Government House,

Bloemfontein, at 11 A.M. on February 6, 1903, between the Rt. Hon. Joseph Chamberlain and certain ex-burghers of the Orange Free State."

most insolent language, bringing three distinct charges of violation of the terms of peace. This naturally roused Joe's indignation, and he decided to read them a lesson. Their spokesman, one Dr. Hertzog, a Hollander and lawyer of doubtful reputation, found that he had more than met his match. For two and a half hours a most animated discussion took place, and we sat in breathless interest. Dr. Hertzog always seeking to confuse the issue and deliberately avoiding any direct answer; and Joe bringing him up to a short corner, and even refusing to hear him unless he would give a direct answer. Meanwhile, it was interesting and instructive to watch the faces of the Boers, many of whom obviously lost faith in their leader, who was rolled over and flattened out again and again by the hard logic of the Colonial Secretary; but he still persisted, in a way that lost him the sympathy of his friends. It was a hard trial of patience and brain power, but the result was eminently satisfactory, for, when it was over, many of the most prominent men present either came to see the Lieut.-Governor, or wrote, repudiating the terms of the Address and excusing themselves for having signed such a document, which they declared had been sprung upon them at the last moment and they did not know what it contained, while they were entirely satisfied with Joe's assurances as to the future. It is rumoured that the document in question was really framed in Cape Town by the Afrikander Bond and was foisted upon the Boers of the Orange River Colony.[1]

Worsted in the interview and abandoned by many of their own number, the extremists sought to turn the tables by giving a garbled account of the proceedings to the press. This was a most improper course, since the interview was supposedly private. It was also most imprudent. Had its authors waited till Chamberlain had left Bloemfontein the trick might have had at least a local success. As it was, they gave him an unexpected opportunity both of rebuking them publicly for the substance of their petition and of discrediting them for their breach of confidence. It was an opportunity which he did not neglect. Years later, when one of those who had been present recalled the interview and Hertzog's part in it, Chamberlain said, "I mistrusted him from that moment, but I thought very little of his ability."[2]

[1] Mrs. Chamberlain to her mother February 12, 1903.
[2] From the contemporary note of a conversation with Chamberlain at Prince's Gardens, on July 16, 1911, made by Sir Harry Wilson.

Milner had rejoined Chamberlain at Bloemfontein; and the CHAP.
intervals between deputations and official functions were filled XCI.
with further talks between them. These, as Chamberlain's diary ÆT. 66.
shows, ranged over the whole field of South African affairs, from
the great constitutional goal of Federation to the behaviour of
a local magistrate who had scandalised his community by
attending a fancy dress ball dressed, or rather disguised, as a
Kaffir. The last day in Bloemfontein was entirely devoted to
"finishing up things with Lord Milner though, with all they
were both doing up to the last, they were bemoaning that they
could not get enough time together".[1]

Chamberlain made two public speeches in Bloemfontein.
The first is of some interest for the light it throws on his political
philosophy. One passage expresses, in the simplest terms, his
conception of the relations between Colonial Government and
capitalist enterprise. It is an almost classical statement of the
enlightened imperialism of his time.

You want railways and irrigation. But railways and irrigation mean
money and . . . the country by itself, whatever may be its general conditions, cannot find millions and tens of millions. For this you want new
capital to pour into the country, and capital is the greatest coward in the
world. It is always timid and, unless it has confidence in your country
and your institutions, it will not flow here for the improvements so much
desired. And so . . . you want a strong, energetic and progressive government, which has the confidence of the whole people, which must work
hand in hand with them for their benefit.

A second passage went still deeper.

Man does not live by bread alone. Material prosperity is the chief
thing, but it is not altogether sufficient, if it only exists . . . side by side
with political conditions so narrow as to place a large section of the
population in a position of humiliating inferiority under a government
conducted with an irritating opposition to one part of the population.[2]

Here in a sentence is both the expression and the qualification
of what has so often been called Chamberlain's materialism.

[1] Mrs. Chamberlain to her mother,   address of welcome, February 5, 1903
February 12, 1903.   (*Bloemfontein Post*, February 5, 1903).
[2] Speech delivered in reply to an

The second speech was his last in the new Colonies; and, in parts of it, he touched the heights.

. . . The object of my mission has been accomplished beyond my expectations. I came here to learn, and I have learned much. It is not so much that I have gathered new facts . . . but I have now had the advantage of seeing them from a new standpoint. . . . The other day, when we were out upon the veld and in the calm beauty of a summer night, we looked up into the deep blue of your African sky and saw the glorious constellations that studded the heavens. We recognised some of our old favourites, but, in this pure and clearly-defined atmosphere, and in the altered position which they assumed in this Southern hemisphere, they took upon themselves an appearance with which we were not familiar. And so it is with your South African questions. They are the same questions as those with which we have been familiar for a long time at home, but somehow or another, in the atmosphere of London they appear to be different from what they are in the atmosphere of South Africa (*cheers*). . . .

Having admitted that he had learnt much from his visit, he went on to express the hope that the new Colonies had also learned something from him. Then came one of his most brilliant aphorisms on the secret of constitutional government.

. . . Everything depends, in administration and in high politics, upon the extent to which those who govern and those who are governed are able, to some extent at any rate, to put themselves in each other's places. . . .

In a brilliant descriptive passage he looked back on his journey through the former republics.

. . . My visit to these Colonies, measured by days, has been a short one. My time has been well occupied, and my visit has combined an almost infinite variety and many phases of your local life. I have seen the strenuous, I might almost call it the feverish activity, of a great commercial and industrial centre like Johannesburg. I have seen the steadier and slower, but still deep, current of political and social life which runs in centres like these old capitals of Bloemfontein and Pretoria; capitals where the national characteristics and the old traditions of administration are still preserved, and where the old life moves slowly after the new. I have visited a country town such as Potchefstroom, the agricultural

villages of Ventersdorp and Lichtenburg; and I have seen something of   CHAP.
the mystery and the beauty of the solitude of the illimitable veld. I have   XCI.
seen all these things, and they have left pictures on my mind which will   ÆT. 66.
never be effaced. I have had interviews by the hundred, and deputations
by the score. . . .

Recalling the subject-matter of these interviews he plunged
for the next half-hour into practical problems. With the peroration he returned almost to the level of the opening passages.

. . . Let us hope we shall hear no more of the war (*cheers*); that a new
chapter will open in the history of South Africa, a chapter of permanent
peace and prosperity (*cheers*).

Here, surely, that chapter may begin under the happiest auguries. All
your traditions in the Orange River Colony are favourable to union and
to concord. You had, before the war and for many years, a pure, an
efficient, and, on the whole, a liberal Administration (*cheers*).

Let us go back; let us return to the spirit of those older times, to the
happier records of the Administration of President Brand (*cheers*). . . .
You will find in the future no substantial change, no unwelcome innovation. Things will proceed a little faster—I hope they will (*laughter*). I
hope that in the general movement . . . you will share in the more rapid
development of this rich country, but that all you consider most worthy
of preservation in your laws, in your religion, in your administration, in
your customs, those will be carefully safeguarded.

. . . I appeal from this platform to the population of the two Colonies
to help us and your present rulers—but not your tyrants, your friends
(*cheers*)—I call upon you to help us to quench the embers of a strife that
might never have arisen, and which now is happily over. And, if you do
this, it will not be long before you will be again a free State and, at the
same time, a member of the greatest Empire. . . . It is with the prayer
that this great consummation may be speedily effected that I now bid
you farewell. . . .

That night Milner wrote in his diary: "One of the most
successful speeches he has made", and added all too laconically,
"we got home before 12, but sat up for some time talking. Mr.
Chamberlain was interesting on the subject of oratory."[1]

Thus far Milner's hand had only been strengthened by the
tour. But now, Chamberlain was leaving for Cape Colony; and

[1] *Milner Papers* (*South Africa*), vol. ii. p. 441.

Cape politics were the one important subject on which the two men were still sharply divided. Next day, Milner would write:

The Chamberlains have left after a triumphant procession through both the new colonies. They reach the Cape to-night where may good Angels protect them from being beguiled. . . . They will need the whole heavenly host![1]

Certainly the last labour of the tour would be the hardest.

IV

The guiding aims of Chamberlain's mission had been to reconcile Dutch with British and to obtain from each Colony some contribution to the financial burden of Empire. These had nowhere been easy to attain, but, in their pursuit, Chamberlain had, thus far, enjoyed solid advantages. He had played his hand, such as it was, from strength. In Natal, British supremacy was unchallenged; the population was thoroughly loyal; and the Colonial Government had been eager to prove its goodwill. In the Transvaal and the Orange River Colony, Chamberlain had been in conquered territory, administered by his nominees in a spirit even more Imperialist, if that were possible, than his own. The power of the Boers had been broken, and his appeal to them for reconciliation had come with all the aura of a conqueror's magnanimity to a fallen foe. By the same token, his invitation to the Rand magnates to contribute to the cost of the victory had been made irresistible by the knowledge that their present safety and their future prospects were in his hands.

At the Cape, Chamberlain enjoyed no such advantages. The Sprigg Ministry, though elected on the Progressive vote, had become wholly dependent for its parliamentary majority upon the Bond. By an irony, rare even in history, the same events which had extinguished the Boer republics had brought the great Dutch party to power in Cape Colony. The leaders of the Bond pursued a constant aim. Their hopes of an independent Dutch South Africa might be dimmed; but they were determined, whether within the British Empire or outside it, to maintain the supremacy of their nation. They regarded themselves as

[1] Milner to Lady Edward Cecil, February 9, 1903. Quoted from *Milner Papers* (*South Africa*), vol. ii. p. 442.

the trustees of Afrikanderdom, and, recognising that they were
economically the more backward of the two communities,
sought to preserve their identity by deliberately inflaming the
racial issue. Too prudent, as yet, to come far out into the open,
they pursued more insidious tactics. Thanks to their control of
Parliament, their views and sympathies presently permeated
the administration. In a hundred different ways they practised
a deliberate policy of discrimination—in those districts where
they were strong—against the British and, above all, against the
loyal Dutch. Where there were jobs to be given, compensation
to be paid or permits to be granted, the Bondsman, whatever his
war record, seemed all too often to be preferred to the loyalist.
Moreover, to the ill-feeling engendered by unequal treatment
was added the galling slur of the social boycott. The Progressives, of course, made the most of such incidents; but, after
making due allowance for exaggeration, there is still no doubt
that, where the influence of the Bond prevailed, loyalty was at
a discount.

Under such conditions, Chamberlain could rely on nothing
but his personal influence. He could expect no support from the
Cape Government; for the Government was the creature of the
Bond. Nor could the genuine Progressives muster a majority.
It was to the Bond, therefore, and to the Bond alone that he
must look, if he was to obtain from this visit either a contribution or any advance towards reconciliation. A lesser man, or
a more prudent, might well have been daunted by so dark a
prospect. It would have been easy enough to have disclaimed
responsibility for the affairs of a self-governing colony and
passed through the Cape behind a protecting smoke-screen
of platitude. But this could never have been Chamberlain's
way.

On entering the Cape he set three practical aims before
himself. The first was to bring to an end the period of concealed Bond rule through the Sprigg Government. He was
determined to prevent Sprigg from postponing elections any
longer or from passing any further controversial legislation.
Elections would clear the air whatever their outcome. Should
the Progressives win, British supremacy would seem assured.
If the Bond, then at least its leaders would have to come into

the open and accept responsibility for its policies, instead of governing irresponsibly through Sprigg.

His second aim was to affect at least a show of reconciliation between Dutch and English. He could not hope, he did not even wish, to suspend the strife of parties altogether. His purpose was to divert it from the purely racial issue. One means to this end, which he would for a time consider, was a full merger—not a coalition as some authors have stated—of the Bond with the English moderates or "mugwumps", as their opponents called them. Milner regarded such a scheme as impracticable, and, as it proved, he was right; but it would have had the merit of bridging the gap between Dutch and British.

His third aim was contingent upon his second. If he succeeded in bringing the Bond to make a show of reconciliation and loyalty, he could then put their sincerity to the test by asking them to support a contribution.

In the difficult game that faced him at the Cape, Chamberlain had only one strong card. His attitude over the Suspension crisis had given him great authority with moderate opinion. This meant that the Bond could only quarrel with him at the risk of alienating the moderate vote; and elections were near. There was, besides, just a chance that the Bond leaders might be prepared to make substantial concessions in order to secure an amnesty for the rebels.

V

Chamberlain's journey through the Cape was, in effect, a political campaign. We have already discussed its strategic objectives. We must now consider its tactical conduct. The first step was to establish himself as the champion of "loyalist" rights. In this way, he would throw the Bond on to the defensive and rally the Progressives behind him. This would offer by far the strongest bargaining position.

Leaving Bloemfontein on February 9, Chamberlain arrived next morning at Grahamstown, "the City of the Settlers". Grahamstown was a centre of "loyalism" and offered an excellent platform for an opening attack upon the Bond:

There is one thing in this Colony which is patent to all men, and that is that, after a century of British Government, there is still a considerable section of the population which is entirely unsympathetic. Now I ask myself, what is the reason of that. It cannot be the fault of the institutions . . . there is nothing in the laws, there is nothing in the administration to account for the discontent. Their religion is respected; their language has equal rights . . . their education is all that they themselves have asked for; and yet there exists, even to this day, a barrier which it seems almost impossible to remove. . . . As far as I have studied this question—and Heaven knows I have given it many anxious hours—, I believe that this unfortunate, this unhappy result . . . is all due to a propaganda which may have been . . . honestly conducted, but which, in my opinion, has been mischievous in its results and mistaken in its objects. The object has been to exalt racial differences; the result has been to put Dutch and English in this country into opposition, which is quite unnecessary. . . . My object . . . is to secure in this Colony the fusion of races, to make the two peoples into one nation. . . . If I had my way, I would know nothing in this country of Dutch or English. I would hardly use the words. . . . Good citizenship should be the test of everything in South Africa.[1]

He underlined his argument by a brief account of the progress of reconciliation in the former republics. Was the Premier Colony alone to lag behind?

Are you going to be the only colony which is divided against itself, are you, while union is within your grasp, and is, in my opinion, certain to be attained in these new colonies, in which only a few months ago the red flag of war was waving, . . . are you going, instead of following their good example, to stand aside and still have these petty local quarrels and . . . to continue these miserable racial animosities?[2]

Then as "a poor down-trodden taxpayer of the United Kingdom, paying double Income Tax",[3] he spoke of the Cape's Imperial obligation. He reminded his audience that, while theirs was the only Colony which had made a profit out of the war, their contribution of £5000 to the Royal Navy was too small to keep the cruiser *Good Hope* in commission even for six months. He made no definite proposal for a contribution but his meaning was clear enough.

We have a mission, a work in the world. We were not given this Empire for nothing. If we do not discharge it, well, the Empire will fall

[1] Grocott's *Penny Mail*, February 11, 1903.   [2] *Ibid.*   [3] *Ibid.*

to pieces . . . like the great empires of the past. . . . Our World-Wide
Dominion . . . must be based on a community of sacrifice.[1]

The speech was vigorously attacked in the Bond press, while
the Progressives whooped for joy. This was indeed what
Chamberlain had intended. The opening manœuvre had been
successfully accomplished. The next stage was to expose the
Sprigg Ministry's dependence on the Bond and so free his hands
for direct negotiations with that party. Port Elizabeth provided
the platform from which he developed this second phase of his
attack.

What . . . is the situation here in Cape Colony? If we were not dealing
with a very serious question, I should say that, as it presents itself to me,
it is a subject for a comic opera. Here are you, a people that for a generation have enjoyed self-government and all the blessings which that is
supposed to confer. It is understood by most of the Anglo-Saxon races
that self-government is the panacea for all . . . evils. . . . That is the
theory; but here we have found a large section of the population engaged
in a sanguinary rebellion against their own institutions which, by virtue
of their numerical majority, they have practically dominated. . . . But
that is not all. . . . We have Constitutional Government and, under Constitutional Government, we have the Ministry which is placed in power
by a majority of the representatives of the people (no, no). Here you have
the curious and anomalous fact. By some stroke of fate the existing
ministry has been deprived of the support of all its friends, who put them
in power, and enjoys the confidence of those who previously were its
opponents. Yes, but that does not conclude the extraordinary situation
with which I am brought face to face (laughter). Here you have a parliament . . . elected by Constituents, 10,000 of whom have since been dis-
franchised. I am not going to comment (laughter). I merely state them to
you as facts . . . and I say they have a humorous aspect.[2]

This was hard hitting for a Colonial Secretary in a self-governing
Colony. The Cape Ministers in attendance might blush with
embarrassment, but the audience were delighted. Their enthusiasm rose still higher, when a few minutes later, he embarked on
the third and final phase of his political offensive. This took the
form of an appeal to the Bond leaders, which they could only

[1] Grocott's *Penny Mail*, February 11, 1903.
[2] *Cape Times*, February 13, 1903.

reject or ignore at the risk of alienating moderate opinion. He
prefaced this offer with a passionate denunciation of the boycotting of Loyalists which brought the audience to its feet.

I have received evidence, which I cannot ignore, that in parts of this
British Colony at the present time, loyalty involves persecution (*terrific
cheering*). That is an intolerable state of things (*renewed cheering*). It
cannot continue (*renewed loud cheering*). My sympathies in this matter
are not so much excited on behalf of Britons. . . . As a rule they can take
care of themselves. . . . It is with those of the Dutch . . . who have
defended the institutions which they enjoyed in common with us, and
who are, on that account, made the mark for a special crusade; a crusade
which it is our business to see shall not be successful.

Then, in measured terms, came his appeal.

If the aspiration which we know existed in the minds of some, possibly
of many, of our Dutch fellow-subjects—an aspiration for a separate
Republic outside the British Empire; if that aspiration were renounced
for ever; if we knew that the Dutch accepted with absolute sincerity
our idea of a common State, one great difficulty at any rate would be removed. We want someone with authority to tell us that no longer in the
history of this colony shall there be any racial or political or religious
ostracism on the ground of loyalty to its institutions. We want evidence,
and I hope it will be forthcoming, that our Dutch fellow-citizens recognise that in the future their dealing is inseparable from ours, and that
they are ready to share our pride in the Empire to which we all belong;
that they are ready to accept their full share in its obligations as in its
principles. . . .[1]

Here was a definite offer to the Bond leaders of the terms on
which Chamberlain would be prepared to work with them. It
was the decisive statement of his visit to the Cape. The initiative
now lay with the Bond.

VI

While the Dutch leaders revolved the significance of his words,
Chamberlain began the long journey to Cape Town across the
Great Karroo. Mrs. Chamberlain's letters afford the best glimpses
of this stage of the tour.

[1] *Cape Times*, February 13, 1903.

. . . The work, as you will guess, is tremendous . . . but he is getting through it wonderfully well, and, though he is tired, I really believe it is more physical than mental, in spite of the ceaseless strain upon his nerves and his brain; but his hope of success and the encouragement of having already solved some very knotty points in the new Colonies keep him going and save him from too great fatigue of mind. . . . From morning till night—never does he get a moment to sit down quietly—one Address and Deputation—one interview after another—one "quiet" lunch with one or two important people to talk to, succeed each other, sandwiched in between Dinners and public functions. When he is not acknowledging the cheers of the crowds, which assemble even at the stations at which the train does not stop, he is deep in conversation with some one of importance—be it Governor, Prime Minister—other Ministers—Leaders of Opposition—Dutch farmers, or some one else, who either travels with us for the chance of talking with him, or comes on to the train between two stations. And this is the way our week's journey through Cape Colony, en route to Cape Town, is going on. He is like a schoolboy in marking off the days till we sail—and now there is only a fortnight more and we shall be homeward bound. . . . The climate has certainly agreed with him, for he has been extraordinarily well and, except at the end of a hard day's work, he is looking better than when we started. . . .[1]

The first stop after Port Elizabeth was at Graaff Reinet, known, from its setting, as "the gem of the Karroo", and, from its history, as the most discontented community in the Colony for over a hundred years. Here, for the first time in his whole visit, Chamberlain met with a hostile reception. A number of the inhabitants had ridden in Scheepers' Commando and turned out sporting their rebel colours.

. . . The English people, of course, gave us a warm welcome and the visit meant much to them; but one could not but be struck by the difference between this place, and even those in the Transvaal and Orange River Colony, in the general spontaneity of the people. Two-thirds of the houses we passed had stolid, impassive groups on their *stoeps*—who vouchsafed no sign of welcome—while the remaining third were waving flags and handkerchiefs and bowing with all their might. One does not expect the Boers to do all this, but with occasional excep-

[1] Mrs. Chamberlain to her mother, February 12, 1903.

tions, we had hardly ever failed to receive a bow from them; here, even in response to our bows, few hats were raised, though now and then a reluctant dame gave a grumpy nod, or a shaggy farmer pulled at his hat brim in a grudging kind of way. Their curiosity was too great to keep them within doors, but they could not bring themselves to greet us, even though they were citizens of a self-governing British Colony. And in that lies the difference between the new Colonies and the old ones, and marks the difficulty of the situation.

Later in the day, Chamberlain received an Afrikander Deputation. He spoke straight out and rebuked them for the discourtesy of their compatriots who had not acknowledged his bows when he entered the town. He then launched into a vigorous attack against the Bond. It is worth quoting as an example of the man-to-man directness with which he handled such deputations.

I do not consider that some opposition to the Government in the sense of political opposition can be described as disloyalty. . . . But it is to be regretted that political differences here have always been fought out on racial lines. As long as that is the case, there will not be any peace in this country. The object of the Bond has always been to emphasise the differences and not to remove the differences or lessen them. All the questions that they have raised, language, or representation, or questions of appointment, have always been a Dutch agitation as against an English agitation. I shall tell Mr. Hofmeyr, when I see him at Cape Town, that in my opinion an organisation based on this principle is a mischievous organisation, and the proper organisation would be one which shall make the Dutch and English friends. In Graaff Reinet the agitation has always been on these racial lines. If it were confined to ordinary political agitation we might regret it, but after all . . . a considerable number of your citizens, about 100 in number, went out and joined the enemy. You had no complaint against your own Government; you returned a majority of it: you were, therefore, taking up arms against your own Government. All government is impossible if that is to be the case. . . .

What are we to say about the future? I understand there has been a good deal of ill-feeling between those who abstained from taking part in the war . . . and those who were either actively disloyal or sympathised with the enemy. If those who sympathised with the rebellion are not prepared to give up any idea of punishing those who were loyal, how can you expect those who were loyal to the British Government to show any mercy to those who were disloyal? After all, ours is the greater complaint of the two. . . .[1]

When Chamberlain resumed his journey next morning there was a significant addition to his party. With him travelled N. F. De Waal, the Organising Secretary of the Bond. This was Hofmeyr's first reaction to Chamberlain's appeal at Port Elizabeth.

The conversation which followed is important to our story. It marked the first step towards a reconciliation between Dutch and British at the Cape. It also raised Chamberlain's hopes somewhat unduly.

De Waal proved most conciliatory, and Chamberlain presently broached his plan for cutting across the racial division in Cape politics.

It was necessary if reconciliation was to be secured, that in some way or other the issues should be changed, and new lines of party division be found. . . . I said that if the Bond were dissolved it might be possible to form a central or national party in which men like Mr. Hofmeyr might associate with moderate men of English birth and sympathies who had never been members of the previous association; and I suggested Mr. Schreiner and Mr. Graham as examples. Mr. De Waal said that such a radical change could only be effected by one man, viz. by Mr. Hofmeyr, but that, if he accepted such a policy, he, Mr. De Waal would welcome it and give it every assistance in his power.[2]

Encouraged by De Waal's receptive attitude, Chamberlain went on to discuss the question of a financial contribution from the Cape. He had already sounded Sprigg and Graham about this during his visits to Mafeking and Kimberley, and had found them unexpectedly favourable.[3] He now suggested that Cape colony should undertake the maintenance of the South African squadron :

The Capital expenditure of which, including the works at Simons Bay, was about 6 millions, while the annual expenditure was nearly £400,000 per annum.

[1] Chamberlain's Business Diary, vol. ii. p. 113.
[2] Ibid. p. 136, February 14, 1903.
[3] Mafeking, January 28, 1903 (Chamberlain's Business Diary, vol. i. p. 175). Kimberley, January 31, 1903 (Ibid. vol. i. p. 181).

Mr. De Waal thought that this would not be objected to, and that Mr. Hofmeyr would not be disinclined to make such a proposal, although he had not had any personal communication with him on the subject as yet. For himself, he would be glad to support it as a proof of the reality of the assurances given that the Dutch now considered themselves as part of the British Empire and equally bound with all its other members to contribute to its defence and maintenance.[1]

These eminently satisfactory but private statements were duly followed by a striking public declaration. The train halted at Middelburg, where a crowd had gathered to watch the Mayor present the address of welcome. De Waal, although a Hollander by birth, was the leading man in Middelburg and presently rose to speak.

Mr. Chamberlain asked assurances from the Dutch-speaking population that they should abandon the idea of a Dutch Republican South Africa and should in future bear true allegiance to British authority. Well, this assurance was extremely easy to give. . . . He [Mr. De Waal] spoke for himself and for those who worked with him politically when he said that, in the future equally as in the past, there would not be the slightest desire on their part to sever themselves from the British connection. *We propose to prove our loyalty by our acts. We propose to assist in the great future scheme that you [Mr. Chamberlain] have laid down. We wish to show by our lives that we wish to live in amity with our fellow men.* . . . We have now in South Africa one country, one ruler, one flag. Why should it not be possible to become one people.[2]

This clear statement from the Organising Secretary of the Bond caused a profound sensation in London, as well as in Cape Town. De Waal had gone a long way towards supplying the assurances which Chamberlain had called for.

From Middelburg the journey was continued until,

just as a wild and stormy sunset was fading in the west, we drew up at a lonely station on the Karroo . . . even here a crowd from all the country-side was assembled, and, though it was too dark to see their faces, Joe thanked them for coming and said a few words to them. Then they

[1] Chamberlain's Business Diary, vol. ii. p. 136, February 14, 1903.
[2] From the *Cape Times*, February 18, 1903. The portion marked in italics though taken down by the *Cape* *Times* reporter was omitted from the text of the speech subsequently issued by Mr. De Waal. Perhaps he thought he had gone too far.

dwindled away and we were shunted on to a siding, there to pass the night.[1]

Next day, a Sunday, was spent in the house of Mr. Charles Southey, the owner of a well-known stud and ostrich farm. One story of the war, which he heard that day, impressed Chamberlain so much that he afterwards dictated an account of it.

Mr. Pack, formerly tutor in Mr. Southey's family, relates the following facts which are confirmed by Mr. Southey. Mr. and Mrs. Becker, with their son, lived together on a farm, and, on the outbreak of the war, Mrs. Becker did all in her power to keep her husband and son from joining the rebels. But, on one occasion, Mr. Pack found her in tears with a copy of the "Review of Reviews" containing lurid descriptions of the cruelty of the British Govt. and British soldiers to the women and children. She said, "What can I do in face of this? I can no longer ask my men to refuse to join to put an end to such a state of things."

He endeavoured to reassure her, but she said, "it appears in an English paper. It must be true."

When the next commando came round the son joined and was killed shortly afterwards. . . .[2]

Here was the justification, on human grounds, of Chamberlain's bitter attacks at the Khaki Election against the pro-Boers. All through that night, the next day and the night following, the train sped across the Karroo, stopping at occasional wayside stations, where Chamberlain was the object of more or less friendly demonstrations.[3] Early on the morning of February 17, they came by the Hex River Pass into the smiling vales above the Paarl.

It is such a typical old Dutch village and has such a foreign air about it, that it formed a great contrast to all that we had seen elsewhere. . . . Imagine a hot, summer morning—and us emerging from a dusty train, Joe in his grey frock coat and I in white muslin. . . . The Mayor and his wife and little daughter, with a huge bouquet, met us, and then we

[1] Mrs. Chamberlain to her mother, February 13, 1903.
[2] Chamberlain's Business Diary, vol. ii. p. 145, February 16, 1903.
[3] At Beaufort West, for example, only the Resident Magistrate and a handful of Englishmen appeared. The Mayor and the whole Dutch community stayed away.

entered the carriage and, with an escort of Cape Police—who, as usual, smothered us in dust—drove two miles.

Paarl, like Graaff Reinet, is a thoroughly Dutch centre, and has been very much disaffected during the war and even now is not in the least reconciled to the turn which affairs have taken—and so, as at Graaff Reinet, we were unwelcome visitors to many of the inhabitants. They showed it in a different way and a more dignified one, for many of the *stoeps* were deserted as we passed, instead of the curious and hostile groups which we had seen before. But this only had the effect of making the loyalists more enthusiastic, and from them we received the warmest of welcomes.

. . . We were formally received at the Public Garden, where various Addresses, etc., were presented, and I was again laden with flowers. It was very hot and poor Joe was so tired that I wondered how he would ever get through it, but, as usual, he rose to the occasion and it went off very well. . . .[1]

In the evening, the Mayor gave a garden party in Chamberlain's honour; but, though 800 invitations had been issued, only 200 guests came. Reconciliation was still no more than a pious hope; but we may guess that Chamberlain derived a certain caustic satisfaction from this personal experience of the workings of Bond propaganda. It would only strengthen his hand for his negotiations with Hofmeyr.

The last lap of the journey to Cape Town was completed that night. Chamberlain was by now thoroughly exhausted; and to avoid the weariness of an official reception at the station, the train was stopped at Rondebosch, whence the party drove to Newlands, the Governor's summer residence. It was the only time in the whole tour that Chamberlain allowed himself to disappoint the public.

VII

Chamberlain spent a week in Cape Town; a week of intensive political activity both for him and for the leaders of the two great parties in the Colony. His only relaxation was provided by a short week-end spent with Admiral Moore at the naval base of Simonstown.

[1] Mrs. Chamberlain to her mother, March 1903 (undated).

One evening, during this week-end, the conversation turned on Tristan da Cunha, the remote little island in the South Atlantic whose only communication with the world, in those days, was provided by the annual visit of a warship. The Admiral declared that it would be best to remove altogether its handful of inhabitants who, at best, could only eke out a precarious living. Other senior officers present agreed; but Chamberlain suddenly intervened and said: "No; we must hold this island. It would be a mistake to give it up; for some day it may be required as a wireless station." [1] It was a prophetic remark. Wireless was then still in its infancy; but, after the outbreak of war in 1939, a meteorological station was set up on the island and made possible the South Atlantic patrols of the Royal Air Force.

For the rest, the visit to Cape Town was "desperately hard work. . . . Almost every day the Governor and Joe went into Cape Town about 10.30 and did not return until 7 o'clock—deputations, a big lunch at Government House of important people, interviews, etc.—and then a dinner in the evening at Newlands." [2]

On the morning of February 18, the first of the visit, Chamberlain drove through packed and cheering streets to receive the welcome of the Mayor and Corporation in Green Market Square. The vast crowd heard the different addresses with mounting impatience and greeted Sprigg with hisses and catcalls. Chamberlain, however, received a tumultuous ovation. It was a broiling hot day, and contemporary photographs show Monkbretton holding up an umbrella to shield him from the sun while he spoke.

The speech was a clear restatement of his attitude towards Cape politics. He began by defining his aims—"union and conciliation"—

a union which must be, if it is of any value, a union of hearts, not of words only; and a conciliation which, in order to be effective, must be reciprocal, must not be confounded with weakness, and must not involve any desertion of our friends. [3]

[1] Captain Coke to Commander Locker-Lampson, September 8, 1920.
[2] Mrs. Chamberlain to her mother, March 1903 (undated).
[3] *Cape Times*, February 19, 1903.

He went on to speak of his personal impressions of the situation at the Cape. He had high hopes of reconciliation between Dutch and English in the former republics, but

in this colony I confess that my experience has made me less hopeful of immediate and satisfactory results. . . . The antagonism . . . between the two races seems almost to have become chronic and, while we find rebellion exalted into heroism by men in authority, loyalty, if it is not treated as a crime, is, at any rate, discountenanced and ostracised. . . . Meanwhile, an active propaganda is still continued in the press and I am sorry to say in the pulpit, a propaganda whose tendency it is, even if it be not its intention, to intensify the separation between the two races that ought to be united. . . .

Here is the one cloud which darkens the horizon of South Africa. . . . It is not given to one man to conjure such a cloud away but . . . it may not even now be useless to make an appeal . . . to the moderate men of all parties . . . that they shall seek and find some remedy. . . .

The speech was angrily received by the commentators of the Bond press; but, while they wrote their acid "leaders", important negotiations were in progress. The same afternoon, Chamberlain at last came face to face with Hofmeyr.

"Onze Jan", as the Dutch farmers knew him,[1] held no official position in the Bond hierarchy, but he was the real power in the Dutch community. He had done his best to restrain Kruger right up to the outbreak of the war, but, once the die was cast, he had hoped and worked for a Boer victory. It was even said that, when Kruger had asked him if there was any chance of the British giving way to the Boer demands, he had replied, "Not unless you shoot Milner through the head". Hofmeyr was a passionate Dutch nationalist but he recognised the advantages which membership of the British Empire could bring to his people. In his own way, he was an Imperialist and, at the first Colonial Conference of 1887, had taken the initiative in proposing a 2 per cent duty against foreign goods to provide an Imperial Naval Defence Fund.

While Chamberlain was still on his way to Cape Town, Hofmeyr had told the press that it would hardly be worth their

[1] The political world knew him as "the Mole", because of his propensity for working underground.

while to meet. "Mr. Chamberlain", he had said, "can accomplish nothing unless he is prepared to grant a general amnesty, to give universal compensation, and to recall Lord Milner."[1] None the less he had accepted the Governor's invitation to lunch, and afterwards had remained alone with Chamberlain for three hours.

That evening Chamberlain would write of Hofmeyr, "He gave me the impression of being sincere but strongly biased and unable to make allowance for the feelings of those who were opposed to him".[2] Their conversation was cordial, but the crafty old Dutch leader was not prepared to go as far as De Waal had led Chamberlain to hope. He commended Chamberlain's speeches and assured him that he would make a public declaration of the Bond's desire for reconciliation. He rejected, however, the proposal for a realignment of the political parties.

Mr. Hofmeyr . . . evidently did not consider it possible or desirable to make an entirely new start.[3]

He was equally discouraging about the prospects of an increased defence contribution.

He said that he could not with advantage initiate any such proposal. . . . For himself personally, he considered that the Cape Colony might well undertake to find an additional £100,000 a year for the maintenance of the *Good Hope* . . . but . . . he did not believe that any grant of such an amount as had been suggested, viz. £10,000,000, would be possible.[4]

This seemed definite enough, but Hofmeyr's next move showed that he had not altogether closed his mind to the idea of a substantial contribution. He asked Chamberlain bluntly whether a general amnesty could be obtained in return for such a contribution. Chamberlain refused to strike a definite bargain, but hinted that such a proof of loyalty would go far to justify the remission of all penalties imposed upon the rebels.

. . . I told him that, if the British people were satisfied that the Dutch would be loyal in the future, . . . in my private opinion the objection to granting amnesty would also be removed.

[1] *Standard*, Feb. 16, 1903.
[2] Chamberlain's account of the conversation, Business Diary, vol. ii. p.

164, February 18.
[3] *Ibid.* p. 116, February 18, 1903.
[4] *Ibid.*

This talk decided Chamberlain to drop the contribution proposal for the time being. He had put the idea of it into Hofmeyr's
mind, but could not press further for its acceptance without
being drawn into dangerous negotiations over amnesty. These
must turn upon the disfranchisement of the rebels, and even to
have discussed this question would have shaken his credit with
the "loyalists". His immediate aim was to secure public assurances from the Bond leaders of their loyalty and desire for
reconciliation with the British. Once these assurances had been
given, the question of a contribution could be revived as a test of
their sincerity. Accordingly, when Chamberlain met Hofmeyr's
lieutenants, Theron and Malan, next day, he told them that

. . . I had decided to drop the matter altogether and I neither asked for
nor expected anything. . . . If it were dealt with at all, . . . it would
probably come better after my departure, when it could not possibly be
represented as the result of any bargaining or haggling between us.[1]

For the moment deeds were less important than words.
These proved forthcoming beyond all expectation. On the
morning of February 21, Chamberlain received a deputation
from the Bond. The Deputies, led by Hofmeyr, De Waal,
Theron, Sauer and Merriman, assembled in the throne room of
Government House. They had come in such numbers that not
enough chairs could be found in the whole building to seat more
than a few of them; an unexpected discomfort, which, despite the
length of the proceedings, they bore with good humour. After
a short, rather truculent speech, Merriman read the Bond
address. Besides reiterating that party's "firm and unalterable
attachment to the British connection", the text was not in itself
reassuring.[2]

Then Hofmeyr spoke. After briefly defending the record of
the Bond and alleging that many of the charges of boycotting
were exaggerated or invented, he made a significant admission:

We have no doubt that, even if all these cases of pseudo-ostracism or
persecution be deducted, some regrettable instances of offensive conduct

[1] Chamberlain's Business Diary, pp.
191-195, February 19, 1903.
[2] Hofmeyr afterwards told Chamberlain that the address had been drafted
by Merriman. Much contentious matter had already been struck out of it
but if Hofmeyr had had his way, "he
would have cut it much more"
(Chamberlain's Business Diary, vol. ii.
p. 217, February 22, 1903).

remain which cannot be thus got rid of. It would be astonishing, if after the stirring events which recently convulsed the whole country, it were otherwise. . . .[1]

Then came the long-awaited declaration:

But on whatever side such offences are committed, we, one and all here assembled, condemn them utterly and completely. We hold with you, sir, that loyalty is no crime. We beg with you, sir, that no member of the Town Guard, or of the District Mounted Troops should be ostracised or cold-shouldered in society, be injured in his calling or ordinary avocations, be made to feel that he is any the worse off in either a social or business point of view, merely because he had fought for his country. We reprobate all acts of an offensive character; the irritation of loyal subjects by sporting the colours of the late republics, and the wearing of the distinguishing badges of rebel forces or chiefs, or singing songs of a character calculated to breed misunderstanding or suspicion. We are prepared to address an appeal to our people in the spirit of this statement, and to co-operate to the fullest of our power to promote good understanding between, and the happiness and prosperity of both the great European sections of our population under the flag which waves over all of us. . . .[2]

Here was the assurance for which Chamberlain had appealed at Port Elizabeth when he had first entered the Colony. It must have matched his most sanguine hopes, and he responded warmly.

I consider that that statement is admirable in its spirit and is calculated to make more for the peace and goodwill, which ought to prevail among all classes, than anything that has been said or done up to the present time. I accept it as a most hopeful and most happy augury for the future. . . .[3]

The Bond leaders had been induced to play their part. It was now Chamberlain's task to make sure that the Progressives met them at least half-way. In his public speeches he had always spoken as the champion of Loyalist claims. But, in private talks with the Progressive leaders, he was careful to restrain their hopes. The only practical step that he would take on their behalf was to uphold the Loyalists' claim to the right to bear

[1] *Cape Times*, February 23, 1903.   [2] *Ibid.*   [3] *Ibid.*

arms. Its neglect, as he had seen for himself, was their most CHAP. XCI. burning grievance, and one which it would be wise to remedy for reasons of policy as well as of sentiment. For the rest, he was ÆT. 66. deliberately discouraging. He offered no remedy against boycotting. He criticised the Progressives' treatment of Sprigg, and even hinted that in choosing Jameson as their leader they would provoke the resentment of moderate elements. No wonder Jameson would speak of him as "the callous devil from Birmingham".[1] But Chamberlain was right. He judged it necessary to deflate the Progressives for two reasons. First, to win them the moderate vote when elections came. Second, and more immediate, to bring them to a frame of mind where, in public at least, they would accept the Bond leaders' assurances.

Some such pressure was certainly required. The Progressive press had received De Waal's speech at Middelburg with considerable suspicion; and the *Cape Times* had written of Hofmeyr's statement:

We are not of opinion that Mr. Hofmeyr deserves any credit for doing what was his obvious duty and what he ought to have done long ago.[2]

The private view of most Progressives is well expressed in the following letter from Kipling.

KIPLING TO CHAMBERLAIN

February 25, 1903.—Of course it is difficult to believe that Hofmeyr was sincere in his recent promises, and impossible to believe that even he could dam up or divert the waters of strife that he has led in channels of his own crooked digging since 1881. After all, we are only the children of our works.

Such misgivings were natural enough; but, from a political point of view, it was bad tactics to express them publicly. Chamberlain argued the point very frankly with a deputation of the Progressive leaders introduced by Sir Lewis Mitchell.[3]

I quite admit that assurances, after all that has passed, can hardly be accepted as entirely satisfactory. On the other hand, I am certain that it is the best policy of the loyalists in this country to make the most even of assurances. Let us treat it as a matter of business. If a man with whom

[1] Colvin, *Dr. Jameson*, vol. ii. p. 217.   [3] Chamberlain's Business Diary,
[2] *Cape Times*, February 23, 1903.   vol. ii. pp. 179-181.

you have had differences or of whom you have had suspicions in business, were to come to you and to say, "Look here, we have had this difficulty— I intend to pay you £100 in six months' time". You would not turn your back on the offer and say, "You confounded liar, I do not believe a word of what you say".

You would say "I accept your statement certainly. I am glad to hear that you are going to pay the money." And by that means you would make it infinitely more probable that the man would keep his promise than if at the time you showed any doubt of his sincerity. You might retain the idea that you would not obtain your money, but, as a matter of policy, you would not allow that to appear, and you would do your very best to show confidence and trust in the promise which had been made.

May I apply that practically? The other day I had a very long interview with Mr. De Waal, the Secretary of the Bond, who is a very able man and clever politician.

Partly as a result of that interview, Mr. De Waal goes down to Middelburg, where he by his personal influence had invited a great number of the Dutch sympathisers with the rebellion to attend on the platform, and, in their hearing and in face of the public, he makes a very conciliatory and reassuring speech.

Well, I see that one result is that already there is a good deal of fluttering in the dovecotes in the opposite camp. Some of the Dutch are saying that he went too far. He certainly, to some extent, took his life in his hands in making that statement, which was not a popular statement to make; and, whatever the motive was, the policy of a political party is to deal with the matter as a man of business would deal with it. He has given his assurance, and, if I were acting as a political leader on the other side, I would endeavour to make this clear and say, Mr. De Waal has made this assurance and I should make the most of it. Even if the assurance is not fulfilled, your recognition and praise of it would do something to separate Mr. De Waal from the more extreme members of his party and to create within the Bond a nucleus of a moderate section. That being the case, I regret to see in the papers which represent the Progressive Party and views here, a sneering allusion to it and statements that he does not mean it. For my own part I would dismiss all that kind of suspicion. I do not see how we can be harmed by making the most of it and accepting it in terms as cordial as those in which it was uttered. On the other hand, I can see great danger in rejecting a proposal

of that kind—of rejecting and sneering at it. You simply unite the Bond
Party, and Mr. De Waal will find it necessary to take back his words in
order to recover his influence. On this ground, I press upon you that, if
assurances are given you at any time of that kind, even if you retain
perhaps well grounded suspicion in regard to them, I suggest that it is
policy and patriotism not to express that suspicion but on the contrary to
hope that the assurances may be relied upon and therefore to say so. . . .

The passage is important. It shows very clearly that Chamberlain was not taken in by Hofmeyr, as has so often been said,
and that his welcome of the Bond's assurances proceeded from
policy rather than faith.

The Progressive leaders were persuaded by Chamberlain's
advice. At a party meeting, on February 23, they decided to
reciprocate Hofmeyr's assurances publicly. Their intended
statement was communicated to Chamberlain next morning by
Abe Bailey and Walton. He announced it that evening at a
farewell banquet.

When I entered your city the other day, I thought it necessary to say
that here, in the premier Colony of South Africa, was the point of danger.

Now the incidents of the last week, have had the effect of relieving
my anxiety—and I hope I shall go away with the well-grounded hope
that a new era is beginning, a new chapter has been opened, and that
this colony will once more take its proper place and lead the way in a
policy of reconciliation and of union. (*Cheers.*)

On Saturday last I received with the most unfeigned satisfaction the
assurances which were given me then by the trusted leader of a great
party in this country (*loud cheers*)—assurances so full, so definite, and so
authoritative, that I cannot doubt that their publication, their circulation
throughout the country into the agricultural districts, will have its effect
—its natural effect—in stopping any further manifestation of ill-feeling
directed against any man on account of his loyalty (*loud cheers*);—and
that assurance was given to me without any condition, without any
qualification. I say that the leaders of the party to which I refer have
done their duty. (*Loud cheers, and a voice: "Question".*) But, then, there
is always the pessimist, and the pessimists begin to say, "Oh, yes, those
assurances are all very well, but are they sincere? (*a voice: "Yes"*)—they
will either be rejected by the other party, or they will be received with a
grudging and ungenerous acceptance." (*Cries of "No".*)

I have the answer in my hand. (*Hear, hear.*) This morning unsolicited, I received a message on behalf of the other great party in the State (*hear, hear*)—and it is to the following effect: "The Progressive Party accept with pleasure Mr. Hofmeyr's assurance that he, and those associated with him, will do their utmost to allay race feeling in the country and eliminate the racial question from the coming political struggle. (*Loud and prolonged cheering.*) This has always been the aim of the Progressive Party. They accept Mr. Hofmeyr's promise of co-operation in that respect in all sincerity." (*Loud cheers.*) Now I say the other party have done their duty. (*Applause.*) Is it not an advance in Cape politics? (*Hear hear.*) Am I not entitled to be optimistic? . . .[1]

Bond and Progressive had each played their part. It was left to Chamberlain to show that the Imperial Government would not fail in theirs. As if to set a seal upon this formal act of reconciliation, he made an unexpected plea for clemency to political prisoners.

In this Colony . . . I have no authority, no claim and no right to interfere, but I may be permitted, perhaps, in these closing words to express the hope that there should be forthcoming, in the near future, such evidence of a restoration of mutual good feeling throughout the country . . . that the Government may feel justified in cleaning the slate, in restoring to their homes, those whose offences have been purely political. . . . When that time has arrived is . . . a matter not for me but for the responsible Governments of the Colonies concerned, but I cannot resist the hopeful expectation that it may not be long before the echoes of the war will have entirely died down.[2]

This public exchange of assurances between the two great parties at the Cape was the crowning act of the South African tour. It was a triumph for Chamberlain's dialectic skill. Nor were its practical results insignificant. Hofmeyr's statement was duly embodied in a circular and distributed throughout the country by the Bond. Ten days later the old Dutch leader would write:

HOFMEYR TO CHAMBERLAIN

March 4, 1903.—. . . The cause of conciliation is making progress. . . . My circular has by now been spread all over the Colony. I followed it up with a private note to most of our clergy: and, fearing that the rela-

[1] *Cape Times*, February 25, 1903.   [2] *Ibid.*

tives of our political prisoners were among the most bitter on our side, I found an opportunity on Saturday of visiting the gaol at Tokay and inducing its inmates to write to their relatives in the spirit of my circular. They promised to do so. I hope for good results. . . .

These were forthcoming; and, less than two months later, Chamberlain would write to the most serious critic of his Cape policy:

CHAMBERLAIN TO MILNER

April 27, 1903.—I am told that the action taken by Hofmeyr has produced considerable effect in the country districts. The Dutch Church are said to be hostile still, but in many cases the people have settled down and boycotting has received a great check. This was the point which was to me of the greatest importance.

Formal reconciliation between Bond and Progressives had been one of Chamberlain's aims from the start. But it had only been one of them. Now that it was achieved, his mind fastened at once upon the next step. In his reply to Hofmeyr, he reopened the question of a contribution.

CHAMBERLAIN TO HOFMEYR

March 26, 1903.—. . . I desire to thank you for the loyal way in which you are carrying out the policy of conciliation. I know that we must not expect full results immediately and I am sure there will always be mischievous people trying to undo our work. . . .

You have already seen that the amnesty to which you have attached so much importance has been conceded. I hope that your expectation of good results may be justified, but undoubtedly the experience of the past makes one a little afraid lest acts of grace should be construed into acts of weakness. . . .

I observe that "Onsland" is protesting against any further contribution to the expenses of the Empire. Although I decided not to press for such evidence of loyalty, I do desire to repeat to you my firm conviction that some material proof that the Dutch would in future share our pride in possession and the obligations which rest on all who accept the British flag, would do more than anything else to change suspicion into confidence and to convince the people of this country, and through them the British speaking inhabitants of South Africa, that we are at last on the way to become a united people.

I cannot exaggerate my own sense of the moral influence which such a policy would exercise. Its consequences would be far reaching, but, as I have always told you, it must be a voluntary approach on the part of the Dutch, if it is to have its full importance. There can be no question of a bargain. We have done our part without asking for anything in return. A quick response on the part of your friends would fix the situation and have a lasting and beneficial effect.

This appeal failed. The Bond took the short view. Perhaps it was just as well. Had they offered a substantial contribution, they might have rallied the moderate vote; and it would then have been very difficult for Sprigg to refuse to re-enfranchise the rebels. As it was, the moderates joined the somewhat chastened Progressives; the rebels remained without a vote; and the Bond were defeated at the polls in 1904.

Chamberlain never got a contribution from the Cape. But his other aims were fulfilled. He received assurances from Sprigg that elections would be held as soon as possible and that, meanwhile, no controversial legislation would be introduced. He also persuaded Bond and Progressives, as we saw, to pay homage to the principle of reconciliation.

The banquet at which this reconciliation was announced was the occasion of Chamberlain's last public speech in South Africa. More than 500 guests were seated in the Drill Hall and the galleries were thronged with their wives and relations. When Chamberlain rose to speak, he received a tremendous ovation. Wave upon wave of cheers rolled out as he assumed his favourite and well-known attitude, right foot slightly forward and right hand grasping the lapel of his coat. It seemed for a moment as if the cheering would never stop; and he had to raise his hand to plead for silence.

The time of parting has come. . . . The play is over, the curtain has been rung down, and here I stand in front of the footlights of that great theatre of South Africa, which has been the scene of so many an eventful drama, to say to you a few words of thanks. . . . I have crowded into the last two months, work and impressions which might have been expanded into years. The labour has been unremitting. . . .

I came to these shores as an optimist, and I leave them with the firm conviction that Providence, which out of evil still educes good, will evolve some compensation for the sufferings and the misery which a great war involves. . . . I leave this shore more convinced than ever that the forces, the natural forces, which are drawing you together, are more potent than those evil influences which would tend to separate you.[1] The material interests of South Africa weigh heavily in the balance in favour of you.

The first need of the country is development. You want more capital, more confidence, more population, better communications, energy and enterprise everywhere. Above all, South Africa needs the best capacity of all of its children. There are great questions which loom in the near future and upon which your prosperity and position depend. . . . You have to make preparation for that ultimate federation of South Africa which is destined, I hope in the near future, to establish a new nation under the British flag, which shall be daughter in her mother's house and mistress in her own. . . . Your fate is in your own hands.[2]

On the following evening, February 25, Chamberlain went on board the Union Castle liner *Norman*. An hour later, in the failing light, she put out to sea.

VIII

The work was done at last. In two months almost to the day, Chamberlain had visited twenty-nine towns; delivered sixty-four important speeches; received eighty-seven deputations and given more than two hundred and fifty interviews. It had been a Herculean task.

The positive achievements of his mission were considerable. The thorny problems of war damage and compensation had been resolved. The loan for the development of the Transvaal and Orange River Colonies had been secured; and, with it, the terms of the Contribution which these Colonies were to make to the cost of the war. The foundations of self-government in the

[1] This was the sentence which Kipling used as a sub-title to his poem "The Settler".

"Here, where my fresh-turned furrows run,
    And the deep soil glistens red,
I will repair the wrong that was done
    To the living and the dead.
Here, where the senseless bullets fell,
    And the barren shrapnel burst,
I will plant a tree, I will dig a well,
    Against the heat and the thirst."

[2] *Cape Times*, February 25, 1903.

new Colonies had been laid. The broad approach to South African Union had been traced. Countless minor administrative decisions had been taken besides; and, even where no decisions had been reached, the full exchange of views between Milner and Chamberlain would save endless correspondence and ensure a maximum of delegation from Whitehall to Johannesburg. Nor were the moral consequences unimportant. The Loyalists in the old Colonies, the British and the National Scouts in the new, had been reassured. Personal, even friendly, contact had been established between former enemies. In Cape Colony the chasm dividing the two races had been seemingly bridged.

No less impressive was the negative achievement. Never once, in his whole course through the tortuous maze of South African politics, had Chamberlain put himself in the wrong. Never once in all his speeches and interviews had he even laid himself open to serious criticism from any side. The *Daily Telegraph* correspondent, who accompanied him throughout the tour, gave the following measure of its success.

Six years ago there was no name more execrated by one half of the population of South Africa than that of Joseph Chamberlain. At the outbreak of the war the odium had risen higher by several degrees. On Feb. 25, 1903, this same statesman left Table Bay, not merely covered with the praises of his own people, but followed by the respect of those who had been his foes.[1]

The successful completion of the tour was hailed with equal enthusiasm in South Africa, in England and throughout the Empire. Even the foreign press joined in the general congratulations, and one German commentator would forecast "the rise of a British Bismarck wielding policy on a grand scale".[2]

At home, Chamberlain's achievements in South Africa remained above party criticism. "You will have a tremendous reception", wrote Lord Onslow, "on your return both by the public and the House of Commons. The unanimous approval that greeted the announcement of your visit has been accorded to everyone of its results."[3] With a singular sense of historical

---

[1] *Daily Telegraph*, March 16, 1903.
[2] Quoted by *The Times*, March 16, 1903.
[3] Onslow to Chamberlain, January 24, 1903.

perspective, British opinion saw the tour not as an isolated incident but in relation to South African policy as a whole. Opponents judged it a great gesture of reparation, while Unionists held it to be a vindication of the justice and humanity of their cause. Balfour would put the point well when he said:

CHAP.
XCI.

ÆT. 66.

It is the happy revenge of time that the one man who was . . . criticised for what he did in common with the whole of his colleagues in the Government, should now be able to come back with the credit to himself alone of having done so much to wipe out the effects of the war; that he, who was accused of troubling the peace of nations, should now be regarded and justly regarded as a great peace-maker and as the man above all others in this Empire who deserves the blessings which have been pronounced on the peace-maker.[1]

Thus Chamberlain contemporaries. The verdict of history is not substantially different. Events, indeed, belied some of the expectations that had been raised. On leaving Cape Town, Chamberlain had said, "Your material interests tend to bring you together". In the long run this would prove true. But, seen close to, the graph of progress seldom describes a regular upward curve. Chamberlain's visit was followed by an economic blizzard. The harvest failed. Farmers faced starvation; and mounting living costs, coupled with the continued shortage of native labour, threw the Rand into the trough of a depression. The payment of the £30,000,000 contribution was at first postponed, then altogether abandoned. Meanwhile, economic discontent revived nationalist passions and hindered the progress of reconciliation. But, in spite of all, the essential work endured; and, within seven years, a United and self-governing South Africa would arise on the foundations which Chamberlain and Milner had laid together.

But it is not only by the outcome of its several decisions that Chamberlain's visit should be judged. It had a deeper significance. Looking back, we can see that it was a moral necessity. In the eyes of Boer and of Briton, this one man stood like no one else for the British Empire. The South African policy had been his policy from first to last. He carried England's share of the

[1] Speech at a luncheon at the Mansion House, March 20, 1903 (*The Times* report).

responsibility for the war. He had been the organiser of victory. He had granted the terms of surrender. If there was now to be peace under the British flag, if the policy with which he was identified was to lead to the building of a new South Africa, then he must be the peace-maker and the architect. Men's minds are not easily adjusted to the rapid turns of the wheel of history. It needed the symbolism of the Warlord turned Peace-maker to make them understand and accept the revolution in South African affairs. Without it, events alone might, in the end, have pressed the two peoples into the new mould created by the British victory; but the process must have taken longer; and time was of the essence, for, though none of them knew it, the first World War was at hand.

We cannot gauge the exact effect of this symbolism upon the evolution of South Africa. How far, for instance, did Chamberlain's personality or ideas have an influence, direct or indirect, on Botha or Smuts or upon all those men of Boer and British stock, known and unknown, who have built up the Union of South Africa? No one can say for certain. Until psychologists have opened up the secret recesses of the mind, the influence of individuals and ideas upon other men and their actions must remain imponderable. But, if nothing can be asserted, some things may be fairly presumed. In coming to South Africa, Chamberlain had made a generous and human gesture. By a natural process, it called forth a generous and human response. Boer and Briton sat down at the same table. Old enemies shook hands. Forgiveness and reconciliation were on men's lips, if not in their hearts. Oil had been poured on the waters of strife. The effect was certainly not permanent. Antipathies revived; and, a few months later, Botha would describe the visit as a dismal failure. But, for all that, South African politics were never the same again. A new beginning had been made. There would be much backsliding, but no turning back.

The tour was symbolic in another sense, no less significant. It was symbolic of the new spirit and modern method of Chamberlain's Imperial administration. The Colonial Secretary had made use of modern means of travel to come to South Africa and of the modern processes of democracy to reach its peoples. Men could now see for themselves that the representative of the

Imperial Government was a man of flesh and blood like themselves and that the cold calculations of his policy were restrained,
perhaps even inspired, by a moral purpose and a deep humanity.
For the first time in history Downing Street had come to the
Colonies.

BOOK XX

THE ORIGINS OF TARIFF REFORM
(1901–1903)

CHAPTER XCII

DRAGON'S TEETH

September 1901–June 1902

CHAMBERLAIN at the Height of his Power—Unionism at the Cross-
roads—Chamberlain and Defence—Foreign Competition and the
Protectionist Revival—The Atlantic Combine—A Retaliationist
Policy for Shipping—Imperialism and Social Reform—Chamberlain
drops Old Age Pensions—His Passivity Explained—Hicks Beach and
the Growth of Expenditure—His Disagreement with Chamberlain—
Income Tax or Revenue Duties?—The Corn Duty Revived—
Laurier's Suggestion—Balfour's Rebuke—Chamberlain Supports
Laurier—An Open Question.

I

WE have observed, in the foregoing pages, the course of events
which raised Chamberlain to the height of his power and fame.
The Khaki Election had secured his position in the constituencies and in Parliament. The duel with Bülow had made him
the champion of England in the international arena. The
Treaty of Vereeniging had set the seal of success on his South
African policy. To crown it all, his journey to the scene of strife
had raised him above party and completed his triumph.
Liberals might damn the war as "Chamberlain's war". Unionists
might claim the victory as "Chamberlain's victory". But both
sides in politics and the whole British Democracy, at home and
overseas, were united in hailing the peace as "Chamberlain's
peace".

By a natural dispensation, the same events which raised him
to his zenith brought his opponents to their nadir. The glamour
of his achievements was enhanced by the misery of their dissensions. Meantime, his personal ascendancy over the Unionists
was still further marked by the retirement of the great Prime

CHAP.
XCII.

Æt. 65.

Minister, who for so long had moderated his impetuous career. Moreover, as often happens with strong personalities, public opinion drew a sharp distinction between his qualities and the defects of his colleagues; and Moberly Bell, the famous manager of *The Times*, might write at the beginning of 1902:

> Joe is no doubt playing his hand excellently. He is perfectly loyal to the Government and yet somehow manages to keep detached from it. People think and speak of "the Cabinet—and Chamberlain".[1]

The Unionist alliance had now endured seventeen years; and, during fourteen of them, the allies had controlled the destinies of Britain. They might look back with some pride on the long list of their achievements, domestic and Imperial. As Chamberlain said in conversation about this time:

> . . . We have done things worth doing and that will make part of history. . . . At the end of the first Government I was in with Mr. Gladstone, I felt we had done nothing to show as the result, but now we have done a great deal. . . . We have something we can be satisfied to think of.[2]

But, if the allies might dwell on the past with complacency, they could also look forward to the future with confidence. They still commanded an ample majority. Parliament had another five years to run. The country was rich; and they represented its wealth and property. Thus the ponderable factors seemed fair. But it is always dangerous to linger on the summits. The exertion of the climb may tempt the weary mountaineer to bask in the sunshine and enjoy the view. But the weather may break. Night comes on. Danger and death attend upon delay. The forces of Unionism stood at the summit of achievement. Now was the moment, while the political weather was still clear, to decide their next objective and press on towards it.

There was no time to lose. We have reached one of those points in history, when material and ideological forces, long dammed up, suddenly find their spokesmen and break into the main stream of political life. To harness these revolutionary forces to their interest was the task which challenged Chamber-

[1] E. H. C. Moberly Bell, *Life and Letters of C. F. Moberly Bell*, p. 224.
[2] J. Parker Smith, "Memories of Joseph Chamberlain", published in the *National Review*, May 1932.

lain and his colleagues. But it was not to be. Already the worms
were boring at the foundations of the great Alliance; and, in this
year of 1902, while Chamberlain was carried to the summit of
his fortunes, the fate of Unionism was decreed.

II

Imperialism and Social Reform had been the twin pillars of
Chamberlain's policy. "The two", he once said, "must always
go together, as Disraeli saw. In his novels there is always the
double idea, Social and Imperial; in Sybil, for instance, in a
fantastic way." [1] Now, after two and a half years of war waged
for Imperial ends, the country was ripe for a fresh instalment
of Social Reform. Nor were the issues lacking. The demand for
an Eight-hours Day was widespread. The Trade Unions, hamstrung by the Taff Vale Judgment, urgently required remedial
legislation. Above all, the whole Working Class waited with
mounting impatience for the grant of Old Age Pensions. The
cost of such measures would have been small. The political
advantages were obvious. Organised Labour, still too weak to
stand on its own feet, had not yet decided to throw in its lot
with the Liberals.

Here, then, was a great opportunity for Chamberlain to
secure the glitter of his Imperial achievements with the hard
currency of domestic reform. Yet, on this score, he remained
strangely passive. To understand this unexpected change of
attitude we must look back a little. In the last year of peace, as
we have seen,[2] he had committed the Government to the principle of Old Age Pensions. He had also privately told Lloyd
George that he would stand by the Chaplin Committee's recommendation of a pension of five shillings a week for "necessitous
and deserving persons over sixty-five". While the war lasted this
proposal had been considered in abeyance; but in 1901 Chamberlain had shown signs of returning to it. His plan, from the
beginning, had been for state reinforcement of voluntary thrift,
and he deplored the agitation in favour of universal and non-
contributory pensions. Nevertheless, he encouraged the Friendly

[1] J. Parker Smith, "Memories of   the National Review, May 1932.
Joseph Chamberlain", published in   [2] Vol. III. pp. 626-627.

Societies to prepare a scheme,[1] and, in a special postscript to his speech at Edinburgh,[2] held out a hope of action by the Government.

I know it is one of the falsehoods which are told about me—they are like the sands of the sea, you cannot count them—that I have promised Old Age Pensions. I never promised anything of the kind. . . . What I did say, and what I say now, is that the time may come, and will come and ought to come—when the end of the war has arrived—when once more the Government may devote itself to these matters, and that it may be possible to do something to encourage and stimulate the provision for old age which is made by the working class themselves. . . .

This was hardly a revolutionary pronouncement; yet legislation even on these lines would have been hailed as a great advance. Practical proposals were now widely expected, but, instead of pressing on to action, he passed the responsibility for preparing a scheme to the representatives of the Working Class itself. Early in the New Year, he told a Birmingham audience

. . . that nothing can be done and nothing will be done in this direction, desirable as it is, until those great agencies for promoting thrift in this country—the Friendly Societies, the Benefit Societies, the Trades Unions and the Cooperative Societies . . . unite in order to put forward and support a practicable scheme. . . .[3]

This imprudent invitation was attended by inevitable consequences. A few days later, the Committee of the Trade Union and Co-operative Congresses met in London.[4] Amid great enthusiasm the delegates unanimously adopted a resolution in favour of non-contributory Old Age Pensions of five shillings a week for every citizen, male or female, on reaching the age of sixty. No other result could well have been expected from these organisations; but Chamberlain's only reaction was to condemn their resolution as "distinctly hurtful to the cause".[5] Instead of meeting them half-way with a modified scheme, he lapsed into passivity, explaining that

[1] Speech to Annual Conference of National Independent Order of Oddfellows, Birmingham, May 30, 1901—correspondence with Mr. Claverhouse Graham of the Oddfellows and Mr. Medhurst of the Royal Hearts of Oak.
[2] October 25, 1901.

[3] Address as President of the W. Birmingham Relief Fund, January 6, 1902.
[4] January 14, 1902.
[5] Letter to Mr. S. M. Holden of Accrington, published in *Daily Telegraph*, January 24, 1902.

as long as extravagant expectations prevail of what is possible, and as long as the friendly societies continue divided on the question, I do not see how any Government can hope to deal satisfactorily with the question. . . .[1]

He would never give up the idea of Old Age Pensions; and we shall see him return to it with new proposals under very different circumstances. But now, in a fateful hour, he let slip a great opportunity. It would not return.

Whatever its reasons, and we shall seek them presently, the fact by itself is arresting. It meant that Chamberlain had renounced the leadership of the great movement for Social Reform. Under him, it had transcended party dissensions for thirteen years. Now it would turn once more to the Liberal party and find a new leader in the rising Welsh tribune. One day, Old Age Pensions would be among his victories.

What is the explanation of Chamberlain's strange passivity? Had the time come at last, when even he no longer had a social message to deliver? In one sense this was true. Old Age Pensions had certainly never been a burning issue with him. Yet it is hard to believe that he could have lightly abandoned a proposal, which he had been urging for eleven years and which conformed so closely to the Unionist interest as well as to his own inclinations. It would seem, rather, that, on this one question, he had already advanced further than his colleagues or supporters were prepared to follow.

In the past, while it still reflected a predominantly landed interest, the Tory party had not been averse to measures of municipal or state socialism; especially when the burden of them fell chiefly upon the urban middle class. But with the Home Rule split and the Imperial policies of the 90's—both of them Chamberlain's work—that same middle class had become the dominant partner in Unionism. In the House, and still more in the country, business men were now the backbone of the Unionist alliance. Essentially individualists, they were stubbornly opposed to any measures which, by adding to the burden of taxation, might hinder their ability to compete in the markets of the world. At this very time, moreover, they were engaged in

[1] Letter written September 3, 1902, published in *The Times*, September 22, 1902.

a general offensive against the Trades Unions, of which the Taff
Vale Judgment was only one, if the most notable, of their
victories. They were, thus, in no mood to make concessions to
Labour. Yet these were the men who looked to Chamberlain.
He was their foremost representative, and it was upon them
that he relied for the furtherance of his Imperial policies.

The temper of Unionism was thus unfavourable to a programme of Social Reform. More immediately deterrent, perhaps,
were the opinions of the Chancellor of the Exchequer and his
advisers at the Treasury.

III

The Liberal press and the popular cartoonists habitually
represented Chamberlain and Hicks Beach at daggers drawn.
Nor was the legend altogether unfounded. Their personal relations, indeed, were cordial enough; and we have seen that only
the adverse tide of war had prevented them from taking a
holiday together in the West Indies. But there was no common
ground between them to make for friendship. They represented
wholly different schools of thought, almost different epochs.[1]

Hicks Beach has been described as "a difficult horse to go up
to in the stable".[2] His colleagues certainly found him trying;
especially poor Brodrick, already strained by overwork on his
ill-fated Army Scheme.

BRODRICK TO CHAMBERLAIN

September 16, 1901.—. . . About Beach. I want to help him, but he
makes things very difficult—and, though I am very far from wishing him to
leave the Ministry his nerves lately make work increasingly troublesome.

Have you ever thought of Arthur Balfour taking the Exchequer? I
throw this out, because I feel sure we shall have a crisis with Beach in
November.

The same day that this letter was written, Hicks Beach sent
Chamberlain advance copies of two Cabinet memoranda on the

[1] We can still recapture something
of the relationship between them from
a daughter's description: "Difference
of outlook naturally affected their political relations, and the fact that Mr.
Chamberlain's views were the more
calculated to draw popular applause
was of itself sufficient to stiffen instinctive resistance in Sir Michael"
(Lady Victoria Hicks Beach, *Life of Sir
Michael Hicks Beach*, p. 159).
[2] See Viscount Ullswater's *A
Speaker's Commentaries*, vol. i. p. 321.

Growth of Expenditure. These state papers deserve our attention. They mark a turning-point in the history of British financial policy.

The first is an analysis, prepared by the Treasury, of the growth of Government expenditure since the formation of the Unionist Coalition. In the seven years from 1895 to 1902, annual expenditure, not including the cost of the war in South Africa, is shown to have risen from £105,130,000 to £147,549,000, or by 40 per cent. The significance of these figures is underlined by a comparison with earlier years which show an increase of only 5 per cent between 1883 and 1890, and of 15 per cent between 1890 and 1895.

The second memorandum, written by Hicks Beach himself, is a powerful plea for retrenchment. He argues that the growth in the rate of expenditure cannot long be maintained, without departing from the principles of sound finance. Hitherto that growth has been met by the high yield, due to prosperous times, of indirect taxation and of the death duties, and by the increase of the income-tax. The first two are beginning to fail, as a result of the recession of trade. The income-tax "even if wholly continued, cannot in my judgment be increased in peace time".[1] He therefore concludes:

Heavier direct taxation would not then be borne; any attempt to increase the existing indirect taxes would be useless on a falling revenue, and the only possible new indirect taxes which would produce any important amount, without a complete return to a protectionist policy, would be small duties on corn, or meat or petroleum, on the political objections to which I need not dwell.

The inference is clear. A point has been reached where increased expenditure can only be financed either by raising the income-tax or by imposing revenue duties. To the "Gladstonian Garrison" at the Treasury, the mere suggestion of either savoured of immorality.

[1] Elsewhere in the memorandum Sir Michael writes of the income-tax: "I see no hope . . . of a sufficient surplus to take off even a 1d. of the income tax in 1902–3, though we must expect great complaints of its retention at so high a figure as 14d. after the war, properly so called, is over; and it is undoubtedly a very serious matter that . . . our ordinary expenditure would still require the continuance at a war rate in time of peace of a tax which has always been considered our great reserve for time of war". The reader of a later age will variously smile or weep.

The rest of the memorandum is devoted to suggestions for retrenchment in the different departments. Oblivious of the darkening international scene and of the German naval programme, the Chancellor proposes drastic economies in the Navy and Army Estimates. More reasonably, and evidently with an eye on Chamberlain, he calls for ". . . a determined attempt to induce our self-governing Colonies to take their share in the naval defence of the Empire". The Colonial Office is censured for having "gone too fast"; and the survey closes ominously with the statement: "I think we are not now in a position to hold out hopes of additional grants from the Exchequer either in aid of rates or for Old Age Pensions".

The two memoranda were accompanied by a private letter in which the Chancellor spoke of resigning, if his demands for retrenchment were not met.

HICKS BEACH TO CHAMBERLAIN

Private.—September 16, 1901.—. . . We are still in the region of war finance, and . . . I fear that we may have to have a December session before we get out of it. But I shall certainly press, even if we remain in that region, that, so far as expenditure is concerned which is not due to the war, we should abstain from burthening ourselves with further permanent increases in next year's Estimates. And I have thought it only right to give the Prime Minister full and early intimation of the course I may feel bound to take, if the Cabinet take a different view. . . . I should not have said all I have on the subject of our expenditure, both publicly and privately, if I had not felt deeply on a matter for which as Chancellor of the Exchequer I am primarily responsible. I have served many years in office—I have never, so far as I know, tried unduly to insist on my own views. . . . I have frequently been overruled by the Cabinet . . . and have yielded—notably in Brodrick's "army organisation" last spring. But I think you will admit that this has its limits in matters affecting the department for which one is oneself responsible; and I cannot accept, next year, even a more unbearable position than that in which I was placed last session.

Chamberlain was never the irresponsible spendthrift of public money that his enemies pretended. But he could never accept that the energies of a fast-expanding Empire should be confined or endangered by blind regard for the canons of orthodox finance. He did not yet pursue his ideas on this subject to their logical conclusion, but his revulsion from the Chancellor's plea for "economy at any price" was instinctive. He made no attempt to rebut the detailed arguments of the Treasury—they were, indeed, irrefutable within the assumptions of so-called sound finance; but, for all its elaborate courtesy, his reply was a denial of the whole spirit of Hicks Beach's memorandum.

CHAMBERLAIN TO HICKS BEACH

Confidential.—September 30, 1901.—. . . There is much in your minute with which I agree and I sincerely sympathise with you in all the anxieties of your position during the critical time through which we have been passing. I entirely repudiate and dissociate myself from the charges which ignorant critics have sometimes invented against you, and I recognise that you have been very broadminded in regard to all expenditure, however gigantic, for which just and reasonable cause could be shown. I may occasionally have thought that you have refused expenditure which would have been fruitful, but, on the whole, you have been more severely tried by your colleagues than any Chancellor in my time. . . .

I agree that the time will come when popular enthusiasm will no longer support a continuance of war taxation, and there is real fear of a dangerous reaction against military and naval expenditure (including the modest demands of the Colonial Office).

At the same time I would observe that, considering the increase of population and of wealth, I think that even our present burdens are very light, compared with what our forefathers bore in the beginning of the 19th Century, and they are moderate in comparison with the estimates of foreign nations at the present time. Still I believe you are right in thinking that, without a great cause to justify them, the people of this country will expect a reduction, when the present war is over.

But, and this is very important for you to consider, the reaction has not even begun yet. The Opposition would, without a moment's hesitation, join the malcontents of our own party in denouncing us, if there were the slightest ground for saying that we put economy before either the strenuous prosecution of the war or the necessary preparation for future defence. In fact, the failures of the war have produced an uneasy feeling that we are not strong enough and that any contest forced upon us by a European power would find us insufficiently prepared. The mistakes of the Army have, to some extent, encouraged doubts as to Naval efficiency, and I am convinced that any serious conflict between the Government and its Naval and Military advisers on the subject of efficient preparation would be disastrous for the former. *Still more would it be disastrous for the reputation of an individual Minister if he parted from his colleagues because they took the side of the experts. Randolph's case is in point here.*[1] The time may come, and probably will come, when the demands of the experts will be unreasonable, and public opinion, no longer under the influence of the feelings aroused by the war, will be on the side of the economist; but I am firmly convinced that that time has not yet arrived and that it would be a fatal mistake to anticipate it. . . .

There are a number of minor points in your paper which I will not enter upon now, although they must be fully discussed hereafter, but, on the main question, my judgment is that there is serious ground for caution and for careful examination of all new estimates, but there is no necessity for the declaration of a "policy of economy" as a supreme object at the present time, but that, on the contrary, undue stress on this point would be misconstrued and would seriously endanger the position of any Government or Minister that gave to it an exceptional and special prominence.

Chamberlain's reference to Lord Randolph Churchill was fully justified by Beach's use of the threat of resignation; but it touched the Chancellor on the raw. He answered with some asperity:

HICKS BEACH TO CHAMBERLAIN

October 2, 1901.—I am much obliged by your letter. But I fear I cannot say that your conclusions are satisfactory to me. I do not think you quite understand what I desire. . . .

I do not ask for a reduction of our present burthens. That is impossible without a reaction, which, as you say, has not yet visibly begun. But I do ask for a cessation, so far as may be possible, of their increase; and certainly for a much less rate of increase than has prevailed in the past six years. It is true that our present burthens are light, considering the increase of population and wealth, compared with those borne by our ancestors 100 years ago. . . . But the lightness of our taxation has been one of the main causes of a far greater increase in the wealth and comfort

---

[1] My italics.—J. A.

of our population in the last 50 years than any other European nation
has gained: and, if our peace taxation is to grow largely, as it must if
our present rate of increase in expenditure continues, that wealth and
comfort will be so diminished as to cause grave social danger. . . .

Despite its sharpness of tone, this letter marks a retreat from
Hicks Beach's earlier position. There is no further hint of
resignation, and the demand for immediate retrenchment is
abated. "I do not ask for a reduction of our present burthens.
. . . But I do ask for a cessation, so far as may be possible, of
their increase; and certainly for a much less rate of increase."

Chamberlain had won his point. Nevertheless, this correspondence must haved admonished him of the danger of trying the
Chancellor too far. Something would have to be sacrificed to his
plea for economy. The dangers of the international situation
made it hard to contemplate a reduction in the Defence Estimates. The cut, therefore, would have to come in his projects for
Social Reform. Here is the surest explanation of his abandonment of Old Age Pensions. It is difficult to see what else he
could have done in the circumstances. Hicks Beach and the die-
hards were against the measure on grounds of economy. Balfour
and the more progressive elements wanted all available funds
for their rival project of an Education Bill. This, in its way, as
we shall see, was also a great measure of Social Reform, but it
made no appeal to the Working Class as a whole. After a long
spell of circuses, the British Democracy was again hungry for
bread. The failure to provide it would be fatal to Unionism.

There is another and more far-reaching aspect to these
exchanges on financial policy. They show that the resources of
the fiscal system, which had prevailed from the time of Peel,
were exhausted. Neither Social Reform, nor Defence, nor any
of the varied enterprises of a modern state in the new age that
was dawning, could be financed without some transgression of
the canons of liberal economics. The dilemma was plain enough
to Hicks Beach, as his memorandum shows. It was equally plain
to John Morley, when he said: "If you are going to be militant
Imperialists, Free Trade goes".[1] They would have made no
provision for foreign danger or social change. But this could

---

[1] House of Commons, May 23, 1901.

never be Chamberlain's view. The needs of the modern state would have to be supplied. But how was the money to be raised? There were two ways, as Hicks Beach had pointed out: to increase direct taxation, or to impose revenue duties. The letters, just examined, show that Chamberlain thought the country well able to bear an increase in its burdens. One look, however, at the Unionist benches in the House of Commons must have been enough to convince him that there would be no support from that quarter for any taxation which involved a redistribution of wealth.

Was the alternative then to return to customs duties? If the "heretics" were right, these would be paid by the foreigner; if not, the burden would at least be evenly distributed over the whole community. As such, it might be defended on the respectable ground that it would "broaden the basis of taxation"; nor could customs duties strictly be considered as Protectionist so long as they were only raised for purposes of revenue. Was this, perhaps, a way for Unionists to finance Social Reform?

IV

When, in due course, Hicks Beach came to draw up the Budget, he was confronted, despite all economies, with a substantial deficit.[1] The greater part he proposed to cover by loan, but there would still remain a gap of £10,000,000. To bridge it, he resorted with sombre satisfaction to those desperate measures which, as he had warned the Cabinet, would become inevitable, if the growth of expenditure continued unchecked. He clapped an extra 1d. on the income-tax thus bringing it to 1s. 3d. in the £, a figure unprecedented since the Napoleonic Wars. To broaden the basis of taxation he also revived the registration duty of 3d. per cwt. on imported grain and corn and 5d. per cwt. on imported meal and flour. From this last imposition he looked for a yield of £2,650,000.

This Corn Duty deserves our close attention; for it will figure in our story like the grain of mustard seed in the parable. It had first been imposed for revenue purposes by Peel, at the

---

[1] The real deficit was £26,824,000, but Hicks Beach judged it prudent to raise a further £18,000,000 to provide for unexpected contingencies, so that altogether he had to find some £45,000,000.

"WILL HE TRIP, TRIP, TRIP?"

SIR MICHAEL: *I hate this Zollverein music, but I suppose I shall have to dance to it, and then I shall drop my money.*

From the cartoon by F. Carruthers Gould in the *Westminster Gazette*, June 11, 1902

same time that he had repealed the Corn Laws. Experience had
proved it both remunerative and easy to collect; and even
Gladstone, as Chancellor of the Exchequer, had thought it worth
retaining. It had been abolished, however, by Robert Lowe in
1869, in the course of a final orgy of tariff dismantlement. Lowe
had been irked by what he regarded as a tax on "raw material
in its very rawest state" and had hoped that its withdrawal
might lead to an increase in the English depot trade in corn.
His hopes were disappointed by the event; nor was abolition
followed by any fall in the price of bread. The only result had
been an immediate loss to the Exchequer of £900,000.[1]

CHAP. XCII.

Æt. 65.

Hicks Beach introduced the Budget—his seventh and last—
on April 14, 1902. The early part of the speech seemed to excite
little controversy, but, when he announced the revival of the
Corn Duty, a shout of "Well done, Well done!" rang across the
House. It came from Sir Howard Vincent, the leader of the little
group of old-fashioned Tory Protectionists. Protectionism was
by no means as dead among the "Gentlemen of England" as
many might assume; and, that night, George Wyndham would
write to his father:

I must congratulate you on having "lived to see the registration duty
reimposed on corn". . . .

You could not have taken the £2,650,000 on corn without putting
another penny on the income tax. . . .

It is a good Budget; both sound in the revival of a principle and opportune in the moment for applying it.

The delight of the Protectionists gave the Liberals their cue.
They declared that Free Trade was in danger, and Harcourt
condemned the duty as a tax on "the first necessity of the food
of the people". But to the great majority of Unionists these
seemed to be mock heroics. The person of the Chancellor was in
their eyes sufficient guarantee of the "soundness" of the proposal; and, if they needed any argument, it was supplied by
young Mr. Bonar Law, who proved conclusively that the

[1] Strangely enough Chamberlain had apparently had doubts about Lowe's decision several years before. Austen Chamberlain once told my father of a dinner at Highbury, in the 70's or early 80's, when Chamberlain had told Bright that he thought the final dropping of the Corn Duty had been a mistake. Bright had been rather shocked by this unorthodox view.

additional cost to the production of the four-pound loaf would be half a farthing. When the House divided on the resolution only two Unionists [1] voted with the minority. The rest were content to believe with Hicks Beach that

a duty which, when it existed, nobody felt, for the removal of which nobody was grateful because nobody desired it, will no more in the future than in the past have . . . any practical effect on the cost of food.

In the country at large the revival of the Corn Duty aroused little interest. It was condemned by the Cobden Club and the Manchester Chamber of Commerce; but business opinion, as a whole, was more concerned with the increase in the income-tax and the stamp-duty. Press comment was restrained, but there was a prophetic sentence in the *National Review*, then a publication of rising importance:

Though there is no rebate on Colonial corn, such as there ought to be, the slow-moving mother-country is gradually working towards the position in which she will be able to enter into preferential trade relations with the daughter nations.[2]

The first reference to the Corn Duty among Chamberlain's Papers is in the form of a directive to Vince, his chief agent in Birmingham.

CHAMBERLAIN TO VINCE

April 26, 1902.—. . . As regards the "Bread Tax"—"Big Loaf"— "Grinding the Poor"—I think the right line is: "You will be asked to make a sacrifice for a war which you have approved, and in which you have as much interest as any other class. It is doing you the greatest injustice to say that you are not ready to take your full share. If you were not, you would be making a war at other people's expense, which is not a very honourable position."

I do not believe in the argument which some of my friends affect, viz. that the new Tax will cost the working class nothing.

As yet he still regarded the Duty as a domestic and purely financial measure. A few days later, however, an important exchange in the Parliament at Ottawa raised the question to a new level.

---

[1] Messrs. A. Cross and C. H. Seely.   [2] *National Review*, May 1902.

The Colonial Prime Ministers were due to meet in London for CHAP.
XCII.
the Coronation. Accordingly, on May 12, Borden, the leader of
the Canadian Opposition, initiated a discussion on Imperial ÆT. 65.
relations. In the course of his speech, he proposed that the
House should pass a resolution in favour of the establishment
of reciprocal tariff preferences within the Empire, in order to
strengthen the hands of the Canadian Government at the
Colonial Conference. Laurier replied that

he was going to England to discuss them [Commercial relations] on the
invitation of the Imperial Government, and he could not conceive that
Mr. Chamberlain would invite the Colonial representatives to discuss the
subject, unless the British Government had something to propose.

There was now a duty on wheat and flour which placed Canada in a
position to make offers which she could not make in 1897. *A step had
thus been taken which would make it possible to obtain preference for
Canadian goods.*

Sir Wilfrid concluded by announcing amid cheers that he was prepared
to discuss with Mr. Borden the resolution to be adopted unanimously by
the House.[1]

Laurier's statement was received in London on May 13, the
second day of the debate on the Finance Bill. Campbell-
Bannerman at once drew attention to it, as evidence that the
Corn Duty was a first step to a preferential policy. Balfour,
replying for the Government, repudiated Laurier's interpretation. He declared that the tax had no connection, direct or
indirect, either with the Colonial Conference or with the visit of
the Canadian Prime Minister.

We have reached a crucial point in our story. The Prime
Minister of Canada, the greatest of the Colonies, had expressed
the hope that the Corn Tax would lead to reciprocal preferential trade between Canada and the United Kingdom. The
next day he had been sharply rebuffed by Balfour. Chamberlain's mind was not yet set upon Preference, though he already
leaned towards it. He was determined, however, that Laurier's
proposal should not be condemned in advance. To have done so,
indeed, would have been to wreck the prospects of the Colonial
Conference. Matters could not, therefore, remain where Balfour

[1] From the account in *The Times* of May 13, 1902. (My italics.—J. A.)

had left them. Someone would have to reassure Laurier that, on this question of Preference, the Cabinet's collective mind was at least open to persuasion.

On May 16, four days after Laurier's statement, Chamberlain spoke in Birmingham Town Hall.[1] His speech is vital to our study. It is the prologue to the Tariff Reform campaign.

For more than an hour Chamberlain traversed the whole field of politics. He censured the Opposition, discussed the Education Bill and explained the course of events in South Africa. Thence, by a natural order of ideas, he addressed himself to the cost of the war, and so to the provisions of the Budget, and, finally, to the Corn Duty itself. He began by ridiculing the Opposition claim that the duty would lead to a return of the "hungry '40s".

Now the experts . . . tell us that there is grave reason to doubt whether we shall pay it at all, whether it will not fall on the producers in other countries. . . . I am sure I hope they are true. I confess I think there is a certain humour in the thought that those who have denounced us, who have calumniated us in connexion with this war, will have themselves partly to pay for it. But I have not come down here to my own people to defend this tax on the ground that you will not pay any of it. I will assume that you will pay, every one of you, an average of one-eighth of a penny per 4 lb. loaf more than you paid before. (*Laughter.*)

He went on to deride Campbell-Bannerman's warning that the Corn Duty paved the way for Preferential Trade.

. . . Sir Henry Campbell-Bannerman told us that this tax had another and a most dangerous aspect. It was the thin end of the wedge, it was the beginning of a new policy, of which he spoke with bated breath and in tones of horror (*laughter*); and what do you think the new policy is to which he thinks this tax may lead? It is the possibility of preferential relations with our colonies. He quoted a statement of Sir Wilfrid Laurier, the distinguished and patriotic Prime Minister of Canada, in which he referred to the approaching conferences in London, and expressed his hope that they would lead to closer commercial relations. Ah! But here Sir Henry Campbell-Bannerman saw the trail of the serpent. (*Laughter.*) What? Closer relations between the colonies and the mother country!

[1] The annual meeting of the Grand Committee of the Birmingham Liberal Unionist Association.

Cobden, Cobden whom he professes to follow, Cobden the great free trader, made a reciprocity treaty with France; but the idea of a reciprocity treaty with our own children—that fills the mind of Sir Henry Campbell-Bannerman with disgust which he is only able ineffectively to express (*laughter*); and in this he shows once more that lack of imagination, that lack of foresight, which distinguishes, and always has distinguished, the Little Englander or the Little Scotchman. (*Laughter.*) . . .

This was in a tone of banter, but, in what followed, he was never more in earnest in his life.

The position of this country is not one without anxiety to statesmen and careful observers. The political jealousy of which I have spoken, the commercial rivalry more serious than anything we have yet had, the pressure of hostile tariffs, the pressure of bounties, the pressure of subsidies, it is all becoming more weighty and more apparent. What is the object of this system adopted by countries which, at all events, are very prosperous themselves—countries like Germany and other large Continental States? What is the object of this policy of bounties and subsidies? It is admitted; there is no secret about it; the intention is to shut out this country, as far as possible, from all profitable trade with those foreign States and, at the same time, to enable those foreign States to undersell us in British markets. That is the policy; and we see that it is assuming a great development, that old ideas of trade and free competition have changed. We are face to face with great combinations, with enormous trusts, having behind them gigantic wealth. Even the industries and commerce which we thought to be peculiarly our own, even those are in danger. *It is quite impossible that these new methods of competition can be met by adherence to old and antiquated methods which were perfectly right at the time at which they were developed. At the present moment, the Empire is being attacked on all sides and, in our isolation, we must look to ourselves. We must draw closer our internal relations, the ties of sentiment, the ties of sympathy, yes, and the ties of interest. If by adherence to economic pedantry, to old shibboleths, we are to lose opportunities of closer union which are offered us by our colonies, if we are to put aside occasions now within our grasp, if we do not take every chance in our power to keep British trade in British hands, I am certain that we shall deserve the disasters which will infallibly come upon us.* (Cheers.)

. . . *The days are for great Empires and not for little States.* . . .[1]

---
[1] My italics.—J. A.

His meaning was plain enough. Economic isolation was as out of date as diplomatic isolation. In the face of foreign competition, the nations of the Empire must draw closer together if they would survive. Laurier's suggestion, therefore, deserved the most serious consideration. To most people in the spring of 1902 this sounded only common sense. A year later, when he came to draw the conclusions, it would seem revolutionary.

In the country the speech attracted attention; nothing more. Campbell-Bannerman claimed it as proof of the sinister intentions of the Government;[1] but Rosebery, speaking at Leeds a few days later, seemed almost approving.[2] *The Spectator* commented acidly, "Why cannot our statesmen leave the Empire alone?" Leo Maxse, however, wrote in a more prophetic strain:

[The outcome] depends on the energy and will power of one man. . . . Far better that he should leave the government and raise a new standard, than allow the Colonial Premiers to return to their homes with the conviction that the Mother country rates her shibboleths above her children.[3]

Meanwhile, Chamberlain had achieved his immediate purpose. When the House met again after Whitsun, Hicks Beach declared: ". . . I disclaim altogether the interpretation which Sir Wilfrid Laurier has placed upon the corn duty". Nevertheless, he went on to say:

If we could have Free Trade with our Colonies, I do not see why that necessarily involves increased duties on our part against foreign nations; but, if we could have Free Trade with our colonies, even some sacrifice in that direction might be made.

The Corn Duty had been proposed as a revenue duty "absolutely without prejudice to any discussions which may take place between us and the colonial representatives on the question of commercial relations".[4]

Chamberlain was not in the House that afternoon, but Austen rose to answer the many references made to his Birmingham speech. In a conciliatory tone, he pointed out that his father had not gone so far as to advocate the adoption of reciprocal preferences. He had only refused "to be deterred

---

[1] Speech at Darlington, May 24, 1902.
[2] May 30, 1902.
[3] *National Review*, June 1902.
[4] June 9, 1902.

from proposing a tax, which he believed to be good on its own
merits, merely because it might be used, if the people of this
country so willed, to draw closer the ties between the Mother
country and the Colonies".[1]

Further controversy was thus avoided and the question of
reciprocal preferences was left open for the consideration of the
Colonial Conference. As yet, this was all that Chamberlain
desired.

V

Momentous and far-reaching changes were in the air. In the
months between the burial of the Queen and the anointing of
her son, ideas, which until then had been the preserve of
advanced thinkers and of a few far-sighted statesmen, suddenly
became the common stock of the back benches, the platform,
and the press. The Victorian age was over; and the new age,
conceived and long nurtured within the old, slowly struggled
towards the light. But so solid was the social structure through
which it had to break, and so tenacious the habits of mind
which bound it to the old, that its growth would be long
retarded; fatally, as it proved, for the world.

We have followed in some detail the steps by which England
was weaned away from Splendid Isolation. Since Chamberlain's
duel with Bülow, Germany was more and more regarded as the
enemy; and, as the public slowly awoke to the dangers of the
international situation, so its attention was increasingly engaged by the problems of defence. Already, the Navy League
warned against von Tirpitz's naval programme and pleaded for
a stronger battle fleet.

There was also widespread dissatisfaction with the condition
of the Army. The South African War had exposed the utter
inadequacy of a military system dating from the Crimean War;
but few believed that Brodrick's scheme for Army Reform was
suited to our needs. Unlike the military nations of the Continent,
we had no trained reserve of man-power; and this spring saw
the foundation of the National Service League to advocate
compulsory military training for the youth of the country.

There were many, and Lord Roberts was among them, who

[1] June 9, 1902.

believed that Chamberlain should have devoted himself to the reorganisation of the armed forces. Nor was this only the opinion of his friends. So sharp a critic as W. H. Massingham had compared him to Carnot,[1] and even the *Annual Register* had written that "he was looked upon, rightly or wrongly, as the only member of the Cabinet capable of re-organising the naval and military organisation of the country".[2]

It is tempting to speculate that, with better military preparations, we might have averted the first World War, or at least hastened the victory. Yet, there can be little doubt that Chamberlain was right not to seek out a task to which he was never invited. It was his faith, and events would confirm it, that the unity of the Empire was our greatest strength. But, as yet, the Colonies felt no urge to unite in schemes of Imperial defence. Chamberlain already knew their mood. They had rejected his "Kriegsverein" proposals two years earlier;[3] and it would be the same at the Colonial Conference that year. If opinion in the Empire had been different, if the Colonies had been as much concerned with defence as they were with commerce, he might well have chosen the military road. Had it turned out that way, it is pleasing to believe that, as with Gibbon, the organiser of the Edgbaston Rifle Corps might not have been useless to the Minister of Defence.[4]

Anxiety over our military preparations was matched by growing fears for our commercial position. Our steel production had for some time been outstripped by that of the United States and of Germany; and our firms were faced, both at home and abroad, with the competition of giant trusts or cartels, subsidised by their Governments and protected by high tariffs. To quote M. Halévy: "The British manufacturers were fighting in the open and as scattered units a foe secured by strong entrenchments and organised as a disciplined army".[5] The strength of these trusts had been shown in 1901, when Pierpont Morgan's United States Steel Corporation had acquired a majority of the shares of the Leyland Shipping Company. In 1902, the American Tobacco Trust was only just prevented from buying up the

[1] Article in the *Speaker*, July 12, 1902.
[2] *Annual Register*, 1902.
[3] See Vol. III. ch. lxxv. p. 630.
[4] See Vol. I. ch. iv. p. 62.
[5] *A History of the English People.* Epilogue (1895–1905), vol. i. p. 292.

whole British tobacco industry by the amalgamation of the chief British firms. The Imperial Tobacco Company would pay its way handsomely. Its success, indeed, aroused the envy of many business men. Nor were they deterred by the general belief that no trust or cartel could operate successfully without a tariff to keep up domestic prices.

Since the Budget of 1901, indeed, there had been a significant revival of Protectionist agitation. Its chief exponents in the House of Commons formed a little group led by Sir Howard Vincent and Mr. Lowther. Early in the session of 1902, one of them, Mr. Seton-Karr, had moved an amendment urging some measure of agricultural protection to strengthen our domestic food supplies in case of war, but coupled with the grant of preferences in favour of the Colonies. The amendment had been withdrawn in face of the opposition of the President of the Board of Trade; though not before a number of speeches had been made in its support, one of them by Mr. Chaplin, a former member of the Government. Similar tendencies were evident in the press. Sir Vincent Caillard, a former governor of the Ottoman Bank and a financier of international repute, wrote in the *National Review* of the need for an Imperial Tariff.[1] A few weeks later the *Daily Mail* challenged the established fiscal policy in an article headlined "Are the books wrong?" [2]

No single incident gave greater impetus to these new ideas than the formation of the North Atlantic Shipping Combine; an effect of the first great wave of American surplus capital seeking new fields for investment. By April 7, 1902, Pierpont Morgan, the head of the Combine, had gained control of all our best Atlantic shipping, excepting only the Cunard and Allan lines. Our fastest ships were in American hands and might even be transferred to the American flag. Something like a panic ensued. Was it the end of us? "The supremacy of the mercantile marine had slipped from us while we slept." [3] The Government was blamed for not preventing "an intolerable national humiliation", making "Great Britain a mere annex of the United States".[4]

The fears aroused were exaggerated but they were not

[1] *National Review*, February and April 1902.
[2] July 1902.
[3] *Annual Register*, 1902 (published 1903).
[4] *National Review*, June 1902.

groundless. The incident was both a warning and a revelation. In the event, a satisfactory agreement was reached between the Board of Trade and the Combine. It was settled that the British lines absorbed by it should remain British, and that at least one-half of the ships built, in the future, for the Combine should fly the British flag. As a reinsurance, however, the Cabinet also decided to subsidise the Cunard line, to the extent of £150,000 a year, in return for a pledge from its directors that it would remain entirely in British hands.

The Chamberlain Papers show that Gerald Balfour, the President of the Board of Trade, consulted Chamberlain at every step during the negotiations with Morgan. Chamberlain's views on the eventual agreement are an interesting blend of fundamental radicalism and shrewd common sense. They also offer a pungent commentary on the mood of the Cabinet at this time.

CHAMBERLAIN TO DEVONSHIRE

September 22, 1902.—I agree with you that the proposed agreement with Morgan is vague and probably does not amount to much.

But it has the advantage of meeting the fears of some members of the Cabinet that we might be engaging in a contest with the U.S. Government, who would be able to beat us in any Subsidy Competition. This arrangement makes us friends with Morgan & prevents anything in the nature of an international conflict.

Personally I do not share the fears of my colleagues & I think that G. Britain is never so weak as when she is afraid to meet any adversary on equal terms.

But then I am a Jingo, & I never can get any real support, from you or any one else in the Cabinet, in support of my own convinced opinion that we ought not to give way to the bluffing of any Foreign Power & that, if the worse came to the worst, we could hold out, as our ancestors did, against the lot of them.

I think the Morgan Combination is a move in a great commercial war &, if I were dictator, I would meet it with strong measures. As it is, I attach most importance to the agreement with the Cunard Co. which will strengthen them to hold their own in the ensuing fight. The Morgan agreement is a "sop to Cerberus", &, if we are not prepared to fight for all we are worth, it is the best alternative I can suggest.

Quite apart from the Atlantic Combine, Chamberlain was already keenly concerned by the handicap imposed on the British merchant navy and on British trade by foreign shipping subsidies. Evelyn Cecil, then chairman of the Select Committee dealing with this question, found him a strong supporter of retaliationist measures; and we see him urging these upon his colleagues in the Cabinet.

CHAMBERLAIN TO LANSDOWNE

House of Commons, June 10, 1902.—. . . If I were Dictator, I should at once propose—subject to the approval of the Colonies which I think would be given—either (1) That coastal trade—including *grand cabotage* —should be confined to British ships and to the ships of those countries which give us reciprocal privileges . . . or (2) Require that all foreign ships, engaged in trade between a British and any other port, should be subject to all the liabilities as to load-line, number of crew, accommodation, boats etc. to which British ships are subject, or should pay dues or taxes equal to the estimated charge which these liabilities impose.

This letter is significant. It shows how far Chamberlain had already departed from accepted nineteenth-century commercial doctrine.

CHAPTER XCIII

THE COLONIAL CONFERENCE: I. POLITICAL RELATIONS AND DEFENCE

(July 1902)

IMPERIAL Character of the Coronation—The Coronation Postponed—
Imperial Federation *versus* Colonial Nationalism—Salisbury's "last
testament"—Procedure and Personalities of the Conference—
Chamberlain Proposes a Council of Empire—His Proposal Ignored—
The Colonies and Imperial Defence—"The sea is all one . . ."—An
Imperial Reserve—The British Proposals Rejected—Chamberlain
Rebukes the Premiers.

I

BOOK
XX.
1902.

THE time appointed for the Coronation now drew on. Sixty-four
years had passed since London had seen a coronation; sixty-four
years which had witnessed the transformation of an Empire.
When Queen Victoria had come to the throne, Canada had
scarcely begun to spread beyond the provinces of the eastern
seaboard; Australia was best known as a penal settlement; New
Zealand was not yet wrested from the Maoris; and India was
still administered by a trading company. Now the first three had
become strong, self-governing nations, while the Great Dependency had been brought under the Crown. In addition, the
foundations of a new Empire had been laid in the four corners of
the African continent; not least by Chamberlain's efforts.

The Coronation was to be celebrated with extraordinary
magnificence. Above all, it was to be an Imperial occasion. The
Premiers of the self-governing Colonies came as guests of honour
and, with the Princes of India and the rulers of the Protectorates,
mingled with the assembled throng of foreign royalties and
envoys. By a happy stroke of imagination, military contingents

were summoned from every part of the Empire to join in the processions and reviews. The soldiers of the self-governing colonies, veterans of the South African War, bivouacked in the London parks. The hosts of India—Gurkhas, Rajputs and Sikhs—were mustered at Hampton Court; and the public were amazed and delighted by exotic detachments of Hausas from West Africa, gendarmes from Fiji, and Chinese infantry from Singapore.

London rose to the occasion as never before. Every day brought forth its civil festivity or martial review. Theatres and places of entertainment were packed, and the streets were gay with flags and bunting. The most elaborate of these decorations was the Canadian Arch, a structure of wheat sheaves and apples, festooned with electric lights, spanning the whole width of Whitehall. We must mark this arch well. It has a sinister part to play in our story.

With all these festivities there was little rest for the Colonial Secretary. Within the space of a few days, we find him opening the Colonial Troops Institute, presiding at the annual dinner of the Corona Club, and attending an almost continuous series of Courts, banquets and receptions. These multiplied in number, as the distinguished guests assembled, and included a great reception at Prince's Gardens for the royalties of the Empire: among them the Maharajah of Jaipur, a great admirer of Chamberlain, the Sultan of Perak, and Lewanika, the pictur-esque monarch of Barotseland.

All this time there was no respite from work. The debates on the Budget raged in the House of Commons; and, in Committee, the Education Bill dragged its length along. Meanwhile, in addition to current legislation and to the routine administration of the Empire, the Colonial Secretary's agenda was crowded with the problem of the South African settlement and the preparation for the Colonial Conference. When a few days later he wrote, "Just now, with the Colonial premiers here, there is a fearful stress of work", it was no mere figure of speech.[1]

The King was to have been crowned on June 26. Suddenly, towards midday on June 24, London was stunned to learn that he was "suffering from perityphlitis . . . rendering an urgent

[1] J. C. to Lord Alverstone, July 1, 1902.

operation necessary". The operation was performed successfully, but the Coronation was indefinitely postponed. By the
royal wish, the other festivities went forward as arranged; but
the spell was broken; and, for many days to come, the crowds
turned their backs on the parades to stand dense but silent
outside the palace, waiting for the bulletins.

The uneasiness of the sickroom spread to the Coronation
guests. The foreign royalties departed; and it was in an
atmosphere of awkwardness and constraint that the Colonial
Premiers assembled for the opening of the third Colonial
Conference.

II

Few political conclaves have aroused such great expectations
as the Colonial Conference of 1902 or, led on, despite apparent
failure, to such momentous consequences. In the development
of Chamberlain's ideas, it marked a turning-point. He came to it
with an open mind. When it ended, the broad direction of his
future course was set for ever.

The public, both at home and in the Colonies, approached the
Conference in a very different spirit from that of 1897. Then, the
meeting of Premiers had seemed a mere incident of the Diamond
Jubilee celebrations, deserving but little attention. Now, it was
a major event in its own right, coinciding with the Coronation
merely for convenience. As Chamberlain was to say in his
opening speech:

You came here, gentlemen, for two purposes. You have come here to
take your part—and a very prominent part—in the ceremonies of the
Coronation as the representatives of the great nations across the seas
but you have also come for the purpose of a business conference.[1]

This difference of approach sprang from the upsurge of
Imperial sentiment evoked by the South African War. The
unity of the Empire was no longer a theory. It had been proved
in battle. But, though Imperialism was the prevailing faith of
the whole self-governing Empire, it assumed very different
manifestations in its several parts.

At home, most Imperialists still thought of Imperial Federation as the goal. Some looked to its attainment by the creation

[1] Minutes of Colonial Conference, 1902.

of federal political institutions. Others, more concerned by our
declining share of the world's trade, urged the formation of
an Imperial customs union with a common tariff against the
foreigner. Yet others, and they were the majority at this time,
pressed for increased Colonial participation in Imperial Defence.
These were all centralising conceptions. Federal institutions
would, inevitably, have been situated in England. An Imperial
customs union implied a supreme customs authority, and must
have been dominated by the Board of Trade. Colonial participation in Imperial Defence was envisaged in terms of increased
contributions to the Navy Estimates and subordination of the
Colonial armies to the War Office. The truth is that most
Englishmen still thought of the self-governing Colonies as
dependencies. They recognised the King's subjects in these
Colonies as their equals. But, in their hearts, they did not yet
concede that the Colonies, as nations, were equal in status to the
United Kingdom.

In the larger Colonies, in Canada and Australia, the outlook
was very different. The same factors which had revived their
Imperial sentiment had also strengthened their local nationalism. They were proud to belong to the British Empire, but as
Canadians or Australians, not just as individual subjects of the
King. The immense disparity in population, wealth and experience, which separated them from the United Kingdom, robbed
Imperial Federation of its attractions. It would have placed
them under heavy obligations to the Imperial Government,
without giving them equivalent control over its policies. With
the natural inferiority complex of growing nations, they were
both impressed by the power of Downing Street and suspicious
of its intentions. They wanted, therefore, not federation, with
the surrender of power to Downing Street which it would have
implied, but co-operation; equality, not so much between
individual British subjects, as between the different British
nations.

The outlook of the smaller Colonies—New Zealand, the Cape,
and Natal—was intermediate. Their local patriotism was already
strong, but it could hardly be called nationalism. They still
thought of themselves as Englishmen settled overseas and,
though insistent on their own rights, were willing, even anxious,

to join in wider Imperial schemes. The following incident illustrates their attitude. At one point in the Conference, Seddon of
New Zealand launched out, in his rather rambling fashion, into a
description of economic conditions. "In your country?" queried
Sir Wilfrid Laurier. "In our *Colony*", Seddon replied with
dignity.[1]

Such differences of outlook were the chief obstacle to closer
Imperial Union. To reconcile them would entail the sacrifice,
if not of principles, at least of long-cherished prejudices; and,
in countries where public opinion is a deciding factor, such
sacrifices are not easily made.

Salisbury, with his brilliant power of analysis, perceived the
difficulties and judged them still unripe for solution. In the last
great public speech of his life, he earnestly warned against the
dangers of seeking to force the pace of Imperial integration.

There are very important men, men of great intellect and authority,
who think the moment has come for some legislative action on our part,
which should federate the Colonies. I exhort them, before they do so,
carefully to consider what steps they are going to take and what results
they expect to come from them.

We have no power, by legislative action, to affect the flow of opinion and
of affection which has arisen so largely between the mother country and
her daughter states. They will grow in their own power, in their own
irresistible power, and I have no doubt they will leave combinations,
behind them, which will cast into the shade all the glories that the British
Empire has hitherto displayed.

But we cannot interfere by legislative action. . . . All kinds of difficulties are there before us—difficulties as to the burden of finance, difficulties as to the duty of defence, difficulties as to the rights of decision
which the mother country should retain, and . . . I look with some
apprehension upon any attempt to anticipate events or to foreclose
the results, the precious results which, if we are only patient and careful, the future has in store for the Empire.

The tendency of human beings and of statesmen—who are human
beings—is to anticipate all such matters and to think that, because their
own wretched lives are confined to some sixty or seventy years, therefore
it is open to them to force an anticipation of the results which the natural

[1] Conference Minutes, p. 56.

play of forces . . . bring before us. There is nothing more dangerous than to force a decision, before a decision is ready . . . There is no danger that appears to me more serious, for the time that lies before us, than an attempt to force the various parts of the Empire into a mutual arrangement and subordination for which they are not ready and which may only produce a reaction in favour of the old state of things. . . . Remember that . . . there is arising a state of things perfectly new to the world, a condition in which . . . an Empire is slowly arising out of the sea, that it has behind it the feelings and the affections of some of the most vehement races upon the face of the world, that the future destinies of the Empire depend on the prudence and judgment with which these forces are guided, [and] that the guidance of those forces must be, in a country such as ours, largely affected by the trend of popular opinion.[1]

This speech reads almost like a last testament, disinheriting Chamberlain. In the light of events, some may well think it prophetic. Chamberlain would fail in his endeavour; and yet the nations of the Empire have continued to "grow in their own power, in their irresistible power". But this is to oversimplify. Chamberlain wanted, no more than Salisbury, to impose new arrangements upon the Colonies. But what if the Colonies themselves came forward with agreed proposals for strengthening Imperial Unity? What if these seemed good, and only prejudice at home stood in the way of their fulfilment? Might it not, then, become the duty of an English statesman to persuade his colleagues to take the necessary "legislative action", or, if they refused, to appeal over their heads to the broad masses of the people?

III

The proceedings of the Conference of 1902 have never been published.[2] This secrecy has caused some speculation; and it was at one time suggested that publication had been withheld at Chamberlain's instance.[3] No evidence has ever been advanced in support of this rumour, nor is any to be found among the Chamberlain Papers. A more likely explanation is afforded by a

[1] Speech to the Primrose League, delivered at the Albert Hall, May 7, 1902 (from *The Times*, May 8).
[2] A report of tantalising brevity and incompleteness was issued in October 1902 (Cd. 1299).
[3] See Richard Jebb, *The Imperial Conference*, vol. i. p. 339.

letter from the Australian Prime Minister. It was written on his way to the Conference.

SIR EDMUND BARTON TO CHAMBERLAIN

Rome, June 9, 1902.—. . . Some of the questions are at present in a stage which necessitates great delicacy in handling. In a conference the proceedings of which are to be reported, and after a time published, it will perhaps be found impossible for the representatives of self-governing colonies to address you with the absolute frankness which alone will enable you to quite know the reasons why we hold certain views.

A verbatim report, however, was kept of the Conference and is before the present author. It covers 197 pages of printed foolscap and, except for two occasions when the Premiers consulted in private,[1] is a complete record of the proceedings.

The Conference was opened on June 30 and closed on August 11. Altogether there were ten sessions;[2] but a fortnight intervened between the second and the third, while Chamberlain was recovering from severe head injuries. We shall return, in another chapter, to the cab accident which caused them. Here it is enough to note that the Colonial Premiers as well as British public opinion were unanimous in insisting that the Conference could not proceed without him.

The Premiers met in the Secretary of State's room at the Colonial Office, and Chamberlain took the Chair at each session. He was accompanied by his Permanent and Parliamentary Under-Secretaries, Sir Montagu Ommanney and Lord Onslow, while Sir John Anderson of the Colonial Office acted as Secretary. Selborne, Brodrick and Gerald Balfour also took part, with their experts, in discussions affecting their departments.

Laurier had brought with him to London four members of the Canadian Government: the Ministers of Finance, Customs, Defence and the Postmaster-General.[3] Barton was also accompanied by his Minister of Defence, Sir John Forrest. At Laurier's instance, and despite some protest from Seddon who had come alone, these Ministers were admitted to the Conference to

[1] The first of these private consultations concerned defence. It was at the second that the decision was taken not to give the full Minutes to the public.
[2] June 30, July 4, July 18, July 22, July 25, July 30, August 1, August 5, August 8, August 11.
[3] Mr. W. S. Fielding, Mr. W. Paterson, Sir Frederick Borden and Sir William Mulock.

speak, though not to vote, on matters which were their special concern.

Chamberlain dominated the Conference by his personality and prestige. But, except for the opening session, his attitude was one of reserve. At times, he recalled the Premiers to the business in hand or intervened to test a doubtful argument or to put forward some consideration which seemed in danger of being overlooked. Otherwise he listened more than he talked. A great actor in Parliament or on the platform, he was matter of fact and "without atmosphere" in council.

Among the Colonial representatives Laurier and Seddon were outstanding. Silver-haired and silver-tongued, Laurier was the most distinguished of them, both by his extraordinary command of English, not his native language, and by the Gallic precision of his mind. A very shrewd politician of still unsuspected depth, he looked at the Empire from the standpoint of Canadian nationalism and, seeing in it advantages for his people, judged it good, in spite of earlier prejudices. He too spoke seldom at the Conference, and then more often on points of procedure than of substance; yet his interventions were the most decisive.[1]

Seddon was in every way his opposite; a large, robust, restless man, full of ideas, but rambling in exposition sometimes to the point of incoherence. He could count on the whole-hearted backing of New Zealand, where the people had just testified to their faith in "Seddonism", as his peculiar blend of Radicalism and Imperialism was already known, by presenting him with a purse of £2500. Barton, the dignified Australian Premier, was more prudent than forceful, and very conscious of the precarious position of the Australian Commonwealth Government, then still in the making. Of the two South African Premiers, Sir Gordon Sprigg was obliged to return early to the Cape to face the Suspension crisis.[2] Sir Albert Hime, a genial Natal squire, acquitted himself with distinction but felt, like Sprigg, that any initiative

---

[1] The Chamberlain Papers show that Laurier was offered a peerage in the Coronation honours, but declined (telegrams of June 10 and 18). Somewhat earlier (February 19, 1902) Lord Minto had written to Chamberlain: "Sir Wilfrid Laurier . . . has not been at all well and . . . I hear of Tarte speculating . . . to the effect that *he* may be Prime Minister some day!" Minto was well informed: Laurier suffered a serious breakdown in health after the Conference, and was forced to dismiss Tarte soon after his return to Canada.

[2] His place was taken by Mr. Fuller, the Agent-General for the Cape.

on his part should wait upon the Federation of the South African Colonies. Sir Robert Bond, of Newfoundland, was only there by courtesy, as he was himself almost painfully aware. He made only one serious attempt to intervene in the discussions, but it was lunch-time, and the others cut him short.

As in all conferences, much important business was done outside the ordinary sessions. The Premiers consulted privately among themselves, with Chamberlain, and with the other Ministers and permanent officials of the Imperial Government. These private meetings and the general sessions formed the warp and the woof from which the final pattern of the Conference was woven.

IV

Chamberlain's opening speech to the Conference is among his best. Broad principles and detailed proposals are skilfully combined. There is gravity without rhetoric; and the practical issues stand out with diamond clearness. He began by indicating the main subjects to be discussed.

. . . Our paramount object is to strengthen the bonds which unite us, and there are only three principal avenues by which we can approach this object. They are: Through our political relations in the first place; secondly, by some kind of commercial union. In the third place, by considering the questions which arise out of Imperial defence. These three great questions were considered at the last Conference, and, I think, it is clear they must form the principal subject of our deliberations on this occasion, and, indeed, of those of any future conferences which may afterwards be held.[1]

Here we may appropriately consider "these three great questions" under their separate heads.

Political Relations

The most eloquent passage of Chamberlain's opening speech was devoted to the political relations between the Colonies and the Mother Country. His words fell on stony ground, but some part of them must be quoted, if we are fully to understand the tenacity of his ideas. He still spoke of nothing less than the political federation of the Empire.

[1] Minutes of Colonial Conference of 1902, p. 2.

. . . I may be considered, perhaps, to be a dreamer, or too enthusiastic, but I do not hesitate to say that, in my opinion, the political federation of the Empire is within the limits of possibility. I recognise, as fully as anyone can do, the difficulties which would attend such a great change in our constitutional system. . . . But . . . I hold that, as we must put no limits to science, as the progress which has already been made is only an indication of the progess which may be made in the future . . . we have no right to put, by our action, any limit to the Imperial patriotism of the future; and it is my opinion that, as time goes on, there will be a continually growing sense of the common interests which unite us, and also perhaps, which is equally important, of the common dangers which threaten us. . . .

He then proceeded, in a celebrated passage, to renew his suggestion of setting up a Council of Empire.

. . . I would venture to refer to an expression in an eloquent speech of my right honourable friend, the Premier of the Dominion of Canada. . . . "If you want our aid call us to your Councils". Gentlemen, we do want your aid. We do require your assistance in the administration of the vast Empire which is yours as well as ours. The weary Titan staggers under the too vast orb of its fate. We have borne the burden for many years. We think it is time that our children should assist us to support it, and whenever you make the request to us, be very sure that we shall hasten gladly to call you to our Councils. If you are prepared at any time to take any share, any proportionate share, in the burdens of the Empire, we are prepared to meet you with any proposal for giving to you a corresponding voice in the policy of the Empire. . . . I have always felt myself that the most practical form, in which we could achieve our object, would be the establishment . . . of a real Council of the Empire to which all questions of Imperial interest might be referred; and, if it were desired to proceed gradually, as probably would be our course, . . . the Council might in the first instance be merely an advisory council. . . . But, although that would be a preliminary step, it is clear that the object would not be completely secured until there had been conferred upon such a Council executive functions, and perhaps also legislative powers; and it is for you to say, gentlemen, whether you think the time has come when any progress whatever can be made in this direction.[1]

[1] Minutes of Colonial Conference of 1902, pp. 2-4.

Next day, at a dinner given in honour of the Colonial Premiers, Sir Albert Hime seemed to take up this proposal when he expressed the hope "that at some not too distant period they in the Colonies might be thought worthy of some representation in it [the Imperial Parliament]".[1] But, in the Conference, there was no response of any kind. In 1897, the idea of a Council of Empire had provoked long discussions. This time it was not even criticised; it was ignored. Nothing could better illustrate the strength of Colonial aversion to any scheme for Imperial federation. The Premiers were patriots of Empire, but they were Colonial Nationalists first. How far the trend towards Colonial Nationalism had already gone was shown by Sir Edmund Barton:

> . . . I have a colleague who is so very British—although he is an Australian too, like myself—that he objects to the term of nationhood as applied to Australia.
>
> I myself rather revel in that term. I believe in the Canadian nation; I believe in the Australian nation. I believe in the South African nation, because I believe that the strength of the Empire is in the brotherhood of nations come from the same stock.[2]

V

Imperial Defence

With the failure of Chamberlain's proposal to set up a Political Council, Defence and Trade relations remained "the two main avenues "[3] along which the goal of a United Empire might be approached. Of the two, Defence relations were uppermost in the minds of the British Government and of the informed public at home. The reasons for this are not far to seek. For one thing, the experience of the Boer War had made problems of defence the chief topic of the day. For another, the new spirit of Imperialism aroused by that war had found, thus far, a primarily military expression. Last but not least, the growing burden of taxation led men to ask why the Colonies

[1] Speech at the Inner Temple, July 1, 1902 (quoted from *The Times* of July 2, 1902).
[2] Speech at a dinner given by the Imperial South Africa Association, June 20 (from the account in *The Times* of June 21).
[3] Chamberlain on receiving the freedom of the Grocers' Company, August 1, 1902.

should not contribute more towards the upkeep of the fighting services which assured their security as well as England's.

In the Colonies, it was the other way about. There, opinion had always looked on Imperial trade as the main avenue leading to closer Imperial unity, and there was little enthusiasm for strengthening the ties of defence. The Colonies had already begun to build up defence forces of their own. In their hearts, they always meant to rally to the Mother Country in the hour of danger; but they were afraid to commit themselves beforehand to a centralised defence system. They feared that it might draw them, against their will, into an unpopular European war. This fear, a kind of political claustrophobia, had been forcibly expressed by Laurier. Shortly before the Conference he had told the Dominion Parliament that

no scheme of defence applicable to all the Colonies could be devised . . . Canada would discuss the part she would take in her own defence and the Government had given a pledge . . . that it was prepared to carry out its duty on that score. But there was a school in England and in Canada, who wanted to bring Canada into the vortex of militarism, now the blight and curse of Europe. He was not prepared to endorse any such policy.[1]

Chamberlain had already been warned of Laurier's attitude by his old friend, Colonel George Denison, a Canadian nationalist as well as an Imperial patriot. Denison's proposal for circumventing the political objections to "a straight cash contribution" shows how closely the questions of trade and defence were connected in the Colonial mind.

DENISON TO CHAMBERLAIN

Toronto, February 22, 1902.—. . . If Sir Wilfrid [Laurier] agrees to a straight cash contribution for defence, the French [*i.e.* French Canadians] will raise the cry of "tribute", and demagogues will make trouble, and we do not want a French Ireland in Canada between us and the sea. We have therefore suggested the idea of a tariff for defence all around the Empire, and the French Canadians are such strong protectionists that they would agree to that. Monk and Bourassa [Liberal frondeurs] both told me that they thought our proposition would be a good thing for Canada.

[1] Speech delivered in the Dominion House of Commons, May 12, 1902   (from the report in *The Times*, May 13, 1902).

Denison was, in effect, renewing Hofmeyr's proposal of 1887 for a small duty on foreign goods, the proceeds of which could be devoted to the Navy. This proposal might well have proved acceptable to the Colonies, especially as it implied preferential trade between the different members of the Empire. But, for that very reason, Hicks Beach would not have it. Chamberlain felt keenly the difficulty of seeking concessions from the Colonies over defence when he could offer no thing in return, in the sphere of trade; witness his comments on Selborne's plans for increasing Colonial contributions to the Navy:

CHAMBERLAIN TO SELBORNE

Private—Colonial Office, May 29, 1902.—. . . I fear that yours is a counsel of perfection and that we shall not get near to it at present.

It might be different, if Beach were willing to open up the question of Preferential Trade in its widest form, but at present we must take what we can get and proceed slowly.

Despite this warning, Admiralty and War Office determined to launch a major offensive at the Conference. Their aims were, first, to obtain increased contributions from the Colonies, and, second, to extend their own control over the Colonial fighting services.

Despite his private doubts, Chamberlain gave Selborne and Brodrick his full support. In his opening speech, he contrasted the burden of defence borne by the Mother Country with that borne by the Colonies. In the United Kingdom, defence expenditure per head of population amounted to 29s. 3d. a year. In the Australasian Colonies, it was less than 4s., and, in Canada, only 2s. From these figures he drew a homely moral.

. . . Justification of union is that a bundle is stronger than the sticks which compose it, but, if the whole strain is to be thrown upon one stick, there is very little advantage in any attempt to put them into a bundle. . . .

He returned to the subject in his peroration, leading up to the conclusion that the strength of an Empire depended upon the "community of sacrifices" of its members.

... We, in the United Kingdom, for centuries past have been holding
our house like a strong man armed against all our enemies. We have felt,
throughout all the period, the burdens as well as the privileges and
advantages of empire. We see now that all other nations are also arming
to the teeth. I want you to consider for a moment what is the present
position of the smaller nations with whom, in population, you may more
closely compare yourselves. What is the position of such nations in
Europe as Greece, the Balkan States, or Holland, or the South American
Republics? Why, gentlemen, they are absolutely independent nations,
accordingly, they have to bear burdens for their military or naval de-
fences, or for both, as the case may be, to which yours bears no proportion whatever. I point out to you, therefore, that, in the clash of nations,
you have hitherto derived great advantages, even from a purely material
standpoint, from being a part of a great Empire. But the privileges, which
we enjoy, involve corresponding obligations. The responsibilities must be
reciprocal and must be shared in common, and I do not think that any
empire may be said to be on a sure foundation which is not based upon a
recognised community of sacrifices. . . .[1]

At subsequent sessions the Conference was addressed by the
First Lord of the Admiralty and by the Secretary for War.
Selborne expounded the classical Admiralty doctrine that "the
sea is all one and the British Navy therefore must be all one".[2]
It was pointless, he argued, for the Colonies to build navies of
their own. Instead they should increase their naval contributions. The Royal Navy, was, after all, their navy; and special
provision might be made to encourage their young men to enlist
in it.

Selborne's argument was coldly received by the Colonial
Premiers. The truth is that, in their minds, Defence Contributions raised the principle of "no taxation without representation". They could not make large-scale contributions to
Imperial Defence, without claiming a voice in the control of
their expenditure. Such a claim would have been only too
readily granted; but it would have meant participation in some
central defence body; and this, as we saw, they were determined
to avoid from fear of Whitehall domination. The Canadian

[1] June 30, 1902 (Minutes of Colonial
Conference of 1902, pp. 8-9).

[2] Memorandum by Lord Selborne,
August 7, 1902.

Ministers must have had this point in mind, when they wrote that acceptance of the Admiralty proposals ". . . would entail an important departure from the principle of Colonial self-government."[1]

Seddon, for his part, argued that the Colonies could not afford to pay direct contributions. Their Governments already had to bear the heavy expenses of railway construction and other public works, essential to the development of backward countries. There was, however, an indirect way in which they could make a great contribution.

> . . . If we give to the Mother Country advantages which we do not give to other countries, and under which the manufacturers of the Mother Country profit, then I say that is a contribution. Ten per cent. preference on British goods imported into New Zealand means £150,000 a year. . . .
>
> . . . It would be equal to paying the interest on five millions of money at three per cent., and, correspondingly, you might say that the Colony of New Zealand, by paying this, would be paying the interest on five battleships that might cost a million each. . . .

We may be sure that this argument was not lost on Chamberlain.

The outcome of these discussions was scarcely satisfactory to the Admiralty. Canada declined to make any contribution at all towards the Navy. The other Colonies eventually agreed to slight increases in their existing contributions: the Cape and Natal unconditionally; Australia and New Zealand in return for the strengthening of the Australasian squadron.[2]

On the military side, Brodrick urged the creation, in each of the Colonies, of an Imperial Reserve for the Army. This was to be a body, distinct from the local militias, trained and equipped on the same lines as the British regular army, and liable for service overseas. Brodrick based his proposal on a very similar offer of Seddon's; and it was hoped that New Zealand's example would influence the other Colonies.

[1] Memorandum by Canadian Ministers, August 11, 1902 (Minutes of Colonial Conference of 1902, p. 261).
[2] Much of Australian opinion favoured the creation of an Australian fleet, but the Commonwealth Minister of Defence, Sir John Forrest, was a powerful advocate of a single British navy. See his memorandum for Sir E. Barton of March 15, 1902.

CHAMBERLAIN TO BRODRICK

Private—40 *Prince's Gardens, July* 25, 1902.—When you see Seddon, tell him that you attach special importance to his proposal, because you think it will force the hands of the Commonwealth and the Dominion who cannot with decency remain behind after New Zealand has taken the initiative. The result will be similar to that which followed his offer of the latest contingents for the war.

This will be true *and he will like it.*

It was in vain. Canada and Australia both opposed the idea of an Imperial Reserve; Canada even refusing to equip its militia with the rifle in use in the rest of the Empire—an idiosyncrasy which Brodrick not unfairly described as "a little unfortunate". Moreover, it presently transpired that there was more difference between Brodrick's scheme and Seddon's than had at first appeared. Brodrick had proposed that the Imperial Exchequer should bear the cost of the Imperial Reserve, provided its members were liable for service overseas. Seddon agreed in principle, but wished to have it stipulated that the New Zealand Reserve would only be liable for service overseas in China, South Africa and Canada. He was not prepared to accept unconditional liability for service in India and Europe, nor would he agree to the integration of the New Zealand Reserve into Imperial regiments. As a counter-concession, however, he offered to contribute one-third of the total reserve pay from New Zealand funds.

At this point Chamberlain intervened with a compromise proposal. It was made in secret session [1] and no record of it was preserved. There is, however, some indication that it involved entrusting the Colonies with the defence of certain military areas and placing both Imperial and Colonial troops in those areas under a united command responsible to the Government of the Colony concerned. Be this as it may, the following letter suggests that Chamberlain's proposal satisfied neither the War Office nor the Premiers of Canada and Australia. It was not adopted, and Seddon's offer was withdrawn.

BRODRICK TO CHAMBERLAIN

War Office, August 11, 1902.—You will see from the enclosed that our present negotiation with New Zealand is at an end.

[1] August 8, 1902.

The discussion of last Friday was a serious blow to me and lands me in difficulties here, and I should be very much averse to opening fresh negotiations till we have come to an agreement between ourselves.

From what I can gather, neither Canada nor the Commonwealth Government appear likely to support the scheme, as modified by you—so that I fear we shall get nothing.

I realise that you were forced, by your views as to the policy involved, to take the course you did, but, from a Military point of view, it is the wreckage of a scheme which would have saved us heavy expenditure.

There the matter rested.

Apart, therefore, from the slight increase obtained in naval contributions,[1] the Conference had altogether failed to produce any agreed scheme for Imperial Defence. The failure made a deep impression on Chamberlain. Later, he would come to accept the attitude of the Colonies on this subject; but his immediate reaction was to rebuke them.

. . . We are told by the representatives of the Great Dominion of Canada and by the representative of the Commonwealth of Australia, that, in the present condition of public opinion in those Colonies, it would not be practicable to give us the assurance that any such scheme could be carried out. Gentlemen, I regret very much that such should be the case. I am bound to say that, in my opinion, public opinion in these Colonies must be very backward. I think it will have to progress, and that it will, in the natural course of things, progress, especially as the dangers, which lie all around you, are better appreciated. I know very well, of course, that, at the present time, these great Colonies have been free from anything in the nature of an attack upon themselves—it is all very well to rest upon that, but you may easily be too optimistic, and I think that anyone, who takes even a superficial view of the present state of the world, must feel that it is desirable that all, in proportion to their means, should be fully prepared for any emergency. . . .[2]

[1] They amounted altogether to about 1 per cent of U.K. expenditure on the Navy.   [2] Minutes of Colonial Conference of 1902, p. 99.

CHAPTER XCIV

THE COLONIAL CONFERENCE: II. RECIPROCAL PREFERENCE

(July 1902)

PREFERENCE, a Constitutional Issue—Canada Calls for Reciprocity—
Dualism of Chamberlain's Approach—His Private Initiative;
Laurier's Response and Hicks Beach's Veto—Chamberlain Defines
his Attitude Towards Empire Commercial Relations—Laurier Asks
for Reciprocity—Fielding and Paterson Demolish the Board of Trade
Arguments—Private Meeting of Chamberlain and the Canadian
Ministers—They begin Negotiations with the Board of Trade—An
Unexpected Conflict of Principle—Preference by Reducing Duties or
by Raising Them?—An Inconclusive Resolution—Canada's Warning
—The Lesson of the Conference.

I

Commercial Relations

THE Colonial Premiers were as positive in their approach to the
problems of commercial relations as they had been negative
to those of Imperial Defence. This time, it was the Imperial
Government which was on the defensive, while the same
Canadian Ministers, who had refused to contribute a penny
towards the Royal Navy, were the head and front of the Colonial
initiative. The course which they pressed upon the Imperial
Government was that of reciprocal fiscal preferences between
the Colonies and the United Kingdom.

This question of Imperial Preference will occupy henceforward the greater part of our story. It is time, therefore, to
determine its real nature, still unrevealed to Chamberlain.
At bottom, despite all appearances to the contrary, it was a
constitutional question, not one of economics.

429

Until the repeal of the Corn Laws in 1848, the Colonies had granted and enjoyed a substantial measure of Preference in their trade with the United Kingdom. Thereafter the preferences had been cancelled, and with them the last economic links of Empire. "Colonies", Turgot had written, "are like fruits, which cling to the tree only till they ripen"; and the latter-day disciples of the great rationalist administrator had thought it not only natural but desirable that the British Colonies should grow to full independence and break away from the Empire. Cobden had even written in 1842: "The Colonial system, with all its dazzling appeals to the passions of the people, can never be got rid of except by the indirect process of Free Trade which will gradually and imperceptibly loose the bonds which unite our colonies to us by a mistaken notion of self-interest". The centrifugal process, indeed, went very far. Much further than was generally understood, when the Imperialist revival began in the 80's. At home and in the Colonies, that revival at first took the form of a movement for Imperial federation. But, in fact, the federal idea was already out of date. The Colonies had travelled too far along the road to nationhood.

The growth of Colonial nationalism, though scarcely realised by many Colonials and still incomprehensible to English opinion, made federation impossible; for federation implies a surrender of national sovereignty. It was on this rock, as we have seen, that Chamberlain's proposals for Kriegsverein and Zollverein had foundered. There could not be a union for defence without a central defence authority. In the same way, there could not be a customs union without a central customs authority; and fiscal autonomy was among the first attributes of nationhood. Here, then, was the fundamental conflict of ideas between the Mother Country and the Colonies. To opinion at home, conscious of the dependence of the Colonies upon the United Kingdom especially in matters of defence, federation seemed to be the natural way of rationalising Imperial relations. The Colonies recognised the logic of the argument, only to reject it. It would have meant Empire in the old sense. They wanted full nationhood within the Empire.

This conception of full nationhood within an Empire was wholly new to the world; something never yet dreamed of, nor

attempted. What would it mean in practice? What would be
the relation between the different parts? How could such conflicting aims be reconciled? British Imperialists had scarcely
even formulated these questions. But, in the Colonies, the leaders
were already groping towards an answer, though by the light of
instinct rather than reason. What they wanted was not a
rationalisation of the Imperial structure, but a harmonisation
of the aims of its component parts: a permanent alliance of the
British nations operative in every sphere of life. Despite the
misgivings of minorities, the will to such an alliance was strongly
rooted in the sentiments, the race consciousness, and the traditions, as well as in the interests of the British element in the
Colonies. The problem was to find means of giving it practical
expression.

In the political sphere, these had already been found in the
Colonial Conference itself. Here was consultation on the highest
Imperial level, but without any surrender of sovereignty. In the
sphere of defence, the Colonies meant to proceed along similar
lines. They would build up armies and navies of their own; but
they wished to do so in the closest understanding with the War
Office and the Admiralty. They looked forward to joint staff
talks, to the employment of British advisers, to some standard-
isation in training and equipment, and, indeed, to all other
measures which would enable them to assimilate, without compelling them to obey, the experience and wisdom of Whitehall.

But for young communities in that peaceful age, the problems
of trade bulked much larger than those of politics or defence.
They were nations still in the making; and, for them, any alliance
was necessarily unconstructive, even unreal, so long as it lacked
an economic foundation. But what form was this to take? They
would not accept a customs union. Complete Free Trade was by
definition promiscuous, and was, therefore, excluded as the basis
of an alliance. There remained the way of Preference; of giving
English goods access to the Colonial markets, not, indeed, on
equal terms with the goods of the importing Colony itself, but
on better—that is preferential—terms than those accorded to
the foreigner.

This conception of reciprocal Preference, of discrimination in
favour of the British and against the foreigner, exactly expressed

the relationship which the Colonies wished to develop with the Mother Country; and this in all spheres of life, not merely in the commercial. Preferences thus came to symbolise a new constitutional relationship—the Commonwealth relationship as we have since learnt to call it. That it was an economic symbol need not surprise us, "for where your treasure is, there will your heart be also". Economic interests would play their part, and a vital one, in focusing attention on the issue; but it was as transcendent as any in that age.

II

The idea of Imperial Preference had been actively revived after the first Colonial Conference of 1887.[1] Seven years later the Ottawa Conference had passed a resolution in favour of the preferential principle by a decided majority. As a result, in 1897, the Canadian Government had taken the first practical step towards it, by giving a unilateral preference of 25 per cent to British imports. At the second Colonial Conference, a few months later, the other Colonies had resolved to follow Canada's example. Nothing had come, as yet, of their resolution; but this had been for reasons largely outside their control. The federation of Australia had involved the reconstruction of the Australian tariff; and this was still under discussion. In the Cape and Natal the question had been postponed by the war.

Opinion in all the Colonies, however, remained strong for Preference. In New Zealand, Seddon had responded to the invitation to the third Colonial Conference by offering a preference on all goods carried in British ships. About the same time the Government of the Cape made a significant enquiry.

SIR W. HELY-HUTCHINSON TO CHAMBERLAIN
(Telegram)

January 29, 1902.—. . . Ministers would like to be informed in strict secrecy whether in Mr. Chamberlain's opinion England is likely to consent to any modification of the policy of Free Trade which for half a century has prevailed there.

In Canada, Ministers still kept silent; but, all over the Dominion, Chambers of Commerce and Boards of Trade passed

[1] See Vol. III. p. 178.

resolutions, urging the Imperial Government to grant a preference whenever it imposed a duty on goods of a kind produced
in the Empire.[1] These resolutions were important. They raised
a new issue; the issue of reciprocity.

At the Conference of 1897, the Colonial Premiers had not
demanded reciprocal preferences from the United Kingdom.
For one thing, there had been no sufficient English tariff on
which such preferences might have been granted. For another,
English attachment to Free Trade was such that, short of a full
Zollverein, there could be no question of putting on a duty
against the foreigner to take it off in favour of the Colonies.
The Premiers, indeed, had regarded their offer of preferences
primarily as a return for the burdens of defence, already carried
by the Mother Country on their behalf. They had hoped that
their offers might lead to reciprocity; but they had not felt in
a position to claim it.

This was still the official view of most of the Colonies in 1902;
and naturally so, seeing that they had not yet given effect to the
resolution of 1897. In Canada, however, matters had gone much
further. In 1900 the Dominion Government had voluntarily
raised the initial preference on British goods from 25 to $33\frac{1}{2}$ per
cent. This was a generous gesture, but it had met with some
criticism from Canadian manufacturers and from certain
American interests afraid of sharper English competition. The
inference of this criticism was plain. Either the Canadian
Government must reduce or even abandon its preference, or it
must obtain counter-concessions from the United Kingdom.
Most Canadians preferred the latter alternative; but, until 1902,
it had been difficult to see what form such counter-concessions
could take. With the imposition, however, of the Corn Duty, the
Imperial Government was at last in a position to give a preference to Canada's most important industry. Laurier, as we
saw, had at once expressed a hope that such a preference would,
in fact, be introduced. Balfour had denied that this was the
Government's intention; but Chamberlain, at Birmingham, had

---

[1] Sir W. Laurier laid before the Conference a selection of such resolutions
from the Boards of Trade of Toronto,
Montreal, Windsor, Strathroy, Kings-
ton, Halifax, British Columbia, Ross-
land, Saint John, and from the Cham-
bre de Commerce of Montreal (Minutes
of the Colonial Conference of 1902,
App. XV. pp. 442-448).

insisted that the question should not be prejudged; it was a matter for the Colonial Conference to decide. Reciprocity was thus the question of the hour.

III

How far was Chamberlain's mind already made up on this question of reciprocal Preference? Nothing in our story is harder to assess; but the evidence suggests that, after long reflection, the process of reaching a decision had begun. Twelve years had passed since Chamberlain had promised Denison to study the whole question and, if he came to the conclusion that Preference was in the interests of the Empire, to "take it up and advocate it".[1] Now, a few weeks before the Conference met, the two men lunched together. Later Denison recorded the following impressions of their talk:

He argued the matter with me, bringing forward any number of objections which I answered as well as I could. I soon came to the conclusion that he was quietly taking my measure and testing my knowledge of the question. I then warmed up in my arguments . . . and soon came to the conclusion, from a mischievous expression in his eye, that he was not as much opposed to me as his remarks would lead one to think. When leaving I felt that although he did not say a word in support of my plan, yet he was not altogether unfavourable.[2]

This was one side of the picture. At the same time, however, Chamberlain was also studying the reports prepared by the Board of Trade, and consulting in private with Sir Robert Giffen, a former Permanent Under-Secretary of that department. Although more broadminded than many of the experts, Giffen was a staunch exponent of orthodox economic doctrine. He set little value upon the adoption of Preference by the Colonies, and was consistently opposed to any thought of reciprocity by the United Kingdom.

These consultations and enquiries seem to have produced a certain dualism in Chamberlain's approach to the problem. As an Imperialist, he was naturally sympathetic to a policy on which the Colonies had set their hearts and which might help to

[1] See Vol. II. p. 408.
May 4. 1902. Colonel George T.

Denison, *The Struggle for Imperial Unity*, ch. xxvi. p. 298.

build up trade within the Empire. As an economist, however, he still doubted whether Preference could be defended as a strictly business proposition. It was an awkward dilemma; and the inaccurate, or at least incomplete information with which he was supplied by the Board of Trade, led him inevitably to an awkward approach.

CHAP.
XCIV.
Æt. 65.

IV

Between Chamberlain and Laurier there was mutual respect, but little sympathy. In later years the Canadian Premier once observed:

Chamberlain was the first English statesman whom we came to know intimately. I was much impressed by his force and directness. He was ambitious, but not for himself alone. Unfortunately our views often clashed. . . .[1]

Chamberlain's opinion of Laurier was expressed a few days after the Conference in the following letter:

CHAMBERLAIN TO AUSTEN

Highbury, August 25, 1902.—. . . As you know, I do not entirely trust Laurier. . . . His ideal is an independent Canada and he is certainly not an Imperialist in our sense. . . .

As a result, perhaps, of this uneasiness between the two men, negotiations over Preference were opened through the intermediary of Colonel Denison.[2] In the course of a conversation at the Colonial Office,[3] Lord Onslow also being present, Chamberlain had suggested to Denison that Canada should put certain British manufactures, particularly cottons and calicoes, on the Free list, and that in return Canadian wheat should be exempted from the Corn Duty. As Chamberlain saw it, the Free Traders would find it hard to oppose such a plan, since it would be a move towards freer trade between Britain and Canada. He therefore asked Denison to put it to the Canadian Ministers, saying, "It will be the thin end of the wedge and Preferential Trade will follow".

[1] Skelton, *Life and Letters of Sir Wilfrid Laurier*, vol. ii. p. 297.
[2] The following account is derived from Colonel Denison's *The Struggle for Imperial Unity*, pp. 331-334, supple-mented by an unpublished letter of June 3, 1920, from Colonel Denison to Mr. J. L. Garvin.
[3] June 13, 1902.

It so happened that, at this time, Denison's relations with the Canadian Ministers were strained. As a result, he had no contact with Laurier and did not tell him of Chamberlain's proposal until the eve of the Conference. As soon, however, as he was informed of it, Laurier saw its advantages and instructed the Canadian High Commissioner to make a formal offer at the Colonial Office.

In this offer, Laurier asked for immediate legislation to exempt Canada from the Corn Duty. He wanted a decision before the House rose. But this was more than Hicks Beach would accept. The Chancellor had several times disclaimed that the Corn Duty was a first step towards Preference, and he would not now ask Members to reduce it in Canada's favour. For the moment, therefore, Chamberlain's initiative came to nothing. But it was not without importance. It gave a lead to the Canadian Ministers, and encouraged Laurier to come out with definite proposals at the Conference.

v

Chamberlain defined his attitude to the problems of commercial relations in his opening speech to the Conference. As he saw it, there were two salient features in the economic position of the Empire:

. . . If we chose . . . the Empire might be self-sustaining; it is so wide, its products are so various; its climates so different that there is absolutely nothing which is necessary to our existence, hardly anything which is desirable as a luxury which cannot be produced within the boundaries of the Empire itself.[1]

[But] . . . the Empire at the present time, and especially the United Kingdom which is the great market of the world—derives the greatest part of its necessaries from foreign countries, and exports the largest part of its available . . . produce also to foreign countries.

He went on to draw the conclusion:

Now, I confess, that, to my mind, that is not a satisfactory state of things and I hope you will agree with me that everything, which can possibly tend to increase the interchange of products between the different parts of the Empire, is deserving of our cordial encouragement.[2]

[1] Minutes of Colonial Conference of 1902, p. 6.   [2] *Ibid.*

His ideal, as always, was Free Trade within the Empire.

We feel confident—we think that it is a matter which demands no evidence or proof that . . . it would enormously increase our inter-Imperial trade; that it would hasten the development of our Colonies; that it would fill up the spare places in your lands with an active, intelligent and industrious, and above all a British population; that it would make the mother country entirely independent of foreign food and raw material.[1]

At the same time, he recognised the convenience, perhaps the necessity, in new countries with scattered populations, of raising revenue by indirect taxation.

But in my mind, whenever customs duties are balanced by excise duties, or whenever they are levied on articles that are not produced at home, the enforcement of such duties is no derogation whatever from the principles of Free Trade as I understand it. If then even with this limitation, which is a very important one, . . . the proposal [for Empire Free Trade] were accepted, I think it would be impossible to overestimate the mutual advantage which would be derived from it.[2]

From this statement of his ideals—and they were still essentially the ideals of a federalist and a Free Trader—he went on to review the moves that had already been made to promote inter-Imperial trade. The Canadian preferences had now been in operation for more than five years, but

. . . I have to say to you that, while I cannot but gratefully acknowledge the intention of this proposal and its sentimental value as a proof of goodwill and affection, yet that its substantial results have been altogether disappointing to us.[3]

Then, speaking from the brief prepared for him by the Board of Trade, he argued that,

in spite of the preference which Canada has given us, their tariff has pressed and still presses, with the greatest severity, upon its best customer and has favoured the foreigner who is constantly doing his best to shut out her goods. . . . While we may most readily and most gratefully accept from you any preference which you may be willing voluntarily to accord to us, we cannot bargain with you for it; we cannot pay for it, unless you go much further and enable us to enter your home market on terms of much greater equality . . .

[1] Minutes of Colonial Conference of 1902, p. 6. [2] *Ibid.* [3] *Ibid.*

VI

The next session of the Conference was occupied with defence. Two days later Chamberlain suffered his cab accident. It was, thus, not until July 18 that the question of commercial relations was fully discussed by the Premiers. It was Chamberlain's first day of business after his accident; and the Minutes of the session leave little doubt that he was not his usual self. He was supported, or perhaps embarrassed, by the presence of Gerald Balfour, the President of the Board of Trade, and a strong delegation from that department. It included Sir Francis Hopwood, the Permanent Under-Secretary, and two eminent pundits of economic orthodoxy, Sir Robert Giffen and Sir Alfred Bateman. Laurier, on his side, was attended by his two colleagues Paterson and Fielding, the Canadian Ministers of Customs and Finance; a more effective reinforcement, as we shall see.

In contrast to the abortive wrangles on defence, the debate on commercial relations yielded positive results at an early stage. Seddon declared that New Zealand would give a preference of 10 per cent to British goods. The representatives of the Cape and Natal offered a preference of 25 per cent. These Colonies would, in each case, only be giving practical expression to the resolution of 1897. They made no demands, therefore, for reciprocal treatment.

Everyone knew, however, that reciprocity was the real issue. The proposals made by the other Premiers had only served to set the stage for the contest between the English and the Canadian delegations. Laurier opened the debate. In words, which must have surprised and delighted Chamberlain, he summarised the economic problem facing the Empire. One passage is still so true today that it is a duty to quote it.

. . . On the part of the Colonies there is a desire for closer trade with the Mother Country. There is a question of sentiment in it; there is also more than a question of sentiment—there is a question of business. . . . Foreign nations . . . are practically engaged in developing a commercial war. . . . I speak of our neighbour, the United States, whose tariff is absolutely prohibitory. Their policy is to sell to the foreign nations as much as they can and not to buy. That has been their tendency ever since the civil war and it is becoming more and more their tendency; . . . but . . . they would have no ground at all for objection if, within the British Empire, we made a mutual trade arrangement. That is a thing that is conceded by all nations, that, within an Empire, we are entitled to try to develop ourselves. The Americans have done it; the Germans have done it; and I am pretty sure that, if we were to adopt such a policy, the United States would, no doubt, in their Press demur to our course, but I feel that before the eyes of the civilised world they would not have a ground—a just ground—of complaint. . . .[1]

From this premise Laurier turned to Chamberlain's criticism that the preferences thus far accorded by Canada did not justify reciprocal treatment by the United Kingdom. This, he said, was an open question, but, provided the principle of reciprocity was accepted he was prepared to concede that the degree of Preference was a matter for discussion.

Assuming it to be fair on our side . . . to make the preference, which we have given, more effective than it is supposed to be at present, the question would remain whether or not the Imperial authorities are disposed, or that they could carry a concession made to us. There would be two ways of doing it. It could be done, first of all, in the way of imposing new duties to make concessions, and I grant that would be the most difficult thing to do. . . . *But, upon the lines of existing duties, I put the question whether it would not be possible that the Colonies should be given a preference.*[2] You have the wine duties, and, if I remember right, the wine duties—when Mr. Cobden was negotiating a treaty with France— afforded a basis for the negotiation of that treaty. . . .

. . . Now you have imposed grain duties. I know it is a delicate subject, but I do not see from what point of view the policy could be objected to, if a preference were to be given to the Colonies upon the grain duties . . . The consumer could not object, because it would be to some extent reducing what little burden there is against him . . . The Colonies would be thereby enabled to furnish more and more of the grain consumed.

[1] Seddon had been equally vigorous in denouncing the fear of retaliation by the United States which had been expressed in some quarters: "There is too much made of this fear of irritating. . . . This retaliation and this bogus irritation. . . . The policy of these other nations is such that they cannot go further than they have gone up to the present time. We have nothing to fear in the way of retaliation at all. . . . They only give us raw products because Britain is the best market for them" (Minutes of Colonial Conference of 1902, p. 49).

[2] My italics.—J. A.

. . . Putting the thing in a concrete form, I would like . . . to know, if . . . we can hope or expect that the Imperial authorities would be in a position to enter into a discussion of that view.

We have come to the crux of the argument. Laurier's question could not be evaded; but it caught Chamberlain singularly unprepared. His mind was still torn between the statistics of the Board of Trade and his own leanings towards a policy which might make for closer Imperial Union. His reply shows him almost thinking aloud. It is, nevertheless, a milestone on the road to Tariff Reform. He would accept the principle of reciprocal Preference, provided it was a step towards freer trade within the Empire and provided the Canadian Ministers could substantiate their claim that it was a paying proposition.

. . . We are well aware absolute Free Trade within the Empire is not practicable at the present moment. The objection would not come from us; the objection would come from the Colonies. . . .

Then the question is, can we make any approach to it? and I attach the greatest importance to what we do. It is not with me, primarily, a question of money sacrifice; it is primarily a question of the unity of the Empire, and I am firmly convinced that unity cannot be effectually secured in the future, unless we can improve and extend our inter-commercial relations, and, therefore, I am not looking at the matter as a mere question of accurate balance sheets, so much on one side and so much on the other, so much sacrifice to be met by an exactly parallel sacrifice on the other side. I should regard the object as of so much importance that we need not look too closely into the exact benefits we have obtained.

In order to secure some advance towards Free Trade within the Empire there are two ways . . . a fixed preference given on either side, or both sides, upon all the taxable goods. . . . A Free Trade list, . . . by testing the tariffs and trying to find a number of articles at present dutiable which might be made free. In either case, ... we should be making an advance towards Free Trade, and I think that, if a substantial advance could be made in that direction, the Mother Country ought to be prepared to do something in return. I am speaking of my own private and personal conviction on the subject. What can the Mother Country do? She can, of course, allow a rebate on such articles as are already taxable in her tariff. . . . I think that is a matter which is worthy of discussion; which can be treated upon its merits. Of course, we have to present a proposal of that kind to our Parliament; we should have to show very clearly what was the corresponding offer made on the part of the Colonies.

. . . The difficulties . . . which would prevent, at all events at the present time, anything like absolute Free Trade in the Colonies, exist also here with regard to any proposal to change in any degree our existing fiscal system. . . . But I do not, myself, regard this as being an insuperable obstacle, and I think that any proposal, having that as one of its collateral consequences, should be fully and freely discussed.[1]

The principle of reciprocity was thus provisionally conceded. Laurier had broken through the English front. He now handed over the pursuit to his economic advisers, Fielding and Paterson.

For the rest of the morning, these two gentlemen rebutted and utterly demolished the criticism levelled against the Canadian preferences. Gerald Balfour and the Board of Trade pundits were silenced; while Chamberlain had been so badly briefed on the whole subject that, at times, he was almost made to seem ridiculous. The following dialogue gives some idea of the discussion.

MR. PATERSON: ". . . The trade of Great Britain with Canada had been steadily declining—it came from 43,000,000 dollars down to 29,000,000 dollars. When the preference was given that decline was immediately arrested, and there has been an upward movement since, till . . . this year . . . the imports from Great Britain have reached 49,000,000 dollars, which . . . is an increase in trade of 20,000,000 dollars, or as near as may be 70 per cent. . . . That, in Canada, does strike us as rather favourable to the Mother Country. . . ."

MR. CHAMBERLAIN: "Of course, Mr. Paterson, the object which you had in view and which we expected when the preference was given, was that it would have the effect of transferring trade from the foreigner to the Mother Country."

MR. FIELDING: "Or preventing the further decline, Mr. Chamberlain, which is just as effective."

MR. CHAMBERLAIN: "Or preventing the further decline? Well, what we find in looking into these figures is that, although . . . our trade with Canada has very considerably increased, it has not increased at the expense of the foreigner; on the contrary, the foreigner has increased in

---

[1] Minutes of Colonial Conference of 1902, pp. 50, 51, 52.

even greater proportion, and, therefore, we attribute the increase not to
the preferential tariff, but to . . . the increased prosperity of Canada."

MR. FIELDING: "But think, Mr. Chamberlain; ask the question: if the
preference had not been there, what would the condition have been?"

MR. CHAMBERLAIN: "I think that our feeling is that the preference did
exactly what you say: it arrested a decline but it has not, unfortunately
—as we hoped it would do—increased the consumption."

MR. FIELDING: "But it has increased the consumption over what it
would be to-day if there was no preference, and that is the material
question."

MR. CHAMBERLAIN: "That is so." . . .[1]

Paterson and Fielding then proceeded to attack the Board of
Trade's argument that the Canadian tariff was prohibitive.
They showed that Canada's total imports were continually in-
creasing and suggested that, if, in spite of the preference, the
British manufacturer was being beaten by his foreign com-
petitor, it was hardly Canada's fault.

MR. FIELDING: "If our tariff were so high that we were shutting out
imports, there would be room for criticism. . . . But in most lines there is
no competition from abroad. If goods are coming in, one parcel from the
United States paying $3 duty, while another of like character from Great
Britain is admitted for $2, and if, under these circumstances, the United
States manufacturer is taking the lead, is this to be considered the fault
of the Canadian tariff? Does it not rather show that some persons over
here are a little slow?"

MR. CHAMBERLAIN: "I quite agree." [2]

Finally, Paterson demonstrated that the statistics produced
by the Board of Trade were largely irrelevant. The Board had
compared the total of British imports into Canada with the total
of imports into Canada from foreign countries. The proper comparison,he suggested, should leave out of account those imports
—chiefly raw materials—which the United Kingdom had never
attempted to sell to Canada. If the enquiry was thus restricted—
i.e. to a comparison between British imports and those foreign
imports which competed against the British—it would be found
that, in the four years during which the preference had been

---

[1] Minutes of Colonial Conference of 1902, pp. 52, 53.　　[2] *Ibid*. p. 57.

operating, imports from the United Kingdom had increased by 59 per cent, as against an increase on the part of all other countries of only 47 per cent. Canada might, therefore, claim that the preference "has not only wholly arrested the decline as we look at it, but has promoted trade and cannot fail to promote trade".

At this point the Conference was mercifully adjourned. The discussion, however, left a profound impression on Chamberlain's mind. His faith in the Board of Trade was permanently impaired.

VII

On the morning of July 22, at Laurier's request, Chamberlain received the Canadian Ministers, in private. The Conference was due to meet within half an hour. There was thus no time for detailed discussion; nor was there any need. It is clear, from the subsequent exchanges at the Conference, that Chamberlain and Laurier now agreed that the principle of reciprocity should be put to the test of detailed negotiations between the Canadian delegation and the Board of Trade. It was time to decide what further preferences Canada could offer the United Kingdom in return for exemption from the Corn Duty.

Accordingly, when the Conference reassembled, Chamberlain suggested a definite course of action.

It appears to me that, while we are agreed generally, we have not yet been able to make any approach to a definite settlement. . . . Therefore, if we are to do anything, I think our first business is to come to close quarters which we can only do, if the representatives of the several Colonies concerned would agree to meet privately representatives of the Home Government and discuss these matters with them.

The general principle is that we do desire to increase inter-Imperial trade and are willing to consider Preference as one of the means by which that increase can be accomplished." [1]

Gerald Balfour and the other Premiers were surprised by this proposal and at first demurred. They had hoped to conclude the discussion of commercial relations by passing a general resolution in favour of Preference. But Chamberlain and Laurier knew

[1] Minutes of Colonial Conference of 1902, p. 62.

their own minds and would have their way. As Laurier put it:

If we pass a resolution, it must contain the basis of some practical scheme. . . . I think, therefore, that a great deal of good would be come to by these negotiations . . . with the Board of Trade in order to see how far we can agree. . . . If we cannot agree upon the general terms, we will have to see whether we can agree upon the line of specified articles, and, if we cannot agree upon anything at all, what is the good of passing any resolution? [1]

The argument was unanswerable; and it was, therefore, agreed that negotiations should go forward.[2]

Thus far, the discussion of commercial relations had made steady progress towards agreement. But, with the opening of practical negotiations, an unexpected conflict of principle emerged. When the Canadian Ministers came to make detailed proposals, they found that to give a preference to the United Kingdom exporter by further reducing their duties would, in many cases, deprive the Canadian manufacturer of the protection of the Canadian tariff. They decided, therefore, that, in such cases, they would give the preference not by reducing the duty in favour of the United Kingdom but by raising it still further against the foreigner. A formal proposal to this effect was therefore placed before the Conference. It offered the United Kingdom exporter

the existing preference of $33\frac{1}{3}$ per cent and an additional preference on lists of selected articles—(a) by further reducing the duties in favour of the United Kingdom; (b) *by raising the duties against foreign imports*; (c) *by imposing duties on certain foreign imports* now on the free list.[3]

This proposal came as an unpleasant surprise to Chamberlain. As yet, he had always thought of mutual preferences in terms of the reciprocal reduction of duties. This would have been a step towards freer trade, and, as such, might have been commended to Parliament on the most orthodox economic grounds. The Canadian proposal, however, was distinctly protectionist. It

---

[1] Minutes of Colonial Conference of 1902, p. 68.
[2] The Australian Ministers had similar conversations though of a more exploratory character. The Premiers of New Zealand, the Cape and Natal had

already made firm offers of Preference and, in the absence of their economic advisers, were not prepared to undertake detailed negotiations.
[3] Minutes of Colonial Conference, p. 127. (My italics.—J. A.)

involved the granting of Preference not by reducing but by increasing duties. Canada, of course, might do as she pleased. But for the United Kingdom to accept such a proposal, as part of a mutual trade agreement, would be not merely to countenance but to encourage Protection in the Colonies.

The discussion of the Canadian proposal showed that the Canadian attitude was shared by the other Colonies. All the Premiers were agreed that their offers of Preference would, in many cases, have to take the form of raising the duty against the foreigner rather than of reducing it in favour of British imports. Against this Chamberlain argued that, where a duty was already prohibitive, there would be little advantage to the United Kingdom in making it still more prohibitive to foreign exporters. But once again he had been badly briefed by the Board of Trade; and Fielding easily showed that his argument did not apply to Canada. The statistics proved that Canada was already importing "vast quantities of goods" from England and from foreign countries. By raising the duty against the foreigner, Canada would not, indeed, increase her total imports but she could "turn the trade" from the foreigner to the United Kingdom.

The discussion that morning was once again inconclusive. Chamberlain had submitted a draft resolution, but he had assumed in it that Preference would take the form of a reduction of duties; and it had, therefore, to be withdrawn. In the end, it was agreed that Laurier and the other Premiers should meet privately to prepare a second draft.

This was submitted to the Conference on August 8. Most of it was unexceptionable and would be accepted. But on one point it went too far. It expressly committed the United Kingdom to granting

preferential treatment to the products and manufactures of the Colonies by exemption from or reduction of duties now or hereafter imposed.

This was more than Chamberlain could accept. For one thing, he thought it "a retrograde step" for the United Kingdom to promise reciprocity before specific trade agreements had proved its value. They would have to move from the particular to the general. For another, he could not hope, with Hicks Beach still in office and Balfour's new Cabinet not yet formed, to secure the

necessary authority from the Cabinet. The Premiers had, therefore, to modify their text and, instead of binding the Imperial
Government to the introduction of reciprocal preferences, they
had to content themselves with urging these upon it. In its final
form the resolution ran:

1. That this Conference recognises that the principle of preferential
trade between the United Kingdom and His Majesty's Dominions beyond
the Seas would stimulate and facilitate mutual commercial intercourse,
and would, by promoting the development of the resources and industries
of the several parts, strengthen the Empire.

2. That this Conference recognises that, in the present circumstances
of the Colonies, it is not practicable to adopt a general system of Free
Trade as between the Mother Country and the British Dominions beyond
the Seas.

3. That with a view, however, to promoting the increase of trade
within the Empire, it is desirable that those Colonies which have not
already adopted such a policy should, as far as their circumstances
permit, give substantial preferential treatment to the products and
manufactures of the United Kingdom.

4. *That the Prime Ministers of the Colonies respectfully urge on His
Majesty's Government the expediency of granting in the United Kingdom
preferential treatment to the products and manufactures of the Colonies
either by exemption from or reduction of duties now or hereafter imposed.*

5. That the Prime Ministers present at the Conference undertake to
submit to their respective Governments at the earliest opportunity the
principle of the resolution and to request them to take such measures as
may be necessary to give effect to it.[1]

On the face of it, this seemed to mark little advance on the
resolution of 1897; but the Canadian Ministers left no doubt in
Chamberlain's mind that they expected action to result from it.
In a covering memorandum they issued a plain warning.

The Canadian Ministers desired to have it understood that they took
this course [of submitting the resolution] with the strong hope and expectation that the principle of preferential trade would be more widely
accepted by the Colonies, and that the Mother Country would, at an early
day, apply the same principle by exempting the products of the Colonies
from Customs duties.

[1] Minutes of Colonial Conference of 1902, p. 189. (My italics.—J. A.)

If, after using every effort to bring about such a readjustment of the fiscal policy of the Empire, the Canadian Government should find that the principle of preferential trade is not acceptable to the Colonies generally or the Mother Country, then Canada should be free to take such action as might be deemed necessary in the presence of such conditions.[1]

As if to underline this warning and prove their independence, the Canadian Ministers left a few days later for Paris. Their purpose was to conclude a trade agreement with the French Government. Meanwhile, their negotiations with the Board of Trade remained in suspense.

VIII

The further labours of the Conference need not detain us. These, which we have discussed, were the great issues; the rest seem trivial by comparison. The meagre results disappointed Chamberlain. His idea of a Council of Empire had been ignored. His appeals for Colonial contributions to Imperial Defence had been rejected. The trade negotiations remained inconclusive. But the lesson of the Conference was plain. Reciprocal Preference offered the only line of approach to closer Imperial Union which the Colonies were prepared to consider. And their conception of Preference was a protectionist conception. Here at last Chamberlain came face to face with the great problem of his time. There could not be a closer union of the Empire without a fiscal revolution at home.

The opening moves of this revolution would not be long delayed. We shall discuss them in some detail, but first we must consider two contemporary developments destined in different ways to sharpen the main issue. These were the reconstruction of the Government and the controversy aroused by Balfour's Education Bill.

[1] Minutes of Colonial Conference of 1902, App. XVII. p. 452.

CHAPTER XCV

BALFOUR BECOMES PRIME MINISTER

(July 1902)

CHAMBERLAIN's Cab Accident—A Shower of Tributes—Salisbury Resigns—The King Sends for Balfour—Balfour Secures Chamberlain's Support—Resignation of Hicks Beach—Salisbury and Chamberlain —Chamberlain and the Premiership—Chamberlain and Balfour— Reconstruction of the Ministry—Buckle Urges Chamberlain to Take the Exchequer—Ritchie Chosen—"The prisoner of the Government" —Political Consequences of the Cab Accident—Chamberlain's Grand Design.

I

BOOK XX.

1902.

ON the morning of July 7, the Colonial Secretary reviewed the contingent of the West African Frontier Force brought to London for the Coronation. Under the watchful eye of their British officers and non-commissioned officers, the veterans of the Ashanti wars were marshalled in the Quadrangle of the Colonial Office. They made a brave show: white-turbaned Hausas in their flowing robes, and men of Sierra Leone and the Gambia with their gold-tasselled tarbooshes, scarlet and khaki tropical uniforms, and sandalled feet. On the stroke of noon Chamberlain stepped into the Quadrangle, impeccably attired in top-hat and frock-coat with a pink orchid in his buttonhole. Accompanied by the senior staff of the Office, he passed slowly down the dusky ranks, examining the unfamiliar uniforms and satisfying a still youthful curiosity with insistent questions. Then in ringing tones he harangued the troops, dwelling, in the approved style, on their loyalty to the King and telling them "that even now you may have some opportunity of seeing the King's face before you return to your homes".

Chamberlain was on the eve of his sixty-sixth birthday; and

448

his secretary, Lord Monkbretton, noted that "he was never in better form". Looking back, Monkbretton would wonder whether he was ever quite the same man again.

That same afternoon, Chamberlain left the Colonial Office in a hansom-cab to go to the Athenæum. His purpose was to support the claims of a friend, whose election to that assembly was in question. The day had been very hot; and the glass window, fitted in the front of the cab to protect the occupant from rain, was folded back under the roof and secured by a leather strap. Whitehall had been watered, shortly before, to lay the dust, and the wood pavement was slippery. The driver, therefore, went slowly; but, as he came to the great Canadian arch, the horse shied at the tinkling gewgaws, with which it was festooned, slipped on the wet pavement, plunged and fell. Chamberlain was projected violently forward. In the same instant the strap, which secured the window, yielded to the shock, and the heavy glass pane crashed down upon his forehead. Half stunned and with blood pouring into his eyes, he stumbled into the street and asked a passer-by to help him to the Colonial Office. A crowd quickly collected. A policeman bound up the wound with a handkerchief and, calling another cab, hurried Chamberlain off to Charing Cross Hospital.

The cut was found to be a deep one, stretching for three and a half inches from the centre of the forehead towards the right temple. The glass pane had penetrated to the bone and caused a slight indentation of the skull. Three stitches were put in at once, Chamberlain refusing an anaesthetic. The loss of blood was regarded as serious—"I never knew I had so much blood to lose", he would say—but the pulse was normal, and it was thought, at first, that he had escaped shock or concussion.

Monkbretton and Cochrane, his Parliamentary Private Secretary, were the first to receive the news. They went at once to the hospital and found Chamberlain inclined to make light of the incident. He held out his hand saying, "See, it does not shake". Mrs. Chamberlain arrived soon afterwards. Driving in the Park with her mother, she had been astonished and alarmed to read a poster announcing "Chamberlain in Hospital". She had hurried to her husband's bedside and was now relieved to find him wreathed in a cloud of smoke from one of his black cigars.

Next day, his birthday, he sat up in bed to read the news-papers and the many letters and telegrams—from the King and from Roberts among others—which showered upon him. That evening, he was to have attended a dinner given by the Prince of Wales in honour of the Colonial Premiers. In his absence, Mrs. Chamberlain went alone and, on her way home, drove to the hospital. There was no porter at the door, and, though the coachman rang the bell several times, no one answered. Deciding to investigate for herself, Mrs. Chamberlain pushed the swing-door open and walked in. There was no one about. Trusting to her memory, she made her way through the wards to her husband's room. There was no night nurse to be found; but Chamberlain was fast asleep; and, after sitting by him for half an hour, she returned to the carriage. A weird picture this, of the Edwardian lady driving from a Royal banquet to watch over the statesman, asleep in a deserted hospital.

Chamberlain returned to Prince's Gardens on the following day. He could wear no hat, but, in his immaculate way, had caused the bandages on his head to be covered with a black silk wrap. With his customary punctuality, he wrote at once, though with a shaky hand, to thank the hospital authorities and send a donation of fifty guineas "in the hopes that it may serve to relieve others in worse case than myself". But the doctors now took a more serious view of his condition than they had at first. He had lost more than a pint of blood, and they suspected that he was also suffering from shock. They insisted, therefore, that he should keep his bed and give up all work and interviews for at least a fortnight.

II

By a compensating process, Chamberlain's accident raised him to new heights in the esteem of his countrymen. It was more than mere sympathy for bad luck. It was as if the danger, through which he had passed, had suddenly reminded them how indispensable he had become.

The day after the accident, *The Times* devoted almost the whole of its second "leader" to him. Here we may well recall a few sentences from it. They show better than anything else the position which he held in the eyes of his contemporaries.

The sooner the Colonial Secretary is at work again the better for the nation and for the Empire, but we sincerely trust that he will himself realise the unwisdom of premature exertion after an ordeal of this kind. . . . Mr. Chamberlain's health is, in a very real sense, an Imperial asset, never of greater value to us than at present, when so many Imperial problems pregnant with great issues seem ripening for settlement, or for that fruitful discussion which leads to settlement. The esteem in which his countrymen at home hold him has long been very high, and it has broadened and deepened, as the events of the last few years have brought out his great qualities more and more clearly. His insight, his grasp of the essential features of large questions, and his contempt for shams and irrelevancies, his strong common sense, his resourcefulness in administration, and his readiness in debate, his large and noble patriotism, and, above all, his high courage and unyielding tenacity of purpose in good and in evil fortune, have won for him, in spite of occasional mistakes, their admiration, their gratitude and their affection. Amongst his countrymen beyond the seas he enjoys—and deservedly enjoys—a popularity greater than any other Imperial statesman has ever commanded.[1]

Such praise had seldom been read in living memory outside the obituary columns; but, though it was the most eminent tribute, it was by no means the only one nor even the most fulsome. A few days later,[2] *The Spectator*, never a friend, joined in the chorus. Some of its comments are also worth quoting. They supply a good picture of Chamberlain, as he seemed to many moderate men.

As it turned out the accident . . . did not seriously injure Mr. Chamberlain, but it set everybody considering what, if he were disabled even for a time, would be the result. Though we by no means agree with all Mr. Chamberlain's policy, . . . we cannot doubt that his disappearance from the scene, even for a time, would have been a heavy blow, both to the Cabinet and the Empire. As regards the latter point, there is in fact no serious controversy. From every side, the vast body of British Colonies and dependencies send up evidence of profound confidence in their present manager; confidence not born, we think, wholly of the recent explosion of Imperial feeling . . . but of a sense that, in Mr. Chamberlain, they have a Secretary for the Colonies who really studies them, consults

[1] *The Times*, July 8, 1902.   [2] *The Spectator*, July 12, 1902.

their feelings and devotes his whole capacity and attention to making them prosperous. That has not been the unbroken record of the heads of the department. . . . His despatches, and still more his speeches, have soothed the pride of the Colonists, and have so modified the general opinion, especially in Canada and Australia, that all thought of quitting the Empire has died away. . . . No doubt Mr. Chamberlain was fortunate in the incidents of the war which stirred the patriotism of race . . . but still it is true that when he took office the great Colonies were in a criticising mood, and that now they are sending men to die in defence of the Empire. . . .

It is as a member of the Cabinet that Mr. Chamberlain is now a subject of controversy. His enemies declare that he is much too dominating and pugnacious; that he presses his undoubted influence too hard; that he is too often in favour of a policy of action; and especially that, when he makes speeches on Foreign Affairs, he leaves an impression, most galling to the greater states, that he rather despises them. This impression is extraordinarily prevalent on the Continent, where Mr. Chamberlain is regarded as a potential enemy of the first class. Some little bit of this accusation is probably true . . . and, though his temperament is, in a perplexed world like the present, sometimes a little dangerous, it must not be forgotten that it is the temperament of strength, and that what British Cabinets want is usually a tonic. . . . The man who can lend force to a British Cabinet and make that force visible in his speeches is invaluable . . . and, though Mr. Chamberlain may never be Premier, he will never, while he lives, lose his influence over his countrymen, or cease to be regarded as a great reserve force against a day of peril.

III

While Chamberlain still lay confined to bed, a fateful transaction was accomplished. Lord Salisbury resigned and, having assured Balfour's succession to the Premiership, sloped away from the political scene with characteristic insouciance. He had been aware for some time that his powers were failing; [1] and, since the winter, it had been generally known that he would

[1] He confessed to the Speaker that he found himself dropping off to sleep in Cabinet (see Viscount Ullswater's *A Speaker's Commentary*, vol. i. p. 320) and, if Lord James is to be believed, "his memory failed and his public utterances were lamentable, both in matter and in delivery" (see Lord Askwith's *Lord James of Hereford*, p. 267).

soon retire. And yet the news came as something of a shock to the public. He had held office for so long; longer, indeed, than any Prime Minister since Lord Liverpool.

Salisbury restored his seals of office [1] to the King on the morning of Friday, July 11. No public announcement of his resignation was made, until after the week-end; and he does not seem either to have consulted his colleagues or even to have notified them beforehand of his decision. It has sometimes been suggested that he deliberately chose to resign, while Chamberlain was *hors de combat*, in order to smooth Balfour's path to power. There is no evidence whatever to support this theory. The most that can be said is that he evidently did not regard the temporary incapacity of his strongest colleague as a valid reason for postponing his resignation.

On the afternoon of Salisbury's resignation, the King sent for Balfour to form the new Ministry. The messenger from the Palace found him at the House of Commons, but Balfour felt it impossible to accept the Royal commission without first consulting Chamberlain. Accordingly, he drove at once to Prince's Gardens, where the Chamberlains were still as ignorant as the general public of what had taken place. Chamberlain was asleep, when Balfour called; and it was only when Mrs. Chamberlain understood the cause of his visit that she agreed to disregard the doctor's orders and wake her husband. At Chamberlain's bedside, Balfour received the fullest assurance of his support. There is no record of their conversation, but a few days later, Lord Esher, a close friend of Balfour's, would write:

... Joe Chamberlain was more seriously hurt than was known. Very nearly killed, in fact. The skull was bruised at a very thin place, and he has not been able to read or think since.

He saw Arthur Balfour, however, and expressed his complete loyalty to him. He was so touched by Arthur's loyalty to him all through the most difficult moments of the South African war, that he determined—at any cost—that Arthur should succeed Lord S. [Salisbury] and that he would serve under him. It is a pretty story, and quite true.[2]

[1] The office of Prime Minister was not yet constitutionally recognised, but Salisbury was concurrently Lord Privy Seal.

[2] See *Esher: Journals and Letters*, vol. i. p. 340.

Later that same evening, Balfour saw the Duke of Devon-shire, still the titular leader of the Liberal Unionist party, and, after some discussion on the Education Bill, told him of the King's invitation. He was favoured with a gruff and inarticulate reply, which was certainly interpreted and no doubt intended to signify assent.[1] Next day, July 12, Balfour kissed hands.

Having made sure of the Liberal Unionist leaders, Balfour next tried to secure the continued adherence of Hicks Beach. Beach enjoyed great prestige in the Conservative party and, as Balfour himself had written, had "earned a greater financial reputation than any Chancellor since Mr. G."[2] But, for some time past, Beach had felt that his ideals of statesmanship, and in particular of "sound finance", no longer commanded the full agreement of his colleagues. Above all, he feared Chamberlain's influence; and, when Balfour pressed him to remain at his post, he asked for assurances with regard to those policies on which he and Chamberlain were most at odds. Balfour would dearly have liked to retain Beach's support, holding that the resignation of the Chancellor might be a blow to confidence. But his relations with Chamberlain came first. He declined, therefore, to commit himself.

BALFOUR TO HICKS BEACH

July 13, 1902.—As regards Merchant Shipping, Colonial Customs, and Sugar, I do not *think* there is any reason to anticipate a fundamental diver-gence of view between yourself and any member of the Cabinet. But these are questions in which Chamberlain is particularly mixed up, either by virtue of his office, or by the direct commission of the Cabinet—and so long as he is confined to bed and forbidden to do anything but the merest routine, I do not see how I *can* say anything definite. I hope he will be well enough to come to Cabinet Thursday. I will not commit you to-morrow.[3]

---

[1] The Duke undoubtedly felt piqued that neither Salisbury nor the King had consulted him, before a final de-cision was taken. He had been offered the Premiership in 1880 and again in 1886, when Salisbury himself had offered to serve under him. By 1902, his ambition was probably extinct, but he felt that his claims to the succession should have received some formal ac-knowledgment (see *Life of the Duke of Devonshire*, by B. Holland, vol. ii. p.
280; *Lord James of Hereford*, by Lord Askwith, p. 267; and especially the Duke's letter of July 11, 1902, to Lansdowne, quoted in *Lord Lans-downe*, by Lord Newton, p. 241).
[2] Balfour to Lady Hicks Beach, quoted in *The Life of Sir Michael Hicks Beach*, by Lady Victoria Hicks Beach, vol. ii. p. 173.
[3] See Lady Victoria Hicks Beach's *Life of Sir Michael Hicks Beach*, vol. ii. p. 174.

But Hicks Beach proved inexorable. Salisbury's retirement gave him an opportunity to go without causing a crisis; and he resigned "in a good hour for himself".[1] His resignation marks the end of the great era of Victorian finance.

Salisbury's retirement and Balfour's succession were made public on Monday, July 14. The same day, Balfour summoned the Unionist Members of Parliament to a conference at the Foreign Office. His acceptance of the Premiership was unanimously approved; and the Duke of Devonshire gave a special pledge of loyalty on behalf of the Liberal Unionists. Austen Chamberlain read out a message from his father.

. . . I am to say how greatly disappointed my father is that he cannot be here to-day to welcome Mr. Balfour to the leadership (*cheers*)—and to say with what pride and pleasure he will give all the assistance in his power to Mr. Balfour in the responsible task which lies before him. (*Renewed cheers.*) . . . My father bids me to say to you, Mr. Balfour, that you will find in him a colleague equally attached to you by private friendship and public regard, and, in offering you his own support, he feels that he may speak also in the name of the whole of the Liberal Unionist Party in the House of Commons. (*Hear, hear, and cheers.*)[2]

IV

Salisbury's aloofness was proverbial. He and Chamberlain were never intimate. But the old Prime Minister was careful to keep their alliance in repair and always showed the younger man the greatest personal consideration. He succeeded where Gladstone had failed; and the comparison of their relations with Chamberlain throws an interesting light on their qualities of leadership. Gladstone persistently underestimated the Birmingham manufacturer and his hold over the British democracy. Where concessions had to be made, he seldom concealed his reluctance in yielding. Nor did he ever encourage those private contacts which alone might have led to better understanding. In the event, his failure to conciliate Chamberlain wrecked both his party and his policy.

Salisbury never made the same mistakes. He recognised Chamberlain's power and paid the price of their alliance, in

---

[1] See Lady F. Balfour's *Ne Obliviscaris*, p. 366.   [2] *The Times*, July 15.

terms of social reforms, without haggling. At the same time, he left Chamberlain a very free hand in the Empire, shrewdly recognising that it was a field where the latter's reforming energies could only promote those interests which, at home, they might have threatened. Only over Foreign Policy were they seriously at odds. Even then it was an undeclared war; and, though the struggle was keen, neither allowed it to mar their general understanding. In later years Vince, Chamberlain's chief agent in Birmingham, remembered hearing from his chief that

Lord Salisbury, unlike Mr. Gladstone, gave him reasonable opportunity of expressing his views on any important point of policy, before the final decision was taken. He had found, in short, that his position, as a Liberal member of a Unionist administration, was far more comfortable and required less sacrifice of independence than his former position, as a Radical member of a Liberal administration.[1]

Nor was it otherwise in their personal relations. The Chamberlains were frequent guests at Hatfield; and Salisbury, for all that he was reputed the most reluctant "diner-out" in London, was more often seen at Prince's Gardens than in any other house outside his chosen circle. Now, the Patrician and the Tribune were come to the parting of the ways; and, here, we may fittingly transcribe the letters which marked the close of their memorable partnership.

DOWNING STREET, S.W.
July 10, 1902.

MY DEAR CHAMBERLAIN—I know that one of the results of your lamentable accident is that for some days you must not attend to business.

But I do not think that prohibition should prevent me from writing to say that, after some communication with the King, I have arranged to wait upon him at Buckingham Palace tomorrow in order to place my seals in his hands.

From something you said to Cranborne, I gather that this step on my part will not surprise you. For some little time back, I have felt my strength was no longer equal to the demands of my official duty; and I have been only prevented from retiring earlier, first by the fear that it

[1] Unpublished letter of C. A. Vince to Commander Locker-Lampson, April 9, 1920.

might be inconvenient, if I did so while the war was going on, and later by the King's lamentable illness.

I cannot sever our connection of many years without thanking you most warmly for the steady forbearance and loyal support which you have uniformly shown me and which have made a somewhat difficult condition of things both easy and agreeable. I am terminating our official relations with very great regret.—Yours very truly, SALISBURY.

Salisbury's letter is in his own hand;[1] but Chamberlain was not yet in a fit state to write, and his reply was dictated to his wife. He at once assured Salisbury of his loyalty to his nephew.

40 PRINCE'S GARDENS, S.W.

Private *July* 11, 1902.

MY DEAR SALISBURY—I thank you very much for your letter. When I spoke to Cranborne some months ago, I had no anticipation of any early change, but the newspapers were saying silly things about me, and I wished you to know that, if at any time you contemplated retirement, my supposed ambition would not prevent me from giving to Arthur any support that it might be in my power to render.

I cannot be surprised that after such long and strenuous service you should desire relief, but I sincerely regret that the time for parting has come.

I have always felt that it was owing in great measure to the consideration which you showed us at the critical time of the Home Rule business, that we were able successfully to tide over the difficulties of a most exceptional situation.

For that, and for all your other kindness to me I am very grateful, and am always,—Yours very truly, J. CHAMBERLAIN.

With this went a letter from Mrs. Chamberlain. It reveals the gravity of Chamberlain's condition and adds warmth to the rather formal exchange between the two men.

40 PRINCE'S GARDENS, S.W.

Private *July* 11, 1902.

DEAR LORD SALISBURY—I have ventured to intervene and, much against his will, to persuade my husband to dictate the enclosed letter to

[1] Though dated July 10, this letter does not appear to have reached Chamberlain until the afternoon of July 11. According to Mrs. Chamberlain's recollection, it had not been received at the time of Balfour's visit.

me, instead of writing it with his own hand as he wished to do, feeling sure that you would forgive me, and would understand that it was yielding to my entreaties only which induced him to do it.

It is most important, at the present moment, that he should be spared all effort, for his accident was a very severe one, and absolute rest is required, else I should have been the first to wish him to tell you, in his own handwriting, of the deep regret which he feels at the news which your letter contained and of his sincere gratitude for all the kindness you have shown him. The years that he has worked with you and under you have been very full ones, and he has always relied on your kindness and sympathy. To sever the link of active work together is a great break to him, but I need hardly say that his allegiance will be most heartily given to your successor.

May I too be permitted to say that I am grateful to you from my heart, for, at a dark moment of his political career, your support gave him and all those associated with him the help which was most needed.

We greatly regret that we must lose the pleasure of our visit to you next Sunday at Hatfield. I am glad, however, to say that the report of the doctors is a very good one, and I hope that a few more days of absolute quiet will enable him to resume his work before long.—Believe me, Very truly yrs,

MARY E. CHAMBERLAIN.

V

Balfour's succession to the Unionist leadership had been too long expected to cause any great sensation. At home, the prevailing sentiment was one of approval that the Premiership had returned to the House of Commons. Abroad, there was general relief that Chamberlain had not become Prime Minister. Foreign opinion, however, expected that he would dominate the new Cabinet; and the *Neue Freie Presse* hazarded the guarded prediction: "It is not impossible that the Balfour Cabinet may merely pave the way for that of Mr. Chamberlain".[1]

Chamberlain's loyal acceptance of Balfour's leadership was praised on all sides, as the press and the private letters of the time still show. Unionists, indeed, could not help contrasting it with the unseemly struggle for power which had rent the Liberal party after Gladstone's retirement. But some of Chamberlain's

---

[1] *Neue Freie Presse*, July 14, 1902.

friends feared that his influence might suffer from his allowing
himself to be passed over. Maxse even went so far as to write:
"Mr. Chamberlain's conduct has been morally magnificent, but,
with great respect, we must say that it is not politics".[1]

There can be no doubt that King Edward was constitutionally
correct in sending for Balfour. Balfour was already First Lord
of the Treasury and had been, since 1891, the leader of the
Conservative party in the House of Commons. Nevertheless, we
are bound to ask ourselves whether matters might not so have
been arranged that the Premiership had passed to Chamberlain.
Of the two men, he was incomparably the more popular in the
constituencies, while, in the House, the diamond quality of his
debating power was generally recognised as superior to Balfour's
supple steel. The Conservative leaders might still prefer a Cecil,
but the great majority of back benchers and party organisers
would have been for Chamberlain. They knew that he had been
the organiser of the electoral victories of 1895 and 1900. Above
all, they acknowledged him as the leader of Imperialism, the
dominant movement of the day, which still spanned the latent
antagonism between Labour and the Middle Class.

These powerful claims had been publicly canvassed earlier
that year in the *Nineteenth Century* and the *National Review*.
They found a ringing echo among Imperialists of every shade
of opinion. The following extract from the *African Review*[2] is a
good illustration of the mood and the hopes of those who looked
to Chamberlain as their leader.

. . . It so happens that apart from this local question—the settlement
of South Africa—all the great questions which cry aloud for immediate
solution, Imperial reciprocity, the creation of an Imperial Army and
Navy, are at one and the same time Colonial questions, and questions
which would need to receive their impetus from the man at the head of
the Cabinet. Who is better fitted, therefore, to take the lead than Mr.
Chamberlain? Again, who but Mr. Chamberlain could enter upon the task
of reforming the various departments, getting rid of unprofitable servants, and breaking the power of retrograde permanent officials? Such
work as this belongs necessarily to the supreme head of an Administration; the Prime Minister must in any case initiate it, and we can see no

[1] *National Review*, August 1902.
[2] *African Review*, March 15, 1902.

possible Prime Minister, other than Mr. Chamberlain, on either side of the House, capable of attempting, much less accomplishing, this Herculean task. To pretend, as Mr. Chamberlain's rancorous detractors pretend, that the Colonial Secretary would in any way push his claims to the Premiership is absurd. We need no assurance from *The Spectator* or another to convince us that between Mr. Chamberlain and Mr. Balfour there is not, and never has been, anything in the nature of a personal rivalry. Mr. Balfour, though not the strongest of men or the wisest of Ministers, is a patriot and a gentleman. His mind, essentially academic—and in this, as in many other regards, his strength and his weakness are very much Lord Rosebery's strength and weakness—is too keen not to tell him that Mr. Chamberlain is the man marked out by his qualities to lead the nation at this crisis in its affairs. We believe the King will send for Mr. Balfour to form the next Ministry, but we also believe Mr. Balfour will tell the King that Mr. Chamberlain is the nation's choice. . . . Mr. Chamberlain is no ephemeron, no mere man of the hour. He is the man of tomorrow and the day after tomorrow.

The agitation in favour of Chamberlain's claims was powerful and persistent; but there is nothing to show that he ever encouraged it. All the evidence, indeed, points the other way. At the end of February 1902, when the first articles appeared, he sent for Balfour's Private Secretary, J. S. Sandars,[1] and told him categorically that he was not a candidate for the Premiership.

MEMORANDUM ON A CONVERSATION WITH MR. CHAMBERLAIN [2]

10 *Downing Street.*—About 5.30 today—Tuesday, Feb. 25 [1902]—Mr. Chamberlain asked me to come into his room [House of Commons]. He said he had been much concerned by statements in the St. James' Gazette and other papers—the net effect of which was that he had claims to be the next Prime Minister. He went on to say that these statements were not confined to mere newspaper gossip, but that he had been approached —not by Liberal Unionists—but by Tories—"your people", some of them, who had expressed their wish that he should succeed Lord Salisbury.

[1] According to Sir Sidney Lee, Sandars was in very confidential relations with his chief, on occasion even representing his views to the King (see Sir Sidney Lee's *King Edward*, p. 49).

[2] See Blanche Dugdale's *Arthur James Balfour*, vol. i. pp. 336-337.

Mr. Chamberlain then went on further to say, in most emphatic tones, that I was to understand that he was *"not a candidate"* for that office— "I have my own work to do and it is not done yet and I am quite content to stay where I am. It is true that I once said that I meant to be the next Prime Minister in succession to Mr. Gladstone, but circumstances have entirely changed, and I frankly recognise that such is the case. I say again what I have said before, I shall be quite willing to serve under Balfour —but mark, I would not serve under anyone."

All this was said with great earnestness and almost passionate emphasis, and the impression he made on me was that he was talking *through me* not only to A. J. B. but to other persons who might be interested in the political drama.

Our conversation ended with Mr. Chamberlain begging me to remember that he had always been most deeply touched by A. J. B.'s splendid and unselfish loyalty towards himself, and that every member of his family shared his feelings.

It was an interesting conversation—Mr. Chamberlain being to all appearances determined to commit himself.

That this conversation reflected Chamberlain's innermost mind would appear from the following extract:

MRS. CHAMBERLAIN TO HER MOTHER

March 11, 1902.—I send you the article which has appeared in "The National Review", written anonymously by an enthusiastic admirer. The suggestion it makes one is now hearing on all sides, and it is one that I deprecate. While, of course, it is flattering when coming from friends, it raises a question which is not to be even considered under circumstances as they are. The Opposition are only too glad to fan the flame, and thus try to create dissension within the ranks of the Government which, happily, they are powerless to do. I hope it will blow over as so many surmises do, but "The Nineteenth Century" has a less discriminating article in the same sense, and another review, I am told, has the same.

It is hard to believe that Chamberlain had for ever abandoned all thought of the Premiership. He was still the same man who had once remarked that the Premiership was the only political position worth having; but there were now very valid reasons why he could not press his claims and must even disavow their promotion by others. Had he cared to put matters to the test, he might have secured the support of a majority of Unionists in the House and in the country. But it would have been to grasp Dead Sea fruit; for the minority would have remained irreconcilable. Despite all his services to Unionism, there were still forces in the alliance, more influential perhaps than numerous, which deeply resented his ascendancy. They could not forget that he was alien to their most cherished traditions by his social origins, his Nonconformist upbringing, and his Radical past. Similar objections could have been and, indeed, were urged against Disraeli. But there was an essential difference between the two men. Disraeli, for all his racial and personal exoticism, identified himself with the British governing class and made himself the interpreter of their interests and their dreams. Not so Chamberlain. He might count many friends among the great families, but he was never their man. That very spring, the controversy over the Education Bill had sharply reminded Conservatives how close was his connection with the forces of Dissent. To the end, he would remain the representative of the middle classes from which he had sprung. It was not for nothing that, in an age when every successful brewer bought an estate and posed as a country-gentleman, Chamberlain still preferred to make his home in a Birmingham suburb.

In the House, Unionist opposition to Chamberlain came chiefly from the die-hards round Hicks Beach and from a group of younger men, Salisbury's sons among them, who deplored what they affected to regard as Chamberlain's "materialism". Behind these elements lurked the deeper and more calculating antagonism of the powerful forces centred upon Hatfield, the Palace and, above all, the Treasury. For all their mutual respect and long collaboration, Salisbury was the most implacable opponent of Chamberlain's ambitions. It was not merely that he wished to keep the Premiership in the hands of the Cecil connection. There were weightier reasons which would, in any case, have opposed him to Chamberlain's succession. His genius was of the negative kind. He knew that concessions had sometimes to be made, but he regarded it as the function of the Conservative party to delay and wear down each innovation, until it could be assimilated with the least possible change into the body politic. Between this philosophical Conservatism and Chamberlain's constructive Radicalism there could be compromise but not synthesis. Salisbury had always known this. He had, therefore, regarded Chamberlain as a force to be used in the service of the Conservative interest, but never allowed to become its master.

The long-drawn difference between the two men, over the projected German alliance, had deepened still further Salisbury's patient subtle antagonism to Chamberlain. The old Prime Minister always regarded the conduct of Foreign Affairs as the first business of statesmanship; and, as long as his strength endured, he had remained his own Foreign Secretary. As such, he had been deeply shocked not so much by the aims of Chamberlain's Foreign Policy—they were not very different from Balfour's—as by his methods. We may well believe that he never forgave Chamberlain for the Leicester speech; and his resentment can only have increased if, as is likely enough, he learned of the frankness with which Chamberlain criticised his policy in conversation with German diplomats.

Splendid Isolation had been abandoned even before Salisbury retired; but, though Chamberlain's ideas on Foreign Policy would be accepted, his methods were remembered against him. Much was made of his unpopularity abroad; and there can be little doubt that forces were at work, in the Foreign Office and the Palace, to exclude him from the conduct of affairs which they regarded as their special preserve.

To the number of these hostile forces must be added the Treasury. Its officials, at this time, enjoyed a prestige only comparable to that of the priesthood in an earlier age. They already suspected Chamberlain of economic heresy and disapproved of him as the author of expensive measures. The power of the permanent officials is often over-estimated, but their influence is all-pervading; and there is no doubt that, at the Treasury, they were already assiduous in spreading the legend that Chamberlain was "unsound".

VI

For the future of the Government and of Unionism, everything now depended on the continuing co-operation between the new Prime Minister and his more active and famous lieutenant. And yet it would have been hard to find two men with less in common. Disraeli once remarked with disapproval that Balfour "sat upon his spine". By temperament he was a dilettante; and politics, though he gave his life to them, never wholly absorbed him. His heart, if he had one at all, was in philosophy, and his detachment from the main business of his life sprang from a profound scepticism of the value of all human endeavour. This cold outlook was matched and, perhaps, induced by a subnormally low vitality. With his back to the wall, Balfour could be a skilful fighter, but no man was ever more reluctant to take up a challenge, still less to provoke a quarrel. Chamberlain once said of him: "Arthur hates difficulties: I love 'em". Balfour returned the compliment when he remarked: "The difference between Joe and me is the difference between youth and age: I am age".

There was also a sinister side to Balfour's character. His charm and accessibility covered a streak of ruthlessness. When he thought it necessary, he could sacrifice friends with complete detachment; and no one was more skilful in beguiling the suspicions of rivals or opponents with personal amenities. Chamberlain, for one, would pay dearly for mistaking Balfour's friendliness for friendship.

Great changes were in the air when Balfour was called to the summit of political life; but no one was ever less a democratic leader than this study dialectician. Wise in counsel, brilliant in debate, charming in company, he left a popular audience equally unkindled and unconvinced. The more sophisticated might appreciate the delicate precision of his intellect; but the masses were chilled by his lack of passion and sensed his lack of faith.

If he had a political faith at all, it was that "Delay is as important as progress". But the only fundamental principle, which guided his policies, was to preserve the unity and, if possible, maintain the power of the Conservative party. He could never, like Chamberlain—or, for that matter, like Disraeli or Gladstone—bring himself to look on party as a mere instrument for furthering ideas. He regarded himself, first and foremost, as the trustee of the Conservative interest. In this he was Salisbury's legitimate heir, and, as such, shared the secret antagonism which we have already discerned in his uncle's attitude to Chamberlain.

Chamberlain and Balfour entered upon their partnership as the best of friends. Each felt the anomaly of their new relationship, and did his best to smooth the other's path. But there was no natural affinity between them; and, if at times they seemed intimate, it was from propinquity rather than inclination. Had their rôles been reversed they might have made a formidable team. As it was, the internal balance of their combination was too unsteady. A man of Chamberlain's stature could only concede the forms of power to a brilliant junior, if he could be sure of the substance.

We have dwelt at some length on this question of the succession, for it is of vital importance to our story. The position of Prime Minister is by far the most powerful under the British constitution. Sheltered from the direct blasts of criticism by the doctrine of collective responsibility, the Prime Minister, nevertheless, concentrates in his own hands all the essential levers of power. His official connections with the Monarchy and the Church, his supervision as First Lord of the Treasury of the whole civil service, and his virtual monopoly of patronage give him a range of influence which dwarfs that of any other office. Still more decisive is his authority over the Cabinet. The doctrine of collective responsibility, reinforced by the sanction of the Premier's power to dismiss, will compel the conformity of all but the strongest colleagues. It can seldom be imposed upon the Prime Minister himself. Powerful Ministers may, upon a given issue and by skilful combination, force a political crisis; but the Prime Minister, by the mere threat of dissolution, can force a crisis at any time. No less important are his negative powers. As chairman of the Cabinet, he determines the order of business and the priority of the issues raised by his colleagues. His is the power to approve or disapprove, and almost infinite are the resources by which he can postpone decision. Greatest of all is his authority, when he is at the same time the leader of the Conservative party. For all the laxity of its discipline, the Conservative party is authoritarian in structure and tradition; and its leader enjoys the undisputed control of the party machine. This was the prize which had eluded Chamberlain.

The most prophetic comment on the change in the Unionist leadership was contained in an anonymous article in the *Fortnightly*. It appeared under the title "From Amurath to Amurath". The author began by describing Salisbury as "the last of the Barons", and predicted that his analytical and negative qualities would be continued in Balfour. Regretting that Chamberlain had not been chosen as Prime Minister, he wrote:

> The country is full of a vague desire for great change, but Mr. Balfour is made Prime Minister precisely because it is desired by the ruling families that the minimum of change should be made. If that desire is to prevail, it will not take long to prove that the new ministry is fundamentally out of harmony with the temper of the country.[1]

Balfour's succession was, perhaps, inevitable, but it was a reactionary step. It was taken to bar the way to Chamberlain. It would end by opening it to Lloyd George. Looking back, we can have little doubt that Balfour would have served even the narrow interest of party far better, if he had followed the advice of the *African Review* and told the King that "Mr. Chamberlain is the nation's choice".

VII

The doctors had ordered Chamberlain a fortnight's complete rest; but he could not keep his bed at such a time. Within a week, he insisted on attending Balfour's first Cabinet.[2] Then, after a three-day cruise on board the Admiralty yacht *Enchantress*, he resumed the Chair at the Imperial Conference.[3] A week later, he was back in the House and introduced the Colonial Estimates with his usual clearness and force.[4]

Meanwhile, the new Prime Minister was confronted with the need and opportunity to reconstruct the Government. Chamberlain by his own wish would remain at the Colonial Office. He never hesitated over this decision and let it be known through *The Times*, on the same day that Balfour's succession was announced.

---

[1] *Fortnightly*, August 1902. Notes, in the possession of the present writer, show that Mr. Garvin was the author of this article.

[2] July 17, 1902.
[3] July 22, 1902.
[4] July 29, 1902.

Mr. Chamberlain has no thought of leaving the Colonial Office, his view being that the work he has undertaken for the welding together of the Empire is, as yet, by no means accomplished. He has put his hand to the plough with regard to the reconstruction of South Africa and to other great Colonial problems, which are now prominently before us, and he is quite content for the present to prosecute his task to its completion.[1]

The news, though unofficial, was received with relief and delight by the Colonial Premiers. Barton declared that it "would be accepted throughout the Empire as of 'good augury'", and went on to say, in terms verging on *lèse-majesté*, that

there would have been universal mourning on the part of all the Colonies at the retirement of the statesman who had made the Colonial Office the symbol, or at any rate one of the chief symbols, of the Empire's power.[2]

Chamberlain's friends at home, however, did not all share this enthusiasm. One dissenting view, coming as it did from the influential editor of *The Times*, is worth quoting:

G. E. BUCKLE TO CHAMBERLAIN

July 22, 1902.—. . . Many of your friends, whose desire is that the Empire should have the benefit of your invaluable services for as long a time as possible, are wondering whether it would not be prudent for you to husband your strength, and take some post less exhausting than that which you have occupied with so much distinction for the last seven years. More than once in the last year or two, you have confessed to me that you felt very tired and could wish (but for patriotic considerations) that the other side could come in for a short time and give you a holiday. You have now an honourable opportunity of passing to an office, the Chancellorship of the Exchequer, where you would still, by the power of the purse, largely control Colonial policy, and might steadily supervise the work of your successor at the Colonial Office. Of course, there is no one who could completely take the place you have filled for the last seven years. But you have laid down lines from which no successor could depart; you could secure a successor (perhaps Austen) in harmony with your ideas; and the Colonies would have a guarantee, in your presence at the Exchequer, that continuity would be preserved.

[1] July 15, 1902.
[2] Speech at a lunch given in honour of the Colonial Premiers at Lloyd's Registry, July 14, 1902.

Of course you may have already weighed all these considerations and made up your mind. . . . But I do feel very strongly that it would be a most serious misfortune for the Empire, if you continued in your present post and then broke down in a year or two from overwork and had to seek premature retirement.

Wise after the event, we can see that this was the right advice. At the Exchequer, Chamberlain might have initiated his fiscal revolution without even causing a Cabinet crisis. He would certainly have been spared the sorry imbroglio over the Budget of 1903. After the resignation of Hicks Beach, his appointment would have seemed a natural step; and Balfour could scarcely have hoped—and might not even have wished—to resist it. Some, no doubt, would have thought it daring, but this in itself might have been an asset, serving to revive the waning reputation of the Unionist regime. But there is nothing to show that Chamberlain ever seriously considered Buckle's proposal. He still did not see that the fiscal question would soon become the central issue of his life. Besides he had other plans.

Meanwhile, the post of Chancellor had to be filled; and it was of the utmost importance to Chamberlain, already groping towards fiscal innovations, that it should be filled by a friend. The names of Lord George Hamilton and of Brodrick were at first widely canvassed. Hanbury was also mentioned, though the very suggestion led the Treasury to threaten resignation in a body.[1] Later speculation centred chiefly on Austen Chamberlain and C. T. Ritchie. In an evil hour for Chamberlain, as for Balfour, the lot fell upon Ritchie.

Ritchie was of Dundee and the jute trade. He had entered Parliament in 1874—two years before Chamberlain—and had been in turn Secretary at the Admiralty, President of the Local Government Board, President of the Board of Trade, and Home Secretary. He had first attracted attention in 1881, when, as a Fair Trader, he had moved a resolution condemning Free Imports in a world which refused Free Trade. By a strange irony, it had fallen to Chamberlain, then Gladstone's President

[1] Moberly Bell to L. S. Amery, July 18, 1902: "The Treasury, I believe, threaten resignation in a body if Hanbury is made Chancellor of the Exchequer".

of the Board of Trade, to oppose the resolution in the name of economic orthodoxy.

Ritchie looked a big strong man, but with a sallow face and black beady eyes. He was given to "heavy and affected pleas-antry",[1] and made himself unpopular by "his habit of forcing his claims for preferment whenever he thought there was any chance of their being overlooked".[2] His lack of *savoir-faire* sometimes led him into ridiculous situations; and once, when the Queen received him standing, he was said to have offered her a chair. Lord George Hamilton described him as "a middle class merchant of curt and ungracious manner";[3] and Balfour's secretary, Sandars, wrote of him: "Ritchie had the *anima naturaliter vulgaris*. . . . His abilities were of the second class, but he was a hard-working minister of pedestrian methods."[4] Yet history may be kinder to Ritchie's memory than his contemporaries have been. Events would show that, however disagreeable, he was energetic, determined, and shrewd.

Ritchie's appointment as Chancellor attracted little attention. The country was bored with the familiar figures of the Unionist regime; and the critics were unanimous in urging Balfour to revive its fading popularity by a transfusion of younger blood. Chamberlain shared this opinion, but, when he and Balfour came to discuss possible changes, it was only to discover the truth of Napoleon's dictum—"*Les hommes sont rares*". The following extract from one of Balfour's letters illustrates their difficulties and the characteristic difference in their approach:

BALFOUR TO CHAMBERLAIN

Confidential.—10 *Downing Street, July* 25, 1902.—I have been thinking over our conversation of yesterday, and perhaps you will not mind read-ing the following observations upon it. . . .

You laid great and proper stress upon the desirability of making the changes bulk as largely as possible in the public eye. I think the con-siderations you brought forward have great weight. But there is another way of approaching the subject, which I should like you to think over.

---

[1] Unpublished Papers of J. Sandars.
[2] *Ibid.*
[3] *Ibid.* In his published Memoirs Lord George passed a kinder judgment

(see *Parliamentary Reminiscences and Reflections*, p. 329).
[4] Unpublished Papers of J. Sandars.

The first question I ask myself is: What men are there who, if introduced into the Cabinet, would add to its distinction and efficiency? There really are only two—Austen and George Wyndham, both of them in their respective ways quite first-rate—, both of them speakers on whom you and I shall have largely to rely,—now that Beach has gone—, in general debate. But is there a third? I think not. So that, if we added anybody else to our numbers, it would probably be a source, in the long run, of weakness rather than of strength, and would involve us in the same problems over which we are now puzzling.

Surely we should know better where we were as regards new Candidates for Cabinet office, if we waited till George Curzon came back,—a period which would afford a natural termination to George Hamilton's work at the India Office. New geniuses may show themselves among our unofficial independent members, and we shall be able to see how the new members to our Bench approve themselves in office. I enclose the last scheme which has occurred to me, and which involves a full clearance except for George Hamilton.

The Duke, I understand, is *quite* ready to leave the Education Office now.

Austen and George Wyndham were duly admitted to the Cabinet. Austen became Postmaster-General, a negative appointment. He was still too junior to carry much weight in Cabinet on his own, and his office was not one from which he could bring his father much support. Wyndham was Balfour's protégé, sharing some of his brilliance but with more zest for living and a less calculating mind. He retained the Chief Secretaryship, but, despite promising beginnings, his patron would rue the appointment.

The promotion of these two young men was justified by their ability; but it savoured of nepotism and was not enough to raise the stock of the administration. Yet, for the rest, reconstruction was conspicuous by its absence. Lord James was discarded; an injury for which he would in time exact full repayment. Lord Londonderry became President of the Board of Education, a Caligulan appointment only palliated by the ability and scholarly distinction of his Parliamentary Secretary, Sir William Anson. Lord Cadogan retired from the Irish Viceroyalty, but his successor, Lord Dudley, was not even in the Cabinet.

The changes in the lower ranks were equally uninspiring, though one deserves attention. Bonar Law was made Parliamentary Under Secretary to the Board of Trade; the reward for his defence of the Corn Duty during the Budget debates.[1] No place, however, was found for any of the Tory "frondeurs", among whom young Winston Churchill was already prominent. A note of Mr. Garvin's suggests that Chamberlain mentioned Churchill's claims on this occasion, but that the Whips thought it would be good for the unpopular young man to wait.

The reconstruction of the Government was received with universal disappointment or indifference. *The Spectator*[2] described the changes as "a half-hearted and perfunctory patching in lieu of a real remaking". The *Fortnightly* condemned them as "commonplace, pointless and inept".[3]

One pathetic consequence of the reshuffle of the junior posts was the dismissal of Chamberlain's old friend, Jesse Collings. The honest fellow was reluctant to be turned out to grass, and wrote in sorrow to his chief.

JESSE COLLINGS TO CHAMBERLAIN

August 13, 1902.—Balfour's letter came upon me so suddenly and unexpectedly that, when I saw you with it, I was quite unable for the moment to realize what it meant to me.

My principal feeling at the time was a hope that matters could be allowed to remain as they were for a short time, perhaps till Xmas—so that there might be a resignation instead of a dismissal. If I had known Balfour's intention a little earlier, I think this view might have been urged with some reason. From our conversation, however, I got the impression that the question had already been finally settled; that it was then too late and that Balfour's letter was only a formality. I am sorry for it, but it can't be helped, and the question is what is best to be done to meet the new conditions.

I have been looking into my affairs and find that my financial position makes it most difficult if not impossible for me to remain in Parliament.

Knowing as I well do the extraordinary amount of work, worry and anxiety you have had during the past two or three years, which, together with the extra strain and holdback inseparable from your accident, form a weight that few other men could bear (supposing that you are satis-

[1] April 22, 1902.   [2] August 16, 1902.   [3] *Fortnightly*, August 1902.

factorily bearing it about which I am not sure), I am reluctant to trouble you with my concerns, but as the head of the party, I must not contemplate any step without your knowledge and advice.

I shall be willing to do what you think best, but I feel very stranded now. However we must go "where the road leads" and fortunately "every hour has its end".

This parting with his Sancho must have been a poignant moment for Chamberlain. It was without political significance, but it was a painful reminder of the extent of his political isolation. There was no one to take even Collings' place.

The failure to find "new men" is remarkable in so consummate a politician as Chamberlain. The truth is that, in the years of the Unionist alliance, he had neglected to provide himself with staunch allies or loyal henchmen. It would prove a fatal oversight. His personal prestige was at its height but, except for his son, he could not count on a single whole-hearted adherent in the Government. Friends he had enough in the ordinary sense, but there was not one of them who would rank the attachment above the ties of office or of loyalty to the Prime Minister.

Looking back, we can see that, for all the spectacular triumphs of this year, the old foundations of Chamberlain's political power were crumbling away. In 1886, he had held the balance in the fight against Home Rule. In 1895, he had been the unquestioned leader of the Liberal Unionists in the constituencies. In 1900, he had been "the organiser of victory" at the Khaki Election, as well as in South Africa. These things had made him indispensable to his colleagues. But now the war was over and Liberal Unionism was moribund. The Whigs had merged insensibly with the Tories. The more Radical sort had died out or, with the Education Bill, would drift back to the Gladstonian fold. Thus at the zenith of his fame Chamberlain stood alone. A strong tide had borne him thus far, and presently another, still mightier, would carry him out into uncharted seas. Meanwhile, though the world might think him the master of the Government, he was more nearly its prisoner.

VIII

On August 9, the same day that the changes in the Government were announced, the King was crowned at last. Chamberlain took his place in the Abbey "in his uniform as a Brother of Trinity House, looking significantly upon the scene—the man who had done more than all men living to build up the sense of Imperial Unity upon which the whole feeling of King Edward's coronation is based".[1]

He was by now regarded as fully recovered from his accident, but there can be little doubt that the shock of it, coming as it did at the end of a period of prolonged overwork, was much more serious than had at first been thought. He carried the scar on his forehead to the grave, and it showed red when he was tired. Otherwise no permanent ill effects were apparent. Nevertheless, the question has often been asked: did he come back to work too early? Certainly it was at this time that the press first noticed his age; and Monkbretton would recall, at a distance of some twenty years, that he was "never so quick or elastic again", and would speak of "the bent knee and flat tread of old age".[2]

The accident may have had another and more sinister consequence. The period of Chamberlain's weakness coincided both with the reconstruction of the Ministry and with the critical debates on Preference at the Colonial Conference. There is nothing to show that this weakness influenced his attitude in these decisive transactions. But, on one point, a doubt seems to have lingered in his mind. Had he been in his normal health, he might have opened himself more fully to Balfour, not on any particular issue but on his whole conception of the political future. It was a decisive moment and more complete possession of each other's minds might have welded their association into a firm alliance. At the least, it would have helped to avoid later misunderstanding.[3]

IX

Chamberlain had lost the great prize of the Premiership with all its opportunities for constructive action. But he was still the most famous figure in British politics. His physical and mental powers were unimpaired, and he might reasonably look forward to another decade of active life. How, then, did he conceive his

[1] *Daily Telegraph*, August 11, 1902.
[2] Note of a conversation between Lord Monkbretton and Mr. Garvin (undated).
[3] Mrs. Chamberlain's recollections.

LIFE OF JOSEPH CHAMBERLAIN

BOOK
XX.
1902.

part in the political future? For once, we can answer with some certainty. His papers show that he was already revolving a new design to further his dominant ideal of a United Empire. Only one phase of it would be fulfilled, but it remains the most daring, the most original, and the most mature of all his political conceptions.

Imperial sentiment was at its height. Nevertheless, the long awaited Colonial Conference had done little to bring the vision of a United Empire nearer to reality. The Colonies still declined to contribute to the cost of Imperial Defence. The United Kingdom was equally unwilling to sacrifice its long-standing fiscal policies on the altar of Imperial Trade. Chamberlain, for his part, was already convinced that both sides would have to make concessions on these counts. He had said as much more than once; but as yet his arguments had proved unavailing. Advocacy, however, is only a part of the statesman's business. Far more important is the chemistry by which opposing elements can be combined. Chamberlain's plan was essentially chemical in its conception. He would raise the temperature of Imperialism to a point, where the prejudices and objections which still separated the Colonies from the Mother Country would be dissolved like impurities in a crucible.

The means which he chose to this end involved a sensational departure from established precedent. He would visit each of the self-governing Colonies in turn. This was not altogether a new plan. It had been in his mind when he first went to the Colonial Office in 1895.[1] But, then, it would have been premature. In those days, he was still unknown to the Colonies, and had not yet established his later ascendancy over the Unionist Cabinet and parties. Now, he would go out as the most powerful member of the Imperial Government and with seven years' experience of Colonial administration.

In these circumstances each visit must go far to create the atmosphere in which opposing interests might be reconciled. It would enable him, by more direct contact with the Colonial leaders, to diffuse his outlook among them and influence their

[1] "It is an open secret that when Joseph Chamberlain became Colonial Secretary in 1895, he cherished the idea of initiating a new departure in Down-ing Street by taking long Colonial tours to see for himself" (*National Review*, December 1902).

counsels. It would also give him the opportunity, in his public speeches, to rouse the Colonial peoples to a new understanding of the privileges and responsibilities of Empire. Nor was this all. He would return from each visit to plead Imperial policies at home, with a new and almost irresistible authority. In the Colonies, he would speak for England. In England, he would speak for the Empire. It was a grand design and would have raised him above party, above country even, to an Imperial position from which he might have carried his Imperial policies against all opponents.

X

Chamberlain broached his design to Balfour, when the latter became Prime Minister. It was virtually the condition of his remaining in the Cabinet; and Balfour whole-heartedly approved. Next, Chamberlain sounded the Colonial Premiers at the Conference, and was encouraged by their replies.

We have already discussed, in another context, the particular considerations which led Chamberlain to choose South Africa as the object of his first visit. We have also considered in some detail the visit itself and its place in the development of British policy in South Africa. Here our purpose is only to explain the more general, political motives which led to the first of Chamberlain's projected Empire tours.

CHAMBERLAIN TO MILNER

Colonial Office.—Private and Personal.—September 4, 1902.—I am seriously contemplating an early visit to South Africa and I want your frank opinion on the subject, I am led to this intention by several reasons. In the first place I want a holiday, or, if that is impossible, at least a change of thought and some relief from the constant pressure almost hour by hour to which I have been subject during the last seven years. I am thankful to say I am very well, and, if I were alone concerned, I should probably go on—at all events until I broke down; but my wife is anxious and has made me promise to endeavour to get some relaxation. Her anxiety has naturally been increased by my late accident which was a very serious one. I do not feel any ill effects now, but I lost an immense amount of blood and for some time afterwards I found that I must limit my work.

So much for the personal side. But I am also actuated by political motives of great importance. *I think that the time has come, when, if a further marked advance is to be made in the relations between the Mother country and the Colonies, I must take some new steps of a rather sensational kind, and, accordingly, when Balfour became Prime Minister I told him that I had it in my mind to make a visit to all the self-governing Colonies.*[1] I do not propose to do this in a single year but to take them in turn in successive years if circumstances and my health would permit.

I have been most warmly invited by the representatives of Australia, New Zealand and Canada, who assure me that the novelty of a visit from an acting Secretary of State would touch the sentiment of the Colonists and would strengthen the hands of their representatives in drawing more tightly the bonds which already unite us.

I should have, in this case, to forgo attendance in Parliament for at any rate a certain portion of each Session, but I think this could be accomplished, if not without inconvenience, at all events without serious danger. In carrying out this intention I propose to begin with South Africa. . . .

Chamberlain's plan was enthusiastically received by Milner, as we saw. It was discussed and approved by the Cabinet on October 21.

BALFOUR TO THE KING

10 *Downing Street—October* 21, 1902.—Mr. Balfour, with his humble duty to Your Majesty, begs respectfully to say that at Cabinet today three questions were discussed all of first rate importance. . . .

The second subject discussed was one on which Mr. Chamberlain desires to address himself directly to Your Majesty, as it concerns his special relations with the Colonies. Mr. Balfour will, therefore, say no more than that he entirely approves Mr. Chamberlain's scheme. . . .

The public announcement issued a few days later was followed by invitations to Chamberlain to extend his journey to Australia and Canada.

LORD TENNYSON (ACTING GOVERNOR-GENERAL OF AUSTRALIA) TO CHAMBERLAIN
Telegram

October 30, 1902.—Prime Minister in speaking of your intended visit to South Africa expressed the opinion that, if you could possibly

[1] My italics.—J. A.

extend it to Australia, the results would be of the highest benefit to that country.

You would receive hearty welcome from all parties and classes, and the good understanding, which is the root of the unity of the Empire, would be greatly promoted.

SIR WILFRID LAURIER TO CHAMBERLAIN

November 17, 1902.—A rumour has spread in this country that, after your visit to South Africa, you would likely extend your trip to Australia. I am voicing the whole public opinion of this country in asking you, if such is your intention, that you will also visit Canada, where you would be sure to meet a very cordial welcome. . . .

These, for the time being, had to be declined. But Balfour, in a speech at the Guildhall, made it clear that he regarded the South African tour as only the first of the series:

Let us lay it down that this visit of the greatest of Colonial Ministers to our Colonies is only to be the first of a long succession of such visits.[1]

[1] Guildhall, November 9, 1902. A very different view was privately expressed by Hicks Beach. "I am glad that Joe is going to South Africa. I hope he will keep his optimism under control, and will not make this a precedent for visiting Canada and Australia, with which he has nothing to do. A Colonial Secretary has no right to leave England for visits of that kind—even if it didn't place him, in the eyes of foreigners and Colonials, in something of a Royal position as compared with his colleagues, as representing this country by himself." (Lady Victoria Hicks Beach, *Life of Sir Michael Hicks Beach*, p. 182.)

CHAPTER XCVI

THE EDUCATION BILL OF 1902

(September 1901–December 1902)

BACKGROUND to the Education Bill—Education and the Cabinet—
Devonshire Differs from Chamberlain—Morant at Highbury—"Local
Option"—Salisbury Against the Bill—Attitude of the Conservative
Party—Chamberlain's Opposition Withdrawn—The Letter to Dr.
Glover—Balfour Goes Back on "Local Option"—Nonconformist
Agitation—The North Leeds By-election—Chamberlain's Despairing
Mood—His Efforts for Compromise—The Birmingham Bishopric—
The Birmingham Revolt—The Revolt Quelled—Chamberlain Defends
the Closure on the Third Reading—Passage and Consequences of the
Bill.

I

BOOK
XX.
1902.

WE noted in an earlier chapter that, among the causes of
Chamberlain's abandonment of Old Age Pensions, was the existence of a rival measure of Social Reform. This was an Education
Bill sponsored by Balfour himself and enthusiastically supported
by a majority of the Tory party. The merits of the educational
controversy are now of little interest, but its political implica-
tions were momentous; not least for Chamberlain. It would
foster the reunion of the Liberal party and would estrange a
powerful section of the Unionist following in the constituencies.
We must, therefore, devote some little space to the issues involved; and if at times the subject-matter may seem dry, the
patient reader will none the less be rewarded by some curious
sidelights on the contemporary conduct of our affairs.

The Education Bill was, at bottom, only another manifestation
of the revolution then in progress in British political thought. As
such it was in line with the abandonment of diplomatic isolation
and with the onslaught already preparing against Free Trade.

478

For some years, the belief had been spreading that the confusion of our educational system was in part responsible for
the decline of our commercial supremacy, and the apparent
exhaustion of the national genius for invention. As a result,
there had grown up a movement for educational reform which
found its inspiration in the more logical and centralised educational systems of Germany, France and Switzerland. Two of its
exponents will detain us; for, though they worked separately,
they worked to the same end.

Sidney Webb, then at the height of his period of Bismarckian
state socialism, was Chairman of the London County Council,
and, through his friend Graham Wallas, controlled the London
School Board. He was also a leading member of the Fabian
Society and a tireless author of articles on every aspect of social
reform. Robert Morant was that dangerous combination, a man
of high ideals with a remarkable aptitude for intrigue. After a
varied career in Siam, he had joined the Department of Education, where he had become a passionate advocate of educational
reform. Like Sidney Webb, he wished to see the existing patchwork of educational authorities replaced by a system which
would bring elementary, secondary and higher education under
the control of a single local authority, responsible in its turn to
a single government department.

Webb and Morant both succeeded in capturing the confidence
of Sir John Gorst, the Vice-President of the Council and, under
the nominal supervision of the Duke of Devonshire, the Minister
responsible for the Education Department. Webb plied him with
private memoranda and prodded him with published articles.
Morant became his secretary and his chief adviser, thanks to
Gorst's dislike of Kekewich, the Permanent Under Secretary.
Such were the two men who were to guide the educational
policy of the Unionist administration.

We have already observed how the Cockerton Judgment had
challenged the status of a great part of the secondary education of the country. The Act of 1901 had only been a stopgap.
The Government had still to decide what authority was to be
made responsible for secondary education. Two solutions were
possible. The School Boards might be empowered to administer
secondary as well as primary education. Alternatively the

School Boards might be abolished, and the local control of all education, primary as well as secondary, entrusted to the County Councils.

The School Boards were strongholds of Radicalism and Nonconformity, and, as such, traditionally hostile to the Established Church. It was, therefore, out of the question for a Conservative Government to adopt the first alternative. Nor, indeed, would such a solution have been logical; for, now that the County Councils were elected on a democratic franchise—as they had not been at the time of Forster's Education Act—, there was little justification for the direct election of an entirely separate local body to administer education. Gorst and Morant, therefore, decided for the second alternative: to abolish the School Boards and bring all education under the control of the County Councils. The problem was how to secure the necessary political support to overcome the resistance which the School Boards must inevitably offer to their intended abolition. On this subject Morant wrote:

> The only way to get up steam for passing any Education Bill at all, in the teeth of School Board opposition, will be to include in it some scheme for aiding denominational schools.[1]

This Machiavellian advice was to plunge the nation into fierce religious controversy. For the reformers, the denominational aspect was but a side-show. For the public at large and for many of the political leaders, it would be the main issue.

The situation was ripe for a denominational conflict. By an interesting but not unnatural process, the growing popular indifference to religion had strengthened the hands of the extremists in Church and Chapel. Within the Establishment, the High Church was in the ascendant. Among the Nonconformists, the dominant influence lay with the highly organised Federation of Free Churches. Between these two opposing elements the future of the educational system had for some time been a cause of contention.

The Education Act of 1870 had been a great victory for the Nonconformists. By the Cowper-Temple Clause, it had virtually endowed the Free Churches by instituting in the Board Schools

[1] Bernard M. Allen, *Sir Robert Morant*, p. 153.

precisely that Bible-reading and simple form of prayer which was the essence of Nonconformist teaching. The advantage thus derived by Nonconformity became ever more apparent, as the mounting costs of education and the impoverishment of the Established Church threatened the continued existence of many of the Voluntary Schools. The Nonconformists might even hope that the Voluntary Schools would presently die a natural death and that the whole school-population of the country would then be brought up on the Cowper-Temple teaching, scarcely distinguishable from Nonconformity itself.

But the danger to its schools aroused the militant spirit of the Establishment. The Bishops pleaded with the Government for help and mobilised the Anglican sentiments of the Tory party. They enjoyed the sympathy of Balfour and other members of the Cabinet. In the House, their cause was championed by Lord Hugh Cecil and his group of friends who, as we saw, affected to deplore the influence of Chamberlain's "materialism".

It was on this Anglican element that Morant and Webb counted. The bait, which they set for it, was rate aid for the Voluntary Schools. Having reached this decision, Morant came to the conclusion that Balfour would be the most suitable political instrument for carrying his reforms into law. At a lunch, specially arranged by Bishop Talbot, Morant won Balfour completely for his views. Balfour decided to take personal charge of the Bill and shortly afterwards invited Morant to prepare a draft.

II

The Cabinet met to determine its Education policy on November 5, 1901; a meeting which revealed deep differences of opinion.[1] Balfour urged that, in view of the strong Anglican concern over the future of the Voluntary Schools, legislation should not be limited to secondary education. Chamberlain, however, vigorously opposed his suggestion that the Voluntary Schools should receive aid from the rates. His reasons were political and are cogently expressed in a letter written only two days later to Selborne, who had taken the opposite view.

[1] *Memoirs of Sir Almeric Fitzroy*, p. 13.

CHAMBERLAIN TO SELBORNE

Colonial Office, November 7, 1901.—. . . The question of Education is a very delicate one in the case of the Radical Unionists. If you were to promote a Bill giving Rate aid to denominational schools, I think you would lose Birmingham and the Birmingham influence, whatever that may be worth, to the Unionist Party.

You are perfectly consistent in your views, but you may on that very account be unaware of the strong feeling of the other section of the Party with whom I am constantly brought into contact. . . .

At this stage, the majority of the Cabinet sided with Chamberlain, variously moved by the desire to maintain the coalition or to avoid adding to the rates. A Cabinet Committee was, therefore, appointed, with instructions to prepare a Bill which would unify both primary and secondary education but excluding any proposal of rate aid for the Voluntary Schools.

But when the Cabinet Committee met to draw up the Bill, they found it impossible, on both technical and political grounds, to exclude the Voluntary Schools altogether from rate aid. Technically, the situation would be inconsistent, since the local authorities could hardly claim control over Voluntary Schools for which they accepted no responsibility. The political objections to such a measure were succinctly summarised by Balfour:

The Radicals would oppose it, because its effect would be to abolish School Boards and to repeal the Cowper-Temple clause. The friends of the Denominational Schools would oppose it, since it would wreck their last hopes of saving these schools from ruin. The teachers would be hostile, as they desire a Bill which would place increased means at the disposal of school managers.[1]

The deliberations of the Cabinet Committee were attended by a fateful political consequence. Devonshire sided with Balfour against Chamberlain.

DEVONSHIRE TO CHAMBERLAIN

December 3, 1901.—. . . Whatever may be the difficulties or objections to Rate aid for the Voluntary schools, I am more and more convinced that we cannot pass a Bill without it. . . .

[1] Balfour's Cabinet memorandum, December 12, 1902.

Thus, on an issue which touched Liberal Unionist voters to the quick, the Whig leader prepared to abandon his party's ancient alliance with the Nonconformists. It was not yet an open rift, but it prepared the way for the final separation eighteen months later. That would be the final result. At this stage, however, the Duke conceived of himself not as Chamberlain's opponent, but as a mediator between Chamberlain and Balfour. In a long conversation, he sought to reconcile their conflicting interests. Chamberlain made it clear that his objections were not to the principle of rate aid itself. He had accepted the dual system in 1891, and knew that there could be no return to his own plans for purely secular education. But he was convinced that the Radical Unionists in the constituencies could not be persuaded to accept rate aid for the Voluntary Schools. He held therefore that, on political grounds, the Liberal Unionist party could not afford to concede the point.[1]

The Duke was profoundly impressed by the nature and force of these arguments. He communicated his impressions to Balfour, who dispatched the persuasive Morant to Birmingham to discuss the details of the Bill with Chamberlain. According to Morant's notes,[2] written for Balfour's benefit, their discussion was vigorous and prolonged. Chamberlain left no account of it, but Morant would look back upon it as one of the most interesting encounters of his life. He would also claim it, with less justice, as his greatest dialectical triumph.

Chamberlain recognised that some provision would have to be made for the Voluntary Schools. His objection to rate aid was that the increase in the education rate would be a continual reminder to the Nonconformist ratepayer that he was being taxed to subsidise the Church Schools. The same objection would not attach to grants from the Exchequer, since the purposes for which national taxation was levied were not specified at the time of their collection. Chamberlain, therefore, confronted Morant with a counter-proposal.

CHAMBERLAIN: "Why not do as was done in 1870, and promise addi-

[1] *Memoirs of Sir Almeric Fitzroy*: December 11, where he quotes from a conversation with Balfour, who had just received an account from the Duke of his talk with Chamberlain.
[2] Bernard M. Allen, *Sir Robert Morant*, pp. 166-169. The meeting took place on December 12, 1901.

tional grants to Voluntary Schools out of State funds, thus avoiding recourse to the rates?"

MORANT: "Because your War has made further recourse to State grants impossible." [1]

It was a shrewd thrust, and Chamberlain made no attempt to parry it. Like most of his colleagues, he was so much under the influence of Hicks Beach's insistence on retrenchment that he abandoned the one solution which might have made the Bill acceptable to the Radical Unionists. It is not the least irony of the Education battle that Balfour would several times have recourse to Exchequer funds before his Bill became law.

Morant's rejection of Chamberlain's counter-proposal left the two men as much opposed as ever. Their discussion seemed likely to end in deadlock. At this point, however, Morant mentioned a proposal which Devonshire had put to the Cabinet Committee, as a means of meeting Chamberlain's objections. This was:

That no local authority should take the place of the School Board, or give aid to the Voluntary schools from the rates, unless it passed a specific resolution that it desired to do so. [2]

If such a clause were inserted into the Bill, the local authority would then have the "option"—as the jargon of controversy had it—whether or not to subsidise the Voluntary Schools. It followed from this that, where the local authority was controlled by a Nonconformist majority, the existing situation might remain unchanged. Here was a basis for compromise upon which Chamberlain would later try to build. For the time being, however, he remained obdurate.

Mr. Bernard Allen is mistaken in believing that Morant secured Chamberlain's acquiescence to Balfour's proposals. [3] The events of the next few days show clearly that the Colonial Secretary did not yet regard the concession of rate aid to the Voluntary Schools as inevitable. He still hoped that it might be possible to limit the proposed legislation to secondary education and to preserve the *status quo* in elementary education until the state of our finances should allow the Exchequer to make direct grants to the Voluntary Schools.

[1] Quoted from *Sir Robert Morant*, by Bernard M. Allen, p. 168.
[2] *Ibid.* p. 165.   [3] *Ibid.* p. 169.

In his continued opposition to the Bill, Chamberlain had powerful allies; among them the Prime Minister, Hicks Beach, and Lord George Hamilton. Salisbury was a staunch friend of the Voluntary Schools, but he was strongly opposed to their receiving rate aid on the ground that it would destroy the voluntary principle itself:

The moment that any school has the right to receive rate aid by asking for it, from that moment the subscriptions to that school will absolutely cease. The only motive that keeps the stream of school subscriptions running is the belief that, if they are not paid, the school will perish. . . .[1]

He recommended using "the rates as an exception, having recourse to them only in the cases where the schools must fall if not aided and entirely within the discretion of the local authority. . . ." If, by this means, the Voluntary Schools could be preserved, then

Other questions would lose their practical importance. . . . We could go on for many years without settling the demand for united educational authorities, without abolishing School Boards, and even without remedying the injustice of the Cowper-Temple clause.[2]

For once in his life Chamberlain must have given thanks for Salisbury's philosophic Conservatism.

In putting his views before the Cabinet, Salisbury was careful to judge the education proposal on its own merits. But it is probable that more deep-seated considerations underlay his opposition to it. He belonged to a generation accustomed to think of politics in denominational terms. He was a Conservative, but he was also a Churchman; and it must have seemed to him one of the greatest merits of the Unionist alliance that it had divided the political allegiance of the Nonconformists. The value of this division to the Anglican interest had been proved by the Education Act of 1891, when Chamberlain had accepted as permanent the dualism of the educational system. The Act might have been a concession on the part of Conservatism. It had certainly been a victory for the Establishment. Now, however, the strangely assorted partnership of educational reformers and militant Churchmen threatened to alienate

[1] Memorandum by Lord Salisbury circulated to the Cabinet, December 17, 1901.   [2] Ibid.

Chamberlain's followers and reunite Nonconformity under the Liberal banner. The old Prime Minister might well fear that his life's work was in danger.

The meeting of December 13 found the Cabinet still deeply divided. It was decided—by a majority of 10 to 8, according to one account[1]—to confine the main Bill to secondary education. In this Salisbury and Chamberlain were said to have been supported, among others, by Hicks Beach, Lord George Hamilton, Ritchie, James and Selborne. Balfour and the Duke were the chief protagonists of the broader measure, and carried with them Hanbury, Long, Gerald Balfour, Londonderry and Lansdowne. In the Cabinet, as in the House, the conflict was to some extent one between generations.

Chamberlain's objections had been sustained. But one of Balfour's intimates would note in his diary next day: "A crisis in the Cabinet may have been averted but a crisis in the party is rendered imminent".[2] Balfour remained staunch for the more comprehensive measure, despite his uncle's opposition; and it was soon clear that neither the Educationalist nor the Anglican interest would agree to a Bill confined to secondary education.

Chamberlain's situation was unenviable. If the broader Bill were introduced, the bulk of his Radical Unionist following would be alienated. If it were not introduced, the Government would be faced by a revolt of the Conservative party with which the Leader of the House and a number of Ministers would be in sympathy. As the leader of a minority party in the coalition, Chamberlain could not hope to maintain his veto on rate aid indefinitely. In the end he would have to yield or resign. Resignation was out of the question. For one thing, his concern in the matter was purely tactical; he cared nothing for the issues at stake. For another, he could not honourably withdraw before the end of the war in South Africa. Besides, resignation over the Education Bill would have been political suicide. None of the Tories and only a handful of the Liberal Unionists would have followed him. The time for reunion with the Liberals was long past. In the circumstances, his most hopeful course was to accept the main principles of Balfour's Bill and insist on such modifications as might gild the pill for the Radical Unionists.

[1] *Memoirs of Sir Almeric Fitzroy*, December 14, 1902.   [2] *Ibid.*

Accordingly, he took advantage of his victory at the Cabinet of CHAP. December 13 to resume negotiations with the Duke.

CHAMBERLAIN TO DEVONSHIRE

Highbury, December 14, 1901.—. . . I ought to say, in the first place, that I am convinced that the right policy for the Government was to say from the outset, in plain and unmistakable language, that they did not intend to deal with Primary Education in the next Session. Unfortunately, the idea has been allowed to gain consistence that we contemplate a large and comprehensive measure and it is possible that our own friends are now so possessed with this notion that they will refuse to consider any Bill which is limited to Secondary Education only.

If this is your opinion and if you think that we must have a Bill dealing with Primary Education, then I suggest the following as the lines on which it might be drawn.

1. Abolish School Boards.

2. Set up a Municipal authority for Education on the lines of your draft.

3. Give powers to this Authority (or rather to the authority which elects it) to make such grants to such schools for such times and under such conditions, as may be agreed upon between the new Authority and the Managers of any Voluntary School in its district.

4.   .   .   .   .

5. If it is necessary to carry out this scheme to abolish the Cowper-Temple Clause, let it go—although I would rather not raise this thorny subject if it could be avoided.

The tone of the letter is firm, but the concessions offered were considerable. By points (1) and (2) Chamberlain agreed to the establishment of a unitary system of education, while by point (5) he accepted the abolition of the Cowper-Temple Clause which had virtually endowed Nonconformity. The only counter-concession which he asked for was contained in point (3). This would confer upon the new educational authority the free choice, or "option", as to whether or not to give rate aid to the Voluntary Schools and on what conditions. This "Local Option" clause was essential to Chamberlain. It might enable him to draw the sting of Nonconformist criticism.

The letter had its desired effect. For some time yet, various alternative proposals were canvassed; but, during the Christmas recess, we find Balfour and Chamberlain joining hands to repel an attack by Hicks Beach on the principle of "Local Option".

BALFOUR AND CHAMBERLAIN

January 1, 1902.—*Balfour to J. C.*—. . . Beach . . . also sent a suggestion in connection with the Education Bill having for its object to compel Voluntary Schools, in any arrangement that may be come to with the local authority, to pay a certain proportion of the annual charge. I have replied to him that, whatever may be said for this as a practical proposal, it violates the theory of our Bill, which is, that the local authority is to be trusted. If we abandon this principle in a direction hostile to Voluntary Schools by inserting one qualification, we shall certainly be required by our own friends to insert other qualifications in order to give protection to Voluntary Schools against partisan County Councils. Howsoever the Bill may emerge from Committee, I am disposed to think that it should be introduced at all events in its simple and logical form.

January 3, 1902.—*J. C. to Balfour.*—I entirely agree with what you say in regard to the Education Bill. It will be much easier to fight, if it is based on some principle which we can hold up as against amendments from either side.

With the New Year, Conservative pressure on the Cabinet was increased; and the Whips Office reported that "it would be hazardous to ignore the feeling of the great bulk of the Party, in favour of rate aid to the Voluntary Schools, for the sake of removing the scruples of a few Radical Unionists in the Midlands".[1] Meanwhile, the tension in the Cabinet seems to have persisted; and the Duke, on hearing of a case of suicide, might ask, "Had he anything to do with the Education Bill?"

In all his life Chamberlain never yielded more reluctantly. He fought hard to secure the widest possible interpretation of "Local Option"; and so little was he reconciled to the Bill that, as late as March, he remarked to a colleague: "We could easily engineer a demonstration of the County Councils against being asked to take over Elementary Education".

In the end he had his way over "Local Option" and, with this,

[1] *Memoirs of Sir Almeric Fitzroy*, January 20, 1902, p. 72.

gave his grudging assent to the Bill. It was introduced into the House by Balfour on March 24.

III

Ministers were somewhat reassured by the first reactions to the Bill. On the Liberal side it was commended by Haldane,[1] and welcomed by the *Manchester Guardian*. Most gratifying of all, the National Union of Teachers gave it their unanimous approval. The attitude of the Nonconformists, however, was threatening from the start. Rev. Hugh Price Hughes, the Wesleyan leader, declared that it might be the duty of Nonconformists to refuse to pay the Education rate. A few days later,[2] at the conference of Free Church Councils, it was decided to launch a campaign against the Bill. The leading spirit of this agitation was Dr. Clifford, the minister of Westbourne Park Baptist Chapel. These things seemed to confirm Chamberlain's apprehensions. No less ominous, from his point of view, were the reactions of the Bill's supporters. They showed no lack of enthusiasm but were almost unanimous in condemning the "Local Option" clause.

The agitation of the Free Churches presently disturbed the Liberal Unionists. Their concern found its first expression in a letter addressed to Chamberlain by Dr. J. G. Glover, a veteran of the National Education League. Glover's tone was friendly, but he voiced the feelings of an important section of Chamberlain's followers when he wrote:

Our Conservative allies in Unionism cannot expect that we should renounce, on a vital question like education, the essential principles of Liberalism—representation with taxation, the soundest education of the people without waste of public money, and the liberation of teachers from educational tests.[3]

Chamberlain's reply was gentle in form but firm in substance. Despite all his misgivings he had decided to support the Government, and, once committed, there was no better fighter. He has so often been accused of inconsistency and worse in his attitude

---

[1] House of Commons, March 24.
[2] April 15.
[3] Dr. Glover's letter of April 17 and Chamberlain's reply of April 22 were published together in *The Times* of April 24, 1902.

to education that we must quote from this letter at some length. It is a convincing justification of the compromises with his early principles which he had come to accept.

CHAMBERLAIN TO DR. GLOVER

April 22, 1902.—. . . I must once more go back to the agitation in 1870 in which we both took part. At that time, we put forward, as the only absolutely fair and logical system, the entire separation between religious and secular education. We argued that the State should secure the latter, while leaving the former to be provided by the religious organisations at their sole cost and responsibility. According to this view, the Voluntary Schools would have become in fact Board Schools, or, if they were closed, other schools would have been provided by the Board in their place. The local authority would have controlled the secular teaching, while making arrangements under which every religious organisation desiring it would have an opportunity of teaching its own tenets to such of the children as were allowed by their parents to receive it.

This was the theory, and the Second Board of Birmingham, of which I was the Chairman, endeavoured to put it into practice. The system did not succeed and was ultimately abandoned, against the advice of Dr. Dale and others, owing to the overwhelming pressure of the Nonconformists themselves, who refused to accept an entirely Secular system.

I do not believe that this plan, just and logical as I believe it to be, has now any better chance of success than it had 30 years ago; and we have, as practical educationists, to consider what can be substituted for it. As far back as 1891, I told my constituents in a public speech that I no longer thought that the extinction of the Voluntary Schools, painless or otherwise, was possible. I pointed out the enormous expense which would be involved in allowing them to be closed and in supplying the necessary buildings to take their place, and I suggested that the utmost we could now do was to ask that they should be content to receive on their committees of management some representatives of the ratepayers and parents of the children.

This object has been secured in the Bill. . . .

I have assumed that the option given in the Bill to adopt part 3 will be generally exercised. As the Bill is drawn, however, the local authority may, in any district in which the majority of ratepayers object to give aid to Volun-

tary Schools, refuse to adopt this portion of the Bill and leave matters as they are at present. . . .[1]

I trust that I have said enough to convince you that, whatever may be the defects of the Bill, the promoters have been actuated mainly by a sincere desire to simplify, coordinate and develop our educational system; and that, in endeavouring to effect this, they have not failed to keep in mind the principle of popular and representative control.

If they have been unable to exclude sectarianism altogether, . . . that is due to the inherent and inevitable difficulties of the situation. The denominational schools exist, they provide accommodation at the present time for the great majority of the children at school, and, if reform is to wait until they have all disappeared, not only will it be indefinitely delayed but it will be so costly when it comes as to provoke a serious and most regrettable reaction.

This letter, reprinted as a pamphlet, did much to allay Liberal Unionist anxieties. The rank and file of the party were content to follow their leader, while the more critical sort found some comfort in the "Local Option" clause.

The Bill was read a second time on May 8,[2] by a majority of 402 to 165.[3] This was a parliamentary triumph for the Government. The news from the constituencies was less heartening, but there was no reason to believe that Ministers would have to face anything more serious than the increased activity of their professional opponents. Indeed, the only disturbing consequence of the Bill was the opportunity which it gave the Liberals to close their ranks. But, now that the end of the war was approaching, Liberal reunion had become sooner or later inevitable.

Speaking at Birmingham a few days later,[4] Chamberlain dealt with the Education Bill in no apologetic manner. His whole tone suggests that he was satisfied that the opposition within the Unionist ranks had been broken. He began with a devastating description of the existing conditions of education.

[1] My italics.—J. A.
[2] It was in this debate that Lord Hugh Cecil made the speech of his career. Chamberlain described it as "a lay sermon but the finest thing he had ever heard" (see *Memoirs of Sir Almeric Fitzroy*, p. 84).
[3] The Irish Nationalists voted with the Government in the interests of the Roman Catholic Voluntary Schools. Balfour, as we shall see, had always counted on the Irish to prevent any future Liberal Government from trying to put the clock back.
[4] May 16, 1902.

We have a system, which is no system at all, which is a state of anarchy and confusion. . . . The authorities, which collect the taxes or the rates, are not the authorities which spend the taxes or the rates. There is no efficient control over the secular education. . . . You have the secular education of the country in a vast number of schools starved and inefficient owing to the inability of the managers or persons in charge to provide the necessary funds. Who suffers by that? not the managers but the children of the people. . . . All these things constitute a national weakness and a national danger in view of the competition to which we are subjected.

IV

After the second reading of the Bill, Ministers had hoped that the worst was behind them. Their hopes were premature. Within a few weeks the temperature of the controversy was to be dramatically heightened by the proceedings during the Committee stage.

On July 9, while Chamberlain still lay in Charing Cross Hospital after his cab accident, Mr. Hobhouse, a prominent Conservative member, moved that the "Local Option" clause be struck out. Under his amendment it would be made compulsory, instead of optional, for all County Councils to give rate aid to the Voluntary Schools. Balfour announced that the Government would leave the decision to a free vote. He added, however, that he had personally come round to the view that "Local Option" would only lead to bitter religious controversy at every local election, and that he would, therefore, support the amendment. The discussion was heated and long-drawn. In the end, the closure was applied, and the "Local Option" clause was deleted by 271 votes to 102.

There can be little doubt that, in the interest of education, the decision of the Committee was right. Educationalists of all parties were at one in condemning the "Local Option" clause; and its widespread exercise would only have perpetuated the patchwork system of the past, which it was the first aim of the Bill to reform. But the clause had been inserted to meet Chamberlain's objections to the Bill. It had been the condition of his agreement that the measure should go forward. In Chamberlain's condition immediate consultation was impossible; and Balfour might plead overwhelming pressure from the Tory benches in his defence. The fact remained, however, that, in allowing a free vote at all, Balfour had gone back on his bargain with Chamberlain. It was left to Austen to enter a silent protest by casting his vote with the minority.

In the "Local Option" clause, Chamberlain had seen a useful instrument for disarming the violence of his opponents and allaying the anxieties of his supporters. Nonconformists might disapprove the Bill, but they could hardly raise a great agitation against it so long as they had powers to modify or suspend its local application. Under "Local Option" the controversy would be transferred from the national arena to the parish pump; and where none could be compelled all might still be persuaded. But, with the excision of the clause, this one safeguard was removed; and it was not long before Chamberlain's grimmest predictions were fulfilled.

The spectre of compulsion stirred the Nonconformist conscience to its depths. The leaders of Dissent and their supporters in Parliament prophesied, or threatened, a wholesale boycott of the rates. The correspondence columns were swollen by their busy pens, while in a hundred cities platform and pulpit echoed their denunciations.

The Government now fed fuel to the flames by their amendment to Clause 6. Under this, the Councils were to be compelled to pay for the upkeep of the Voluntary Schools, but were not to have full control of them. By statutory provision two-thirds of the managers of these schools were to be appointed by the "foundation authority"—*i.e.* the Church—and only one-third by the local authority. It needed no great demagogy to suggest that the ancient principle of "no taxation without representation" was at stake.

Henceforth the Nonconformist agitation knew no bounds. Nor were its triumphs merely rhetorical. On July 30 the Radicals won a resounding victory in the by-election at North Leeds. The seat had returned a Conservative at five successive elections; and, in 1900, the Conservative majority had exceeded 2000 votes—a substantial margin for the small electorates of those days. Now the Radical candidate was returned by 758 votes. He was a Baptist and had fought the election almost entirely on the Education issue. A few weeks later, the Opposition all but repeated this success at the by-election at Sevenoaks, justly considered an impregnable Tory stronghold. Their attack was concentrated once again upon the Education Bill. It failed, but by so close a shave as to send a shiver down the backs of Unionist organisers all over the country.

In the recess, while Unionists relaxed on moor and links, the Nonconformist orators were on the warpath. Nor did they lack allies. The Liberal factions rallied to oppose the Bill, some from conviction, others delighting in the opportunity to close the party's ranks. Yet others, like Gladstone in 1885, welcomed an issue which might postpone the consideration of social questions subversive of the deepest Liberal principles. By a typically British combination, the Liberal lead was followed by the Labour movement. Labour's chief men were, many of them, Dissenters and Chapel preachers. Still smarting under the injustice of the Taff Vale decision, and disappointed in their hopes of Old Age Pensions, they were already preparing to transfer their adherence to the Liberal camp. They now took the plunge. In the first week of September, the Trade Union Congress condemned the Education Bill by an overwhelming majority. The event passed almost unnoticed, but it was fateful for Unionism.

All through August and September, the agitation against the Bill surged and grew. It reached its climax in a great demonstration on Woodhouse Moor outside Leeds. There, from five separate platforms, the patriarchs of Nonconformity admonished and exhorted a vast concourse, assembled by special excursion trains from all over the country. The tides of emotion thus released rolled on, flooding into every part of the land. Not even Birmingham would be spared.

Chamberlain's view of the situation during these months is best told in his own words. For the only time in his political life, his mood verges on despair.

CHAMBERLAIN AND EDUCATION

J. C. to Balfour, August 4, 1902.—My unfortunate accident, among many other inconveniences, has prevented me from following closely the debates on the Education Bill. . . .

From what I hear and read, I fear that things are not going well and I
confess that I am exceedingly anxious as to the future. The predictions
of evil, which I pressed so earnestly upon the Cabinet before the Bill was
introduced, appear to me to be in course of realisation, and even the
passage of the Bill is not at all likely to be an end of our difficulty. . . .

I trouble you now, however, because I think it is right that you should
know exactly how matters stand at the present time. When you first
introduced the Bill, its reception was on the whole a good deal better than
I had expected, and I began to hope that my fears would prove to have
been excessive. That is not now the case. . . .

To my mind it is clear that the Bill has brought all the fighting Nonconformists into the field and made of them active instead of merely
passive opponents. Their representations and appeals to the old war
cries have impressed large numbers of the middle and upper working
classes who have hitherto supported the Unionist Party without joining
the Conservative organisation. The transfer of their votes will undoubtedly have immense importance at a general election, and, after
Leeds,[1] I do not think that any seat, where there is a strong Nonconformist electorate, can be considered as absolutely safe.

I hear that Middleton considers that the Corn Tax was an important
factor. In my opinion it was only a convenient instrument used by the
Nonconformist Party to support their own grievance. By itself I do not
believe it would affect anything but an infinitesimal number of votes. . . .

I recognise that it may be too late for any compromise at all and that
there is nothing for us but to go to what I believe is certain political
destruction. . . .

I cannot be hopeful of any solution, and I am perfectly ready to accept
your decision, but at least let us face the situation with the full knowledge of what will happen if we continue on our present lines. . . .

J. C. to Balfour, August 31, 1902.—. . . I know that you are alive to the
seriousness of the position and will only say on this head that, in my
judgment, we are rapidly running on to the rocks, and that, if, after all,
the Bill is passed in the present stage, it will be the death knell of the
Voluntary Schools—and probably also of the Government. . . .

J. C. to Balfour, September 9, 1902.—. . . I am always ready to accept
your decision . . . and I agree that the Bill does not justify on its merits

[1] The by-election of July 30, see p. 493.

the extraordinary opposition which has been carried on against it. I am not, perhaps, so much surprised as you may be at the character of this opposition, having had more intimate acquaintance with the methods and prejudices of the fighting Nonconformists. Meanwhile there is no doubt as to the damage done. Within the last few days, I have been told by a local agent that we should lose at least two seats in Birmingham, if there were a general election now, and the reports from other districts are not more satisfactory. . . .

J. C. to Devonshire, September 22, 1902.—The political future seems to me—an optimist by profession—most gloomy. I told you that your Education Bill would destroy your own Party.

It has done so. Our best friends are leaving us by scores and hundreds and they will not come back.

I do not think that the Tories like the situation but I suppose they will follow the Flag. The Liberal Unionist will not.

We are so deep in the mire that I do not see how we can get out. If we give way now, those who have sacrificed much to be loyal will naturally be furious, while our enemies will not be appeased.

If we go on, we shall only carry the Bill with great difficulty—and, when it is carried, we shall have sown the seeds of an agitation which will undoubtedly be successful in the long run.

After all, we have done some good work in the last seven years and ought to be satisfied. I wonder how much mischief the Opposition will be able to do, when they at last seize the opportunity which we have so generously presented to them.

J. C. to Devonshire, October 3, 1902.—. . . As regards concessions on the Education Bill, it is no use proposing them without knowing how they will be received both by our own friends and by the enemy or the more moderate of them.

I believe a compromise might have been arranged but I fear it may now be too late.

If none is possible, I see no chance of getting the Bill through till next year unless the guillotine is used.

The worst of the business is that after the Bill has passed the agitation will continue in its most serious form. What are you going to do with Town Councils that refuse to act and ratepayers who refuse to pay? D—n the Bill!

CHAMBERLAIN PASHA GETS NEWS OF A RISING IN THE BIRMINGHAM BALKANS.

From the cartoon by F. Carruthers Gould in the *Westminster Gazette*, October 5, 1902

J. C. to Brodrick, October 5, 1902.—. . . We have a charming prospect before us! Why could we not "let it alone" and leave the reform of primary education to our successors?

These extracts show Chamberlain's deepening pessimism. But it was not his way to regard any situation as beyond remedy. To the end he plied Balfour with suggestions for bringing about a compromise between moderate Churchmen and moderate Nonconformists. His main plan was to give the local authorities full control of secular instruction in the Voluntary Schools, while leaving religious teaching to the representatives of the "foundation". To achieve this end, he proposed that the Councils should appoint a majority, instead of a minority, of the Voluntary School managers. All the denominations, moreover, should be given the right to give religious teaching in all schools to such children as wanted it.

But Balfour would not make the necessary concessions. He had courage in his cold, detached way and was peculiarly insensitive to the temper of public opinion. Moreover, he was by now convinced that the right course for the Government was to press on with the Bill and get it out of the way as soon as possible. His letters to Chamberlain are conciliatory in tone but uncompromising in substance. One extract gives their essence:

BALFOUR TO CHAMBERLAIN

North Berwick, September 3, 1902.—. . . Unfortunate as a defeat on it [the Bill] would be, and reluctant as I am that the Government should go out before you have been able to settle South Africa and before we have done one or two other legislative matters which require to be dealt with, anything would be better than the kind of concession which permanently conciliates no opponent, but does permanently endanger all confidence among your friends. . . .

. . . Let me . . . say, in conclusion, that, much as I feel the burden of this unhappy controversy, there is nothing connected with it which gives me more pain than the reflection that the difficulties and dissension, which have occurred, have produced their bitterest fruit among the section of the party which look to you as their leader.

I earnestly hope that the dissatisfaction, which has been caused, is not as deep-seated as you suppose, and as I fear. . . .

V

An incidental circumstance provides some light relief from this bitter controversy. In his search for a compromise between Churchmen and Nonconformists, Chamberlain had consulted Dr. Gore, the High Church Bishop of Worcester. The two men became firm friends, and their conversations presently extended to a subject which Chamberlain had very much at heart. From civic pride, he had for some time been working for the creation of a bishopric of Birmingham. This project was maturing, and he was now concerned to find a suitable incumbent. "If we are going to have a Bishop in Birmingham", he once observed to Bishop Gore, "I want him to be the best Bishop of the lot." [1] Gore was already keen to leave Worcester for Birmingham. He wrote to Chamberlain:

DR. GORE TO CHAMBERLAIN

Worcester, August 30.—*Private.*—. . . As to the Birmingham Bishopric, I should like to say in confidence that my strong desire is, if the Bishopric is founded, to take that part of the diocese myself and give up Worcester for a new man. I wish this because all my interests are in municipal work and life. And I am so keen about the Bishopric that I am giving the whole of my private capital, £10,000, "pour encourager les autres". But I must feel my way. The Low Church influence is very strong in Birmingham, and I am in their eyes more than suspect.

Here was a man after Chamberlain's own heart; and he seems to have determined that Gore should be the first Bishop. In the end he had his way; and it fell to him, as senior member for Birmingham, to introduce the motion for the foundation of the Bishopric. It is not the least of the ironies of his astonishing career—and one which he often referred to with amusement—that the Unitarian and former apostle of Disestablishment should have taken the lead both in founding an Anglican diocese and nominating its first incumbent.

VI

Meanwhile, the Nonconformist agitation had spread to Birmingham. A new Education League stirred memories of an

---

[1] Recalled by Mrs. Joseph Chamberlain in conversation with the author.

earlier fight; and the survivors or descendants of those who had marched with Chamberlain in 1870 prepared to renew the battle. Only this time Chamberlain was not with them. By an irony of fate, he was now called upon to play the part of Bright and to mediate between a Prime Minister loyal to the Establishment and the Nonconformist supporters of his Ministry.

The correspondence columns of the Birmingham press show that discontent had for some time been growing in the Midland capital. For several weeks discipline was preserved by Chamberlain's immense prestige, efficiently seconded by the inconspicuous yet powerful Birmingham "machine". But, at length, the swollen torrent burst its banks. The Nonconformists broke into open revolt; and Chamberlain was compelled to defend his base in Birmingham as never again in his political life.

On the last day of September, a conference of Birmingham Liberal Unionists unanimously carried a resolution condemning the Education Bill in the strongest terms. They demanded that a majority of the managers of the Voluntary Schools be selected by the local authority, and that the appointment of teachers should not be subject to any religious test. The conference had been convened by Messrs. Ansell and Titterton, two of Chamberlain's leading supporters. Liberal Unionist Headquarters might claim that the meeting had not been wholly representative; but many of the most prominent Liberal Unionists in Birmingham were associated with it; and some of them afterwards declared that they would leave the party, unless substantial concessions were made to meet their point of view. The Opposition naturally made the most of such a situation, and employed every art to incite the "rebels" to break with Unionism. But Radical editors were not much exaggerating when they spoke of "the Birmingham Revolt".

Chamberlain, at Highbury, realised at once that the challenge was too grave to be ignored. He must reassert his authority, if he was to retain his position not only in Birmingham but in Parliament and in the country. Accordingly, that same night, he made it known that he would call a meeting of officers and chief supporters of the Birmingham Liberal Unionist Association to discuss the Education Bill.

The meeting was arranged for October 9. Meanwhile, Chamberlain sent for Morant to impress upon him, and through him upon Balfour, the absolute necessity of making some concession to the Nonconformists. There is no record of his conversation with Morant, but the next day he wrote a revealing letter to Balfour's secretary:

CHAMBERLAIN TO J. S. SANDARS

I had an interview with Morant yesterday. . . . I wish we had begun business a little earlier, I am afraid things are in an awful tangle and I am quite certain from the inquiries I have made and the indications of feeling which I have from every quarter, that with our present policy we are running straight on to the rocks. . . . Nothing would induce me to withdraw the Bill for a second time. I would rather resign. . . . *What is wanted is to make it absolutely clear that the complete control of the secular education goes to a representative authority; while at the same time the denominational character of the Voluntary Schools is preserved.*[1]

I do not think it impossible to secure this result, but, if Balfour nails his flag to the mast on Tuesday at Manchester, I consider the Unionist cause is hopeless at the next election, and we shall certainly lose the majority of the Liberal Unionists once and for all.[2]

This was no attempt to make Balfour's flesh creep. Chamberlain meant every word. How grave a view of the situation was taken at Highbury is shown in the following purely personal letter:

MRS. CHAMBERLAIN TO HER MOTHER

October 7, 1902.—Work begins in earnest for Joe this week, for he has various very important affairs on hand. The progress of the Education Bill is anything but cheering. An honest attempt to make things better and easier than they are, both for Churchmen and Nonconformists, it pleases neither; and for the Liberal Unionist party it promises to be disastrous. We hear of one after another refusing to support it, and Joe thinks that the party is really on the verge of being broken up by it. Once broken it will not reunite—and he fears it is now too late to save it. It is a disappointment after sixteen years to have the rank and file revert

---

[1] My italics.—J. A.

[2] Quoted from *Sir Robert Morant*, by Bernard M. Allen, pp. 190-191. Mr. Allen does not give a date for the letter, but from internal evidence it must have been written on October 8 or 9. Morant signed his name in the visitors' book at Highbury, but omitted to put the date.

to their old friends, from whom they are really separated by many more
things now than Home Rule. He means to try and save some brands from
the burning and, on Thursday night, is to have a conference with the
Liberal Unionists here on the subject.

Chamberlain was in no position to press Balfour for concessions. He had made up his mind not to break with the
Conservatives over Education. They knew it; and he was thus
bound hand and foot to the Prime Minister's car. He would,
therefore, come before his critics with empty hands. Nor could
he play to any great extent upon their fears. In the past, indeed,
he had sometimes restored discipline in the Liberal Unionist
ranks by appealing for solidarity with the Conservatives to keep
the Home Rule party out of office. But now the fear of Home
Rule was waning; and his agents reported that this argument
alone would no longer avail. In these circumstances the conference might well seem an awkward corner to turn. He would not
lead "the rebels" against the Bill: he could offer them no
definite concessions. There was nothing for it but to throw the
whole weight of his personal prestige into the scales and make
the issue one of confidence.

VII

The conference assembled in the dingy Liberal Unionist
offices in Edmund Street, at 8 o'clock on the evening of October
9. Invitations had been confined to the officers of the party and
the Liberal Unionist members of the local councils and the
School Boards. Altogether 105 persons were present, including
Ansell and Titterton, the leaders of the revolt. Chamberlain was
supported by his two sons, Austen and Neville, and by his
principal henchmen, Jesse Collings, Powell Williams and his
cousin William Kenrick.

Birmingham took an unusual interest in the proceedings. A
large crowd gathered to watch the party leaders assemble, and,
despite incessant rain, waited for nearly three hours until the end
of their deliberations. The press was present during Chamberlain's opening speech, but was then invited to withdraw so
as to allow greater freedom of discussion.

The rights and wrongs of the Educational controversy have
been obscured by the passage of the years. But Chamberlain's

speech remains a masterpiece of platform tactics. As such it still compels our attention. Never, in his whole career, had he spoken at such a disadvantage, nor perhaps with greater skill. It was a difficult audience which confronted him; respectful, but deeply worried by issues of principle and knowing him too well to be easily spell-bound. He stood before them with empty hands; all his instincts opposed to the course which he had to defend.

He began with a show of firmness.

I may say at once, and in order that we may have a clearer idea of the issues to be discussed, that the Government will not withdraw this Bill. Therefore if this Bill should be defeated—which I don't think is possible —but if it should be defeated, it will mean the resignation of the Government.[1]

Having sounded this note of warning, he appealed to the audience's loyalty to him and to the Unionist cause.

They [the Radical Press] head their notices "*Revolt in the Liberal Unionist Party*" (*laughter*). "*Mutiny against Mr. Chamberlain*" (*laughter*). They say the time is coming when I shall be stoned in my own city (*more laughter*) and they predict with apparently good faith, which makes me say that they are silly (*laughter and applause*)—they predict that my political extinction is imminent (*renewed laughter*). Well gentlemen, I beg you to pay no attention whatever . . . to my personal position. I have been threatened many times. I have not been made afraid (*applause*). But the time is coming when the question of whether or not I continue in political life is a matter of absolute indifference to me; but what is of consequence . . . is that the cause and objects to which I have given my life, that they should continue as they are now, strong in the hearts and determination of the British people. If, long after I am forgotten, those principles for which I take no credit—since, indeed, I have no pretence to have initiated them— . . . if they remain, it matters nothing about myself or about any individual who has been concerned in promoting them. I hope the differences, if differences there be, between us at the present time may be composed. But if not, . . . then, gentlemen, at least let us agree to differ upon this one contested and complicated point. . . . Let us consent to that, but let us never consent to do anything

[1] This and subsequent extracts of Chamberlain's speech of October 9, 1902, are taken from the *Birmingham Post*.

that would assist the intrigues of those who . . . would hand over Ireland to the Home Rulers, would transfer the settlement of . . . South Africa . . . to the discretion and patriotism of the Pro-Boers, who would leave our interests in the hands of the Little Englanders, who would depend for our reforms upon the framers of the Newcastle Programme.

These words wrung from his audience the response which he sought. The critical mood was momentarily dispelled; they hung on his words. Having disarmed the meeting, he now deliberately sought to reduce the temperature of the discussion. Oratory was abandoned and his tone became conversational, matter-of-fact. He asked that the dissentients should

be definite in their accusations. We want chapter and verse . . . we want to know to what clause, to what line or word do you take exception and . . . what amendment would satisfy you. . . . We don't want the ordinary platform oratory (*hear, hear*). . . . What we want is more facts and fewer phrases (*hear, hear*).

To illustrate the need for formulating precise accusations, he examined some of the general objections raised by the opponents of the Bill. He pressed no particular thesis but contented himself with asking questions and pointing out difficulties. At times his technique was purely Balfourian; and it is tempting to imagine that he deliberately chose to inflict upon his audience the same sort of elusive, intangible argumentation he had for so long endured at the hands of the Prime Minister. He dwelt, for instance, on the accusation that the Bill was contrary to the principle of "No taxation without representation":

The advocates of the Bill assert—and I defy anyone to contradict them —that there is representation. . . . You may argue that it is not sufficient in amount, that it is unsatisfactory in its character, that it is not adequately secured—you may argue all these things; you may be right, you may be wrong; but at least you cannot appeal to that great principle of taxation and representation. It is evidently only a question of degree, and what I ask from this meeting is that you shall tell me what particular form of representation you desire—how much of what kind and under what security.

The principle of Religious equality, the appointment of teachers, and the powers of the local authority were subjected to the same inconclusive but dissolvent treatment. Otherwise, he made much of the Government's readiness to make reasonable concessions though, apart from a guarded reference to "the right of entry", he put forward no proposals himself. He did, however, invite the audience to subscribe to a principle which he regarded as setting the limits within which concessions might be made:

> Popular control of secular education, denominational control of religious education in Voluntary Schools; once you accept that principle, to my mind the way is clear.

Only towards the end did he depart from his factual tone. He had been defending the right of the denominations to control religious education in the Voluntary Schools. Suddenly he broke off:

> Believe me, gentlemen, if in this discussion we could hear a little more about the children and a little less about the sects, we should make greater progress. . . . I attach the greatest importance to those conscientious scruples which I know exist. . . . Yet, if I had to fight this question in the open, if I had to go to my constituents, or to the country, it is not upon these lines, these paltry questions of sectarian competition that I should argue the question. But I should argue it from the point of view of the children themselves—the future citizens of this country.

The words were not mere rhetoric; they were a warning to those who might dare to challenge him on a great social issue.

The speech was followed by two hours of discussion in which the Birmingham leaders voiced their uneasiness and objections. Chamberlain then put to the meeting four skilfully worded questions which were answered in the desired sense by an overwhelming majority. At Titterton's request, a further question was put, asking whether the local authority should not have the right to appoint a majority of the Voluntary School managers. This question was also answered in the affirmative by a similar majority. It contained the substance of the "rebels" case, but its significance was lost in the general satisfaction which Chamberlain's speech had given. The truth is that the audience, as so often in England, had been more impressed by his general attitude towards the issues at stake than by his specific arguments. It is a deep British instinct that, if a man's attitude is

sound, the rest will follow. Ansell and Titterton declared themselves unconvinced; but it was generally agreed at the end that
less than 10 per cent of the meeting were with them.

The conference was a triumph of personality and dialectic
skill. As one of the Liberal Unionist critics afterwards admitted,
"the revolt so to speak is stifled. Mr. Chamberlain has won a
great victory." [1] A split in the party had been averted, and,
though a section would continue to oppose the Bill, there was no
likelihood of another open crisis.

Later, when the spell of the meeting was broken, many had
second thoughts. What concessions had Chamberlain offered?
Some of his supporters pressed him on the point, but he evaded
them with a show of firmness.

CHAMBERLAIN TO DOWSON

Highbury, October 13, 1902.—I do not know what you mean by "the
amendments which I indicated". In my opinion the Bill gives full popular
control of secular education. I asked the dissentients where it failed, and
stated that, if they could show this, the greatest consideration would be
given to their complaints and every effort made to meet them.

Having explained my views, you will understand that it is impossible
for me to discuss the question in private correspondence.

I regret that we should be so widely apart as your paper shows us to
be, but this cannot be mended and we must be content to be personal
friends and political opponents.

I note with regret that the modern Unitarians are rapidly becoming
the mere creatures of the political orthodox Dissenters, who, as my father
always said, are infinitely more illiberal than the Church in its worse
times.

VIII

Chamberlain's victory over the Birmingham dissentients
marked the turning-point in the Education battle. The Liberal
party and the extreme Nonconformists were not to be reconciled. But, henceforth, numbers of moderate men, otherwise
supporters of the Government, decided to follow Birmingham's
example and not press their opposition to the Bill beyond
reasonable limits. The great reform was thus secured; and the

[1] *Daily News*, October 11, 1902.

Government survived a crisis which, in the test of an election, might have proved fatal.

From this time the tide began to turn. Balfour, influenced no doubt by Chamberlain's conversation with Morant, spoke at Manchester [1] in a conciliatory tone. Thereafter, when the House reassembled, the Government made some show of concession. Nothing of substance was yielded, but, at the instance of Chamberlain and other Birmingham members, a number of amendments were accepted on points of detail. These were at least evidence of the Government's goodwill; and their importance was exaggerated by the protests which they drew from Churchmen. Notable among such amendments was that introduced by Colonel Kenyon-Slaney. It gave the control of religious instruction to the managers of the Voluntary Schools instead of to the local clergyman. This led to a violent outcry on the part of many Churchmen; and poor Kenyon-Slaney was bombarded with abusive letters threatening his life in this world and his soul in the next. One reverend gentleman even declared

the amendment to be the greatest betrayal since the Crucifixion and added that he would have preferred the Colonel should have seduced his wife rather than come to Parliament with such a proposal.[2]

Balfour welcomed, and may even have stimulated, such counter-agitation. It made the Government seem adherents of a middle course. Meanwhile, other forces worked to the same end. Haldane's speeches and Sidney Webb's articles came by a cumulative process to influence thoughtful men. Gradually, the great body of moderate opinion rallied to the Government.

The Opposition were, nevertheless, determined to talk out the Bill in Committee. Every form of obstruction was attempted; and Chamberlain estimated that twice as many amendments had been introduced as against Gladstone's Home Rule Bill. Some indication of Liberal tactics is afforded by the detail that Sir William Harcourt, then in his seventy-fifth year, intervened altogether 150 times in the discussion of the Bill.[3] At length, the Government determined to apply the closure. It was the last serious contest in the history of this protracted struggle. Once

[1] October 14, 1902.
[2] *Memoirs of Sir Almeric Fitzroy,* vol. i. p. 112, November 27, 1902.
[3] Gardiner, *Sir William Harcourt,* vol. ii. p. 545.

again, Chamberlain came to Balfour's support. Hitherto he had
taken no part in the Education debates, but he now agreed to
wind up for the Government. On the evening of November 11,
he spoke for nearly an hour, strictly limiting himself to the
theme of the closure, and carefully avoiding any comment on
the substance of the Bill itself. For the most part, he justified the
Unionist decision by the very arguments which the Liberal
leaders had used in supporting the closure on the Home Rule
Bill in 1892. Throughout he was on the attack; and the speech
is full of ironic, but not unkindly, sallies against the Liberal
leaders. Much of the humour was merely topical, but one thrust
will bear quotation.

There had recently appeared in the *Church Times* an article
unusually abusive of members of the Government. Lloyd
George, quoting from it in the debate, had jocularly suggested
that such abuse reflected on the quality of denominational
education. Chamberlain had not forgotten the Kynoch debate.
He found the opening irresistible:

The hon. member introduced there a most striking and interesting
theory. He said that these personalities were connected with dogmatic
instruction. That leads up to a very interesting problem. What I am led
to believe is that, if any man uses scurrilous language, if he attacks my
character when he should only attack my political opinions, he must
have been brought up in a denominational school. (*Laughter and cheers.*)
I have a conclusive argument against the theory of the hon. member.
The hon. member, according to "Dodds Parliamentary Companion", was
brought up in a Church School. How in the circumstances can he explain
the moderation and the courtesy of his language and the entire absence
of any personality? (*Laughter and cheers.*) The theory is ingenious but
I cannot think it will be generally accepted (*laughter*).[1]

With the closure, the outcome of the Bill was no longer in
doubt. Nevertheless, opposition was sustained to the end; and
the closing scenes were made dramatic by the collapse of the
Primate, stricken by a mortal illness during his speech on the
Third Reading. The Bill did not receive the Royal Assent until
December 18. By that time, as we shall see, Chamberlain had
already left the battlefield. No doubt he left it with relief. His

[1] *The Times*, November 12, 1902.

intervention in the fight had been decisive, but, when he counted
the cost to his party, he could have little heart to celebrate
the victory.

The Nonconformists and their Liberal allies had been defeated. Nor was there much prospect of reversing the defeat;
for the Irish members, as Catholics, supported the Bill; and the
Liberals scarcely expected to be returned with a majority
independent of the Irish vote.[1] Organised resistance therefore
degenerated into a guerilla, which was gradually suppressed
by the Board of Education's firm administration of the Bill.
Nevertheless, the continued agitation, especially at local
elections, helped to erode the Government's majority. It would
contribute powerfully to the Unionist defeat in 1906.

[1] Balfour, writing to Chamberlain,   this view that his work would be
September 3, 1902, evidently shared   secured from reversal by the Irish.

CHAPTER XCVII

PREFERENCE AND THE CABINET—THE TURNING-POINT

(September 1902–February 1903)

STATE Socialist Character of Education Bill—Nonconformity's Last Stand—A Deathblow to Liberal Unionism—Chamberlain Henceforward a Conservative—Balfour's Obligation—"Changing the issue" —Chamberlain Decides for Preference—Fielding at Highbury—His Negotiations with Chamberlain—The Cabinet of October 21— Ritchie's Reservations—The Cabinet of November 19—A Provisional Decision—"I can leave for South Africa with an easy conscience" —Tariff Reform: A Broadening Conception—Influences of South African Tour—The Turning-Point and Milner's Judgment—A Prophet from the Wilderness.

I

THE Education Act of 1902 has been described as one of "the two or three greatest constructive measures of the twentieth century".[1] It has certainly stood the test of time. Its main provisions have never been reversed; and the principles which underlie them have informed all the subsequent reforms of our educational system.

The perspective of politics is very short. To most public men of the day, the passage of the Bill appeared as a great victory for the Establishment over Nonconformity. It was for this, indeed, that the rank and file of the Conservative party had been induced to fight. Yet the real victors were those, on all sides in politics, who represented the growing reaction to the individualism of the previous century. Public controversy might centre on such questions as "Local Option" and the appointment of Managers, but, as Sidney Webb wrote, the real significance was that

[1] R. C. K. Ensor, *England, 1870–1914*, p. 355.

509

for the first time the Bill definitely includes *as a public function*[1] education as education—not primary education only, or technical education
only, but anything and everything that is education from the kinder-
garten to the University.[2]

Salisbury and Hicks Beach had recognised the state socialist
character of the Bill. They had resisted it in Cabinet on the
grounds that the expenditure involved must dangerously
increase the burden upon the ratepayer or the taxpayer; and
Balfour's determination to press on with it was not the least
of the causes which determined the resignation of the Chancellor. Years later, indeed, Balfour himself would admit: "I did
not realise that the Act would mean more expense and more
bureaucracy".[3] Here is one of the many ironies in our story.
Balfour, acting in the interests of the Establishment, introduced
a measure which otherwise ran counter to all his political
opinions. Chamberlain, who represented the rising spirit of
"State Socialism" more than any other statesman of his day,
was compelled to resist it by a sectarian interest, with which he
no longer sympathised.

Earlier in this work, Mr. Garvin described Chamberlain's
agitation against the Education Bill of 1870 as Nonconformity's
"last fight for the leadership of National Politics".[4] Thereafter
the Nonconformists had abandoned hope of political supremacy.
They had remained a powerful political interest in the nation;
but on the defensive. By 1902, the initiative had passed to
frankly secular forces; and, to complete Mr. Garvin's metaphor,
the great agitation against Balfour's Education Bill may fitly
be described as Nonconformity's Last Stand. Rosebery was not
far wrong when he said:

If the Nonconformists of England submit tamely to the enactments of
this Bill, I will not say that they would be weakened religiously; but I will
say this—that in my judgment, politically they will have ceased to exist.[5]

The Nonconformist conscience has remained a powerful and
pervasive influence; but never again would a nation-wide

---

[1] Author's italics.
[2] *Daily Mail*, October 17, 1902.
[3] Quoted from *A History of the English People*, by E. Halévy, Epilogue, vol. i. (1895–1905), p. 207.
[4] *Ibid.* vol. i. p. 143.
[5] On receiving a Nonconformist deputation at Spencer House, December 8, 1902.

political movement gather round the Chapel. The truth is that, as a political interest, Nonconformity had lost its *raison d'être*. The disabilities, under which the Dissenters had lain, had all been removed. The long fight against religious discrimination had been won; and only old men could still remember the injustices of an earlier age. Henceforth the congregations of Chapel as of Church would be subjected to the stresses and strains of a new age no longer thinking in denominational terms.

Chamberlain was well aware of the decline of Nonconformist power. He never abjured his own Dissenting background, nor abandoned his theoretical belief in Secular Education and Disestablishment. But his first loyalty was to other causes. Besides, he considered that the Nonconformists had betrayed their own deepest interest when, in their majority, they had supported Gladstone's policy of Home Rule for Ireland. He gave vent to his feelings on this subject a few weeks before he left for South Africa. It was at the end of a private conversation with R. W. Perks, a prominent Nonconformist and Liberal member of parliament, from whose pen we have the following account:[1]

I went to see Mr. Chamberlain on behalf of the Parliamentary committee of the Wesleyan Methodist Church in regard to [Maltese affairs]. ... After fully discussing the ... position, I rose to go when Mr. Chamberlain said to me quite suddenly, "Sit down again, for I want to tell you something which I wish you to remember". He was not well and I wondered much what he was going to say, for he spoke very quietly and earnestly. He then said, "You Nonconformists, Perks, made a great mistake in 1886 when they followed Mr. Gladstone and refused to listen to me. Had they supported me, they would have had Disestablishment long ago. Now they have got nothing." He then added, "When Mr. Gladstone suddenly sprang his Irish policy upon the country after consulting Morley, it was not so much to satisfy Ireland that he did so, as to prevent me placing the Disestablishment of the Church of England in the forefront of the Liberal programme, as Mr. Gladstone knew and feared I

---

[1] In a letter from R. W. Perks to J. L. Garvin. Perks gives no date for the conversation but says that it took place "in his [Chamberlain's] room at the House of Commons ... a few weeks before he started on his last (*sic*) journey to South Africa". It must have been during the autumn of 1902 while the Education Controversy was still at its height.

meant to do", and then he repeated what he said before, "You Nonconformists have got nothing—nothing".[1]

Looking back over the broad panorama of the years, the decline of Nonconformity appears as a historical development determined by economic and social forces. So in a sense it was; but the form of this development would powerfully influence the substance of many other things. The chain of cause and effect seems to be fashioned in accordance with immutable laws, yet, when the forging of the individual links is examined, the process is seen to be more unpredictable. Within each human being the pressure of social and economic forces comes up against the counter-pressures of those instincts and habits of mind which also make up the personality. Inside each man a battle is fought; and on the outcome of the mass of such battles depends the form of the general historical development. Nor is this question of form unimportant; for, in the long view, the incidental effects of one development are seen as the prime causes of another. So it was with the decline of Nonconformity and its effects upon Chamberlain and, through him, upon much else in our national life.

Chamberlain's Radical Unionist followers were for the most part Nonconformists who, apart from denominational differences, saw eye to eye with their Conservative allies. Their alliance had endured sixteen years; concessions had been made on either part; and the line of distinction between them had ceased to be clearly defined. But, with the Education Bill, memories of their earlier antagonism had been revived. In the breast of each Nonconformist Liberal Unionist interest and emotion contended, and new political loyalties clashed with old sectarian ties. The outcome of each clash varied from individual to individual. Some relapsed into Liberalism. Others retired from public life altogether. Yet others followed Chamberlain and continued their support of the Unionist alliance. Thus the Radical Unionist section was broken. Nor were those who

[1] The letter goes on to give interesting confirmation of Chamberlain's allegation that Gladstone had launched the Home Rule policy to head off Chamberlain's plan for Disestablishment: "The next morning I repeated to Sir Henry Fowler . . . what Mr. Chamberlain said and asked him 'Do you think this is correct?' To which Fowler replied, 'I am inclined to think it is—at all events I should not be at all surprised, if that was Mr. G's main object'."

LEFT IN CHARGE

JOE (*to the nipper*). "NA' THEN, HAWSTIN, I'M AGOIN' IN YER TER SEE SOME PALS, AND YORE
GOT TER MIND THE BLOOMIN' BARRER TILL I COMES BACK, AND YOU WATCH AS 'OW THE MOKE
DON'T DO A BUNK—SEE?"

From a cartoon in the *Daily Dispatch*, November 19, 1902

followed Chamberlain ever the same men again politically. By preferring Unionism to Nonconformity, they underwent, as it were, a chemical change, discarding with their sectarian loyalties the only principle which distinguished them from their Conservative allies. The Liberal Unionist party continued to exist in name for some years to come; but henceforth its independence would be purely formal. The Coalition had become an Amalgamation; and the Radical Unionists, like the Whigs before them, were for all practical purposes absorbed into the Conservative party.

For Chamberlain, this development was of the highest consequence. It meant that he no longer had an independent following in the country. Liberal Unionism was dead. There could be no reconciliation with the Liberals. For better or for worse he was now a Conservative.

One other personal aspect of the controversy claims our attention. The Education Bill was one of the few causes on which Balfour ever set his heart; and its passage may well be reckoned as his most enduring political achievement. Yet it is doubtful whether the Bill could have been carried without Chamberlain's support. The Government were assured of a majority in Parliament, but if Chamberlain had openly opposed the Bill, their position would have become precarious. They might have felt compelled to test their mandate in a general election and they would, then, almost certainly have faced defeat. As it was, Chamberlain gave Balfour his unflinching support; and the proofs of his public loyalty were only underlined by the vehemence of his private disapproval. At the height of the controversy, less than a week after the Birmingham "revolt", he went out of his way to pay a remarkable tribute to Balfour:

I look back upon the long roll of industrious men who have filled in this country the position of leaders of the House and of Prime Ministers of the Kingdom, and I know of none who have earned in greater degree, who have more deservedly earned, the confidence and the regard of the House of Commons, than my friend Mr. Balfour. . . . As none know so well as his colleagues . . . Mr. Balfour . . . possesses qualities which that assembly always appreciates. Unfailing courtesy, which can never be exhausted, is joined in him to those great qualities of firmness, courage, and sincerity which the House of Commons always applauds and always approves. I congratulate him from my heart upon the great position which he has earned, which is deserved by him by his character and by his talents. . . .[1]

Such loyalty was a great source of strength to the Government, and dispelled the rumours fomented by the Opposition. As some shrewd politicians saw, it also placed Balfour under a serious obligation towards Chamberlain.[2]

II

The battle over Education exercised an important influence upon the conduct of Chamberlain's main campaign; the struggle for Imperial Unity. It was the reverse in a minor theatre of operations which gave added urgency to the need for a success on the main battle-front. Lord George Hamilton, Chamberlain's colleague in the Cabinet, would later write:

The first changes propagated the second. If we had had no Education Bill of 1902, we should have had no Tariff Reform in 1903.[3]

This is to put too much on tactics. Chamberlain was a great political tactician; but he never embarked upon a major political campaign for purely tactical reasons. He had sincere and deep-seated motives for entering upon his new course. Yet there can be no doubt that tactical considerations lent an edge to his resolve. The agitation against the Education Bill had reunited the Liberals. It had cost the Government dear in by-elections, and had wrought havoc in the ranks of Unionist Nonconformity. These things convinced Chamberlain of the political necessity of "changing the issue".[4] By this he meant that the Unionist party must call off the electorate from the Education controversy and turn their attention to something more attractive. What was this new issue to be?

Imperial Unity had long been the transcendent purpose of

[1] Speech at the Mansion House, responding to "the House of Commons", October 15, 1902 (quotation from *The Times* of October 16).

[2] Cf. Lord George Hamilton, *Parliamentary Reminiscences and Reflections*, p. 317: "Throughout this period he [Chamberlain] behaved with great constancy and loyalty and thus placed Arthur Balfour under serious obligation to him for the attitude he assumed during the whole of this controversy".

[3] *Ibid.* p. 315.

[4] Unpublished Papers of J. S. Sandars.

Chamberlain's life; and, in this year, as we have seen, he had decided to pursue it by successive visits to the self-governing Colonies. Such visits, however, could only be the means to his end. They would create the atmosphere in which practical unifying measures might be taken. But these practical measures had still to be defined.

Hitherto, Chamberlain's proposals for closer Imperial Unity had been rejected by the Colonies. Staatsverein, Kriegsverein and Zollverein had been considered only to be refused. At the Conference of 1902, however, the Colonies had made a proposal of their own. Laurier, with the full support of the other Premiers, had invited the Imperial Government to adopt a policy of reciprocal Imperial Preference. Nor was this an academic initiative. The Canadian Premier had issued a plain warning that, if the Imperial Government declined his invitation, Canada must regard herself as free to withdraw the substantial preferences she had already granted to the United Kingdom exporter. In the context of contemporary Canadian politics, this implied that Canada would then have to seek prosperity in some special economic arrangement with the United States.

The Conference had thus brought matters to a head. Laurier had raised the issue of Imperial Preference in such a form that no British Government could afford to ignore it. A decision would have to be taken for Preference or against, before the normal course of Imperial relations could be resumed. And, in the first instance, the responsibility for taking that decision would rest with the Colonial Secretary.

The moment of decision, like the point of crystallisation, is seldom easy to determine. When the Conference rose, on August 11, Chamberlain's mind was not finally made up. For the rest of the month he was at Highbury relaxing. In those days the die was cast.

The decision was momentous; for a policy of Preference on Colonial terms must challenge the long-established principles of the British fiscal system. We often pride ourselves as a nation upon our political empiricism, but, at this time, in economic matters our fathers clung to abstract doctrines with an almost religious fervour. A man who set himself against the sacrosanct canons of Free Trade would be taking his political life in his hands. There is no reason to believe that Chamberlain did not fully appreciate the significance of his long-matured decision. His hesitations over Preference in the past and his unwonted reserve on the subject during these months, when it engrossed his mind, all suggest that he was well aware of the dangers of his new course. He moved, therefore, with caution.

III

On the last day of August, Fielding visited Chamberlain at Highbury. His ostensible purpose was to reassure the Imperial Government about the course of the trade negotiations between Canada and France.

CHAMBERLAIN TO AUSTEN

Highbury, September 1, 1902.—Mr. Fielding, Canadian Minister of Finance, was with me yesterday, sent specially by Sir W. Laurier to inform me of their doings in France. His statement is perfectly satisfactory. They want France to give them lower duties on certain articles and in return they are prepared to make concessions on wines and other specialities which do not concern us. They have made it quite clear that they will grant no advantages, which would have the effect of transferring to France any trade that can possibly be given to the Mother country. . . .

Fielding was, after Laurier, the ablest of the Canadian Ministers; and Chamberlain had been much impressed by his handling of the Canadian case at the Conference. "I . . . was particularly struck", he afterwards wrote to Minto, "by Mr. Fielding's ability and courage. The latter quality is really what most politicians are deficient in." [1]

As far as we know, Fielding's visit to Highbury was the only occasion on which Chamberlain had discussions with any of the Canadian Ministers between the adjournment of the Conference and their return to Canada. We shall, therefore, tentatively ascribe to it the conclusion of an important and curious arrangement between the two men.

There is no record of their conversation; but, in the light of what has gone before and of certain letters which will be set

---

[1] Chamberlain to Lord Minto (Governor-General of Canada), October 7, 1902.

out here in their due order, we may reasonably conclude that matters took the following course. Fielding declared that the Canadian Government was ready to give further extensive preferences to British goods imported into Canada, along lines suggested by his conversations with the Board of Trade. He asked, in return, that the United Kingdom should grant Canada a rebate on the Corn Duty. Chamberlain replied that he was personally in favour of remitting the Corn Duty in Canada's favour, and undertook to urge this course upon the Cabinet. He, also, agreed to let Fielding know, during the autumn, what the Cabinet's decision was likely to be. This advance information would enable the Canadian Government to prepare the necessary counter-concessions in time for the presentation of their own Budget. It would also help Laurier to decide his tactics in dealing with Mr. Tarte, who had split the Canadian Cabinet by launching a public campaign in favour of high tariffs. This domestic crisis in Canada raised tactical issues which would play much the same part in Laurier's calculations as had the Education Bill in Chamberlain's.

From Highbury, Fielding returned to Paris and, for the rest of the month, was engaged in negotiations there and in London. His talks with the French Government were inconclusive, and he returned to Canada in October. On his way back, he passed through London and wrote to Chamberlain as follows:

FIELDING TO CHAMBERLAIN

Hotel Cecil, October 4, 1902.—*Confidential.*—The postponement of the consideration of our French business leaves the deck clear for any action that may be possible in Great Britain respecting the British preference.

You were kind enough to say that, at an early period in the Autumn, you would likely be able to give me an intimation as to the probabilities of action by the Imperial Government on this subject. I shall be much obliged if you will bear this in mind and favour me with information as soon as you are in a position to give it.

Tariff questions are exciting considerable attention in Canada at present and, until we know what is to happen in Great Britain, we shall hardly be in a position to deal with such questions.

I think it probable that you are fully possessed of our views on the subject, and that further personal communication is not necessary. But if the business should take such a shape that you thought good ends could be served by one of us coming over again, we should try to arrange for this, although it would not be very convenient, for, from now until the opening of Parliament we shall be much pressed. However, we recognise the importance of the business, and would put everything else aside to assist in bringing about a satisfactory arrangement.

On a corner of the covering docket of this letter, Chamberlain scrawled the single word "Ritchie". It is most unlikely that this was an instruction to his office. His way in such matters was more precise. Was he merely jotting down a passing reflection? Or did the note register a decision to discuss the matter with Ritchie? Whatever the explanation, he must by now have recognised that much would depend on the attitude of the Chancellor of the Exchequer.

Chamberlain first raised the question of remitting the Corn Duty in Canada's favour at the Cabinet of October 21. No minutes were kept in those days of the discussions nor even of the decisions of the Cabinet. The only available records, which may claim authority, are the private papers of Ministers taking part and the Prime Minister's routine letters to the Sovereign. The latter, written on the same day as the Cabinet meeting and by its Chairman, may justly be considered the most responsible.

BALFOUR TO THE KING

10 *Downing Street, October* 21, 1902.—Mr. Balfour with his humble duty to Your Majesty begs respectfully to say that at Cabinet today three questions [1] were discussed—all of first-rate importance. . . .

The third subject was the most important of all, and Mr. Balfour only permitted its discussion on the distinct understanding that no premature decision was to be taken upon it. It is suggested that, while retaining the shilling duty on corn, as regards *foreign* importation, our *Colonies* should be allowed to import it free. There is a very great deal to be said in favour of this proposal. But it raises very big questions indeed—colonial and fiscal —and the Government which embarks upon it provokes a big fight. On the whole Mr. Balfour leans towards it; but it behoves us to walk warily.

The discussion on this occasion was apparently general and inconclusive. The gravity of the issue was stressed; and it

[1] The second question was Chamberlain's proposal to visit South Africa.

was agreed to consider the whole question again at a later date.

Meanwhile, Fielding returned to the charge. The note of urgency in his letter was evidently dictated by the need to counteract Tarte's "unauthorised" Tariff campaign.

FIELDING TO CHAMBERLAIN

*Ottawa, November 3, 1902.—Personal.—*I have read with mingled pleasure and regret the announcement of your intended early departure for South Africa: pleasure because this is a further evidence of your determination to give the closest personal study to important colonial questions, and because I am sure that your visit to South Africa will have very beneficial results, and regret because I fear this move is taking you away from England at a time when there are questions to be considered in which we are much concerned, and in which we are relying upon your help and co-operation. We are naturally anxious to know what the effect of your absence will be on the scheme of preferential trade, which we endeavoured to press upon you recently.

Owing to various circumstances, tariff questions have of late received much attention in Canada. Before we can intelligently shape our own course for the approaching Session of Parliament, we should know what is likely to be the fate of our recent proposals. When I last had the pleasure of discussing the question with you, you were good enough to say that, probably during the Autumn, you would be able to advise us confidentially as to the action likely to be taken by your Government. May we still hope to be favoured with such an intimation, or will your departure for South Africa necessitate the postponement of the consideration of the question until your return?

I do not wish to be unduly pressing in a matter which I know is one that presents many difficulties. But the situation here makes it very important to us to know, at the earliest possible moment, the mind of the Imperial Government on the trade question.

It is possible that, as the matter progresses, there may be occasion for confidential communications by cable. In event of the necessity arising for that, it would be a convenience to have a code number which I could use for communicating with you.

The request for a code number illustrates the very personal nature of the arrangement between the two men. Chamberlain

wished to comply with it and was only prevented by the
pointed disapproval of Sir John Anderson, head of the private
office, who represented that it would be encouraging Fielding to
go behind the Governor-General's back.

Before the Canadian proposal was again discussed in Cabinet,
Ritchie circulated his colleagues with a memorandum setting
out his objections to it. A copy of this memorandum, bearing
Chamberlain's pencilled annotations, is among the Chamberlain
Papers. It is a frank statement of the Treasury's position; the
voice is Ritchie's voice but the hands are the hands of Sir
Francis Mowatt. It is an important document in our story, and
as such must be quoted at some length. Chamberlain's comments are shown in brackets opposite the relevant quotations:

CABINET MEMORANDUM BY C. T. RITCHIE

November 15, 1902.—*Confidential.*—The proposal with regard
to Colonial preference, which we shall have to discuss when we
next meet, is of so important a character that I think it will be
convenient for me to put on paper certain considerations which
I wish to place before my colleagues in connection with the
subject.

We are asked to decide some months before the Budget that
the Corn tax shall be continued. Of course, I cannot yet say how
I shall stand next year, but I have every hope that I shall be in
a position to make substantial reductions of taxation. The tax
that has the first claim to be reduced is the income tax, but I
doubt whether it will be possible to make the reduction appreci-
able without making some remission of taxation on commodities:
for imagine how difficult would be the position of our friends in
the constituencies, if it could be said that we had taken millions
of pounds off the taxation of the rich and nothing off that which
falls on the poor. The choice in reducing indirect taxation will lie
between the tea duty and the Corn duty. I am told that the Corn
duty tells heavily against us in the constituencies; Middleton
tells me it is the one thing he is afraid of at an election, and that,
(He is an ass) if he were the agent of the Liberal Party, he would undertake to
"sweep the country" on that issue. We can, of course, make out
a good case for its continuance. Bread is not appreciably dearer,

but, whenever any change takes place and prices rise, the Corn
duty is sure to get the blame, and, if the employment of labour
were at the same time to fall off, the result would be disastrous
to us politically.

But, assuming that the tax remains, we must not shut our
eyes to the difficulties which present themselves in the way of
according preferential treatment to Canada, by admitting her
grain duty-free into this country. . . .

After what the First Lord and the late Chancellor of the Exchequer said a few months ago, it would be a strong order to
turn the tax to account for differentiation purposes; and it seems
to me to be very difficult for us to get over these pledges. But
for the moment I will put them aside, and assume that we are
free to act as we please.   (We are)

Let us first be quite clear what preferential treatment involves. It involves the imposition of a charge on the taxpayers
of the United Kingdom, in order to benefit our kith and kin
beyond the sea. Don't let us be under any delusion about
that. . . .

The reply to this objection is that the Colonies, in return for
being preferentially treated, will give preference to British
goods; but what may we expect to obtain from this preference?
An unknown doubtful gain to certain British producers in
return for an indubitable loss inflicted on British consumers. . . .

It is extremely probable that any advantage, which the
Colonies might gain, would be at the expense of our trade with
foreign countries, which now take more than twice as much of
our exports as are sent to the Colonies; and a slight differentiation of duties might easily diminish the trade of the United
Kingdom with foreign countries by a much larger amount than
could be counter-balanced by any possible increase of trade
with the Colonies, whose markets this country already to a large (Not Canada)
extent commands.

The grant of preferential treatment to Canada, which is the
immediate question under consideration, may seem a small
matter in itself, when regard is had merely to the amount involved in this particular concession, or when it is viewed as
assistance rendered by the richest country in the world to a

(We can maintain
the principle.
Preference only
given when our
own interests lead
us to impose
duties.)

comparatively undeveloped Colony. But does anybody think we could stop there? It would be an impossibility, not to say an injustice. From the moment that the new policy is announced, it would be open to any Colony to promise some preference to British goods in return for its being accorded preferential treatment itself. Mr. Seddon and others would at once be coming forward and knocking at the door of the Imperial Exchequer with specious proposals. Powerful forces would be set to work, not only to extend the area of preference, but to raise the rate of taxation. For, while a revenue tariff is easily kept moderate, it is certain that, as Hicks Beach said the other day, "any system of preference requires to be based on high duties".

. . . We shall be driven to tax foreign foodstuffs and raw materials, in order to be able to differentiate the tax in favour of some of our Colonies. Taxation on such articles, however moderate it may be, must tend to enhance the cost of production, must handicap British producers and manufacturers in the keen and growingly keen competition with Germany and the United States, and must increase the difficulties already experienced by them in maintaining their hold on home and foreign markets. . . .

It is also to be considered what effect the policy of Colonial preference will have abroad, and especially in the United States, with whom we desire to preserve the most friendly relations. They certainly would have no right to resent such a policy, but this consideration would not prevent them from retaliating in whatever form they thought would be most injurious to us. . . . I am as anxious as any of my colleagues can be to promote the idea of Imperial unity, but in doing this we must be careful not to lay ourselves open to the charge of endangering British interests.

(Are we always
to be frightened
by this bugbear?)

In placing these considerations before my colleagues, my object is not, at least for the present, to ask them to come to a decision adverse to any form of reciprocity for the preferential treatment accorded to us by our Colonies, but to point out some of the difficulties in the way of the special form of preference that has been suggested, and to impress upon them the impolicy of making any

communication to Canada, which would bind us to continue the CHAP.
imposition of a tax which circumstances between now and the time XCVII.
of the Budget might show it would be wise to abandon.[1]

ÆT. 66.

The memorandum made Ritchie's position perfectly plain. He was a declared opponent of Preference; but he did not ask *"at least for the present"* that the Cabinet should

come to a decision adverse to any form of reciprocity for the preferential treatment accorded to us by our Colonies.

What he did ask was that no communication should be made to Canada,

which would bind us to continue the imposition of a tax which circumstances between now and the time of the Budget might show it would be wise to abandon.

These two points are important to our narrative. They explain and, in large measure, justify Ritchie's subsequent behaviour.

The Cabinet returned to the question on November 19. The exact nature of the proceedings on that occasion was later the subject of considerable controversy. Accounts of very varying accuracy have appeared from the pens of the chief protagonists or their biographers. The present author, coming last into the lists, has had the advantage of perusing all the submissions of his predecessors. He believes the following to be the most authoritative account yet published of what really happened.

The evidence deserves to be considered in some detail. Balfour's report is tantalisingly short but quite clear.

BALFOUR TO THE KING

10 *Downing Street, November* 19, 1902.—Mr. Balfour with his humble duty begs respectfully to inform Your Majesty that only two subjects were discussed in Cabinet today (1) . . . (2) the advisability of giving to the Colonies a preferential abatement on the Corn Tax. . . .

In respect to the second question, the discussion was long and elaborate: but no argument was advanced on either side with which Your Majesty is not already familiar. The Cabinet finally resolved that, *as at present advised,*[2] they would maintain the Corn Tax; but that a preferential remission of it should be made in favour of the British Empire.

[1] My italics.—J. A.   [2] My italics.—J. A.

Balfour's letter, written on the same day, is conclusive evidence on two points. First, that the discussion was "long and elaborate".[1] Second, that the sense of the Cabinet was definitely in favour of maintaining the Corn Tax, while remitting it in respect of Colonial produce. It even seems likely that this impression was confirmed by a "provisional Cabinet vote".[2]

The majority of the Cabinet were, thus, in favour of Chamberlain's proposal. The composition of the minority has since been a subject of dispute. Chamberlain, along with other Ministers, believed that the Duke had accepted his proposal;[3] and some colour may have been lent to this belief by the Duke's jocular remark "that it was time for some of them to resign their membership of the Cobden Club, to which he and Chamberlain still belonged".[4] The Duke's recollection, however, would not confirm this view. Balfour of Burleigh was held by some to be irreconcilable; and, indeed, he afterwards told Austen Chamberlain that, at the time, he had expected that his would be the only resignation.[5] There is no doubt, however, that Ritchie was

[1] This would seem to refute the later recollections of Lord George Hamilton and Lord Balfour of Burleigh, that the question was not seriously considered. Cf. Lord George Hamilton (*Parliamentary Reminiscences and Reflections*, p. 318): "Before Chamberlain left he raised an informal and brief discussion upon our fiscal system . . ." and Lord Balfour of Burleigh (memorandum of 1911 quoted by Lady Frances Balfour in *Lord Balfour of Burleigh*, p. 119): "But the subject was not very seriously discussed in all its bearings. . . ." Lord George and Lord Balfour were both writing some years after the event and may in retrospect have confused the Cabinet of November 19 with that of October 21, when the discussion was both general and inconclusive. The reverse confusion was certainly made by Austen Chamberlain, who was convinced, until shown copies of Balfour's letters to the King, that a definite decision had been taken at the first Cabinet. He even recalled saying afterwards to Walter Long: "Our decisions today will make history" (unpublished memorandum of A. Chamberlain, March 4, 1931). All of which only shows how wishful memory can be!

[2] Cf. the Cabinet crisis of 1903. No. 7 —*Balfour to Devonshire* (recapitulat-

ing Chamberlain's part in the events leading up to the crisis of September 1903), *August 27, 1903*—. . . "The matter [Preference] had been formally raised by the Colonial Ministers; it had been brought prominently before the Cabinet over the Tariff controversy with Germany; and had even been put to *a provisional Cabinet vote* in connection with the shilling duty on corn". There is nothing to show to what session of the Cabinet Balfour was referring, but unless it was that of March 15, 1903, which for other reasons seems unlikely, it almost certainly must have been that of November 19, 1902, since Chamberlain, to whose part Balfour is specifically referring, was out of the country between these two sessions.

[3] See Chamberlain's letter to Bernard Holland of October 1, 1910: "As to [the Duke's] attitude . . . I, in common with others of his colleagues, thought that he had accepted my original proposal at the Cabinet which was held just before my departure to South Africa".

[4] Austen Chamberlain's unpublished memorandum: "The Origins of the Tariff Reform Movement", March 4, 1931.

[5] *Ibid.*

the chief, and perhaps the only vocal, opponent of the proposal. CHAP.
That his opposition was not withdrawn was always freely XCVII.
admitted by Chamberlain. Æt. 66.

CHAMBERLAIN TO DEVONSHIRE

Highbury, September 21, 1903.—What did I ask of you before I went
to South Africa? That you should retain the shilling duty on corn and
give a drawback to Canada. *I thought you had all, except Ritchie, accepted
this policy.*

He elaborated this view, some years later, in answer to enquiries from the Duke's biographer.

CHAMBERLAIN TO BERNARD HOLLAND

Highbury, October 1, 1910.—As Mr. Balfour has since publicly stated
in the House of Commons, before I left for South Africa the new departure
in fiscal policy had been explained to and accepted by the majority of
the Cabinet. How many members differed has, as he said, since become
a matter of dispute, but there is no doubt whatever that, at that
time, the majority of the Cabinet and all its most important members
accepted the policy. The exception was Ritchie. . . .

Why then did Ritchie not resign or, at least, threaten to
resign? In fairness to him it must be said that there was no
reason why he should. He had not asked, *"at least for the present"*,
that the Cabinet should *"come to a decision adverse to any form
of reciprocity for the preferential treatment accorded to us by our
Colonies"*. The only point for which he had pressed was that no
communication should be made *"to Canada which would bind
us to continue the imposition of a tax which circumstances between
now and the time of the Budget might show it would be wise to
abandon"*. Now, there is abundant evidence that this point was
conceded. On this the testimonies of Balfour of Burleigh and of
Austen Chamberlain are agreed.

Balfour of Burleigh.—. . . It was felt to be quite premature to attempt
to settle the Budget for the ensuing year eight months in advance. Most
undoubtedly, Mr. Ritchie took this position himself; and equally without
doubt, a majority of the members of the Cabinet *sympathised with him
to that extent.*[1]

[1] Memorandum by Lord Balfour of Burleigh (1911), quoted from *Lord Balfour of Burleigh*, by Lady F. Balfour, p. 119. My italics.—J. A.

Austen Chamberlain.—. . . It will be observed that the Cabinet took a final decision, *subject only to the necessary reservation that it might be revised if in the four or five months which must precede the introduction of the Budget in the following spring, new and unexpected circumstances arose.*[1]

The conclusive evidence, however, is that no official communication was ever made to the Canadian Government. Chamberlain, indeed, wrote privately to Fielding on the following day; but his letter makes it clear that Ritchie's reservations were allowed. He would naturally write with caution about a matter connected with the Budget, but he was evidently not sanguine enough about the prospects of his proposal even to mention the decision of principle which the Cabinet had undoubtedly taken.

CHAMBERLAIN TO FIELDING

November 20, 1902.—Private.—I duly received both your letters on the subject of our Budget arrangements, but have been unable to reply as we have been so full of work over the Education Bill that it has been impossible to secure a full discussion on the subject. *Even now we cannot come to a positive decision. The Chancellor of the Exchequer is naturally unwilling to commit himself positively to any course of action until the time for introducing the Budget is nearer and he knows what his position will be.*[2]

There is, as you must have seen while you were with us, a very strong party determined to resist with all their strength any alteration of our system in the way of preferential tariffs. They will be assisted on the present occasion by the unpopularity of the Corn Tax in some important districts of the country, and they will undoubtedly urge its entire repeal.

I have not concealed from you my own personal impression that it would be worth while to risk this, for the sake of establishing the principle that we intend wherever possible to treat the colonists better than foreigners, but it is impossible to say at present which way the ultimate decision will go.

Under these circumstances, I suggest for your consideration that you

[1] Austen Chamberlain, "Origins of the Tariff Reform Movement" (unpublished memorandum, March 4, 1931).   My italics.—J. A.
[2] My italics.—J. A.

might prepare your Budget on alternative lines, fixing, in the first place,
your tariff as you would propose it should stand in the event of the Corn
Tax being entirely repealed, and taking power to alter this tariff and to
give certain additional advantages to the mother country, provided that
His Majesty's Government here find it possible to give you a preference
by allowing corn to come in free from the Colonies while maintaining the
duty against all others. This would be a clear indication of your policy
and would, I think, strengthen the arguments of those who desire to
meet you.

I am leaving for South Africa on Tuesday, but hope to be back in time
to take part in the final discussions on the Budget.

Please treat this letter as entirely confidential between us. . . .

All this makes it clear that the Cabinet's decision was provisional. The Prime Minister weighed the written word carefully, and it was not for nothing that, in his letter to the King,
he had used the phrase *"as at present advised"*. Ritchie was
therefore under no obligation to stake his opinions or his career
on a decision that was still hypothetical. A view contrary to his
own might have been accepted in principle, but, so long as his
reservation was allowed, the matter could not be regarded as
closed.

We may therefore conclude that the proceedings of the
Cabinet of November 19 took the following form. Chamberlain
again raised the question of granting Canada a preference on the
Corn Tax and, in view of the importance he attached to the
question, asked for a decision before he left for South Africa. A
"long and elaborate" discussion ensued; and a majority of the
Cabinet, perhaps after a vote, accepted his proposal. Ritchie,
who had been in the minority, now protested that it would be
premature to decide details of the Budget so far in advance.
This apparently reasonable protest was sustained, and it was,
therefore, decided to take no decision entailing action. The new
policy was thus accepted subject to a practical reservation; and
such dissentients as there were did not deem it necessary or
prudent to press their opposition.

Chamberlain had only secured a provisional decision, and his
letter to Fielding shows that he knew it. He did not forget
Ritchie as Lord Randolph "forgot Goschen". Nevertheless, he

was entitled to expect that the Prime Minister and his chief colleagues would stand by the policy which they had in principle accepted. He might well exclaim that night as he came home: "Ritchie has been overruled on the Corn Tax. Now I can leave for South Africa with an easy conscience."[1]

IV

Chamberlain sailed from England determined to secure a preference for Canada on the Corn Tax. He came back three months later aiming at nothing less than the full reform of the established fiscal system. In the interval, his particular design had matured into a general conception. Two factors influenced this broadening process.

The long years of office had encroached on his championship of the British democracy. He could still speak to the masses like no one else in England; but, since 1895, he had been urging the Government's policies upon them and not their claims upon the Government. We have already seen how the great movement for Social Reform was passing beyond him. He was losing touch with the people, and, at the height of his fame, the roots of his power were beginning to decay.

Now all that was changed. Daily contact with the people of South Africa might exhaust his body; it brought him measureless refreshment of mind. His ideas of Imperial Union had been slowly elaborated in the calm of his room at the Colonial Office or of the library at Highbury. He had developed them in the clash of minds around the conference table or in private conversations. But it was only now, as he tested them against the great sounding-board of mass opinion, that he realised their elemental force. The South African tour was like an election campaign, fought on the Imperial issue. Here was a faith that appealed both to the rugged individualism of the class from which he had sprung and to the more collective spirit already stirring. Here, in those masses to whom his Imperialism made so powerful an appeal, was the advance guard of a new people's movement. Once again he found himself a people's leader, and rose, like Antaeus, refreshed from the touch of the earth.

[1] Mrs. Chamberlain in conversation with the author.

The more compelling his vision, the greater was his need to devise practical measures for its fulfilment. Nor were opportunities lacking for meditation. There were the nights when he smoked his cigars on *Good Hope's* deck under the starlit tropic sky. There were the long waggon treks across the silent veld and the endless train journeys over the Great Karroo. It was between these moments of reflection and the stormy enthusiasm of his meetings that the practical issue of Preference and the dream of a united Empire were integrated to become a policy.

By a curious accident, a first-hand account has survived of the first occasion on which Chamberlain divulged this new policy to any living man. It was in Milner's house in Johannesburg, during the negotiations over the Transvaal contribution. A member of one of the many deputations which came to see Chamberlain—"a representative of the working class"—had referred to "the bread tax" recently "imposed" in England. The matter had gone no further and the deputation had in due course withdrawn leaving Chamberlain alone with Milner and Sir Percy Fitzpatrick. Tea was brought in and presently Chamberlain remarked to Milner: "It was rather curious that that man should have raised this question of the duty on wheat". The sequel is best told in Fitzpatrick's own words.[1]

. . . Mr. Chamberlain followed up his puzzled reflection by giving a very full outline of his scheme for Tariff Reform and Imperial Preference. . . .

Sipping his tea slowly, and clearly prompted by the accident of this Labour representative's suggestion, he seemed to be working out the details of the policy as he spoke—as though thinking aloud. He began by saying that this 1/- duty upon wheat was the beginning and nucleus of a policy of Imperial Preference and Empire development, by means of which the resources of the Empire would be gradually and surely developed, so that the essentials for life, industry, and trade within the Empire should be available for the Empire, assured as to quantity and regularity of supply, and gradually reduced in cost by reason of the development, which would take place under a defensive tariff against the outer world and a preferential abatement in favour of all parts of the

---

[1] "The Turning Point", an article by Sir P. Fitzpatrick, *The Times*, November 28, 1923. The quotations from the article published here are taken from Fitzpatrick's own typescript, which is somewhat fuller than the printed version.

Empire. He spoke of the enormous possibilities of Canada, Australia and New Zealand in the matter of food supplies, etc., of the illimitable quantity and variety of products from different parts of Africa and the world wide possessions of the British Empire. It was a spell-binding experience. He spoke like a seer—as one quietly, unemotionally, slowly, describing a vision as it unfolded itself to him. He seemed to know the resources and potentialities of the Empire in its most distant parts, and its infinite variety of climate, conditions and soil; of how obvious it was that the superabundance in one portion should make good the shortage in another; of how it would absorb the surplus population; of how a sane, business-like, practical policy, free of all fanaticism and prejudices, made the proper course seem so obvious and simple. . . .

I do not know for how long he spoke. I was divided between the fascination of his slowly unfolded vision and the intense concentrated attention given to him by Lord Milner.

Memory cannot be relied upon to reproduce his own words uttered 20 years ago . . . hence, little but a general outline can be attempted.

At one time, when he seemed to have finished thinking aloud, he spoke of himself as though a period or stage in his career had been reached, and a stage in the essential work completed, where it was open to him to make a choice. I gained the impression that it would be a simple matter for him to be Prime Minister and to carry on without disturbing accepted policies or taking risks; but he dismissed the idea as insufficient warrant for one who was actuated by purpose and conviction, and by the desire to achieve, to do something positive for the Empire. Such a position was admittedly full of honour, the greatest in the world to which a representative could be called; but what was there in it, he asked, for one who felt that there was so much to be done? What had deterred many men from backing their faith was the fear of personal risk. Position, safety, administration, do not attract, he seemed to say; there was something great to be done for the Empire, and he was willing to risk a fall. They had made a beginning (meaning the wheat tax), and from that he would go on. There might be checks; there was sure to be an outcry. Perhaps it might not be adopted at the first attempt—the first General Election—but at the next it would triumph; for, after all, it was only the application of sane, business principles to the greatest business organisation in the world—the British Empire! There were people who regarded Free Trade as a religion—a revealed religion! Fanatics. They would not be converted. It was not a religion; it was not even a fact! But they did not realise it. The Empire was unorganised. Potentially greater than anything in the world! Yes, greater than anything created by the wit and hand of man, but unorganised!

The Mother Country could learn a great deal from the Dominions, who, however extreme in some things, had applied business principles to the practical facts and circumstances of their case as they saw them; but the Mother Country was face to face with a world very different from what it had been 50 years ago—even less than that—and very different from the world in which the present system of tariffs was a practical and profitable one. Other countries had armed themselves with their tariffs, but we stood unarmed and defenceless; and the Nations, which were our competitors, were day by day closing in upon us, invading our home markets, shutting off the avenues of trade. All were equipped with the armour of defensive and offensive tariffs, and, unless something was done, we should be hopelessly cut off—"hemmed in and helpless in an ever closing ring of armed opponents".

At another time, he referred to America as the greatest Free Trade area in the world—its 45 states with no tariff barriers; and yet the most heavily armed against the outer world! And why, he asked, should the British Empire, potentially far greater, neglect to march with the times and equip itself for defence? Why should we not have employment for many men? Why let our people go under foreign flags to fill with the best the unoccupied, undeveloped spaces in other lands, when a little thought would provide better for them within the Empire?

The "Common Sense of Business" was the basis of it all. "Defence" and "Construction" were the dominant notes. . . .

. . . The sequel was not less interesting and impressive. When Mr. Chamberlain left the room to get a short rest before resuming his arduous round of meetings and functions that evening, I asked Lord Milner for some explanation, and, to my great surprise, learnt that this was the first he had heard of Mr. Chamberlain's policy and intentions.

That explained the significance of his unbroken silence and intensely concentrated attention. . . .

. . . That he should be reluctant to pass judgment on the spot—bearing in mind the time, his own position, and all the circumstances—did not seem unreasonable. He was reluctant! And yet . . . he did answer. . . .

. . . The judgment was not passed lightly or hurriedly, but in fragments, as though he too, in turn, were thinking aloud; and he dealt with various points as they came back to him. In his judgment, Mr. Chamberlain was too sanguine, and under-rated the fanatical devotion to so-called Free Trade. The fact that the position in the Old Country and throughout the world and the policies of all countries, had completely changed, was not realised by a very large section who still held the conviction that Free Trade—whatever it might mean—was something sacred, a policy for all time and all circumstances. "Not one General Election will be required to convert people to this new Tariff policy—several! Two or three, perhaps more. It will take years. He is too old to undertake the task, and complete it." Lord Milner added then very gently that he did not think Mr. Chamberlain was very soundly posted or that he thoroughly understood the magnitude and financial intricacies of this question; that he was not definite or clear in mind as to some of the facts and some of the most important details; that he was not ready with the constructive measures; that it did not appear that he had anyone to work this out for him; and that he was insufficiently prepared to face the opposition which the proposal would unquestionably arouse. . . . It was not an undertaking for one man; it called for the most thorough preparation and an organisation of well-informed workers; in fact it needed to be worked out in detail, with the most thorough preparation, before it was launched as a policy. . . .

"He is too old—too old. If he were 20 years, even 10 years younger he would carry it. He is wonderful for his age; but this task is bigger than he realizes."

Too old? Perhaps. And yet it was only now that he reached his full maturity. At sixty-seven he would develop new powers. The last lingering restraints would be abandoned. There would be a broadening of character and a new stirring of imagination. His oratory would reach to its greatest heights. Above all, he would become a leader as never before. With the strength of maturity might also go its weakness. Prudence would decline as self-confidence grew. Judgment would be impaired by the very brightness of vision. The edge of persuasion would be dulled by the habit of command. We know little of the inward development which he now underwent. He was not given to introspection, least of all in his writing. But all his life hereafter is witness that this was the time of a great inward change. Perhaps something of it was due to the long, slow treks across the lonely, silent and illimitable veld. Since time immemorial, it is to the wilderness that men have gone to see visions and dream dreams. One man had set out from England on board *Good Hope*. A new man was now returning, and he too would be a prophet.

END OF VOL. IV

PRINTED BY R. & R. CLARK, LTD., EDINBURGH